A Grammar of Sochiapan Chinantec
Studies in Chinantec Languages 6

SIL International and
The University of Texas at Arlington
Publications in Linguistics

Publication 135

Publications in Linguistics is a series published jointly by SIL International and the University of Texas at Arlington. The series is a venue for works covering a broad range of topics in linguistics, especially the analytical treatment of minority languages from all parts of the world. While most volumes are authored by members of SIL, suitable works by others will also form part of the series.

Series Editors

Donald A. Burquest
University of Texas
at Arlington

Mildred L. Larson
SIL International

Volume Editors

Rhonda L. Hartell
Marilyn Mayers

Production Staff

Bonnie Brown, Managing Editor
Laurie Nelson, Production Editor
Karoline Fisher, Compositor
Hazel Shorey, Graphic Artist

A Grammar of Sochiapan Chinantec
Studies in Chinantec Languages 6

David Paul Foris

A Publication of
SIL International
and
The University of Texas at Arlington

© 2000 by SIL International
Library of Congress Catalog No: 97–62237
ISBN: 1–555671–052–6
ISSN: 1040–0850

Printed in the United States of America
All Rights Reserved

10 09 08 07 06 05 04 03 02 01 10 9 8 7 6 5 4 3 2 1

No part of this publication may be reproduced, stored in a retrieval system, or transmitted in any form or by any means—electronic, mechanical, photocopy, recording, or otherwise—without the express permission of SIL International, with the exception of brief excerpts in journal articles or reviews.

Copies of this and other publications of SIL International may be obtained from

International Academic Bookstore
SIL International
7500 W. Camp Wisdom Rd.
Dallas, TX 75236-5699

Voice: 972-708-7404
Fax: 972-708-7433
Email: academic_books@sil.org
Internet: http://www.sil.org

Contents

Acknowledgments ix

Abbreviations xi

Map. xiv

1 Introduction. 1
   1.1   The people and their culture 1
   1.2   Data and methodology. 5
   1.3   Salient linguistic characteristics. 6

2 Phonology. 9
   2.1   Vowels 10
   2.2   Diphthongs and triphthongs 11
   2.3   Nasalization 14
   2.4   Consonants 14
   2.5   Stress and tone. 16
   2.6   Whistle speech 21
   2.7   Intonation 25
   2.8   Orthography 25

3 Lexical Formation Strategies 27
                3.1–3.4 Stem formation processes
   3.1   Phonological modification of the root 27
   3.2   Affixation 29
   3.3   Compounding 35
   3.4   Classification of compounds 42
             3.5–3.6 Binomial and polynomial expressions
   3.5   Binomial expressions 45
   3.6   Nonpermutable polynomials 52
   3.7   Residue 53

4 The Verb 55

4.1–4.7 Dynamic verbs

4.1 Inflectional rules 57
4.2 Inflection set paradigms 65
4.3 Verbs which inflectionally distinguish between singular and plural subjects 74
4.4 Disyllabic verbs 77
4.5 Stable and unstable nuclei 83
4.6 Internal inflection of verbs. 88
4.7 Verb prefixes 100
4.8 Derivational prefixes 121
4.9 Binomial verbs 126
4.10 State verbs 127
4.11 State verbs versus adjectives 132

5 The Verb Phrase 137

5.1–5.8 The verb phrase adverbs

5.1 The discontinuative 139
5.2 The perfect aspect 139
5.3 The evidential adverb 142
5.4 The terminative adverb 143
5.5 The nonentailment adverb 146
5.6 The neoteric adverb 146
5.7 The negative constituent 148
5.8 The verb phrase intensifier $lí^{LM}$ 157
5.9 The verb phrase constituents and binomial verbs 157

6 The Noun Phrase 161

6.1–6.2 The noun phrase head

6.1 The base 162
6.2 The categorizers 173

6.3–6.4 The possessive construction

6.3 Possession of inalienable nouns 176
6.4 Possession of alienable nouns 180
6.5 The noun phrase modifier 184
6.6 The deictic constituent 188
6.7 The relative clause constituent 195
6.8 The evaluative constituent 196

6.9–6.11 The quantifier

6.9 The specific quantifier phrase 198
6.10 The approximate quantifier phrase 218
6.11 The indefinite quantifier phrase 219

	6.12 Coordination of noun phrases	223

7 The Prepositional Phrase. 225
   7.1 Inalienable nouns as prepositions 226
   7.2 Co-occurrence restrictions. 227
   7.3 Prepositions with *bíʔ^H* (affirmation) 230
   7.4 Prepositions with a deictic complement. 231
   7.5 Prepositional phrases as complement 232
   7.6 Prepositions with adverbs 233

8 The Clause 237

                                               8.1–8.6 The primary constituents
   8.1 The predicate 237
   8.2 Valence 239
   8.3 Split-ergativity 250
   8.4 Direct and inverse cross-referencing 259
   8.5 Passive constructions. 270
   8.6 Antipassive constructions 282

                                          8.7–8.14 The secondary constituents
   8.7 The recipient/source and benefactive constituents. 287
   8.8 The manner constituents 288
   8.9 The locative constituent. 292
   8.10 The comitative constituent 293
   8.11 The temporal constituent 300
   8.12 The instrumental constituent. 304
   8.13 The illocutionary constituent 306
   8.14 The vocative constituent 306

9 Complex and Compound Sentences 309

                                                 9.1–9.2 Relative clauses
   9.1 The restrictive relative clause 310
   9.2 Nonrestrictive relative clauses 319
   9.3 Complementation 319
   9.4 Purpose clauses 322
   9.5 Result clauses 323
   9.6 Cause clauses 324
   9.7 Conditional constructions 325
   9.8 Concessive clauses 329
   9.9 Substitutive clauses 332
   9.10 Comparative constructions 333
   9.11 Coordination of clauses. 338

10 Interrogative Constructions. 341
   10.1 Yes/no questions. 341

10.2 Tag questions 344
10.3 Information questions 345
10.4 Indirect questions 351
10.5 Rhetorical questions 353

11 Illocutionary Adverbs and Particles 355
11.1 Illocutionary adverbs 358
11.2 Illocutionary particles 365
11.3 Co-occurrence of illocutionary markers 377
11.4 A comparison of implications 379

12 Topic-Comment and Focus. 383
12.1 The topic-comment construction 383
12.2 Focus 391

References 397

Index. 401

Acknowledgments

First of all, I would like to thank my wife, Christine, who has taken time to read and comment on various drafts of the manuscript and has contributed useful insights from her own grasp of the Chinantec language and culture.

I am obliged to Mary and Kevin Salisbury, who provided the initial impetus to write this grammar in 1979 (or perhaps I should say that I lay the blame at their feet). When I indicated in an after-dinner discussion that I had thoughts of starting work on a practical grammar to accompany the Chinantec-Spanish dictionary which I was then and still am compiling, they suggested that I discuss the project with Dr. Andrew Pawley of the Linguistics Department at Auckland University. Dr. Pawley willingly accepted me into the linguistic fold at A.U., even though he himself left for 'greener pastures' at Australia National University soon thereafter. What started as an M.A. thesis grew, as the intricacies of this exotic language mandated, into a more thorough description.

I gratefully acknowledge the contribution of Dr. Scott Allan and my colleagues at A.U., Mary Salisbury and Simon Corston, as well as Jim Rupp, Dr. Barbara Hollenbach, and Dr. Doris Bartholomew of the Mexico Branch of the SIL International, who have read and discussed portions of this work with me and have provided helpful insights and encouragement.

This grammar would never have been possible if it were not for the gracious people of San Pedro Sochiapan, Mexico, who welcomed my family and me into their homes and lives. Many Chinantec people have assisted in my acquisition and analysis of their language; those who have been the main contributors to this particular work are Marcelino Flores Mariscal, Miguel Martínez Donato, Francisco Feliciano Cruz, and Wilfrido Flores Hernández.

During the final revision of this book I have been greatly assisted by Wilfrido Flores Hernández, who lived with us in New Zealand for eight months during the final revision of the grammar, and who has greatly enriched our lives by his sunny personality. He patiently explored with me the complexities of Chinantec verbal morphology and discussed with me the implications of various syntactic structures and the nuances of his language. Wilfrido's visit to New Zealand was funded in part by a research grant from Auckland University which is gratefully acknowledged.

In particular, I would like to thank my supervisor, Dr. Frantisek Lichtenberk, for his encouragement, constructive comments, and professional support throughout this project. His insights and suggestions have greatly enhanced my understanding of grammatical analysis and the application of these principles to this fascinating language.

Abbreviations

A	subject of (di)transitive verb	BEN	benefactive
		BN	base nucleus
ADJ	adjective	C	consonant
ADV	adverb	CATEG	categorizer
ADVP	adverb phrase	CAUS	causative
AFF	affirmation	CECIL	Computerized Extraction of Components of Intonation in Language
AH	accessibility hierarchy		
AL	alienable		
ALT	alternative	CES	cessative
AMB	ambulative	CEXP	contraexpectation
AMP	amount phrase	CLASS	classifier
AN	animate	CNEG	contraexpectation negative
ANDT	andative		
ANTP	anticipative	COM	comitative
APP	appositional constituent	COMM	commentative complement;
APP^QP	approximate quantifier phrase	COMP	complementizer
ASN	associate nucleus	COM^AMP	complex amount phrase
ASNT	assentive	CONJ	conjunction
ASSR	assertion	CONT	continuous
ASUM	assumption	CRD^AMP	coordinate amount phrase
ATT	attainment		
ATTN	attenuative	CTOP	contraexpectation topic

xi

DA	ditransitive animate direct	INDEF	indefinite
DAI	ditransitive animate inverse	IND^QP	indefinite quantifier phrase
DEIC	deictic	INDB	indubitative
DES	desiderative	INDQ	indefinite quantifie
DET	determiner	INST	instrumental
DII	ditransitive inanimate inverse	INT	intentive
		INTENS	intensifier
DI	ditransitive inanimate direct	INTERR	interrogative
DIM	diminutive	INTRP	interruptive
DIR	directional (andative or venitive)	INTRV	intransitivizing
		IO	indirect object
DISC	discontinuative	IQ	interrogative quantifier
DIV	divisor	IQH	indefinite quantifier head
DO	direct object	LIM	limiter
EVAL	evaluative	LIT.	literally
EVID	evidential	LOC	locative
EXCL	exclamative	MA	manner
EXCM	exclamation	MASC	masculine
EXH	exhortative	MOD	modifier
EXPC	expectation	MODR	moderative
EXPL	explication	MOT	motion
FEM	feminine	MP	measure phrase
FR	fraction	ms	milliseconds
FUT	future	N	noun
G	glottal	NA	nasalization
H	head	NEG	negative
HAB	habitual	NEO	neoteric
HOD	hodiernal past (since midnight)	NON	nonentailment
		NP	noun phrase
HORT	hortative	NUM	numeral
I	inverse	O	object
IA	intransitive animate	OO	oblique object
II	intransitive inanimate	P	plural
ILLOC	illocutionary	P	predicate
IMP	imperative	PASS	passive
IMPR	improbability	PAST	remote past
IMPRS	impersonal	PH	phrase
IN	inanimate	POSS	possessive
INAL	inalienable	POSS^NP	possessor noun phrase
INCL	inclusive	PP	prepositional phrase

Abbreviations

PPAS	posture passive	T	tone
PR	partative	TA	transitive animate direct
PREP	preposition	TAI	transitive animate inverse
PRES	present		
PREVEN	preventative	TEMP	temporal
PRF	perfect	TI	transitive inanimate
PROG	progressive	TOP	topic
PROH	prohibitive	TRM	terminative
PRT	partitive	unrd	unrounded
PSR	possessor	V	verb
PV	preverb	V	vowel
Q	quantifier	vd	voiced
QH	quantifier head	VEN	venitive
QL	qualifier	VER	verification
QUOT	quotative	vl	voiceless
RC	relative clause	VOC	vocative
rd	rounded	VOCP	vocative phrase
S/SUBJ	subject	VOS	verb-object-subject
S	singular	VP	verb phrase
SC	Sochiapan Chinantec	VSO	verb-subject-object
SIA	state intransitive animate	1	first person
SII	state intransitive inanimate	2	second person
SIL	Summer Institute of Linguistics	3	third person (proximate)
		3i	third-person obviative
Sp.	Spanish	3>2, etc.	inverse cross referencing
SQP	specific quantifier phrase	H	high tone
STA	state transitive animate	M	mid tone
STI	state transitive inanimate	L	low tone
SUPL	supplication	?	question intonation
T	temporal constituent		

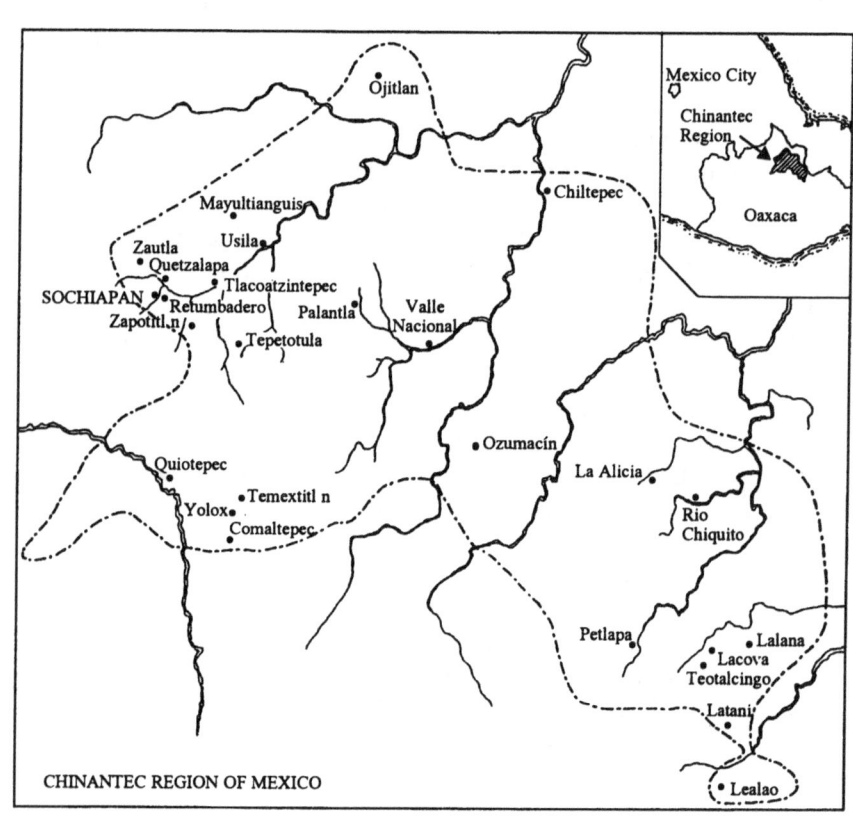

1
Introduction

Sochiapan Chinantec is a language spoken in the northeast quadrant of the State of Oaxaca in southern Mexico. It is one of fourteen Chinantec languages based on intelligibility testing done by Egland (1978) and the most northwestern Chinantec language. According to Egland, Tlacoatzintepec is the closest Chinantec language to Sochiapan. The people of Sochiapan understand 66 percent of the speech of Tlacoatzintepec, whereas the people of Tlacoatzintepec understand 74 percent of the speech of Sochiapan (Rensch 1989:2). The Chinantec languages comprise one of the major branches of the Otomanguean stock of Mesoamerican tone languages.

The region traditionally inhabited by Chinantec speakers is referred to as 'the Chinantla.' According to Bevan (1938), the name 'Chinantla' derives from Nahuatl *chinamitl* 'enclosed place', an appropriate term for this area, which is enclosed by high mountains, making access difficult. Soon after the Spaniards arrived in Mexico, an epidemic of measles and swelling of the glands (mumps?) devastated the Chinantec people. The town of Usila, for example, which originally had a population of 16,000, was left with 400 inhabitants. Although early records indicate that the Chinantecs used to have many fiestas with dances and songs, nowadays, indigenous dances and songs have, for the most part, disappeared.

1.1 The people and their culture

My family and I had the privilege of living in the town of San Pedro Sochiapan for various periods between 1970–86 while studying the Sochiapan

Chinantec language. San Pedro Sochiapan is the municipal town; it has four smaller towns within its jurisdiction: San José Retumbadero, San Juan Zautla, San Juan Zapotitlán, and Santiago Quetzalapa. The inhabitants of Sochiapan readily identify the inhabitants of the other four towns by their accents. No study has been made of the phonology or grammar of these dialects.

Topography and climate. Sochiapan is located in the District of Cuicatlán, Oaxaca, at a median elevation of 4,000 feet above sea level at latitude 17° 49' and longitude 96° 40'. The elevation, climate, flora, and fauna are typical of a cloud forest (Gary Ross, personal communication). The terrain is extremely mountainous with steep limestone cliffs dropping from about 4,000 ft. to 1,800 ft. to the Rio Hormiga. The rainy season extends from mid-June to mid-September, during which nightly rains of two to twelve cms are common. Rarely is there more than a month between rains even in the driest time of the year. In the winter months of December and January, there may be occasional nighttime frosts. During the hottest time of the year, just prior to the rainy season, daytime temperatures are around 30°–35°. Humidity is high throughout the year.

Until recently, overland travel from Sochiapan meant a 40 km. hike over mountainous terrain to a dirt road used principally by lumber trucks. Traffic being sparse, one generally had to walk an additional eight kms. to the nearest town of Concepción Pápalo; once there, one could get a ride in a truck down to the district capital, Cuicatlán, where both bus and train are available. In 1986, construction of a road was begun towards Sochiapan which has since been completed. Trucks now regularly make the six-hour trip from Cuicatlán to San Pedro.

History. Before 1850, San Pedro Sochiapan was a small town or ranch under the jurisdiction of Santa Ana de Tecomaltepec; but after the majority of people in Tecomaltepec died in an epidemic in the mid-19th century, the people abandoned the town and moved to the less affected town of Sochiapan. Sochiapan is now divided into two boroughs—San Pedro and Santa Ana—reflecting the amalgamation of the two communities. Despite intermarriage, even to this day there is a slight dialect difference between the people of the two boroughs.

The town's name, San Pedro Sochiapan, reflects Catholic and Nahuatl influence. San Pedro is the Patron Saint of the town, while Sochiapan derives from Nahuatl *xochitl* 'flower'. The people call their town $?a^L lí^{HL}$, a compound of $?á^M$- 'foliage' and $lí^{HL}$ 'flowers'. They call their language $hú^H hma^M$, the first syllable of which is the compound form of $hái^{HL}$ 'word, message'. The etymology of the second syllable, however, is unknown.

Economy and agriculture. The inhabitants of Sochiapan practice swidden (slash and burn) agriculture. Formerly, after one crop was harvested, the land would lie fallow for five to seven years. But now that artificial fertilizers are being used, some land is used again after only two or three years of lying fallow. There is no plowing of the land. A few people have begun to make small terraces for garden plots adjacent to their homes.

The staple food is maize, which is used in a variety of ways and at various stages of maturity. In addition, various types of beans, squash, bananas, and citrus are cultivated, along with leaf cabbage, head cabbage, sweet potato, and cassava.

Chickens, turkeys, and a few ducks roam freely through the town during the day and find their own way home in the evening. Pigs are kept in town, either on a tether or in an enclosure. A few people keep goats, but this has not proven popular. Some people have become adept beekeepers, using commercial-type hives. Several people have cattle in private paddocks. Most families now have a horse, mule, or burro.

Coffee is presently the only cash crop; however, with the road all the way to Sochiapan, it will probably become economical to transport and sell other crops such as bananas and oranges. Sugar cane is grown and processed to make crude sugar; or the juice is allowed to ferment, producing an alcoholic beverage, which is occasionally distilled to produce rum.

The traditional house was enclosed by split balsa slats, tied together with vines; the roof was thatched with sugar cane leaves. Due to the steady improvement of the local economy over the past few years, walls may now be rough-sawn boards, locally manufactured concrete blocks, or, rarely, adobe bricks. Roofs are usually corrugated iron, although some are made of locally manufactured cedar slats. Flat roofs are of poured concrete. Generally, the interior is one large room used for cooking and sleeping, although many families now construct a separate cooking hut to prevent the blackening of the main dwelling by smoke from open-hearth cooking fires. Very few houses have anything other than tamped-earth floors.

Cotton was traditionally grown and spun. Men wore a simple white shirt and pants. Women wore a simple skirt and a colorful *huipil*—a long, heavy tunic made by stitching together three woven panels of homespun, decorated profusely with stylized birds and geometric patterns. Weaving was done on a back-strap loom, a craft no longer practiced by the young women of Sochiapan, although it is still practiced in the nearby town of Quetzalapa. Most clothing is now either bought ready-made or sewn on treadle sewing machines from lengths of fabric.

Social infrastructure. Extended family units often share a single dwelling with up to four generations living together.

Marriages were traditionally arranged by parents, sometimes without the knowledge of their children; at other times, a boy would ask his parents to speak with a particular girl's parents and arrange a marriage. Most young people now decide among themselves whom they wish to marry, although the final decision still generally rests with the parents. It is considered improper for marriage partners to be more closely related than third cousins, and even that is regarded as barely acceptable. A betrothal gift is usually given by the boy's parents to the girl's parents; if the relationship later breaks up, the gifts are not returned. Newlyweds generally live at the boy's house. If husband and wife separate, a mutually agreeable arrangement is made for the children.

Children are treated almost as adults and are quickly given the responsibilities of washing their own clothes, carrying water and firewood, weeding gardens, minding younger siblings, and making tortillas.

For entertainment, little boys play with homemade tops; little girls make pretend kitchens and dolls of rags. Teenage boys and men (but not girls and women) play basketball. In recent years, volleyball has become popular and is played by both genders, often in mixed teams. Property is handed down from father to son. Community decisions were traditionally made in town meetings by the men, although widows also attended and occasionally spoke on issues. Such participation by women is now becoming more common.

Town officials are democratically elected for one three-year term and serve without pay. Reelection of the town president is prohibited by law. The town secretary is the only nonelected official. He is paid a wage and may serve under various administrations. All young men must serve as police for four years, with duties ranging from apprehending criminals to carrying official letters to other towns. In addition, young men serve another three years on the school committee, assisting the teachers in a variety of ways, such as in transporting school supplies, painting the school, and cutting the lawn. These duties generally alternate on a yearly basis, beginning with police duty.

Each group of young officials meets early in the morning for about an hour to see if there is any task for that day, either for a few individuals or for the whole group. If there are no assignments, they disperse to do their own work. These duties are generally unpaid, but major undertakings by the whole group may result in a small gratuity to buy a soft drink and some fresh baked bread.

Education. There has been a government school in Sochiapan for many years. When my wife and I arrived in Sochiapan in 1970, the local primary school offered only two grades. Later, the remaining four years of primary education were added. Because the medium of education was (and still is) purely Spanish, the children generally take four or five years to complete the first two grades. The typical primary school graduate is between 15 and 18 years old. The first year of secondary school became available in 1993.

Although a few teachers speak the local language, they generally avoid using it in school to avoid being considered incompetent in Spanish by the other teachers.

Four primers are available in Sochiapan Chinantec. The first three teach reading and writing in Chinantec; the fourth is a 'bridge' primer for developing reading ability in Spanish and gives practice in using a small bilingual (Spanish-Chinantec) dictionary. A full Spanish-Chinantec dictionary is still in preparation. A teacher's guide has also been prepared, designed for use by those who have taken the 15-week literacy course. About 250 adults have completed this course, many having been taught in our absence by the people of Sochiapan themselves.

Religion and the supernatural. The Chinantec were traditionally animistic. According to Bevan (1938), animal sacrifice was practiced in some Chinantec communities and in others, human sacrifice. The pre-Columbian practices of the communities in and around Sochiapan are unknown.

Many folk stories exist which refer to the sun and moon as male and female deities, respectively. Monkeys are believed to be humans who were out in the open when the sun deity first climbed into the sky and shone on the earth; all those who were struck by sunlight became monkeys.

Catholicism was introduced throughout the Chinantla soon after the Spanish conquest, but a syncretism of Catholicism and animism developed. In Sochiapan, the images in the Catholic Church were referred to as 'gods' in Chinantec. In 1970, a parish priest, Father Luis Pacheco, began to promote Bible studies. When he left the area a year later, the next parish priest forbade Bible studies, but a handful of people continued and later organized themselves as a Protestant fellowship. Presently, about two-thirds of the community consider themselves Protestants.

Belief in the supernatural is integral to the fabric of life. Some men, particularly those who are bald, are reputed to command the power of the thunder spirit and are able to cause illness and death. Some women, particularly those with unusually long hair, are reputed to command the power of the rainbow spirit in a similar fashion. Many stories exist of men and women who have the power to transform themselves into a puma, buzzard, snake, rat, or coati. Stories of spirit manifestations, particularly on New Year's Eve, are common. Many spirits are considered just mischievous, although others are regarded as evil. Animal sacrifices to such evil spirits to gain healing from serious illness is practiced to this day.

1.2 Data and methodology

This study stems from sixteen years (1970–86) of involvement in the Chinantec community—working on a phonemic analysis (Foris 1973), developing an alphabet, and producing an array of literacy materials, most of which are bilingual (Chinantec-Spanish). My wife and I analyzed various aspects of the syntax, two of which studies are published (Foris 1978 and 1980). Approximately six years were spent in actual residence in the village. When outside of the village, one or more language assistants often lived with our family and assisted us in the language study.

A bilingual Chinantec-Spanish dictionary (the computer database includes English as well) is currently being compiled. It has nearly 5,000 main entries.

Data for this study have been drawn from a collection of folklore, procedural texts, historical commentary, biographical, and autobiographical materials, the Chinantec New Testament (1986), and field notes. Several oral and written texts were processed in 1973 using a computer program of the Linguistics Project of the University of Oklahoma, under grant GS1605 of the National Science Foundation. FIESTA, an interactive concordancing program developed for personal computers by the Summer Institute of Linguistics, has facilitated searches for grammatical patterns and illustrations in oral and written texts gathered since 1973.

Two recent field trips—in August 1991 and in August 1992—enabled me to clarify many issues in the grammatical analysis. The data and analysis have been finally checked with Wilfrido Flores Hernández, a native speaker of Chinantec, who lived with us in New Zealand from February to October 1993.

In an attempt to make this grammar of Sochiapan Chinantec as accessible as possible to readers of any theoretical persuasion, I have sought to produce a model-neutral description. The occasional use of 'process terminology' is more a matter of convenience than a tacit agreement with that methodology.

1.3 Salient linguistic characteristics

Apart from verbs, which may have several prefixes, most Sochiapan Chinantec words are monosyllabic. Only prefixes occur, whether inflectional or derivational.

Chinantec is a numeral-classifier language. Nouns which require classifiers when enumerated are mainly those which refer to small inanimate items of specific shapes. Complex numerals are based on a vigesimal system.

There are two genders: animate and inanimate. Descriptive adjectives, deictics, and quantifiers agree with the head of the noun phrase as to animacy. Intransitive verbs agree with their subject as to animacy, and transitive verbs agree with their object in an ergative pattern.

By change in tone, stress, nucleus, or a combination of these, verbs are indexed for person-of-subject and for direct or inverse cross-referencing; they are inflected for tense, aspect, mood, motion, and voice, often in combination with a prefix.

Introduction

Sochiapan Chinantec has two ways of forming passives, one of which can be used to express impersonal passives. The language also has an antipassive construction.

A variety of first- and second-person pronouns enables the speaker to express her/his attitude to self and/or the addressee; in addition, there is a so-called 'fourth-person' pronoun used for keeping track of two third-person participants in discourse.

Speaker attitude toward the proposition or addressee is conveyed by a rich array of illocutionary adverbs and particles.

In the relative clause construction, the determiner of the domain noun generally occurs within the restrictive clause, a possibility not mentioned in Keenan's typology (1985b:145).

Certain features of Sochiapan Chinantec offer counter-examples to generalizations made in the literature, such as Dixon's claim (1987:3) that "absolutive is the unmarked case from an absolutive-ergative system," Noonan's claim (1985:135) that all languages have at least two complementation strategies, and Li and Thompson's claim (1976:484) that in topic-comment constructions, so-called double-subject constructions are always in the order: NP1 (topic), NP2 (comment), V.

Chinantec is principally a VSO language, although VOS order is not uncommon where the verb is inflected for inverse cross-referencing.

Chinantec is typical of VO languages (Greenberg 1966) in that demonstratives, descriptive adjectives, relative clauses, and possessor follow the noun; however, numerals and some evaluative adjectives precede the noun.

In Sochiapan Chinantec, up to seven tones and two stresses—ballistic and controlled—are distinguished in monosyllabic words or in the final syllable of polysyllabic words. Ballistic stress is characterized by a rapid enunciation of the syllable, whereas controlled stress prolongs the enunciation of the syllable. This differs from vowel length in that the entire syllable (any nonplosive onset, nuclear and nonnuclear vowels) is compressed or prolonged. In nonfinal syllables, only three tone distinctions occur and stress distinctions are absent.

Whistle speech, based on thirty-one etic tone-stress distinctions, is used to communicate complex messages with minimal ambiguity.

Except for chapter 2, Chinantec examples are cited in this study in phonemicized orthography. Furthermore, in this orthography, the letter /H/ represents high tone, /M/ mid tone, and /L/ low tone. Double letters /MH LM HL ML/ represent glides. Ballistic stress is marked by an acute accent over the nuclear vowel (for example, $táu^M$ 'banana'); controlled stress is unmarked.

2
Phonology

Sochiapan Chinantec syllable structure was described in Foris 1973. This chapter presents an updated description.

The majority of Sochiapan Chinantec words consist of a single syllable; a small percentage are disyllabic, and less than a dozen are trisyllabic. In polysyllabic words, nonfinal syllables display a more limited inventory of tones and segmental combinations than final syllables and lack contrastive stress. Monosyllabic words have the same characteristics as final syllables.

The two kinds of stress found on final syllables—ballistic and controlled—are marked by the presence or absence of acute accent over the nuclear vowel. Tones are written as the final constituent of their syllable and are represented by raised letters.

The essential components of a final syllable are a vowel nucleus and a tone, either of which can be simple or complex. Most syllables have a consonantal onset. The structure of the final syllable can be diagrammed as in (1), where G is a glottal consonant, C is a nonglottal consonant, V is a vowel, and T is a tone. The glottal and nonglottal consonants constitute the syllable onset. The vowels and tone constitute the syllable nucleus which may be open or checked by glottal stop /ʔ/. The optional vowels of the nucleus may be realized only by /i u ɯ/. There seems to be no limitation on the occurrence of final glottal stop with other elements of a word-final syllable.

(1)
$$\text{(G) (C) (V) } \overset{T}{V} \text{ (V) (ʔ)}$$

In nonfinal syllables of polysyllabic roots, there is a strong tendency to disallow glottal closure and complex tones.

(2) /mi^M ɲiɨ^L/   pig   /ʔi^H mii ʔ^MH/   bread
     /tu^M héɯ^HL/   police   /ku^L ðiɐ^M hẽ^M/   suddenly
     /mi^H hlɯ^M kɛi ʔ^LM/ scissors   /tsii^H kɐ^M lú ʔ^L/ type of caterpillar

There are a few exceptions. For example, older speakers say *huɯ^MH kuí^M* 'sugar' with a rising tone on the nonfinal syllable, but the younger generation says *huú^H kuí^M*.[1] Prefixes, however, are strictly open syllables and have only simple tones. Disregarding these exceptions, the nonfinal syllable can be diagrammed as in (3), although a glottal consonant is rarely realized concurrently with a nonglottal consonant, and the first of two vowels is always either /i/ or /ɯ/, and never /u/.

(3)   T
        (G) (C) (V) V

2.1 Vowels

Seven vowels are distinctive in simple syllable nuclei:[2] close front unrounded /i/, close back unrounded /ɯ/, close back rounded /u/, close-mid back unrounded /ɤ/, open-mid front unrounded /ɛ/, open-mid back rounded /ɔ/, and open central unrounded /ɐ/.

(4) /ʔi ʔ^LM/   (my) nose   /ʔɯ ʔ^LM/   (s/he) injects
     /ʔu ʔ^LM/   (my) fingernail   /ʔɛ ʔ^M/   (her/his) nose
     /ʔɤ ʔ^M/   (her/his) fingernail   /ʔɔ ʔ^L/   (s/he) dislikes
     /ʔɐ ʔ^M/   crack (noun)

(5) Vowels

	Front unrd	Central unrd	Back unrd	rd
Close	i		ɯ	u
Close-mid			ɤ	
Open-mid	ɛ			ɔ
Open		ɐ		

---

[1] The word *huɯ^MH kuí^M* 'sugar' derives from *huɯ^MH* 'powder' and *ʔna^H kuí^M* 'sugar cane'. This compound may be in the process of being assimilated to the normal pattern for a single word. There are no known polysyllabic words consisting of a single morpheme that allow a tone glide on the nonfinal syllable.

[2] Phonetic symbols and description are taken from the revised IPA (Ladefoged 1990). The diacritic · represents 'voiceless', + marks 'advanced', − marks 'retracted', and ˜ marks 'nasalazation'.

Phonology

The vowel /i/ is found following all consonants except /ɣ/, /ɯ/ is found following all consonants except /ß ɸ r z̞ ɣ/, /u/ is found following all consonants except /ɸ r ɣ/, and /e/ is found following all consonants except /ŋ ɣ/.

The vowel /ɔ/ is found following all consonants except /m ß ɸ/ and has an offglide to open-mid central unrounded vowel [ɜ] in open syllables, as in /kɔᴹ/ [kʰɔɜᴹ] '(he) plays', where [ɜ] represents a slightly lower position than that given in the IPA chart (Ladefoged 1990:551).

The vowel /ɐ/ is found following all consonants except /ɸ/, where /ɐ/ represents an open central unrounded vowel that is lower than that given in the IPA chart.

The vowel /ɤ/ is marginal to the system, occurring only following /m k h ʔ/ and never in combination with other vowels. /ɤ/ never occurs in nonfinal syllables. Only thirty words with this vowel have been found; for example, /kɤᴸ/ 'money', /hɤᴴ/ '(her/his) word, message', /ʔɤʔᴹ/ '(her/his) fingernail'. The only example of /ɤ/ following /m/ is the word /mɤᴹᴴ/ 'nut' (from Spanish *nuez*). In some idiolects this vowel is even more marginal, with /ɯɛ/ corresponding to /ɤ/ in all but a handful of words. For example, almost all known speakers utilize /ɤ/ in /hɤᴴ/ '(her/his) word, message', but many speakers say /ʔɯɛʔᴹ/ instead of /ʔɤʔᴹ/ '(her/his) fingernail'.

If the marginal vowel /ɤ/ is disregarded, the Sochiapan Chinantec vowel system corresponds to Crothers' (1978) Type 6.1—six vowels, five of them peripheral /i u ɛ ɔ ɐ/, one of them interior /ɯ/.

2.2 Diphthongs and triphthongs

The three close vowels /i ɯ u/ may combine with each other or with /ɛ ɔ ɐ/ to form complex nuclei of two or three vowels.

The vowel /i/ can precede /i u ɛ ɔ ɐ/ and follow /ɛ /, /u/ can precede /ɯ u ɛ ɔ ɐ/ and follow /ɐ ɔ/, and /ɯ/ can precede or follow /ɛ ɐ/. In triphthongs the first and third vowels are always one of the close vowels /i ɯ u/ and the middle vowel never is. There are five permissible triphthongs: /iɛi iɐu uɐɯ uɔu ɯɛɯ/.[3]

When /i/ is the first of two or three vowels, it is realized as [j] or results in either palatalization or retraction of the onset consonant and is lost. /k/ preceding /i/ is fronted to [k̟], and /i/ is realized as [j]. When /s ts l n/ precede /i/, however, /i/ is lost and the consonant is palatalized to [ʃ tʃ ʎ ɲ], respectively, and when /t n/ precede /i/, /i/ is lost and the consonants are retracted to [t̠ n̠], respectively.

---

[3]The sequence /ɯɛɯ/ collocates only with /k/, and only four words that utilize this sequence are known: *kɯɛɯᴸ* 'eat! (2 IMP)', *kɯɛ́ɯʔᴸ* '(your) money', *kɯɛɯʔᴸᴹ* '(it) is closed', and *tsiᴴkɯɛ́ɯʔᴹᴸ* 'stuck (IN)'. The sequence /uɐɯ/ is known to occur in only one word, the verb *kuɐ̈ɯᴹᴸ* 'abandon' when inflected for inverse cross-referencing (§8.4), as in *kuɐɯᴹᴴ* '(I) will abandon (you)'.

(6) /ké?ᴹ/ [kʰé?ᴹ] type of vine /kié?ᴹ/ [kʰʲé?ᴹ] (s/he) splits
    /sɛᴴ/ [sɛᴴ] (I) will sprinkle /siɛᴴ/ [ʃeᴴ] manioc
    /tsɛᴴᴸ/ [tsɛᴴᴸ] (we) will grab (you) /tsiɛᴴᴸ/ [tʃeᴴᴸ] (s/he) will offend (me)
    /lé?ᴸᴹ/ [lé?ᴸᴹ] (it) will roll down /lié?ᴸᴹ/ [ʎé?ᴸᴹ] (s/he) will wash hands
    /ŋúᴸ/ [ŋúᴸ] meat /ŋiúᴸ/ [ɲúᴸ] (s/he) will vomit
    /tɐᴹᴴ/ [tʰɐᴹᴴ] work /tiɐᴹᴴ/ [tʰaᴹᴴ] dad (VOC)
    /nɐᴹᴴ/ [nɐ̃ᴹᴴ] open /niɐᴹᴴ/ [nã ᴹᴴ] (I) will open

Of the vowels that may follow /i/, /ɐ/ is fronted to [a], /ɛ/ is raised to [e], and /ɔ/ is raised to [o], while /i u/ are unaffected.

(7) /miɪᴹ/ [mʲíᴹ] year /tsiɪᴸ/ [tʃíᴸ] wind
    /?iúᴹ/ [?ʲúᴹ] sun /siu?ᴹᴴ/ [ʃu?ᴹᴴ] crisp
    /tiɛᴴ/ [tʰeᴴ] (I) shave /?iɛ?ᴹ/ [?ʲe?ᴹ] stem
    /siɛᴴ/ [ʃeᴴ] manioc /?iɐᴹ/ [?ʲaᴹ] hello
    /tiɐᴹᴴ/ [tʰaᴹᴴ] father /kiɐᴴ/ [kʰʲaᴴ] dirty
    /?niɔᴸ/ [?nõə̃ᴸ] (s/he) wants /ŋiɔᴴ/ [ɲõə̃ᴴ] (I) know
    /?iɛi?ᴹᴴ/ [?ʲei?ᴹᴴ] excessively (full) /θiɐuᴹᴸ/ [θʲauᴹᴸ] (it) is left over

The sequence /ii/ does not contrast with simple /i/ following alveolars or velars, nor does /iɛ/ contrast with /ɛ/ following velars. The sequences /ii iɛ/ are interpreted as such because the onset consonant in these contexts has the same phonetic quality as when preceding sequences /iɐ iɔ iu/.

(8) /tsɐᴴᴸ/ [tsɐᴴᴸ] (it) will run out /kiẽᴴ/ [kʰʲẽᴴ] (I) will tie together
    /tsiiᴴᴸ/ [tʃiᴴᴸ] (I) will loan /tsiɐᴴᴸ/ [tʃaᴴᴸ] (I) will tell
    /ŋiúᴸ/ [ɲúᴸ] (s/he) will vomit /ŋúᴸ/ [ŋúᴸ] flesh
    /kɔ̃ᴴ/ [kʰɔ̃ᴴ] (I) will put down /ŋiiɪᴸ/ [ɲiíᴸ] sit down!
    /kiɔ̃ᴴ/ [kʰʲɔ̃ᴴ] steep

In the absence of a consonantal onset, the /i/ as the first element of a complex nucleus has more oral friction than when following a consonant.

Phonology   13

(9)   /iɛᴹ/   [jeᴹ]   tick   /iɛi↑ᴴᴸ/ [jei↑ᴴᴸ]   (you) will
      /iɔ́↑ᴹᴸ/   [jɔ́↑ᴹᴸ]   (s/he) spreads,   extinguish
                               smears

When /u/ is the first of two or three vowels, it is realized as labialization
of the onset consonant, which may only be /k h ʔ/.

(10) /kuúᴹ/   [kʰwúᴹ]   maize   /kuɛ́↑ᴸᴹ/ [kʰwɛ́↑ᴸᴹ] church
      /kuɔ↑ᴹ/   [kʰwɔ↑ᴹ]   scar   /huɯᴸᴹ/   [u̯ʷɯᴸᴹ]   road
      /huɛ́↑ᴹ/   [u̯ʷɛ́↑ᴹ]   rotten   /ʔuɛ́ᴸᴹ/   [ʔʷɛ́ᴸᴹ]   earth
      /ʔuɛ̃ᴸ/   [ʔʷɛ̃ᴸ]   shoddy   /ʔuɐᴴ/   [ʔʷɐᴴ]   soft
      /ʔuɔ̃uᴸᴹ/ [ʔʷɔ̃ũᴸᴹ]   (I) skin

In the absence of a consonantal onset, /u/ is realized as [w] and has more
oral friction than otherwise.

(11) /uúᴸ/   [wúᴸ]   (s/he) will   /uɛ̃ᴸᴹ/   [wɛ̃ᴸᴹ]   (my)
                               climb   mouth
      /uúɯ↑ᴹ/   [wúɯ↑ᴹ]   smooth

When /ɯ/ follows an open vowel in an unchecked syllable, it is realized
as [ɣ] in the absence of nasalization (or nasal consonant onset) and as [ŋ] in
the presence of such nasal elements. The presence of [ɯ ɯ̃] after open vowels in only checked syllables contributes to this interpretation that [ɯ ɯ̃ ɣ ŋ]
are all allophones of /ɯ/.⁴

Further evidence that [ɣ ŋ] are allophones of /ɯ/ is found in verbs which
index the second person by glottal closure. For example, although [ɣ] occurs
in /hɐɯᴸᴹ/ [hɐɣᴸᴹ] 'we cut (a field)', [ɯ] occurs in /hɐɯ↑ᴸᴹ/ [hɐɯ↑ᴸᴹ] 'you
cut a field'. Similarly, [ŋ] occurs in /ʔẽɯᴹᴸ/ [ʔeŋᴸᴹ] 'we jump' but when the
verb is indexed for second-person present by glottal closure, the nasalized
allophone [ɯ̃] occurs in /ʔẽɯ↑ᴸᴹ/ [ʔãɯ̃↑ᴸᴹ] 'you jump'.⁵

(12) /uúɯᴸ/   [wúɯᴸ]   difficult   /kuɯ̃ᴹᴸ/   [kʰwɯ̃ᴹᴸ]   s/he disposes (AN)
      /huɯᴸᴹ/   [u̯ʷɯᴸᴹ]   road   /ʔuɯ̃↑ᴴ/ [ʔʷɯ̃↑ᴴ]   dark-brown (AN)
      /kɛ́ɯ↑ᴴ/   [kʰɛ́ɯ↑ᴴ]   (I) cinch   /ʔlɛ́ɯ↑ᴴ/ [ʔlɛ̃́ɯ̃↑ᴴ] bad, evil (AN)
      /kɛ́ɯᴹ/   [kʰɛ́ɣᴹ]   cage   /hɛ́ɯᴴᴹ/   [ɐ̯ɐ́ɣᴴᴸ]   word

---

⁴This interpretation of [ɣ] and [ŋ] as allophones of /ɯ/ is mentioned in Foris 1973 as an alternative analysis to positing postnuclear /ɣ/ and /ŋ/.
⁵The sequence /ɛɯ/ has a very limited distribution; for most speakers it only follows /k/. A
few speakers use /ɛɯ/ in place of /aɯ/ following /h/, but for only selected lexemes. For example, although most people say /hɐ́ɯᴴᴸ/, a few say /hɛ́ɯᴴᴸ/ 'word, message'. Some speakers use
/ɛɯ/ in place of /ɯ/ following /k/ as in /kúɯ́ᴴ/ or /kɛ́ɯᴴ/ 'rock'. The sequence /ɯɐ/ has been
found in only the one word /hɯɐ↑ᴹ/ 'look!'.

/ŋɐɯLM/ [ŋɐ̃ŋLM] (we) ask /nɐ́ɯM/ [nɐ̃́ŋM] weed
/kɐ́ɯH/ [khɐ̃́ŋH] rock /ʔɐ̃ɯML/ [ʔɐ̃ŋML] (it) bounces

2.3 Nasalization

Syllable nuclei are oral or nasal. Any combination of nuclear segments may occur in the presence or absence of nasalization, and all are affected by it. However, nasalization is marked only over the stressed vowel.

(13) /kɐM/   candle   /kɐ̃M/   (I) pluck
      /tsiiLM/   (s/he) sifts   /tsiĩLM/   (my) head
      /tuɯL/   to, at, from   /tũɯL/   is turn of
      /ʔɛʔH/   (I) am embarrassed   /ʔɛ̃ʔH/   (I) leave (some food)
      /ʔɤʔM/   (her/his) fingernail   /ʔɤ̃ʔM/   type of snake
      /hlɐɯLM/   (s/he) replaces (a lid)   /hlɐ̃ɯLM/   (s/he) is hit by
      /ʔliɐɯLM/   (I) push (you)   /ʔliɐ̃ɯLM/   (s/he) wears
                                                          (a prosthesis)

When a nasal /m n ŋ/ occurs in the syllable onset, the following nucleus is always nasal, resulting in the neutralization of this feature in the nucleus. In the transcription, it is left unmarked in this context.

(14) /muLM/   [mũLM]   bone   /nɔM/   [nɔ̃ɔ̃M]   rat
      /ŋɯL/   [ŋɯ̃L]   (s/he) will extend
                        (border of field)

2.4 Consonants

A simple onset may consist of any one of eighteen consonants: bilabials /p ɸ β m/, interdentals /θ ð/, alveolars /t ts s ʐ r l n/, velars /k ɣ ŋ/, or glottals /ʔ h/.

(15) Consonants

	Bilabial	Interdental	Alveolar	Velar	Glottal
Plosive	p		t	k	ʔ
Affricates			ts		
Fricative vl	ɸ	θ	s		h
vd	β	ð	ʐ	ɣ	
Nasal	m		n	ŋ	
Lateral			l		
Flap			r		

Phonology

/p t k/ are voiceless stops which vary from unaspirated to slightly aspirated. The stops towards the back of the mouth are progressively more aspirated as in /pɐ^{MH}/ [pɐ^{MH}] 'big', /tɐ^{MH}/ [tʰɐ^{MH}] 'work', /kɐ^{LM}/ [kʰɐ^{LM}] 'crooked'.

/ts/ is the only affricate: /tsɐ́u^M/ 'people', /tsō^M/ 'true'.

The voiceless bilabial fricative /ɸ/ occurs only in words borrowed from Spanish: /ɸɛ́^{L}/ 'Felix' (Sp. *Felix*), /ɸiɛ^H/ 'Alfred' (Sp. *Alfredo*).

/θ/ is a voiceless interdental fricative: /θúɨ^L/ 'bottle', /θɔ̄^{H}/ 'type of grass'.

/β ð ɣ/ are voiced fricatives and are all marginal to the system. Of native Chinantec words, /β/ has been found in seven words, /ð/ in about forty, and /ɣ/ in five. For example, /βíʔ^L/ 'brown eyed', /ðɛ̄^{L}/ 'baby maize', /ðɔ̄^{M}/ '(s/he) twists', /ɣɔ̄^{L}/ 'two (AN)'. In addition, there are several words borrowed from Spanish: /βɛ́ʔ^L/ *(Roberto)* 'Robert', /ðɛ́ʔ^L/ *(Adela)* 'Adele', /ɣɐ́u^L/ *(Gregorio)* 'Gregory'. Examples of contrasts between the voiceless stops and voiced fricatives are presented in (16).

(16) /piʔ^{MH}/ small   /βíʔ^H/ (affirmation)
      /pɐ^{MH}/ big (IN)   /βɐ^{MH}/ godfather (from Sp. *compadre*)
      /tɐʔ^H/ (I) block (you) /ðɐʔ^H/ (I) chew
      /kɐu^L/ cooked (IN)   /ɣɐu^L/ (we) two

/z/ is a voiced slightly retroflexed fricative: /zɛ́ʔ^M/ 'green (IN)', /zɐ́u^L/ 'sweet (IN)'.

The nasals /n ɲ/ contrast in all environments except before /ii/. Preceding /ii/, the contrast is neutralized to /ɲ/.

(17) /niɐ^{LM}/ [nā^{LM}]   (s/he) opens   /ɲiɐ^{LM}/ [ɲā^{LM}] come in
      /niɛ^H/   [nē^H]   dark color   /ɲiɛ^H/   [ɲē^H]   high
      /niɔ^M/   [nɔ̃ɔ̄^{M}]   be present (PL) /ɲiɔ^H/   [ɲɔ̃ɔ̄^{H}] (I) know
      /niu^{ML}/ [nū^{ML}]   she stretches   /ɲiu^{ML}/ [ɲū^{ML}] (s/he) vomits
                                                   /ɲii^H/   [ɲī^H]   (my) face

/l/ is a voiced lateral: /lí^{HL}/ 'flower', /ʔlɐ^H/ 'corpse'.

An alveolar flap /r/ occurs in onomatopoeic words, in one expletive, and in words borrowed from Spanish: /trí^H/ 'chirp (of cricket)', /réi^{HL}/ (emphasis), /kɔ^{M}rɔ^{H}né^H/ 'crown' (Sp. *corona*).

The glottals /ʔ h/ may occur as simple syllable onsets or preceding nasals or the lateral. The glottal fricative /h/ is the voiceless counterpart of the phoneme it precedes.

(18) /ʔɐ́u^M/   medicinal herb /ʔmɛ́^{M}/   wood
      /ʔnú^M/   you (SG)   /ʔɲɐ^{MH}/   spotted cavy
      /ʔlɐ́u^M/   cliff   /hú^{HL}/ [u̥ú^{HL}] mosquito
      /hmɯ^M/   [m̥mɯ̃^{M}]   blood   /hnɔʔ^H/ [n̥nɔ̃ʔ^H] we

/hŋiu^HL/ [n̥n̥ʲũ^HL] hairy   /hliɛ^L/ [ɬʎe^L] deep
/hɐʔ^LM/ [ɐ̥ɐʔ^LM] fist   /hẽ^L/ [ɛ̥ɛ̃^L] bed
/huɔ́u^LM/ [u̥ʷɔ̃u^LM] tough   /hiẽ^L/ [ii̥ẽ^L] odor

The complex onsets /ßř tř kř/ have been introduced from Spanish: /ʔɐ^Mßři^MH/ 'April' (Sp. *abril*), /tř5^H/ 'Petrona' (Sp. *Petrona*), /křɛi^MH/ 'cross' (Sp. *cruz*).

2.5 Stress and tone

Chinantec exhibits complex interaction between tone and stress, which results in fourteen tone-stress patterns for final syllables and three for nonfinal syllables.[6]

Stress on final syllables. Monosyllabic words and final syllables in polysyllabic words carry either ballistic stress, characterized by brevity and high intensity, or controlled stress, characterized by length and medium intensity.[7] Syllables with ballistic stress are hereafter referred to as BALLISTIC SYLLABLES, those with controlled stress as CONTROLLED SYLLABLES. Ballistic syllables are marked by an acute accent over the nuclear vowel, controlled syllables are unmarked.

Ballistic syllables are characterized by an initial surge and rapid decay of intensity, with a resultant fortis articulation of the consonantal onset. Ballistic syllables are also shorter in duration than those with controlled stress. When syllables begin with the semivowels [j w], there is greater friction in the articulation of the semivowels if receiving ballistic stress than if receiving controlled stress. Controlled syllables generally display a more gradual surge and decay of stress, as well as a longer duration of the maximum stress.

In both ballistic and controlled syllables, high and high-falling tones have the greatest intensity, low and low-rising tones have the least. Stress graphs produced with CECIL for isolated words within a word list show that, although stress varies in intensity from syllable to syllable, the average intensity of ballistic syllables is greater than that of controlled syllables.

Controlled syllables whose nuclei consist of a single vowel give the impression that the vowel is lengthened, and syllables whose nuclei contain two or three vowels have all vowel segments lengthened. Because this lengthening in controlled syllables is relative to that of ballistic syllables, it

---

[6]Tone and stress analysis has been carried out using CECIL. CECIL stands for Computerized Extraction of Components of Intonation in Language. It consists of SIL speech-analysis software and a small hardware component (JAARS International, Inc.) that plugs into the computer for analyzing and displaying elements of pitch, stress, and timing. CECIL can accept data for analysis from either microphone or tape recorder.

[7]INTENSITY is used in Chinantec phonological studies to refer to air pressure which presumably has its primary source in the lungs.

Phonology   17

is preferable to talk in terms of ballistic and controlled stress rather than of vowel length.

A comparison of the duration of vowel segments in ballistic and controlled syllables is presented in (19), and shows that controlled syllables last approximately three times as long as ballistic syllables and that the nuclear (open) vowel in controlled syllables lasts about one and a half times as long as peripheral (close) vowels. In ballistic syllables, two patterns emerge; the nuclear vowel is equal in length with a preceding peripheral vowel, but one and a half times as long as a following peripheral vowel.[8]

(19)   Duration of vowel segments (in milliseconds)

		Pre-nuclear peripheral	Nuclear	Post-nuclear peripheral	Total
/hɐʔ^H/	basket	—	342	—	342
/hɐ́ʔ^H/	fly	—	111	—	111
/θiɔʔ^L/	(you) serve up	132	223	—	355
/θiɔ́ʔ^L/	(s/he) will serve up	066	067	—	133
/tsɐɯʔ^{LM}/	(s/he) burns	—	249	192	441
/tsɐ́ɯʔ^{LM}/	(s/he) will burn	—	090	053	143

Stress on nonfinal syllables. Only the three simple tones occur on nonfinal syllables. Based on graphs produced with CECIL, nonfinal syllables are brief in duration, similar to syllables with ballistic stress, but lack the intensity of a ballistic syllable. The intensity of nonfinal syllables closely approximates that of controlled syllables with simple tones, low tone having the least intensity, high tone the greatest.[9]

Stress graphs of affixed roots[10] with controlled stress indicate that when both prefix and root have the same simple tone, the stress on the prefix varies from slightly less than that of the root to about one and a half times the intensity of the root. Those affixes that occur on roots with ballistic stress, however, have a relative intensity that varies from about half to nearly equal the intensity of the root, but never exceeding it. For example,

---

[8]The first two words were spoken in isolation in a word list, the following four were spoken as pairs in a language practice tape. Words with final glottal were chosen as it is easier to determine syllable closure.

[9]Merrifield (1968:14) identifies two syllable types for Palantla Chinantec: stressed and unstressed, where "the stressed syllable is the last toned syllable of a phonological word." The stressed syllables are of two types, ballistic and controlled. Prefixes would be an example of unstressed syllables. If stress is regarded as intensity, however, these labels do not accurately portray the situation for Sochiapan Chinantec. Measurements using CECIL show that the intensity of prefixes approximates that of a contiguous controlled syllable of the same level tone. In this respect they cannot be called 'unstressed'. The relevant distinction appears to be between final and nonfinal syllable types.

[10]The affixed roots that were chosen were clause medial to lessen any possible influence from utterance initial or utterance final intonation.

the word /kɐᴸkɐᴸ/ 's/he tore' displayed a slightly greater stress on the final syllable; the length of the nonfinal syllable was 151 ms, and that of the final syllable was 270 ms.

Tone on final syllables. Final syllables display both simple (level) and complex (contour or sequence of) tones.

The three simple tones are: high /ᴴ/, mid /ᴹ/, and low /ᴸ/. The four complex tones include two upglides /ᴹᴴ ᴸᴹ/ and two downglides /ᴴᴸ ᴹᴸ/. The complex tones roughly span the distance in pitch for which each is named, that is, tone /ᴹᴸ/ is a glide from /ᴹ/ to /ᴸ/. All Chinantec syllables have one of the simple tones or tone sequences.

Simple tones are typically level in pitch. Exceptions are that mid tone descends slightly in pitch when occurring with controlled stress and that low tone descends markedly when occurring with ballistic stress in an open syllable. The step from low to mid tone is generally greater than that from mid to high. Measurements in several sentences show that there is generally a difference of three to four semitones between low and mid tones and two to three semitones between mid and high tones in normal unemotional speech. Utterances which had only high and low tones averaged a span of five semitones.

In each of the four tone sequences, the sequence begins on or close to the indicated pitch, but does not quite reach the final pitch. When tone /ᴴᴸ/ follows a /ᴴ/, it begins slightly higher than /ᴴ/. Ballistic /ᴸᴹ/ shows the shallowest tone contour, having a pitch rise of only a half to one semitone.

Foris 1973 stated that stress contrasts are limited in the presence of tone sequences. Further investigation, however, has shown that such a limitation exists only in certain idiolects. For example, all seven tones occur in both ballistic and controlled syllables in the speech of Marcelino Flores Mariscal. Ballistic /ᴹᴴ/ appears to be a predictable perturbation of ballistic /ᴸᴹ/, occurring when contiguously following a syllable with tone /ᴴ/ or when marking question intonation. This is true of disyllabic roots as in /kuᴴiɛ́iʔᴹᴴ/ 'nighthawk', and there are no known examples of a monosyllabic root with unperturbed ballistic /ᴹᴴ/. Native speakers react to ballistic /ᴹᴴ/ as distinct from ballistic /ᴸᴹ/ so I treat it as phonemic, although largely predictable.

A comprehensive study was done of all possible combinations of consonants, vowels, and tones in monosyllabic roots. There are several combinations that yield eleven and twelve semantic distinctions. Most combinations yielded seven or eight semantic distinctions. Both very low yield and very high yield distinctions are uncommon. A few combinations yielded only one or two meanings, such as the combination /pɐɯʔ/ which yielded the unique word /pɐɯʔᴸ/ 'bald, bare'.

Phonology

Two sequences have been found that display fourteen tone-stress patterns, /tɐ/ and /ʔiã/. The *tɐ* set is as listed in (20).

(20) /tɐᴴ/   (I will) be prompt   /téᴴ/   entire
      /tɐᴹ/   (I) am prompt   /téᴹ/   recently
      /tɐᴸ/   (her/his) foot   /téᴸ/   a weaving
      /tɐᴴᴸ/   (we) will fight   /téᴴᴸ/   (we) will carve
      /tɐᴹᴸ/   (we) fight   /téᴹᴸ/   (we) carve
      /tɐᴹᴴ/   work   /téᴹᴴ/   will (s/he) weave?
      /tɐᴸᴹ/   ladder   /téᴸᴹ/   (s/he) will weave

Another example of ballistic /téᴹᴴ/ is found in /ɲiᴴtéᴹᴴ/ '(s/he) wants to weave', where the verb is prefixed by /ɲiᴴ-/ to mark intent.

Tone and stress are particularly susceptible to variation among individual speakers. This may be due to the fact that historically the town of San Pedro is an amalgamation of two towns which were evidently of slightly differing dialects. These slight differences are still reflected in the choice of tone and stress patterns that modern speakers make for individual words, some speakers lacking contrasts that others have. For example, although all speakers appear to have both the tones /ᴴᴸ/ and /ᴴ/, some pronounce words such as /kuéʔᴴᴸ/ 'soil' and /ʔéuʔᴴᴸ/ 'compost' with a simple high tone as /kuéʔᴴ/ and /ʔéuʔᴴ/. Some speakers appear to completely lack the contrast between ballistic and controlled tone /ᴹᴸ/.

Tone on nonfinal syllables. Only the three level tones occur in nonfinal syllables.[11] Both high and mid tones are level and of brief duration like that of ballistic /ᴴ ᴹ/ in final syllables, but of less intensity. Low tone is brief like the ballistic /ᴸ/ of final syllables, but lacks the sharp downglide that characterizes this tone in open syllables; it is like controlled /ᴸ/ in both degree of intensity and level pitch.

Since the controlled ballistic contrast is neutralized in nonfinal syllables, it can be left unmarked. Because of the brevity of these syllables, however, nonfinal syllables with high and mid tones tend to be identified by native speakers with ballistic /ᴴ ᴹ/, while those with low tone are identified with controlled /ᴸ/.

---

[11] When teaching Chinantecs to write tone, initial literacy trials showed that if two key words were given for each emic tone, one for the open syllable and one for the closed syllable, the students could more readily compare a new word (one for which the tone symbol was not yet known) with the key words to determine which tone-stress symbol was appropriate. If a closed syllable was compared to only key words with open syllables (or vice versa), the students would assert that there was no match. As a consequence, the literacy books utilize twenty-eight key words for teaching tone-stress, even though there are only thirteen or fourteen emic tone-stress patterns on final syllables.

Tone and stress on borrowed words. Borrowed words that have been assimilated into Chinantec are usually monosyllabic and display the same range of tone-stress variations as native Chinantec words. Generally, with names, only the Spanish stressed syllable is retained and modified to fit the Chinantec phonology.

(21) /βέʔᴸ/   *Roberto*   Robert   /ɸiɛᴴ/   *Alfredo* Alfred
     /kɇ́ᴴ/   *Carlos*   Charles   /ðiɔ́ᴸᴹ/   *diós*   god
     /miᴹᴴ/   *Carmelo*   Carmelo   /liɇ̃ᴹᴴ/   *Julián* Julian

Examples of assimilated polysyllabic words are presented in (22).

(22) /mɇᴹzɛ́iᴸ/   *María*   Mary   /ðɇᴹβiᴹᴴ/ *David* David
     /βiᴹnɇᴴðíʔᴸ/   *Bernadino*   Bernard

Recent borrowings are similarly modified to fit Chinantec phonology, but tone-stress follows a pattern not entirely consistent with the above description of nonfinal syllables. For a Spanish word that is stressed on any nonfinal syllable, the syllable corresponding to the stressed syllable of the Spanish word is given high tone with the intensity similar to that of a ballistic syllable, but with length similar to that of a controlled syllable. Chinantec speakers associate it with a controlled /ᴴ/, a tone that is not normally permitted in a nonfinal syllable. In the conventional orthography, this stressed syllable is written as controlled /ᴴ/.

Borrowed words of up to four syllables exist. Any syllables which precede or follow the stressed syllable of the borrowed word take tone-stress that is normally associated with nonfinal syllables for native words: all syllables that precede the stressed syllable are given a tone /ᴹ/; all syllables which follow the stressed syllable are tone /ᴴ/, but they are briefer and slightly lower in pitch than the tone /ᴴ/ of the stressed syllable. In the phonemicized orthography, all syllables which follow the stressed syllable are written as ballistic /ᴴ/.

(23) /liᴴtrɔᴴ/   *litro*   liter
     /sɯᴹmɇᴴnɇᴴ/   *semana*   week
     /puᴹyɇᴴðɇᴴ/   *pulgada*   inch
     /tɔᴹnɛᴹlɇᴴðɇᴴ/   *tonelada*   ton
     /kiᴴlɔᴴ/   *kilo*   kilo
     /miᴹnuᴴtɔᴴ/   *minuto*   minute
     /rɇᴹsɛᴴnɇᴴ/   *docena*   dozen
     /kiᴹlɔᴴmɛᴴtrɔᴴ/   *kilómetro* kilometer

2.6 Whistle speech

Tone has a high functional load in Chinantec; almost all verbs mark the difference between present and future simply by a change in the tone and stress.

These tone and stress contrasts are utilized in whistle speech to facilitate long distance communication. In addition, falsetto speech is used as an alternative to whistling for reasons described below.

The three forms of whistle speech and falsetto speech described in this section are almost entirely the domain of the men in the Sochiapan Chinantec community. When I have tried to get female language associates to whistle tones on words, the usual reaction has been that they are incapable of whistling. If an effort was made, it was done with great mirth and some embarrassment. Nonetheless, most women understand whistle speech.

When men wish to communicate over a distance, they use one of four methods: (1) whistling by putting the tongue against the alveolar ridge for close-by communication (up to 10 meters); (2) bilabial whistling for mid- to far-distance (up to 200 meters); (3) fingers-in-mouth whistling for far-distance, sometimes audible more than a kilometer away, depending on terrain and background noise; and (4) falsetto speech for mid- to far-distance (up to a kilometer). There are three verbs for the different styles of whistling: /sie^M/ (close-by), /huɯ^{LM}/ (mid-distance), and /huɔ^M/ (far-distance). Falsetto speech (the verb /ʔɔ́ʔ^{LM}/ 'shout') is used in place of whistling in the following situations: (1) the person is unable to whistle (e.g., dry mouth); (2) the person is in danger; (3) the person is acting authoritatively, for example, a member of the police force walking through town summoning the inhabitants to a town meeting; or (4) as part of the training to understand whistle speech.

With respect to the final point above, in observing my main language associate training his son to understand whistle speech, he would whistle to him from about 7–10 meters, then speak to him using falsetto, immediately followed by a whistled repetition of the same utterance.

When a young man begins his first tour of obligatory town duty (§1.1), he is given a test to see if his whistle can be heard over a set distance of about a kilometer; if not audible, he is fined the equivalent of three days' wages. In the early morning the village comes alive with whistled messages as people communicate with one another their plans for the day.

Virtually anything that can be expressed by speech can be communicated by whistling. The most complex example that I had interpreted for me was on the occasion that the supply plane was due to come in. Because of heavy rains, I checked the dirt airstrip for erosion and saw that it needed extensive repairs. I went to the town president and explained the need for immediate repairs, a job that was the responsibility of the town police in those days. The town is set on a horseshoe-shaped hillside; his house is at one end of the 'arm' with the town hall at the center about one-half a kilometer away. He put his fingers in his mouth and whistled to get their attention. They responded that they were listening, and he whistled a long message. I asked for the interpretation, which he gave as the following: "The plane will be here soon. The airstrip needs to be repaired. Get the picks, shovels, and wheelbarrows and fix it right away."

I have not purposefully collected data in an attempt to analyze whistle speech. The incidental information that I have gathered, however, is sufficient for me to present the salient characteristics as follows:

1. Syllable-final glottal stop is incorporated into whistle speech, interrupting the air flow. This effectively doubles the fourteen tone-stress distinctions to twenty-eight on final syllables; nonfinal syllables allow only three tone-stress distinctions (see footnote 9). Thus, in effect, thirty-one tone-stress distinctions are utilized in whistle speech.

2. All whistled utterances end with the whistling of the word /réi^{HL}/, which might be glossed as a radio operator's 'over!'.

3. Looking at tone and stress on syllables with CECIL, it has become apparent that concomitant tone on nonobstruent voiced onsets such as nasals and fricatives is ignored in whistle speech, as is the tone of peripheral vowels of the syllable nucleus.

The figures in (24)–(27), created using CECIL, present pitch (tone) and intensity (stress) contours of words superimposed on each other. The pitch frequencies are measured in hertz (HZ, cycles per second), but the intensity scale is not labeled since it can vary considerably from utterance to utterance depending on the proximity of the speaker to the microphone and the speaker's focus on the work (interested/bored). Tone appears to be quite stable, generally varying less than a semitone from utterance to utterance for words of the same phonemic tone. The significance of the intensity graph lies in the point of maximum intensity and its intersection with the tone graph.

The figure in (24) presents the tone and intensity of the word /lé^L/ 'ear of maize' when spoken. It illustrates that words with a nonobstruent voiced onset and ballistic tone /^{L}/ in open syllables have a tone contour that is an almost perfect sine wave. The tone starts high at the beginning of the /l/ with minimal intensity, falls, and then rises again to a point slightly higher than the starting point. The point of highest pitch approximates the point of maximum intensity, and then both pitch and intensity fall away together.

Phonology

(24) Tone and intensity contours of /léL/ 'ear of maize' when spoken

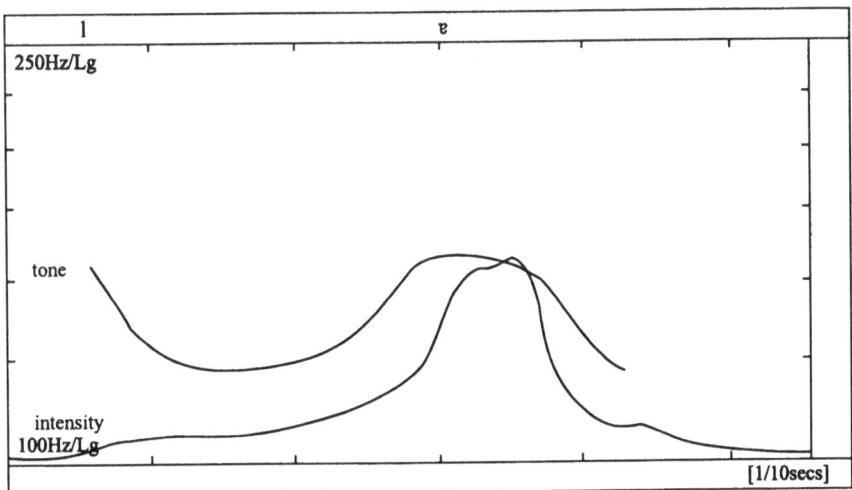

Figure (25) presents the corresponding contours for this same word when whistled. It shows that only the final falling component of tone is whistled; that is, the point from maximum stress onwards. The pitch of the consonantal onset /l/ is not whistled.

(25) Tone and intensity of /léL/ 'ear of maize' when whistled

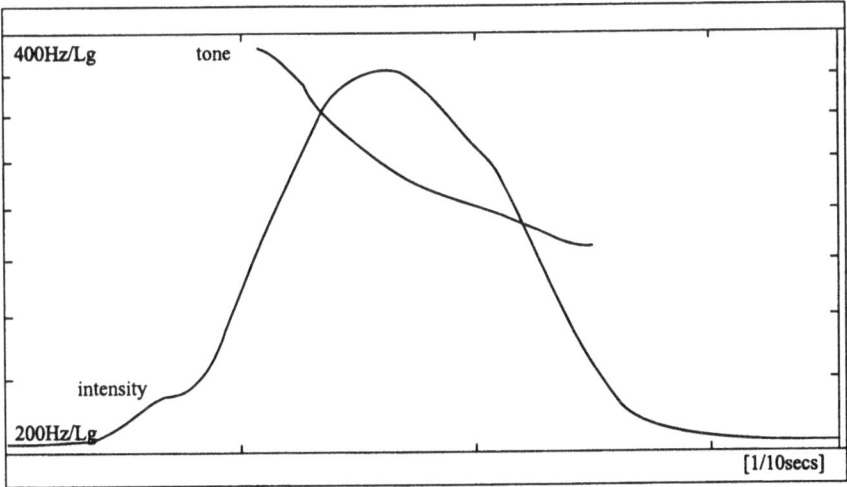

The contours of (24) and (25) are typical of other words like /lé̠ᴸ/ 'ear of maize' with nonobstruent voiced onsets and tone /ᴸ/, when spoken and whistled. Syllables with obstruent onsets, however, such as the word /hɔ́ᴸ/ 'child (VOC)', yield only a falling tone trace when spoken, as in (26).

(26)   Tone and intensity contours for /hɔ́ᴸ/ 'child' when spoken

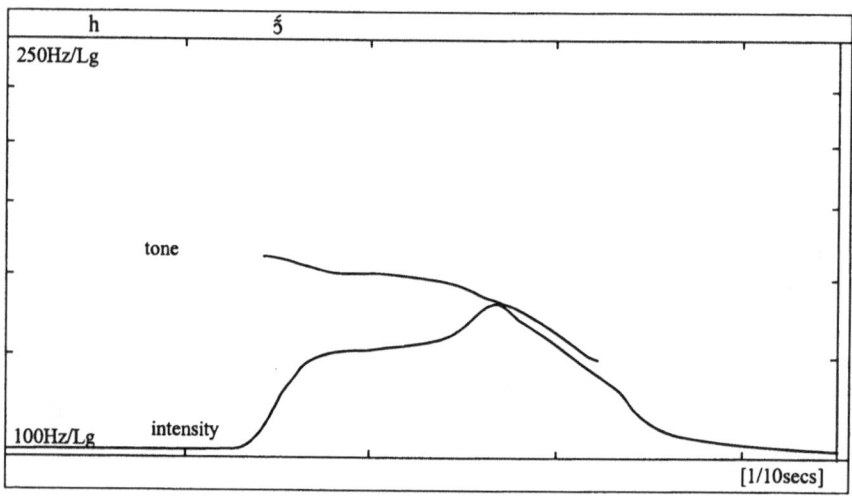

A comparison of the tone tracings of whistled speech and of spoken words demonstrates that emic tone is the domain of the nuclear vowel and not of the peripheral vowels. The figure in (27) shows the tone and stress of /ʔɯɛ́ᴴᴸ/ 'let's sing' when spoken where pitch rises at the beginning of the nucleus during the production of the peripheral vowel /ɯ/, reaching its peak at the start of the vowel /ɛ/, which is also the point of maximum stress. When words of this type are whistled, however, only the falling component is realized.

Phonology 25

(27) Tone and intensity contours of /ʔɯé^{HL}/ 'let's sing' when spoken

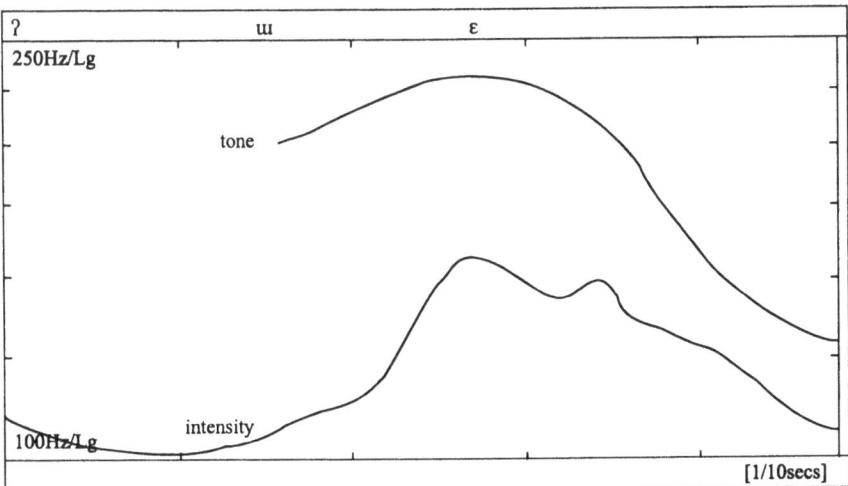

2.7 Intonation

Very little study of Sochiapan Chinantec intonation has been undertaken. Two patterns that are immediately apparent, however, are question and anger intonation.

In a question introduced by a question word, the intonation is the same as for a statement. One way of forming a yes/no question, however, is by placing the first syllable of the first word on a higher than normal pitch while preserving its general configuration as level, upglide, or downglide. The stress of this first syllable also increases slightly, but the distinction between ballistic and controlled syllables is still apparent. The remainder of the utterance is as for normal statements.

Anger intonation is marked by the use of a higher register for all the tones in the utterance and by a diminishing of the span between each of the tone levels and the corresponding tone sequences.

2.8 Orthography

The Sochiapan Chinantec data in chapters 3–12 of this study are presented in a conventional orthography. The chart in (28) summarizes the phonetic sounds and lists their phonemic equivalents. To facilitate comparison with previously published grammars in related Chinantec languages, the conventional orthography follows their precedent for the most part. However, nasalization of the syllable nucleus is marked by tilde over the nuclear vowel except when a nasal occurs in the onset, in which case the following nucleus is always nasalized so it is not marked.

(28)   Phonetic and practical equivalents

Vowels

Phonetic	Phonemic	Conventional
[ɐ a]	/ɐ/	a
[ɛ e]	/ɛ/	e
[ɤ]	/ɤ/	ë
[i j ʲ]	/i/	i
[ɯ ɣ ŋ̍]	/ɯ/	ï
[ɔ ɔə o oə]	/ɔ/	o
[u w ʷ]	/u/	u

Consonants

Phonetic	Phonemic	Conventional
[β]	/β/	b
†*[kʰ k̬ʰ]	/k/	k
[ts]	/ts/	c
*[tʃ]	/tsi/	ci
[ð]	/ð/	d
[ɸ]	/ɸ/	f
[ɣ]	/ɣ/	g
[ʔ]	/ʔ/	ʔ
(voiceless counterpart of following phone)	/h/	h
[l]	/l/	l
*[ʎ]	/li/	li
[m]	/m/	m
[n]	/n/	n
*[n̠]	/ni/	ni
[ŋ]	/ŋ/	ŋ
*[ɲ]	/ŋi/	ŋi
[p]	/p/	p
[z̠]	/z̠/	r
[ɾ]	/ɾ/	ř
[s]	/s/	s
*[ʃ]	/si/	si
†[tʰ]	/t/	t
†*[t̬ʰ]	/ti/	ti
[θ]	/θ/	θ

*See §2.2
†See §2.4

3
Lexical Formation Strategies

This chapter addresses the ways that Sochiapan Chinantec extends its lexicon through word (stem) formation and by use of nonpermutable binomial and polynomial expressions.

3.1-3.4 Stem formation processes

Sochiapan Chinantec uses phonological modification of the root, affixation, and compounding of roots and stems for stem formation. These three processes are presented here in turn.

3.1 Phonological modification of the root

There are a few words formed by phonological processes that seem totally idiosyncratic, involving any of the following: suprasegmental modification of the root (that is, a change in tone, stress, or nasalization), vocalic change, or the addition of glottal closure of the syllable. The input root is always a noun, the derived stem is either a noun, an adjective, an intransitive verb, or a transitive verb.[12]

---

[12]Inalienable nouns are marked for person of possessor; thus, '3' indicates that the possessor is inanimate third person, and '1P/3' indicates that the possessor is either animate first-person plural or third person (either animate or inanimate).

(29) change in tone and stress
hnai^{MH} lid (3) → hnai^{LM} close (TI)   N → V
ʔmá^M tree, wood → ʔma^M paralyzed   N → ADJ

(30) addition of nasalization
ci^{fH} head (1P/3) → cĩ^{fH} prime, supreme   N → ADJ

(31) change in tone and addition of nasalization
tiú^{ʔHL} breast (1P/3) → tiũ^{ʔM} nurse (TA)   N → V
láu^M skin → láũ^L naked   N → ADJ

(32) addition of glottal closure
kuo^M hand (1P/3) → kuoʔ^M branch (3)   N → N
kuo^M hand (1P/3) → kuoʔ^M thrust hand inside (TI)   N → V

(33) change in tone, stress, and addition of glottal closure
hmái^M water → hmaiʔ^{MH} broth, sap (3)   N → N
ɲiú^M fellow → ɲiuʔ^{HL} male   N → ADJ
no^H fat → noʔ^L greasy   N → ADJ
ʔo^L mouth (1P/3) → ʔóʔ^{LM} shout   N → V

(34) changes in vowel, tone, stress, and glottal closure   N → ADJ
ɲif^H salt → ɲieʔ^H salty

The noun ʔɲie^{HL} 'rope' yields several related verbs, each one exhibiting a variety of modifications.

(35) ʔɲie^{HL} rope → ʔɲiéi^{LM} tie up (TA)
    → ʔɲiéiʔ^{LM} tether (TA)
    → ʔɲieiʔ^{LM} tie together (TI)
    → ʔɲie^M tie up (TI)
    → ʔɲieʔ^M retie (TI)
    → ʔɲiéiʔ^{ML} tie to (something) (DI)

It is difficult to say categorically that the derivational process is N → ADJ and N → V rather than ADJ → N and V → N. In (29), it is perhaps easier to see hnai^{MH} 'lid' as deriving from the verb hnai^{LM} 'shut, close' than the other way around. It is hard to imagine, however, the derivation of kuo^M 'hand' in (32) from an unusual verb such as kuoʔ^M 'thrust hand into'. There are no comparable verbs from which other body parts such as ta^L 'foot' or ci^{fH} 'head' might be derived. Among all the phonological irregularity it would be gratifying at least to posit a common source (that is, nouns) for the derived adjective and verb stems.

3.2 Affixation

The causative prefix and a set of posture-orientation prefixes function to form derived stems.

má^M- (causative). The causative prefix *má^M-* is generally productive, combining with many, but not all adjectives[13] and a few nouns and adverbs, resulting in transitive verbs which are generally causative in implication. It, rather than the following root, inflects for person and tense, as in the case of other disyllabic verbs (§4.4). For example, *má^M-* marks a derived verb as third-person present tense, while *ma^L-* marks it as third-person future. Past tense is marked by prefixing *ka^L-* (remote past) or *li^M-* (hodiernal past) to the derived future stem.

(36)   ka^L-ma^L-ciú^{LM} cú^M má^{LM} kiú^{HL}
      PAST-CAUS-good^TI^3 3   food   have^STI^1PL
      She prepared our food.

The adjective roots of most derived transitive verbs do not undergo any modification.

(37)   háu^M empty (IN) → má^{M}háu^M tidy up (TI)
      cõ^M true (IN) → má^{M}cõ^M assess, judge (TI)
      ciú^{LM} good (IN) → má^{M}ciú^{LM} prepare (TI)
      hue?^{LM} large (IN) → má^{M}hue?^{LM} enlarge (TI)

There are, however, some derived transitive verbs in which the adjective roots undergo tone and stress changes, and occasionally nasalization as well.

(38)   cõ^L accused (AN) → má^{M}cõ^{HL} capture (TA)
      tié?^{L} castrated (AN) → má^{M}tiẽ?^{M} castrate (TA)

Transitive verbs derived from adjectives are illustrated in (39) and (40).

(39)   hlá?^{H} ré^M hmá^L má^{LM} má^M-ciú^{LM} ?iá^{H}tï^{LM}
      really well be^tasty^SII food   CAUS^PRES-good^TI female^teacher
      The food which the lady teacher prepares is really delicious.

---

[13]Adjectives are marked for animacy when there are separate animate (AN) and inanimate (IN) forms as in *tiáu^M* 'white (AN)', *tiáu^M* 'white (IN)'. An adjective for which only one form exists is not so marked, as in *dáï^L* 'red'.

(40) né^{LM} bí?^{H} ma^L-hue?^{LM} fé^L cio^L
today AFF CAUS^FUT-large^TI Felix cut^field^3
Shortly, Felix will enlarge the area of his field.

I have found only two transitive verbs derived from adverb roots; má^{M}ré^M of (41b) is illustrated in (42).

(41) a. uóu?^{LM} far away → má^{M}uóu?^{LM} move away (IA)
b. ré^M well → má^{M}ré^M arrange, adjudicate (TI)

(42) cáu^{HL} cá^M hmí^H tiáu?^{H} ?ŋiu^{L}mí^{H}ŋií^M má^M
crime^3 person TRM occupy^IA^PRES^3P jail   PRF

ná^H-má^M-ré^M cá^{L}tã^{MH} ta^{L}né^{LM}
PROG-CAUS^PRES-well^TI authorities now
The crimes of those who were in jail are now being adjudicated by the town authorities.

Transitive verbs derived from nouns are relatively uncommon; most appear to undergo tone and stress changes, but in a few derived verbs the root remains unaltered. A sentential example using the derived transitive verb in (43a) is given in (45).

(43) a. ?ma?^{MH} price, wage → má^M?ma?^{H} pay (TI)
b. co^L crime, sin → má^{M}cõ^{HL} punish (TA)

(44) li^{MH} signal, proof → má^{M}li^{MH} demonstrate (TI)

(45) ?liáu^L kïe^L ka^L-ma^L-?ma?^{H} ie?^{L} ciáu^L
plentiful^IN money PAST-CAUS-wage^TI elder yesterday
The old man paid a large wage yesterday.

The causative prefix má^M- can be affixed to inalienable nouns which refer to items associated with human usage or that can be owned; that is, not kinship terms, bodily excretions, or body parts (§6.2). For example, the noun ?ŋiú^{HL} 'house (1P/3 POSS)' can become the verb má^M?ŋiú^{HL} 'acquire a house'.[14]

(46) ?ŋiú^L ní^M bí?^{H} má^M ka^L-ma^L-hŋiú^{HL} cú^M
house that AFF PRF PAST-CAUS-house^TI^3 3
He has acquired that house.

---

[14]Even though native speakers find the verbalizing of inalienable nouns by má^M- to be grammatical, they regard it as an unusual construction.

(47) ʔŋiúᴸ nĩᴹ bíʔᴴ máᴹ máᴴ-ʔŋiúᴸᴹ   hnáᴴᴸ
     house that AFF PRF CAUSˆFUT-houseˆTIˆ1S I
     I will now acquire that house.

In Foris 1980 I proposed that inalienable nouns could also be verbalized by the intransitivizing prefix *lĩᴹ*-, as in (48). I now realize that illocutionary particles such as *iáʔᴸ* (ASSR) can intrude between *lĩᴹ* and the inalienable noun, as in (49). Since illocutionary particles cannot intrude between affix and stem (§11), example (49) must be analyzed as the verb *lĩᴹ* 'become' followed by *ʔŋiuᴸᴹ* 'house (1S)' as complement.

(48) ʔŋiúᴸ nĩᴹ bíʔᴴ máᴹ kaᴸ-lĩᴸ-ʔŋiuᴴᴸ   hnáᴸᴹ
     house that AFF PRF PAST-INTRV-houseˆ1S I
     That house is the house that became mine.

(49) ʔŋiúᴸ nĩᴹ bíʔᴴ máᴹ kaᴸ-lĩᴸ   iáʔᴸ hŋiuᴸᴹ hnáᴴᴸ
     house that AFF PRF PAST-becomeˆIIˆPRESˆ3 ASSR houseˆ1S I
     That house is the house that became mine.

Posture-orientation prefixes. These prefixes are described in greater detail in the discussion of verb structure in §4, but must be mentioned here along with *ʔíᴴ-* (progressive motion) in their role as derivational affixes.[15] These prefixes are presented in (50) with their meanings when not used derivationally.

(50) *cíᶠᴴ-* (vertical, sustained, indefinite, singular)
     kuáᴴ- (sitting, indefinite, singular)
     díᴴ-   (vertical singular)
     ráᴴ-   (horizontal singular)
     ʔúᴴ-   (containing singular)
     náᴴ-   (plural)
     ʔíᴴ-   (motion)

When these prefixes function derivationally, the root to which they are affixed may undergo phonological changes in tone, stress, vowels, and nasalization. They can combine with verbs, adjectives, adverbs, or nouns to produce adjectives, adverbs, and nouns. The classes of base roots and the resultant classes of derived stems produced by this set of derivational prefixes are listed in matrix (51), where rows indicate base classes and columns derived classes.

---

[15]Because of limited output of this derivational process it may be best regarded as nonproductive, "serving simply to analyze existing word forms in the lexicon" (Anderson 1985:56).

(51)
	N	ADJ	ADV
N	X	X	X
V	X	X	X
ADJ		X	X
ADV			X

As derivational prefixes, they individually exhibit varying degrees of semantic bleaching. Sometimes it is no longer clear why one prefix is preferred over another. In many derived stems, for example, the posture distinction between $kuá^H$- (sitting singular) and $dí^H$- (vertical singular) seems to be lost, both prefixes simply marking singular in contrast to $ná^H$-, which regularly marks plurality on the same root.

The apparently idiosyncratic preference for $kuá^H$- (sitting singular) or $dí^H$- (vertical singular) can be seen in the way they combine with the verbs $ʔíe^M$ 'nominate, appoint (TA)' and $ʔlá ʔ^H$ 'earn (TI)', respectively.

(52) $kuá^H ʔíe^H$ nominated singular
      $ná^H ʔíe^H$ nominated plural

(53) $dí^H ʔlá ʔ^H$ indentured singular
      $ná^H ʔlá ʔ^H$ indentured plural

In other instances some recognizable semantic content remains in the prefixes, as can be seen, for example, in the adverbs $rá^H ʔí^L$ 'lying face down', $kuá^H ʔí^L$ 'squatted, crouched, cowering', $dí^H ʔí^L$ 'leaning over, bent (while standing)', where the root $ʔí^L$ is not a free morpheme.

Of the seven derivational prefixes in this set, $cí^H$- (upright sustained singular) is the most productive; $dí^M$- (vertical singular) and $ʔú^H$- (containing singular) have maintained their posture orientation the most, and $ná^H$- (plural) consistently marks the derived stem as plural. Each prefix is discussed in turn below.

$cí^H$- (vertical, sustained, indefinite, singular). When $cí^H$- functions as a progressive prefix, it marks the posture of the subject/agent as either upright, indefinite, or participating in some kind of sustained action (for example, the pushing and shoving of a crowd). Being the least specific of the posture-oriented prefixes, in its derivational function it forms a wide variety of stems.

(54) a. $ʔméi ʔ^{LM}$ blink (TI) → $cí^H ʔmí ʔ^H$ shut-eyed (N)
     b. $hã^M$ get ahead (IA) → $cí^H há^L$ ahead (ADV)
     c. $ʔnái̯^L$ widow(er), orphan (ADJ AN) → $cí^H ʔnái̯^L$ incomplete (ADJ)

d. ŋa^M   pass through (TI) → cif^Hŋa^M excessively (ADV)
e. ŋif^H   first (ADJ IN) → cif^Hŋif^H incessantly (ADV)
f. cõ^L   detained (ADJ AN) → cif^Hcõ^L forcibly (ADV)[16]
g. ʔniéi^M struggle (N) → cif^Hʔniéi^M forcefully (ADV)

(55) cif^H-ʔniéi^M   ʔniáuʔ^LM   kuoʔ^HL   ʔnú^M
     INDEF-struggle be^necessary^SII go^nonhome^IA^FUT^2S you^S

ca^Lʔáu^M
tomorrow
You must go tomorrow without fail.

kuá^H- (sitting indefinite). As a progressive aspect prefix, kuá^H- marks the subject/agent of the verb as animate singular, and either seated or with posture unspecified. When used derivationally, it appears that mainly adjective stems result (but note above the adverb kuá^Hʔĩ^L 'crouched'). A few derived stems retain the 'seated' denotation, but usually the posture is irrelevant. In all cases, however, the derived adjective is animate singular.

(56) a. ciã^L leave (TA) → kuá^Hciã^H consecrated (ADJ)[17]
     b. kiãʔ^ML choose (TA) → kuá^Hkiã́ʔ^H chosen (ADJ AN)
     c. ŋif^H first (ADJ IN) → kuá^Hŋif^H preeminent (ADJ AN)[18]

(57) ʔĩ^L   bíʔ^H lĩ^L   hã^M   cá^M kuá^H-ciã^H ŋif^Hk^M dió^LM
     that^AN AFF be^IA^PRES^3 one^AN person INDEF-leave towards God
     That (person) is a person consecrated to God.

dí^H- (vertical singular), i.e., vertical to the earth's plane.[19]

(58) hũʔ^ML fold (TI) → dí^Hhũʔ^L valley (N)
     cáu^M person (N) → dí^Hcáu^M bodily (ADV)
     tĩ^L intact (IA) → dí^Htĩ^L reliable (ADJ AN)

---

[16]The implication of (54f) and (54g) may be identical: a person is being forced to do something against her/his will; however, (54g) may alternatively imply that s/he is determined to do something.
[17]dí^H- (vertical) can substitute for kuá^H- in both (56a) and (56b), expressing the explicit vertical orientation of the person or animal concerned, although kuá^H-, by virtue of its nonspecific orientation, is the more common prefix of the two.
[18]In (56c), since those in authority (preeminent) are generally seated while exercising their power, the sense of 'seated' is retained.
[19]dí^H- can substitute for kuá^H in (56a) and (56b), expressing the explicit vertical orientation of the subject.

(59) ka^L-ma^L-hnia^{LM} cú^M ʔi^L θẽʔ^M dí^H-cáu^M
     PAST-CAUS-appear^TA^3 3   COMP   stand^SIA^3 upright-person
     He presented (himself), standing bodily (i.e., not as a spirit-being or in a vision).

rá^H- (horizontal singular). As a progressive aspect marker, rá^H- denotes that the subject/agent is in a flat or horizontal position. This orientation is preserved in only some derived stems.

(60) kã^{LM} side, edge (N) → rá^{H}kã^M sideways (ADV)
     hua^M ash (N) → rá^{H}huá^{HL} ashen, grey (ADJ IN)
     hua^M ash (N) → rá^{H}huá^M speckled grey (ADJ AN)
     lïʔ^{LM} disk, hoop (N) → rá^{H}lïʔ^M round (ADJ IN)[20]
     hliu^{LM} crooked (ADJ IN) → rá^{H}hliu^{LM} crooked (ADJ IN) (e.g., a path)
     θa^M be altered, be changed (II) → rá^{H}θa^M loose (cash), change
                                                                      (ADJ IN)

(61) tiá^M ki^H hná^{HL} kïe^L rá^H-θa^M
     not   bring^STI^1S   I   money   flat-be^altered
     I didn't bring any change.

ʔu^H- (containing singular). As a progressive aspect marker, ʔu^H- denotes that the subject is enclosed, held, or contained. This denotation carries over in its role as derivational prefix as well, as seen in (62).

(62) ta^{MH} work (N) → ʔu^{H}ta^{MH}/ʔu^{H}tá^H certainly (ADV) (lit., contains work
                                            in the sense of worthwhile, worth the effort)
     cií^H head (1P/3) → ʔu^{H}cií^H hat
     cií^H head (1P/3) → ʔu^{H}cií^{HL} hat (1P/3)

ná^H- (plural).

(63) hni^{ML} enclose (TI) → ná^{H}hni^M sections, rooms (N)
     ŋó^{HL} son-in-law (1P/3) → ná^{H}ŋó^{MH} be brothers-in-law (SIA)
     ʔe^M hang, suspend (II) → ná^{H}ʔe^M identically (ADV)
     hnie^M cloud (N) → ná^{H}hnie^M cloudy (ADJ IN) (many clouds)
     ŋií^H first (ADJ IN) → ná^{H}ŋií^H preeminent (ADJ AN P)
     ʔŋiéiʔ^{ML} tie up (TI) → ná^{H}ʔŋiei^{MH} tied up (ADJ IN) (several items)
     θa^M alter, change (II) → ná^{H}θa^M unequal (ADJ IN)

---

[20]Alternatively, rá^{H}lïʔ^M may derive from lïʔ^{LM} 'roll (II)'.

(64) kǎu^M hmái^H ná^H-hnie^M bí?^{H} né^{LM}
one^IN day INDEF^P-cloud AFF today
It is a cloudy day today (there are many clouds in the sky).

?í^H- (motion). As a verbal prefix, ?í^H- marks progressive motion of unspecified direction. The sense of progressiveness appears to be largely retained when functioning as a derivational prefix, but not motion. Only a few examples of word formation with ?í^H- are known.

(65) tǎ^H complete (ADJ) → ?í^{H}tǎ^H full (moon) (ADJ AN)
tiá^L intensively (ADV) → ?í^{H}tiá^L continuously (ADV)

(66) hlǎ?^{H} ?í^H-tiá^L má^M ka^L-ŋï?^{LM} cá^{M}huú^M
really motion-INTENS PRF PAST-assemble^IA^3 townsfolk
The townsfolk have been assembling continuously.

In addition to examples where the root is readily identifiable, there are several other words which appear to utilize this set of derivational prefixes, but the root is not identifiable as a free morpheme. All are adverbs.

(67) cií^H?lí?^{H} on tiptoe
dí^H?iũ?^{H} upside down
rá^{H}siã^M lying crosswise
?í^{H}siã^M stooping

3.3 Compounding

Compounding is the most productive word formation process in Sochiapan Chinantec. Compound stems are found for most word classes: nouns, adjectives, adverbs, prepositions, and conjunctions. No examples of compound verb stems have been found. Except for certain words such as ti^{LM} 'teacher', hmái^M 'water', and hái^{HL} 'word', which combine with a fairly wide range of nouns and adjectives, compounding does not appear to be a productive process. The phonological, syntactic, and semantic rules presented here are nonproductive, serving only to analyze existing lexemes. The majority of Chinantec compounds yield nouns, regardless of the elements of which the compound is composed. This section is organized around the types of phonological modifications that occur in the formation of compounds. In the following section, the structural classification of compounds is addressed.

Stems may undergo modification by both affixation and compounding, but there are some differences between the two processes. Although phonological modification of the root occurs occasionally with the derivational process of affixation, when compounding occurs, phonological modification of both roots is prevalent. The nonfinal root is more frequently affected than the final root, resulting in a typical nonfinal syllable with (1) deletion of glottal closure, (2) neutralization of syllable stress, and (3) a strong tendency to disallow tone glides. If a glide is neutralized, the resultant level tone is usually the higher component, e.g., /LM/ → /M/ or /HL/ → /H/. In addition, there may be an accompanying tone change, e.g., /M/ → /H/ or vowel change in one or both of the roots. When a nonfinal root already has the tone and segmental characteristics of a nonfinal syllable, it only undergoes stress neutralization.

There are only a few compound words in which a nonfinal syllable retains its vowel glide, as in hui^{MH} 'powder' + $ʔná^Hkuú^M$ 'sugar cane' → $hui^{MH}kuú^M$ 'sugar', but in this case a special condition exists: a nonfinal syllable of the second root is deleted. Moreover, a number of speakers eliminate the tone glide and say $hui^Hkuú^M$. There may be phonological pressure in this direction to increase the differentiation between sugar and the substance called $hui^{MH} kuú^M$ 'maize powder', that is, corn-borer droppings which are used to make a type of porridge.

The majority of compound stems consist of two roots; only a few consist of three roots. These latter stems, however, can be analyzed as a compound of two elements, a root plus a compound stem which itself consists of two roots.

There are (at least) nine patterns of phonological modifications of compounds, seven of which involve more phonological modification than just simply neutralizing the stress of the nonfinal syllable.

Noun roots which undergo phonological modification as the nonfinal element of a compound differ from inalienable nouns which have an inanimate possessor. The noun $táu^M$ 'hole', for example, has two other related forms, to^H and $tá^M$. to^H is an inalienable noun which exhibits a final-syllable stress and does not form a compound, as in $to^H hmá^H$ 'seed-hole'; whereas $tá^H$ is a compounding root which lacks contrastive stress, as in $tá^Mʔláu^M$ 'cave' (formed from $ʔláu^M$ 'cliff').

Other nouns with their alienable, inalienable, and compounding forms are listed in (68).

(68) $hái^{HL}$ $hë^H$ $hú^H$-   word, message
      $ʔio^{MH}$ $ʔio^H$ $ʔiá^H$-   weed
      $láu^M$ lo^L $lá^M$-, or $hú^M$-   skin, hide

The following examples illustrate the types of phonological modifications that may occur. Input stem classes and resulting word classes are supplied to illustrate the variety of compounds that exist within each phonological process.

1. The most common phonological modification in compounds involves a tone-stress change on one or both roots. The class of input stems and resulting forms found for this pattern include $[N-N]_N$, $[N-ADJ]_N$, $[N-PREP]_N$, $[V-N]_N$, $[V-PREP]_N$, and $[V-ADJ]_{ADV}$.

Lexical Formation Strategies   37

(69) $h\tilde{o}^M$ child (1P/3) + $r\tilde{a}i?^{MH}$ kinsman (1P/3) → $h\tilde{o}^H r\tilde{a}i?^{MH}$ sibling
      [N-N]$_N$
      $c\acute{a}i?^L$ roof (3) + $\eta ie?^M$ within → $ci^L \eta ie?^M$ attic [N-PREP]$_N$
      $?o^L$ mouth (1P/3) + $?\eta i\acute{u}^L$ house → $?o^L?\eta i\acute{u}^{HL}$ doorway [N-N]$_N$
      $?m\acute{a}^M$ wood + $ti\acute{e}i^M$ narrow → $?m\acute{a}^M ti\acute{e}i^{HL}$ rod [N-ADJ]$_N$

The noun ti^{LM} 'teacher, master' productively combines with many other nouns as the first root, involving a tone and stress change on ti^{LM}.[21]

(70) ti^{LM} + si^{fM} book → $ti^M si^{fM}$ secretary
      ti^{LM} + $?m\acute{a}^M$ wood → $ti^M?m\acute{a}^M$ carpenter
      ti^{LM} + $mi^{fH}\eta i^{fM}$ metal → $ti^M mi^{fH}\eta i^{fM}$ mechanic

2. The second pattern of modification involves a vocalic change in the first root and, for some stems, tone or stress change in one or both roots. Such shifts, however, are not regular to the point of being able to predict the syntactic class of the derivative.

The input and resulting classes for this pattern are [N-N]$_N$, [N-V]$_N$, [N-ADJ]$_N$ [V-N]$_N$, [ADJ-ADJ]$_{ADJ}$, [ADJ-N]$_{ADJ}$, [ADV-ADV]$_{ADJ}$, [ADV-V]$_{ADV}$, [N-ADV]$_{ADV}$, [ADJ-N]$_{ADV}$, [ADV-ADJ]$_{ADV}$, and [ADV-V]$_{ADV}$. Example (71) shows vocalic, stress, and tone changes to the root when compounded.

(71) $l\acute{a}u^M$ skin + $?o^L$ mouth (1P/3) → $l\acute{u}^M?o^L$ lip (1P/3) [N-N]$_N$
      $l\acute{a}u^M$ skin + ηie^M stretch (TI) → $l\acute{a}^M \eta ie^M$ rubber band [N-V]$_N$
      cio^M lake + si^{fM} fire → $cia^L si^{fM}$ conflagration [N-N]$_N$
      $k\ddot{i}e^L$ money + $d\acute{a}i^L$ red → $k\acute{u}^H d\acute{a}i^L$ coin [N-ADJ]$_N$
      $hm\acute{a}i^M$ liquid + $to?^M$ bee → $hmi^M to?^H$ honey [N-N]$_N$
      $ci\acute{a}u^L$ yesterday + $?lo^{LM}$ late (II) → $cia^L?lo^H$ yesterday evening
      [ADV-V]$_{ADV}$

The noun $h\acute{a}i^{HL}$ 'word', productively combines with many adjectives and a few nouns, involving a tone and stress change on $h\acute{a}i^{HL}$.[22]

---

[21] The compounding of ti^{LM} with various nouns may be a relatively recent phenomenon, as many speakers still utilize the noncompounded forms and regard the two elements as separate words.

[22] Such compounds with $h\acute{a}i^{HL}$ appear to follow the rules for compounds, but when native speakers write their language, they react to most sequences of hu^H- plus an adjective as separate words, whereas hu^H- plus a noun (such as the first example in (72) is readily accepted as a compound word. That the negative $ti\acute{a}^M$ 'not' can be inserted between hu^H plus an adjective, as in hu^H-$ti\acute{a}^M$-$c\tilde{o}^M$ 'untruth', but not other compounds of the form [N-ADJ]$_N$, appears to lend support to native-speaker intuition. Another consideration is that native speakers may be unduly influenced by Spanish. Since Spanish does not exhibit any phonological changes characteristic of compounding in N-ADJ sequences involving *palabra* 'word', and because *palabra* and its following ADJ modifier are written as separate words, Chinantec speakers may feel a (subconscious) desire to separate the Chinantec roots into two words to parallel the Spanish.

(72) *háï^{HL}* word + *to?^{M}* bee → *hú^{H}to?^{M}* boast (noun)
      háï^{HL} word + *cõ^M* true → *hú^{H}cõ^M* truth
      háï^{HL} word + *?ṹ^H* complex → *hú^H?ṹ^H* sarcasm, proverb
      háï^{HL} word + *te^L* ignorant → *hú^{H}te^L* erroneous teaching

3. The third compounding pattern involves a vowel change on the first root, and tone, stress, and vowel change on the second root. Only one example is available.

(73) *mí^{H}hla^M* knife + *keï?^{LM}* close (II) → *mí^{H}hlí^{M}kéï?^{LM}* scissors
      [N-V]$_N$

4. The fourth compounding pattern involves a tone-stress change and loss of glottal closure on the first root.

(74) *tu?^{LM}* bag + *cio^H* heneken → *tú^{M}cio^H* sack [N-N]$_N$
      kuá?^{HL} soil + *kiéi^M* dry → *kuá^{H}kiéi^M* desert [N-ADJ]$_N$
      ?mï?^{LM} cloth + *ɲie^M* stretch → *?mí^{M}ɲie^M* undershirt [N-V]$_N$

5. The fifth compounding pattern involves a loss of glottal closure on the first root together with vowel or tone-stress changes or both. The compounds found are [N-N]$_N$ and [N-ADJ]$_N$.

(75) *ma?^{M}* viper + *tá?^{H}* bamboo → *mí^{M}tá?^{H}* coral snake [N-N]$_N$
      ka?^{M} lizard + *ré?^{M}* green → *ki^{L}ré?^{M}* type of green lizard [N-ADJ]$_N$

6. The sixth compounding pattern requires the second root to be nasalized. Only one example is available.

(76) *cá^M* person + *ta^{MH}* task → *cá^{M}tã^{MH}* authorities [N-N]$_N$

7. Because of the scarcity of stems that are comprised of a root plus a stem, and the fact that each of them appears to be unique in the type of phonological change involved, they are grouped together here. The compounds have the form [N-[V-N]$_{ADJ}$]$_N$ or [ADV-[ADV-V]$_V$]$_{ADV}$, respectively.

(77) *?má^M* wood + *ɲii?^{LM}* ignite (II) + *sí^M* fire → *?má^{M}ɲií^{M}sí^M* match
      kãu^M simply + *diá^M* not + *hã^M* wait (TA) → *ku^{L}diá^{M}hã^M*
                                                                    suddenly

8. Some stems are compounds of an identifiable free root plus another morpheme for which the meaning may be inferred, although it never occurs

Lexical Formation Strategies

on its own. In (78), those roots which are affixed with a hyphen are found only as a bound form.

(78) $cá^M$ person + $-dãu^{LM}$ old → $cá^M dãu^{LM}$ old person
      $?í^L$ tortilla + $-mii?^{MH}$ foreign → $?í^H mii?^{MH}$ bread
      $hái^{HL}$ word + $-mii?^{MH}$ foreign → $hu^H mii?^{MH}$ Spanish
      $hmái^M$ water + $-mii?^{MH}$ foreign → $hmí^M mii?^{MH}$ ocean
      $kuú^M$ maize + $-mii?^{MH}$ foreign → $kuú^M mii?^{MH}$ wheat, rye

There are other compounds in which neither morpheme is a free root, but one morpheme keeps recurring, and so the meaning may be inferred. The ancillary morpheme on its own, however, is meaningless (a 'cranberry' morpheme). For example, the morpheme $mí^H$- appears to mean 'metallic', but the morphemes $-ŋií^M$, $-hma^M$, $-hla^M$, $-tái^L$, and $-?u^{LM}$ are meaningless on their own. An exception is the word $mí^H cií^H$ 'axe', which is a compound of $mí^H$- 'metallic' and $cií^H$ 'head'.

(79) $mí^H ŋií^M$ bell, metal $mí^H hma^M$ shovel
     $mí^H hla^M$ knife $mí^H tái^L$ machete
     $mí^H ?u^{LM}$ chisel

The final group of words discussed in this section is a mixture of (1) compounds formed from an identifiable free root plus a bound morpheme for which the meaning may be inferred, and (2) compounds for which neither root occurs as a free morpheme, but one root keeps recurring. The factor that unifies this group of words is that they share many of the characteristics of what Welmers (1973:459-74) describes as "ideophones" for various African languages (see also Schachter 1985:21).

Almost all Chinantec ideophones are manner adverbs, representing specific sounds and imparting a vividness or picturesqueness to the utterance. Some ideophones are onomatopoeic such as $pã?^L$ 'glug' (the sound of swallowing water), but with other ideophones, such as hla^L 'thud' (the sound of a galloping horse or running feet), it is difficult to see the correlation between the phonetics of the word and the sound to which it refers.

Phonologically, all ideophones have only simple tones, usually low tone; other adverbs, however, have either simple tones (e.g., $kái^M$ 'later') or glides (e.g., $lí^{LM}$ 'very'). A few ideophones are anomalous as to the sequence of phonemes which occur. All five words that begin with the sequence *pou*, for example, are ideophones, as in $póu^L$ 'thump, bang' and $póu^H$ (noise of snakes at night). The adverb $uá^H θř^L$ (defecate noisily), for example, has the unique sequence /θř/ (a voiceless interdental fricative, followed by a flapped r), which is found only in onomatopoeic words.

All manner adverbs that have *uá^H*- 'quite' as their first root are ideophones, but words such as *uá^Hhĩʔ^H* 'even though' and *uá^Hlíʔ^L* 'never' have *uá^H*- as their first root and are not ideophones. *uá^H*- 'quite' conveys a sense of intensity to a punctiliar event. Only three ideophones compounded with *uá^H*- occur in my data, but it is likely that more exist. The final syllables of these forms, in (80), do not occur as free roots.

(80) *uá^Hhua^L* thud (sound of falling onto weeds or soft ground)
      uá^Hpṍ^L boom (sound of a heavy door banging shut)
      uá^Hθřḭ^L (noise of explosive defecation)

(81) *kãu^M*   *uá^H-hua^L*   *ka^L-tá̰ʔ^L*   *ʔnú^M*
     simply   quite-thud   PAST-fall^IA^2S   you^S
     You fell with quite a thud.

Some ideophones may repeat, a feature not found with other adverbs. *põuʔ^L* 'thud, thump', for example, may occur on its own or be repeated.

(82) *ka^Lla^L*   *põuʔ^L*   *ka^L-tá̰ʔ^L*   *háʔ^L*
     really   thud   PAST-fall^IA^3S   animal
     The animal fell with a real thud (when it was shot).

(83) *põuʔ^L*   *põuʔ^L*   *ɲi^LM*   *huʔ^MH*
     thump   thump   walk^IA^PRES^3S   armadillo
     The armadillo walks thump thump.

Several ideophones are optionally prefaced by *pa^Li^L*- 'quite', resulting in a trisyllabic stem which is not found in other adverbs. *pa^Li^L*- conveys a sense of intensity and iterativity in contrast to *uá^H*- 'quite' which conveys a sense of intensity to a punctiliar event.

(84) *ka^Lla^L*   *pa^Li^L-põuʔ^L*   *hmu^M*   *cú^M*   *ta^MH*   *kioʔ^MH*
     really   quite-thump   do^TI^PRES^3   3   work   have^STI^3
     S/he really thumps and bangs around when working.

(85) *kuá^H-hmu^M*   *cá^M*   *cō^L*   *pa^Li^L-tḭ̃^L*   *ʔɲiu^Lmí^Hɲi^M*
     INDEF^PROG-do^TI^3   person   accused   quite-crash   jail
     The accused is banging and crashing around in the jail.

(86) *ka^Lla^L*   *pa^Li^L-pã̰ʔ^L*   *nä̰ïʔ^L*   *cú^M*   *hmái^M*
     really   quite-glug   swallow^TI^PRES^3   3   water
     S/he really glugs down the water.

Lexical Formation Strategies

Ideophones such as $hlié^L$ 'snort', $pã?^L$ 'glug', $póu^L$ 'bang', and $põu?^L$ 'thud', which exist as free roots, undergo no phonological modification when compounded with pa^Li^L- 'quite'. Nonadverb roots which otherwise are not ideophones, however, undergo tone and stress changes when compounded with pa^Li^L-.

(87) $huá^{ML}$ shake (II/TI) → $pa^Li^Lhua^L$ clatter
 $siu?^{MH}$ crisp, dry (ADJ IN) → $pa^Li^Lsiu?^L$ rustle
 $tĩ^{ML}$ fight (IA) → $pa^Li^Ltĩ^L$ rumble, crash, bang

All ideophones with pa^Li^L- 'quite' which have been found to date are listed in (88).

(88) $pa^Li^L?ne?^L$ creak (of house in an earthquake)
 $pa^Li^Lhaï?^L$ swish (of timber being cut)
 $pa^Li^Lhla^L$ thud (of galloping, running feet)
 $pa^Li^Lhlia?^L$ slap (slap on the face)
 $pa^Li^Lhlié^L$ snort, snuffle (of pig)
 $pa^Li^Lhlo?^L$ bubble (of boiling water)
 $pa^Li^Lhua^L$ clatter (of putting dishes away)
 $pa^Li^Lpã?^L$ glug (of swallowing water)
 $pa^Li^Lpóu^L$ bang (of furniture, utensils, fireworks)
 $pa^Li^Lpõu^L$ clatter (of working energetically)
 $pa^Li^Lsiĩ^L$ snuffle (of heavy breathing when asleep)
 $pa^Li^Lsiu?^L$ rustle (of walking through dry leaves)
 $pa^Li^Ltĩ^L$ rumble (of thunder, drums)

Two known ideophones may also be used in a way which does not represent a sound: $póu^L$ 'thump' may function as an intensifier with sense 'tremendously', and $póu^H$ (of snake at night) may function like an adjective with the sense 'jiggly' (due to fattiness).

(89) $ó^{LM}$ $θe?^M$ $káu^M$ $?má^M$ pa^{MH} $póu^L$
 yonder stand^SII one^IN tree   big   tremendously
 Over there stands a tremendously big tree.

(90) $nĩ^M$ $kuá^H$-ha^{LM} $cá^Mmi^L$ $póu^H$ $hmí?^H$ $?í^L$
 there INDEF^PROG-come^IA^3S woman jiggly rump^3 that^AN
 Here comes that woman with a jiggly rump.

No single phonological or syntactic criterion distinguishes a Chinantec ideophone. Rather, a set of partially overlapping features help to identify them: (1) the first root may be $uá^H$- 'quite' or pa^Li^L- 'quite', (2) the root is most likely a manner adverb referencing a kind of noise, (3) it may be repeated, (4) it has simple tones, usually low, and (5) it may have anomalous phonological features. As Welmers remarks, "the borderline between the normal lexicon and ideophones may not be sharply defined in all respects" (1973:467). The only feature common to all ideophones is humor—a mischievous twinkle to the eye, a smile, or outright laughter inevitably accompanies their use as even serious situations (for example, a prisoner trying to break out of jail) are made light of.

9. In the ninth and final compounding process, the only phonological change is stress neutralization of nonfinal syllables. Both elements may occur as free roots, but the meaning of the whole is not readily predictable from the component parts. Nor can any other lexeme be inserted between the two elements that make up the compound.

(91) $\textit{ʔmá}^M$ wood + si^H saddle → $\textit{ʔmá}^M si^H$ chair [N-N]$_N$
$mí^H ŋií^H$ metal + $há^H$ tooth (1P/3) → $mí^H ŋií^M há^H$ saw [N-N]$_N$
$hŋií^M$ vein (1P/3) + mu^H bone (1P/3) → $hŋií^M mu^H$ body (1P/3)
[N-N]$_N$
$cá^M$ person + $lái^H$ illustrated → $cá^M lái^H$ doll [N-ADJ]$_N$
si^M fire + $kuïʔ^{LM}$ squeeze (TI) → $si^M kuïʔ^{LM}$ flashlight [N-V]$_N$
$ʔŋiu^L$ within + $mi^L kuú^M$ world → $ʔŋiu^L mi^L kuú^M$ heaven
[PREP-N]$_N$
ku^L simply + $tí^L$ be complete (II) → $ku^L tí^L$ certainly [ADV-V]$_{ADV}$
$ní^H$ when (FUT) + $huáʔ^L$ say (TI^FUT^3) → $ní^H huáʔ^L$ if
[CONJ-V]$_{CONJ}$

3.4 Classification of compounds

This section follows Anderson's (1985:46–52) formal structure classification of compounds—modified-modifier, modifier-modified, verb-object, and subject-predicate—ending with a discussion of coordinate compounds.

Modified-modifier compounds. The second element of this type of compound modifies the first, paralleling normal NP structure (§6). They function as nouns, adverbs, or adjectives.

(92) $hmái^M$ liquid + $toʔ^M$ bee → $hmí^M toʔ^H$ honey [N-N]$_N$
$hmái^M$ liquid + $ráu^L$ sweet → $hmí^M ráu^L$ refreshment [N-ADJ]$_N$
$ʔu^{LM}$ glass + $hnióʔ^{LM}$ see far (SIA) → $ʔú^M hnióʔ^{LM}$ telescope,
binoculars, microscope,
magnifying glass [N-V]$_N$
$cáïʔ^L$ roof (3) + $ŋieʔ^M$ within → $cí^L ŋieʔ^M$ attic [N-PREP]$_N$

ciáu^L yesterday + *ʔlo^{LM}* become late (II) → *cia^{L}ʔlo^H* yesterday evening [ADV-V]$_{ADV}$
ʔu^{MH} be contained (II) + *niéi^M* darkness → *ʔú^{M}niéi^M* dawn [V-ADJ]$_{ADV}$
hmái^H day + *tí^M* prior → *hmí^{H}tí^M* previously [N-ADV]$_{ADV}$
ta^L while + *né^{LM}* today, now → *ta^{L}né^{LM}* immediately [CONJ-ADV]$_{ADV}$
mí^{M}niáu^L yellow + *réʔ^M* green → *mí^{M}nia^{L}réʔ^M* chartreuse [ADJ-ADJ]$_{ADJ}$
mí^{M}niáu^L yellow + *hlái^M* egg → *mí^{M}nia^{L}hlái^M* egg-yolk yellow [ADJ-N]$_{ADJ}$

Modifier-modified compounds. Most modifier-modified compounds involve the quantifier *kåu^M* (meaning 'one') which functions both adjectivally and adverbially (meaning 'simply, just') when preceding the element it modifies.[23]

(93) *kåu^M* one + *hmái^H* day → *ká^{M}hmái^H* long ago [ADJ-N]$_{ADV}$
kåu^M simply + *hueʔ^{LM}* large → *kú^{M}hueʔ^{LM}* preferably [ADV-ADJ]$_{ADV}$
kåu^M simply + *tí^L* be complete (II) → *ku^{L}tí^L* certainly [ADV-V]$_{ADV}$
kåu^M simply + *diá^M* not + *hã^M* wait (TA) → *ku^{L}diá^{M}hã^M* suddenly [ADV-[ADV-V]$_V$]$_{ADV}$
kåu^M simply + *ré^M* well → *ká^{M}ré^M* alike [ADV-ADV]$_{ADJ}$
kó^{LM} periphery + *huú^M* town → *kú^{M}huú^M* foreign [N-N]$_{ADJ}$
co^M straight + *ta^{MH}* work → *cú^{M}ta^{MH}* upright [ADJ-N]$_{ADJ}$
ni^H when (FUT) + *huáʔ^L* say (TI^FUT^3) → *ni^{H}huáʔ^L* if [CONJ-V]$_{CONJ}$

Verb-object compounds. Verb-object compounds are uncommon.

(94) *kai^{LM}* tear (TI) + *ʔáu^M* herb → *ká^{H}ʔáu^M* chicken [V-N]$_N$

Subject-predicate compounds. In subject-predicate compounds, the noun which functions as the subject precedes the verb, unlike the unmarked VSO structure of Chinantec. Those compounds that consist of two elements all have the form [N-V]$_N$.

(95) *ʔmá^M* wood + *cã^{LM}* dance → *ʔmá^{M}cã^{LM}* (toy) top

---

[23] *kåu^M* may also follow the noun it modifies, meaning 'other, next', as in *sií^M kåu^M* '(the) other book', and *mií^M kåu^M* 'next year', but in this position it does not form compounds.

Coordinate compounds. Coordinate compounds consist "of two (or more) members of the same lexical class" (Anderson 1985:50). The other important characteristics of coordinate compounds is that (1) neither element can be identified as the center; that is, one element cannot be identified as the modified element, and the other as modifier; and (2) they can be assigned a unitary meaning; that is, they are not merely logical conjunctions. For example, the difference between (96) and (97) is that the former has *ʔŋiú^L* 'house' as its center, whereas the latter has no center.

(96) *ʔŋiú^L* house + *mí^{H}ŋií^M* metal → *ʔŋiú^{L}mí^{H}ŋií^M* jail

(97) *hŋií^M* vein (1P/3) + *mú^{LM}* bone (1P/3) → *hŋií^{M}mu^H* body (1P/3)

Although Anderson (1985:50) observes that such compounds "may function as a member of the same class as its members, or as a member of other classes," only nouns have been found to form such compounds in Sochiapan Chinantec, and the compounds function solely as nouns.

(98) *kuáʔ^{HL}* soil + *ʔué^{LM}* land → *kuá^{H}ʔué^{MH}* planet
      ʔŋá^H forest + *máʔ^L* mountain → *ʔŋá^{H}máʔ^L* world
      kuaʔ^{MH} gourd + *uõ^M* plate → *kuá^{H}uõ^M* gourd bowl, crockery

3.5–3.6 Binomial and polynomial expressions

The term BINOMIAL is used by Kikuchi (1985) to refer to constructions consisting of two juxtaposed words of the same word class, some of which are frozen in a strict order, and others which are not. I have called constructions with more than two juxtaposed words of the same word class POLYNOMIALS. The features which distinguish binomial and polynomial expressions from compounds in Sochiapan Chinantec are:

1. The potential for pause between the elements of a binomial,
2. Some binomials permit reversal of the elements, a feature which cannot occur in compounds,
3. No compounds of three members of the same lexical class exist, whereas such polynomial expressions are found which function as a single lexeme.
4. Unlike compounds, binomial nouns may be comprised of two inalienable nouns or two alienable nouns, but not a mixture of both, and
5. Stress neutralization, simplification of tones and loss of glottal closure do not occur in the nonfinal base of binomial expressions, except in the case of binomial verbs. The two verb bases do not form a compound, however, as an adverb may be repeated with both bases.

Both binomials and polynomials serve to extend the Chinantec lexicon. The following discussion centers primarily around the identification and structure of irreversible binomials, followed by a brief look at the structure of nonpermutable polynomials.

Binomials are far more common than polynomials in Sochiapan Chinantec. They can be regarded as idioms, but they function as lexemes with the identifiable part-of-speech characteristics of word classes. I do not discuss idiomatic expressions such as *a stitch in time saves nine* or *kick the bucket*, nor do I discuss idioms which function as a nominal like those in (99).

(99) a. *mí^{H}ɲif^M hmu^M cú^M ?ué?^{L}*
    metal   do^TI^PRES^3 3   symbol
    typewriter

b. *tu?^{LM} tio?^{LM} ta^L cú^M*
    bag   contain^II^PRES^3P foot^3 3
    shoes

3.5 Binomial expressions

A Chinantec coordinate phrase requires a coordinator such as *?ï^L* 'and' or *hï^L* 'also, and' (§6.12), whereas elements are simply juxtaposed in binomial expressions. The contrast is illustrated in (100).

(100) a. *la^L hãu^M ka^L-huá?^{L} hméi^M cú^M hï^L mí^{H}θiú^{HL} cú^M*
    idea that^IN PAST-say^TI^3 father^3 3   and   mother^3 3
    That is what (both) her/his father and mother said.

b. *la^L hãu^M ka^L-huá?^{L} hméi^M mí^{H}θiú^{HL} cú^M*
    idea that^IN PAST-say^TI^3 father^3 mother^3 3
    That is what her/his parents said.

In discussing translation problems, Kikuchi (1985) uses two terms which are useful in talking about binomials. She labels English expressions such as brothers and sisters as PREFERRED EXPRESSIONS since the elements may be reversed with no appreciable change of meaning. Through repeated usage, preferred expressions can turn into irreversible CONVENTIONAL EXPRESSIONS. I do not here attempt to evaluate the degree of conventionalization of the preferred expressions in (101), but have found that Chinantec speakers readily understand them when reversed, although they regard the reversal as highly amusing. Note that both components of an inalienable binomial expression decline for person.

(101) a. dí^{H}ʔio^L ŋiú^{H}de^{ʔL}
       grandmother^1P grandfather^1P → our grandparents

   b. ŋieʔ^M mí^{M}θiúʔ^M
      father^2 mother^2 → your parents

   c. cá^{M}mï^L cá^{M}ŋiuʔ^M
      woman   man → ladies and gentlemen, people

   d. cii^L ʔlaʔ^{MH} cii^L náï^M
      DIM cricket DIM grasshopper → hopping insects

Kikuchi identifies two subtypes of CONVENTIONAL EXPRESSIONS: (a) those which "cannot be interpreted literally and have unique conventional interpretations" (Kikuchi 1985:62), such as *spic and span*, and (b) those which have a conventional meaning in addition to a literal meaning, such as *oil and water*, which has its literal meaning and the conventional meaning "incompatible" (p. 64). Most Chinantec binomials appear to have only conventional meanings.

Irreversible Sochiapan Chinantec binomials are found for the open-class parts of speech: nouns, adjectives, adverbs, and verbs. Binomial nouns exhibit a new meaning which is more often than not transparently derived from the parts. Binomial adjectives, adverbs, and verbs usually denote an intensification of the attribute or action. Binomial verbs also convey a durative, intensity, iterative, or complete-affectedness sense as well. Binomial verbs frequently acquire a meaning that is not readily transparent as the sum of the parts. Binomial adverbs are unlike the other binomials in that the two bases of which they are composed are not necessarily themselves adverbs.

Binomial nouns. There are alienable and inalienable binomial nouns. As mentioned above, the nonfinal base of a binomial noun does not undergo any of the phonological modifications that regularly occur in compounds.

(102) mí^{H}θioʔ^{MH} source + sï^M fire → generator
       kuaʔ^{MH} gourd + ʔia^{LM} jar → kitchenware
       ʔŋiú^L house + kú^{H}hẽ^M sheet metal → iron-roofed house
       hmï^L rain + cii^L wind → gale
       mï^L-hmá^L fruit-tasty + mï^L-ráu^L fruit-sweet → edible fruit
       cá^{M}kuuï^M person^hand + cá^{M}ta^L person^foot → assistant (1P/3)[24]

---

[24]cá^{M}kuuï^M is clearly a compound stem of cá^M 'person' + kuo^M 'hand, arm (1P/3)' due to the vowel and tone-stress change from kuo^M to kuuï^M. No phonological changes occur with the final root of cá^{M}ta^L, but being the second component of a juxtaposition, with parallel semantics, it too is a compound stem.

Lexical Formation Strategies 47

The measurement *káM táuM* 'one span' normally refers to the distance from fingertip to mid-chest, with outstretched arm. When this measurement is repeated, *káM táuM káM táuM*, the meaning is 'from one side through to the other'.

(103) *ŋaM   hoʔH káM táuM káM táuM*
       pass^TI^PRES light one span one span
       The light passes from one side through to the other.

Binomial adjectives. There are two types of binomial adjectives, those that require a repetition of the NP head, and those that do not. The former type is an AB AC doublet, in which A is the repeated noun, and B and C are semantically similar adjectives. Binomial adjectives which require a repetition of the head noun differ from apposed NPs (chapter 9) in that they often denote plurality as well. Most binomial adjectives of this type consist of two synonymous adjectives, as in (104).

(104) a. *piʔMH   siūH*
         small   little → tiny (AN^P)

   b. *háʔL   piʔMH   háʔL   siūH*
      animal small   animal little^AN
      tiny animals (refers mainly to insects)

   c. *cáM   piʔMH   cáM   siūH*
      person small   person little^AN
      tiny people (i.e., toddlers)

(105) a. *ʔŋáH   náïM*
         undomesticated wild → wild/savage (AN^P)

   b. *háʔL   ʔŋáH   háʔL   náïM*
      animal undomesticated^AN animal wild → wild animals

(106) a. *ʔlaʔL   ʔóLM*
         bad   repugnant → despicable, contemptible, repulsive (IN)

   b. *ʔiL   ʔlaʔL   ʔiL   ʔóLM*
      thing   bad^IN   thing repugnant^IN → despicable thing (s)

The first base of some binomial adjectives appears to be *kúM* 'just, simply'. Unlike modifier-modified compounds with *kúM*, however, the modified noun is repeated.

(107) cáᴹ   kúᴹ   cáᴹ   lā́uᴸ
person just person bare^ᴀɴ
entirely bare person

Repetition of the noun with each base of the binomial adjective is not obligatory with those binomials whose first base is *kúᴹ*. The longer form conveys a stronger sentiment.

(108) a. cáᴹ   kúᴹ   huẽʔᴹ
person just large^ᴀɴ
mighty, powerful person (e.g., God)

   cáᴹ   kúᴹ   cáᴹ   huẽʔᴹ
person just person large^ᴀɴ
mighty, powerful person

b. cáᴹ   cíʰ   huíᴸ
person silly pitiable
abject person

   cáᴹ   cíʰ   cáᴹ   huíᴸ
person silly person pitiable
abject person

Binomial adverbs. Monomial manner adverbs may precede the element they modify, follow it, or both precede and follow it. No example of a binomial adverb that must precede the element it modifies is known, but both other types have been found.

ʔiúᴹ kuóʔᴸᴹ 'incessantly (lit., day will arrive)' is a binomial, not a compound, because when occurring with it, the adverb *kúᴹ* 'simply' is repeated with both bases forming an AB AC doublet in which the modifier is repeated rather than the head.

(109) hlã̄ʔʰ   kúᴹ   ʔiúᴹ   kúᴹ   kuóʔᴸᴹ ʔíʰ-θauᴸᴹ ʔmaʔᴹʰ
really simply day simply arrive ᴍᴏᴛ-rise^ɪɪ price
Prices are incessantly rising.

This adverb, when unmodified can precede or follow the element it modifies.

(110) ʔiúᴹ   kuóʔᴸᴹ   ʔŋaᴹ   cúᴹ
day arrive ask^ᴛɪ^ᴘʀᴇꜱ^3   3
S/he is incessantly asking.

(111) cá^{M}mi^L ʔí^L hmí^{fH} cá^M-hïe^L ʔiú^M kuó?^{LM} hue^{MH}
woman that^AN TRM   ANDT^PRES-see^TA^3 day arrive judge

ʔí^L
that^AN
That woman used to go incessantly to see that judge.

Many binomial adverbs appear to require the presence of a repeated modifier, never occurring without them as in la^L ʔuá^M la^L hma^M 'night and day', la^L koʔ^L la^L ŋieʔ^L 'inside out', and ha^H huú^M ha^H ʔŋiú^L 'up and down the streets'.

(112) hmu^M cú^M ta^{MH} la^L ʔuá^M la^L hma^M
do^TI^PRES^3 3   work even night even day
S/he works night and day.

(113) kuoʔ^M cú^M liei^{MH} la^L koʔ^L la^L ŋieʔ^L
know^TI^PRES^3 3   law   even outside even inside
S/he knows the law inside out.

(114) ʔe^L ta^{MH} tí^H ŋíʔ^H ʔniu^{LM} ha^H huú^M ha^H ʔŋiú^L
what? work PRES walk^IA^PRES^2S 2S   among town among house
Why are you constantly walking up and down the streets?

Binomial verbs. Many binomial verbs (§4.9) are formed from two semantically related verbs, the first of which usually undergoes the phonological modification of a normal nonfinal syllable. Phonologically and semantically then, they function as single lexemes. Syntactically, however, the two bases function as separate words in that the innermost prefix or adverb that occurs with the first base is obligatorily repeated with the second base as in (115).

(115) a. hláʔ^H ré^M má^M lí^M-ʔlí^M lí^M-liéiʔ^{LM} ieʔ^L hõ^M
much well PRF   HOD-speak^TI HOD-tell^DA^3 elder child^3
The old man really admonished his child well.

b. ka^L-mí^L dí^M ní^{H}huáʔ^L ʔi^L lí^{HL} ʔi^L tiá^M
PAST-ask^TI^3 he if   COMP be^able^II^FUT COMP not

ʔá^H tiá^M ŋá^{HL} dí^M la^L hãu^M
step^on^TI^FUT not   pass^by^TI^FUT^3 he idea that^IN
He asked if it would be possible that he not go through those experiences.

Binomial verbs convey aspectual nuances of intensity, durativity, iterativity, or complete-affectedness. Examples of binomial verbs are listed in (116).

(116) cii^M remove (TI⌢S) + $?ué?^{ML}$ remove (TI⌢P) → cif^M $?ué?^{ML}$
　　　　　　　　　　　　　　　　　　　　　　　　　　extract (TI PL)
　　　$?a^M$ step on (TI) + ηa^M pass by (TI) → $?á^M$ ηa^M experience (TI)
　　　$?ẽ^M$ desire (TI) + $h\tilde{a}^M$ await (TA) → $?é^M$ $h\tilde{a}^M$ anticipate (TA)
　　　$?le?^{LM}$ speak (TI) + $liéi?^{LM}$ tell (TA) → $?lí^M$ $liéi?^{LM}$ admonish
　　　　　　　　　　　　　　　　　　　　　　　　　　　　　　　　(TA)
　　　$?ma^{LM}$ store (TI) + hni^{LM} enclose (TI) → $?má^M$ hni^{LM} conceal (TI)
　　　$\theta ai?^{LM}$ inform (TA) + cia^{LM} relate (TI) → θi^M cia^{LM} proclaim (TI)

Certain verbs, such as $?a^M$ 'step on' and $ki\tilde{u}?^{LM}$ 'strike' (with an instrument), form the first element of several binomial verbs.

(117) $ki\tilde{u}?^{LM}$ strike (TA) + $p\tilde{a}^{ML}$ hit (TA) → $ki\acute{u}^M$ $p\tilde{a}^{ML}$ beat up (TA)
　　　$ki\tilde{u}?^{LM}$ strike (TA) + $h\tilde{i}^M$ scold (TA) → $ki\acute{u}^M$ $h\tilde{i}^M$ discipline (TA)
　　　$ki\tilde{u}?^{LM}$ strike (TA) + $t\tilde{a}i?^{ML}$ obstruct (TA) → $ki\acute{u}^M$ $t\tilde{a}i?^{ML}$
　　　　　　　　　　　　　　　　　　　　　　　　　　　　　argue with (TA)
　　　$ki\tilde{u}?^{LM}$ strike (TA) + $hu\acute{o}u^{LM}$ hurl down (TA) → $ki\acute{u}^M$ $hu\acute{o}u^{LM}$
　　　　　　　　　　　　　　　　　　　　　　　　　　　　　curse (TA)
　　　$ki\tilde{u}?^{LM}$ strike (TA) + $hna?^{ML}$ whack (TA) → $ki\acute{u}^M$ $hna?^{ML}$ malign
　　　　　　　　　　　　　　　　　　　　　　　　　　　　　(TA)

The first base of a binomial verb may also be one of a set of preverbs (PV). Preverbs are semantically empty, but function syntactically like the first base of a binomial verb. They are often used in lieu of a semantically similar second verb stem with which to form a binomial. They have pragmatic force, however, as indicated in (118).[25]

---

[25]The occurrence of the same motion, mood, aspect, or tense prefix on two or successive verbs is one of the characteristics of a serial verb construction. There are several characteristics of Chinantec binomial verbs, however, which differentiate them from serial verb constructions: (1) When the first base has several prefixes, only the innermost prefix is repeated; (2) only two bases ever occur in sequence, whereas serial verb constructions may consist of two or more (Foley and Olsen 1985:18); (3) Foley and Olsen (p. 19) observe that "the second verb in a serial construction is 'always in some sense a further development, result or goal' of the first verb in the construction" (quoting from Lord 1974), whereas the first base of Sochiapan Chinantec binomial verb construction is nearly synonymous with the second base or is a semantically empty preverb; and (4) the existence of binomial nouns, adjectives, and adverbs, provides a ready syntactic pattern for the interpretation of binomial verbs.

Lexical Formation Strategies

(118) $kí^M$ (neutral or mildly approbative)
 $pí^M$ (deprecatory evaluation by speaker)
 $kuú^M$ (desired effect achievable)
 $tú^M$ (desired negative effect achievable)
 $kí^M$ (undesirable effect achievable)
 $tí^M$ (neutral goal)
 $ciú^M$ (neutral or mildly negative goal)
 $\theta iú^M$ (negative goal)

(119) a. $\text{?}liáu^L$ $kí^M$ $kí^{ML}$ $tiú^L$ $kio\text{?}^{MH}$ $\text{?}ái^M$
 soldier PV^PRES remove^TI^PRES^3 rifle have^STI^3 thief
 The soldiers remove the thieves' rifles.

 b. $kí^M$ $cái\text{?}^{ML}$ $cú^M$ $\text{?}\eta ie^{HL}$
    PV^PRES wind^up^TI^PRES^3 3   rope
    S/he winds up the rope (quality of action unspecified).

 c. $pí^M$ $cái\text{?}^{ML}$ $cú^M$ $\text{?}\eta ie^{HL}$
    PV^PRES wind^up^TI^PRES^3 3   rope
    S/he winds up the rope (doing a messy job every time).

 d. $né^{LM}$ $ká\text{?}^L$ $kuú^M$ $\eta ï\text{?}^{ML}$ $\text{?}liáu^L$
    today precisely PV^PRES assemble^TA^PRES^3 soldier

    $cá^M$ $cií^H$ $cá^M$ $ho\text{?}^H$
    person supreme person have^STA^3
    The captain assembles his unit promptly (lit., precisely today) (complete-affectedness and/or iterative).

 e. $tá^H$ $ní^M$ $hlá\text{?}^H$ $kuú^M$ $\text{?}liá^{ML}$ $cá^Hmí\text{?}^H$
    Gustavo that really PV^PRES shove^TA^PRES^3 children

    $rāï\text{?}^{MH}$
    companion^3
    That Gustavo really shoves around his companions (iterative).

 f. $hlá\text{?}^H$ $lí^H$ $tú^M$ $lí^H$ hua^{ML} $cú^M$ $\text{?}ú^Hcií^{HL}$
    really NON PV^PRES NON shake^TI^PRES^3 3   hat^3

    tu^{MH}
    Anthony
    They are tossing Tony's hat around.

g. *la^L*   *ná^H-kí^M*   *ná^H-hmi^{ML}*   *ná$^{\prime M}$*   *rẽ$^{\prime M}$*
apparently PROG^P-PV PROG^P-attack^TA^2 you^P companion^2

la^{L}hmĩ$^{\prime H}$ *hmu^M*   *cái^M*
like   do^TI^PRES^3   dog

Apparently, you are attacking your companions as if you were a dog (metaphorically, e.g., by gossip).

h. *hãu^M*   *ʔŋiú^L*   *hãu^M*   *né^L*   *ka^L-kí^M*   *ká^M-kuõ^L*   *bí$^{\prime H}$*
then   house   that^IN   TOP   PAST-PV   PAST-run^II   AFF

Then as for that house, it fell to pieces.

i. *tí^M*   *hĩ$^{\prime ML}$*   *cú^M*   *hõ^M*
PV^PRES turn^back^TA^PRES^3 3   child^3

S/he corrects her/his child (iterative).

j. *hlá$^{\prime H}$*   *ŋii^L-tí^H*   *ŋii^L-ŋi^{LM}*   *ŋiú^{M}mí$^{\prime H}$*   *nĩ^M*   *ha^H*   *ŋiú^L*
really AMB-PV AMB-walk^IA^3S boy   that among house

That boy is constantly walking back and forth between the houses.

k. *ti^{LM}*   *mĩ^L*   *ciú^M*   *ŋii$^{\prime ML}$*   *cá^M*   *cãu^H*
master medicine PV^PRES check^TA^PRES^3 person sick

hãu^M   *cio$^{\prime HL}$*   *nĩ^{H}huá$^{\prime L}$*   *ʔĩ^M*   *mĩ^{H}uĩ^L*
then   find^TI^FUT^3 if   which illness

hau^M   *cú^M*
take^TA^PRES^3^i>3 3

A doctor investigates the patient thoroughly to find whatever illness s/he may have (lit., whatever illness takes her/him).

l. *má^M*   *θiú^M*   *má^M*   *ʔíe^M*   *cú^M*   *pé^H*   *ʔliá^M*
PRF   PV^PRES PRF indicate^TI^PRES^3 3   Peter because

ka^L-pã^L   *hõ^M*
PAST-strike^TA^3 child^3

They are criticizing Peter because he struck his child (iterative).

3.6 Nonpermutable polynomials

There are a few nonpermutable polynomial expressions, all of which are nouns. The preferred expression *dí^{H}ʔio^L ŋiú^{H}deʔ^L* ('grandmother' +

Lexical Formation Strategies

'grandfather') 'grandparents' may occur in nonpermutable polynomials. Those presented in (120) all denote plurality; the polynomial in (121) does not.

(120) a. *hméi^M*   *dí^H?io^L*   *ŋiú^{H}de?^{L}*
      father^1P   grandmother^1P   grandfather^1P
      our ancestors

     b. *cá^M?ãu^{LM}*   *dí^H?io^L*   *ŋiú^{H}de?^{L}*
        ancestor   grandmother^1P   grandfather^1P
        our remote ancestors (more remote than a.)

     c. *cá^M?ãu^{LM}*   *hméi^M*   *dí^H?io^L*   *ŋiú^{H}de?^{L}*
        ancestor   father^1P   grandmother^1P   grandfather^1P
        our remote ancestors (more remote than b.)

(121) *la^L*   *hãu^M*   *tí^M*   *hmu^M*   *hméi^M*   *dí^H?io^L*
      idea   that^IN   DISC   do^TI^PRES^3   father^1P   grandmother^1P

     ŋiú^{H}de?^{L}   *dí^M*
      grandfather^1P   we^INCL
      That is what our ancestors used to do.

(122) *hui^{LM}*   *ko^H*   *hui^{LM}*   *?ŋiú^{HL}*
      path   community   path   house^3
      home town (1P/3)

hui^{LM} ko^H hui^{LM} ?ŋiú^{HL} 'home town' is an unusual polynomial because it forms an AB AC doublet. A few speakers apply phonological compounding rules to the repeated element *hui^{LM}* 'path' of this polynomial, reducing it to an irreversible binomial.

(123) *huú^M-ko^H*   *huú^M-?ŋiú^{HL}*
      path-community   path-house^3
      home town (1P/3)

3.7 Residue

In addition to the above methods used to expand its lexicon, Chinantec also makes extensive use of metaphor, especially metaphors based on the heart.

(124)   *kiéi^M* dry + *cí^L* heart → be thirsty (IA)
        hŋi?^{LM} kill^self + *cí^L* heart → be preoccupied (IA)

These metaphors are free expressions, not compounds, because phonological compounding rules do not apply, and an adverb may be inserted between the elements of the metaphor.

(125) kiéi^M líˆ^LM cíˆ^L cú^M
     dry   very heart 3
     S/he is very thirsty.

With over 150 examples of 'heart' metaphors collected so far, this merits a separate study.

4
The Verb

Chinantec syntactically encodes two main types of verbs: DYNAMIC and STATE.[26] All Sochiapan Chinantec verbs are inflected for animacy, person-of-subject, and transitivity. An ANIMATE VERB is indexed for animate subject if intransitive, or animate direct object if either transitive or ditransitive. Conversely, an INANIMATE VERB is indexed for inanimate subject if intransitive, or inanimate direct object if either transitive or ditransitive. If the object of a transitive verb is animate, it is further inflected for direct or inverse cross-referencing. Dynamic verbs, but not state verbs, are additionally inflected for tense, mood, motion, and aspect; and some dynamic verbs are inflected for passive voice.[27]

The description of verbs is set forth in this chapter in ten sections. The first seven sections present the complex inflectional details of Sochiapan Chinantec dynamic verbs. This is followed by discussion of derivational prefixes (§4.8), binomial verbs (§4.9), and state verbs and how adjectives differ from state verbs (§4.10).

4.1–4.7 Dynamic verbs

Most nonderived, phonologically simple Sochiapan Chinantec dynamic verbs have a high degree of inflectional complexity, inflecting by tone,

---

[26]Givón (1984:53) distinguishes semantically INSTANTANEOUS verbs, ACTIVITY/PROCESS verbs, and STATES. Chinantec dynamic verbs include both INSTANTANEOUS and ACTIVITY/PROCESS verbs.
[27]The citation form for verbs is the third-person present tense, unless otherwise indicated.

stress, and segmental changes to mark transitivity, animacy, person-of-subject, person-of-object, motion, tense, aspect, and mood. Number of subject or object (in a few verbs) is marked by suppletive forms. Motion, tense, aspect, and mood are usually marked by a prefix in conjunction with internal inflection. Derived dynamic verbs only inflect for animacy of subject or object and person-of-subject.

The analysis of this complex inflectional system is based on a corpus of 607 dynamic verbs. It is unclear whether all inflectional paradigms have been accounted for,[28] but there are three major classes of Sochiapan Chinantec dynamic verbs.

1. Class A verbs have distinct inflectional sets for each of the four person-number categories third person, second person, first-person singular, and first-person plural.

2. Class B verbs have distinct inflectional sets only for third person versus nonthird person, with all nonthird forms exhibiting a single tone-stress combination which differs from all third-person tone-stress combinations.

3. Class C verbs have only one inflectional set for all four person-number categories.

Verb classes A, B, and C are illustrated in (126)–(128), respectively, with tense, aspect, and related categories distinguished along the vertical axis and categories of person distinguished along the horizontal axis.

(126) Class A: $\textit{ʔlia}^{LM}$ push (TI)

	3	2	1S	1P
PRES	$\textit{ʔlia}^{LM}$	$\textit{ʔliaʔ}^{LM}$	$\textit{ʔliá}^{ML}$	$\textit{ʔliá}^{ML}$
FUT	$\textit{ʔliá}^{LM}$	$\textit{ʔliáʔ}^{H}$	$\textit{ʔliá}^{HL}$	$\textit{ʔliá}^{HL}$
PAST	$\textit{ʔliá}^{L}$	$\textit{ʔliáʔ}^{H}$	$\textit{ʔliá}^{L}$	$\textit{ʔliá}^{HL}$
AMB	$\textit{ʔlia}^{MH}$	$\textit{ʔliaʔ}^{MH}$	$\textit{ʔliá}^{HL}$	$\textit{ʔliá}^{HL}$
HORT	$\textit{ʔlia}^{MH}$	xxx	$\textit{ʔliá}^{HL}$	$\textit{ʔliá}^{HL}$
EVID	$\textit{ʔlia}^{MH}$	$\textit{ʔliaʔ}^{MH}$	$\textit{ʔliá}^{HL}$	$\textit{ʔliá}^{HL}$
HOD	$\textit{ʔliá}^{LM}$	$\textit{ʔliáʔ}^{H}$	$\textit{ʔliá}^{L}$	$\textit{ʔliá}^{HL}$
ANDT	$\textit{ʔliá}^{M}$	$\textit{ʔliáʔ}^{H}$	$\textit{ʔliá}^{L}$	$\textit{ʔliá}^{HL}$
PROH	—	$\textit{ʔliá}^{M}$	—	—

---

[28] The 607 dynamic verbs and seven state verbs in the main verb corpus have been carefully checked. A secondary corpus of 322 dynamic verbs and 19 state verbs has been partially checked. The verb analysis does not generally draw on the verbs in the secondary corpus; but portions of the secondary corpus is sometimes used to give a more comprehensive picture than would otherwise be possible from the primary corpus alone. In such instances, verbs have been carefully checked with respect to the point being discussed.

The Verb   57

(127) Class B: ɲiiʔ^{ML} light, ignite (TI)

	3	2	1S	1P
PRES	ɲiiʔ^{ML}	ɲii ʔ^{MH}	ɲii ʔ^{MH}	ɲii ʔ^{MH}
FUT	ɲii ʔ^{L}	ɲii ʔ^{MH}	ɲii ʔ^{MH}	ɲii ʔ^{MH}
PAST	ɲii ʔ^{L}	ɲii ʔ^{MH}	ɲii ʔ^{MH}	ɲii ʔ^{MH}
AMB	ɲii ʔ^{H}	ɲii ʔ^{MH}	ɲii ʔ^{MH}	ɲii ʔ^{MH}
HORT	ɲii ʔ^{H}	xxx	ɲii ʔ^{MH}	ɲii ʔ^{MH}
EVID	ɲii ʔ^{H}	ɲii ʔ^{MH}	ɲii ʔ^{MH}	ɲii ʔ^{MH}
HOD	ɲii ʔ^{L}	ɲii ʔ^{MH}	ɲii ʔ^{MH}	ɲii ʔ^{MH}
ANDT	ɲii ʔ^{L}	ɲii ʔ^{MH}	ɲii ʔ^{MH}	ɲii ʔ^{MH}
PROH	—	ɲii ʔ^{MH}	—	—

(128) Class C: kuõu^{LM} sleep (IA)

	3	2	1S	1P
PRES	kuõu^{LM}	kuõu^{LM}	kuõu^{LM}	kuõu^{LM}
FUT	kuóu^{LM}	kuóu^{LM}	kuóu^{LM}	kuóu^{LM}
PAST	kuóu^{M}	kuóu^{M}	kuóu^{M}	kuóu^{M}
AMB	kuõu^{MH}	kuõu^{MH}	kuõu^{MH}	kuõu^{MH}
HORT	kuóu^{M}	xxx	kuóu^{M}	kuóu^{M}
EVID	kuõu^{MH}	kuõu^{MH}	kuõu^{MH}	kuõu^{MH}
HOD	kuóu^{M}	kuóu^{M}	kuóu^{M}	kuóu^{M}
ANDT	kuóu^{M}	kuóu^{M}	kuóu^{M}	kuóu^{M}
PROH	—	kuóu^{M}	—	—

4.1 Inflectional rules

There are a total of thirty-one prefixes that affect the tone-stress inflection of the verb. The future and present tenses and the second-person imperative are marked purely by tone-stress inflection. The second-person prohibitive is marked by the prohibitive adverb lí^{M} plus tone-stress inflection of the verb.

There are a few automatic tone-stress perturbations on monosyllabic verbs and the final syllable of disyllabic verbs. When referring to the stress and tone of a syllable, the symbols b and c in conjunction with the tone letters represent ballistic stress and controlled stress, respectively. These perturbations are as follows.

1. When a monosyllabic verb with tone-stress b^{LM} follows a verb phrase adverb, or a prefix with tone-stress b^{H}, b^{LM} is perturbed to b^{MH}. The same is true of disyllabic verbs where the final syllable has a tone-stress b^{LM}.

(129) a. *sé^{LM}*   *cú^M cáu^M hmái^M*
      spray^DA^FUT^3 3   people water
      S/he will spray people (with) water.[29]

   b. *hmí^H sé^{MH}*   *cú^M cáu^M hmái^M*
      TRM   spray^DA^FUT^3 3   people water
      S/he intended to spray people (with) water (but didn't).

In addition, the ambulative (AMB) prefix *ɲii^L-* induces the same perturbation of b^{LM} to b^{MH} despite its low tone. Since *ɲii^L-* governs the tone-stress of the verb, there are no minimal pairs to demonstrate this perturbation; however, there are no verbs with tone-stress b^{LM} following *ɲii^L-*.

(130) *ɲii^L-có?^{MH}*   *cú^M mí^{H}tiei^{MH} ho?^{H}*   *ti̱^{L} ó^{LM}*
      AMB-distribute^TA^3 3   cat   have^STA^3 at yonder
      S/he is walking around distributing her/his cats over there.

I, therefore, write the underlying tone-stress b^{LM} for b^{MH} in all verbal inflection charts. The tone-stress b^{MH} is used in examples, however, following native-speaker perception of a difference between b^{LM} and b^{MH}.

2. There are two tones which appear to be affected by the andative-past prefix *ɲif^H-* 'went' (which is optionally preceded by the past prefix *ka^L-*): tone-stress b^L in the verb is perturbed to b^{HL}, and c^L is perturbed to c^{HL}. By applying this rule to arrive at the underlying tone-stress, all seventeen directional prefixes (ten andative and seven venitive) induce the same tone-stress inflection on the verb.

(131) a. *ka^{L}kua^{L}kiá̱^{L}*   (s/he) arrived carrying (TI)
          ka^{L}ɲif^{H}kiá̱^{HL}   (s/he) went carrying (TI)

       b. *ka^{L}kua^L?a̱^{L}*   (s/he) arrived stepping on (TA)
          ka^{L}ɲif^H?a̱^{HL}   (s/he) went stepping on (TA)

Inflection of class A verbs. Of the four grammatical persons which are distinguished inflectionally in class A verbs, the third-person paradigm is potentially the most complex and exhibits the greatest variety of inflectional paradigms, decreasing in turn for the second-person, 1S, and 1P paradigms,

---

[29]In Chinantec, the third-person pronoun *cú^M* is indeterminate both as to gender (masculine, feminine) and number (S, P). Glosses of examples that are drawn from text material reflect the implicit gender and number. Elicited material either reflects the normal social roles or, when such roles are ambivalent, the gloss 's/he' is provided; often 'they' could be equally implied.

The Verb 59

respectively. Of the 607 dynamic verbs in the corpus, 311, or 51 percent are class A verbs.

The inflectional matrix for class A verbs is set out in (132) below. Some cells in the matrix are dependent, that is, their form is the same as a form elsewhere in the paradigm for that same grammatical person. Such cells are cross-referenced to the cell that shares the same tone-stress. Other cells disallow any form; these are indicated by xxx. Cells for which the inflection is not the same as a form elsewhere in the verb matrix are indicated by +. With but seven known exceptions, the continuous is not able to be directly prefixed to the dynamic verb root. Since the innermost prefix always governs the tone-stress inflection of the verb, and since the continuous generally cannot occupy that position, its nongoverning nature is indicated by —. The same holds true for three of the four prohibitive cells.

The leftmost column, labeled inflectional parameter, sets out the three nonaffixed tenses first, followed by the motion, mood, and tense parameters from innermost prefix to outermost, finishing with the prohibitive. The inflectional parameters which are grouped together are members of the same distribution set and cannot co-occur. If an inflectional parameter consists of a set of prefixes, the number of prefixes in that set is supplied immediately following the name given to that parameter (for example, progressive-5).

This 64-cell matrix of class A verbs shows that there are 18 independent cells, 33 dependent cells, 7 nongoverning cells, and 6 nonfunctional cells.

(132) Class A verb inflection matrix

Inflectional parameter	3(S)	2(S)	1S	1P
PRES	+	+	+	+
FUT	+	+	+	+
IMP	xxx	PAST	xxx	xxx
PROG-5	PRES	PRES	PRES	PRES
AMB	+	+	FUT	FUT
ANDT-10	+	PAST	PAST	FUT
VEN-7	ANDT	PAST	PAST	FUT
MOT	PRES	PRES	PRES	PRES
INT	FUT	FUT	FUT	FUT
CONT	—	—	—	—

Inflectional parameter	3(S)	2(S)	1S	1P
PAST	+	+	+	FUT
HOD		PAST	PAST	FUT
EVID	+	AMB	FUT	FUT
HORT	+	XXX	FUT	FUT
EXH[30]	XXX	PAST	XXX	FUT
PROH	—	+	—	—

If the order in which the prefixes affix to the verb stem is disregarded, the above matrix can be reorganized to gain a more symmetrical grouping as in (133).

(133) Class A verb inflection matrix, reorganized

Inflectional parameter	3	2	1S	1P
PRES	+	+	+	+
FUT	+	+	+	+
PAST	+	+	+	FUT
AMB	+	+	FUT	FUT
HORT	+	XXX	FUT	FUT
EVID	+	AMB	FUT	FUT
HOD	+	PAST	PAST	FUT
ANDT	+	PAST	PAST	FUT
PROH	—	+	—	—
PROG	PRES	PRES	PRES	PRES
MOT	PRES	PRES	PRES	PRES
INT	FUT	FUT	FUT	FUT
VEN	ANDT	PAST	PAST	FUT
EXH	XXX	PAST	XXX	FUT
IMP	XXX	PAST	XXX	XXX
CONT	—	—	—	—

In the examples given in (134) of Class A verb paradigms, the order of the tenses is the same as that shown in (133). Those inflectional parameters which

---

[30] The form of the verb for the exhortative is the same as for the imperative, both of which are derived from the past, but with the morphological glottal which marks second person omitted.

The Verb

utilize a stem from another part of the paradigm are not included. These examples show the possible variety of tone-stress paradigms found in class A monosyllabic verbs without the segmental elements and the prefixes. For consistency in comparison, the verbs are TI and they do not undergo phonological changes in the root.

(134) Examples of tone-stress inflection on class A transitive inanimate verbs

$hl\tilde{\imath}^{ML}$ 'cover'	3	2	1S	1P	$hu\acute{o}\textrm{\textipa{P}}^{ML}$ 'whip'	3	2	1S	1P
PRES	bML	bML	bML	bML	PRES	bML	bLM	bLM	bLM
FUT	bL	bHL	bHL	bHL	FUT	bL	cMH	cMH	cMH
PAST	bL	bL	bL	bHL	PAST	bL	cL	bLM	cMH
AMB	bHL	bHL	bHL	bHL	AMB	bL	bLM	cMH	cMH
HORT	bHL	xxx	bHL	bHL	HORT	bHL	xxx	cMH	cMH
EVID	bHL	bHL	bHL	bHL	EVID	bHL	bLM	cMH	cMH
HOD	bL	bL	bL	bHL	HOD	bL	cL	bLM	cMH
ANDT	cLM	bL	bL	bHL	ANDT	bL	cL	bLM	cMH
PROH	—	bL	—	—	PROH	—	bLM	—	—

$t\tilde{o}^{M}$ 'confess'	3	2	1S	1P	hmu^{M} 'make'	3	2	1S	1P
PRES	cM	cML	cM	cML	PRES	cM	cLM	cM	bML
FUT	cL	cHL	cH	cHL	FUT	cL	bH	cH	bHL
PAST	cL	cL	cL	cHL	PAST	bL	cL	bLM	bHL
AMB	cH	cHL	cH	cHL	AMB	cH	cMH	cH	bHL
HORT	cH	xxx	cH	cHL	HORT	cH	xxx	cH	bHL
EVID	cH	cHL	cH	cHL	EVID	cH	cMH	cH	bHL
HOD	cL	cL	cL	cHL	HOD	bL	cL	bLM	bHL
ANDT	cL	cL	cL	cHL	ANDT	bL	cL	bLM	bHL
PROH	—	cL	—	—	PROH	—	bM	—	—

If a verb has b^{ML}/c^{LM}, c^{ML}, or b^{LM} for 1PL^PRES, it is usually a class A verb. A few class C verbs also exhibit the tones b^{ML}, c^{ML}, and c^{LM} for 1PL^PRES. If a verb cannot collocate with $l\tilde{\imath}^{M}$- (hodiernal past), it is a class C verb; however, if it can collocate with $l\tilde{\imath}^{M}$- but exhibits the same tone-stress for the present of the 1P, 1S, second and third person, it is a class C verb. Otherwise, it is a class A verb.

Initially, when researching the verb paradigms, there appeared to be an almost overwhelming variety of tone-stress combinations for each grammatical person and inflectional parameter. Further research has shown that much of this variety is due to four main factors: free variation, speaker preference, generational preference, and verb-specific aspectual nuances. Some, but not all, verbs mark the aspectual difference of 'frequency' and 'degree of affectedness' (permanent versus temporary) by a change in the tone-stress. Many other variations have been found in the third-person, second-person, 1S, and 1P paradigms. The reasons why some verbs have alternate tone-stresses and others do not, and why only some of the verbs which have alternatives convey aspectual differences must await future research.

The 'standardized' tone-stress given in the following paradigms is the tone-stress that is most widespread; that is, there is no alternative in some verbs and is a valid possibility, although perhaps not the preferred choice, in other verbs. This approach has helped reduce the proliferation of paradigms, but the picture is still by no means simple.

Inflection of class B verbs. A typical class B verb is characterized by a single form for all cells in the nonthird-person part of the verb matrix. There are seven known exceptions to this generalization.[31] Of the 607 dynamic verbs in my corpus, 139, or about 23 percent are class B verbs. The reorganized matrix for class B verbs is set out in (135).

(135) Class B verb inflection matrix

Inflectional parameter	3	Non-3
PRES	+	+
FUT	+	PRES
PAST	+	PRES
AMB	+	PRES
HORT	+	(PRES)
EVID	+	PRES
HOD	+	PRES
ANDT	+	PRES
PROH	—	PRES
PROG	PRES	(PRES)
MOT	PRES	PRES
INT	FUT	PRES
VEN	ANDT	PRES

---

[31]The exceptions for class B and class C verbs, and the details of unusual and/or alternate paradigms for second person, first-person singular, and first-person plural are left to the Chinantec-Spanish dictionary, which is in preparation.

The Verb 63

Inflectional parameter	3	Non-3
EXH	xxx	(PRES)
IMP	xxx	(PRES)
CONT	—	—

Although the hortative, prohibitive, imperative, and exhortative forms in the column labeled 'Non-3' are identical to any nonthird-person present form, the hortative can only be used with the first person, the prohibitive and imperative can only be used with the second person, and the exhortative can only be used with the second-person and first-person plural; this is indicated in (135) by parentheses around the referent.

Two examples of tone-stress paradigms found in class B monosyllabic verbs are given in (136). Both verbs are TI and do not undergo phonological changes in the root.

(136) Examples of tone-stress inflection on class B transitive inanimate verbs

rau?^{LM} 'embroider'	3	Non-3	*cü?*^M 'wreck'	3	Non-3
PRES	cLM	bH	PRES	cM	cMH
FUT	bLM	bH	FUT	cL	cMH
AMB	cMH	bH	AMB	cH	cMH
PAST	cL	bH	PAST	cL	cMH
HORT	cMH	(bH)	HORT	cH	(cMH)
EVID	cMH	bH	EVID	cH	cMH
HOD	bLM	bH	HOD	cL	cMH
ANDT	bH	bH	ANDT	cL	cMH

A tone H, HL, or MH in the 1P^PRES is usually diagnostic of a class B verb. A few class C verbs also exhibit these tones in the 1P^PRES. If the verb in question cannot collocate with *lî*^M- (hodiernal), it is a class C verb; however, if it can collocate with *lî*^M-, it is a class B verb.

Inflection of class C verbs. The typical class C verb is characterized by a single tone-stress paradigm for all grammatical persons, that of the third person.

The quickest diagnostic of a class C verb is to check the tone-stress of the 1P^PRES which exhibits seven possible tone-stresses: b^M, c^M, b^L, c^L, b^{ML}, c^{ML}, or c^{LM}. The four level tones are unique to class C verbs in the 1P^PRES; the three contour tones are also found in class A verbs. If a verb cannot collocate with *lî*^M- (hodiernal), it is a class C verb. If it can collocate with *lî*^M-, but exhibits the same tone-stress for the present of the 1P, 1SG, second and third person, it is a class C verb. Otherwise, it is a class A verb. Of the 607 dynamic verbs in the corpus, 146, or 24 percent are class C verbs.

The matrix for Class C verbs is given in (137). Unlike class A and B verbs, the hortative is found with all persons. The prohibitive and imperative of class C verbs is generally dependent on the presence of the hortative prefix, which governs the tone-stress inflection, indicated by —. The referent for the exhortative is in parentheses to indicate that it is used only with the second person and first-person plural.

(137) Class C verb inflection matrix

Inflectional parameter	All grammatical persons
PRES	+
FUT	+
PAST	+
AMB	+
HORT	+
EVID	+
HOD	+
ANDT	+
PROH	—
PROG	PRES
MOT	PRES
INT	FUT
VEN	ANDT
EXH	(PAST)
IMP	—
CONT	—

An example of the hortative used as the imperative of a Class C verb is shown in (138). The sense of this construction is subjunctive in force rather than a true imperative.

(138) kuí͡ʰ-hẽʔᴹ   nǔᴹ   rẽʔᴹ   hëʔᴸ   hmí͡ᴹ-ŋíᴸ
HORT-meet^TA^2 you^s sibling^2 gully water-chayote
(May you) meet your sibling at Chayote gully.

The prohibitive of most class C verbs requires the hortative prefix kuí͡ʰ- on the verb, as in (139). Because it is the innermost prefix and therefore influences the tone-stress on the verb, I do not list the prohibitive in the inflectional paradigm; it would be redundant.

(139) *lî́*^{M} *kuî́*^{H}-*kấi*^{M} *nú*^{M} *ŋiú*^{H}
PROH HORT-get^behind^IA^2 you^s friend
Don't get behind, mate.

The few irregular class C verbs which have an imperative inflection and those where the tone-stress of the prohibitive must be supplied because it does not require *kuî́*^{H}-, will be noted in the forthcoming Chinantec dictionary.

Three examples of tone-stress paradigms found in class C monosyllabic verbs are set out in (140). All three are intransitive animate (IA) and do not undergo phonological changes.

(140) Examples of tone-stress inflection of class C verbs

rãʔ^{LM} 'fly'	All persons	*sõ*^{M} 'descend'	All persons	*kuõu*^{LM} 'sleep'	All persons
PRES	cLM	PRES	cM	PRES	cLM
FUT	cHL	FUT	cHL	FUT	bLM
PAST	cLM	PAST	cM	PAST	bM
AMB	cHL	AMB	cH	AMB	cMH
HORT	cLM	HORT	cM	HORT	bM
EVID	cMH	EVID	cM	EVID	cMH
HOD	cLM	HOD	cM	HOD	bM
ANDT	cLM	ANDT	cM	ANDT	bM

Of the 146 class C verbs in the corpus, 140 cannot take the hodiernal past prefix or the set of directional prefixes. All intransitive inanimate (II) verbs are defective. The defective non-II verbs do not appear to form a semantic class. Examples are: *kấi*^{M} 'get behind (IA)', *huế̃ʔ*^{M} 'be frightened (IA)', *hẽʔ*^{M} 'meet (TA)', *loʔ*^{M} 'harvest (TI)', *rố̃ʔ*^{LM} 'manage (TI)', and *ʔî́*^{ML} 'believe (TI)'.

In addition, there are three irregular verbs which do not meet the criteria of a class C verb: a single tone-stress paradigm for third person, second person, 1S, and 1P. They are *rố̃ʔ*^{LM} 'manage (TI)', *tióʔ*^{LM} 'manage to (TI)', and *coʔ*^{M} 'finish (TI)'. Details will be provided in the dictionary.

4.2 Inflection set paradigms

In this section, the various paradigms found in the inflection sets for all persons and tenses of classes A, B, and C verbs are charted; the paradigms are labeled P1, P2, etc.

In the charts, tone-stress alternatives which are not in parentheses are valid for all verbs; alternatives in parentheses are only valid for some verbs.[32] The row labeled *Quant* indicates the number of verbs in the corpus which follow that paradigm. The row labeled *V-Chng* indicates the number of verbs of that paradigm which exhibit vocalic change with respect to the nucleus of the 3-PRES base form. The symbol *xx* indicates that no form exists for any verb which follows that paradigm. Defective paradigms are characteristic of class C verbs.

Inflection set I-a paradigms. Inflection set I-a is the set of third-person tone-stress paradigms for class A and B verbs; and the set for all grammatical persons for class C verbs. Seventy-four inflection set I-a tone-stress paradigms have been identified and are charted in (141).

(141)   Inflection set I-a paradigms

	P1	P2	P3	P4	P5	P6	P7	P8	P9	P10
PRES	bH	bH	cH	bM	bM	bM	bM	bM	cM	cM
FUT	bH	bH	cH	bM	bM	cL	bHL	bHL	cM	cL
PAST	bH	cMH	cH	bM	bM	bM	bM	bM	cM	bL
AMB	bH	bH	cH	bM	bHL	bHL	xx	bHL	cH	cH
HORT	bH	bH	cH	bM	bM	bM	bM	bM	cM	cH/(cHL)
EVID	bH	cMH	cH	bM	bM	bHL	bM	bHL	cM	cH
HOD	bH	cMH	cH	bM	bM	cL	xx	bM	cM	bL
ANDT	bH	xx	cH	bM	bM	bM	xx	bM	cM	bL/(cLM)
Quant	3	6	9	2	2	1	5	4	9	19
V-Chng	1	0	1	0	0	1	0	1	0	17

---

[32]The tone-stress paradigms have been organized on the following basis: ballistic stress (b) precedes controlled stress (c); the three level tones precede the two falling tones, followed by the two rising tones so that the order of priority is H, M, L, HL, ML, MH, LM. The columns are ordered on the basis of the tone-stress found in the first row (present), then the second row is taken into consideration, etc.

The Verb

	P11	P12	P13	P14	P15	P16	P17	P18
PRES	cM/(bML)	cM/(cML)	cM	cM	cM	cM	cM	cM
FUT	cL/(bL)	cL	bHL	cHL	cHL	cHL	cHL	cHL
PAST	cL/bL	cL	bLM	cM	cM	cL	cL	cHL
AMB	cH/bHL	cH/(cHL)	xx	cH	cHL/(cH)	cH	cHL	cHL
HORT	cH/bHL	cH/(cHL)	cM	cM	cM	bM	cM	cHL
EVID	cH/bHL	cH/(cHL)	xx	cM	cHL/(cH)	cH	cM	cH
HOD	bL/cL	cL	xx	cM	cM	xx	xx	xx
ANDT	bL/cL	cL/(cM/cH)	xx	cM	cM/(bH)	xx	xx	xx
Quant	2	50	1	13	23	1	1	1
V-Chng	2	5	0	1	17	0	1	0

	P19	P20	P21	P22	P23	P24	P25	P26	P27
PRES	cM	cM	cM	bL	bL	cL	bML	bML	bML
FUT	cHL	bLM	bLM	bL	bL	cL	bL	bL	bL
PAST	bLM	bL	bL	bL	bL	cL	bL	bL	bL
AMB	xx	bLM	bLM	bHL		cHL/(cH)	bHL	bHL	bHL
HORT	cM	bLM	bLM	bL	bHL	cL	bHL	bHL	bHL
EVID	cHL	cHL	cMH	bL	bHL	cL	bHL	bHL	bHL
HOD	xx	bLM	bLM	bL	xx	cL	bL	bL	bL
ANDT	xx	bLM	bLM	bL/(cLM)	xx	cL	cH	bM	bL
Quant	1	2	1	4	1	7	1	4	64
V-Chng	1	1	1	0	0	2	1	1	14

	P28	P29	P30	P31	P32	P33	P34	P35	P36	P37
PRES	bML	bML	bML	bML	bML	bML	bML	bML	bML	bML
FUT	bL	bL	bL	bL	bL	bL	cL	bHL	bHL	bHL
PAST	bL	bL	cL	cL	cL	cL	cL	bM	cL	bHL
AMB	bHL	bHL	bHL	bHL	bHL	xx	bHL	xx	bHL	bHL
HORT	bHL	bHL	bHL	bHL	bHL	bHL	bHL	bM	bHL	bHL
EVID	bHL	bHL	bHL	bHL	bHL	cMH	bHL	xx	cMH	bHL
HOD	bL	bL	bL	bL	bL	xx	xx	xx	xx	xx
ANDT	cMH	cLM/(bL)	bM	bL	cLM	xx	xx	xx	xx	xx
Quant	1	30	1	2	5	1	2	1	3	5
V-Chng	0	0	1	2	1	1	0	0	0	0

	P38	P39	P40	P41	P42	P43	P44	P45	P46
PRES	cML	cML	cML	cML	cMH	bLM	bLM	bLM	bLM
FUT	cL	cHL	cHL	cHL	cMH	cL	cMH	bLM	bLM
PAST	cL	cM	cL	cHL	cMH	bLM	cMH	bL	cL
AMB	cH/cHL	xx	xx	cHL	cMH	cHL/(bLM)	xx	bLM	xx
HORT	cH/cHL	cM	cHL	cHL	cMH	cHL	cMH	bLM	bLM
EVID	cH/cHL	xx	cH	xx	cMH	bLM	bLM	bLM	xx
HOD	cL	xx	cL	xx	cMH	bLM	xx	bLM	xx
ANDT	cL/(cM/cH)	xx	xx	xx	cMH	bL	xx	cL	xx
Quant	58	2	1	2	4	11	2	1	1
V-Chng	14	0	1	1	2	11	2	1	0

	P47	P48	P49	P50	P51	P52	P53	P54	P55
PRES	bLM	bLM	cLM	cLM	cLM	cLM	cLM	cLM	cLM
FUT	bLM/(cL)	bLM	cHL	cHL	bL	cL	cMH	bLM	bLM
PAST	bLM	bLM	cLM	cLM	bM	cL	bLM	bM/(cM)	bM
AMB	bLM/(cHL)	bLM	cHL	cMH	xx	cMH	xx	cMH	cMH
HORT	bLM/(cHL)	bLM	cLM	cLM	cMH	cHL	cMH	cMH	bM
EVID	bLM/(cHL)	bLM	cMH	cMH	xx	cMH	xx	cMH	cMH
HOD	bLM	bLM	cLM	cLM	xx	bLM	xx	xx	bM
ANDT	cL/(bLM)	bLM	cLM	cLM	xx	bL	xx	xx	bM
Quant	88	3	1	5	1	1	6	11	2
V-Chng	63	0	0	0	1	1	6	3	1

	P56	P57	P58	P59	P60	P61	P62	P63	P64	P65
PRES	cLM	cLM	cLM	cLM	cLM	cLM	cLM	cLM	cLM	cLM
FUT	bLM	bLM	bLM	bLM	bLM	bLM	bLM	bLM	bLM	bLM
PAST	cM	bL	bL	bL/(cL)	bL	cL	cL	cL	cL	cL
AMB	cMH	cMH	cMH	cMH	cMH	xx	xx	cMH	cMH	cMH
HORT	cM	bM	cMH	cMH	cMH	bM	cMH	bHL	bLM	cMH
EVID	cMH	cMH	cMH	cMH	cMH	cMH	cMH	cMH	cMH	cMH
HOD	cM	bM	bLM	bLM	bLM	xx	cL	cL	bLM	bLM
ANDT	cM	bM	cH	bM/(cM)	cLM	xx	xx	xx	bLM	bH
Quant	1	1	2	34	1	1	3	2	1	18
V-Chng	1	0	1	5	0	1	1	2	1	10

The Verb

	P66	P67	P68	P69
PRES	cLM	cLM	cLM	cLM
FUT	bLM	bLM	bLM	bLM
PAST	cL	cL	cL	cL
AMB	cMH	cMH/(bHL)	cMH/(bHL/cHL)	cMH/(cHL)
HORT	cMH	cMH/(bHL)	cMH/(bHL/cHL)	cMH/(cHL)
EVID	cMH	cMH	cMH/(bHL/cHL)	cMH/(cHL)
HOD	bLM	bLM/(bL)	bLM	bLM
ANDT	cH	bL/(cM/cLM)	cL/(bL/bLM/cM/cLM)	cLM/(bM/cM)
Quant	3	26	15	5
V-Chng	1	18	7	1

	P70	P71	P72	P73	P74
PRES	cLM	cLM	cLM	cLM	cLM
FUT	bLM	bLM	bLM	cLM	cLM
PAST	bLM	bLM	cLM	cL	cLM
AMB	cMH	cMH	xx	xx	cMH
HORT	cMH	cMH	cLM	cLM	cLM
EVID	cMH	cMH	xx	cLM	cLM
HOD	bLM	bLM	xx	xx	cLM
ANDT	cM/cL	bM	xx	xx	cLM
Quant	14	1	1	1	2
V-Chng	0	1	0	1	0

Paradigm P12 in (141) is representative of how alternative paradigms have been combined. Included in P12 are verbs in which the PRES may have (1) only tone-stress c^M, or (2) either c^M or c^{ML}, with one verb preferring c^M and another c^{ML}; similar choices are found for the AMB, HORT, EVID, and ANDT. If c^{ML} is the preferred option for the PRES, then the tendency is that c^{HL} will be the preferred option for the AMB, HORT, and EVID. Similarly, if c^M is the only or the preferred option for the PRES, then c^H tends to be the only or the preferred option for the AMB, HORT, and EVID. However, there are verbs in which the opposite holds true. In the ANDT, generally tone-stress c^L is preferred, and in many verbs it is the only option; in some verbs, however, c^M is the preferred option. A preference for c^L or c^M in the ANDT does not appear to correlate to the remainder of the paradigm.

Two I-a paradigms, P2 and P64, occur exclusively with the 3P of verbs which exhibit an inflectional distinction between 3S and 3P. The paradigms P1 and P26 occur in both the 3P and nondifferentiated third person.

Several of the inflection set I-a paradigms are unique to either class A, B, or C verbs. For example, paradigms P10, P29, and P67 are unique to class A verbs; paradigms P9, P22, P48, P65, and P66 are unique to class B verbs; and P7, P14, P36, P37, P50, P53, and P54 are unique to class C verbs. There is also a fair degree of overlap, however, as illustrated in (142). Because of this overlap, the third-person paradigms of all three verb classes are combined into the single inflection set I-a.

(142) Inflection set I-a paradigms shared by class A, B, and C verbs

Class A	Class B	Class C
	P3	P3
P8		P8
P12	P12	P12
P15	P15	P15
	P24	P24
P27		P27
P32		P32
P38	P38	P38
	P42	P42
P43		P43
P47	P47	
P59		P59
P68	P68	
P69	P69	
P70		P70

Inflection set I-b paradigms. Inflection set I-b in (143) is the set of second-person paradigms for class A verbs and the set of nonthird-person paradigms for class B verbs. Inflection set I-b is not relevant to class C verbs. Thirty-nine of these paradigms have been identified.

(143) Inflection set I-b paradigms

	P1	P2	P3	P4	P5	P6	P7	P8	P9	P10
PRES	bH	cH	bHL	cHL	bML	bML	bML	bML	bML	bML
FUT	bH	cH	bHL	cHL	bHL	bHL	bHL	bHL	bHL	bHL
PAST	bH	cH	bHL	cHL	cH	cH	cH	bM	cM	cM
AMB	bH	cH	bHL	cHL	bHL/cMH	bHL	bHL/(cMH)	bHL	bHL	bHL
PROH	bH	cH	bHL	cHL	bM	cM	bL	bM	bL	cL
Quant	31	72	9	8	7	1	10	1	4	1
V-Chng	17	40	1	0	7	0	9	1	4	1

The Verb

	P11	P12	P13	P14	P15	P16	P17	P18	P19
PRES	bML	bML	bML	bML/(cLM)	bML	bML	bML	cML	cML
FUT	bHL	bHL	bHL	bHL		bHL	bHL	bHL	cHL	cHL
PAST	bL	bL	cL	cMH	cMH	cLM	cLM	cH	cH
AMB	bHL	bHL	bHL	bHL	bHL	bHL	bHL	cHL	cHL
PROH	cM	bL/(bM)	cM	cM/(bM)	bL	bL	cL	cH	cL
Quant	2	35	1	5	1	3	1	6	13
V-Chng	0	1	0	0	0	2	1	6	7

	P20	P21	P22	P23	P24	P25	P26	P27
PRES	cML	cML	cML	cML	cML	cML	cML	cML/(cLM)
FUT	cHL	cHL	cHL	cHL	cHL	cHL	cHL	cHL
PAST	cM	cM	cM	cL	cMH	cMH/(cLM)	cLM	cLM
AMB	cHL	cHL	cHL	cHL	cHL	cHL/(cMH)	cHL	cHL
PROH	cM	bL	cL	cL	cL	cMH	cL	cLM
Quant	9	1	27	32	17	3	23	6
V-Chng	2	1	7	13	0	0	7	0

	P28	P29	P30	P31	P32	P33
PRES	cMH	bLM	bLM	bLM/(cLM)	cLM	cLM
FUT	cMH	cMH	cMH/(bH)	cMH	bH	bH
PAST	cMH	bL/cH	cL/(cH)	bLM/(cLM)	bH	bM
AMB	cMH	cMH/bLM	cMH/(bLM/cHL)	cMH/(bLM)	cMH	cMH
PROH	cMH	bLM	bLM	bLM/(cLM)	bM	bM
Quant	26	1	36	3	26	11
V-Chng	0	1	17	3	8	11

	P34	P35	P36	P37	P38	P39
PRES	cLM	cLM	cLM	cLM	cLM	cLM
FUT	bH	bH	bH	cH	cMH	cMH
PAST	bL	cL/(cH)	cMH	bL/(cL)	cL	cL
AMB	cMH	cMH	cMH/bH	cMH/(bHL)	xx	cMH/bLM
PROH	bM	bM/(cM)	bM	cLM	cLM	bL
Quant	15	7	2	3	2	1
V-Chng	10	5	0	2	2	1

Inflection sets I-c and I-d paradigms. Inflection sets I-c and I-d apply only to class A verbs, corresponding to the 1S and 1P paradigms, respectively. There are seven I-c (1S) paradigms as in (144), and three I-d paradigms as in (145).

(144) Inflection set I-c (1S) paradigms

	P1	P2	P3	P4	P5	P6	P7
PRES	cM	cM	bML	cML	cML/(cLM)	bLM	cLM/(cML)
FUT	cH	cH	bHL	cHL	cHL/(cMH)	cMH	cMH/(cHL)
PAST	cL	bLM	bL	cM	cL/(bLM)	bLM	bLM/(cLM)
Quant	25	33	69	8	10	36	129
V-Chng	4	21	3	0	3	3	18

(145) Inflection set I-d (1P) paradigms

	P1	P2	P3
PRES	bML/cLM	cML	bLM
FUT	bHL	cHL	cMH
Quant	131	144	38
V-Chng	23	31	3

From the paradigms of inflection sets I-a, I-b, I-c, and I-d given above, it can be seen that there are certain constraints. No more than eleven of the thirteen possible tone-stresses occur with any given inflectional parameter; and the tone-stresses b^{ML} and c^{ML} are unique to the present tense in every inflection set. These are charted in (146).

(146) Tone-stress inflections found with each inflectional parameter

Inflectional parameter	Tone-stress inflections, inflection set I-a
PRES	bH cH bM cM bL cL bML cML cMH bLM cLM
FUT	bH cH bM cM bL cL bHL cHL cMH bLM cLM
PAST	bH cH bM cM bL cL bHL cHL cMH bLM cLM
AMB	bH cH bM bHL cHL cMH bLM
HORT	bH cH bM cM bL cL bHL cHL cMH bLM cLM
EVID	bH cH bM cM bL cL bHL cHL cMH bLM cLM
HOD	bH cH bM cM bL cL cMH bLM cLM
ANDT	bH cH bM cM bL cL cMH bLM cLM

Tone-stress inflections, inflection set I-b

PRES	bH cH	bHL cHL bML cML	cMH bLM cLM
FUT	bH cH	bHL cHL	cMH
PAST	bH cH bM cM bL cL	bHL cHL	cMH bLM cLM
AMB	bH cH	bHL cHL	cMH bLM
PROH	bH cH bM cM bL cL	bHL cHL	cMH bLM cLM

Tone-stress inflections, inflection set I-c

PRES	cM	bML cML	bLM cLM
FUT	cH	bHL cHL	cMH
PAST	cM bL cL		bLM cLM

Tone-stress inflections, inflection set I-d

PRES		bML cML	bLM cLM
FUT		bHL cHL	cMH

Summary of verb tone-stress paradigms. After running a statistical count on the combination of the inflection set paradigms and transitivity types found in each class of verbs, the following observations are noted.

For class A verbs, the total number of paradigms found for each person category is 27 for I-a (3), 36 for I-b (2), 7 for I-c (1S), and 3 for I-d (1P). Furthermore, inanimate verbs (TI and DI) are more common than type animate verbs (TA and DA), 52.7% and 36.1%, respectively.

For class B verbs, only those which exhibit second-person paradigms P1 or P2 potentially undergo vocalic change as part of the inflection. The total number of paradigms found for each person category are 20 for I-a (3), and 5 for I-b (non-3), (not including the exceptions for nonthird person outlined above). In class B, animate verbs (TA and DA) are more common than inanimate verbs (TI and DI), 53.3% and 39.6%, respectively—the opposite of class A verbs.

For class C verbs, inflection set I-a is used for all grammatical persons. A total of 40 paradigms have been identified, 7 of which are found only in the final syllable of disyllabic verbs (P3, P4, P24, P42, P46, P73, and P74). Class C verbs are predominantly intransitive inanimate (II)—68.5%; all II verbs are class C. The proportion of IA verbs—19.2%—is significantly greater than that of either TA or TI verbs—4.8% and 5.5%, respectively; in contrast, IA verbs comprise a small percentage of class A and B verbs. There are no known examples of class C ditransitive verbs. The majority of class C verbs, including the II verbs, are defective in that they cannot collocate with the hodiernal or directional prefixes. Some II verbs are defective for additional inflectional parameters such as the ambulative and/or the evidential.

Class A verbs are referenced in the manner presented in (147a). Thus, for example, ʔí^ML 'count' is (TA)–A.38.26.6.2. Class B verbs are referenced in the manner presented in (147b). Thus, caïʔ^LM 'rewrap' is (TI)–B.65.1. Class C verbs are referenced in the manner presented in (147c).

(147) a. Verb paradigm reference—Class A verbs

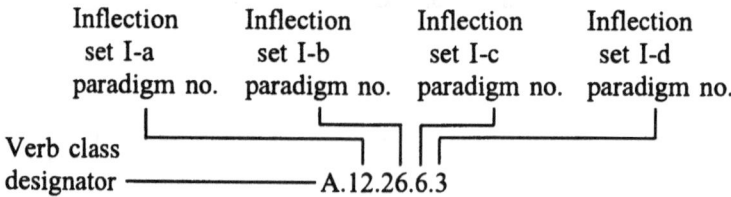

b. Verb paradigm reference—Class B verbs

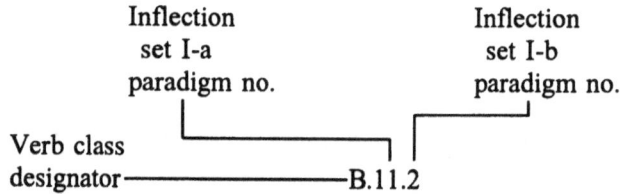

c. Verb paradigm reference—Class C verbs

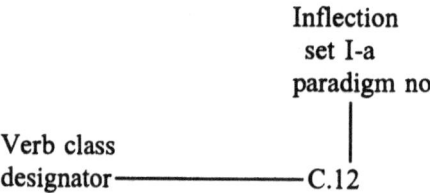

4.3 Verbs which inflectionally distinguish between singular and plural subjects

Some verbs, including all the motion verbs, make a six-way distinction of person and number for the subject: 3S, 2S, 1S, 3P, 2P, and 1P. This six-way distinction is accomplished in a variety of ways and most such verbs are a combination of stems within the class A, B, C system.

Each verb's paradigmatic combination can be referenced according to the system presented in example (147). For example, the verb ʔí^ML 'enter (TI)' is referenced as A.32.31.6.x/A.64.31.x.3. The slash means there are two stems; the first stem (which is singular) is a class A verb and only inflection sets I-a,

The Verb

I-b, and I-c can occur, with their respective paradigms P32, P31, and P6; similarly the second stem (which is plural) is a class A verb and only inflection sets I-a, I-b, and I-d can occur, with their respective paradigms P64, P31, and P3. In the first stem, inflection set I-d does not occur, and in the second stem, inflection set I-c does not occur. The inflection of $\textipa{?í}^{ML}$ is illustrated in (148).

(148) $\textipa{?í}^{ML}$ enter (IA)-A.32.31.6.x/A.64.31.x.3

	3S	2S	1S	3P	2P	1P
PRES	$\textipa{?í}^{ML}$	$\textipa{?ú?}^{LM}$	$\textipa{?ú}^{LM}$	$tãu\textipa{?}^{LM}$	$t\tilde{o}\textipa{?}^{LM}$	$táu\textipa{?}^{LM}$
FUT	$\textipa{?í}^{L}$	$\textipa{?u?}^{MH}$	$\textipa{?u}^{MH}$	$t\tilde{o}\textipa{?}^{LM}$	$t\tilde{o}\textipa{?}^{MH}$	$tau\textipa{?}^{MH}$
PAST	$\textipa{?i}^{L}$	$\textipa{?ú?}^{LM}$	$\textipa{?ú}^{LM}$	$tãu\textipa{?}^{L}$	$tiõ\textipa{?}^{LM}$	FUT
AMB	$\textipa{?í}^{HL}$	$\textipa{?u?}^{MH}$	FUT	$tãu\textipa{?}^{MH}$	$t\tilde{o}\textipa{?}^{MH}$	FUT
HORT	$\textipa{?í}^{HL}$	XXX	FUT	$tiõ\textipa{?}^{LM}$	XXX	FUT
EVID	$\textipa{?í}^{HL}$	AMB	FUT	$tãu\textipa{?}^{MH}$	AMB	FUT
HOD	$\textipa{?í}^{L}$	PAST	PAST	$tiõ\textipa{?}^{LM}$	PAST	FUT
ANDT	$\textipa{?i}^{LM}$	PAST	PAST	$tiõ\textipa{?}^{LM}$	PAST	FUT
PROH	—	$\textipa{?ú}^{LM}$	—	—	$t\tilde{o}\textipa{?}^{LM}$	—

Most motion verbs exhibit one stem for 3S, 2S, 1S, and 1P which inflects like a class A verb, and a different stem for 2P and 3P which inflects like a class B disyllabic verb (see §4.4). All the verbs which follow this pattern are motion verbs.

(149) ηi^{LM} walk (IA)-A.59.1.3.1/α.B.1.1

	3S	2S	1S	1P	3P	2P
PRES	ηi^{LM}	$\eta í\textipa{?}^{H}$	$\eta í^{ML}$	$\eta í^{ML}$	$\eta ii^{L}táu\textipa{?}^{H}$	$\eta ii^{L}táu\textipa{?}^{H}$
FUT	ηi^{LM}	$\eta í\textipa{?}^{H}$	$\eta í^{HL}$	$\eta í^{HL}$	$\eta ii^{L}táu\textipa{?}^{H}$	$\eta i f^{H}táu\textipa{?}^{H}$
PAST	ηi^{L}	$\eta í\textipa{?}^{H}$	ηi^{L}	FUT	$\eta ii^{L}táu\textipa{?}^{H}$	$\eta ii^{L}táu\textipa{?}^{H}$
AMB	ηi^{MH}	$\eta í\textipa{?}^{H}$	FUT	FUT	$\eta ii^{L}táu\textipa{?}^{H}$	$\eta ii^{L}táu\textipa{?}^{H}$
HORT	ηi^{MH}	XXX	FUT	FUT	$\eta ii^{L}táu\textipa{?}^{H}$	XXX
EVID	ηi^{MH}	AMB	FUT	FUT	$\eta ii^{L}táu\textipa{?}^{H}$	AMB
HOD	ηi^{LM}	PAST	PAST	FUT	$\eta ii^{L}táu\textipa{?}^{H}$	PAST
ANDT	ηi^{M}	PAST	PAST	FUT	$\eta ii^{L}táu\textipa{?}^{H}$	PAST
PROH	—	ηi^{M}	—	—	—	$\eta ii^{L}táu\textipa{?}^{H}$

For other verbs the picture is more complex, with up to three suppletive stems occurring. Based on the stems, the division is not strictly between singular and plural subjects; paradigmatically, however, it is possible to treat a verb such as $kiau^{LM}$ in (150) as a combination of two class A verbs, with 3S, 2S, 1S, and 1P forming a full class A verb, and 3P with 2P forming a truncated class A verb with only inflection sets I-a and I-b occurring.

(150) $kiau^{LM}$ lie down (IA)-A.56.12.7.1/A.26.23.x.x

	3S	2S	1S	1P	3P	2P
PRES	$kiau^{LM}$	$\theta\acute{a}\text{?}^{ML}$	θan^{LM}	$\theta\tilde{a}^{ML}$	$ti\tilde{a}\text{?}^{ML}$	$ti\tilde{a}\text{?}^{ML}$
FUT	$ki\acute{o}^{LM}$	$\theta\acute{a}\text{?}^{HL}$	θan^{MH}	$\theta\tilde{a}^{HL}$	$ti\tilde{a}\text{?}^{L}$	$ti\tilde{a}\text{?}^{HL}$
PAST	kiu^{M}	$\theta\acute{a}\text{?}^{L}$	$\theta\acute{a}^{LM}$	FUT	$ti\tilde{a}\text{?}^{L}$	$ti\tilde{a}\text{?}^{L}$
AMB	$kiau^{MH}$	$\theta\acute{a}\text{?}^{HL}$	FUT	FUT	$ti\tilde{a}\text{?}^{HL}$	$ti\tilde{a}\text{?}^{HL}$
HORT	kiu^{M}	xxx	FUT	FUT	$ti\tilde{a}\text{?}^{HL}$	xxx
EVID	$kiau^{MH}$	AMB	FUT	FUT	$ti\tilde{a}\text{?}^{HL}$	AMB
HOD	kiu^{M}	PAST	PAST	FUT	$ti\tilde{a}\text{?}^{L}$	PAST
ANDT	kiu^{M}	PAST	PAST	FUT	$ti\tilde{a}\text{?}^{M}$	PAST
PROH	—	$\theta\acute{a}^{L}$	—	—	—	$ti\tilde{a}\text{?}^{L}$

Several class C verbs exhibit suppletive stems for singular and plural. For example, the inanimate verb 'fall down' has the singular and plural forms $ta\text{?}^{LM}$ (II^S)-C.59 and $su\text{?}^{LM}$ (II^P)-C.70 (see (151a)); and the IA verb 'fall down' has the singular and plural forms $t\tilde{a}\text{?}^{LM}$ (IA^S)-C.59 and $s\tilde{u}\text{?}^{ML}$ (IA^P)-C.38 (see (151b)). A peculiarity of most class C IA plural stems is that the 1P is distinguished from the non-1PL by vocalic change (§4.5); the tone-stress paradigm, however, is the same for both the 1P and non-1P forms.

(151)

a. fall down (II)

	Singular	Plural
PRES	$ta\text{?}^{LM}$	$su\text{?}^{LM}$
FUT	$t\acute{a}\text{?}^{LM}$	$s\acute{u}\text{?}^{LM}$
PAST	$t\acute{a}\text{?}^{L}$	$s\acute{u}\text{?}^{LM}$
AMB	$ta\text{?}^{MH}$	$su\text{?}^{MH}$
HORT	$ta\text{?}^{MH}$	$su\text{?}^{MH}$
EVID	$ta\text{?}^{MH}$	$su\text{?}^{MH}$
HOD	xxx	xxx
ANDT	xxx	xxx

b. fall down (IA)

	Singular	Plural Non-1P	1P
PRES	$t\tilde{a}\text{?}^{LM}$	$s\tilde{u}\text{?}^{ML}$	$sau\text{?}^{ML}$
FUT	$t\acute{\tilde{a}}\text{?}^{LM}$	$s\tilde{u}\text{?}^{L}$	$sau\text{?}^{L}$
PAST	$t\acute{\tilde{a}}\text{?}^{M}$	$s\tilde{u}\text{?}^{L}$	$sau\text{?}^{L}$
AMB	$t\tilde{a}\text{?}^{MH}$	$s\tilde{u}\text{?}^{H}$	$sau\text{?}^{H}$
HORT	$t\tilde{a}\text{?}^{MH}$	$s\tilde{u}\text{?}^{H}$	$sau\text{?}^{H}$
EVID	$t\tilde{a}\text{?}^{MH}$	$s\tilde{u}\text{?}^{H}$	$sau\text{?}^{H}$
HOD	xxx	xxx	xxx
ANDT	xxx	xxx	xxx

Other verbs with suppletive stems, II and IA are shown in (152).

The Verb   77

(152) Verbs with singular and plural suppletive stems

	Inanimate		Animate		
	Singular	Plural	Singular	Plural	
				Non-1P	1P
sprout	ʔia^{LM}	ʔiõ^M			
leave	kuá^{M}ʔaï^{LM}	ʔue^{LM}	kuá^{M}ʔaï^{LM}	ʔuē^{LM}	ʔue^{LM}
stand	tá^{M}θaʔ^H	tá^{M}no^H	tá^{M}θã̄ʔ^H	tá^{M}tõʔ^H	tá^{M}tauʔ^H
die		hṹ^{ML}		cã^M	cau^M

The singular IA verbs tã̄^{ʔLM} 'fall down' and hṹ^{ML} 'die' may also be used for the plural (but the plural forms can never be used for the singular). If the speaker chooses the form for the singular, the individuals are seen as acting independently; if the form based on the plural stem is chosen, the individuals are seen as acting corporately.

(153) a. huõu^{LM} cú^M ka^L-tá̱ʔ^L ʔú^H huï^{LM} ɲií^H
         many^AN 3   PAST-fall^down^IA^3^s   along trail   place

      ka^L-kuō^L kuáʔ^{HL}
      PAST-slip^II   soil
      Many people fell down along the trail where the slip occurred
      (i.e., one by one, as they came to the slip).

   b. huõu^{LM} cú^M ka^L-sū̱ʔ^L ʔú^H huï^{LM} ɲií^H
      many^AN 3   PAST-fall^down^IA^3P   along trail   place

      ka^L-kuō^L kuáʔ^{HL}
      PAST-slip^II   soil
      Many people fell down along the trail where the slip occurred
      (i.e., they were together and fell together).

There are also verbs which exhibit suppletive stems for singular and plural object. These are discussed separately in §4.6.

4.4 Disyllabic verbs

The majority of Chinantec verbs are monosyllabic; of 607 dynamic verbs in the corpus, only about 20 are nonderived disyllabic; that is, the etymology of the final syllable is not recognizable. Disyllabic verbs appear to be restricted to class B and class C, whether derived or not.

The final syllable of disyllabic verbs behaves like a monosyllabic verb, marking the second person by glottal closure and marking animacy by nasalization. The tone-stress paradigms of the final syllable of some disyllabic verbs are also found in monosyllabic verbs. On this basis disyllabic verbs are classified according to their final syllable type. In the majority of disyllabic verbs, the final syllable inflects like a class B verb (the nonthird-person paradigm consists of a single tone-stress for all inflectional parameters for second person, 1S, and 1P, whereas the third person inflects for tense, mood etc.); in a few verbs the final syllable inflects as a class C verb, i.e., the tone-stress inflection found in the third person is also found in the corresponding inflectional parameter of second person, 1S, and 1P.

Regardless of whether the tone-stress of the final syllable inflects like a class B or C verb, the initial syllable of most disyllabic verbs exhibits limited tone-stress inflection for third person, second person, 1S, and 1P in a manner similar to that of class A verbs; this paradigm is labeled α. The tone-stress of the initial syllable is supplied for the independent cells in the matrix in (154). Several cells have alternative tones, in which case the preferred tone is given first.

(154) Inflection of the initial syllable of disyllabic verbs, paradigm α

Inflectional parameter	3	2	1S	1P
PRES	bM	cL/bM	bM/cL	bM/cL
FUT	cL	bH	bH	bH
PAST	FUT	cL	cL	cL/bH
AMB	FUT	PAST	cL/bH	cL
HORT	bH/cL	xxx	FUT	FUT
EVID	bH	FUT	FUT	FUT
HOD	FUT	PAST	PAST	FUT
ANDT	FUT	PAST	PAST	FUT
PROH	—	PAST	—	—

The combination of paradigm α with a final syllable which inflects like a class B or C verb is illustrated in (155a) and (155b), respectively.

(155) a. *dí^{M}ŋiu^L* prop up, support (DI)

	3	2	1S	1P
PRES	dí^{M}ŋiu^L	di^{L}ŋiuʔ^{MH}	dí^{M}ŋiu^{MH}	dí^{M}ŋiu^{MH}
FUT	di^{L}ŋiu^L	dí^{H}ŋiuʔ^{MH}	dí^{H}ŋiu^{MH}	dí^{H}ŋiu^{MH}
PAST	di^{L}ŋiu^L	di^{L}ŋiuʔ^{MH}	di^{L}ŋiu^{MH}	di^{L}ŋiu^{MH}
AMB	di^{L}ŋiu^{HL}	di^{L}ŋiuʔ^{MH}	di^{L}ŋiu^{MH}	di^{L}ŋiu^{MH}
HORT	dí^{H}ŋiu^L	xxx	dí^{H}ŋiu^{MH}	dí^{H}ŋiu^{MH}
EVID	dí^{H}ŋiu^L	dí^{H}ŋiuʔ^{MH}	dí^{H}ŋiu^{MH}	dí^{H}ŋiu^{MH}

The Verb   79

	3	2	1S	1P
HOD	$di^L\eta iu^L$	$di^L\eta iu?^{MH}$	$di^L\eta iu^{MH}$	$di^H\eta iu^{MH}$
ANDT	$di^L\eta iu^L$	$di^L\eta iu?^{MH}$	$di^L\eta iu^{MH}$	$di^H\eta iu^{MH}$
PROH	—	$di^L\eta iu^{MH}$	—	—

b. $má^M?o^L$ assist, help with (TI)

	3	2	1S	1P
PRES	$má^M?o^L$	$má^M?o?^L$	$má^M?o^L$	$má^M?o^L$
FUT	$ma^L?o^L$	$má^H?o?^L$	$má^H?o^L$	$má^H?o^L$
PAST	$ma^L?o^L$	$ma^L?o?^L$	$ma^L?o^L$	$ma^L?o^L$
AMB	$ma^L?o^{HL}$	$ma^L?o?^{HL}$	$ma^L?o^{HL}$	$ma^L?o^{HL}$
HORT	$má^H?o^L$	xxx	$má^H?o^L$	$má^H?o^L$
EVID	$má^H?o^L$	$má^H?o?^L$	$má^H?o^L$	$má^H?o^L$
HOD	$ma^L?o^L$	$ma^L?o?^L$	$ma^L?o^L$	$má^H?o^L$
ANDT	$ma^L?o^L$	$ma^L?o?^L$	$ma^L?o^L$	$má^H?o^L$
PROH	—	$ma^L?o^L$	—	—

Although most of the alternative tones in (154) appear to be in free variation, the 3-HORT with tone c^L implies that the speaker expects prompt compliance, whereas tone b^H implies that compliance is expected as soon as possible (for example, the person concerned may not be present).

(156) a. $kui^{?H}$-$ma^L?ma?^H$ $cú^M$ $kio?^{MH}$ $cá^M$ $lá^M$
   HORT-pay^TI^3   3   have^STI^3 person this
   S/he ought to pay (the wages of) this person (now).

   b. $kui^{?H}$-$má^H?ma?^H$ $cú^M$ $kio?^{MH}$ $cá^M$ $lá^M$
   HORT-pay^TI^3   3   have^STI^3 person this
   S/he ought to pay (the wages of) this person (soon).

A 1P-PAST with tone c^L in the first syllable implies that the action was premeditated, whereas a tone b^H implies nonpremeditated action. For example, in (157a), the event is premeditated; we had planned to do this. In (157b), the event is spontaneous; when we came across Peter on the trail, he needed assistance, and so we gave it.

(157) a. ka^L-$ma^L?ö^H$ $hno?^H$ $pé^H$ $?ú^H$ hui^{LM}
   PAST-help^TA^1P we   Peter   on   trail
   We helped Peter on the trail.

b. *ka^L-má^{H}ʔõ^H*   *hnoʔ^H*   *pé^H*   *ʔú^H*   *huḭ^{LM}*
   PAST-help^TA^1P   we   Peter   on   trail
   We helped Peter on the trail.

In only two disyllabic verbs does the initial syllable inflect as a class C verb (see (158)). This inflection is labeled paradigm β. In both verbs the final syllable also inflects as a class C verb.

Disyllabic verbs which exhibit paradigm β in the initial syllable are inflectionally simple. As with monosyllabic class C verbs, the tone-stress of the third-person β paradigm inflectional parameters is exhibited by the corresponding nonthird-person inflectional parameters.

(158) Inflection of the initial syllable of disyllabic verbs, paradigm β

Inflectional parameter	3	2	1S	1P
PRES	bM	bM	bM	bM
FUT	bH	bH	bH	bH
PAST	PRES	PRES	PRES	PRES
AMB	xxx	xxx	xxx	xxx
HORT	FUT	FUT	FUT	FUT
EVID	xxx	xxx	xxx	xxx
HOD	xxx	xxx	xxx	xxx
ANDT	xxx	xxx	xxx	xxx
PROH	xxx	xxx	xxx	xxx

Both the disyllabic verbs which exhibit paradigm β are IA as in (159).

(159) *ka^L-ʔiá^{M}cĩ^H*   *cú^M*   *ci^L*   *kuá̰ʔ^M*   *ó^{LM}*
   PAST-appear^on^top^of^IA^3   3   top   hill   yonder
   S/he appeared on top of that hill over there.

The combination of paradigm β with a final syllable which inflects like a class C verb is illustrated in (160).

(160) *iá^{M}ʔã^H* be frightened (IA)

	3	2	1S	1P
PRES	*iá^{M}ʔã^H*	*iá^{M}ʔã^H*	*iá^{M}ʔã^H*	*iá^{M}ʔã^H*
FUT	*iá^{H}ʔã^H*	*iá^{H}ʔã^H*	*iá^{H}ʔã^H*	*iá^{H}ʔã^H*
PAST	PRES	PRES	PRES	PRES
AMB	xxx	xxx	xxx	xxx
HORT	FUT	FUT	FUT	FUT

The Verb

	3	2	1S	1P
EVID	xxx	xxx	xxx	xxx
HOD	xxx	xxx	xxx	xxx
ANDT	xxx	xxx	xxx	xxx
PROH	xxx	xxx	xxx	xxx

Class B disyllabic verbs are referenced in the same manner as monosyllabic verbs with the addition of paradigm α or β notation. For example, $má^M?ō^L$ 'assist (TA)'-α.B.24.2 inflects its initial syllable with the tone-stress of paradigm α, is a class B verb, and inflects its final syllable with I-a paradigm 24 and I-b paradigm 2.

There is a limited set of first syllable morphemes found in disyllabic verbs as follows.

1. The causative $má^M$- (§4.8) can be prefixed to state verbs, adjectives, adverbs, and nouns, generally resulting in a transitive verb (see §3.2). There are, however, a few inherently disyllabic verbs which utilize $má^M$- where there is no clear etymology for the final syllable such as $má^M?o^L$ 'assist, help with (TI)'.

2. The first syllable of a few disyllabic verbs appears to derive from the preposition $ŋi^H$ 'on'; as the first syllable, it inflects using paradigm α.

(161) ka^L-$ŋii^L c\tilde{i}^{MH}$ $hná^{HL}$ $hã^M$ $kuá^H huí^M$
        PAST-sit^on^TA^1S   I   one^AN steer
        I sat on (i.e., rode) a steer/bull.

3. A subset of the progressive prefixes (§4.7)—$rá^H$- (singular horizontal orientation), $dí^H$- (singular vertical orientation), and $ná^H$- (plural nonspecific orientation)—is found as the initial syllable of some disyllabic verbs, but the progressive aspectual force is lacking, and they may occur with the progressive prefixes. They inflect using paradigm α.

In transitive verbs, the progressive prefixes mark number and physical orientation of the subject; whereas the morphemes $rá^M$-, $dí^M$-, and $ná^M$- of disyllabic verbs mark the number and orientation of the object. These morphemes are integral to the semantics of several verbs, the final syllable either having no meaning or a different meaning without them; for example, $ŋiu^L$ of $dí^M ŋiu^L$ 'support, brace (DI)' has no meaning on its own. Examples of the verbs $ná^M c\tilde{i}^L$ 'put (plural nonspecific orientation of object) (TI)', $rá^M c\tilde{i}^L$ 'put (singular horizontal orientation of object) (TI)', and $dí^M cií^L$ 'put (singular vertical orientation of object) marked for the progressive aspect (singular vertical orientation of subject) are given in (162).

(162) a. *dí^H-ná^{M}cï̂^{L}*　　　　　*cú^M　sí^M　ŋí^H　hó^{H}ʔmá^M　ó^{LM}*
upright^PROG-put^TI^P^3　3　book　on　board　yonder
S/he is putting the books on that board over there (while s/he is in a standing position).

b. *dí^H-rá^{M}cï̃^{LM}*　　　　*cú^M　sí^M　ŋí^H　hó^{H}ʔmá^M　ó^{LM}*
upright^PROG-lie^TI^s^3　3　book　on　board　yonder
S/he is laying the book on that board over there (while s/he is in a standing position).

c. *dí^H-dí^{M}cïí^L*　　　　*cú^M　sí^M　ŋí^H　hó^{H}ʔmá^M　ó^{LM}*
upright^PROG-stand^TI^s^3　3　book　on　board　yonder
S/he is standing the book on that board over there (while s/he is in a standing position).

In addition, disyllabic verbs formed with these morphemes are able to be affixed directly with the past tense prefixes *ka^L-* (PAST) or *lǐ^M-* (HOD), whereas verbs affixed with any of the progressive prefixes cannot. See (163a) and (163b), respectively.

(163) a. *hã́u^M　ka^L-ra^{L}ca^M　　hná^{HL}　cú^M　ŋí^H　hē^L*
so　PAST-lie^TA^3 > 1　I　3　on　bed
So they laid me down on top of the bed.

b. *hã^M　ʔliáu^L　má^M　lǐ^M-di^{L}cïí^L　　cá^{M}tã^{MH}　cáĩ$^{?L}$　ʔŋiú^L*
one^AN soldier　PRF　HOD-stand^TA^3　authority　roof^3　house
The authorities stood a soldier on the roof of the house.

In disyllabic intransitive verbs, the orientation of the subject is marked by the first syllable *dí^M-* (vertical) or *rá^M-* (horizontal), but it appears that grammatical number is no longer implicit even though *dí^H-* is strictly singular when it occurs as a progressive aspect prefix. For example, the verb *dí^{M}hŋí^{LM}* 'kneel' can collocate with the progressive plural prefix *ná^H-*.

(164) *ná^H-dí^{M}hŋí^{LM}　　cáu^M　ta^L　ŋí^H　mi^{L}hmú^L*
PROG^P-kneel^IA^3　people　before　face^3　bishop
The people are kneeling in front of the bishop.

4. There are two other syllables with obscure etymologies which are found as the first syllable in disyllabic verbs: *iá^M-* and *ʔiá^M-*; for example, *ʔiá^{M}cï̃^{H}* 'appear on top of (IA)' (see (158) above) and *iá^{M}ʔã^H* 'be frightened by (TA)' (see (159)).

4.5 Stable and unstable nuclei

About 37 percent of the 614 verbs in the data exhibit varying degrees of change in their nuclei as they are inflected for person, tense, motion, mood, and aspect. I have chosen the nucleus as found in the 3-PRES as the base form because it is the citation form[33] and because it is also the only relevant grammatical person for intransitive inanimate verbs. A base form is needed in order to describe the types of vocalic changes that take place.

Some of the nuclei in Chinantec appear to be stable, while others have the potential of undergoing change. By stable I mean that if one of the nuclei in (165) is found in third-person present, it will be found throughout the entire verb paradigm. The nucleus *ieï* is tentatively included in the list of stable nuclei; no verb has yet been found in which *ieï* occurs in the third-person present.

(165) Stable nuclei

> *eï*   *iau*
> *ii*   *(ieï)*
> *ou*
> *ue*
> *uï*
> *uu*

The unstable nuclei (that is, those having the potential for change) are listed in (166). The nuclei *ë* and *ïa* are uncommon, so a verb may yet be found in which they undergo some form of modification. They are included in the list of unstable nuclei because many speakers utilize the unstable diphthong *ïe* in place of *ë* and/or *ïa*.

(166) Unstable nuclei

> *a*   *aï*   *iei*
> *e*   *au*   *uaï*
> *(ë)*   *ei*   *uou*
> *i*   *ia*
> *ï*   *ie*
> *o*   *io*

---

[33]When a Chinantec speaker is presented with a Spanish infinitive, the Chinantec equivalent is generally supplied in the third-person present, although occasionally the third-person future may be given. Wilfrido Flores Hernández, my principle language assistant in analyzing verb paradigms, intuitively considers the third-person present to be fundamental in determining a verb's tone-stress paradigm and vocalic changes; however, the precise interaction of tone-stress inflection and changes in the nucleus remains elusive.

```
u    iu
     (ïa)
     ïe
     ua
     uo
```

Two generalizations from the lists above are: (1) if the nucleus is simple, it is unstable, and (2) geminate vowels (*ii, uu*) are stable.

As a verb is inflected for person, tense, motion, mood, and aspect, some unstable nuclei do not change, others undergo only one change from the third-person base form, and others may undergo two or even three changes. Two factors which condition whether or not change will occur, and the degree of change which occurs are the preceding consonant and the tone-stress paradigm.

Unstable nuclei which do not undergo change. There are 142 class A verbs, 74 class B verbs, and 113 class C dynamic verbs in the corpus which have unstable nuclei but do not exhibit any change in the nucleus.[34] There are no known instances of a given unstable nucleus which is preceded by the same consonant and shares the same tone-stress paradigm, that undergoes different changes in the nucleus or some kind of change in one instance and no change in another.

Although the conditioning factors of preceding consonant and tone-stress paradigm may be of equal importance in determining vocalic change, I have treated the preceding consonant as primary in the present analysis because it is easier to list all the consonants which occur with any given vowel than it is to list all the tone-stress paradigms.

Nuclei which undergo one change. There are 115 class A verbs, 55 class B verbs, and 17 class C verbs in the corpus which exhibit one change in the nucleus. After charting these verbs, it was apparent that the degree of vocalic change is not based solely on the consonant preceding the nucleus; for example, the nucleus *a* may change to *aï* or *ia* following *k, n,* or *θ*. Similarly, the degree of vocalic change is not based solely on the tone-stress paradigm; for example, the nucleus *e* may change to *aï* or *ei* with tone-stress paradigm B.15.1.

Example (167) illustrates changes in the nucleus of a class A verb, *kauʔ^{LM}* 'utilize (TI)'-A.67.7.7.1, which exhibits change in four cells in the verb matrix: 3-FUT, 3-HOD, 2-PAST, and 1S-PAST.

---

[34]The various charts and tables from which the conclusions regarding unstable nuclei are drawn can be seen in full in my dissertation (1993).

The Verb

(167)
	3	2	1S	1P
PRES	kauʔ^{LM}	káuʔ^{ML}	kauʔ^{LM}	káuʔ^{ML}
FUT	kóʔ^{LM}	káuʔ^{HL}	kauʔ^{MH}	káuʔ^{HL}
PAST	kauʔ^{L}	koʔ^{H}	kóʔ^{LM}	FUT
AMB	kauʔ^{MH}	káuʔ^{HL}	FUT	FUT
HORT	kauʔ^{MH}	xxx	FUT	FUT
EVID	kauʔ^{MH}	AMB	FUT	FUT
HOD	kóʔ^{LM}	PAST	PAST	FUT
ANDT	káuʔ^{L}	PAST	PAST	FUT
PROH	—	káuʔ^{L}	—	—

Example (168) illustrates a class B verb, ŋaï^{LM} 'cross (over) (IA)'-B.66.2, which exhibits change in two third-person cells and the nonthird-person cells.

(168)
	3	Non-3
PRES	ŋaï^{LM}	ŋa^{H}
FUT	ŋáï^{LM}	ŋa^{H}
PAST	ŋa^{L}	ŋa^{H}
AMB	ŋaï^{MH}	ŋa^{H}
HORT	ŋaï^{MH}	(ŋa^{H})
EVID	ŋaï^{MH}	ŋa^{H}
HOD	ŋáï^{LM}	ŋa^{H}
ANDT	ŋa^{H}	ŋa^{H}
PROH	—	ŋa^{H}

With respect to vocalic change, there are two types of class C verbs: (1) those which exhibit a change in one of the nonthird-person paradigms which is retained throughout the entire paradigm for that person and the tone-stress and segmental elements are independent features; and (2) those which exhibit a change in one or more of the third-person cells, which is then exhibited by the corresponding inflectional parameter for the nonthird-person paradigms. The majority of class C verbs are of this type. In both types of class C verbs, the tone-stress paradigm found in the third-person is the same for all grammatical persons.

Nuclei which undergo two changes. There are eight class A verbs and two class C verbs in the corpus which exhibit two vocalic changes. The nature of the change is conditioned by the preceding consonant alone. To determine if one, two, or three changes take place, however, the tone-stress paradigms must also be taken into account. One example of class A verbs and one of class C verbs are given in (169) and (170), respectively, to illustrate the changes which may occur. Where alternate forms are supplied, the first form is the preferred one.

(169) *haʔᴹ* clean, weed (TI)-A.21.31.6.3

	3	2	1S	1P
PRES	*haʔᴹ*	*háïʔᴸᴹ*	*háïʔᴸᴹ*	*háïʔᴸᴹ*
FUT	*háïʔᴸᴹ*	*haïʔᴹᴴ*	*haïʔᴹᴴ*	*haïʔᴹᴴ*
PAST	*háïʔᴸ*	*héiʔᴸᴹ*	*háïʔᴸᴹ*	FUT
AMB	*háïʔᴸᴹ/héiʔᴸᴹ*	*haïʔᴹᴴ/héiʔᴸᴹ*	FUT	FUT
HORT	*héiʔᴸᴹ/haʔᴴ*	xxx	FUT	FUT
EVID	*haïʔᴹᴴ/haʔᴴ*	AMB	FUT	FUT
HOD	*héiʔᴸᴹ*	PAST	PAST	FUT
ANDT	*héiʔᴸᴹ*	PAST	PAST	FUT
PROH	—	*háïʔᴸᴹ*	—	—

In class C verbs, the tone-stress of the third-person inflectional parameter is identical for all grammatical persons; consequently, only the tone-stress paradigm for third person is given in full. However, the nucleus of second person, 1S, and 1P may differ from that of third person. Because the nucleus which occurs in the present of second person, 1S, and 1P is found throughout the remainder of the paradigm for each person, respectively, only the form for the present of each nonthird person is supplied. The symbol <~ indicates that the tone-stress is taken from the form to the left, and the segmental elements are taken from the form above.

(170) *loʔᴹ* harvest (TI)-C.15

	3	2	1S	1P
PRES	*loʔᴹ*	*lãᴹ/lõᴹ*	*loᴹ*	*loᴹ/lauᴹ*
FUT	*loʔᴴᴸ*	<~	<~	<~
PAST	*loʔᴹ*	<~	<~	<~
AMB	*loʔᴴᴸ*	<~	<~	<~
HORT	*loʔᴹ*	<~	<~	<~
EVID	*loʔᴴᴸ*	<~	<~	<~
HOD	xxx	xxx	xxx	xxx
ANDT	xxx	xxx	xxx	xxx

Nuclei which undergo three changes. There are 19 class A verbs in the corpus which exhibit three changes. No class B or C verbs have been found which exhibit three changes. The nature of the changes can be determined from the preceding consonant alone; to determine if one, two, or three changes take place, however, the tone-stress paradigm must also be taken into account. Note the example in (171) which illustrates three changes in a class A verb nucleus.

(171) *tóᴸᴹ* toast, roast (TI)-A.43.34.2.2

	3	2	1S	1P
PRES	*tóᴸᴹ*	*tauʔᴸᴹ*	*toᴹ*	*tauᴹᴸ*
FUT	*tauᴸ*	*táuʔᴴ*	*toᴴ*	*tauᴴᴸ*
PAST	*tóᴸᴹ*	*tiáuʔᴸ*	*tóᴸᴹ*	FUT
AMB	*tioᴴᴸ*	*tauʔᴹᴴ*	FUT	FUT
HORT	*tioᴴᴸ*	XXX	FUT	FUT
EVID	*tóᴸᴹ*	AMB	FUT	FUT
HOD	*tióᴸᴹ*	PAST	PAST	FUT
ANDT	*tiáuᴸ*	PAST	PAST	FUT
PROH	—	*táuᴹ*	—	—

Degrees of vocalic change. Vocalic changes in the nucleus are only potential; some verbs which employ one of the unstable nuclei do not exhibit any change, while other verbs may have one or more changes. For example, the unstable vowel *o* in the verb *tóᴹᴸ* 'put, stick on (TI)' does not change anywhere in the verb matrix; in the verb *tóᴸᴹ* 'throw (TA)', however, there is one vocalic change (*o → io*); and in the verb *tóᴸᴹ* 'throw (TI)' three changes of the nucleus *o* occur, with *o, io, au,* and *iau* occurring in various cells of the matrix.

After comparing the base nuclei of verbs which undergo no change with those which undergo one to three changes, and comparing the environment with the nature of the changes which occur, it is evident that neither the consonant which precedes the nucleus nor the tone-stress paradigm alone is sufficient to predict whether one, two, or three changes will occur for a given nucleus, or the nature of the change, or even if change will occur at all. By taking into account both the consonant preceding the nucleus and the tone-stress paradigm, however, it appears that the degree and nature of vocalic change can be determined. For example, when the nucleus *aï* is preceded by *n,* the tone stress paradigm A.27.30.6.3 is associated with one vocalic change, the paradigm A.47.18.7.2 is associated with two changes, and the paradigm A.43.33.2.1 is associated with three changes.

Although the two conditioning factors of the preceding consonant and the tone-stress paradigm determine the absence or presence of change in the nucleus and the degree of that change if it occurs, there appear to be no rules for determining precisely which cell in a verb's matrix will exhibit change.

The interaction of tone-stress and vocalic change. At this stage of my analysis, it is unclear whether the utilization of a particular tone-stress paradigm for a grammatical person triggers vocalic change, or if vocalic change influences the choice of a particular tone-stress paradigm. The only issue that is clear is that some tone-stress paradigms for a particular grammatical person are associated with change in the nucleus, whereas other tone-stress paradigms are associated with the absence of change.

4.6 Internal inflection of verbs

Each of the eight parameters outlined in §4.1 that occasion inflection of the dynamic verb root is discussed in more detail in the following subsections.

4.6.1 Inflection for transitivity. There does not seem to be any rule for predicting the changes that occur on a verb root when the valence (degree of transitivity) is altered. Even though some tone-stress paradigms appear to be unique to intransitive verbs (e.g., C.54), transitive verbs (e.g., A.47.19.7.2), and ditransitive verbs (e.g., A.58.37.5.2), there are many paradigms that are not valence specific. For example, the verbs $kué^{ML}$ 'sneeze (IA)', $kuí^{ML}$ 'discard (TI)', and $?ó^{ML}$ 'excavate (DI)' all share the same paradigm A.29.12.3.1; and $hmi?^{LM}$ 'urinate (IA)', $?lia^{LM}$ 'push (TI)', and cia^{LM} 'measure (DI)' all share the same paradigm A.59.32.3.1. Thus the precise relationship between tone-stress paradigms and a verb's valence, if there is any, is unclear.

Inflectionally related verbs[35] of differing valence appear to follow separate tone-stress paradigms, often with vocalic differences as well. The examples in (172) give only the third person, with inflections for future, present, remote past, and the hortative, which is sufficient to demonstrate the existence of different paradigms.

(172)
		PRES	FUT	PAST	HORT
a.	suckle (IA)	$tiú?^{ML}$	$tiú?^{L}$	$tiú?^{L}$	$tiú?^{HL}$
	suckle (TA)	$tiũ?^{M}$	$tiũ?^{L}$	$tiũ?^{L}$	$tiũ?^{HL}$
b.	lower (IA)	$sõ^{M}$	$sõ^{HL}$	$sõ^{M}$	$sõ^{M}$
	lower (TA)	$sió^{LM}$	$sió^{LM}$	$sió^{LM}$	$sió^{MH}$
c.	laugh (IA)	$\eta áï^{ML}$	$\eta áï^{L}$	$\eta áï^{L}$	$\eta áï^{HL}$
	laugh at (TA)	$\eta áï^{LM}$	$\eta áï^{LM}$	$\eta áï^{LM}$	$\eta áï^{MH}$
d.	run (IA)	$kuõ^{M}$	$kuõ^{L}$	$kuóu^{L}$	$kuõ^{H}$
	disarray (TI)	$kuõ^{ML}$	$kuõ^{L}$	$kuõ^{L}$	$kuõ^{HL}$

---

[35] The term "inflectionally related" refers to a verb's syntactic/semantic counterparts; that is, forms which are not just synonyms, but are syntactically in complementary distribution. This may involve differences in transitivity valence (animacy, number, or cross-referencing). Some TA verbs have inflectionally related forms for subject ≠ object, subject = object (reflexive), and subject ⇆ object (reciprocal). The term "inflectionally related" does not imply that the verbs share the same tone-stress inflectional paradigm, although they may; if so, they generally differ vocalically.

In (172a), the intransitive form of the verb 'suckle' is not nasalized, but the transitive counterpart is nasalized to mark an animate object.

In (172b), the transitive form of the verb 'lower' is palatalized; the intransitive form is not.

In (172c), there is no phonological difference between the two verbs 'laugh' and 'laugh at', only tone-stress inflectional differences.

In (172d), there are both tone-stress and vocalic differences between the verbs 'run' and 'cause to run, disarray' (for example, the knocking over and scattering of a stack of bricks).

Although the object of most transitive verbs is generally present, some transitive verbs such as $kú?^M$ 'eat' and $?le?^{LM}$ 'speak' regularly omit the object. There is no change in the internal inflection (tone, stress, or nucleus) of the verb when this occurs as in (173).

(173) $hlá?^H$ $ué^L$ ka^L-$?lé?^L$ ti^{LM} $(hái^{HL})$
       really long^time PAST-speak^TI^3 teacher word/message
       The teacher went on speaking (the message/lesson) for ages.

4.6.2 Inflection of ditransitives. Chinantec ditransitives cross-reference three nominal constituents directly, without prepositions.[36]

The animacy of the DO and the person of a recipient IO affects the paradigm of the ditransitive verb, yielding four subtypes of verbs: ditransitive inanimate direct (DI), ditransitive inanimate inverse (DII) where the recipient is the same as the subject, ditransitive animate direct (DA), and ditransitive animate inverse (DAI); for the direct-inverse contrast, see §8.4. Examples of each subtype, respectively, are given in (174)–(177).

(174) P   S   IO   DO   T
       $kué?^{LM}$ $cú^M$ $hõ^M$ $kïe^L$ $ca^L?áu^M$
       give^DI^FUT^3   3   child^3 money   tomorrow
       S/he will give her/his child money tomorrow.

(175) P   S   IO   DO   T
       $kué^{LM}$ $cú^M$ $hná^{HL}$ $kïe^L$ $ca^L?áu^M$
       give^DII^FUT^3>1 3   I   money   tomorrow
       S/he will give me money tomorrow.

---

[36]Sochiapan Chinantec ditransitives commonly exhibit both the IO and DO constituents within a single clause, unlike Tepetotutla Chinantec which evidently prefers a kind of clause chaining, expressing the two objects in conjunction with separate verbs (Westley 1991:24–25).

(176) P   S   IO   DO
       kuẽ^L cú^M hõ^M hã^M mí^{H}tiei^{MH}
       give^DA^FUT^3 3   child^3 one^AN cat
       S/he will give her/his child a cat.

(177) P   S   IO   DO
       kue^L cú^M pé^H hná^{HL}
       give^DAI^FUT^3>1 3   Peter I
       S/he will give me (to) Peter (in marriage).

Ditransitive verb arguments (subject, direct object, indirect object) and their permutability are discussed in §8.1.

Some combinations of the inflection-set paradigms appear to be unique to ditransitive verbs; for example, A.58.37.1.2 (kue$^{?LM}$ 'give (DI)'), and B.24.28 (dí^{M}ŋiu^L 'brace (DI)'). The majority of ditransitive verbs, however, are not identifiable as ditransitive simply by means of their tone-stress paradigms.

Some verbs may be used either transitively or ditransitively with no change in the internal inflection; other verbs appear to be only transitive or ditransitive. There is no semantic difference for most verbs which may be used transitively or ditransitively (see (178)); however, a few verbs with transitive and ditransitive counterparts differ semantically (see (179)).

(178) a. P   S   DO   IO
        má^M dí^H-to?^{M} cú^M θié^L lái^H ?ái^M
        PRF upright^PROG-put^DI^P^PRES^3   3   noose neck^3 thief
        He is already (standing) putting the nooses (around) the thieves' necks.

      b. P   S   DO
         má^M dí^H-to?^{M} cú^M má?^{L} kuá^L
         PRF upright^PROG-put^TI^P^PRES^3 3   squash   chilacayote

                  L
         ŋiéi?^{L} ?ŋiu^{L}kuî^L
         inside crib
         S/he is already putting the chilacayote squash in her/his (storage) crib.

(179) a. ?íe^L cú^M pé^H
         slander^TA^FUT^3 3   Peter
         S/he will slander Peter.

The Verb   91

    b. ʔi̯e^L   cú^M pé^H ca^Lkuá^H hoʔ^H
      show^DA^FUT^3 3   Peter horse   have^STA^3
      S/he will show Peter her/his horse.

4.6.3 Inflection for reflexives. Chinantec reflexive verbs are transitive or ditransitive. The internal inflection of reflexives differs from that of the nonreflexive counterpart, both direct and inverse. Compare the reflexive forms of 'kill' in (180a) and the nonreflexive direct and inverse TA forms in (180b) and (180c).

(180)   a. *hŋïʔ^{LM}* kill oneself, commit suicide (TA)-A.68.20.4.2

	3	2	1S	1P
PRES	hŋïʔ^{LM}	hŋïʔ^{ML}	hŋïʔ^{ML}	hŋïʔ^{ML}
FUT	hŋíʔ^{LM}	hŋïʔ^{HL}	hŋïʔ^{HL}	hŋïʔ^{HL}
PAST	hŋïʔ^L	hŋïʔ^M	hŋïʔ^M	FUT
AMB	hŋïʔ^{MH}	hŋïʔ^{HL}	FUT	FUT
INT	hŋíʔ^{LM}	FUT	FUT	FUT
HORT	hŋïʔ^{MH}	xxx	FUT	FUT
EVID	hŋïʔ^{MH}	AMB	FUT	FUT
HOD	hŋíʔ^{LM}	PAST	PAST	FUT
DIR	hŋïʔ^L	PAST	PAST	FUT
PROH	xxx	hŋïʔ^M	xxx	xxx

    b. *hnïʔ^M* kill (TA)-A.12.26.7.2

	3	2	1S	1P
PRES	hnïʔ^M	hnïʔ^{ML}	hnïʔ^{LM}	hnïʔ^{ML}
FUT	hnïʔ^L	hnïʔ^{HL}	hníʔ^{MH}	hnïʔ^{HL}
PAST	hnïʔ^L	hnïʔ^{LM}	hníʔ^{LM}	FUT
AMB	hnïʔ^H	hnïʔ^{HL}	FUT	FUT
INT	hnïʔ^L	FUT	FUT	FUT
HORT	hnïʔ^H	xxx	FUT	FUT
EVID	hnïʔ^H	AMB	FUT	FUT
HOD	hnïʔ^L	PAST	PAST	FUT
DIR	hnïʔ^M	PAST	PAST	FUT
PROH	xxx	hŋïʔ^L	xxx	xxx

c. *hna?ᴹ* kill (TAI)-A.12.22.7.2

	3	2	1S	1P
PRES	*hna?ᴹ*	*hna?ᴹᴸ*	*hnaï?ᴸᴹ*	*hna?ᴹᴸ*
FUT	*hna?ᴸ*	*hna?ᴴᴸ*	*hnaï?ᴹᴴ*	*hna?ᴴᴸ*
PAST	*hna?ᴸ*	*hna?ᴹ*	*hnáï?ᴸᴹ*	FUT
AMB	*hna?ᴴ*	*hna?ᴴᴸ*	FUT	FUT
INT	*hna?ᴸ*	FUT	FUT	FUT
HORT	*hna?ᴴ*	xxx	FUT	FUT
EVID	*hna?ᴴ*	AMB	FUT	FUT
HOD	*hna?ᴸ*	PAST	PAST	FUT
DIR	*hna?ᴹ*	PAST	PAST	FUT
PROH	xxx	*hŋa?ᴸ*	xxx	xxx

Reflexive verbs optionally take as the DO a reflexive pronoun (§6.1), which agrees in person and number with the subject.

(181) *kaï?ᴸᴹ*   *cúᴹ (?ŋáᴹ) ɲiɩᴴháuᴹ nɩ̂ᴴ   máᴴ*
       cover^DA^PRES^3 3   self^3S blanket   when^FUT PRF

   kaᴸ-niéiᴹ
   PAST-become^dark^II
   S/he covers (herself/himself) with a blanket at night.

The presence of the reflexive pronoun appears to add an element of contrastiveness: s/he does it to self rather than to someone else; or, s/he does it to self rather than permit someone else to do it to her/him.

4.6.4 Inflection for reciprocals. Chinantec reciprocal verbs imply that the subjects, which must be plural animate, are doing something to one another.

The internal inflection of reciprocal verbs is distinct from that of their nonreciprocal counterparts. All the reciprocal verbs that have been identified inflect as class A or C. Since the subject must be plural, they inflect only for 3P, 2P, and 1P. Compare the paradigms of the nonreciprocal verbs for 'kill' in (180) above with the paradigm in (182).

(182) *hɲí?ᴹᴸ* kill (one another) (TA)-A.27.12.x.1

	3	2	1S	1P
PRES	*hɲí?ᴹᴸ*	*hɲí?ᴹᴸ*	xxx	*hɲí?ᴹᴸ*
FUT	*hɲí?ᴸ*	*hɲí?ᴴᴸ*	xxx	*hɲí?ᴴᴸ*
PAST	*hɲí?ᴸ*	*hɲí?ᴸ*	xxx	FUT
AMB	*hɲí?ᴴᴸ*	*hɲí?ᴴᴸ*	xxx	FUT

The Verb 93

	3	2	1S	1P
INT	hŋíʔ^L	FUT	XXX	FUT
HORT	hŋíʔ^{HL}	XXX	XXX	FUT
EVID	hŋíʔ^{HL}	AMB	XXX	FUT
HOD	hŋíʔ^L	PAST	XXX	FUT
DIR	hŋíʔ^L	PAST	XXX	FUT
PROH	XXX	hŋíʔ^L	XXX	XXX

A sentential example of *hŋíʔ^M* 'kill (one another) (TA)' is given in (183).

(183) hŋíʔ^{ML} cáu^M ʔliá^M táïʔ^M ʔué^{LM}
       kill^TA^PRES^3P people   because   dispute^TI^PRES^3 land
       People kill (each other) because they dispute over land.

With TI reciprocal verbs an overt object is common (see (184)); but an object need not be present (see (185)).

(184) hlá̋ʔ^H ka^L-huőʔ^L cú^M hú^H-ʔla^L ʔi^L
       really   PAST-discuss^TI^3P   3   word-bad^IN   COMP

       ka^L-tḯ^H pé^H
       PAST-regard^TA^3   Peter
       They really discussed bad things (gossip) about Peter.

(185) ti^L ó^{LM} bíʔ^H ná^H-huőʔ^{ML} cú^M
       at   yonder   AFF   PROG^P-discuss^TI^3P   3
       They are having a discussion over there.

With TA and DA reciprocal verbs, an overt DO is grammatical, but is generally regarded as superfluous. Examples of TA and DA reciprocal verbs are shown in (186) and (187), respectively.

(186) tḯ^{ML} cáu^M (cá^M hã^M cá^M hã^M)   ʔliá^M
       fight^TA^PRES^3P   people   person   one^AN   person   one^AN   because

       hlá̋ʔ^H
       quarrelsome^SIA^3
       They fight (each other) because they are quarrelsome.

(187) hná̋ʔ^M cáu^M kḯ^H (cá^M hã^M cá^M hã^M)
       strike^DA^PRES^3P   people   rock   person   one^AN   person   one^AN

nî̗ᴴ   máᴴ   kaᴸ-hẽʔᴹ
when   PRF   PAST-meet^TA^3
They throw rocks (at one another) whenever they meet.

4.6.5 Marking for animacy. Most intransitive verbs mark an animate subject by nasalization of the verb nucleus (57 out of 76 verbs in the corpus). Nearly all transitive and ditransitive verbs inflected for direct cross-referencing exhibit nasalization of the verb root to mark a third-person animate object (141 out of 143 verbs). Morphological nasalization does not occur with the inverse system.

Although animacy tends to entail nasalization, especially for transitive and ditransitive verbs, the presence of a nasalized verb nucleus does not necessarily entail animacy. Morphological nasalization to mark animacy is obscured when the final syllable begins with a nasal consonant, or when nasalization of the nucleus is integral to the verb.

4.6.6 Inflection for person-of-subject. Intransitive animate verbs mark person-of-subject by internal inflection. In addition, intransitive animate, transitive inanimate, and ditransitive inanimate verbs which do not already end in glottal closure as part of the verb root are usually indexed for second-person subject by the addition of glottal closure; however, transitive and ditransitive animate verbs are not. In (188), the first three verbs exhibit morphological glottal for the second-person subject; in the fourth verb, $tiúʔ^{ML}$ 'suckle (IA)', the glottal is part of the verb root, neutralizing the indexing for second person. All four verbs are IA and inflected for the PRES.

(188)	run	whistle	sneeze	suckle
3	$ku\tilde{o}^M$	huo^M	$kué^{ML}$	$tiúʔ^{ML}$
2	$ku\tilde{o}uʔ^{LM}$	$huouʔ^{LM}$	$kuéʔ^{ML}$	$tiúʔ^{ML}$
1S	$ku\tilde{o}^M$	huo^M	$kué^{ML}$	$tiúʔ^{LM}$
1P	$ku\acute{\tilde{o}}u^{ML}$	$huóu^{ML}$	$kué^{ML}$	$tiúʔ^{ML}$

4.6.7 Inflection for subject-and-object. A transitive or ditransitive animate verb is indexed for either the direct or the inverse cross-referencing system by the presence or absence of morphological nasalization, respectively. In addition, there is frequently a change in the verb nucleus and occasionally a change in the tone-stress inflection; such inflectional change generally affects only the 2-PAST, but occasionally it may affect the whole verb paradigm.

In the direct system, either the agent (subject) is nonthird person, and the patient (object) is third person; or, the agent is third-person proximate, and the patient is third-person obviative. The term proximate refers to the first third-person participant introduced in a series of clauses; obviative refers to the next third-person participant introduced (usually in the patient role).

In the inverse system, if the patient is nonthird person, then any person may be the agent (other than self), or if there are two third-person participants, then the agent must be third-person obviative, and the patient must be third-person proximate. In examples, the inverse system is indicated by the use of an arrow, where the agent is shown to the left of the arrow and the patient is shown to the right; for example, 1S > 2 means there is a first-person singular agent and a second-person patient/recipient. Details and examples of the direct and inverse systems, and their interaction with accusativity and ergativity are given in §8.4.

Examples of the direct system, inanimate and animate, respectively, are seen in (189). Examples of the inverse cross-referencing system are given in (190).

(189) a. hlã$?^H$ ré^M pá^{ML} cú^M láu^M
      really well hit^TI^PRES^3 3   skin
      He really plays the drums well.

   b. pã^{ML} cú^M hõ^M ?liá^M tiá^M ne$?^L$
      hit^TA^3^PRES 3   child^3 because not be^obedient^SIA^3
      S/he hits her/his children because they are disobedient.

(190) a. kũ^L ca^L?áu^M bí$?^H$ po^{ML} cú^M hná^{HL}
      each tomorrow AFF hit^PRES^TA^3 > 1 3   I
      S/he hits me every day.

   b. má^M ɲií^H-pou^{MH} hná^{HL} ?nú^M
      PRF   INT-hit^TA^1S > 2   I   you^s
      I am about to hit you.

In (189b), the verb 'hit' is inflected for the direct system and is nasalized to mark an animate third-person object. In (190a) and (190b), the verb 'hit' is inflected to mark the inverse system, which involves the absence of nasalization and, for this verb, a change of the nucleus from a to o or ou.

An example of two third-person participants in which the first and second verbs are inflected for the direct system (indicating that the subject of the second clause is co-referential with the subject of the first clause) is:

(191) ka^L-hĩ^L má^{M}réi^L pé^H tĩ^{L}la^L tiá^M ka^L-pã^L iá$?^L$ cú^M
      PAST-scold^TA^3 Mary   Peter   but   not   PAST-hit^TA^3 ASSR 3
      Mary scolded Peter, but she didn't hit him.

An example of two third-person participants in which the first verb is inflected for the direct system and the second for the inverse system (indicating that the subject of the second clause is *not* co-referential with the subject of the first clause) is:

(192) ka^L-hi̠^{L} má^{M}réi^L pé^H ti̠^{L}la^L tiá^M ka^L-po^L iá$^{\jmath L}$
      PAST-scold^TA^3 Mary   Peter   but   not   PAST-hit^TA^3¹>3 ASSR

      cú^M
      3

Mary scolded Peter, but he didn't hit her.

4.6.8 Inflection for number. All class A verbs differentiate between 1S and 1P subjects by internal inflection regardless of their transitivity, but only a few differentiate between 3S and 3P and between 2S and 2P. This has already been discussed and illustrated in §4.1 and §4.3 above.

A few TI and TA verbs use suppletive forms to mark the number of the object; for example, the verbs tó̠^{ML} (TI^S)-A.47.23.1.2 and sú$^{\jmath ML}$ (TI^P)-A.38.26.7.2 'cause/make to fall down'. An example of each, respectively, is given in (193) and (194).

(193) ŋif^H-tó̠^{MH} cú^M ká^{H}ʔáu^M kuá^H-ci̠^{MH} ʔiú$^{\jmath H}$
      INT-make^fall^TA^S^3 3   chicken   sit^PROG-sit^IA^3   perch
S/he wants to make the chicken sitting on its perch fall (off).

(194) ka^L-sũ$^{\jmath L}$ cú^M cii^{L}ma$^{\jmath M}$ ciu^L sí̠^{M}
      PAST-make^fall^TA^P^3 3   ant   midst   fire
S/he made the ants fall into the fire.

This agreement of a verb with its object as to number is discussed further in §8.3.

4.6.9 Echo. Merrifield (1968:30ff.) described an inflectional category for Palantla Chinantec which he termed "echo", in which verbs form pairs with one denoting a first time action and the other a related action which is subsequent to the first. The same inflectional category is found in Sochiapan Chinantec, as illustrated in (195)–(197). The echo form tends to have glottal closure and a more complex nucleus, but there do not appear to be any definitive characteristics.

The Verb 97

(195) Transitive inanimate verbs

    hmu^M   s/he makes   *hmou?^{LM}*   s/he fixes
    ʔmï^{LM}   s/he sews   *ʔmaï^{LM}*   s/he mends

(196) Transitive animate verbs

    ʔna^M   s/he sells   *ʔnï̈ʔ^{ML}*   s/he resells
    lã^{ML}   s/he buys   *ló^{LM}*   s/he buys secondhand

(197) Transitive animate verbs

    ha^{LM}   s/he comes   *hấuʔ^{ML}*   s/he returns here

4.6.10 The present and future tense inflection. Sochiapan Chinantec verbs distinguish the present and future tenses purely by internal inflection of the verb root. What I have labeled as present and future tenses, Rupp (1989:6) for Lealao Chinantec, and Anderson (1989:8) for Comaltepec Chinantec, refer to by aspectual names, i.e., the progressive and the intentive, respectively. In Sochiapan Chinantec, however, the progressive is clearly marked by a set of posture-oriented prefixes, and the intentive by the prefix *ŋi^H-*.

The verbal inflection I have called present may mean either a present actuality or habitual aspect with certain verbs. The majority of dynamic verbs permit only the habitual sense. There are five classes of verbs which permit either meaning:

1. verbs of cognition, such as *ŋí^{ML}* 'understand (TI)', *ʔnauʔ^M cí^L* 'cogitate (IA) (lit., search heart)';
2. attitudinal verbs, such as *heiʔ^{LM}* 'like (TI)', *kái^{ML}* 'be compatible (IA)', *huéʔ^M* 'fear (IA, TA, TI)';
3. accompaniment/transportation such as *kã^{ML}* 'take with (TI)', *hó^{LM}* 'take home (TA)';
4. verbs of speech, such as: *huáʔ^{ML}* 'say (IA)', *léiʔ^{LM}* 'speak to (TA)', *cia^{LM}* 'relate, tell (TI)'; and
5. the verbs *kuí^{ML}* 'discard (TI︵P)' and *súʔ^{ML}* 'sow, make fall (TI︵P)'.

Examples from each set of verbs which can mean both present process and habitual aspect when inflected for the present are given in (198)–(202), respectively.

(198) a. ŋí^ML   hná^HL hái^HL ʔi^L
      understand^TI^PRES^3 I   word COMP

      dí^H-ʔle^ʔLM   cá^M   ó^LM
      upright^PROG-speak^TI^3 person yonder
      I understand what that person over there is saying.

   b. ŋí^ML   hná^HL hú^Hmii^ʔMH
      understand^TI^PRES^3 I   Spanish
      I understand Spanish (habitual, i.e., whenever I hear it).

(199) hā^LM   cú^M tá^Hla^L lí^HL   má^LM
      wait^IA^PRES^3 3   while finish^II^FUT   food
      S/he waits/is waiting while the food finishes (cooking).

(200) ká^ML   cú^M si^M ʔŋiú^HL ti^LM
      take^TI^PRES^3 3 book house^3 teacher
      S/he takes/is taking the books to school.

(201) ʔí^M   hái^HL huó^ʔLM   ʔno^ʔM
      which^IN? word   discuss^TI^2 you^P
      What things do you discuss/are you discussing?

(202) kuí^ML   cú^M má^Hki^LM ká^Hʔŋiu^MH ʔŋiú^HL
      discard^TI^PRES^3 3 rubbish   back^3   house^3
      S/he discards/is discarding rubbish at the back of her/his house.

The inflection I have labeled future conveys a definite sense of futurity, sometimes with a sense of intent, sometimes without.

(203) hŋï^ʔL   cú^M mí^Mŋií^L ca^Lʔáu^M
      kill^TA^FUT^3 3 pig   tomorrow
      S/he will kill the pig tomorrow.

(204) ʔnú^ʔLM   ŋiú^Mmí^ʔH ní^M hmái^M ní^Hhuá^ʔL ʔi^L
      suffocate^TA^FUT^3 boy   that water if   COMP

            ca^L-liáu^ʔL   kua^L
            ANDT^FUT-bathe^IA^3 river
      That boy will drown if he goes swimming in the river.

When the future occurs with certain adverbs, such as the perfect má^M (§5.2), the temporal reference is future.

(205) máᴹ hmuᴸ   cúᴹ ʔíᴴmiiʔᴹᴴ
    PRF make^TI^FUT^3 3   bread
    S/he is about to make bread.

When a verb inflected for the future occurs with some of the other adverbs, there may be aspectual or modal connotations which do not necessarily have a future temporal reference. For example, when the terminative adverb hmi^H_i (§5.4) occurs with the future, unfulfilled desire (206) or polite request (207) can be expressed.

(206) hmíᴴ láᴴᴸ   hnáᴴᴸ   kắuᴹ   hmíᴹráuᴸ ʔiᴸ hmíᴴ
    TRM buy^TI^FUT^1s I   one^IN soda   and TRM

    aïʔᴹᴴ
    drink^TI^FUT^1s
    I was going to buy a soda and drink it (but didn't).

(207) hmíᴴ míᴴᴸ   hnáᴴᴸ kắuᴹ   ʔiᴸ   kiắᴴᴸ
    TRM ask^TI^FUT^1s I   one^IN tortilla have^STI^2
    I was wanting to ask you for a tortilla (i.e., I want one, but I'm not sure if you will give it to me).

4.6.11 Inflection for the imperative mood. The imperative mood is marked on class A and B verbs by internal inflection alone. The imperative is based on the form of the 2-PAST minus the morphological glottal closure of the final syllable which indexes second-person subject on certain verbs. However, if glottal closure forms part of the final syllable, neutralizing the morphological glottal, the form of the imperative is identical to that of the 2-PAST.

In (208), the first three verbs illustrate the loss of morphological glottal closure when the verb is inflected for the imperative, and the fourth verb, *tiúʔᴹᴸ* 's/he suckles (IA)', illustrates how inherent glottal closure is retained.

(208)   Derivation of the imperative

	run (IA)	sneeze (IA)	slash (TA)	suckle (IA)
3-PRES	kuõᴹ	kuéᴹᴸ	háiᴸᴹ	tiúʔᴹᴸ
2-PRES	kuõuʔᴸᴹ	kuéʔᴹᴸ	haïʔᴸᴹ	tiúʔᴹᴸ
2-FUT	kuốuʔᴴ	kuéʔᴴᴸ	háiʔᴴ	tiúʔᴴᴸ
2-PAST	kuốuʔᴸ	kuéʔᴸ	héiʔᴸ	tiuʔᴸᴹ
2-IMP	kuốuᴸ	kuéᴸ	héiᴸ	tiuʔᴸᴹ

In imperatives, second-person singular pronouns are usually omitted; however, second-person plural pronouns are usually retained. An example of each, respectively, is given in (209) and (210).

(209) nia^MH   ʔo^L ʔŋiú^HL
      open^TI^IMP doorway
      Open the door!

(210) ré^M hïe^L   ná ʔ^M
      well look^TI^IMP you^P
      Look closely!

A few class C verbs form a true imperative the same way as class A and B verbs (§4.1). The functional equivalent to the imperative for the majority of class C verbs is formed by prefixing the hortative kuí^H- and generally retaining the second-person pronoun, as illustrated in (211).

(211) kuí^H-káï^HL   nú^M kiú ʔ^H mí^H mí ʔ^H   lá^M
      HORT-get^on^with^TA^2 you^s   accompany^STA^2 little^girl^this
      You must get on with (i.e., make friends with) this little girl.

4.7 Verb prefixes

The thirty-one verbal prefixes which have been identified fall into ten ordered constituent sets; these are set out in (212), counting back from the verb stem.

(212) VERB → (INJUNCTIVE) (EVIDENTIAL) (PAST) (CONTINUOUS)
             (INTENTIVE) (MOTION) (VENITIVE) (ANDATIVE)
             (AMBULATIVE) (PROGRESSIVE) VERB STEM

Six of the ten constituents have a variety of manifesting morphemes; for example, the injunctive constituent includes the hortative (HORT) prefix kuí^H-, and the exhortative (EXH) prefix ma^L-.

A maximum of five prefix constituents can occur together in a single verb, although rarely do more than three occur. The example in (213) illustrates this maximum; included are the evidential, past, continuous, motion, and progressive prefixes, respectively.

(213) ŋi^H-ka^L-ta^L-ʔí^H-ci^H-ʔó ʔ^LM   dáï^M   pi ʔ^MH ʔŋiu^L
      EVID-PAST-CONT-MOT-suspend^PROG-cry^IA^3   baby   little   inside

The Verb

    mí^Mtiéi^M
    shawl
The little baby in the shawl was evidently constantly crying nonstop (while) hanging (there).

In (213), the prefix *ɲíʃ^H-* connotes that the speaker could hear the action; *ka^L-* marks the event as at least one day prior to the speech act, *ta^L-* marks the event as continuous enough to be regarded as a state, *ʔí^H-* connotes that the noise of the crying was progressive or constant, and *ciʃ^H-* connotes that the subject is suspended above terra firma.

There are certain features which I believe give grounds for distinguishing between verbal prefixes and adverbs which are part of the verb phrase. Prototypical verbal prefixes are those elements which:

1. occur in a fixed order;
2. occur only on verb roots;
3. occasion inflection of the verb root; and
4. can collocate only with a dynamic verb root.

State verbs must first be made dynamic by the causative *má^M-* or be marked for the inception of the new state by the continuous *tá^M-* before they can take these prefixes.

The pre-head verb phrase elements (chapter 5) differ from the prefixes in the following ways:

1. their order is not entirely fixed;
2. they can function outside of the verb phrase, acting as modifiers of other parts of speech, which prefixes cannot; and
3. they do not occasion any inflection of the verb.

Some elements may fail one or two of these criteria for identifying prefixes; however, an element can still be considered to be a prefix if it fulfills the majority of the criteria, or adjacent clearly defined elements require the one in question to function as a prefix.

4.7.1 The progressive aspect prefixes. The first constituent to the left of the verb stem consists of a set of posture oriented prefixes which generally connote progressive aspect (PROG), but at times may be closer to continuous aspect in connotation. Even though this set of prefixes does not meet all the criteria that I have set up as diagnostic of a prefix, I consider them to function as verbal prefixes on the basis that other morphemes which do fulfill all the criteria for prefixes are able to precede the progressive morphemes.

There are five progressive prefixes which can collocate with dynamic verbs; four specify the posture of singular subjects, the fifth is used whenever the subject is plural, neutralizing the posture distinctions: rá^H- (flat or horizontal (S)), dí^H- (upright (S)), kuá^H- (sitting or indefinite (S)), cií^H- (upright, sustained or indefinite (S)), and ná^H- (nonspecific (P)).

Each of these prefixes has been grammaticized from various posture-oriented verbs. The phonological shape of the prefix is often only suggestive of its origin, as can be seen in (214). Each is discussed in turn below.

(214)   Derivation of the progressive prefixes

Verb   Prefix

ró^LM   lying flat (S)   > rá^H-/rá^M-   flat or horizontal (S)
θeʔ^ML   stand (IN^S)   > dí^H-   upright (S)
θẽʔ^M   stand (AN^S)   > dí^H-   upright (S)
kua^LM   sit (AN^S)   > kuá^H-, ɲii^L- sitting or indefinite (AN^S)
cii^MH   stand (IN^S)   > cií^H-   upright or indefinite (S)
cii^H   stand (AN^S)   > cií^H-   upright or indefinite (S)
nio^M   be present (P)   > ná^H-   indefinite (P)

1. rá^H- or rá^M- 'flat or horizontal' collocates with both animate and inanimate verbs. There does not appear to be any difference in meaning between the two variants, although rá^M- tends to occur more frequently when the following syllable is on a low or low-rising tone. The verb must have as its subject/agent either a singular animate or inanimate nominal, or an inanimate mass nominal. Examples of each are given, respectively, in (215)–(217).

(215)   hláʔ^H   rá^H-ʔuó^H   ɲiú^M   nĩ^M   ʔliá^M
        really   flat^PROG-be^tired^SIA^3 fellow that   because

        ɲiéi^H   kú^Hkiú^L
        Go^nonhome^PAST^IA^3S   Santa^Maria
        That fellow is lying around exhausted because he went to (and returned from) Santa Maria.

(216)   má^M   rá^M-kau^LM   ciáu^M   kioʔ^MH   ieʔ^L   pé^H
        PRF   flat^PROG-burn^II cut^field   have^STI^3 elder   Peter
        Old man Peter's cut field is burning.

(217)   ré^M   bíʔ^H   rá^H-ʔmá^H   kéi^HL   pé^H
        well   AFF   flat^PROG-hide^II   money^3   Peter
        Peter's money is well hidden.

The Verb

2. $dí^H$- 'upright, perpendicular to the earth's plane' appears to collocate almost exclusively with animate verbs as in (218), but does occur occasionally with inanimate verbs as in (219); $dí^H$- readily collocates with inanimate state verbs as in (220).

(218) $dí^H$-ko^M $mí^Hmí?^H$ ti^L $ó^{LM}$
         upright^PROG-play^IA^3   girl   at   yonder
         The (little) girl is playing over there.

(219) $má^M$ $dí^H$-hmu^M ta^{MH} řefřigeřadoř $kiõ^{MH}$
         PRF   upright^PROG-do^TI^3   work   refrigerator   have^STI^1S
         My refrigerator is now functioning.

(220) $má^M$ $dí^H$-$?ú^H$ ka^M $?ŋiú^{HL}$ $ie?^L$ tu^{MH}
         PRF   upright-shine^SII   candle   house^3   elder   Anthony
         A candle is now burning in old man Anthony's house.

3. $kuá^H$- (nonsecond person) and $ŋii^L$- (second person) (sitting or indefinite) collocates with only animate verbs.

(221) $?e^L$ $ŋii^L$-$hmu?^{LM}$ $nú^M$ $ŋiú^H$
         what?   sit^PROG-do^TI^2   you^S   friend
         What are you sitting (there) doing (my) friend?

(222) $lá^M$ $má^M$ $kuá^H$-$?í^{ML}$ $hná^{HL}$ $kǎu^M$ si^{fM}
         here   PRF   sit^PROG-read^TI^1S   I   one^IN   book
         I'm sitting here reading a book.

4. The prefix $cí^H$- (upright, sustained or indefinite) collocates with either animate or inanimate verbs; it is preferred over $dí^H$- (upright) for inanimate verb which may reference either a singular noun or a group of objects viewed as a singular entity, such as a field of maize.

(223) ti^L $ó^{LM}$ $cí^H$-$?é^{ML}$ $hmái^M$ $ŋi^{fH}$
         at   yonder   sustain^PROG-sound^II   water   place

         $cí^H$-$?e^M$ $lá?^H$
         sustain^PROG-be^suspended^II   trough
         Over there is the sound of water where a (raised) trough is situated.

5. The prefix $ná^H$- marks both the progressive aspect and plurality of the subject, but does not denote any specific posture. $ná^H$- may replace any of

the singular, posture specific prefixes. Examples of ná^H- with inanimate and animate verbs are given, respectively, in (224) and (225).

(224) má^M   ná^H-su?^LM   mi^L   má^H   ?liá^M   tiá^L
       PRF   PROG^PL-fall^II^P   spherical   mango   because   intensely

       líi^LM   ha^LM   ci^fL
       very   come^PRES^II   wind
       The mangoes are falling now because the wind is blowing so intensely.

(225) ná^H-hmu^LM   hno?^H   ta^MH   kio?^MH   ie?^L
       PROG^P-do^TI^PRES^1P   we   work   have^STI^3   elder
       We are working for the old man.

4.7.2 The ambulative prefix ŋii^L-. The probable source of ŋii^L- (AMB) is the verb ŋi^LM 'walk'. It is used when the direction of the motion is unknown, insignificant, or suppressed for some reason. If no other tense-designating prefix occurs with ŋii^L-, the connotation may be either actual present or habitual aspect.

(226) ?e^L   ta^MH   ŋii^L-ŋí?^H   nu^M   ŋi^fH   lá^M
       what?   work   AMB-walk^IA^2S   you^s   place   this
       Why are you walking around here? (actual present)

(227) ŋii^L-huï^MH   cu^M   ha^H   ?ŋiu^L   ?i^L   té?^ML
       AMB-whistle^IA^3 3   among   house   COMP   call^TA^PRES^3

       räï?^MH
       companion^3
       He walks around in the streets calling his companions/peers (habitual, but not right now).

By metaphorical extension the ambulative can also collocate with the verb ŋi^LM 'walk' when it references an inanimate nominal.

(228) hlá?^H   ?í^Mtäï^LM   ŋii^L-ŋi^MH   třëi^MH   ó^LM
       really   slowly   AMB-walk^II^s   train   yonder
       That train over there is moving very slowly (present). *or* That train over there moves very slowly (habitual).

When a verb is inflected for second person and affixed with ŋii^L-, the tone-stress of the verb generally disambiguates between the second-person progressive (sitting unspecified) and the ambulative.

(229) a. ʔe^L ta^{MH} ŋii^L-hmuʔ^{LM} nú^M ŋiú^H
what? work sit^PROG-do^TI^2 you^s friend
What are you sitting (there) working on (my) friend?

b. he^L ta^{MH} ŋii^L-hmuʔ^{MH} nú^M ŋiú^H
what? work AMB-do^TI^2 you^s friend
What are you walking around working on (my) friend?

4.7.3 The andative and venitive prefixes. The third-order andative and fourth-order venitive prefixes have functional and etymological similarities. The general term for both sets is directional prefixes since motion is seen as taking place with reference to the speaker as the deictic center.

To establish the andative as the third-order prefix, an example of the second-order ambulative ŋii^L- being preceded by an andative is shown in (230).

(230)   cá^M-ŋii^L-liáuʔ^{HL} cú^M kua^L
ANDT^PRES-AMB-bathe^IA^3 3   river
S/he goes to the river to swim around.

The order venitive-andative is illustrated by (231) where the andative prefix ŋif^H- 'go (PAST)' is preceded by the venitive prefix kua^L- 'come (PAST)', resulting in kuá^{M}ŋif^H- 'went and returned'. When these two prefixes co-occur, neither of the past tense prefixes can occur.

(231)   má^M kuá^M-ŋif^H-héiʔ^{MH} cú^M ʔiá^H
PRF VEN^come^PAST-ANDT^go^PAST-weed^TI^3 3   weed^3

kuú^M
maize
S/he has returned from weeding her/his cornfield.

There are ten distinct andative prefixes (ANDT) denoting motion away from the speaker as deictic center, as well as marking person, tense, and mood, as listed in (232).

(232) The andative prefixes

	3	2	1S	1P
HAB	cá^M-	kua^L-	ɲif^M-	cá^M-
PRES	há^M-	kua^L-	ɲif^M-	cá^M-
FUT	ca^L-	kuá^H-	ɲif^H-	cá^H-
PAST	ɲif^H-	ɲif^H-	ɲif^H-	ɲif^H-
IMP	xxx	kuá^M-	xxx	xxx
ATT	cia^L-	cia^L-	xxx	xxx

Most motion verbs consist of pairs that are oriented towards 'home' or 'nonhome'. Home is the place where a person lives and works for himself which could be his house, hometown, ranch, or cornfield. Nonhome is elsewhere.

There are two possible verbs that could have become grammaticized into the set of andative prefixes (apart from the prefix $há^M$- (3-PRES), the etymology of which is unknown): cau^{LM} 'go (home)' or $cã\textasciitilde^{LM}$ 'go (nonhome)'. Native speaker reaction favors the paradigm of cau^{LM} 'go (nonhome)' as the source of the andative prefixes, even though the formal correspondence between the set of andative prefixes and the paradigm for $cã\textasciitilde^{LM}$ 'go (home)' appears to be greater than with the paradigm for cau^{LM} 'go (nonhome)'. Full paradigms can be found in Foris 1993:163.

The Chinantec present can include both actual present and habitual aspect, but a distinction is made between these two aspects in the third-person andative prefixes. The form $há^M$- is used to mark the actual present, and $cá^M$- is used to mark the habitual aspect.

(233) má^M há^M-kiãu^M   cú^M kuo^H   kio?^{MH}
      PRF   ANDT^PRES-bring^TI^3 3   firewood have^STI^3
      S/he is on her way to bring back her/his firewood.

(234) hmáï^H la^L lá^M má^M cá^M-héi^L   cú^M ciá^M hɲiéi^M
      time   about this PRF   ANDT^PRES-slash^TI^3 3   field^3 bean
      About this time of year people go to cut (the jungle to make) their beanfields.

The attainment prefix cia^L- (ATT) in (232) is treated as a subset of the andative prefixes. When a verb is affixed with this prefix, the actual journey to the point of the action is not in mind, as it is with both the andative and venitive prefixes. Instead, the subject is visualized as undertaking (or undergoing) the action from the moment of arrival. The prefix cia^L- (ATT) derives from $ciau^{LM}$ 'arrive (nonhome) (IA)'. The form of the verb is the same as

The Verb

when affixed for the andative. cia^L- is restricted in its distribution, occurring only with second and third person.

When cia^L- occurs with a verb inflected for the third person, it is obligatorily found in conjunction with the hortative prefix kui^H- and indicates a wish is being expressed by the speaker, which can function as an indirect command, as in (235). If the subject is inanimate, however, a wish is being expressed which is generally adversative, as in (236).

(235) kui^H-cia^L-lia^{LM} cu^M ma^{LM} $?i^L$ $ku?^L$
HORT-ATT-buy^TI^3 3   food COMP eat^TI^FUT^3
May they attain the purchasing of food to eat (i.e., I am telling you to tell them to go and buy some food to eat).

(236) kui^H-cia^L-kai^H $?a^H$ cu^M
HORT-ATT-be^torn^II shirt^3 3
May his shirt attain (the state of) being torn (e.g., when he climbs the tree which he insists on climbing).

The only prefix that is able to occur with kui^H- (HORT) and cia^L- (ATT) when both are present, is the intentive $ɲi^H$-.

(237) kui^H-$ɲi^H$-cia^L-$cu?^H$ cu^M $?ɲiu^{LM}$ na^H
HORT-INT-ATT-ruin^TI^3 3   house^IS I
May they keep wanting to attain the ruination of my house.

When cia^L- (ATT) is affixed to a verb inflected for the second person, the sense is of a gentle imperative or a polite request. The second-person pronoun is obligatory, as in (238). A verb affixed with the second-person imperative andative prefix kua^M-, however, requires the omission of the second-person singular pronoun as in (239).

(238) cia^L-$hĭe^H$ nu^M $re?^M$
ATT-see^TA^2 you^s sibling^2
Go see your sibling.

(239) kua^M-$hĭe^H$ $re?^M$
ANDT^IMP-see^TA^2 sibling^2
Go see your sibling!

There are seven distinct venitive prefixes (VEN) denoting motion towards the speaker as deictic center, as well as marking person, tense, and mood, shown in (240).

(240) The venitive prefixes

	3	2	1S	1P
HAB	há^M-	ɲia^L-	há^M-	há^M-
PRES	ha^L-	ɲia^L-	ha^L-	ha^L-
FUT	ha^L-	ɲiá^H-	há^H-	há^H-
PAST	kua^L-	kua^L-	kua^L-	kua^L-
IMP	xxx	ɲiá^M-	xxx	xxx

There are two verbs that could have become grammaticized into the nonpast venitive prefixes: hã́u$^{?ML}$ 'come (home)' and ha^{LM} 'come (nonhome)'. The past venitive prefixes are most likely derived from either kuã$^{?LM}$ 'arrive (home)' or kuã^{ML} 'arrive (nonhome)'. Considering the speaker as the deictic center, it is logical to regard hã́u$^{?ML}$ 'come (home)' and kuã$^{?LM}$ 'arrive (home)' as their sources. However, native speaker reaction favors the paradigms of ha^{LM} 'come (nonhome)' and kuã̂^{ML} 'arrive (nonhome)' as the sources.

The original verbs that became grammaticized into the andative and venitive prefixes are difficult to determine categorically. What is important is the function these prefixes serve in indicating the directionality of motion.

When verbs are prefixed for direction, the sense is motion towards or away from the speaker as the deictic center, not the sense of motion towards home or nonhome. If the direction of motion is indeterminate, either ɲii^L- (AMB) or ʔi^H- (MOT) is used.

A verb inflected for third person and directionality exhibits a single form regardless of the andative or venitive prefix used. This is illustrated by the verbs in (241). In the first row of each partial paradigm, the verb is not affixed for directionality, in the second row it is affixed for the andative, and in the third row it is affixed for the venitive. As can be seen, a verb affixed for directionality undergoes tone-stress inflection (with reference to the third-person present citation form as the base), and sometimes change in the nucleus as well.

(241)
a. la^{LM} buy (TI)

		FUT	PRES	HOD	PAST
	buy	lá^{LM}	la^{LM}	liá^{LM}	la^L
ANDT	go buy	ca^{L}lia^{LM}	cá^{M}lia^{LM}	ɲi^{fH}lia^{LM}	ɲi^{fH}lia^{LM}
VEN	come buy	ha^{L}lia^{LM}	há^{M}lia^{LM}	kua^{L}lia^{LM}	kua^{L}lia^{LM}

The Verb

		FUT	PRES	HOD	PAST
b. $tó^{LM}$ toast, roast (TI)					
	toast	tau^L	$tó^{LM}$	$tió^{LM}$	$tó^{LM}$
ANDT	go toast	$ca^L tiáu^L$	$cá^M tiáu^L$	$ŋií^H tiáu^{HL}$	$ŋií^H tiáu^{HL}$
VEN	come toast	$ha^L tiáu^L$	$há^M tiáu^L$	$kua^L tiáu^L$	$kua^L tiáu^L$

c. $tú^{ML}$ drop (TI)

		FUT	PRES	HOD	PAST
	drop	$tú^L$	$tú^{ML}$	$tú^L$	$tú^L$
ANDT	go drop	$ca^L tu^{LM}$	$cá^M tu^{LM}$	$ŋií^H tu^{LM}$	$ŋií^H tu^{LM}$
VEN	come drop	$ha^L tu^{LM}$	$há^M tu^{LM}$	$kua^L tu^{LM}$	$kua^L tu^{LM}$

A verb inflected for any of the nonthird persons and directionality is always identical to a form elsewhere in the verb's paradigm; for the nonimperative correlates, see the descriptions for class A, B, and C verbs in §4.1.

When a verb is affixed with the imperative directional prefixes $kuá^M$- (ANDT) or $ŋiá^M$- (VEN), the verb is inflected identically as for the simple imperative (which is derived from the past).

(242) $ŋiá^M$-$ʔliá^H$ $tiá^L$ $kĩ^H$ $lá^M$ $ŋiú^H$
 VEN^IMP-push^TI^IMP^2 SUPL rock this friend
 Please come and push this rock, mate.

When a verb is not affixed for directionality, $lí^M$- (HOD) or ka^L- (PAST) are generally obligatory to mark the past tense. When affixed for directionality and past tense, $lí^M$- (HOD) is obligatorily absent, and ka^L- (PAST) may optionally precede the directional prefix; however, it appears that the more remote in time the event is from the time of the speech act, the more likely ka^L- (PAST) will be used. Examples of the use of directional prefixes are given in (243)–(248).

(243) Andative future

 $ʔí^H$ $hã^M$ $cáu^M$ $tiá^M$ $tió^{ʔLM}$ $ʔi^L$
 not^even one^AN person not be^able^TI^PRES^3 COMP

 ca^L-$kiãu^M$ $ʔi^L$ $cĩ^H$ cii^{LM} $hná^{HL}$
 ANDT^FUT-bring^TI^3 thing place^STI^3 head^IS I
 No one is able to go and bring the thing which my head rests on.

(244) Andative present

cau^{LM} cá^{M}mï^L ʔí^L má^{ʔL} ʔi^L
go^nonhome^PRES^IA^3S woman that^AN mountain and

cá^M-ʔniauʔ^M hʔ^M kúʔ^M
ANDT^PRES-search^for^TI^3 edible^plant eat^TI^PRES^3
That woman goes to the mountains and searches for plants to eat.

(245) Andative past

hmḯ^{H}háu^M ka^L-ŋif^H-ʔi^{LM} cú^M siáʔ^L ŋieʔ^M hē^L
then^PAST PAST-ANDT^PAST-enter^TI^3S 3   again under bed
Then he went and got under the bed again.

(246) Venitive present (actual)

há̊u^M ka^L-θá^{HL} hnoʔ^H cú^M ʔi^L ha^L-ká̊^{HL}
then PAST-tell^DI^1P us   3 COMP VEN^PRES-bring^TA^1P

cá^M cō^L bfʔ^H hnoʔ^H
person suspect AFF us
Then we told them that we were coming back bringing the suspect (i.e., we are on our way to where he is staying, then we will return with him).

(247) Venitive habitual

há^M-hā^M cú^M cá^M cá̊u^H ʔŋiú^{HL} tí^{M}mí̊^{L}
VEN^HAB-bring^TA^3 3   person sick house^3 doctor
They come bringing sick people (here) to the clinic.

(248) Venitive past

kí^H křisto dá^M kuā^L ʔi^L kua^L-kā^{LM}
because Christ VER come^IA^PAST^3S and VEN^PAST-bring^TI^3

hú^H-ciú^{LM}
word-good^IN
Because Christ came and brought the good news.

4.7.4 The motion prefix. The progressive motion (MOT) prefix *ʔí^H*- denotes an event as progressive and in motion. Like the ambulative prefix *ŋii^L-*, *ʔí^H*- (MOT) does not imply a direction; reference to a deictic center is absent. Generally, *ʔí^H*- implies that the subject, singular or plural, is walking along while fulfilling the action of the verb. The form of the verb is the same as for the present.

(249) háu^M huóu^LM cá^Mmï^L hmï^H ʔí^H-ʔó?^LM   ʔi^L ʔí^H-ʔo^M
      so   many^AN woman TRM MOT-shout^IA^3 and MOT-cry^IA^3

      ʔi^L   ka^L-tï^H   cú^M
      COMP PAST-concern^IA^3   3

So, many women were walking along shouting and crying because of him.

When ʔí^H- is affixed to a verb which references an inanimate subject, simple progressive motion is denoted.

(250) hlá?^H ré^M ʔí^H-cau^LM   ʔmá^Mlï?^LM lá^M
      really well MOT-go^II^3S wagon   this
      This wagon really moves along well.

(251) má^M ʔí^H-?mu?^LM mu^M ó^LM   ciu^L   hmáï^M
      PRF   MOT-sink^II   boat yonder within water
      That boat over there is sinking beneath the water.

ʔí^H- (MOT) is the first prefix to the left of the verb which is able to occur with the set of progressive prefixes.

(252) ʔí^H-cif^H-la?^LM   hmáï^M co?^M   ʔláu^M
      MOT-sustain^PROG-flow^II   water   side^3 cliff
      The water is steadily flowing down the cliff face.

ʔí^H- (MOT) is also able to occur with the andative and venitive prefixes. An example of ʔí^H- with a fourth-order venitive is shown in (253).

(253) ó^LM   bï?^H má^M ʔí^H-há^M-héi?^LM   cú^M huï^LM
      yonder AFF   PRF   MOT-VEN-slash^TI^3 3   trail
      From over there they are coming along slashing (the overgrowth beside) the trail.

In some contexts the two nondirectional motion prefixes ɲii^L- (AMB) and ʔí^H- (MOT) are interchangeable.

(254) hlá?ʰ ʔíᴹtáïᴸᴹ ɲiiᴸ-ɲiᴹᴴ   caᴸkuáʰ óᴸᴹ
      really slowly AMB-walk^IA^3S horse yonder
      That horse walks very slowly (habitual). or That horse is walking very slowly (actual present).

(255) hlá?ʰ ʔíᴹtáïᴸᴹ ʔíʰ-ɲiᴸᴹ   caᴸkuáʰ óᴸᴹ
      really slowly MOT-walk^IA^3S horse yonder
      That horse is walking very slowly (actual present only).

If the action referred to by the verb can be iterative in nature, however, then ɲiiᴸ- is used to convey the sense of motion between the points where the action of the verb takes place, whereas ʔíʰ- denotes that the action is carried out while in motion.

(256) máᴹ ɲiiᴸ-huïᴸᴹ   gááuʰ haʰ   ʔɲiúᴸ
      PRF AMB-whistle^IA^3 Gregory among house
      Gregory is walking along whistling in the streets (i.e., he walks some distance, stops to whistle, then walks further and whistles again).³⁷

(257) máᴹ ʔíʰ-huïᴸᴹ   gáuʰ   haʰ   ʔɲiúᴸ
      PRF MOT-whistle^IA^3 Gregory among house
      Gregory is walking along whistling in the streets (i.e., he is walking and whistling at the same time).

4.7.5 The intentive prefix ɲiiʰ-. When the intentive (INT) ɲiiʰ- occurs with an animate verb, it is generally intentive or desiderative in its implication. It derives from the verb ʔniᴸ 'want, intend'. The inflection of the verb for the intentive is the same as for the future for each grammatical person, respectively.

(258) a. hniˬ   cúᴹ hmáiᴹ kuᴸléᴸ
         transport^TI^FUT^3 3 water later
         S/he will haul water later.

      b. ɲiiʰ-hniˬ   cúᴹ hmáiᴹ kuᴸléᴸ
         INT-transport^TI^3 3 water later
         S/he intends/wants to haul water later.

With an inanimate intransitive verb, ɲiiʰ- always implies imminence.

(259) máᴹ ɲiiʰ-iéiᴹᴴ   bíʔʰ síᴹ kiúᴴᴸ
      PRF INT-be^extinguished^II AFF fire have^STI^1P
      Our fire/lamp is about to go out.

---

³⁷huïᴸᴹ 'whistle' denotes communicating in whistle speech (see §2.6).

ɲíí^H- (INT) is able to occur with the future directional prefixes. An example of ɲíí^H- preceding fourth-order ha^L- (VEN) is given in (260).

(260) ɲíí^H-ha^L-ʔíʔ^M cú^M hmí^Mráu^L
  INT-VEN^FUT-drink^3 3 soda
  S/he wants to come drink a soda.

It appears that ɲíí^H- (INT) cannot collocate with the fifth-order motion prefix ʔí^H-, probably because of the clash between the progressive connotation of ʔí^H- and the future connotation of ɲíí^H-. In order to group together the four prefix constituents which denote movement (motion, venitive, andative, and ambulative) I have assigned ʔí^H- (MOT) to fifth-order and ɲíí^H- (INT) to sixth-order, rather than the other way around.

Since the intentive ɲíí^H- is homophonous with the first-person future directional, there is potential ambiguity; however, usually a difference in the internal inflection of the verb and/or the context clarifies which prefix is occurring. Compare (261) and (262) using the verb hmu^M 'make, do'.

(261) ɲíí^H-hmu^H hná^HL má^LM
  INT-make^TI^1S I food
  I want to eat. (lit. I want to make a meal.)

(262) ɲíí^H-hmú^MH hná^HL má^LM
  ANDT^FUT-make^TI^1S I food
  I am going to eat (actual movement). or I am going to prepare food to eat.

In (261), the intentive prefix does not entail movement, although movement is not precluded; and in (262) the andative prefix indicates the necessity of motion to another location, but intent or desire is not entailed. For example, it is possible to combine (262) with a negated version of (261).

(263) ɲíí^H-hmú^MH hná^HL má^LM uá^Hhinʔ^H ta^L tiá^M
  ANDT^FUT-make^TI^1S I food even^though while not

  ɲíí^H-hmu^H ná^H
  INT-make^TI^1S I
  I will go eat/prepare food, even though I don't want to.

4.7.6 The continuous prefix tá^M-. The continuous (CONT) prefix tá^M- marks continuous aspect. It inflects for the present, past, and future; the past form being tá^M-, which is the only form found with dynamic verbs. It must be preceded by the past tense prefix *ka^L-* (PAST), and generally is followed by one of the progressive prefixes as illustrated in (264b).

(264) a. *ná^H-hïé^ML   cú^M lio^MH kio?^MH*
PROG^P-watch^TI^3 3   cargo have^STI^3
They are watching their cargo.

b. *lí^H   ka^L-ta^L-ná^H-hïé^ML   cú^M lio^MH kio?^MH*
NON PAST-CONT-PROG^P-watch^TI^3 3   cargo have^STI^3
They just stood watching their cargo (i.e., as the truck went off with their cargo inside).

When *tá^M-* (CONT) is directly affixed to a dynamic verb, there is tone-stress inflection, and occasionally change in the nucleus as in (265b).

(265) a. *ka^L-kuá^L   cú^M ŋif^H ?má^Msi^H*
PAST-sit^IA^3 3   on chair
S/he sat on the chair.

b. *lí^H   ka^L-ta^L-kuá^HL   ?ŋá^M bí?^H cú^M ŋiéi?^L*
NON PAST-CONT-sit^IA^3 alone AFF 3   inside
S/he just remained sitting alone inside.

The internal inflection of dynamic verbs which can be directly affixed with *tá^M-* (CONT) is not equivalent to that of any other inflectional parameter. There are, however, only seven such verbs known (semantically, only three verbs): *kua^LM* 'sit (IA)', *θá?^ML* 'grab, hold (TI)', *θã?^ML* 'grab, hold (TA)', *θãu?^ML* 'grab, hold (TAI)', *ká^ML* 'carry (TI)', *kã^ML* 'carry (TA)', and *kãu^ML* 'carry (TAI)'. Because these make up only one percent of the dynamic verbs in the corpus, I prefer to treat them as irregular verbs in the forthcoming Chinantec dictionary. When any of the verbs glossed 'carry' are affixed directly with *tá^M-*, the sense becomes 'be responsible for'.

The construction of *tá^M-* (CONT) plus progressive prefix can also function as an alternative to the passive (PASS) formed with the directional prefixes (§8.5). Example (266) illustrates a normal passive construction, and the posture passive (PPAS) construction, respectively.

(266) a. *ka^L-ha^L-?ĩ^HL   cá^Mhuú^M ciáu^L*
PAST-PASS-count^IA^3 townsfolk yesterday
The town inhabitants were counted yesterday (i.e., the census was taken).

The Verb 115

b. *ha^H cá^M rē^M co^L bí?^{H}*
   among person owe^TI^PRES^3 offense AFF

   ka^L-ta^L-dí^H-ʔĩ^{HL} cú^M
   PAST-CONT-upright^PROG-count^IA^PPAS^3 3
   He was counted among those guilty of offenses.

The position of *tá^M-* as the seventh-order prefix is established by being able to precede sixth-order *ŋií^H-* (INT).

(267) *lĩ^H ka^L-ta^L-ŋií^H-ku?^{L} cú^M ʔí^L*
      NON PAST-CONT-INT-eat^3 3   tortilla
      For no obvious reason s/he remained hungry (lit., wanting to eat tortillas).

tá^M- appears to derive from *táu^L* 'be situated, be standing (SII^P/SIA^P)'.

4.7.7 The past tense prefixes. There are two prefixes that make up the eighth-order set of prefixes: *lĩ^M-* generally marks a verb for the hodiernal past (HOD), an event that has occurred earlier in the day of the speech act, and *ka^L-* generally marks the remote past (PAST), an event prior to the day of the speech act. In addition, the past is marked on the verb by internal inflection (see §4.1). Exceptions to these prototypical functions are discussed later in this section. Examples of the use of *lĩ^M-* and *ka^L-*, respectively, are given in (268) and (269).

(268) *kú^{H}pi?^{MH} bí?^{H} lĩ^M-kú?^{LM} hná^{HL} má^M?mái^L*
      little   AFF   HOD-eat^TI^1S I   earlier^today
      I ate only a little (food) earlier today.

(269) *ŋií^H hue?^{LM} bí?^{H} ka^L-ká?^{HL} hno?^{H}*
      place large^IN AFF   PAST-dig^TI^1P we
      We excavated a large area.

In the nonthird-person paradigms of class A and B verbs, the hodiernal past and remote past are not distinguished by internal inflection, the prefixes alone marking the past event as hodiernal or remote. Only in the third person, and only in about 40 percent of the verbs, does internal inflection occur. The examples in (270) illustrate, respectively, (1) no difference in the verb between hodiernal and remote past, (2) inflectional differentiation by tone-stress, (3) differentiation by vocalic change, and (4) differentiation by a combination of tone-stress and vocalic change.

(270) a. lî̂ᴹhã̄ᴸ   s/he took (TA)
         kaᴸhã̄ᴸ   s/he took (TA)

      b. lî̂ᴹʔî́ʔᴸᴹ   s/he hid (IA)
         kaᴸʔî́ʔᴸ   s/he hid (IA)

      c. lî̂ᴹtiéʔᴸ   s/he called (TA)
         kaᴸtéʔᴸ   s/he called (TA)

      d. lî̂ᴹkiéiʔᴸᴹ s/he cut (TI)
         kaᴸkieʔᴸ   s/he cut (TI)

The majority of class C verbs, such as taʔᴸᴹ 'fall (II)', kä́i̯ᴹ 'fall behind (IA)', and hué̯ʔᴹ 'fear (TI/TA)', do not take lî̂ᴹ- (HOD), but occur only with kaᴸ- (PAST) even though the event may have just occurred. The prefix kaᴸ- is optional for the class C verb hṹᴹᴸ 'die (IA)', the past being marked by internal inflection alone, hũᴸ 's/he died'. The more remote the event is in time, the greater the likelihood that kaᴸ- will be used.

None of the motion verbs can be affixed with lî̂ᴹ- (HOD), and may or may not occur with kaᴸ- (PAST); the past tense of these verbs is generally marked by internal inflection alone. When kaᴸ- (PAST) is used with a motion verb, it specifies a deliberate act, although its absence does not necessarily imply that the act was nondeliberate.[38]

(271) miiᴹ   ká́ᴹ-cá́ᴸᴹ   bíʔᴴ   ɲiéiᴴ   hná́ᴴᴸ
      year   PAST-finish^II AFF   go^nonhome^IA^PAST^IS   I

      mî̂ᴹʔiaʔᴸᴹ
      Zapotitlán
      I went to Zapotitlán last year.

Although the prototypical use of lî̂ᴹ- (HOD) is to mark the 'past-of-today', it can also be used to mark past in the past, denoting one past event as preceding another past event; the event of the verb marked with lî̂ᴹ- (HOD) temporally precedes the event of the verb marked with kaᴸ- (PAST), but the two past events generally occur on the same day.

(272) laᴸ   má́ᴹ   lî̂ᴹ-hɲiʔᴸ   cúᴹ   mî́ᴹɲiiᴸ   hmî̂ᴴ
      apparently PRF   HOD-kill^TA^3   3   pig   when^PAST

---

[38] When kaᴸ- (PAST) is preceded by a high tone and followed by a mid or rising tone, it optionally permutes to ká́ᴴ-; and when preceded by a high or mid tone and followed by a low or rising tone, it optionally permutes to ká́ᴹ-.

The Verb   117

        káʰ-ciáu^MH   *hnoʔ^H*
        PAST-arrive^nonhome^IA^IP we
        Apparently, they had just killed a pig when we arrived.

    Although *lĩ^M-* (HOD) generally refers to an event since midnight just prior to the time of the speech act, and *ka^L-* (PAST) refers to an event prior to midnight, there is some flexibility in the use of *lĩ^M-* in the midnight hours; an event that took place late at night, say at 11 p.m., may be referred to at 2 a.m. with *lĩ^M-* due to the brevity of time since the event. By sunrise, however, the event at 11 p.m. would be referred to with *ka^L-*.

    lĩ^M- (HOD) may also be used in a manner similar to the English historic present; the speaker chooses *lĩ^M-* as if the events had just occurred earlier in the day. The following extract is from a hortatory monologue where one of the elders of San Pedro berates the inhabitants of a neighboring town, Retumbadero, for their apparent ingratitude after San Pedro helped them several years earlier to become a legally established township.

(273) *káu^M ʔi^L ciu^MH lĩ^M-hmú^L cá^M θiã^M ha^H huú^M*
       one^IN thing good HOD-do^TI^3 people exist^SIA^3 among town

       lá^M
       this
       The people of this town did a big favor (for you).

    ka^L- is able to contiguously precede the past forms for the venitive and andative prefixes, and the ambulative prefix. *lĩ^M-* is unable to precede any other verbal prefix. Both *lĩ^M-* and *ka^L-* may be preceded by the ninth-order evidential *ɲii^H-;* see (276) and (277), respectively, in the next section. An example of *ka^L-* (PAST) preceding seventh-order *ta^L-* (CONT) is given in (274).

(274) *ka^L-ta^L-ʔi^H-cá^Mhéi^ML ʔmá^M ci^Mhíeʔ^M ué^L   lĩ^LM*
       PAST-CONT-MOT-spin^II wood clacker   long^time very
       The wooden clacker went on spinning for a long time.

    4.7.8 The evidential prefix *ɲii^H-*. The ninth-order constituent *ɲii^H-* denotes that there is audible evidence for the action encoded by the verb, as in (275). (In contrast, the evidential adverb *la^L* is nonspecific as to the source of information; see §5.3.)

(275) *ɲii^H-hmu^H   cú^M ʔi^Lráu^L   ti^L ó^LM*
       EVID-make^TI^3 3   crude^sugar at yonder
       Evidently, they are making (crude) sugar over there.

The evidential (EVID) ɲif^H- is able to precede either eighth-order past tense prefix.

(276) ɲif^H-lí^H-ʔlé^ʔMH   cá^M   lí̂^L   ta^MH   má^Mʔmáï^L
EVID-HOD-speak^TI^3 person be^IA^3 authority earlier^today
Evidently, the mayor was speaking earlier today (i.e., I could hear his voice over the loud speaker but couldn't understand what he was saying).

(277) ɲif^H-ka^L-hɲiú^L   pé^H   ʔmá^M   ciáu^L
EVID-PAST-plane^TI^3 Peter wood yesterday
It sounded like Peter was planing boards yesterday.

The only prefixes closer to the verb root which ɲif^H- (EVID) cannot contiguously precede are ɲif^H- (INT) and ta^L- (CONT). However, ɲif^H- (EVID) is able to collocate with them if ka^L- (PAST) also occurs.

(278) lí̂^H   ɲif^H-ka^L-ta^L-ɲif^H-ʔï̂^L   ie^ʔL   hmí^Mráu^L
NON EVID-PAST-CONT-INT-drink^TI^3 elder refreshment
Apparently, the old man was just left wanting to drink a soda pop.

4.7.9 The injunctive prefixes. The tenth and last order of prefixes, the injunctive constituent, consists of the hortative (HORT) kuí̂^H- and the exhortative (EXH) ma^L-. The hortative is generally used to express wishes or desires, and in some constructions it is analogous to the imperative (§4.6.11); apart from class C verbs, it is restricted to first- and third-person subjects. The exhortative is similar to the hortative in function, but also connotes that motion is necessary for fulfillment of the injunction; it occurs only with first-person plural and second-person subjects. Examples of kuí̂^H- (HORT) preceding ninth-order ɲif^H- (EVID) and sixth-order ɲif^H- (INT) are given, respectively, in (279) and (280).

(279) kuí̂^H-ɲif^H-ʔo^H   dáï^M
HORT-EVID-cry^IA^3 baby
Let the baby keep on crying (i.e., child not visible).

(280) kuí̂^H-ɲif^H-ʔau^L   dáï^M
HORT-INT-cry^IA^3 baby
Let the baby keep on acting like it wants to cry (i.e., the child is acting like it is about to burst into tears, but since it isn't ours, let's not get involved).

The Verb   119

As one of the outermost (tenth-order) prefixes, $kuí^H$- shows a mixture of prefix-like and adverb-like qualities. In the examples I have treated it as prefix or adverb according to context.

The first-person singular and plural hortative of class A and B verbs exhibit the same form of the verb as for the future of their respective paradigms. The tone-stress inflection of the verb for the third-person hortative is not identifiable with any of the other inflectional parameters. Examples of $kuí^H$- (HORT) with first-person singular, first-person plural, and third person are given, respectively, in (281)–(283).

(281) $kuí^H$-$ŋii$ʔ^{MH} $hná^{HL}$ ʔ$ŋiu^{LM}$
       HORT-go^home^IA^FUT^1s I   house^1s
       I should go home.

(282) $kuí^H$-$hmú^{HL}$ hnoʔ^H $k\mathring{a}u^M$ ʔ$ŋiú^L$ reʔ^L
       HORT-make^TI^FUT^1P we   one^IN house temporary
       Let's make a temporary shelter.

(283) $kuí^H$-hmu^H $cú^M$ $hu\tilde{e}$ʔ^M $cí^L$
       HORT-make^TI^3 3   large^AN heart^3
       May s/he be patient, forgiving.

An example of $kuí^H$- (HORT) used to form the imperative of a class C verb is shown in (284). Depending on the class C verb, this construction may range in force from subjunctive, expressing wish or desire, to being comparable to a true imperative.

(284) $kuí^H$-$ŋí^{HL}$ ʔnoʔ^M $háï^{HL}$ $lá^M$
       HORT-understand^TI^FUT^2 you^P word this
       May you understand this word/message.

The adverb-like qualities of $kuí^H$ appears to be restricted to formulaic expressions such as $kuí^H$...$kuí^H$ 'whether...or'. Examples of this use are given in (285) and (286).

(285) ʔ$niáu$ʔ^{LM} ʔ$\acute{u}^H$ $nú^M$ ʔ$ua^Lh\tilde{a}^{MH}$ ʔi^L
       be^necessary^SII be^established^STI^2 you^s ready   COMP

       ʔ$lé$ʔ^{HL} $nú^M$ $háï^{HL}$ $kuí^H$ ʔ$nió^L$ $kuí^H$
       speak^TI^FUT^2 you^s   word   HORT want^STI^3 HORT

>   *tiá^M ʔnió^L cú^M ne^L*
>   not want^STI^3 3   hear^TI^FUT^3
> You need to be in a state of readiness to announce the message, whether they want to listen or not.

(286) *kuí^H cá^{H}mí^{ʔH} kuí^H cá^M má^{M}liei^{ʔMH}*
HORT children HORT person mature
whether they are children or adults

The exhortative (EXH) *ma^L-* can occur only with a first-person plural or second-person subject. *ma^L-* probably derives from the uninflected injunction word *má^{LM}* 'come on!' This injunction can often be heard when someone in a group is trying to exhort the group to go and do some project or play some sport together. There is always a sense of motion involved. In (287) the speaker utilizes the injunction *má^{LM}* to exhort a hesitant sick person to accompany him.

(287) *náu^M má^{LM} kí^H ó^{LM} dí^H-té^{ML}*
get^up^IA^IMP come^on because yonder upright^PROG-call^TA^3>2

   cú^M ʔnú^M
   3   you^s
Get up, come on, he's standing over there calling you.

When affixed by *ma^L-*, the form of the verb is the same as when inflected for the future. The prefix *ma^L-* is found most frequently with the motion verbs *cau^{LM}* 'go (nonhome)' and *cã^{ʔLM}* 'go (home)' inflected for the first-person plural.

(288) *káu^M ma^L-cáu^{ʔHL} hno^{ʔH} kiú^{HL}*
simply EXH-go^home^IA^1P we   have^STI^1P
Let's get going home!

When *ma^L-* occurs with a nonmotion verb, the future andative prefix *cá^H-* 'go (1P)' may also occur; in this context, *cá^H-* is generally altered phonologically to *cí^H-*.

(289) *háu^M ma^L-cí^H-ne^{ʔMH} dí^M*
so   EXH-ANDT^FUT-see^TI^1P we^INCL
So let's go take a look.

Even when *ma^L-* (EXH) occurs directly affixed to a nonmotion verb, movement to the location where the action will take place is implied.

(290) ma^L-hlai^{MH} dí^M mí^H sií^M kuo^H
      EXH-cover^DI^1P   we^INCL flat paper firewood
      Let's go cover the firewood with a sheet (of plastic).

Examples of ma^L- (EXH) with a second-person subject are rare. The form of the verb is the same as for the imperative.

(291) ma^L-pá^L ʔnú^M hŋiéi^M
      EXH-strike^TI^2   you^s   bean
      Let's (go and) have you thresh the beans.

The prefix ma^L- (EXH) is assigned to the same distribution set as kuí^H- (HORT) purely on a semantic basis. The only prefix which ma^L- can collocate with is the first-person plural future andative cá^H-.

4.8 Derivational prefixes

There are two derivational prefixes, the causative (CAUS) prefix má^M- and the continuous (CONT) prefix tá^M-. There is also a verb lí^M 'become, happen', which appears to be becoming grammaticized into a derivational prefix, which I have labeled a 'pseudo-activizer'. Each of these is discussed in turn below.

The causative derivational prefix. The causative prefix má^M- can collocate with many state verbs and dynamic verbs, but not all. It can also be used to derive verbs from adjectives, adverbs, and nouns (see §3.2).

When dynamic verbs are derived from state verbs by má^M- (CAUS), they function as any nonderived dynamic verb and can be affixed by any of the inflectional prefixes, but there is no concomitant inflection of the root to mark tense, mood, aspect, or motion as occurs in dynamic verbs. The prefix má^M- itself inflects like the first syllable of disyllabic verbs to mark person, tense, motion, and mood, although in a limited fashion. Examples (292)–(294) illustrate third-person present, third-person future, and third-person hodiernal past, respectively.

(292) hlá^{ʔH} ré^M má^M-tí^{LM} cá^M ní^M hëH
      really   well   CAUS^PRES-be^complete^TI^3   person   that   word^3
      That person really keeps her/his word.

(293) ma^L-tí^M cú^M hõ^M sií^M
      CAUS^FUT-be^able^DI^3   3   child^3   book
      S/he will teach her/his child books (i.e., how to read).

(294) má^M lí^M-ma^L-tí^M   cú^M cá^Hmí?^H sii^M
      PRF HOD-CAUS-be^able^DI^3 3 children book
      S/he has just taught the children to read.

A derived dynamic verb with the intentive prefix ɲíí^H- is as follows.

(295) ?e^L   láï?^LM   ɲíí^H-má^H-tí̧^HL   nú^M cá^Hmí?^H sii^M
      what? be^gained^SII INT-CAUS-be^able^DI^2 you^s children book
      Why do you intend to teach children to read?

When *má^M-* (CAUS) derives a dynamic verb from a state verb or dynamic verb, often there is an increase in that verb's transitivity valence, e.g., intransitive verbs become transitive, and transitive verbs become ditransitive. A state intransitive verb in (296a) becomes a dynamic transitive verb in (296b).

(296) a. tiá^M tí^L   kïe^L   kiõ^MH   hná^HL
         not be^complete^SII money have^STI^1S I
         I don't have enough money.

      b. tiá^M má^M-tí^LM   cú^M hái^HL kio?^MH
         not CAUS^PRES-be^complete^TI^3 3 word have^STI^3
         S/he doesn't keep her/his word.

A dynamic intransitive verb in (297a) becomes transitive in (297b).

(297) a. ku^L ní^M bí?^H ka^L-táu?^L   hái^HL ní^M
         about that AFF PAST-end^II   word that
         That's the end of that story.

      b. má^M ka^L-ma^L-táu?^LM   cú^M hái^HL kio?^MH
         PRF PAST-CAUS-end^TI^3 3   word have^STI^3
         S/he has finished her/his story.

A state transitive verb in (298a) becomes a dynamic ditransitive in (298b).

(298) a. tí̧^M   cú^M hú^Hmii?^MH
         be^adept^at^STI^3 3 Spanish
         S/he is adept at Spanish.

      b. má^M-tí̧^M   cú^M hõ^M hú^Hcõ^M
         CAUS^PRES-be^adept^at^DA^3 3   child^3 truth
         S/he teaches her child the truth.

The Verb

A few verbs, when affixed with *má*^{M}- (CAUS), may retain their same valence but with a semantic shift, as shown in (299).

(299) a. *ʔliãu*^{L} *hmái*^{H} *ka*^{L}-*lé*^{L} *hno*ʔ^H *ʔú*^{H} *hui*^{LM}
    many^IN day PAST-delay^IA^IP we   on   trail
    We spent many days on the trail (unintentionally).

b. *tiá*^{M} *ka*^{L}-*ma*^{L}-*lé*^{HL} *iá*ʔ^L *hná*^{HL}
    not PAST-CAUS-delay^IA^IS ASSR I
    I didn't delay (intentionally).

The continuous derivational prefix. Not all state verbs can take the continuous (CONT) prefix *tá*^{M}-, but it appears that most, if not all, dynamic verbs can be stativized by *tá*^{M}-. There is no change in valence. When *tá*^{M}- (CONT) is affixed to a state verb, it marks a change of state; when affixed to a dynamic verb, it marks the inception and continuance of a state-like condition. These observations are elaborated and illustrated below.

The continuous *tá*^{M}- does not follow the tone-stress inflectional pattern of first syllables in disyllabic verbs (§4.4). There are only four tone-stress inflections for tense and mood, regardless of the grammatical person. These are listed in (300).

(300) Inflection of the continuous prefix

    PRES *tá*^{M}-
    FUT   *tá*^{H}-
    PAST *ta*^{L}-
    HORT *tá*^{H}-

When *tá*^{M}- is prefixed to a state verb and inflected for the present, the state is seen as holding true from time to time (habitual). When inflected for the past, it is optionally preceded by the remote past prefix *ka*^{L}- but the hodiernal past prefix *lí*^{M}- cannot occur with *tá*^{M}-. Examples (301)–(304) illustrate the use of *tá*^{M}- inflected for the present, future, past, and hortative, respectively.

(301) *tá*^{M}-*rãu*ʔ^{MH} *ie*ʔ^L *pi*ʔ^{MH} *ó*^{LM} *kãu*^{M} *tiú*^{L}
    CONT^PRES-possess^flat^STI^3 elder little yonder one^IN rifle
    That little old man over there has a rifle (which is in a horizontal position and which he has borrowed for a prolonged period).

(302) táH-rãuʔMH   ŋiúMmíʔH míHtáïL
       CONT^FUT-possess^flat^STI^3 boy   machete
       The boy will acquire a machete (horizontal orientation of the object possessed).

(303) (kaL)-taL-rõL   cúM   ʔuéLM
       (PAST)-CONT-lie^SIA^3 3   ground
       S/he ended up flat on the ground.

(304) kuíH-táH-rõL   ŋiúMmíʔH ŋiíH héiLM hnáHL
       HORT-CONT-lie^SIA^3 boy   on   bed^IS I
       Let the little boy continue to lie on my bed.

When the state verb root collocates with *táM-*, it frequently undergoes tone, stress, or vocalic change, or a combination of these. Examples are: *rõLM* → *táMrõHL* 'be present (horizontally) (SII^S)' and *θẽʔM* → *táMθãʔH* 'stand (SIA^S)'. An example of a verb root which does not change phonologically is *caíʔMH* 'possess (group of plants) (STI^P)' → *táMcaíʔMH* 'derive, gain (e.g., money, abstract qualities) (STI^P)'. Other state verbs, such as *kioʔMH* 'have (STI)' and *θiaLM* 'exist (SII)', do not take the continuous *táM-*.

The use of *táM-* (CONT) with dynamic verbs has been discussed and illustrated in §4.7. The event encoded in a dynamic verb affixed with *táM-* is regarded as having persisted for such a prolonged period that it is like a state.

(305) uéL   líLM kaL-taL-díH-hiML   cáiM
       long^time very PAST-CONT-upright^PROG-bark^IA^3 dog
       The dog went on barking for a long time.

When either a continuous prefix or progressive prefix is affixed to a state verb, the sense is continuous; however, there are functional differences: (1) the progressive prefixes indicate that the subject is singular or plural and, if singular, give the physical orientation of the subject, but the continuous prefix does not; and (2) the continuous prefix is inflected for tense and mood but the progressive prefixes are not.

The continuous prefix and the set of progressive prefixes supplement each other by being able to co-occur. Normally the progressive prefixes cannot occur with any of the other verbal prefixes that have a future connotation, such as the intentive *ŋiíH-*, or a past connotation, such as the remote past *kaL-* and the hodiernal past *líM-*. The set of progressive prefixes can occur, however, with the continuous inflected for the past.

The Verb

(306) *(ka^L)-ta^L-kuá^H-ʔleʔ^{LM}*   *ieʔ^L*   *ʔŋiu^{LM}*   *hná^{HL}*
(PAST)-CONT-sit^PROG-speak^TI^3   elder   house^3   I
The old man kept on speaking in my house (while sitting) (i.e., continuously, not iteratively).

The pseudo-activizer. At first glance, *lḯ^M* appears to function like the causative *má^M-*, deriving dynamic verbs from state verbs. In other Chinantec languages, the cognate has been analyzed as an activizing prefix; for example, in Tepetotutla Chinantec (Westley 1991:18) and in Comaltepec Chinantec (Anderson 1989:13). In Sochiapan Chinantec, however, *lḯ^M* is an intransitive inanimate verb meaning 'occur, happen, become', not an affix. *lḯ^M* takes only complements as its subject. The complementizer *ʔi^L* 'that, which' is not found in any text material between *lḯ^M* 'become, happen, occur' and a state verb, but if inserted, the construction is accepted as grammatical by native speakers.

(307) *ka^L-lï^L*   *(ʔi^L)*   *θai^{LM}*   *cú^M mï^L*   *má^H*
PAST-happen^II   (COMP)   like^STI^3   3   spherical   mango
It happened (that) s/he came to like mangoes.

There are, however, several textual examples of *lḯ^M* 'become, happen, occur' followed by *ʔi^L* (COMP) when there is a dynamic verb in the complement.

(308) *ka^L-lï^L*   *ʔi^L*   *ŋií^H-kuóu^{MH}*   *hná^{HL}*
PAST-happen^II   COMP   INT-sleep^IA^IS   I
I became very sleepy.

Also, illocutionary particles such as *iáʔ^L* (ASSR) can intrude between *lḯ^M* 'occur, happen, become' and the verb.

(309) *ka^L-lï^L*   *iáʔ^L*   *θai^{LM}*   *cú^M mï^L*   *má^H*
PAST-happen^II   ASSR   like^STI^3   3   spherical   mango
S/he really did come to like mangoes.

Illocutionary particles do not intrude between affixes or between an affix and stem (see chapter 11), so the construction in (309) must be analyzed as the verb *lḯ^M* followed by a complement clause.

There is evidence that *lḯ^M* is becoming grammaticized as a prefix. When it occurs with certain verbs such as *hnió^L* 'want (STI)' or *tí^L* 'complete (SII)', none of the illocutionary particles nor the complementizer *ʔi^L* can intrude. Based on a limited random sampling, there appear to be more verbs which permit such intrusion than those that do not.

4.9 Binomial verbs

Many verbs form couplets to express intensity, iterativity, persistence, or complete-affectedness of an action. The nature of the two bases which comprise binomial verbs are discussed in §3.5. They are not compounds, as almost any of the prefixes and verb phrase adverbs can be repeated with both bases. Nor are they serial verbs, as illustrated in §3.5. The purpose of this section is to illustrate how affixation works with binomial verbs.

The first base of a binomial verb can take any permissible combination of prefixes. The second base, however, takes only the innermost prefix (or adverb, if no prefix occurs) that occurs with the first base. Examples of both a preverb and a phonologically modified verb functioning as the first base, respectively, are given in (310) and (311). In (310), the preverb $\textit{ʔiú}^M$ is of unknown etymology; its presence denotes iterativity of the second base verb mi^{LM} 'ask (TI)'. In (311), the first base verb $\textit{ʔlí}^H$ derives from $\textit{ʔleʔ}^{LM}$ 'speak'.

(310) $cá^M$ $má^Mlieiʔ^{MH}$ $ʔí^L$ $né^L$ ka^L-$ɲi^{fH}$-$ʔiú^M$
person elderly   that^AN TOP PAST-ANDT^PAST-PV

   $ɲi^{fH}$-mi^M la^L $lá^M$
   ANDT^PAST-ask^TI^3 idea this
That old man, he went and kept on pleading in this manner.

(311) $ɲi^{fH}$-ka^L-$ʔlí^H$ ka^L-$liéiʔ^{LM}$ $ieʔ^L$ $hõ^M$ $ué^L$ $lí^{LM}$
EVID-PAST-speak PAST-admonish^TA^3 elder child^3 long^time very
Evidently (i.e., by the sounds of it), the old man kept on admonishing his child for a very long time.

Examples (312)–(315) illustrate the following prefixes, occurring with a binomial verb: a first-order progressive prefix, a directional prefix, the eighth-order prefix ka^L- (PAST), and the tenth-order prefix $kuí^H$- (HORT), respectively.

(312) $hláʔ^H$ $ná^H$-$tí^M$ $ná^H$-$ʔóʔ^{LM}$ $cá^Hmíʔ^H$
really PROG^P-PV PROG^P-shout^IA^3 children
The children are yelling and shouting.

(313) $ʔniáuʔ^{LM}$ $kuá^H$-$ciú^H$ $kuá^H$-$haʔ^{MH}$ $ʔnú^M$ $hái^{HL}$ $lá^M$
be^necessary^SII ANDT^FUT-PV ANDT^FUT-spread^3 you^s word this
You must keep on going everywhere announcing this message.

The Verb 127

(314) ciú^Hha^{MH} lî^{MH} bí?^H ka^L-kiu^L   ka^L-po^L   cú^M hno?^H
publicly very AFF PAST-smite PAST-hit^TA^3>1 3   we
They kept on beating us publicly.

(315) huo?^H   ?nú^M cá^M   cá^Hŋiú^H   ?i^L   kuî^H-tî^H
tell^DA^FUT^2 you^s person young^men COMP HORT-PV

       kuî^H-hî?^{HL}   cú^M ?móu^{LM}
       HORT-correct^TA^3 3   self^P
Tell the young men that they must keep on controlling themselves.

When a disyllabic verb forms the second base, it is unable to take any adverb or prefix; instead, the first syllable of the disyllabic verb affixes to the verb or preverb (PV) of the first base. For example, in (316) the preverb ki^M is used in the first base with the verb $di^Mhŋi^{LM}$ 'kneel', and the binomial verb is di^Mki^H $di^Mhŋi^{LM}$ 'kneel (repeatedly)'.

(316) ka^L-di^Lki^L di^Lhŋií^{LM} di^M ta^L   ŋií^H   cú^M
PAST-PV   kneel^IA^3 3   before face^3 3
They kept kneeling repeatedly before him.

In (317) the second base consists of a derived dynamic verb using the causative ma^L-; the derivational prefix is required on the first base as well.

(317) ná^H-má^M-kí^M   ma^L-kiẽ^M   cú^M dió^{LM}
PROG^P-CAUS-PV CAUS-important^TA^3 3   God
They are praising and honoring God.[39]

4.10 State verbs

State verbs are syntactically distinct from dynamic verbs in the following ways: (1) they cannot be directly affixed with the tense, mood, and motion prefixes without first being prefixed with either the causative or continuous (§4.3); and (2) they do not inflect by tone-stress or vocalic change for tense, mood, or motion. Dynamic verbs, on the other hand, exhibit both of these features.

Not all semantically state verbs are syntactically distinct from dynamic verbs. Some verbs that appear to describe a state do not require a derivational prefix to collocate with the tense, mood, and motion prefixes. For example, the verb $ŋi^{ML}$'s/he understands' is syntactically a dynamic

---

[39]Since this binomial verb is in the present tense, the causative prefix should be inflected to $má^M$- on the second base, as it is on the first base. This appears to be one of the few instances where tonal dissimilation occurs, a process not yet studied, but it appears to be limited to elements within a syntactic unit.

verb, with the past tense $ka^L\eta i^{HL}$'s/he understood (TI)', whereas the verb $tí^M$'s/he is able (STI)' is syntactically a state verb, requiring the causative $má^M$- before being affixed with ka^L- (PAST) to give $ka^L ma^L tí^M$'s/he taught'.

There are a few state verbs that have only one form for all grammatical persons, e.g., $tó?^M$ 'brag (SIA)' and $?ó^M$ 'hate (STA)'. However, many intransitive animate state verbs appear to inflect for 1P and non-1P; e.g., $\theta iõ^M$ 'live (SIA)' gives nonfirst plural $\theta iã^M$ and first plural $\theta iáu^M$.

Transitive state verbs can inflect for the same range of person-of-subject as class A dynamic verbs, e.g., $?nió^L$ 'want (STI)' gives third person $?nió^L$, second person $?náu?^M$, first singular $?nó^{LM}$, and first plural $?náu^M$. Some transitive state verbs display only one contrastive inflection for person-of-subject, but it is the third-person form that is distinctive rather than the first-person plural as for the SIA verbs; e.g., $?nio^L$ 'want, love (STA)' gives third person $?nio^L$ and nonthird person $?no^L$.

There appear to be at least four subclasses of state verbs: posture (including posture possessives), nonposture possessives, existentials, and others. These subclasses are established on the basis of the affixibility of the continuous prefix, the causative prefix, and the progressive prefixes; see (§§4.7–4.8). Each subclass is discussed in turn below.

Posture state verbs. Posture state verbs indicate the orientation of the subject (if intransitive) or the object (if transitive). They (1) permit affixation with the continuous prefix, (2) do not permit affixation with the causative prefix, and (3) permit affixation of all the transitive possessive verbs and those intransitive possessive verbs which reference plural or mass nominals with the progressive plural $ná^M$-. (When the transitive possessive verbs are prefixed with $ná^H$-, the connotation is that there is more than one possessor.)

The known posture state verbs, possessive and nonpossessive, are listed in (318). Number (S versus P) of subject or object is implicit in the verb stem, which is uncommon in Chinantec verbs. The intransitive and transitive counterparts are adjacent.

The verbs $cií^H$ 'stand (SIA^S)' and $cí^H$ 'stand (SIA^P)' do not appear to have a phonologically related counterpart which expresses possession of an animate entity; instead, the verbs $\theta éi?^{LM}$ 'possess (STA^S)' and $tió?^{LM}$ 'possess (STA^P)' are their semantic counterparts for expressing possession of animate entities.

The Verb

(318) Posture state verbs

Intransitive	Transitive

$rõ^{LM}$	lie (S)	$rãu?^{LM}$	possess (horizontal) (S^IN)
$\theta e?^M$	stand (S^IN)	$\theta éi?^{LM}$	possess (vertical) (S^IN)
$\theta \tilde{e}?^M$	stand (S^AN)	$\theta éi?^{LM}$	possess (vertical) (S^AN)
ci^{MH}	stand (P^IN)	$caï?^{MH}$	possess (vertical) (P^IN)
$cĩ^H$	stand (P^AN)		
cii^{MH}	stand (S^IN)	$ciei?^{MH}$	possess (vertical) (S^IN)
cii^H	stand (S^AN)		
nio^M	be extended (P^IN)	$nió?^{LM}$	possess (extended) (P^IN)
hna^H	be planted (P^IN)	$hnau?^{LM}$	possess (mass) (P^IN)
$?a^{MH}$	hold liquid (S/P^IN)	$?au?^{MH}$	possess (liquid) (S/P^IN)
$?u^{MH}$	hold solid (S^IN)	$?aï?^{MH}$	possess (mass) (S^IN)
$tio?^L$	contain (P^IN)	$tiau?^{MH}$	possess (confined) (P^IN)
$tiõ?^M$	live at (P^AN)	$tiõ?^{LM}$	possess (P^AN)

When a posture state verb is affixed with the continuous (CONT) $tá^M$-, there is often internal inflection of the verb root. Examples of the posture state verbs $\theta e?^M$ 'stand (SII)' and $\theta éi?^{LM}$ 'possess (vertical) (STI)' affixed with $tá^M$- (CONT) are given, respectively, in (319) and (320).

(319) ha^H $huú^M$ $bi?^H$ $tá^H$-$\theta a?^H$ $?\eta iú^{HL}$ ti^Mmi^L
       among town   AFF   CONT^FUT-stand^SII   house^3   doctor
       The doctor's house (i.e., clinic) will stand in the middle of the town.

(320) $li?^L$ ka^L-ta^L-$\theta éi?^{LM}$ $cú^M$ $sü^H$ ni^M
       when?   PAST-CONT-possess^upright^STI^3   3   radio   that
       When did s/he acquire that radio (standing) there?

Nonposture possessives. The nonposture possessives $kio?^{MH}$ 'have (STI)' and $ho?^H$ 'have (STA)' are discussed extensively in §6.4. They do not permit direct affixation with $tá^M$- (CONT) nor with the progressive prefixes; they do permit affixation with $má^M$- (CAUS).

When a state verb is prefixed with $má^M$- (CAUS), it becomes a dynamic verb stem and is able to be prefixed by any semantically appropriate dynamic verb prefix. In the interlinear glosses, such derived verbs are no longer marked as 'state'. Examples of affixation with the causative are given in (321) and (322).

(321) má^M ka^L-ma^L-kio?^MH   cú^M ?ué^LM háu^M
      PRF PAST-CAUS-have^TI^3 3   land that^IN
      S/he has acquired that land.

(322) kuí^H-ma^L-ho?^H   cú^M mí^Mŋií^L ?í^L
      HORT-CAUS-have^TA^3 3   pig   that^AN
      May s/he acquire that pig.

Existentials. Existential state verbs do not permit affixation with the continuous *tá^M-*, but do permit affixation with the causative *má^M-* (except for the inanimate *θia^LM* 'exist') and the progressive plural prefix *ná^H-*.

There are three existential state verbs: *θia^LM* 'exist (SII)', 'have (STI)'; *θiã^M* 'exist, be present (SIA)', 'have (STA)'; and *θiá̰^LM* 'not exist, be absent (SIA)'. Although transitive examples are found for the first two existentials, they are uncommon. There is also an existential possessive related to *θia^LM* 'have (STI)' which is *θio?^M* 'possess (mass) (STI)'.

When *θiá̰^LM* 'not exist, be absent' is affixed with *má^M-* (CAUS) and takes an oblique object with the preposition *ŋií^Hkõ^M* 'towards', it means 'disregard, neglect'; see (325) below. *θiá̰^LM* is the only known negative verb in Chinantec.

The causative is found with both the positive and negative animate existentials, but not the inanimate existential. Examples of the existentials with the causative are given in (323)–(325) and with the progressive plural *ná^H-* in (326)–(327).

(323) ?e^L   láï?^LM   ka^L-ma^L-θiã^M   cú^M káu^M ?i^L káu^H
      what? be^gained^SII   PAST-CAUS-live^TI 3   one^IN thing foolish
      Why ever did s/he live so foolishly?

(324) tiá^M ?niáu?^LM   iá?^L ma^L-θiá̰^LM   cú^M ca^L?áu^M
      not be^necessary^SII   ASSR CAUS^FUT-be^absent^IA^3 3 tomorrow
      S/he must not absent herself tomorrow (i.e., s/he must not give excuses for not fulfilling her/his obligations).

(325) ?e^L   láï?^LM   ka^L-ma^L-θiá̰^LM   cú^M ŋií^Hkõ^M
      what? be^gained^SII   PAST-CAUS-be^absent^IA^3 3   towards

      ŋií^Mkuo^M
      spouse
      Why did s/he neglect her/his spouse (e.g., give excuses for not assisting with any chores)?

The Verb

(326) hlá?ʰ réᴹ máᴹ náᴴ-θiaᴸᴹ táuᴹ taᴸnéᴸᴹ
really superb PRF PROG^P-exist^SII banana now
It's superb that bananas are now in abundance.

(327) hmḭʰ náᴴ-θiãᴹ cáᴹ ʔḭᴸ laᴸ kūᴸ ʔiᴸ
TRM PROG^P-live^SIA^3 people that^AN about only COMP

tjᴸᴹ cḭᴸ dióᴸᴹ
reach^TI^PRES^3 heart^3 God
Those people were living in a way which was pleasing to God.

Other state verbs. This fourth group of state verbs do not exhibit the same degree of semantic cohesiveness as is found within each of the first three groups. Included in this group are verbs such as ʔõᴹ 'hate (STA)', ʔnioᴸ 'love (STA)', ʔnióᴸ 'want (STI)', ŋiiᴸᴹ 'know (STI)', ʔniaʔᴸ 'lack, require (SIA)', ʔåuᴸ 'care for (STA)', tõʔᴹ 'brag (SIA)', huoᴹᴸ 'be pitiable (SIA)', tḭᴹ 'be able, be adept at (STI)', tḭᴸ 'be complete (SII)', tḭᴸ 'be complete (SIA)', and rēᴹ 'owe (STI)'.

This group of state verbs are distinguished by the following: (1) they do not permit direct affixation with the continuous táᴹ-, (2) some, but not all, permit affixation with the causative máᴹ-, and (3) they permit affixation with the progressive prefixes.

With reference to point (1), if a state verb is first affixed for the progressive aspect (§4.7), it can then be further affixed with the continuous, marking the inception of a new state.

Although the criterion in (2) is not definitive, there appears to be nothing gained by further distinguishing between those verbs which can take the causative and those which cannot; no obvious semantic subclasses emerge. Of the verbs given above, ʔõᴹ 'hate', ʔnioᴸ 'love', ʔnióᴸ 'want', ŋiiᴸᴹ 'know', tõʔᴹ 'brag', huoᴹᴸ 'be pitiable', tḭᴹ 'be able, be adept at', and tḭᴸ 'be complete' are able to take the causative; the others cannot. For example, the implication of (328) is that a conscious decision was made by the agent to actively benefit the patient on a particular occasion.

(328) hlá?ʰ kaᴸ-maᴸ-ʔnioᴸ cúᴹ räïʔᴹʰ
really PAST-CAUS-want^TA^3 3 relative^3
S/he really showed love to her/his relative.

With reference to point (3), the label progressive for the prefixes in §4.7 is more appropriate to the sense conveyed when they are affixed to dynamic verbs; when affixed to state verbs the sense is more 'continuous'. Generally, with the progressive prefixes, there is also the sense that the state, although continuous at the time of the speech act, has not or will not always hold true.

(329) náʰ-tíᴸ   bíʔʰ   ʔmĩᴹɲieᴹ   tioʔᴴᴸ
PROG^P-be^complete^SII AFF stretchy^fabric put^PRES^TI^P

tãᴹ   hnáᴴᴸ
foot^IS I
My socks are all accounted for.

(330) ʔliáuᴸ   kïeᴸ   kuáʰ-rẽᴹ   hnáᴴᴸ
much^IN money INDEF^PROG-owe^STI^IS I
I owe a lot of money.

In addition to the progressive prefixes in §4.7, there are two other progressive prefixes which are found exclusively with state verbs: ʔúʰ- 'holding, containing' (from ʔuᴹʰ 'enclose, contain (SII)') and ʔáʰ-/ʔáᴹ- 'open' (from ʔóᴸᴹ 'open (SII)'); ʔáʰ- and ʔáᴹ- appear to be completely substitutable for one another, with no difference in meaning. The inclusion of ʔúʰ- and ʔáʰ-/ʔáᴹ- with the other progressive prefixes is based on their similarity to these posture-oriented verbs. Examples of ʔúʰ- 'holding' and ʔáʰ-/ʔáᴹ- 'open' are given, respectively, in (331) and (332).

(331) ɲiíʰ   nĩᴹ   ʔúʰ-ʔõᴹ   ʔlaʰ   séᴸᴹ
place that containing^PROG-be^buried^SIA^3 corpse Joseph
That is where Joseph's remains are buried.

(332) máᴹ   ʔáʰ-naᴹʰ   ʔoᴸtáᴹkiéᴹ
PRF open^PROG-be^open^SII window
The window is already open.

4.11 State verbs versus adjectives

In other Chinantec languages the question has been raised as to the validity of the grammatical class 'adjective'. For example, in describing Lealao Chinantec, Rupp states: "For the most part, the class of Chinantec stative roots corresponds to the class of adjectives of the Indo-European languages" (1989:5). This section specifically addresses this issue from the point of view that in Sochiapan Chinantec, adjectives form a separate syntactic class.

Adjectives resemble state verbs in the following ways.

1. Adjectives can function predicatively in a stative construction. Examples (333) and (334) contain state verbs, while (335) and (336) contain predicate adjectives.

The Verb   133

(333) θia^LM   bí?^H   táu^M
       exist^SII   AFF   banana
       There are bananas.

(334) tiá^M tí^L   bí?^H kie^L   kiõ^MH   hná^HL
       not   be^complete^SII AFF   money   have^TI^IS I
       I do not have sufficient money.

(335) ráu^L   bí?^H   táu^M
       be^sweet^SII   AFF   banana
       The banana(s) is(are) sweet.

(336) tiá^M ciu^MH   iá?^L   tu?^LM nî^M
       not   be^good^SII ASSR   bag   that
       That bag is damaged.

2. Many adjectives, like state verbs, can be made into dynamic verbs by the use of *má^M-* (CAUS). This similarity is not of great significance, however, as verbs can also be derived from nouns and adverbs by *má^M-*; see §3.2. Examples of derived dynamic verbs based on an adjective and on a state verb are given in (337) and (338), respectively.

(337) ka^L-ma^L-kiẽ^M   cú^M   hméi^M
       PAST-CAUS-important^TI^3 3 father^3
       S/he honored her/his father.

(338) ka^L-ma^L-tî^M   cú^M cáu^M   lá?^L   ?î^LM   sií^M
       PAST-CAUS-able^DI^3 3   people how   read^TI^FUT^3   book
       S/he taught them how to read.

Adjectives differ from state verbs in the following ways.
1. There are at least two incontrovertible adjectives that always precede nouns, but cannot be utilized in a stative construction: the evaluative adjectives *uí^H* 'nice, pleasant, desirable, useful' and *?ná^H* 'crude, rough, undesirable, despicable'. These words alone validate the existence of the syntactic class of adjectives.
2. Although adjectives can function predicatively, as in (335) and (336), if a state verb and an adjective co-occur in a sentence, the adjective cannot exchange places with the state verb.

(339) a. nio^M   sií^M dáï^L
          be^present^SII^P   book   red
          There are (some) red books.

b. *dǽi̯ᴸ sii̯ᴹ nioᴹ
   red   book be^present^sɪɪ^ᴘ
   Red books there are.

Other state verbs can be substituted for *nio*ᴹ 'be present (sɪɪ^ᴘ)' in (339a) with no loss of grammaticality; for example, *ti*ᴸ 'be complete, be whole (sɪɪ)', *hniá*ᴸ 'be visible (sɪɪ)', and most of the posture state verbs. Similarly, many other adjectives could be substituted for *dǽi̯*ᴸ 'red'; for example, *pïe?*ᴴ 'hefty', *?mai̯*ᴹᴴ 'new', *kuo*ᴹ 'long', etc.; however, no substitution of state verbs or adjectives for their counterparts in (339b) results in a grammatical utterance.

3. When functioning predicatively, many descriptive adjectives exhibit a special form for 1ᴘ, as is common among sɪᴀ verbs (see §4.10).

(340) a. *pï*ᴸ   *há?*ᴸ
         be^strong^sɪᴀ^3 animal
         The animal is strong.

      b. *pe*ᴸ   *hno?*ᴴ
         strong^sɪᴀ^1s   we
         We are strong.

The 1ᴘ form is not available when an adjective is functioning as a modifier.

(341) a. *há?*ᴸ *pï*ᴸ   *bí?*ᴴ *la*ᴸᴹ
         animal strong   ᴀꜰꜰ   this^one
         This animal is strong.

      b. **hno?*ᴴ *pe*ᴸ   *bí?*ᴴ *la*ᴸᴹ
         we   strong^sɪᴀ^1ᴘ ᴀꜰꜰ   this^one
         We strong (are) these ones.

Examples of other adjectives which have a special 1ᴘ form when functioning predicatively are listed in (342), together with the corresponding non-1ᴘ forms. The non-1ᴘ forms are the same whether the adjective is functioning descriptively or predicatively.

The Verb

(342)   Non-1P   1P
      Inanimate Animate

      $hl\ddot{\imath}?^{MH}$ $hl\acute{\ddot{\imath}}?^{H}$ $hl\acute{a}\ddot{\imath}?^{H}$ wet
      $ci\acute{a}u^{L}$ $ci\acute{a}u^{L}$ $ci\acute{a}u^{L}$ warm
      $li\acute{a}?^{M}$ $li\tilde{a}?^{M}$ $li\acute{a}u?^{M}$ black
      $p\tilde{\imath}^{L}$ $p\tilde{\imath}^{L}$ pe^{L} strong
                    $hu\tilde{\imath}?^{L}$ $hua?^{L}$ lazy

4. There is evidence that neutralization of the distinction between state verbs and descriptive adjectives is not complete when adjectives are functioning predicatively. Strings of two or more descriptive adjectives are grammatical; see §6.5. Such strings are still possible in the stative construction, although fewer combinations are grammatical.

(343) $hl\acute{a}?^{H}$ $r\acute{a}u^{L}$ $\eta ie?^{H}$ mi^{L} $d\acute{u}?^{L}$ $n\hat{\imath}^{M}$
      really be^sweet^sII be^salty^sII spherical candy that
      That candy is really sweet and salty.

A string of state verbs or a mixture of state verbs and adjectives, however, is not grammatical. It would appear then, that the distinction between state verbs and adjectives is largely neutralized in a stative construction, although not fully, as seen in (343).

5. State verbs are able to participate in a relative construction (§9.1) introduced by the complementizer hi^{L} when modifying inanimate and animate nouns, but adjectives cannot.

(344) $h\eta i\acute{e}i^{M}$ $?i^{L}$ θia^{LM} hmi^{fH} $\eta i\acute{\imath}^{H}?i\acute{u}^{M}$
      bean COMP exist^sI occasion spring
      beans which are available in spring

(345) $?m\tilde{\imath}?^{LM}$ $?i^{L}$ nio^{M} $\acute{o}^{LM}$
      clothes COMP be^present^sII^P yonder
      the clothes which are lying over there

(346) $c\acute{a}i^{M}$ $?i^{L}$ $\theta i\tilde{a}^{M}$ ha^{H} $?\eta\acute{a}^{H}$
      dog COMP exist^sIA^3 among jungle
      the dog(s) which live in the jungle

(347) $mi^{M}\eta i\acute{\imath}^{L}$ $?i^{L}$ $r\acute{o}^{LM}$ ciu^{L} $h\tilde{e}^{M}$
      pig   COMP lie^sIA^3 middle mud
      the pig which is lying in the middle of the mud puddle

In all of the above constructions, the complementizer hi^L is optional; however, if the complementizer is present, substituting any inanimate or animate adjective for the state verbs in examples (344)–(347) results in an ungrammatical construction.

(348) *$hŋiéi^M$ $ʔi^L$ $θíʔ^L$ ($hmí^H$ $ŋif^Hʔiú^M$)
bean COMP young^IN (occasion spring)
beans which are young/tender (in spring)

(349) *$ʔmïʔ^{LM}$ $ʔi^L$ $kiá^H$ ($ó^{LM}$)
clothes COMP dirty^IN (yonder)
the clothes which are dirty (over there)

(350) *$cái^M$ $ʔi^L$ $kiá^H$ ($θiã^M$ ha^H $ʔŋá^H$)
dog COMP dirty (live^SIA^3 among jungle)
the dog which is dirty (living in the jungle)

If the complementizer $ʔi^L$ is deleted from (348)–(350), the utterances are grammatical: 'the tender beans (in spring) ', 'the dirty clothes (over there)', and 'the dirty dog (living in the jungle)', respectively.

In summary, state verbs cannot function in a post-nominal position as descriptive adjectives, but adjectives can function predicatively in a pre-nominal position. Therefore, although the distinction between descriptive adjectives and state verbs is somewhat tenuous when an adjective is functioning predicatively, there are sufficient differences to merit treating them as separate syntactic categories.

5
The Verb Phrase

The main purpose of this chapter is to describe the adverbs which function within the verb phrase (VP) and their relationship to one another. The verb phrase adverbs differ from the verb prefixes (§4.7) in the following ways:

1. they have some, albeit limited, possibility of permutation of order;

2. they can function outside of the verb phrase, acting as modifiers of other parts of speech, which the prefixes cannot;

3. they do not occasion any internal inflection (tone, stress, or vocalic change, or a combination thereof) of the verb; and

4. they can directly modify state verbs.

As will be seen, there are some words that may fail one or more of the criteria set up above. I still consider them to be verb phrase adverbs, however, if they fulfill the majority of the criteria; or if adjacent elements require them to be classified as adverbs.

Adverbs which function within the verb phrase can be distinguished from clause level adverbs by the following criteria:[40]

1. Both prefixes and adverbs that are part of the verb phrase share the common characteristic of occurring with both bases of a binomial verb (see §4.9 and §5.9). The ability to occur with both bases of a binomial verb marks these constituents as more closely bound to the verb than adverbs

---

[40]Both Rupp (1989) for Lealao Chinantec and Anderson (1989) for Comaltepec Chinantec treat the perfect, the negative, the terminative, and the nonentailment as prefixes. Co-occurrence and ordering of the various elements is not discussed in any detail. I believe there are sufficient grounds for treating these elements as adverbs in Sochiapan Chinantec and for establishing the unmarked order of these and other adverbs.

which cannot. Those adverbs which cannot occur with the second base of a binomial verb are considered to be outside of the verb phrase.

2. Adverbs which precede the verb phrase head and can be followed by an illocutionary adverb or particle such as $bí?^H$ (AFF) are outside of the verb phrase. The illocutionary adverbs and particles are unable to intrude between the verb and its affixes or between the verb and the adverbs that are part of the verb phrase; when illocutionary adverbs and particles follow a verb phrase, they have the entire verb phrase in their scope (chapter 11).

The adverbs that comprise the clausal constituents include, among others, the manner adverb $hlá?^H$ 'really', the temporal adverbs $hmí^H$ 'when (past)' and $ní^H$ 'when (future)'; these always precede the verb phrase. There are other temporal, locative, and manner adverbs which may precede or follow the verb phrase; see chapter 8. No systematic analysis of these clause-level adverbs has yet been undertaken for Sochiapan Chinantec.

The constituents of the Sochiapan Chinantec verb phrase are given in (351), followed by two examples with a verb phrase (enclosed in brackets).

(351) VERB PHRASE → (NEGATIVE) (NEOTERIC) (NONENTAILMENT)
       (TERMINATIVE) (EVIDENTIAL) (PERFECT)
       (DISCONTINUATIVE) HEAD (INTENSIFIER)

(352) VP [NEG   NON   TRM   H   ]
       $tiá^M$ $lí^H$ $hmí^H$ kue^{LM} $cáu^M$ $má^{LM}$ $?i^L$
       not   NON   TRM   give^TI^PRES^3 people   food   COMP

       $ku?^L$ $cú^M$
       eat^TI^FUT^3   3
       People would not freely give any food for her/him to eat.

(353) VP [TRM   EVID   PRF   DISC   H   ]
       $hmí^H$ la^L $má^M$ $tí^M$ hmu^M $cú^M$ $ka^Llá^M$ ta^{MH}
       TRM   EVID   PRF   DISC   do^TI^PRES^3 3   some   work
       Apparently, s/he had begun doing some work.

The implication in (353) is that the person was young and had finally reached the age of working regularly, but is no longer around. Generally, this would imply an untimely death, although it could mean that the person has left town.

The Verb Phrase

5.1–5.8 The verb phrase adverbs

As illustrated in (351), the verb phrase consists of seven optional pre-head constituents, the head of the verb phrase, and one optional post-head constituent. The pre-head verb phrase constituents are discussed first, followed by the single post-head constituent.

5.1 The discontinuative

The first-order verb phrase constituent is the discontinuative (DISC) adverb $tí^M$. The discontinuative marks an event as no longer true. $tí^M$ collocates with a dynamic verb in the present tense or with a state verb. It can precede the set of progressive prefixes, the ambulative, and the present tense directional prefixes. Examples of the discontinuative directly preceding the verb, collocating with a directional prefix and with a state verb are given in (354)–(356), respectively.

(354) $tí^M$ hmu^M $hná^{HL}$ ta^{MH} $kio?^{MH}$ $cú^M$
      DISC do^TI^PRES^1S I   work   have^STI^3   3
      I used to work for her/him.

(355) $tí^M$ $há^M$-$hã^M$ $cú^M$ $cá^M$ $cã̂u^H$ $ɲií^H$ $lá^M$
      DISC VEN^PRES-take^TA^3 3   people sick   place   this
      They used to bring sick people to this place.

(356) $tí^M$ $\theta ái^{LM}$ $mí^H mí?^H$ $ní^M$ $kó?^{LM}$ $ca^L kuá^H$
      DISC like^STI^3 girl   that   handle^TA^PRES^3 horse
      That little girl used to like handling horses.

The discontinuative, the constituent closest to the VP head, meets criterion (2) above as being able to function outside of the VP. This is shown in (357) where it collocates with an inalienable noun which results in an equative clause (§8.1).

(357) $tí^M$ $?ɲiu^{LM}$ $hná^{HL}$ $?ɲiú^L$ $ní^M$
      DISC house^1S   I   house   that
      That house used to be my home.

5.2 The perfect aspect

The second-order verb phrase constituent is the perfect (PRF) aspect marker $má^M$. It collocates with the nonaffixed verb stem in the present and future tenses, and with most of the prefixes discussed in chapter 4.

má^M (PRF) has been written in Sochiapan Chinantec literature as a prefix. It would appear better on syntactic grounds, however, to consider it as an adverb for the following reasons:

1. When *má^M* contiguously precedes the verb, it does not occasion any internal inflection of the verb and, in fact, can occur with the verb inflected for either present or future.

2. *má^M* can permute with the seventh-order negative *tiá^M*. When the negative adverb precedes the perfect adverb, as in (358), the meaning is 'not yet' (a statement of fact); but when the order is reversed as in (359), the meaning is 'still not' (implying surprise or irritation). Examples of the unmarked (more common) order and the marked order, respectively, are given in (358) and (359).

(358) tiá^M má^M ŋa^M cú^M ʔí^H ká^M hō^H háï^{HL}
      not   PRF   answer^TI^PRES^3 3   not^even one^IN portion word
      S/he is not yet answering (with) even a single word.

(359) la^L má^M tiá^M ŋa^M hā́u^M bíʔ^H cú^M ʔí^H kā́u^M
      as   PRF   not   answer^TI^PRES^3 then AFF 3   not^even one^IN

      háï^{HL}
      word
      Like before, s/he is still not answering (with) a single word.

3. *má^M* can collocate with adverbs and inalienable nouns.

(360) cá^H-hḯ^{HL} dí^M ciáu^M kiú^{HL} ʔi^L rō^{LM} ɲif^H
      ANDT^FUT-burn^TI^1P we   cutting have^STI^1P COMP lie^SII place

      má^M uóu$^{?L}$
      PRF   far
      We will go burn one of our further cuttings.

(361) ʔí^H ka^{L}la^L tï^L ʔi^L kioʔ^{MH} cá^M má^M rē̃ʔ^M iáʔ^L
      even^to even   at thing have^STI^3 person PRF   relative^2 ASSR

      náʔ^M náH-ʔāï̃ʔ^{LM}
      you^P   PROG^P-steal^TI^2
      You are even stealing those things that belong to those who are now your relatives.

má^M (PRF) plus a verb inflected for the future tense marks a situation as imminent. *má^M* plus a verb inflected for the present tense marks a situation

The Verb Phrase 141

as inchoative; the focus is on the recent inception and current relevance, either actual present or habitual. *má^M* plus the past prefixes, whether hodiernal or remote, marks a situation as recent and perfective. Examples of each use are given in (362)–(365), respectively.

(362) *má^M tiú^{LM} ieʔ^L sé^{LM} hó^H ʔmá^M kiá̰^{HL} nú^M*
   PRF   cut^TI^FUT^3 elder Joseph flat wood have^STI^2 you^s
   Old man Joseph is about to cut boards for you.

(363) *má^M lẽ^L hná^{HL} ʔi^L ɲie^H hmái^H*
   PRF   think^TI^PRES^1S I   COMP go^nonhome^IA^FUT^1S fiesta
   I now think that I will go to the fiesta (present).

(364) *má^M kú^M ɲiú^{M}mí^{ʔH} lí^H*
   PRF   eat^TI^PRES^3   boy   tepejilote
   The boy now eats tepejilote (a bitter edible palm) (habitual).

(365) *má^M ka^L-hɲií^L cú^M kuú^M ti^L huí^{LM} kua^{L}uõu^M*
   PRF   PAST-sow^TI^3 3   maize   at   path   Quetzalapa
   S/he has just/already sown maize (in her/his field) by the trail to Quetzalapa.

má^M (PRF) with a state verb generally implies that the opposite condition was true until recently, an implication that is also true when *má^M* occurs with verbs in the present (see (364)).

(366) *má^M ɲii^{MH} hná^{HL} huí^{LM} ti^L híʔ^{LM}*
   PRF   know^STI^1S   trail   to   at   Usila
   I now know the way to Usila.

má^M can occur with most of the inflectional prefixes and both of the derivational prefixes. Examples of *má^M* with a first-order progressive prefix, the fifth-order motion prefix, and the ninth-order evidential prefix are given, respectively, in (367)–(369).

(367) *má^M dí^H-ʔleʔ^{LM} ti^{LM} tu^{MH}*
   PRF   upright^PROG-speak^TI^3 teacher Anthony
   The teacher Anthony is now standing (there) speaking.

(368) *tá^{H}la^L má^M ʔí^H-tiáu^{ʔH} hnoʔ^H hãu^M huí^{LM}*
   while   PRF   MOT-be^present^IA^1P we   then   trail
   While we were already on the trail at that time,...

(369) ʔla^H ti^{LM} hë^H dió^{LM} má^M ŋif^H-téʔ^{HL} cá^M nĩ^M
     deceased master word^3 God PRF EVID-call^TA^3 person that^AN
     It sounds like that person is now calling on the deceased prophet.

Examples of *má^M* (PRF) with the causative and continuous derivational prefixes are given, respectively, in (370) and (371).

(370) má^M má^M-siǔʔ^H cú^M cii^L táʔ^M piʔ^{MH} ŋif^H sĩ^{M}ʔia^{LM}
     PRF   CAUS^PRES-dry^TA^3   3   DIM crayfish little on clay^dish
     S/he is now toasting the little crayfish in the clay dish.

(371) má^M tá^H-rãuʔ^{MH} ŋiuʔ^{LM} hná^{HL} kǎu^M
     PRF   CONT^FUT-possess^horizontal^STI^3 father^is I   one^IN

     sǔ^H ʔmaï^{MH}
     radio new
     My father is about to acquire a new radio.

A future perfect is constructed by using a verb inflected for the past tense and preceded by the perfect adverb on a high tone. The words *nĩ^H* 'when (FUT)' and *nĩ^{H}huáʔ^L* 'if' in (372) and (373) are optional.

(372) (nĩ^H)   má^H ka^L-hŋĩʔ^L cú^M mí^{M}ŋif^L né^L
     (when^FUT) PRF PAST-kill^TA^3 3 pig   TOP
     When the pig has been killed,...

(373) (nĩ^{H}huáʔ^L) má^H ka^L-ʔiõ^M ʔiá^H kuú^M
     (if)   PRF PAST-sprout^II^3 weed^3 maize
     If the weeds have sprouted in the cornfield...

The position of *má^M* as a second-order adverb can be seen in (374), where *má^M* precedes first-order *tĩ^M* (DISC).

(374) hmĩ^H má^M tĩ^M hmu^M ʔla^H pé^H ka^{L}lá^M ta^{MH}
     TRM PRF DISC do^TI^PRES^3 deceased Peter some work
     The deceased Peter had begun to do some work.

5.3 The evidential adverb

The third-order verb phrase constituent is the evidential (EVID) adverb *la^L*. It is nonspecific as to the source of information, unlike the evidential prefix *ŋif^H-* which requires that the source of information be audible. Nevertheless,

The Verb Phrase

if there is no obvious source of information (as in (377)), the speaker is assumed to have heard the information that s/he is expressing.

la^L can denote sources of information other than audible; examples of visual and taste perception are given in (375) and (376). Sometimes, as in (375), la^L may imply surprise or, as in (376), contraexpectation. An example of la^L preceding second-order $má^M$ (PRF) is given in (377).

(375) la^L $kuá^M$-$ŋie^H$ $hmî^L$ ha^H $niéi^M$
      EVID VEN^PAST-go^II rain among darkness
      It looks like it rained during the night.

(376) la^L hma^M $bí?^H$ sandia
      EVID be^tasty^SII AFF   watermelon
      Watermelon is tasty after all.

(377) la^L $má^M$ $lî^M$-$kiéi?^{LM}$ $gáu^H$ $mí?^H$ ta^L
      EVID PRF   HOD-slash^TI^3   Gregory little leg^3
      Apparently, little Gregory has just slashed his leg.

5.4 The terminative adverb

The fourth-order verb phrase constituent is the terminative (TRM) adverb $hmí^{tH}$. When $hmí^{tH}$ (TRM) combines with a verb in the present tense, the implication is that the situation is no longer true, resembling the implication of $tî^M$ (DISC) with the present (§5.1). $hmí^{tH}$, as in (378), however, generally refers to a more recent situation than that referred to by $tî^M$, as in (379). The choice of adverb is dependent on the larger discourse context.

(378) $hmí^{tH}$ tiu^{LM} $cú^M$ $?má^M$ la^L $kǎu^M$ $lá^M$
      TRM   cut^TI^PRES^3 3 wood   about   one^IN this
      They used to cut logs (into boards) in this area (relatively recent past).

(379) $tî^M$ tiu^{LM} $cú^M$ $?má^M$ la^L $kǎu^M$ $lá^M$
      DISC   cut^TI^PRES^3 3 wood   about   one^IN this
      They used to cut logs (into boards) in this area (relatively distant past).

Alternatively, $hmí^{tH}$ (TRM) can imply that, although the former situation is not currently true, it may become true again; whereas $tî^M$ implies that the former situation is unlikely to ever hold true again. The truth condition of both the terminative and the discontinuative adverbs is absolute; neither permits the addition of 'and s/he still does'. It is possible for both $tî^M$ and $hmí^{tH}$

to co-occur, indicating even more strongly the improbability of the former situation recurring.

(380) hmḯ^H tḭ^M ta^LM   cá^Mmi^L ʔáu^HL ŋif^Mkuo^M
       TRM DISC weave^TI^PRES^3 woman pants^3 spouse^3
       The women used to weave their husband's pants.

hmḯ^H (TRM) with a verb in the future tense generally marks either a change in plans due to extenuating circumstances or unfulfilled potential. It may also have an optative connotation, encoding a very polite request. These two nuances of meaning are illustrated in (381) and (382), respectively.

(381) hmḯ^H hú^HL   hná^HL ciáu^M   ca^Lʔáu^M
       TRM burn^TI^FUT^1s I   cuttings tomorrow
       I was going to burn the cuttings tomorrow (but no longer will).

(382) mḭ^L   bíʔ^H hmḯ^H lá^HL   hná^HL ka^Llá^M
       medicine AFF TRM buy^TI^FUT^1s I   some
       I would like to buy some medicine.

hmḯ^H (TRM) plus the intentive (INT) prefix ŋif^H- generally marks a change in intention.

(383) tiá^M hmḯ^H ŋif^H-kué^MH   ʔnú^M cá^M ʔḭ^L ʔi^L
       not TRM INT-give^DI^3>2 you^s person that^AN thing

       mḭʔ^LM
       ask^TI^PRES^2
       That person was not intending to give you the thing you were asking for (but s/he did).

In addition, hmḯ^H (TRM) is able to collocate with the motion, past, ambulative, and directional prefixes; see, e.g., (384) and (386).

The temporal adverb hmḯ^H 'when (PAST)' and the terminative adverb hmḯ^H have probably both derived from the temporal noun hmáḯ^H 'day, time, occasion, fiesta'. Although homophonous, they can be easily disambiguated. The temporal adverb for 'when (PAST)' can be replaced by the phrase hmáḯ^H ʔi^L 'time that', but the terminative adverb cannot. The second hmḯ^H in example (384) can be readily rephrased as in (385). If, however, the first instance of hmḯ^H is replaced with hmáḯ^H ʔi^L, the result is ungrammatical. (The implication of the terminative hmḯ^H in both examples is that consequently, he no longer plays the guitar.)

The Verb Phrase   145

(384)   hmĩ́ʰ   ʔíʰ-kauʔᴸᴹ   tū́ᴸᴹ   ʔlaᴴ   séᴸᴹ   hmĩ́ʰ
        TRM   MOT-play^TI^3 guitar deceased Joseph when^PAST

        kaᴸ-tã́ʔᴸ
        PAST-fall^IA^3
        The late Joseph was walking along playing his guitar when he fell.

(385)   hmĩ́ʰ   ʔíʰ-kauʔᴸᴹ   tū́ᴸᴹ   ʔlaᴴ   séᴸᴹ   hmáïʰ   ʔiᴸ
        TRM   MOT-play^TI^3 guitar deceased Joseph time   COMP

        kaᴸ-tã́ʔᴸ
        PAST-fall^IA^3
        The late Joseph was walking along playing his guitar at the time he fell.

When the terminative occurs with a verb in the past tense in a complex sentence, it marks the clause as temporally antecedent to the subordinate clause. Combined with the perfect *máᴹ*, the sense is pluperfect.

(386)   hmĩ́ʰ   máᴹ   lĩ́ᴹ-ʔȭᴴ   hnoʔᴴ   ʔlaᴴ   hmĩ́ʰ
        TRM   PRF   HOD-bury^TA^1P we   deceased when^PAST

        ká́ᴴ-cióᴹᴴ   mí́ᴹcáuᴹ
        PAST-arrive^nonhome^IA^3S   priest
        We had already buried the deceased when the priest arrived.

The terminative *hmĩ́ʰ* is able to modify a nominal predicate (see §8.1) as can most of the other VP adverbs. (None of the verbal prefixes can occur in this type of construction.)

(387)   P   S
        hmĩ́ʰ   ʔuéᴴᴸ   tuᴹᴴ   ʔuéᴸᴹ   óᴸᴹ
        TRM   land^3   Anthony land   yonder
        That land there used to be Anthony's (land).

An example of *hmĩ́ʰ* preceding third-order *laᴸ* (EVID) is:

(388)   hmĩ́ʰ   laᴸ   ɲiʰ-θiauᴸ   cúᴹ   ʔmáᴹ   nĩ́ᴹ
        TRM   EVID   INT-raise^TI^3   3   log   that
        Apparently, s/he was wanting to raise that log up.

5.5 The nonentailment adverb

The fifth-order verb phrase constituent is the nonentailment (NON) adverb *lḯH*. *lḯH* marks an action or state as having no causal antecedent and often can be represented by the gloss 'just'. It is able to collocate with a wide variety of other verb phrase adverbs and verbal prefixes. Two examples of the many possibilities are in (389) and (390).

(389) *ʔaL   lḯM   lḯH   kuḯH-lḯHL   ʔnoʔM   laL   nḯM*
      MODR PROH NON   HORT-think^TI^FUT^2 you^P   idea that
      Don't just think such things (without any reason).

(390) *lḯH   hmḯH   náH-tắïʔML   bíʔH   cúM   háiHL*
      NON   TRM   PROG^P-obstruct^DI^3   AFF   they word
      They used to just constantly argue (for no reason).

The numeral *kắuM* 'one (IN)' frequently occurs with *lḯH*, functioning adverbially as an intensifier; *kắuM* is glossed 'simply' when it collocates with *lḯH*.

(391) *tiáM   kắuM   lḯH   mḯHL   hnáHL   kïeL*
      not   simply NON   request^TI^FUT^1S   I   money
      I don't just simply ask for handouts.

An example of *lḯH* preceding fourth-order *hmḯH* (TRM) is:

(392) *lḯH   hmḯH   hnáʔML   bíʔH   cáHmíʔH   nḯM   kḯH   nḯH*
      NON   TRM   throw^DI^PRES^3   AFF   children those   stone   when^FUT

      máM   kaL-hẽʔM
      PRF   PAST-meet^TA^3
      Those children just used to throw stones at each other whenever they met.

5.6 The neoteric adverb

The sixth-order neoteric (NEO) adverb *táM* denotes that the situation encoded by the verb has occurred sometime within the past few days or weeks, but not today. Generally, the meaning of *táM* can be expressed by 'recently'. *táM* usually occurs with the verb inflected for the past. Of the two past tense prefixes, only the remote past *kaL-* may occur with the neoteric adverb.

(393) tá^M ka^L-hẽ?^M   hná^HL tî^Mmî^L ?maï^MH ?í^L
     NEO PAST-meet^TA^1S I   doctor   new   that^AN
     I recently met that new doctor.

Verbs which are able to mark the past by internal inflection alone can also be modified by áá^M.

(394) tá^M ŋau^L   bí?^H cú^M ?ŋo^Lhmáï^M
     NEO go^nonhome^IA^PAST^3S AFF 3   Mexico^City
     S/he has recently gone to Mexico City.

Other prefixes and adverbs may occur with tá^M (NEO).

(395) tá^M la^L ka^L-hmou?^L   bí?^H cú^M mí^Hθio?^MH sí^M kio?^MH
     NEO EVID PAST-repair^TI^3 AFF 3   source   fire have^STI^3
     Apparently, he recently repaired his generator.

Establishing the neoteric adverb tá^M as sixth-order is somewhat problematic. It may precede fourth-order hmí^H (TRM) as in (396). It is also possible to construct utterances with the tá^M preceding the fifth-order nonentailment adverb lí^H, as in (397), but such utterances are considered marginally grammatical. Reversing the order of these two constituents results in an ungrammatical construction; therefore, tá^M is considered to precede the fifth-order nonentailment constituent.

(396) tá^M hmí^H ŋi^Η-có^MH   bí?^H cú^M hmáï^H kua^Luóu^M
     NEO TRM INT-go^nonhome^IA^3S AFF   3   fiesta Quetzalapa
     Recently, s/he was wanting to go to the Quetzalapa fiesta (but s/he changed her/his mind).

(397) tá^M lí^L ka^L-ráï^LM   bí?^H cú^M ?mi?^LM kiõ^MH
     NEO NON PAST-wash^TI^3 AFF   3   clothes have^STI^1S
     S/he recently just washed my clothes (where lí^H means 'for free').

The problem deepens, however, when trying to establish the relationship of the neoteric constituent to the negative, the remaining constituent which precedes the VP head. The negative constituent may precede the fifth-order nonentailment constituent, but cannot occur with the neoteric constituent. Due to the semantic dissimilarity, it seems implausible to put the neoteric and the negative constituents into the same distribution class. At this point in my analysis, I have tentatively assigned the neoteric constituent to the sixth-order on the basis that this is the furthest position to the left in which it can yield a marginally grammatical construction. The negative then is the seventh-order constituent.

5.7 The negative constituent

The seventh and final constituent of the verb phrase consists of a negative phrase; its structure is given in (398).

(398) NEGATIVE PHRASE → (MODERATIVE) HEAD (ATTENUATIVE)

The head element of the negative phrase consists of one of a set of six modal adverbs, all of which are negative in one way or another. There are three simple adverbs: the negative (NEG) *tiá^M* 'not', the prohibitive (PROH) *lí^M* 'don't', and the improbability (IMPR) *uú^M* 'improbable, unlikely'. The other three are compound words with the improbability *uú^M* as the second element, and one of the three simple adverbs as the first element. The resulting forms are an interruptive (INTRP) *tiú^{M}uú^M* 'no longer, never', a cessative (CES) *lí^{M}uú^M* 'cease', and a preventative (PREVEN) *su^{L}uú^M* '(please) don't'. I analyze these as compounds rather than separate constituents of the negative phrase for the following reasons.

1. The first syllable of the preventative, *su^L-*, never occurs as a free morpheme.

2. The negative *tiá^M* generally changes phonologically to *tiú^M* when conjoined with *uú^M*, and the prohibitive *lí^M* optionally changes to *lú^M*.

3. Five of the six members of this constituent set (excluding the improbability *uú^M*) may be modified by the attenuative adverb *ŋa^L*, which may be glossed as '(not) much, (not) often'. Four of the six members (excluding the improbability *uú^M* and the preventative *su^{L}uú^M*) may be modified by the moderative (MODR) *ʔa^L*. In other words, the only time that either the moderative or the attenuative adverbs may modify the improbability *uú^M* is when it occurs with *tiá^M* (NEG) or *lí^M* (PROH). The attenuative and the moderative are discussed at the end of this section.

The negative *tiá^M*. *tiá^M* is the most common of the negative adverbs, functioning in a manner similar to the English 'not', and is able to modify elements other than verbs as in (404). Any dynamic or state verb may be negated by *tiá^M*. There does not appear to be any co-occurrence restrictions between *tiá^M* and the verb prefixes or other constituents of the verb phrase, except for the neoteric adverb *tá^M*.

(399) tiá^M kuʔ^{HL} hná^{HL} ʔẽ^M
       not   eat^TI^PRES^IS I   chili
       I do not eat chili.

(400) tiá^M lí^H ka^L-ŋiéi^H   iá?^L ?nú^M kua^Ltá^L
not NON PAST-go^nonhome^IA^2S ASSR you^s Cuicatlán
You didn't just fruitlessly go to Cuicatlán (e.g., the person went to obtain justice at the district court and was successful).

(401) tiá^M kuí^H-má^Hkau^M   cú^M hno?^H
not HORT-deceive^TA^3>1   3   us
May s/he not deceive us.

If *tiá^M* modifies a verb inflected for the second-person future, it may connote a mild prohibition; for example, in (402), the speaker assumes that the addressee may at some future date be tempted to climb the tree, so is being forewarned against the action.

(402) tiá^M uú?^HL   nú^M ?má^M ní^M
not climb^TI^FUT^2 you^s tree that
Don't (ever) climb that tree.

The negative *tiá^M* is heard more frequently as *diá^M* in the speech of older people. Among the young people *diá^M* is rarely heard, but when used it seems to have a more moderate negative connotation. *tiá^M* exhibits two of the features that distinguish adverbs from prefixes.
1. It is permutable with fifth order *lí^H* (NON). In (400), *tiá^M* precedes *lí^H*, which is the more common order. When these elements permute, a change of meaning results. Compare (400) with (403).

(403) lí^H tiá^M ka^L-ŋiéi^H   bí?^H ?nú^M kua^Ltá^L
NON not PAST-go^nonhome^IA^2S AFF you^s Cuicatlán
You just didn't go to Cuicatlán (i.e., you had the opportunity, but chose not to go).

2. It is able to function outside of the verb phrase, having the entire clause in its scope. In (404), the normal predicate-subject order is changed to subject-predicate, with the subject nominal *kïe^L* 'money' being fronted for focus. If it were only the nominal being negated, then a construction such as found in (405) should be grammatical, but it is not. It can be made grammatical by bringing the clause into the scope of *tiá^M* 'not' as in (406).

(404) tiá^M kïe^L θia^LM   kiõ^MH hná^HL
not money exist^SII have^STI^IS I
I don't have any money.

(405) *ʔnióᴸ cúᴹ tiáᴹ kïeᴸ máᴸᴹ bíʔᴴ ʔnióᴸ cúᴹ
      want^STI^3 3 not money food AFF want^STI^3 3
      S/he wants not money, s/he wants food.

(406) tiáᴹ kïeᴸ ʔnióᴸ   cúᴹ máᴸᴹ bíʔᴴ ʔnióᴸ cúᴹ
      not money want^STI^3 3   food AFF want^STI^3 3
      S/he doesn't want money; s/he wants food.

The prohibitive $lî^M$. The prohibitive (PROH) $lî^M$ is generally used when the addressee is obviously about to undertake an undesirable action.

(407) lî̧ᴹ kiéiʔᴸ   ʔmáᴹ ní̧ᴹ
      PROH cut^TI^PROH^2 tree that
      Don't cut down that tree!

Unlike the other adverbs in this set, $lî^M$ occasions an internal inflection of the verb; see §4.1.[41] Verbs that lose the morphological glottal closure of the final syllable to mark the second-person imperative likewise lose the glottal when occurring with $lî^M$ (PROH). The forms of the verb hmu^M 'do, make (TI)' inflected for second person are as in (408).

(408) PRES   FUT   PAST   AMB   IMP   PROH
      hmuʔᴸᴹ   hmúʔᴴ   hmuʔᴸ   hmuʔᴹᴴ   hmuᴸ   hmúᴹ

Also verbs which have glottal closure of the final syllable as part of the verb root, masking the morphological glottal, inflect to mark the prohibitive by either tone-stress, vocalic change, or a combination of these when occurring with $lî^M$. The forms of the verb $ʔïʔ^{ML}$ 'drink (TI)' inflected for second person are shown in (409).

(409) PRES   FUT   PAST   AMB   IMP   PROH
      ʔúʔᴹᴸ   ʔúʔᴴᴸ   ʔíʔᴸ   ʔúʔᴴᴸ   ʔíʔᴸ   ʔúʔᴸ

Despite the prefix-like characteristic of the prohibitive $lî^M$ in governing the tone-stress inflection of the verb, its classification as an adverb is apparent by the following.

1. The prohibitive precedes other adverbs of the verb phrase; it may precede either fifth-order $lî^H$ (NON), as in (410), or second-order $má^M$ (PRF), as

---

[41]Merrifield (1968:31) states that in Palantla Chinantec the direct imperative (positive imperative) is based on the completive form, and the negative imperative (which I have called the prohibitive) is based on the progressive form; in both cases minus the morphological second-person glottal. The formation of the (positive) imperative for Sochiapan Chinantec parallels that of Palantla, but the form of the prohibitive in Sochiapan Chinantec appears to require a tone-stress inflection not predictable from other forms.

The Verb Phrase

in (411). When it does occur with any other verb phrase adverbs, the prohibitive verb inflection is used.

(410) lĩ̵ᴹ   lĩ̵ᴴ   hmúᴹ   ná?ᴹ   liú?ᴴ   ɲiíᴴkṍᴹ   cúᴹ
      PROH   NON   make^TI^PROH^2   you^P   nuisance towards   3
      Don't just make yourself a nuisance to her/him.

(411) ?aᴸ   lĩ̵ᴹ   máᴹ   ?úʔᴸ   hmĩ̵ᴹráuᴸ   nĩ̵ᴹ
      MODR   PROH   PRF   drink^TI^PROH^2   refreshment   that
      Don't drink that soda yet.

2. The prohibitive adverb lĩ̵ᴴ and the negative adverb tiá̵ᴹ both form compounds with the improbability adverb uúᴹ in the same manner: lĩ̵ᴹuúᴹ/lú̵ᴹuúᴹ and tiá̵ᴹuúᴹ/tiú̵ᴹuúᴹ, respectively.

When the prohibitive is used with a verb inflected for the second persons of the various verb prefixes, only the present tense directional prefixes can co-occur. In this case, the verb is inflected not for the prohibitive as occurs in (410) and (411), nor for the andative as might be expected since the directional prefix is contiguous to the verb, but rather for the imperative.

(412) ?aᴸ   lĩ̵ᴹ   kuaᴸ-kuõ?ᴴ   caᴸkuáᴴ
      MODR   PROH   ANDT^PRES-pull^TA^IMP   horse
      Don't go (and) pull that horse.

Although the prohibitive is most commonly found in association with the second person, it is able to function as a prohibition for third person. The co-occurrence of the hortative (HORT) prefix kui̵ᴴ- is obligatory, in which case the verb is inflected as for the 3-HORT.

(413) ?aᴸ   lĩ̵ᴹ   kui̵ᴴ-sõᴹ   cúᴹ
      MODR   PROH   HORT-go^down^IA^3   3
      They ought not to go down!

Although it is possible to construct grammatical sentences for the 1SG and 1PL in the same manner as for the third person, apparently such sentences would not be spoken aloud, but merely thought to oneself.

(414) ?aᴸ   lĩ̵ᴹ   kui̵ᴴ-tá?ᴹᴴ   hnáᴴᴸ   ɲiíᴸ   láᴹ
      MODR   PROH   HORT-fall^IA^1S   I   place   this
      I had better not fall here.

The improbability adverb uúᴹ. In clauses that lack any negative element outside the verb phrase, the improbability (IMPR) adverb uúᴹ (or uĩ̵ᴹ) 'unlikely' has an adversative or pessimistic connotation. It appears to be constrained in its use, always appearing in rhetorical questions with the verification illocutionary particle $dá^M$ (§11.2) and with the verb inflected for the future. It is difficult to map the gloss 'improbable, unlikely' to the Chinantec construction without losing the rhetorical sense, as can be seen in (415) and (416).

(415) $ma^Lcá^{HL}$ $má^{LM} ni̯^M kiá^{HL}$ $kí^H$ $ʔí^M$ $dá^M$ $uú^M$
finish^TI^IMP food that have^STI^2 because which^AN? VER IMPR

$kuʔ^L$
eat^TI^FUT^3

Finish your food, who (else) is likely to eat it (i.e., it is unlikely anyone else will eat it)?

(416) $ʔí^M$ $dá^M$ $cá̯ʔ^M$ $uú^M$ hmu^L $ʔi^L$ li^L
which^AN? VER person IMPR make^TI^FUT^3 COMP become^II^FUT

$ʔiú̯^M$ $ci̯^{LM}$ $hná^{HL}$
be^happy^SII heart^1S I

Who (else) would be likely to make me happy (i.e., it is unlikely anyone else would be able to make me happy)?

$uú^M$ does not occur with any other verb phrase adverbs. The only verb prefixes with which it may occur are the future directionals (§4.7).

(417) $kuá^M$-$ʔi̯ʔ^{MH}$ $háʔ^L$ $hmäï^M kí^H$ $ʔí^M$
ANDT^IMP-give^drink^DA^2 animal water because which^AN?

$dá^M$ $uú^M$ ca^L-$ʔi̯ʔ^H$
VER IMPR ANDT^FUT-give^drink^DA^3

Go give the animal water to drink, who (else) is likely to give it (water to drink)?

When a clause is introduced by a clause level negative adverb such as $sa^Lhü^L$ 'neither' or $hü^Lhuáʔ^{HL}$ 'not as if', the improbability adverb may gain a positive affective connotation, depending on the context. The restrictions mentioned earlier in this section no longer pertain.

(418) $sa^Lhü^L$ $uú^M$ $ʔau^L$ $cú^M$
neither IMPR cry^IA^FUT^3 3
...neither will they be likely to cry.

(419) *hū^Lhuá?^{HL} hmá̈^H uú^M kú?^M lí^H iá?^L cú^M la^{LM}*
not^as^if day IMPR eat^TI^PRES^3 *tepejilote* ASSR 3 this^one
It's not as if this is the season one is likely to eat *tepejilote* (a type of bitter edible palm).

uú^M (IMPR) occurs more frequently as the second element in compound negative adverbs, see below.

The interruptive *tiú^Muú^M*. The interruptive (INTRP) adverb *tiú^Muú^M* 'no longer, never' is a compound of the negative adverb *tiá^M* and the improbability adverb *uú^M*. Although generally the stressed vowel of the nucleus of the first morpheme *tiá^M* assimilates to that of the second morpheme *uú^M*, the interruptive is occasionally heard as *tiá^Muú^M*. The interruptive marks a state or event as no longer true.

(420) *tiú^Muú^M hmu^L cú^M ta^{MH} hã́u^M kiú^{HL}*
INTRP do^TI^FUT^3 3 work that^IN have^STI^1P
S/he won't do that job for us (i.e., s/he has done work for us before, but won't any more).

The interruptive appears to collocate with most other verb phrase adverbs and verbal prefixes.

(421) *tiú^Muú^M ká^M-hí?^{LM} cá^Mmi^L ?í^L ?ŋiú^{HL}*
INTRP PAST-return^home^3 woman that^AN house^3
That woman never returned home.

(422) *tiú^Muú^M lí^H ŋií^H-kó?^{MH} hná^{HL} mi^L láu^M*
INTRP NON ANDT^FUT-play^TI^1S I spherical hide
I won't just go play basketball any longer (i.e., I won't play as frequently *or* I won't play unless there is some prize).

When the interruptive is used with a verb inflected for the second-person future, a mild prohibition results, imploring the addressee not to repeat a particular action, even when there may not be any evidence that the addressee had any such intent.

(423) *tiú^Muú^M uú?^{HL} nú^M ŋií^H ?ã́i?^H ní^M*
INTRP climb^TI^FUT^2 you^s place dangerous that
(Please) don't climb that dangerous place again.

Like *tiá^M* (NEG), *tiú^Muú^M* (INTRP) is able to have the entire clause in its scope. In (424), the verb alone lies within the scope of the interruptive, but in (425) it is the entire clause. In (424), the unmarked predicate-subject order is a simple statement, whereas in (425) the subject-predicate order is contrastive—that particular medicine, in contrast to other medicines. Example (425) also hints that there is an alternative medication with similar properties.

(424) tiú^M uú^M θia^LM iá?^L mí^L hǻu^M
INTRP exist^SII ASSR medicine that^IN
There is no more of that medicine.

(425) tiú^M uú^M mí^L hǻu^M θia^LM iá?^L
INTRP medicine that^IN exist^SII ASSR
There is no more of that medicine.

tiú^M uú^M has a form which is more frequently heard among older speakers; diú^M uú^M (or less frequently diá^M uú^M), based on the variant of the negative diá^M used by older speakers.

The cessative lí^M uú^M. The cessative (CES) lí^M uú^M is a compound of the prohibitive adverb lí^M and the improbability adverb uú^M. The cessative implies that the addressee is in a particular state, presently engaged in an action, or has done something before and is being told to terminate that state or activity. lí^M uú^M occasions the same internal inflection of the verb as does lí^M (PROH) when there is no verb prefix. The same co-occurrence constraints that apply to lí^M also apply to lí^M uú^M.

(426) ?a^L   lí^M uú^M hmú^M   co^L
MODR CES   do^TI^PROH^2 wrong
Stop doing improper things!

(427) lí^M uú^M lí^H ra^L ci^LM   ná?^M ?éi?^LM ŋif^H kṍ^M cáu^M
CES   NON   apply^TI^PROH^2 you^P measure towards people
Stop making unfounded judgments of people.

When the cessative is used with a verb inflected for the second person, of the various verb prefixes, only the present tense directional prefixes can co-occur. The verb is inflected for the imperative, not the prohibitive nor the future.

(428) lí^M uú^M ŋia^L-tǻi^H   hmái^M ?la?^L ŋif^H lá^M
CES   VEN^PRES-dump^TI^IMP water bad^IN place this
Stop coming and dumping dirty water here.

The cessative is able to occur with the third person only if the hortative kui^H- also occurs. The internal inflection of the verb is as for the third-person hortative.

(429) li^Muu^M kui^H-$héi?^{MH}$ $cú^M$ $\eta ií^Hne^M$ $hná^{HL}$
  CES   HORT-weed^TI^3 3   field^IS I
  May s/he never again weed my field.

The cessative has the optional variant $lú^Muú^M$, in which the vowel of the first morpheme has assimilated to that of the second.

The preventative $su^Luú^M$. The preventative (PREVEN) adverb $su^Luú^M$ is a compound of the morpheme su^L, which is of uncertain origin, and the improbability adverb $uú^M$. $su^Luú^M$ is a milder prohibition than li^M; it may be used in an attempt to dissuade someone from initiating a course of action or from repeating an action; in either case the speaker believes that action by the addressee is imminent.

$su^Luú^M$ (PREVEN) follows the same co-occurrence restrictions and requires the same internal inflection of the verb as $li^Muú^M$ (CES) and li^M (PROH). For example, if there is no intervening prefix between $su^Luú^M$ and the verb as in (430), or if an adverb occurs between the preventative and the verb as in (431), the verb inflects as for the prohibitive li^M.

(430) $su^Luú^M$ $hmú^M$ la^L ni^M
  PREVEN do^TI^PROH^2 idea that
  (Please) don't do that!

(431) $su^Luú^M$ li^H $?lé?^M$ $hú^H$-$?la?^L$ $\eta iú^H$
  PREVEN NON say^TI^PROH^2 word-bad friend
  (Please) don't say bad things, (my) friend!

The moderative adverb $?a^L$. The moderative (MODR) adverb $?a^L$ may precede and modify four of the six negative adverbs; excluded are the improbability $uú^M$ and the preventative $su^Luú^M$. The presence of the moderative does not appear to affect the collocation restrictions of those adverbs with which it may occur, and the pragmatic effect is to moderate or lessen the force of the negative statement. There is no appreciable semantic difference in an utterance whether $?a^L$ is present or absent.

The moderative is often found with the negative $tiá^M$.

(432) $?a^L$ $tiá^M$ $kuóu^{LM}$ $iá?^L$ $hná^{HL}$ $?nú^M$
  MODR not know^TA^IS>2 ASSR I   you^S
  Why, I certainly don't know you!

The interruptive *tiúᴹuúᴹ* is infrequently found modified by the moderative.

(433) ʔaᴸ tiúᴹuúᴹ kaᴸ-hniaᴸ iáʔᴸ cáᴹ ʔíᴸ
MODR INTRP PAST-appear^IA^3 ASSR person that^AN
Why, that person never reappeared!

The prohibitive *líᴹ* occurs more commonly with *ʔaᴸ* (MODR) than without.

(434) ʔaᴸ líᴹ hmúᴹ ʔiãᴹ ʔõʔᴹ ŋíʔᴴkõᴹ hnáᴴᴸ
MODR PROH do^TI^PROH^2 cruel heart^2 towards I
Why, don't be mean to me!

The cessative *líᴹuúᴹ* is occasionally found modified by the moderative.

(435) ʔaᴸ líᴹuúᴹ ŋiaᴸ-ʔuᴸᴹ siáʔᴸ ʔŋiuᴸᴹ hnáᴴᴸ
MODR CES VEN^PRES-enter^IA^PROH^2 again house^IS I
Don't ever come into my home again!

The attenuative adverb *ŋaᴸ*. The attenuative (ATTN) adverb *ŋaᴸ* '(not) much, (not) often' may occur following any of the negative adverbs, apart from the improbability *uúᴹ*. The effect is to diminish the force of the negative. Its presence does not appear to affect the collocation restrictions of the negative adverbs. Examples of the attenuative with each of the negative adverbs are given in (436)–(440).

(436) tiáᴹ ŋaᴸ cauᴸᴹ cúᴹ kuaᴸtáᴸ
not often go^nonhome^IA^PRES^3S 3 Cuicatlán
S/he doesn't often go to Cuicatlán.

(437) líᴹ ŋaᴸ kuóᴸ ŋíʔᴴ kuoᴴ
PROH often go^nonhome^IA^PROH^2S place firewood
Don't go to get firewood frequently!

(438) tiúᴹuúᴹ ŋaᴸ cáᴹ-ʔniaʔᴹ cúᴹ háʔᴸ
INTRP often ANDT^PRES-search^TA^3 3 animal
S/he doesn't often go hunting for animals any more.

(439) líᴹuúᴹ ŋaᴸ kúʔᴹ hláïᴹ
CES often eat^TI^PROH^2 egg
Stop eating eggs (so) much!

The Verb Phrase 157

(440) su^Luú^M ŋa^L kõʔ^L   mí^Htiei^{MH} mî^Hmíʔ^H
     PREVEN much play^with^TA^PROH^2   cat   girl
     (Please) don't play too much with the cat, little girl!

The attenuative and moderative elements may co-occur. For example:

(441) ʔa^L tiú^Muú^M ŋa^L ró̰ʔ^{LM}   ieʔ^L ní^M lio^{MH}
     MODR INTRP   much manage^TI^PRES^3 elder that cargo
     That old man sure can't manage (to carry) much cargo any more!

5.8 The verb phrase intensifier *lḭ̂^{LM}*

The intensifier *lḭ̂^{LM}* 'much, very' is the only adverb that may occur after the verb phrase head as part of the verb phrase.

As mentioned above, and discussed in chapter 11, the illocutionary particles and adverbs have within their scope any preceding syntactic unit, and are not able to intrude within that unit. Since no illocutionary particle or adverb is able to come between the head of the verb phrase and *lḭ̂^{LM}*, I consider *lḭ̂^{LM}* to be part of the verb phrase. Examples of *lḭ̂^{LM}* both without and with an illocutionary particle (the affirmation particle *bíʔ^H*) are given in (442) and (443), respectively.

(442) má^M ŋi^H-aï̃ʔ^{MH}   lḭ̂^{LM} hná^{HL} hmḭ̂^Mhma^L
     PRF INT-drink^TI^1S very   I   potable^water
     I am really wanting to drink some (potable) water.

(443) má^M ŋi^H-kuóu^{MH} lḭ̂^{MH} bíʔ^H cú^M
     PRF INT-sleep^IA^3 very   AFF   3
     S/he is very sleepy.

By comparing (442) and (443), it can be seen that the tone-stress of *lḭ̂^{LM}* 'much, very' optionally permutes to a ballistic mid-rising tone when it follows a syllable with a high or mid-rising tone.

5.9 The verb phrase constituents and binomial verbs

As mentioned earlier, one of the features that distinguishes adverbs which function within the verb phrase from those which function at the clause level is that the former are obligatorily repeated with the second base of a binomial verb, whereas the latter cannot be repeated. Examples of the second-order perfect *má^M*, fourth-order terminative *hmḭ̂^H*, and seventh-order prohibitive *lḭ̂^M*, repeated with both bases of a binomial verb, are given in (444)–(446).

(444) má^M kí^M má^M huá^{ML} cú^M hmu^M ciei$^{?LM}$
      PRF   PV^PRES PRF   shake^TI^PRES^3   3   palm^mat outside
      S/he is shaking the grass mats outside.

(445) hmḯ^H kí^M hmḯ^M ʔo^M lḯ^{LM} hó̰^{LM} hná^{HL}
      TRM   PV^PRES TRM   cry^IA^PRES^3   much child^1s   I
      My child used to keep crying incessantly.

(446) lḯ^M θí^M lḯ^M ciá^M háï^{HL} ní^M má^{H}na^{MH}
      PROH tell PROH relate^TI^PROH^2 word this CEXP
      However, don't spread this word around.

In contrast, the clause level adverb hlá$^{?H}$ 'really' can occur only with the first base of a binomial verb.

(447) hlá$^{?H}$ tí^L ʔó$^{?LM}$ cá^{H}mí$^{?H}$ ha^H ʔŋiú^L
      really PV^PRES shout^IA^PRES^3   children among   house
      The children really yell and shout in the streets.

When nonentailment lḯ^H is modified by káu^M 'simply' and occurs with a binomial verb, only lḯ^H appears on both bases.

(448) káu^M lḯ^H tú^M lḯ^H ʔió^{LM} cú^M rāï$^{?MH}$
      simply NON PV^PRES NON malign^TA^PRES^3 3   peer
      S/he just keeps on maligning her/his peers.

Similarly, when any of the negative adverbs are modified by the moderative ʔa^L, only the negative adverb is repeated with the second base.

If a negative is modified by the attenuative ŋa^L '(not) much', the presence of the attenuative bars the repetition of the negative with the second base. The effect of the attenuative is seen in (449b).

(449) a. tiá^M kí^M tiá^M pá^{ML} ieʔ^L hõ^M
         not PV^PRES not hit^TA^PRES^3 elder child^3
         The old man doesn't beat up his child.

      b. tiá^M ŋa^L kí^M pá^{ML} ieʔ^L hõ^M
         not much PV^PRES hit^TA^PRES^3 elder child^3
         The old man doesn't beat up his child much.

When any of the three compound negatives occurs with a binomial verb, only the final syllable is repeated with the second base; this is illustrated in

The Verb Phrase   159

(450) with the cessative *lĩᴹuúᴹ*, which is reduced to *uúᴹ* preceding the second base; the meaning is as if the full cessative has been repeated.

(450) *lĩᴹuúᴹ*   *túᴹ*   *uúᴹ*   *ʔiõᴸ*   *rẽʔᴹ*
       CES   PV^PRES   (IMPR)   malign^TA^PROH^2   peer^2
       Stop maligning your peers.

6
The Noun Phrase

The Sochiapan Chinantec noun phrase has been described previously in Foris 1980. This chapter supersedes that analysis. The structure of the noun phrase (NP) is set out in (451).

(451) NOUN PHRASE → (QUANTIFIER) (EVALUATIVE) (HEAD)
$(\begin{Bmatrix} \text{MODIFIER} \\ \text{POSSESSOR} \end{Bmatrix})$ (DEITIC) (RELATIVE CLAUSE)^n

Potentially, up to six of the NP constituents may co-occur, but more than four is uncommon in natural discourse. All but the evaluative and possessor constituents agree with the head as to animacy. At the discourse level, the head of the NP can be omitted when information is assumed to be shared by both speaker and addressee or when there is ellipsis under co-referentiality.

The modifier constituent includes the possessor since the two may not co-occur; however, the possessor constituent must be expressed by a nominal, and the modifier by an adjective, so on this basis I have subdivided them.

Relative clauses are discussed in detail in §§9.1–9.2; because the possessor of alienable nouns is expressed by means of a relative clause, however, the possessor relative clause construction is dealt with in this chapter, in §6.4. The superscript ^{n} accompanying the relative clause constituent in (451) indicates that there may be multiple relative clauses with the same head noun; in practice, it is rare to find more than two.

All but the evaluative and deictic constituents have the potential of being internally complex; if one of the NP constituents is complex, other co-occurring constituents tend to be simple.

A subject NP with quantifier (Q), head (H), modifier (MOD), and deictic (DEIC) constituents is illustrated in (452).

(452)   NP [Q   H   MOD   DEIC]
        ka^L-$cä^L$ $tá^H$ $niá^L$ $ká^H?áu^M$ $pi?^{MH}$ $?í^L$
        PAST-die^IA^3P entire five chicken little that^AN
        All those five little (baby) chicks died.

An object NP with quantifier, head, deictic, and relative clause (RC) constituents is illustrated in (453).

(453)   NP [Q   H   DEIC RC   ]
        $niéi^M$ $ná?^M$ $ká^M$ $hõ^H$ $hái^{HL}$ $lá^M$ $kiõ^{MH}$ $hná^{HL}$
        hear^TI^IMP^2 you^P   one^IN piece word this have^STI^IS I
        Listen to this brief message of mine.

An object NP with quantifier, evaluative, head, and deictic constituents is illustrated in (454). The verb $kué^H$ is marked for inverse cross-referencing by the code 2 > 1, indicating that the agent is second person and the patient is first person; see §8.4.

(454)   NP [Q   EVAL   H   DEIC]
        $kué^H$ $?ni^{LM}$ $mái^L$ $uí^H$ $mí^L$ $ni^M ráu^L$ $ní^M$
        give^DI^IMP^2>1 three^IN sphere nice spherical orange that
        Give (me) three of those nice oranges.

6.1–6.2 The noun phrase head

The head of the NP consists of an optional categorizer and an obligatory base, in that order.

6.1 The base

The base element may consist of a noun stem, nouns in juxtaposition, an idiom, or a pronoun. A noun stem may be a single root, usually monosyllabic, or be a derived (§3.2) or compound (§3.3) stem. Juxtaposed nouns (nonpermutable binomials and polynomials) are discussed in §3.5 and §3.6. Idioms which can function as an NP head are discussed below.

The Noun Phrase   163

Nouns are divided into four main classes based on two parameters: alienable (AL) versus inalienable (INAL), and animate (AN) versus inanimate (IN).

Inalienable nouns are nouns that are obligatorily possessed. They sometimes have an alienable counterpart. They include kinship terms, part-whole relationships such as body parts or parts of other entities, e.g., mu^{MH} 'leaf (3 POSS)', and some items commonly associated with humans, such as $cái^{HL}$ 'dog (3 POSS)', or bodily excretions such as $\mathit{?ma}^L$ 'excrement (3 POSS)'. The person and number of the possessor of inalienable nouns is indicated by inflection of the possessed noun and optionally by a following NP or pronoun.

Alienable nouns are those that may optionally be possessed by means of a relative clause (see §6.4). Alienable nouns do not inflect to agree with the person of the possessor.

Animacy is not marked on nouns. Descriptive adjectives, anaphoric deictic adjectives, quantifiers, and numerals agree with the head of the noun phrase as to animacy. Intransitive verbs agree with their subject as to animacy, and transitive verbs agree with their object, giving an ergative pattern; see §8.3.

The animacy of nouns closely follows the real world except for $mi?^{LM}$ 'thunder', $hmi^M ki^H$ 'rainbow', $\theta i^{?M}$ 'moon', $\mathit{?iú}^M$ 'sun', and $ci^H hmai^{MH}$ 'stars', which are spirit beings in Chinantec mythology and are treated grammatically as animate.[42] Plant life and body parts are regarded as inanimate. The four main noun classes are represented in (455).

(455) $mí^M ni^L$ pig (AL^AN) $hméi^M$ father (INAL^AN^3 POSS)
        ki^H rock (AL^IN) ci^H head (INAL^IN^3 POSS)

Nouns may be further subclassified as count and mass nouns, contingent nouns, and vocative nouns. All others are referred to as common nouns.

Count and mass nouns. Mass nouns such as kuo^H 'firewood', $hmái^M$ 'liquid, water', and $\mathit{?mái}^M$ 'excrement (AL)', require a preceding mensural classifier to be counted.

(456) $tú^L$ $p\tilde{i}e?^H$ $\mathit{?ma}^L$ $ca^L kuá^H$
        two^IN   pile   excrement^3   horse
        two piles of horse manure

---

[42]There is a tendency for some of the younger speakers to choose inanimate verbs and adjectives to collocate with 'sun' and 'moon'. Traditionally, thunder is a spirit animal; the rainbow is another spirit animal, a bird-like being with a colorful, fanned tail similar to that of a turkey; the moon is a female deity; the sun a male deity; and the stars are believed to be the spirits of dead babies

Count nouns, however, may be quantified by a quantifier phrase (§§6.9–6.11), either with or without a co-occurring mensural classifier; see (457a) and (457b), respectively.

(457) a. ʔnį͡ᴸᴹ   mí͡ʔᴹ   lá͡ᴸ
    three ͡ IN basket maize ͡ ear
    three baskets of ears (maize)

b. ʔnį͡ᴸᴹ   lá͡ᴸ
    three ͡ IN maize ͡ ear
    three ears (maize)

Count nouns which refer to entities with a particular shape require either a co-occurring mensural classifier or a sortal (shape oriented) classifier to be quantified; see (458a) and (458b), respectively.

(458) a. tü͡ᴸ   kuó͡ᴹ   ŋif͡ᴹhmu͡ᴸ
    two ͡ IN box   lemon
    two boxes of lemons

b. tü͡ᴸ   mái͡ᴸ   ŋif͡ᴹhmu͡ᴸ
    two ͡ IN sphere lemon
    two lemons

Contingent nouns. There is a small set of nouns that cannot occur as the head of an NP unless some kind of modifier co-occurs, the most common being a deictic adjective or a descriptive adjective. Because of these restrictions and because their semantic content is relatively general, I call them contingent nouns.

There are four contingent nouns: ʔi͡ᴸ 'thing IN', cá͡ᴹ 'person AN', ŋif͡ᴴ 'place IN', and la͡ᴸ 'manner, idea IN'. The contingent noun cá͡ᴹ 'person' has a morphemic variant cáu͡ᴹ 'person', which functions like a common noun. The contingent noun ʔi͡ᴸ 'thing IN' and the complementizer ʔi͡ᴸ (COMP) are separate morphemes; they can occur contiguously as shown in (459).

(459) θiã͡ᴹ   cá͡ᴹ   kú͡ʔᴹ   ŋif͡ᴹhmu͡ᴸ ʔi͡ᴸ huá͡ʔᴸ   ʔi͡ᴸ
    exist ͡ SIA ͡ 3 person eat ͡ TI ͡ PRES ͡ 3 lemon   and say ͡ STI ͡ 3 COMP

   ʔi͡ᴸ   háu͡ᴹ   bí͡ʔᴴ   hmu͡ᴹ   ʔi͡ᴸ   θiã͡ᴹ   cú͡ᴹ ré͡ᴹ
    thing that ͡ IN AFF do ͡ TI ͡ PRES ͡ 3 COMP exist ͡ SIA ͡ 3 3 well
   There are people who eat lemons and say that such things give them good health.

The Noun Phrase   165

Examples (460) and (461) illustrate a contingent noun with a deictic adjective and a descriptive adjective, respectively.

(460) θāï^{LM} hná^{HL} cá^M nî^M
      like^STA^1S I   person that
      I like that person.

(461) ʔi^L siá$^{?L}$ bíʔ^H θāï^{LM} hná^{HL}
      thing different^IN AFF   like^STI I
      I like something different.

Vocative nouns. All kinship terms[43] have a vocative form. The vocative forms are presented as part of the paradigm of inalienable nouns in §6.3, and the vocative constituent of the clause is discussed in §8.14.

Generally, vocative nouns do not occur as the head of an NP which functions as a subject or object. They usually occur sentence initial, but may also occur sentence final.

(462) hó^L hã^M cá^M kú^{M}huú^M má^M kuá^M
      child^VOC one^AN person stranger PRF   arrive^nonhome^PAST^3S
      Son, a stranger has arrived.

(463) ʔiá^M nú^M hó^L
      hi   you^s child^VOC
      Hi, son (said by priest to a new acquaintance).

Vocatives can also be used referentially with an affectionate connotation.

(464) tiá^M né^H ʔa^L lá$^{?L}$ lî^{ML} mî^H nî^M bíʔ^H
      not know^STI^1P just how think^TI^PRES^3 mother^VOC that AFF
      Who knows (lit., we don't know) how mom there feels?

Idioms. There are idioms which have the surface form of a clause but which function as the head of an NP. Some idioms function as alienable nouns as in (465), others as inalienable nouns as in (466). A sentential example of (465) is is given in (467).

(465) mí^{H}ŋií^M hmu^M cú^M ʔué$^{?L}$
      metal   make^TI^PRES^3 3   symbol
      typewriter

---

[43]The term 'kinship' is used to cover all interpersonal relationships; included are terms such as 'friend', 'servant', 'boss/master', and 'countryman'.

(466) tu$?^{LM}$ tio$?^{LM}$ ta^L cú^M
      bag put^in^PRES^3P foot^3 3
      her/his shoes

(467) má^M ka^L-cú$?^L$ mí^{H}ɲi^M hmu^M cú^M ?ué$?^L$ hấu^M
      PRF PAST-break^II metal   make^TI^PRES^3 3   symbol that^IN

      kiö̃^{MH} hná^{HL}
      have^STI^IS I
      My typewriter has broken (lit., the typewriter that I have has broken).

Pluralization. The noun *cá^M* 'person' is the only nominal root found thus far which can be pluralized, together with compounds based on *cá^M*. The singular and plural forms of this noun and its compounds are given in (468).

(468) Singular   Plural

      cá^M/cá$?^M$ person   cáu^M people
      cá^{M}mí$?^H$ child   (cá^M) cá^{H}mí$?^H$ children
                                               (cá^M) cá^{H}ɲiú^H young men
                                               (cá^M) cá^{H}mái̵^{HL} young women
                                               cá^{M}tã̵^{MH} authorities

Strictly speaking, *cá^M* (or *cá$?^M$*) is not singular, but implies singularity unless the context marks it as plural; the noun *cáu^M* 'people', on the other hand, implies plurality unless the context marks it as singular as in (470). The nominals *cá^{H}ɲiú^H* 'young men' and *cá^{H}mái̵^{HL}* 'young women' are likewise context dependent; in an unmarked context they imply plurality, but can be singular in a marked context. The full binomial expressions *cá^M cá^{H}ɲiú^H* and *cá^M cá^{H}mái̵^{HL}*, however, can only be plural. *cá^{M}tã̵^{MH}* is always plural in connotation. Examples (469) and (470) illustrate the implicit singular and plural meanings of *cá^M* and *cáu^M*, respectively.

(469) cá^M ?í^L ka^L-huá$?^L$ ɲi^{H}kö̃^{M} hná^{HL} ?í^L ka^L-ku$?^L$
      person that^AN PAST-say^TI^3 to   I   COMP PAST-eat^TI^3

      kấu^M ?í^{H}mii$?^{MH}$ ki$?^L$ cá^M ɲi^H ?ná^H
      one^IN bread   accompany^STA^3 person at   remainder

      ?í^L
      that^AN
      That person told me that he shared a loaf with the others.

(470) nɨ́ʰhuáʔᴸ máᴴ kaᴸ-hūᴸ   hāᴹ   cáuᴹ   hmuᴹ   cáuᴹ
      if   PRF PAST-die^IA^3 one^AN people do^TI^PRES^3 people

laᴸ láᴹ
idea this
If a person dies, this is what people do.

There are also a few irreversible binomials, such as hméiᴹ mɨ́ʰθiúᴴᴸ 'parents', and polynomials, such as hméiᴹ dɨ́ʰʔioᴸ ŋiúʰdeʔᴸ 'ancestors', which are inherently plural.

Personal pronouns. Chinantec personal pronouns inflect for person and number. For each grammatical person, there exists more than one pronominal form whose use is determined by sociolinguistic factors.[44]

Chinantec pronouns do not inflect for syntactic role. A single set of personal pronouns functions as subject, direct object, indirect object, and oblique object.

Since Sochiapan Chinantec verbs are inflected for person-of-subject, the use of pronouns to mark the subject is partially redundant. In (471) the forms of each pronoun are listed in order of decreasing frequency of usage. The most frequently used pronouns are 'neutral' in social implication. The other pronouns are used by the speaker to denote such sentiments as superiority, familiarity, compliance, deference, resentment, and denigration, as noted in the list. The numbers in parentheses reference the example below which illustrates a specific usage.

(471) Personal pronouns

    1S   hnáᴴᴸ   neutral in social situation, when left-dislocated may be emphatic or in focus (472)
            náᴴ   reticence (473), deferential, defocusing
            náᴸ   compliance (474), reluctance, annoyance[45]
            niaᴹᴴ   familiarity, intimacy, ingratiating, self-pity (475)
            hnáᴸ   emphatic, contrastively with irony (476), always left-dislocated
            niáᴴ   superiority (477), familiarity with resentment

---

[44]Other Chinantec languages do not appear to exhibit such a wide range of pronominal forms. Rupp, for example, states that in Lealao Chinantec "The first-person singular pronoun is also unique in having an emphatic form" (1989:79). Anderson (1989:71–77) describes seven pronouns in Comaltepec Chinantec (including first-person plural exclusive and third-person animal) with six phonologically less prominent forms, but their use appears to be governed syntactically rather than sociolinguistically.

[45]náᴴ is heard more frequently in women's speech when addressing men, or younger women addressing older ones, giving a deferential nuance.

		$hnia^{LM}$	familiarity, confident warm relationship, used mostly by older people (478)
		na^L	compliance with pity⁴⁶ (479)
	1P	$hno?^H$	neutral, exclusive when occurring with di^M (480) but ambiguously inclusive or exclusive when occurring alone (481)
		di^M	inclusive, emphatic, disambiguates (480) and (482)
		$hnio?^H$	familiarity, camaraderie, inclusive or exclusive (483)
		di^{LM}	inclusive (484), familiarity
	2S	$?nu^M$	neutral, emphatic when left-dislocated (485)
		nu^M	interchangeable with $?nu^M$
		$?niu^{LM}$	familiarity (486), intimacy, deprecatory
	2P	$?no?^M$	neutral, left-disclocated for focus (487)
		$na?^M$	hortative (488)
		$?nio?^M$	familiarity, deprecatory (489)
	3	cu^M	nonspecific for number and gender, neutral, affectionate connotation with animals (490)
		di^M	nonspecific for number and gender, emphasis (491), contrastive; di^M and cu^M disambiguate two third-person referents (see §8.4)
		di^{LM}	nonspecific for number and gender, sympathetic (492)

(472) hna^{HL} $bi?^H$ kau^{MH} lio^{MH} ni^M
    I   AFF take^TI^FUT^1s cargo that
    I will take that cargo.

(473) kau^M kui^H-hmu^H na^H $ka^L la^M$ la^L ku^L $ŋi^H$
    simply HORT-do^TI^1s I   some about just place

        li^{HL}
        be^possible^II^FUT
    I'll just simply do whatever is possible.

---

⁴⁶na^L 'I' is a part of Wilfrido's (nineteen years old) vocabulary, semantically distinct from na^L 'I', whereas his father Marcelino does not recognize two distinct lexical forms, using na^L for situations where Wilfrido would prefer to use na^L. On other uses of na^L they agree. It is possible that na^L is idiosyncratic to Wilfrido, or perhaps a new pronoun is coming into use.

The Noun Phrase   169

(474) kuĩʰ-teʔᴴᴸ   nᵃ́ᴸ tĩᴹ cáïᴹ   hoʔᴹ   kuĩʰ-huïᴹᴴ
       HORT-call^TA^1S   I first dog have^STA^1S HORT-whistle^TI^1S

       nᵃ́ᴸ tĩᴹ   tũᴸ   ciiᴹᴴ   ʔiᴸ   teʔᴴᴸ   nᵃ́ᴸ cáïᴹ
       I   first two^IN bursts   and   call^TA^FUT^1S I   dog

       hoʔᴹ   mᵃ́ʰhᵃ̃ᵘᴹ   sȭᴴᴸ   nᵃ́ᴸ
       have^STA^1S   then^FUT   lower^IA^FUT^1S I
       Let me call my dog first; let me first give two whistles to call my
       dog, then I will get down.

(475) ʔeᴸ   maᴸ   huoᴹᴸ   niaᴹᴴ
       EXCM   EXCL be^pitiable^SIA^1S I
       What an unlucky person am I!

(476) hnᵃ́ᴸ maᴸ dᵃ́ᴹ ŋieᴴ   ʔíᴴ   hlᵃ̃́ʔᴴ kiẽᴹ
       I   EXCL VER go^nonhome^IA^FUT^1S   QUERY   really   important

       cᵃ́ᴹ   óᴸᴹ
       person yonder
       What, me go; is that person there so important (that he can't go on
       the errand instead)?

(477) laᴸ   liᴸ   kaᴸ-híeᴸᴹ   niᵃ́ᴴ kᵃ̃ᵘᴹ   ʔŋiúᴸ
       apparently   happen^II^PAST PAST-see^TI´^1S I   one^IN house

       lẽᴸ
       think^TI^PRES^1S
       It so happens that I saw such a house, I believe (i.e., I have
       information you lack).

(478) mᵃ́ᴹ   ŋieᴴ   hniaᴸᴹ laᴸᴹ   kiõᴹᴴ
       PRF   go^nonhome^IA^FUT^1S   I   this^one have^STI^1S
       I'll be on my way now.

(479) hlᵃ̃́ʔᴴ huoᴹᴸ   núᴹ   tiᵃ́ᴹ θiaᴸᴹ   hŋiéiᴹ kiᵃ̃́ᴴᴸ
       really be^pitiable^SIA^2 you^s not   exist^SII bean   have^STI^2

       lᵃ́ᴹ   ciiᴴᴸ   naᴸ   kᵃ́ᴹ   kuaʔᴹᴴ   kiᵃ̃́ᴴᴸ   núᴹ
       here   loan^TI^FUT^1S I   one^IN gourd   have^STI^2 you^s
       You unlucky fellow, you haven't got any (dried) beans; here, I'll
       loan one gourd-full to you.

(480) hnoʔ^H bíʔ^H ka^L-hmú^{HL} ta^{MH} háū^M kí^H tiá^M
we   AFF PAST-do^TI^1P work that^IN because not

   tái^M dí^M la^L hái^{LM}
   be^capable^STI^1P we^INCL nearly all^1P
We (exclusive) did that work, for not all of us (inclusive) are capable.

(481) kuí^H-ʔíe^{HL} hnoʔ^H
HORT-sing^TI^1P we
Let's sing!

(482) kuí^H-ʔíe^{HL} dí^M
HORT-sing^TI^1P we^INCL
Let's sing!

(483) má^M cáuʔ^{HL} bíʔ^H hnioʔ^H la^{LM} na^{MH}
PRF go^home^IA^1P AFF we   this^one ASNT
Let's go home, okay?

(484) ʔmóu^{LM} bíʔ^H di^{LM} ciá^{HL} ré^M sií^M lá^M ca^{L}ʔáu^M
ourselves AFF we^INCL put^TI^FUT^1P well book this tomorrow
We ourselves will put these books in order tomorrow.

(485) ʔnú^M bíʔ^H ka^L-huaʔ^{MH} ʔi^L cáu^{HL}
you^S AFF PAST-say^TI^2 COMP go^nonhome^IA^FUT^1P
You (are the one who) said that we should go.

(486) tiá^H ciíʔ^H ʔniu^{LM} ka^{L}lá^M kïe^L kiõ^{MH} nia^{MH}
ʔ^not loan^TI^FUT^2 you^S some money have^STI^IS I

   ba^{MH}
   cofather
Won't you loan me some money cofather (Sp. *compadre*)?

(487) ʔnoʔ^M bíʔ^H cá^M hláʔ^H ré^M ná^H-ma^L-tiʔ^{MH}
you^P AFF person really well PROG^P-obey^TI^2
You are the ones who really obey (what I say).

(488) tî^M hïʔ^{MH} náʔ^M hǿʔ^{LM}
PV turn^back^TA^IMP you^P child^2
Admonish your children!

The Noun Phrase   171

(489) ʔeᴸ   dáᴹ   hláʔᴴ   ɲíʔᴴ   ʔnioʔᴹ ɲííᴴ tiõʔᴴ   náʔᴹ
       what? VER   really   know^STI^2   you^P   at   stand^SIA^2P you^P

       níᴹ
       there
       What do you know so much about, (you who are) just standing around there?

(490) tiáᴹ   ɲííᴴ-ʔnaᴴ   hnáᴴᴸ   míᴴtieiᴹᴴ   láᴹ   hoʔᴹ   ʔliáᴹ
       not   INT-sell^TA^1S   I   cat   this   have^STA^1S   because

       hláʔᴴ   koᴹ   cúᴹ   kiõʔᴸ   cáᴴmíʔᴴ
       really play^IA^3 3   accompany^STA^3   children
       I don't want to sell this cat of mine, because s/he really plays with the children.

(491) híʔᴴ   dáᴹ   kiẽᴹ   huáʔᴸ   ieʔᴸ   óᴸᴹ   ʔiᴸ
       where? VER   be^worth^SII say^STI^3 elder   yonder   COMP

       kuáᴴciãᴴ   ɲííᴴkõᴹ   dióᴸᴹ   háᴹ   hmuᴹ
       be^consecrated^SIA^3 to   God   why!   do^TI^PRES^3

       bíʔᴴ   díᴹ   coᴸ
       AFF   he   wrong
       What is the point of that old fellow saying he is consecrated to God; he does bad things?

(492) ɲauᴸ   diᴸᴹ   kúᴹhueʔᴸᴹ
       go^nonhome^IA^PAST^3S 3   after^all
       He went after all.

Reflexive pronouns. There are three reflexive pronouns, as given in (493).

(493) Reflexive pronouns paradigm

       ʔuẽᴹ   1S, 2S
       ʔɲáᴹ   3S
       ʔmóuᴸᴹ   1P, 2P, 3P

Reflexive pronouns are used in three ways: (1) to mark an action as reflexive, where the subject acts upon itself as object; (2) to emphasize the referent's identity; and (3) to mark the referent as solitary or unique. The third-person singular form $ʔɲá^M$ is also used adverbially in the sense of 'alone'. An example of each usage is given in (494)–(497), respectively.

(494) $ma^Lʔno^H$ $cá^Mmi^Lkuóu^M$ $rẽʔ^M$ $nú^M$ $la^Lhmí^H$
       love^TA^IMP   human   companion^2   you^s   as

          $ʔno^L$ $nú^M$ $ʔuẽ^M$
          love^STA^2   you^s   yourself
       Love your fellow human beings as you love yourself.

(495) la^L $hãu^M$ $bíʔ^H$ $kiũʔ^{LM}$ $cá^M$ $ʔáʔ^L$ $cá^M$
       manner   that^IN   AFF   undergo^TI^PRES^3   person   wealthy   person

          $ʔma^{LM}$ $ɲií^Hkõ^M$ $ʔɲá^M$ $ʔi^L$ $kioʔ^{MH}$
          keep^TI^PRES^3   towards   self   thing   have^STI^3
       That is what happens to a wealthy person, a person who keeps his possessions to himself.

(496) $ieʔ^L$ ni^M $dá^M$ la^L $má^M$ ka^L-$ciã^L$ $ʔmóu^{LM}$ $bíʔ^H$
       elder   that   VER   apparently   PRF   PAST-leave^TA^3   themselves   AFF

          $cá^Hmíʔ^H$ $hõ^M$ $hãu^M$ $ʔɲá^M$ $bíʔ^H$ $má^M$ $ɲi^{LM}$
          children   child^3   so   himself   AFF   PRF   walk^IA^PRES^3S
       Apparently, that fellow has abandoned his children by themselves, since he is now walking around by himself.

(497) nio^M $ʔɲá^M$ lio^{MH} $kiõ^{MH}$ $hná^{HL}$
       be^present^SII   alone   cargo   have^STI^1S   I
       My cargo is unattended.

The interrogative pronoun. The interrogative pronoun $ʔe^L$ 'what? (IN)' occurs clause initially (see also §10.3).

(498) $ʔe^L$ $hlá ʔ^H$ $hmuʔ^{LM}$ $ʔnú^M$
       what?   really   do^TI^PRES^2   you^s
       What are you so busy doing?

$ʔe^L$ 'what? (IN)' also functions as an indefinite pronoun.

(499) $kuí^H$-hmu^H $cú^M$ $ʔe^L$ hmu^L $bíʔ^H$
       HORT-do^HORT^3   they   what   do^TI^FUT^3   AFF
       Let them do whatever they want.

The Noun Phrase

6.2 The categorizers

The categorizer element modifies the base noun. Some nouns optionally take a categorizer; there is no difference in meaning whether the categorizer is present or not. For example, there is no change of meaning whether no^M 'rat' is modified by the categorizer cii^L (diminutive), or not. With certain other nouns as base, however, there is a difference in meaning between the presence and the absence of the categorizer. For example, when $ma\textit{?}^M$ 'viper, intestinal worm' is modified by the categorizer cii^L (diminutive (AN)), the meaning is 'ant'. The principal reason for not treating all instances of categorizer plus noun as a compound is that generally, neither categorizer nor noun undergo a tone-stress change, nor are there any segmental changes; the presence of either one of these modifications, or both together, are characteristic of compounds.

Some categorizers resemble classifiers (§6.9) in the way they refer to the shape of an entity. There are significant differences, however, between the classifiers and the categorizers.

1. Categorizers are optional with certain quantified nouns, while the presence of a semantically similar classifier is obligatory.

2. When a noun that takes a categorizer is not quantified, the categorizer is optional, but the classifier is ungrammatical.

3. A categorizer and a classifier can co-occur, but a categorizer cannot replace a classifier in a construction nor can it be enumerated by itself as can classifiers.

4. Categorizers can never function as the NP head since they are adjectival; classifiers, however, when used within a quantifier expression, may be used as an NP head.

5. Categorizers frequently define a noun semantically; sortal classifiers generally imply that the entity being enumerated is portable with the choice of classifier governed by the shape of the referent of the NP head.

Although all categorizers have an attributive function similar to the descriptive adjectives which follow the NP head (§6.5), unlike the descriptive adjectives, they cannot be used predicatively, nor can they follow the head of the NP.

The categorizers which have been identified are listed in (500), together with their source (if known). Each is discussed briefly below.

(500) Categorizer   Source

mi^L	spherical (IN)	$m\acute{a}i^L$	sphere
mu^{MH}/mi^{H}	flat (IN)	mu^{MH}	leaf
$ho^{MH}/h\acute{o}^H$	long flat (IN)	ho^{MH}	side
cii^M	diminutive (IN)	—	
cii^L	diminutive (AN)	—	
$\textit{?}n\acute{a}^H/n\acute{a}^H$	odd, irregular	$\textit{?}n\acute{a}^H$	section, end

Categorizer		Source	
cĩ*H*	disused, old, silly (IN)	ce*ʔH*	old (IN)
ŋiú*M*	masculine (AN)	ŋiu*ʔHL*	male (AN)
mĩ*H*	feminine (AN)	mï*L*	female (AN)

The categorizer *mï*^{L} (spherical), more than any other, has the potential of affecting the meaning of the NP head, such as *kĩ*^{H} 'rock' in *mï*^{L} *kĩ*^{H} 'stone' and *uóu*^{M}*hïeʔ*^{HL} 'grapevine' in *mï*^{L} *uóu*^{M}*hïeʔ*^{HL} 'grape'. It is generally used only with small, portable objects. For example, although *mï*^{L} collocates with the noun *kĩ*^{H} 'rock', the larger the rock, the less likely *mï*^{L} will co-occur.

The categorizer *mu*^{MH} (flat), is frequently heard as *mĩ*^{H} in fast speech. When it collocates with *si*^{M} 'book', for example, the meaning is 'paper'. Similarly, the meaning of the noun *kúʰhẽ*^{M} 'can, tin, bucket' changes to 'roofing iron' when preceded by *mu*^{MH}.

(501) a. *tũ*^{L} *kúʰhẽ*^{M}
 two^IN tin
 two buckets

 b. *tũ*^{L} *ho*^{MH} *mu*^{MH} *kúʰhẽ*^{M}
 two^IN side   flat   tin
 two sheets of roofing iron

The categorizer *ho*^{MH} (long flat) is frequently heard as *hó*^{H} in fast speech. It can be used with *ʔmá*^{M} 'wood, tree', for example, to mean 'board'.

(502) a. *tũ*^{L} *ʔmá*^{M}
 two^IN wood
 two trees

 b. *tũ*^{L} *ho*^{MH} *ho*^{MH} *ʔmá*^{M}
 two^IN side   long^flat wood
 two boards

ci^M (diminutive (IN)), has a mildly positive connotation, implying usefulness or desirability; occasionally it can affect the meaning of the noun with which it occurs, such as *ʔlaʔ*^{LM} 'hook' in *ci*^{M} *ʔlaʔ*^{LM} 'coathanger' and *hmu*^{M} 'palm mat' in *ci*^{M} *hmu*^{M} 'fan (woven)'.

cii^L (diminutive (AN)) is used only with small animals and most, but not all, insects. There does not appear to be any positive or negative connotation to this categorizer; the only common component seems to be size, i.e., 'small', such as

The Noun Phrase   175

ciiᴸ uï?ᴴᴸ 'cockroach' and *ciiᴸ kiu?ᴹᴴ* 'hummingbird'. It is optional with most nouns that refer to small animate entities.

The categorizer *?náᴴ/náᴴ* means (odd, irregular (shape), residual). It does not lexically affect the nominals with which it occurs. The variant *náᴴ* 'odd' is preferred when preceded by the evaluative adjective *?náᴴ* 'despicable'. It is mildly negative in connotation in the sense that the entity concerned is not aesthetically pleasing; there is not necessarily any implication as to the entity's usefulness.

(503)   *kiáᴹ   tiáᴸ   ?náᴴ kuoᴴ   niᴹ*
        bring^TI^IMP SUPL   odd   firewood   that
        Please bring that chunk of firewood.

cîᴴ (disused, old, silly) has a mildly negative connotation. It can occur with a variety of inanimate objects; for example, boxes, clothing, machete, or nearly anything whose condition has deteriorated or is held in low regard. The negative connotation is readily neutralized by the positive evaluative adjective *uîᴴ* 'nice, pleasant', as in (505).

(504)   *cîᴴ   ?mï?ᴹᴴ*
        disused   cloth
        old, disused clothes or rags

(505)   *uîᴴ   cîᴴ   kuoᴹ*
        useful   old   box
        useful old box

The categorizers *míᴴ* (feminine) and *ŋiúᴹ* (masculine) are used to specify the gender of the referents of proper names. *míᴴ* is generally obligatory for women's names; *ŋiúᴹ* is entirely optional for men's names. Examples are *míᴴ tuᴹᴴ* 'Antonia' and *ŋiúᴹ tuᴹᴴ* 'Antonio'.

6.3–6.4 The possessive construction

There are two possessive constructions in Chinantec, one for alienable nouns and one for inalienable nouns. An inalienable noun is inherently inflected for person-of-possessor; these nouns include names for body parts, kinship terms, and certain domestic items. The modifier constituent cannot occur, although the deictic and relative clause constituents can. Possession of inalienable nouns is expressed by inflection of the head noun and by an optional possessor NP. If the head of the NP is an alienable noun, it can be followed by a modifier, a deictic, and one or more relative clauses, one of which may express possession of the NP head.

6.3 Possession of inalienable nouns

Inalienable nouns exhibit a three-way contrast to index the person-of-possessor, inflecting for first-person plural or third person (1P/3 POSS) using the same form, first-person singular (1S POSS), and second person (2 POSS). Inflection generally consists of changes in tone-stress. Second person is generally marked by glottal closure of the final syllable. Some nouns exhibit vowel modification or suppletion, but these do not appear to affect the tone-stress pattern.

Some inalienable nouns retain the same tone-stress for all persons and others have a form only for third person. The latter express a part-whole relationship, e.g., hmu^M 'root (of a plant)', or a product-source relationship, e.g., $ho?^H$ 'light (of sun, lantern)'. Inalienable nouns are classified according to their tone-stress paradigms with the 1P/3 POSS form as a given factor (the dictionary citation form).[47] When the tone-stress of the base form is disregarded, the number of paradigms is eighteen since the tone-stress of only the 1S POSS and 2 POSS need to be accounted for. This is true for most of the disyllabic nouns since the form of the nonfinal syllable is specified in the citation form. The inalienable nouns in (506), for example, can be assigned the paradigm [b^{LM}–b^L], where the symbol [b] corresponds to ballistic stress.

(506)   1P/3   1S   2

a. $?iá^{HL}$ $?iá^{LM}$ $?iá?^L$ jar, jug
b. ma^{MH} $má^{LM}$ $má?^L$ food
c. $mi^L?ué^{HL}$ $mi^L?ué^{LM}$ $mi^L?ué?^L$ rib

The eighteen inalienable noun paradigms are listed in (507) with an example given for each. The symbol [c] corresponds to controlled stress.

(507)   1P/3   1S   2

[b^M-c^H] $?ma^L$ $?má^M$ $?ma?^H$ excrement
[b^M-c^M] $?a^H$ $?á^M$ $?a?^M$ clothes
[b^L-b^L] $diá^Hhó^L$ $diá^Hhó^L$ $diá^Hhó?^L$ co-mother
[c^H-c^H] $huú^Mko^H$ $huú^Mko^H$ $huú^Mko?^H$ hometown
[c^M-b^M] $diá^Hhmäï^M$ $diá^Mhma^M$ $diá^Mhmäï?^M$ godmother
[c^M-c^M] lio^H lio^M $lio?^M$ cargo
[c^L-c^L] $di^H?io^L$ $di^M?io^L$ $di^M?io?^L$ grandmother

---

[47] A bilingual Chinantec-Spanish dictionary is in progress. The citation form for inalienable nouns is based on the normal response by speakers of Chinantec when asked in Spanish for the Chinantec equivalent of a noun; for example, if asked for *padre* 'father', the response would be $hméi^M$ which is the form used for 1P/3 POSS.

The Noun Phrase   177

	1P/3	1S	2	
[bLM-bH]	híe?H	híe?LM	híe?H	larynx
[bLM-cM]	kuoM	uóLM	kuõ?M	hand
[bLM-bL]	kuóuHL	kuóuLM	kuóu?L	firewood
[bLM-cHL]	táMmuHL	táMmúLM	táMmu?HL	palate
[bLM-bLM]	hõM	hóLM	hó?LM	child
[cLM-bH]	háH	hãLM	há?H	tooth
[cLM-cH]	?oL	uẽLM	?õ?H	mouth
[cLM-bM]	mĩLθiúHL	mĩLθiaLM	mĩLθiú?M	mother-in-law
[cLM-cM]	hméiM	ɲiu?LM	ɲie?M	father
[cLM-bL]	kuáH	kuaLM	kuá?L	ear
[cLM-cLM]	?ɲiúHL	?ɲiuLM	?ɲiu?LM	house

The vocative form of inalienable nouns. Most kinship terms have a vocative (VOC) form; some like *hóL* 'child (VOC)' function as the vocative for several kinship terms, such as grandchild, daughter-in-law, and son-in-law. The tone-stress of the vocative form does not seem readily derivable from any part of the inalienable noun paradigm and frequently exhibits vowel modification or suppletion. Because of the unpredictability of the vocative form, and the fact that it is relevant only to the kinship terms among the inalienable nouns, it is treated as a distinct (but related) lexeme to avoid complicating the inalienable noun paradigm further. Note (508) which lists the vocative of some kinship nouns along with their other possessive forms.

(508)

1P/3	1S	2	VOC	
hõM	hóLM	hó?LM	hóL	child
diáHhóL	diáHhóL	diáHhó?L	diáHhóLM	co-mother
rãï?MH	rẽ?M	rẽ?M	re?M	relative
cáMkoH	cáMkoH	cáMko?H	cáMkáuL	countryman
hméiM	ɲiu?LM	ɲie?M	tiaMH	father
díH?ioL	díM?ioL	díM?io?L	míH?iõ?HL	grandmother
diáHhmáïM	diáMhmaM	diáMhmáï?M	diõMH	godmother
míHθiúHL	míMθiaLM	míMθiú?M	míH	mother
mĩLθiúHL	mĩLθiaLM	mĩLθiú?M	maL	mother-in-law

Inalienable nouns which have alienable counterparts. Some nouns, principally kinship terms, are exclusively inalienable. Other nouns have both alienable and inalienable counterparts. Some use the alienable form more, and others the inalienable form. When there is a choice between inalienable and alienable counterparts, the inalienable form denotes a closer association between possessor and possessed than when the alienable is used.

Nouns which have both forms refer to entities which are (1) associated with human usage, e.g., $ʔŋiú^L$ 'house', $ká^Hʔáu^M$ 'chicken'; or (2) express a source-product relationship, such as $hái̯^{HL}$ 'word, message' and bodily excretions (human or animal); or (3) express a part-whole relationship, e.g., mu^M 'leaf' and $mú^{LM}$ 'bone'. Not all nouns of these three categories necessarily have both alienable and inalienable counterparts; for example, $tú^M$ 'turkey' has only an alienable form despite being a common domesticated animal like $ká^Hʔáu^M$ 'chicken'.

The inalienable and alienable counterparts of some nouns are given in (509). There is no apparent rule for deriving either the tone-stress or the nucleus of an alienable noun from its inalienable counterpart (or vice versa).

(509)

Inalienable			Alienable	
1P/3	1S	2		
$ʔmú^{HL}$	$ʔmú^{LM}$	$ʔmúʔ^L$	$ʔmu^L$	mucus
$hái̯^{HL}$	$hái̯^{LM}$	$hái̯ʔ^L$	$hái̯^L$	tunic
$hŋiú^{HL}$	$hŋiú^{LM}$	$hŋiúʔ^L$	$hŋiu^M$	hair
$kéi̯^{HL}$	$kéi̯^{LM}$	$kéi̯ʔ^L$	$kéi̯^M$	cage
$náu^{HL}$	$náu^{LM}$	$náuʔ^L$	no^H	grease, fat
$ʔiá^{HL}$	$ʔiá^{LM}$	$ʔiáʔ^L$	$ʔia^{LM}$	jug
$ʔué^{HL}$	$ʔué^{LM}$	$ʔuéʔ^L$	$ʔué^{LM}$	land
$ʔáu^{HL}$	$ʔáu^{LM}$	$ʔáuʔ^L$	$ʔáu^{HL}$	pants
$héi̯^{HL}$	$héi̯^{LM}$	$héi̯ʔ^L$	$hë^L$	bed
$uóu^{HL}$	$uóu^{LM}$	$uóuʔ^L$	u^M	dish
$ʔma^L$	$ʔma^M$	$ʔmaʔ^H$	$ʔmái̯^M$	excrement
cio^L	cio^M	$cioʔ^M$	$ciáu^M$	cuttings
$hë^H$	$hë^M$	$hëʔ^M$	$hái̯^{HL}$	word
$kéi̯^{HL}$	$kéi̯^{LM}$	$kéi̯ʔ^L$	$kïe^L$	money

The possessor noun phrase. When possession is expressed, the possessor noun phrase is optional; it usually occurs, however, especially for first and second-persons.[48] It is omitted only when the context leaves no doubt as to the possessor. Omission of the possessor NP is marked by ∅ in (510b) and (511).

---

[48]In other Chinantec languages, the reverse appears to be true. In Lealao Chinantec, the occurrence of a noun or pronoun possessor evidently provides a component of contrastiveness; that is, 'mine' in contrast with 'yours'. For example, Rupp states that in Lealao Chinantec "If the possessor is first or second person, the corresponding personal pronoun may follow, but since this is redundant, it is added only to give emphasis" (1989:68).

(510) a. *kú?ʰ   ciī?ᴸᴹ   núᴹ*
         ?ˆhurtˆɪɪˆᴘʀᴇs headˆ2 youˆs
         Does your head hurt?

   b. *hã́ᴸ hláʔʰ kuʔᴹ   ciīᴸᴹ   ∅*
       yes really hurtˆɪɪˆᴘʀᴇs headˆ1s (I)
       Yes, my head really hurts.

(511) *ʔíeʰ   náʔᴹ   hóʔᴸᴹ   ∅*
       teachˆᴛɪˆɪᴍᴘ youˆᴘ childˆ2 (youˆᴘ)
       Teach your child(ren)!

When the possessor is first or second person, the head of the possessor NP must be one of the personal pronouns, as in (512), or a reflexive pronoun, as in (513).

(512) *míᴹθiaᴸᴹ hnáᴴᴸ*
       motherˆ1s I
       my mother

(513) *kãuᴹ   ʔiᴸ   ciã́uʔᴹᴸ   ciīᴸᴹ   ʔuḗᴹ*
       oneˆɪɴ thing findˆᴛɪˆᴘʀᴇsˆ3 headˆ1s myself
       something that I think of myself (lit., something that my own head finds)

If the possessor is third person, potentially any NP may occur.

(514) *hoᴸ   cáᴹ   máᴹ hliáʔʰ   ʔíᴸ   hã́ʰ*
       mouthˆ3 person ᴘʀғ   beˆbrokenˆsɪɪ thatˆᴀɴ toothˆ3
       the mouth of that person who has a broken tooth

(515) *hméiᴹ   cáᴹ   ʔíᴸ*
       fatherˆ3 person thatˆᴀɴ
       that person's father

A possessive NP may itself function as the possessor in a larger possessive NP. Of the two possessive constructions, (516a) and (516b), the latter can function as the possessor of *ʔoᴸ* 'mouth' of the former; see (517).

(516) a. *ʔoᴸ   cúᴹ*
          mouthˆ3 3
          her/his mouth

b. *ʔéa^H*   *cú^M*
stomach^3 3
her/his stomach

(517)   POSS_NP [POSS_NP [   ]]
ʔo^L   *ʔéi^H*   *cú^M*
mouth^3   stomach^3 3
entrance to her/his stomach (lit., the mouth of the stomach of her/him, i.e., where the esophagus joins the stomach)

The presence or absence of a third-person possessor has special implications. If the third-person pronoun *cú^M* 's/he' occurs, then subject and possessor are not co-referential.

(518)   *ka^L-kieʔ^L*   *cú^M*   *ta^L*   *cú^M*
       PAST-cut^TI^3 3   leg^3 3
       S/he$_i$ cut her/his$_j$ leg.

If, however, the third-person subject and possessor are co-referential, there are two possible constructions. The most common one involves omission of the pronoun *cú^M* 's/he' as in (519); the other possibility is to mark the possessor by the appropriate third-person reflexive pronoun *ʔŋá^M* 'himself/herself' or *ʔmóu^{LM}* 'themselves' as in (520).

(519)   *ka^L-kieʔ^L*   *cú^M*   *ta^L*
       PAST-cut^TI^3 3   leg^3
       S/he$_i$ cut (her/his$_i$) leg.

(520)   *ka^L-kieʔ^L*   *cú^M*   *ta^L*   *ʔŋá^M*
       PAST-cut^TI^3 3   leg^3   herself/himself
       S/he$_i$ cut the leg (of) herself/himself$_i$.

6.4 Possession of alienable nouns

If the head of the NP is an alienable noun then it is optionally followed by the modifier, deictic, and relative clause constituents.

One of the more frequent relative clauses to occur expresses an owner-item, benefactor-award, source-product, or part-whole relationship. Since its predominant use is to express possession of alienable nouns (owner-item), it is called the possessor relative clause (see also §9.1).

The two possessive words *kioʔMH* (IN) and *hoʔH* (AN) function as the verb in the possessor relative clause.[49] They are classified as state verbs based on their ability to function predicatively, on the similarity of their paradigms to that of transitive state verbs, and because of their ergative pattern of agreement. Both may be glossed as 'have, possess, own, acquire, get, gain, use' depending on context; for consistency, however, 'have' is used as the literal interlinear gloss.

Lyons remarks that "Relatively few languages exhibit what we may call 'have-sentences', i.e., possessive sentences in which the 'possessor' is the surface-structure subject of a verb 'to have' and the 'possessed object' the surface-structure object of this verb" (1968:392). In this respect, Sochiapan Chinantec is of typological interest.

Relative clauses, in general, are optionally introduced by the complementizer (COMP) *hiL* 'that, which'. The possessor relative clause usually lacks *ʔiL* although it occasionally does occur. If an item has two possessors, the complementizer is optional (and usually absent) from the first possessor relative clause, but the second one is usually introduced by *hiL* as in (521) or when any of the verb phrase adverbs precede the verb of the possessive relative clause, the complementizer *ʔiL* optionally occurs as in (522).

(521) *hnáHL   bíʔH   kiōH   máLM   kioʔMH   séLM   hiL   ʔiL*
        I   AFF   bring^STI^1S food   have^STI^3 Joseph   and   COMP

       kioʔMH   kiuMH   nĩM   siáʔL
       have^STI^3   Francis   too   also
       I have brought Joseph and Francisco's food (lit., I am bringing food (that) J. has and that F. has too).

(522) *muM   (ʔiL)   hmĩH   kioʔMH   hãuM   síiHmuMH*
        boat   COMP   TRM   have^STI^3   that^IN Simon
        the boat that Simon once had

As indicated at the beginning of this chapter, the unmarked order of post-NP head constituents is: (MODIFIER) (DEICTIC) (RELATIVE CLAUSE)ⁿ. The deictic constituent can only occur following the modifier constituent. However, the order of the deictic and relative clause constituents is not fixed.

The deictic can occur within the possessor relative clause, as in (523b), or it can precede the possessor relative clause, as in (523c); the latter

---

[49]In Quiotepec Chinantec such words are called "possessive pronouns" by Robbins (1968:68–74) and in Palantla Chinantec they are called "allocational pronouns" by Merrifield (1968:62–63). Anderson (1989:62–65) describing Comaltepec Chinantec and Rupp (1989:68–73) describing Lealao Chinantec, call them "allocational nouns." For further discussion of possessive verbs in Sochiapan Chinantec see Foris 1993:271–73.

occurrence is more common. There is no appreciable difference in meaning between the two.

(523) a. ho?ᴴ   tiéᴸ   bí?ᴴ   caᴸkuáᴴ ?íᴸ
have^STA^3 Stephen AFF horse that^AN
Stephen owns that horse (mentioned earlier).

b. caᴸkuáᴴ ho?ᴴ   ?íᴸ   tiéᴸ
horse have^STA^3 that^AN Stephen
the aforementioned horse (that) Stephen owns

c. caᴸkuáᴴ ?íᴸ   ho?ᴴ   tiéᴸ
horse that^AN have^STA^3 Stephen
the aforementioned horse (that) Stephen owns

A sentential example of the possession of an inanimate alienable noun is given in (524).

(524) kaᴸ-lauᴹ   cúᴹ míᴴtái̯ᴸ ie?ᴸ háuᴹ kiõᴹᴴ
PAST-buy^secondhand^TI^3 3 machete old that^IN have^STI^IS

hnáᴴᴸ
I

He bought that old machete of mine.

Ellipsis of the subject of the possessive relative clause normally takes place if the subject is coreferential with the subject of the matrix clause.

(525) kiõᴴ   hnáᴴᴸ ɲiᴴháuᴹ kiõᴹᴴ
bring^STI^IS I blanket have^STI^IS
I brought my blanket.

Occasionally, ellipsis of the subject occurs if the subjects of the main and relative clause are not coreferential and at least one subject is nonthird person.

(526) kaᴸ-?ái̯ᴸ   cúᴹ kieᴸ kiõᴹᴴ   (hnáᴴᴸ)
PAST-steal^TI^3 3 money have^STI^IS I
S/he stole my money.

When both the main and the relative clause have third-person subjects, and the subjects are not coreferential, the subject of the relative clause is always present.

The Noun Phrase

(527) ka^L-$ki\tilde{e}^L$ $cú^M$ $t\tilde{u}^{LM}$ $kio?^{MH}$ $cú^M$
PAST-play^TI^3 3   guitar   have^STI^3   3
S/he played her/his guitar (someone else's).

For emphasis, a third-person reflexive pronoun may be used as subject of the possessor relative clause.

(528) ka^L-$ki\tilde{e}^L$ $cú^M$ $t\tilde{u}^{LM}$ $kio?^{MH}$ $?\eta\acute{a}^M$
PAST-play^TI^3 3   guitar   have^STI^3   herself/himself
S/he played her/his own guitar.

It is also possible for the third-person proximate pronoun $dí^M$ to occur as subject of the possessor relative clause to mark continuation of the same third-person participant.

Other uses of the possessive verb $kio?^{MH}$. Although the predominant use of the possessive verb $kio?^{MH}$ is to express possession of an inanimate entity, the verb has several other uses.

Within the context of a relative clause (§9.1) $kio?^{MH}$ can also express source-product and part-whole relationships and benefaction. These uses are illustrated in turn below.

(529) $hn\acute{a}^{HL}$ $?nó^{LM}$ $hmaï?^{MH}$ $kio?^{MH}$ $k\acute{a}^H?áu^M$
I   want^STI^1S   broth   have^STI^3   chicken
I want (to eat) chicken soup (lit., I want (to eat) (the) chicken's broth).

(530) $tiá^H$ $kiá?^H$ $nú^M$ llave $kio?^{MH}$ $mi^L$to^H $lá^M$
?^not bring^STI^2   you^s   key   have^STI^3   padlock   this
Didn't you bring this padlock's key?

(531) $tiá^H$ $hmú?^H$ $ka^L lá^M$ mi^L $ki\tilde{o}^{MH}$ $hn\acute{a}^{HL}$
?^not make^TI^FUT^2   some   medicine   have^STI^1S   I
Won't you treat me with some medicine (lit., won't you make (up) some medicine (that) I can have)?

Within the context of a complement clause (§9.2), $kio?^{MH}$ conveys 'partial affectedness'.

If an animate entity is completely affected, the verb is marked to agree in animacy with its object. In (532), for example, the speaker wishes to eat a whole fried chicken.

If a person desires only a portion of chicken, however, the verb 'want' is inflected for an inanimate object, and the inanimate possessive verb occurs in a complement clause such as (533).

(532) hláʔ^H ɲif^H-kū ʔ^{MH} hná^{HL} hã̄^{M} ká^{H}ʔá^M-siú ʔ^H
really   INT-eat^TA^1S   I   one^AN   chicken-fried^AN
I really want to eat a fried chicken.

(533) hláʔ^H ɲif^H-ku ʔ^{MH} hná^{HL} kioʔ^{MH} ká^{H}ʔá^M-siú ʔ^H
really   INT-eat^TI^1S   I   have^STI^3   chicken-fried
I want (to eat) some fried chicken.

6.5 The noun phrase modifier

The modifier constituent of the NP immediately follows the NP head, but it may occur only if the NP head is an alienable noun. For example, (534a) is grammatical since it uses the alienable form of house, but (534b) with the inalienable form is not (the modifier is ieʔ^L 'old'). Moving the modifier ieʔ^L 'old' to any other position in (534b) fails to produce a grammatical NP; deleting ieʔ^L, however, results in a grammatical NP 'that home of mine'.

(534) a. ʔɲiú^L ieʔ^L hã́u^M kiõ^{MH} hná^{HL}
house   old^IN   that^IN   have^STI^1S   I
that old house of mine

b. *ʔɲiu^{LM} hná^{HL} ieʔ^L hã́u^M
house^1S   I   old^IN   that^IN
that old home of mine, my old home

Only descriptive adjectives may function within the adjective phrase as the modifier constituent; the evaluative adjectives uí^H 'desirable, pleasant, useful' and ʔná^H 'undesirable, despicable' occur before the head (§6.8).

The structure of the NP modifier is set out in (535), where ^{n} stands for any number, including zero.

(535) MODIFIER → (ADJECTIVE)^n ADJECTIVE PHRASE

A nonfinal adjective must be simple or compound; the final adjective can become the head of an adjective phrase with up to three optional qualifiers. Theoretically there is no limit to the number of adjectives that may occur following an alienable noun. Adjectives agree with their head as to animacy, and in a limited fashion they agree in number.

The Noun Phrase   185

(536) cáï^M tiáu^M hḯ?^{HL} huo?^{M}
       dog   white^AN skinny   lazy
       a skinny, lazy, white dog

Agreement as to animacy. If the nucleus of the inanimate adjective is oral, the form of most animate adjectives is derived by nasalization of the nucleus.

(537) liá?^{M} (IN) → liá̃?^{M} (AN) black
       kuo^M (IN) → kuõ^M (AN) long

Some adjectives undergo tone-stress modification as well as nasalization of the vowel to produce the animate form.

(538) pa^{MH} (IN) → pã^H (AN) large (S)
       huá^{HL} (IN) → huã^M (AN) grey

There are several adjectives that have only nasalized forms, which are then identical for both inanimate and animate; e.g., dá̃ï^L 'red' and ?mai^{MH} 'new'. There are a few adjectives with an oral nucleus, such as pi?^{MH} 'small', that retain the same form regardless of the animacy of the head noun.

Agreement as to number. There is only one adjective, pa^{MH} 'big', that marks plurality as well as animateness, yielding four different forms. The plural forms are suppletive with respect to their singular counterparts.

(539) pa^{MH} (IN^S)   pã^H (AN^S)   big
       ká?^{H} (IN^P)   ká̃?^{H} (AN^P)   big

Examples of the four forms for 'big' are shown in (540).

(540) a. káu^M ?má^M pa^{MH}
          one^IN   tree   big^IN^S
          a big tree

       b. jã^M no^M pã^H
          one^AN   rat   big^AN^S
          a big rat

       c. tṹ^L ?má^M ká?^{H}
          two^IN   tree   big^IN^P
          two big trees

d. gõ^L no^M ká̰ʔ^H
two^AN rat big^AN^P
two big rats

Ordering of adjectives. Theoretically, there is no limit to the number of adjectives which can occur within the modifier constituent following an alienable noun. A group of three native speakers uniformly considered long strings of adjectives to be grammatical. Similar results were achieved regardless of the animacy of the NP head. In practice, however, it is uncommon to find more than one adjective following the NP head, and rare to find more than two. Apposition is used to further restrict or modify the referent.

There is a relative ordering of the adjectives. By making up strings of several semantically compatible adjectives and testing them with the aforementioned consultants, the preferred order was established. Adjectives were ranked until about thirty positions had been established. Detailed charts showing the ranking of inanimate and animate adjectives are a part of my dissertation. I note here a few observations which came out of the ranking procedures.

Adjectives of adjacent ranking can generally interchange positions, but if there are more than two intervening ranks, then interchanging them results in a construction which is no longer grammatical. In establishing the rank of various adjectives, some occupy the same semantic domain, such as colors and size. There appears to be a tendency for 'general' to precede 'specific'. Finally, there are, as may be expected, semantic restrictions as to which adjectives can co-occur.

Color adjectives. Color adjectives agree with the NP head as to animacy. They may be simple or compound. The simple inanimate color adjectives are as in (541).

(541) liáʔ^M black   tiáu^M white
       dáï^L red   mí^{M}niáu^L yellow
       réʔ^M green   θḯ^{HL} violet
       saʔ^M brown   saïʔ^M brownish
       huá^{HL} grey   ʔlúʔ^H pale, pastel
       hua^{LM} mottled   ʔuéʔ^L variegated
       huõʔ^M faded

The basic color terms (Berlin and Kay 1969 and Comrie 1989:37) appear to be liáʔ^M 'black', tiáu^M 'white', dáï^L 'red', mí^{M}niáu^L 'yellow', réʔ^M 'green', θḯ^{HL} 'violet', and saʔ^M 'brown'. Historically, the term θḯ^{HL} 'violet' may have included 'blue', as predicted by the color hierarchy; however, the Spanish word *azul* has been adopted by Chinantec for colors that are closer to blue.

The Noun Phrase

Most animate color adjectives are derived from their inanimate counterparts by nasalization of the stem, in the same way as other adjectives.

(542) IN   AN
    ré?^{M} →   ré̃?^{M} green
    tiáu^M →   tiã́u^M white
    liá?^{M} →   liã́?^{M} black
    sa?^{M} →   sã?^{M} brown
    ?ué?^{L} →   ?uẽ́?^{L} variegated

The animate forms of the color adjectives may be used to modify inanimate nouns, in which case the color denoted is an approximation, such as liã́?^{M} 'blackish'.

Compounding of two adjectives seems to occur only with the color adjectives. Whichever color is the more dominant is placed first in the compound. mí^{M}niáu^L 'yellow' has the form mí^{M}nia^L- when it occurs first in a compound, following the constraint on nonfinal syllables. dá̈i^L mí^{M}niáu^L 'dark orange' in (543) is not a compound phonologically, but semantically it functions as a compound.

(543) dá̈i^L mí^{M}niáu^L mí^{M}nia^L-dá̈i^L
       red yellow   yellow-red
       dark orange   light orange

Inanimate compound adjectives are formed by using the inanimate form of the adjective in the first part of the compound and the animate form of the adjective in the second part. An example of an inanimate compound adjective is given in (544).

(544) kuo^M pi?^{MH} ré?^{M}-tiã́u^M
      box   small   green^IN-white^AN
      (a) small pale-green box

An animate compound adjective is formed by using the animate forms of the adjectives in both parts of the compound.

(545) cái^M ?uẽ́?^{L}-liã́?^{M}
      dog   variegated^AN-black^AN
      a black-spotted dog (dog with black spots, e.g., a Dalmatian)

The adjective phrase. If more than one adjective occurs in the modifier constituent of a noun phrase, the adjective that is qualified always moves to the final position, even though this displaces it from its normal rank. Only one adjective can be qualified at any one time. In (546), $?ú?^H$ 'fat', modified by $l\tilde{i}^{MH}$ $ku^L t\tilde{i}^L$ 'very absolutely', occurs after $pá^H$ 'big'. If $?ú?^H$ were not qualified, the order would be $?ú?^H$ $pá^H$.

(546) $h\tilde{a}^M$ $mí^M \eta ií^L$ $pá^H$ $?ú?^H$ $l\tilde{i}^{MH}$ $ku^L t\tilde{i}^L$
        one^AN pig   big^AN^s fat   very   absolutely
        an absolutely very fat big pig

The final adjective can be followed by up to three optional qualifiers QL_x, QL_y, and QL_z, in this order. Any one of the qualifiers or combination thereof may occur, except for semantic co-occurrence restrictions. All three qualifiers are shown in (547).

(547) $h\tilde{a}^M$ $mí^M \eta ií^L$ $?ú?^H$ $kú^H pi?^{MH}$ $l\tilde{i}^{MH}$ $ku^L t\tilde{i}^L$
        one^AN pig   fat   slightly   very   absolutely
        a truly very slightly fat pig *or* a quite minimally fat pig

There are three adverbs that may function as the first qualifier QL_x: $kú^H pi?^{MH}$ 'slightly, somewhat', $pí^L$ 'fast', and $sí^M$ 'vivid'. Adverbs $pí^L$ 'fast' or $sí^M$ 'vivid' may occur only if the adjective being modified is one of the color adjectives.

There are three possible adverbs for the QL_y element: $l\tilde{i}^{LM}$ or $l\tilde{i}^{HL}$ 'very' (an intensifier), $sií?^H$ 'very' (diminutive connotation), or $?la?^L$ 'terribly' (an intensifier connotation, such as in English 'terribly big').

The third and last qualifier element, QL_z, has $ku^L t\tilde{i}^L$ or $ku^L t\tilde{i}^{HL}$ 'absolutely, certainly, truly' or $ka^L lá^M$ 'somewhat' (a reserved comment) as its possibilities.

Two of the above qualifiers undergo morphophonemic changes in certain environments. When $kú^H pi?^{MH}$ 'slightly, somewhat' of QL_x occurs with any adverb of QL_y, then its form is $kú^H pí^H$. When $l\tilde{i}^{LM}$ 'very' of QL_y immediately follows any word with a high tone, then its form is $l\tilde{i}^{MH}$. These two processes can co-occur.

(548) $?mu^L$ $kú^H pí^H$ $l\tilde{i}^{MH}$
        sharp   slightly   very
        very slightly sharp *or* barely sharp

6.6 The deictic constituent

There are five deictic adjectives (or demonstratives); three are used spatially, the other two are anaphoric. The two anaphoric deictics agree with the head noun as to animacy. Two of the deictics have been extended metaphorically to temporal deixis.

The Noun Phrase

The spatial deictics. The three deictics *láM* 'this, these', *nĩM* 'that, those', and *óLM* 'yonder' indicate three degrees of distance from the speaker; all three are neutral as to animateness. The deictic *láM* 'this, these', defines a referent as relatively close to the speaker, *nĩM* 'that, those' defines the referent as closer to the addressee than the speaker, or relatively far from both addressee and speaker, and *óLM* 'yonder' defines a referent as remote from both speaker and addressee or even out of sight. The distance which determines the term is relative to both the speaker and the addressee; it is a "person oriented three-term system" (Anderson and Keenan 1985:284). This is illustrated in (549) where the drowning person is slightly closer to the addressee than to the speaker, but *óLM* 'yonder' is used, marking the distance as far from both speaker and addressee. This is also apparent by the use of the andative prefix *kuáM-* 'go' because if the drowning person was close to the addressee, then the andative prefix would not be used.

(549) ʔeL dáM kaL-kiúʔLM ŋiúM óLM kuáM-kuõʔH dáM
what? VER PAST-befall^TI^3 fellow yonder ANDT^IMP-pull^TA^2 VER

tiáL cúM kíH húL dáM cúM líHL
SUPL he because die^IA^FUT^3 VER he be^able^II^FUT
What has happened to that fellow; please go pull him in, otherwise he might die.

An example of *láM*, indicating proximity to speaker and distance from addressee, is shown in (550).

(550) kóʔL hmíH kiẽM sũH láM kiáHL núM
how^much? TRM cost^STI^3 radio this have^STI^2 you^s
How much did this radio of yours cost?

láM is also used at the beginning of a text to refer to the information about to be given.

(551) ʔiL láM káuM háiHL ʔiL náH-ŋiML cáM
thing this one^IN story COMP PROG^P-understand^TI^3 people

huúM láM
town this
This is an account of the beliefs held by the people of this town.

In (552), the deictic *nĩM* marks the referent as relatively far from both speaker and addressee.

(552) ciɨʰ-kueᴹᴸ   ʔmáᴹ kiéɨᴹ nɨ̃ᴹ háṵᴹ tiáᴹ kïʔᴸᴹ
      upright^PROG-prop^II tree dry that so not fall^II^PRES
      That dry tree is being propped up, that's why it's not falling.

The expression háïᴴᴸ nɨ̃ᴹ 'that story/message/account' occurs in the last paragraph of narrative texts to refer to the information that has just been given.

(553) háṵᴹ kuᴸ nɨ̃ᴹ bïʔᴴ tíᴸ   háïᴴᴸ nɨ̃ᴹ
      so just that AFF be^complete^SII story that
      So that is the end of this story.

nɨ̃ᴹ can also be used anaphorically to refer to a person just mentioned in the conversation by the other participant, implying emotional detachment, as if the speaker has little or no knowledge of the referent.

(554) máᴹ húḷ   bïʔᴴ cáᴹ   nɨ̃ᴹ
      PRF die^IA^PAST^3 AFF person that
      That person has died (i.e., the person you just mentioned, whom I don't really know).

nɨ̃ᴹ is also used as a means of disassociating oneself from the referent (not necessarily visible).

(555) tiáᴹ cáᴹmïᴸ nɨ̃ᴹ mɨ́ᴴθiúᴴᴸ iáʔᴸ hnoʔᴴ
      not woman that mother^IP ASSR us
      That woman is not our mother!

Anaphoric deictics. There are two deictics that have only anaphoric reference: ʔɨ́ᴸ 'that, those (AN)' and háṵᴹ 'that, those (IN)'. The referent has either been recently mentioned in discourse and is presumed to be recoverable, or else is of presumed common knowledge to both speaker and listener.

In (556) from a folklore story about the origin of the sun and moon, the deictic ʔɨ́ᴸ is used twice, once to refer to the gods (sun and moon), and once to refer to the buzzard of whom they were asking a favor.

(556) laᴸ nɨ̃ᴹ bïʔᴴ kaᴸ-huáʔᴸ   dióᴸᴹ ʔɨ́ᴸ   kaᴸ-θáïʔᴸ
      idea that AF PAST-say^TI^3 god that^AN PAST-tell^DI^3

      túᴹhueᴸᴹ ʔɨ́ᴸ
      buzzard that^AN
      That is what those gods told that buzzard.

In (557) from a folklore story, a wealthy man offers his two long-time employees the choice of receiving either their wages or good advice. The deictic *háu^M* is used anaphorically three times to refer to the advice. There is a further use of *háu^M* glossed 'then' which refers back to the entire previous proposition: 'If a person accepts that advice...' and could be glossed 'that being so' or 'so then'. I have chosen to gloss *háu^M* by its closest functional equivalent in the examples.

(557) nḯ^{H}huá$^{?L}$ ciá^M ?e^L hú^{H}ciú^{LM} háu^M háu^M tiú^{M}uú^M
      if   person accept^TI^FUT^3 advice   that^IN then   no^longer

   kïe^L kãu^{HL} iá$^{?L}$ cú^M hï^{LM} la^L hú^{H}ciú^{LM} háu^M
   money   take^TI^FUT^3 ASSR he   only   just   advice   that^IN

   bï$^{?H}$ kãu^{HL} cú^M kḯ^H ?i^L háu^M bï$^{?H}$
   AFF   take^TI^FUT^3 he   because thing that   AFF

   ma^L?au^L ?i^L lḯ^H θiã^M cú^M ré^M
   help^TI^FUT^3 COMP be^able^II^FUT exist^STA^3 he   well

   tḯ^M
   capable

If a person accepts that advice, then he will no longer take the money, only that advice, because that is the thing which will enable him to have a prosperous life.

Deictic pronouns. Deictic pronouns are similar in form and meaning to the adjectival deictics already discussed. A comparison of the adjectival and pronominal forms is given in (558). Note that the pronominal forms *ó^{LM}* 'that (distant)' and *?í^L* 'that (AN)' are homophonous with the adjectival forms; *hãu^{LM}* 'that' refers to an abstract or nonvisible animate referent, *?í^L* 'that' refers to a nonvisible animate referent, and *la^{LM}* 'this', *nï^{LM}* 'that', and *ó^{LM}* 'that' can have either an inanimate or animate antecedent.

(558)   this   that   that/yonder   that (IN)   that (AN)

       Pronouns   la^{LM} nï^{LM} ó^{LM} hãu^{LM} ?í^L
       Adjectives lá^M nḯ^M ó^{LM} háu^M ?í^L

The deictic pronouns may be used in place of a lexical NP, functioning as a complement in a verbless equative construction (§8.1). In (559), it is clear that *hãu^{LM}* 'that one' (anaphoric) functions as a pronominal complement.

(559) kä́u^M ce^L kio?^{MH} cá^M?ãu^{LM} bí?^{H} hãu^{LM}
one^IN jar have^STI^3 ancestor AFF that^one^IN
That aforementioned one (is) a jar belonging to the ancestors.

Deictic pronouns can sometimes convey a more vague or general sense than that conveyed by the corresponding adjective. Compare (560) and (561). In (560), the speaker is indicating a desire to travel in the general direction of the previously mentioned path; however, in (561), a precise path is indicated, and hãu^{LM} cannot be substituted for hä́u^M.

(560) huï^{LM} hãu^{LM} cáu^{HL}
path that^one^IN go^nonhome^IA^FUT^1P
The path (is) that aforementioned one; let's go.

(561) huï^{LM} hãu^M tí^L tũ^L kí^{M}lo^{H}mé^{H}tř́ó^H
path that^IN complete^STI^3 two^IN kilometer
That aforementioned path is two kilometers long.

The next three examples illustrate the use of la^{LM} 'this one'. In (562), the pronoun la^{LM} stands for ?ŋiú^L lá^M 'this house'; in (563), la^{LM} 'this one' functions as the complement to an animate referent hná^{HL} 'I'; and in (564), la^{LM} stands for hái^{HL} lá^M 'this word'.

(562) ?ŋiú^L mí?^{H} θe?^{M} ?ia^{L}hä́u^{HL} má?^{L} la^{LM}
house small stand^SII long^ago EXCL this^one
This (is) a small house (which) has stood for a long time!

(563) hná^{HL} la^{LM} cá^M kuá^H-hmu^M ná^H si^M lá^M
I   this^one person sit^PROG-make^TI^IS I   letter this
It is I, the person who is writing this letter.

(564) su^{L}uú^M lí^{ML} ?nú^M ?i^L hú^H-?laï?^{L} la^{LM}
PREVEN think^TI^PRES^2 you^s COMP word-bad this^one

      lí^M-huá?^{LM} hná^{HL} ŋi^{H}kõ^M nú^M
      HOD-say^TI^IS I   to   you^s
Don't think that this which I just told you is bad advice.

Examples of ni^{LM}, ó^{LM}, and ?i^L, respectively, are:

(565) hä́u^M huá?^{L} ti^{LM} mi^L ŋi^H uóu?^{L} bí?^{H} ni^{LM}
then say^TI^PAST^3 master medicine place distant AFF that^one
So the doctor said, "That (is) a distant place."

The Noun Phrase   193

(566) cá^M   lí^H   θéi^M bí?^H ó^LM
      person appear^STA^3 goat AFF that^one
      A person like a goat (is) that (person) (referring to agility in running in rough terrain).

(567) hã^M   cá^M   hmi^H ?á?^L lí^LM bí?^H ?í^L
      one^AN person TRM   rich   very   AFF   that^one^AN
      That one (is) a person (who) was once very wealthy.

Presentatives. Deictics can also be used adverbially as presentatives; that is, elements "which are used to indicate an item's location or to signal its appearance in (or relative to) the observational field of the [speaker]" (Anderson and Keenan 1985:279).

(568) lá^M ró^LM sií^M ka^L-ti^MH   ?i^L rẽ^M   ?nú^M
      here lie^SII book PAST-regard^TI^3 COMP owe^STI^2 you^s
      Here is the book that records your debts.

(569) ó^LM   tiõ?^M   kũ^L   nió^L ?liáu^L
      there stand^SIA^3P   one^AN   group   soldier
      There stands a group of soldiers (distant).

Temporal deixis. When the deictic lá^M 'this' and hãu^M 'that (IN)' occur with temporal nouns, they distinguish, respectively, 'current, present' from 'previous, previously mentioned'.

(570) a. hmáï^H lá^M
         time   this
         this time/day/occasion, presently (versus né^LM today)

      b. hmáï^H hãu^M
         time   hat^IN
         that time/day/occasion (i.e., the day previously mentioned)

      c. mií^M lá^M
         year   this
         this (current) year

Chinantec does not use the deictics to express the concepts of 'next' and 'last'.[50] To express 'next', the numeral kãu^M 'one (IN)' follows rather than

---

[50] In this respect Chinantec is an exception to Anderson and Keenan's observation, "in the great majority of cases, the system of spatial demonstratives is imported directly into the temporal domain without any particular modification" (1985:297).

precedes the temporal nouns such as $sí^M ma^H ná^H$ 'week', $θíʔ^M$ 'month', and $mií^M$ 'year'. Traditionally, the animate numeral $hã^M$ 'one' follows the word $θíʔ^M$ 'month', but this is changing.[50] Examples of the use of 'one' to mean 'next' are given in (571).

(571) a. $sí^M ma^H ná^H$ $ká̃u^M$
       week   one^IN
       next week

     b. $θíʔ^M$ $ká̃u^M$ or $θíʔ^M$ $hã^M$
       month   one^IN   month   one^AN
       next month   next month

     c. $mií^M$ $ká̃u^M$
       year   one^IN
       next year

To express 'last week', 'last month', or 'last year', the verb ca^M 'be depleted (IN)' is used; or, optionally for 'month', the animate form $cá^M$ is used.

(572) $sí^M ma^H ná^H$ $ká^M$-$cá^{LM}$
       week   PAST-be^depleted^II
       last week

The deictic temporal terms 'now' and 'then' are expressed by three forms.

(573) ta^L-$né^{LM}$ $hmí^H$-$há̃u^M$ $má^H$-$há̃u^M$
       while-today   time-that   PRF-that
       now   then (PAST)   then (FUT)

Sochiapan Chinantec lexically expresses temporal deixis two days in either direction from the present.

(574) hau^L day before yesterday
       $ciáu^L$ yesterday
       $né^{LM}$ today
       $ca^L ʔáu^M$ tomorrow
       $ió^{LM}$ day after tomorrow

There are two compound adverbs based on $ciáu^L$ 'yesterday' and one based on $ca^L ʔáu^M$ 'tomorrow' for distinguishing finer points of reference.

---

[50]There is one word for 'month' and 'moon'. The moon is traditionally regarded as a female deity, thus animate numerals are generally used to enumerate months.

The Noun Phrase 195

(575) $cia^L\text{?}áu^{HL}$ yesterday morning
 $cia^L\text{?}lo^H$ yesterday afternoon/evening
 $ca^L\text{?}á^Mniéi^M$ tomorrow morning

There are eight points of temporal deixis during the day.

(576) ha^Lhnia^M after midnight to near daybreak
 $ná^Hhuã^{LM}$ sky lightens just before dawn
 $\text{?}ú^Mniéi^M$ early morning
 $cii^L\text{?}iú^M$ noon
 $ka^L\text{?}láu^L$ late afternoon
 $ka^Lniéi^M$ after dark
 $\text{?}lãu^L$ just before midnight
 $\text{?}ua^M$ late at night, midnight

Temporal adverbial phrases and adverbial clauses are discussed in §8.11.

6.7 The relative clause constituent

The relative clause constituent is the final constituent of the NP; more than one relative clause may occur. The structure and characteristics of relative clauses in general are discussed in §9.1.

When the head of the NP is an alienable noun, it can be followed by a modifier, a relative clause, or both. (577) illustrates the modifier and relative clause constituents co-occurring.

(577) ni^M $ró^{LM}$ $cái^M$ $pã^H$ $\text{?}i^L$ $hmĩ^H$ $\text{?}nió^L$ $kie\text{?}^{HL}$
 there lie^SIA^3 dog big^AN^S COMP TRM want^STI^3 bite^TA^FUT^3

 $\text{?}í^L$ $pé^H$
 that^AN Peter
 There lies that big dog that was wanting to bite Peter.

If the head of the NP is an inalienable noun, the modifier constituent cannot occur (§6.5), but the relative clause constituent may. In (578a), the construction is ungrammatical when a modifier follows an inalienable noun; however, in (578b), the construction is grammatical when a relative clause follows an inalienable noun.

(578) a. *$\theta iã^M$ $hã^M$ $rẽ\text{?}^M$ $hná^{HL}$ $hu\tilde{i}\text{?}^L$
 exist^SIA^3 one^AN relative^1S I lazy
 There is a relative of mine lazy.

b. θiãᴹ   hãᴹ   rẽʔᴹ   hnáᴴᴸ ʔiᴸ   máᴹ   θiãʔᴸᴹ
   exist^SIA^3 one^AN relative^IS I   COMP PRF   hold^STI^3

   siɨᴹ   ŋiɨᴴ   máᴹ   hŋiéiᴸ
   book   at   PRF   six
   There is a relative of mine who is now in grade six.

More than one relative clause can occur; (579) illustrates the chaining of three relative clauses which have the same head/domain noun.

(579)   H   RC[
   hmɨ́ᴴ   θẽʔᴹ   hãᴹ   caᴸkuáᴴ   ʔiᴸ   hmɨ́ᴴ   ʔúʔᴴ
   TRM   stand^SIA^3 one^AN horse   COMP   TRM   be^fat^SIA

              ] RC [   ] RC[
       lɨ̂ᴹᴴ   hoʔᴹ   náᴴᴸ ʔiᴸ   máᴹ
       very   have^STA^IS I   COMP   PRF

                                ]
       kaᴸ-ʔnaᴸ   náᴴ
       PAST-sell^TA^IS I
   I used to have a horse that was very fat, which I have sold.

6.8 The evaluative constituent

The evaluative constituent occurs immediately preceding the NP head. There are two evaluative adjectives, both with strongly emotive connotations: *uɨ́ᴴ* 'nice, pleasant, desirable, useful' and *ʔnáᴴ* 'crude, rough, undesirable, despicable'.

uɨ́ᴴ is found with a wide range of entities, both animate and inanimate, such as money, fruit, chewing gum, salt, baby, and pig. (580) is an example of the use of *uɨ́ᴴ* with an inanimate noun, (581) exemplifies the use of *uɨ́ᴴ* with an animate noun and also shows co-occurrence of the quantifier and evaluative constituents.

(580) tiáᴴ   θiaᴸᴹ   kaᴸláᴹ   uɨ́ᴴ   háuᴹ
       ʔ^not exist^SII some   nice   cotton
       Isn't there some (nice) cotton (i.e., cotton wool)?

(581) hãᴹ   táᴴ   uɨ́ᴴ   ŋiúᴹ   béʔᴸ   nɨ́ᴹ   hóᴸᴹ   hnáᴴᴸ
       one^AN no^more nice   male   Robert that   child^IS I
       That nice Robert is my only child.

The Noun Phrase											197

The evaluative ʔná^H can be used to modify almost any noun. When used with animate (human or non-human) nouns, the connotation is always pejorative. When used with the noun má^{LM} 'food' or any food item, it marks that food as unpalatable or disagreeable. It can be used with food items in a jocular sense, however, with a reverse meaning of 'delicious, palatable' similar to 'terribly nice' in English. An example of ʔná^H 'despicable' with an animate noun is given in (582).

(582) hǎu^M kǎu^M ka^L-pá^L kiõʔ^L haʔ^{LM} bíʔ^H cú^M cií^H
      then simply PAST-hit^TI^3 with   fist   AFF   he   head^3

      ʔná^H lo^H ʔí^L
      despicable mule   that^AN
Then he simply hit that despicable mule's head with (his) fist.

6.9–6.11 The quantifier

The quantifier constituent occupies the leftmost position in the NP. There are three phrases that can function as the quantifier, each having the potential of being internally complex. In an attempt to clarify the overall structure, (583) presents a schematic of each quantifier phrase type.

(583)   QUANTIFIER → { SPECIFIC QUANTIFIER PHRASE
                        APPROXIMATE QUANTIFIER PHRASE }
                        INDEFINITE QUANTIFIER PHRASE

      1. SPECIFIC QUANTIFIER PHRASE →
                        (QUALIFIERS$_{1-7}$) QUANTIFIER HEAD (LIMITER)
                                    { AMOUNT PHRASE
            QUANTIFIER HEAD → { COORDINATE AMOUNT PHRASE }
                                    COMPLEX AMOUNT PHRASE

        a. AMOUNT PHRASE
           { NUMERAL
            INTERROGATIVE } (DIVISOR) (CLASSIFIER) (MODIFIER)
            QUANTIFIER

        b. COORDINATE AMOUNT PHRASE →
                                             { AMOUNT PHRASE$_2$
            AMOUNT PHRASE$_1$ CONJUNCTION { INDEFINITE QUANTIFIER }

        c. COMPLEX AMOUNT PHRASE →
                                       { FRACTION
            AMOUNT PHRASE PARTITIVE { INDEFINITE QUANTIFIER }

2. APPROXIMATE QUANTIFIER PHRASE →
(QUALIFIER$_{1-7}$) QUANTIFIER HEAD$_1$ (ALTERNATIVE)
(QUALIFIER$_x$) QUANTIFIER HEAD$_2$ (LIMITER)

3. INDEFINITE QUANTIFIER PHRASE →
(QUALIFIER$_a$) (QUALIFIER$_b$) INDEFINITE QUANTIFIER HEAD
(QUALIFIER$_c$) (QUALIFIER$_d$) (CLASSIFIER)

(QUALIFIERS$_{1-7}$) stands for seven separate qualifier constituents in the specific quantifier phrase, and in the approximate quantifier phrase. (QUALIFIER$_x$) stands for the optional repetition of the qualifier constituent which immediately precedes the first quantifier head. Examples of each phrase type are given in their respective sections. Details are not repeated when a phrase functions within other phrases.

6.9 The specific quantifier phrase

The structure of the specific quantifier phrase (SQP) is presented in (584) followed by an example in (585).

(584)   SPECIFIC QUANTIFIER PHRASE →
                    (QUALIFIER$_{1-7}$) QUANTIFIER HEAD (LIMITER)

(585) SQP [QL³   QH [   ] LIM   ]
       kũ^L tũ^L kuaʔ^{MH} tá̃^{H} kuú^M
       approximately   two^IN gourd   complete   maize
       approximately two gourds-full of maize

There are three possible constructions that may function as the head of the specific quantifier phrase: a simple amount phrase, a coordinate amount phrase, or a complex amount phrase.

The amount phrase. The simple amount phrase (AMP) has the following constituents: a numeral or interrogative quantifier, a divisor (DIV), a classifier (CLASS), and a modifier (MOD); only the first constituent is obligatory. The structure of the amount phrase is set out in (586).

(586)   AMOUNT PHRASE→
        { NUMERAL
          INTERROGATIVE QUANTIFIER } (DIVISOR) (CLASSIFIER) (MODIFIER)

The Noun Phrase   199

The first constituent of the amount phrase can be a numeral or an interrogative quantifier.

Numerals. Chinantec numerals may be either simple or complex. These are illustrated in (587) and (588), respectively.

(587) $t\tilde{u}^L$ $(l\acute{a}^L)$
  two^IN ear
  two (ears of maize)

(588) $t\tilde{e}?^L$ nio^M $?\eta ia^L$-$l\acute{a}u^L$ ci^{MH} kiu^L-kia^L $(l\acute{a}^L)$
  twice times five-twenties^IN plus twenty-ten^IN ear
  two hundred and thirty (ears of maize)

Numerals agree in animacy with the head noun. Animate numerals agree with the NP head as to person; there is one set for first-person plural, and another set for all other persons (see (593) and (595)). If no classifier or divisor is employed in the amount phrase, the head of the NP is quantified directly, and the numeral must agree with the NP head as to animateness.

(589) SQP [AMP[NUM]] H
         $k\tilde{a}u^M$ $?\acute{\imath}^L$
         one^IN tortilla
  a/one tortilla

(590) SQP [AMP [NUM]] H
         $h\tilde{a}^M$ $ca^L ku\acute{a}^H$
         one^AN horse
  a/one horse

When the amount phrase includes a classifier or a divisor, the numeral quantifies the classifier rather than the head of the NP, and must be inanimate. An example of an inanimate noun enumerated by an amount phrase with a sortal classifier is given in (591), and an example of an animate noun enumerated by an amount phrase with a mensural classifier is given in (592).

(591) SQP [AMP [NUM   CLASS]] H
         $t\tilde{u}^L$ $m\acute{a}i^L$ $k\tilde{\imath}^H$
         two^IN sphere stone
  two stones, rocks

(592) SQP [AMP [NUM   CLASS]] H
   tũ^L nió^L cáu^M
   two͡IN   group   people
two groups of people

The numerals from 'one' to 'ten' are all monosyllabic. There are five allomorphs of 'one (IN)': kǎu^M, ká^M, ku^L, kú^M, and kãu^{LM} and four allomorphs of 'one (AN)': hã^M, hã^{LM}, -hǎu^M, and kú^M. Each has a particular grammatical usage, delineated in Foris 1993:305–06. The numerals from 'eleven' to 'nineteen' are phonological compounds of the numeral 'ten' plus the numerals from 'one' to 'nine'. Cardinal numerals from one to nineteen are listed in (593).

(593)

	Inanimate	Animate non-1P	Animate 1P
one	kǎu^M	hã^M	—
two	tũ^L	gõ^L	gau^L
three	ʔni^{LM}	gǎu^L	gáu^L
four	kiú^L	kiũ^L	kiē^L
five	ʔɲiá^L	ʔɲiá^L	ʔɲiáu^L
six	hɲiéi^L	hɲiéi^L	hɲiáu^L
seven	kiau^L	kiãu^L	kiãu^L
eight	hɲia^L	hɲia^L	hɲiau^L
nine	ɲiu^L	ɲiu^L	ɲie^L
ten	kia^L	kiã^L	kiã^L
eleven	kia^{L}kǎu^M	kiã^{L}hã^M	kia^{L}hǎu^M
twelve	kia^{L}tú^L	kiã^{L}tũ^L	kia^{L}tē^L
thirteen	kia^{L}ʔni^{LM}	kiã^{L}ʔni^M	kia^{L}ʔni^M
fourteen	kia^{L}kiú^L	kiã^{L}kiũ^L	kia^{L}kiē^L
fifteen	kia^{L}ʔɲiá^L	kiã^{L}ʔɲiá^L	kia^{L}ʔɲiáu^L
sixteen	kia^{L}hɲiéi^L	kiã^{L}hɲiéi^L	kia^{L}hɲiau^L
seventeen	kia^{L}kiau^L	kiã^{L}kiãu^L	kia^{L}kiãu^L
eighteen	kia^{L}hɲia^L	kiã^{L}hɲia^L	kia^{L}hɲiau^L
nineteen	kia^{L}ɲiu^L	kiã^{L}ɲiu^L	kia^{L}ɲie^L

The numerals 20 to 200 are based on a vigesimal system. The Chinantec forms are given in (594). These numerals are formed as follows.

(594)   21–39   kiú^L 'twenty' + 'one' to 'nineteen'
         40   'two' 'twenty' (with allomorphs of 'twenty' -ló^{LM} (IN) and -ló^{LM} (AN))
        41–59   'two' 'twenty' + 'one' to 'nineteen' (with the 'twenty' allomorph -la^L)

The Noun Phrase   201

60	ʔnaï̈ʔ^{LM} 'thrice' + nio^M 'times' + 'twenty'
61–69	'sixty' + 'one' to 'nine'
70–79	'sixty' + cï^{MH} 'plus' + 'ten' to 'nineteen'
80	kiéi̯ʔ^L 'four times' + nio^M 'times' + 'twenty'
81–89	'eighty' + 'one' to 'nine'
90–99	'eighty' + cï^M 'plus' + 'ten' to 'nineteen'
100	'five' + 'twenty' (with allomorphs of 'twenty' -láu^L (IN) and -lä́u^L (AN))
101–199	'one hundred' + cï^M 'plus' + 'one' to 'ninety-nine'
200, etc.	'two' to 'nine' + nio^M 'times' + 'one hundred' (cardinal numbers 'two', 'three', and 'four' may be replaced by tẽʔ^M 'twice', ʔnaï̈ʔ^{LM} 'thrice', and kiéi̯ʔ^L 'four times')

(595) Vigesimal numerals

	Inanimate	Animate non-1P	Animate 1P
twenty	kiú^L	kiú^L	kiä́u^L
twenty-one	kiu^{L}kä́u^M	kiu^{L}hã^M	kiu^{L}hä́u^M
forty	tu^{L}ló^{LM}	tũ^{L}lõ^{LM}	tũ^{L}ló^{LM}
forty-one	tu^{L}la^{L}kä́u^M	tu^{L}la^{L}hã^M	tu^{L}la^{L}hä́u^M
sixty	ʔnaï̈ʔ^{LM} nio^M kiú^L	ʔnaï̈ʔ^{LM} nio^M kiú^L	ʔnaï̈ʔ^{LM} nio^M kiä́u^L
sixty-one	ʔnaï̈ʔ^{LM} nio^M kiu^{L}kä́u^M	ʔnaï̈ʔ^{LM} nio^M kiu^{L}hã^M	ʔnaï̈ʔ^{LM} nio^M kiu^{L}hä́u^M
seventy	ʔnaï̈ʔ^{LM} nio^M kiú^L cï^{MH} kia^L	ʔnaï̈ʔ^{LM} nio^M kiú^L cï^{MH} kiã^L	ʔnaï̈ʔ^{LM} nio^M kiä́u^L cï^{MH} kiã^L
seventy-one	ʔnaï̈ʔ^{LM} nio^M kiú^L cï^{MH} kia^{L}kä́u^M	ʔnaï̈ʔ^{LM} nio^M kiú^L cï^{MH} kia^{L}hã^M	ʔnaï̈ʔ^{LM} nio^M kiä́u^L cï^{MH} kia^{L}hä́u^M
eighty	kiéi̯ʔ^L nio^M kiú^L	kiéi̯ʔ^L nio^M kiú^L	kiéi̯ʔ^L nio^M kiä́u^L
eighty-one	kiéi̯ʔ^L nio^M kiu^{L}kä́u^M	kiéi̯ʔ^L nio^M kiu^{L}hã^M	kiéi̯ʔ^L nio^M kiu^{L}hä́u^M
ninety	kiéi̯ʔ^L nio^M kiú^L cï^{MH} kia^L	kiéi̯ʔ^L nio^M kiú^L cï^{MH} kiã^L	kiéi̯ʔ^L nio^M kiä́u^L cï^{MH} kiã^L
ninety-one	kiéi̯ʔ^L nio^M kiú^L cï^{MH} kia^{L}kä́u^M	kiéi̯ʔ^L nio^M kiú^L cï^{MH} kia^{L}hã^M	kiéi̯ʔ^L nio^M kiä́u^L cï^{MH} kia^{L}hä́u^M

hundred	ʔŋia^{L}láu^L	ʔŋia^{L}láu^L	ʔŋia^{L}láu^L
two hundred	tū^L nio^M	tū^L nio^M	tū^L nio^M
	ʔŋia^{L}láu^L	ʔŋia^{L}láu^L	ʔŋia^{L}láu^L

Some examples are:

(596) tu^L-la^L-kia^L-ʔni̵^{LM}
two-twenties-ten^IN-three^IN
fifty-three (IN)

(597) a. ʔnaï̵ʔ^{LM} nio^M kiú^L
thrice times twenty^IN
sixty (IN)

b. ʔnaï̵ʔ^{LM} nio^M kiú̵^{L}
thrice times twenty^AN
sixty (AN)

(598) a. kiéi̵ʔ^L nio^M kiú^L ci^{MH} kia^L-tū^L
four^times times twenty^IN plus ten^IN-two^IN
ninety-two (IN)

b. kiéi̵ʔ^L nio^M kiú̵^{L} ci^{MH} kiã^L-ŋiu^L
four^times times twenty^AN plus ten^AN-nine
ninety-nine (AN)

(599) a. ʔŋia^L-láu^L ci^{MH} kã́u^M
five-twenties^IN plus one^IN
one hundred and one (IN)

b. ʔŋia^L-lã́u^L ci^{MH} hã^M
five-twenties^AN plus one^AN
one hundred and one (AN)

(600) ŋiu^L nio^M ʔŋia^L-láu^L
nine times five-twenties^IN
nine hundred

The words for 'thousand' (mei^{MH}) and 'million' (mí^{M}iãu^{MH}) are adapted from the Spanish terms *mil* 'thousand' and *millón* 'million' and may be used in a combination like the hundreds although they are commonly replaced in everyday speech by their less complex Spanish equivalents.

The Noun Phrase

Interrogative quantifiers. There are three interrogative quantifiers (IQ) which agree in animateness with the NP head: *há?ᴸ* 'how many? (IN)', *hâ?ᴸ* 'how many? (AN)', and *kṍ?ᴸ* 'how many/much? (IN)'. An example of each interrogative quantifier is given in (601)–(603).

(601) Q [IQ   CLASS] H[   ]
       há?ᴸ   *muᴹᴴ mĩ̂ᴴ sií ᴹ   ?náu?ᴹ   ?núᴹ*
       how^many^IN?   leaf   flat book   want^STI^2 you^s
       How many pages do you want?

(602) Q [IQ   ]   H
       hâ?ᴸ   *cáuᴹ   kaᴸ-hĩeᴴ   ?núᴹ*
       how^many^AN?   people PAST-see^TA^2 you^s
       How many people did you see?

(603) Q [IQ   ]   H
       kṍ?ᴸ   *kúᴴhẽᴹ ?náu?ᴹ   ?núᴹ*
       how^many^IN?   bucket   want^STI^2 you^s
       How many buckets do you want?

If a divisor or classifier is present in the amount phrase, only the inanimate interrogative quantifier *há?ᴸ* 'how many? (IN)' may occur, as in (601) above. An example of an interrogative quantifier with a mensural classifier and an animate head noun is shown in (604).

(604) Q [IQ   CLASS] H[   ]
       há?ᴸ   *kuoᴹ   káᴴ?áuᴹ   pi?ᴹᴴ   ?náu?ᴹ   ?núᴹ*
       how^many^IN?   box   chicken   little want^STA^2 you^s
       How many boxes of baby chickens do you want?

há?ᴸ 'how many? (IN)' cannot collocate with those divisors which take only the numeral *káᴹ* 'one'; for example, *káᴹ cóᴴᴸ* 'one half' is grammatical, but **há?ᴸ cóᴴᴸ* 'how many halves?' is not.

If no divisor or classifier occurs, then the interrogative quantifier directly modifies the NP head and must agree with the NP head as to animateness, as in (602) above.

Most of the qualifier elements of the quantifier phrase cannot occur with the interrogative quantifiers, the only permissible qualifier being *kũᴸ* 'approximately, only, amid' of QL₅.

The interrogative quantifiers are discussed further in §10.3.

Divisors. A divisor may be present only if a numeral or an interrogative quantifier occurs. A divisor may consist of two elements, *ʔná^H* 'section' and an apportional divisor; see (608). *ʔná^H* 'section, portion' may modify any of the apportional divisors, or either element may occur without the other. (605) illustrates how the two elements can co-occur, where *θaï ʔ^{MH}* 'wedge' is an apportional divisor.

(605)   *ká^M*   *ʔná^H*   *θaï ʔ^{MH}*   *má ʔ^L*
        one⌒IN section wedge squash
        one section of a wedge of squash

Chinantec divisors are a kind of classifier in that they must agree with the head of the NP as to shape and animacy; or if a classifier occurs, the NP head governs both the divisor and the classifier. Divisors form a separate syntactic class from the classifier constituent and share the semantic component of 'dividing a unit'. All but *cáu^H* 'half' (of an animate entity or group) may precede a classifier.

If a divisor occurs within the amount phrase, the numeral must be inanimate, even if the entity being divided is animate; compare (606) and (607) below. When the numeral is 'one', the allomorph *ká^M* is used.

(606)   SQP [NUM   DIV]   H
           ká^M   *ʔná^H*   *huï^{LM}*
           one⌒IN section path
        half the length of the trail

(607)   SQP [NUM   DIV]   H
           ká^M   *cáu^H*   *cáu^M*
           one⌒IN half people
        half of the people

(608)   Apportional divisors

        kuõʔ^{MH}   'chunk' irregular, of any size, such as of pumpkin, dried meat, or cloth
        kuõʔ^H   'corner', approximately 'one quarter'; it refers to flat objects only, such as tortilla, slice of bread or paper
        ho^{MH}   'half' of sphere or cylinder split along axis
                   'half' (longitudinally) of a long flat object
        huõʔ^H   'piece' small, irregular (torn off, of bread, meat, tortilla), 'sliver' (of glass or pottery), 'chip' (of wood); it can divide only the divisible measure *siẽʔ^L* 'section'

The Noun Phrase 205

$cá^H$	'half' of a linear measure, bundle of objects, container of objects, liquid, or a period of time
$cáu^H$	'half' of an animate entity or group
$có^{HL}$	'half' of liquid, half or portion (of inanimate entities)
$co?^L$	'equal portion', the result of an equal division of a group of entities or of liquid into two or more parts
$\theta\bar{a}\ddot{\imath}?^{MH}$	'wedge' of anything (e.g., squash, cake)

$?ná^H$ 'section, portion' divides anything into roughly equal parts of two or more; it divides long entities transversally. It may subdivide the apportional divisors $kuõ?^{MH}$ 'chunk', ho^{MH} 'half', $huõ?^H$ 'piece', and $\theta\bar{a}\ddot{\imath}?^{MH}$ 'wedge'. The apportionals $cá^H$ and $cáu^H$ can collocate only with the numeral $ká^M$ 'one'; all other apportionals and $?ná^H$ 'section, portion' can collocate with larger numerals.

(609) SQP [NUM   DIV   ] H[   ]
      $n\ddot{\imath}^{LM}$ $kuõ?^H$ $c\ddot{\imath}^H$ $?m\ddot{\imath}?^{LM}$
      three^IN piece disused cloth
      three pieces of rag

Classifiers. Although Chinantec has classifiers, it is not a prototypical numeral classifier language where nearly all nouns require a classifier.[52] In effect, the requirement of a classifier in quantifier constructions forms a cline where some languages require a classifier with most nouns and others where "the classifiers are not compulsory even for the restricted set of nouns that have them" (Greenberg 1974:18). Chinantec lies closer to the latter end of this cline. There is a structural parallelism between the measure construction which occurs with mass and count nouns and those nouns which require a classifier when quantified. An example of each, respectively, is given in (610).

(610) a. $t\bar{u}^L$ $kua?^{MH}$ $\theta\acute{a}\ddot{\imath}^H$
       two^IN gourd sand
       two gourds of sand

     b. $t\bar{u}^L$ $m\acute{a}\ddot{\imath}^L$ $hl\acute{a}\ddot{\imath}^M$
       two^IN sphere egg
       two eggs

---

[52]Lyons defines a "classifier-language" as one in which "classifiers are obligatory in phrases containing numerals" (1977:461). Greenberg remarks that, although this kind of definition may be "a useful starting point for a discussion on...such a view it is not excessive to state that there are no numeral classifier languages" (1974:18).

Based on Greenberg's five "synchronic generalizations that may be made regarding classifier languages proper" (1974:31), Chinantec classifiers occur as follows.
1. Chinantec conforms to the order, quantifier-classifier-noun.
2. Chinantec does not permit any variation in this order.
3. Numeral and classifier are always readily identifiable.
4. The evaluative constituent (§6.8) and the categorizer (§6.2) may occur between the quantifier and the classifier.
5. The anaphoric construction of Q-Cl without overt expression in the noun may occur.

Furthermore, Chinantec classifiers are modifiers, not the head of a NP. The presence of a sortal classifier is determined by the fact that the referential noun is quantified; and the choice of a particular sortal classifier is determined by the nature of the referential noun—the noun's referent must have a particular shape, be inanimate, and generally be portable. Mensural classifiers are less restrictive than sortal classifiers as to shape; otherwise, they behave like sortal classifiers. The quantified noun, not the classifier, is the head element.

As mentioned above, although Chinantec has classifiers, not all nouns require a classifier when they are enumerated. For example, $ʔmá^M$ 'tree' of (611c) does not take a sortal classifier.

(611) a. kia^L $má\ddot{i}^L$ $kj\acute{\tilde{\imath}}^H$
    ten^IN sphere rock
    ten stones

b. kia^L $ma\ddot{i}ʔ^{LM}$ $u\acute{o}u^M$
    ten^IN long^fine vine
    ten vines

c. kia^L $ʔmá^M$
    ten^IN tree
    ten trees

Ellipsis of an enumerated NP head can occur when it has been previously mentioned or is apparent from the extralinguistic context. In (612b), the numeral and sortal classifier form a unit which functions anaphorically, referring to $ŋi^Mráu^L$ 'orange' of (612a). In (613), however, $mí^Htä\ddot{i}^L$ 'machete' does not take a sortal classifier, so it is the numeral that functions anaphorically.

(612) a. $tiá^H$ $θia^{LM}$ $ŋi^Mráu^L$
    ʔ^not exist^SII orange
    Aren't there any oranges?

b. *θia^{LM} kiau^L mái^L*
exist^sii seven^in sphere
There are seven.

(613) a. *tiá^H θia^{LM} mí^{H}tái^L*
?^not exist^sii machete
Aren't there any machetes?

b. *θia^{LM} ʔni^{LM}*
exist^sii three^in
There are three.

Many classifiers have an identical, or nearly identical, form which can function as the head of a NP. Although the classifier and noun lexemes are historically related, the classifiers have a more generic meaning appropriate to their function within the quantifier phrase. For example, the noun *mái^L* as head of an NP has the specific meaning of 'fruit'; as a classifier, however, *mái^L* means 'sphere' and is used with a wide variety of approximately spherical or elliptical entities.

Chinantec has a small closed set of sortal classifiers that are basically shape oriented. The mensural classifiers (measure oriented) are potentially an open set, as many entities can be used in quantifying expressions. Either type of classifier may occur in an amount phrase.

In Chinantec there are five allomorphs for the numeral 'one (IN)'. Many classifiers which are clearly mensural use the allomorphs *káu^M*, *kú^M*, or *ku^L*; generally *káu^M* can be substituted for *kú^M* or *ku^L*. Many classifiers which are clearly sortal take *ká^M*; such classifiers cannot take *káu^M*. The division of classifiers in (616) and (618)–(619) is based on the allomorph of 'one' with which each occurs. Although the distinction between mensural and sortal classifiers is somewhat blurred for some classifiers, their orientation appears to be reflected by the allomorph of 'one' with which it collocates.

Classifiers can be further sub-categorized according to their ability to occur with divisors. There are two divisible classifiers which can be inflected: *tio^{ʔL} kuo^M* 'armload' and *ci^{MH} ci^{L}kuo^M* 'shoulder-load', which are idioms based on a verb plus a body part. The verb is inflected for third-person inanimate, and the body part is inflected for the person of the referent. Both classifiers require the allomorph *káu^M* for 'one'. Examples (614) and (615) have the two inflected mensural classifiers; (615) further illustrates the co-occurrence of an inflected mensural classifier and a divisor.

(614) *tú^L tioʔ^L kuo^M kuo^H*
two^in contain^ti^pres^3 arm^3 firewood
her/his two armloads of firewood

(615) káᴹ   cóᴴᴸ cïᴹᴴ   cïᴸuóᴸᴹ   kuoᴴ
  one^ɪɴ half be^present^sᴛɪ^3ᴘ shoulder^ɪs firewood
  half my shoulder-load of firewood

The uninflected divisible classifiers that have been identified which occur with the allomorphs *kā̌uᴹ* or *kuᴸ* 'one' are set out in (616), except for the time measures, which are set out separately in (618). The allomorph *kā̌uᴹ* 'one' is preferred with all the classifiers derived from Spanish. Most of the classifiers in (616) and (618) are obviously mensural in nature, whereas many of the classifiers in (619) are obviously sortal.

(616) Divisible classifiers which take *kā̌uᴹ* or *kuᴸ* one

liᴴbřáᴴ	pound (Sp. *libra*)
tóᴹnéᴹlaᴴdáᴴ	ton (Sp. *tonelada*)
púᴹgaᴴdáᴴ	inch (Sp. *pulgada*)
piéᴴ	foot (Sp. *pie*)
řáᴹseᴴnáᴴ	dozen (Sp. *docena*)
kiᴴlóᴴ	kilo (Sp. *kilo*)
gřaᴴmóᴴ	gram (Sp. *gramo*)
kúᴹciaᴴřáᴴ	spoon (Sp. *cuchara*)
liᴴtřóᴴ	liter (Sp. *litro*)
meᴴtřóᴴ	meter (Sp. *metro*)
kíᴹloᴴméᴴtřóᴴ	kilometer (Sp. *kilómetro*)
sẽᴹtiᴴméᴴtřóᴴ	centimeter (Sp. *centímetro*)
kuáᴴ	one bottle full (a small beer bottle holding about 1/5 liter, used to measure kerosene; also refers to 1/4 kilo, 1/4 hectare) (Sp. *cuarto*)
θḯᴸ	bottle
kúᴴhẽᴹ	drum (40 liters)
ceᴸ	jug (earthenware, usually used for liquor)
túᴹcioᴴ	sack (traditionally made of sisal)
ʔáᴹřauᴹᴴ	twelve kilos (Sp. *arroba*)
lioᴹᴴ	a ninety-six liter measure for maize, beans, and other dry produce
táʔᴴ	drop of liquid
tóᴸᴹ	patches, plots of maize, beans, or other crops

The mensural classifiers based on time nominals (618) are able to quantify only the word *taᴹᴴ* 'work'. Some speakers prefer *kúᴹ* 'one', and others prefer *kā̌uᴹ* 'one'.

The Noun Phrase

(617) ɲííH-hmúMH hnáHL kǎuM/kúM hmáïH taMH
    INT-doˆTIˆ1S   I   oneˆIN day work
    I will do a day's work.

(618) Divisible classifiers of time which take káũM or kúM one

    miMnuHtóH   minute (Sp. *minuto*)
    oHřáH   hour (Sp. *hora*)
    siMmaHnáH   week (Sp. *semana*)
    hmáïH   day, time, period
    nieM   night
    miíM   year
    θïʔM   month

All the divisible classifiers that have been identified which use the allomorph káM 'one' are given in (619). Some of these, such as *mu*MH 'leaf', are obviously sortal, but semantically it is not readily apparent why some of the other classifiers should be part of the same set.

(619) Divisible classifiers which take káM one

    kuaʔMH   half a gourd shell, about a liter
    kuoM   box as of rifle shells, mangoes, matches
    ʔiẽʔM   bunch of grapes, mangoes, raspberries, or other
                   clusters of fruit or seeds
    ʔmaM   four liter measure (in the shape of a box)
    ʔmíʔM   span; *ʔmíʔM huéʔL* large span (from thumb to little
                   finger or second finger); *ʔmíʔM piʔMH* little span
                   (from thumb to index finger)
    ʔŋieM   load, e.g., of firewood, cane, or other long items
                   that have been tied up with a rope and can be
                   carried with a tumpline or in the arms
    hoMH   a long flat object, e.g., a board
    hõH   piece or section, e.g., of sugar cane, ladder
    huõM   lines, rows
    liáuM   '400' ears of maize, (usually neatly stacked)
    lioMH   load of items (traditionally carried by tumpline),
                   e.g., firewood, blocks of crude sugar
    míHθiõʔMH   source, e.g., plant with shoots or suckers such as
                   banana palms, sugar cane; or groups of plants
                   growing together, e.g., maize, which is planted with
                   four to eight seeds in each hole

mi͂ᴹtáᴹ	large basket, standard measure for measuring bread
mi͂ʔᴹ	small basketful, e.g., of firewood, avocados, and other items traditionally carried in small baskets by means of a tumpline
muᴹᴴ	leaf (i.e., flat and thin), e.g., paper, pages
náʔᴴ	one meter-square carrying-cloth-full, e.g., of avocados, oranges, or other produce
pi̯eʔᴴ	pile, e.g., of meat, maize dough, manure
kéïᴹ	pile of firewood, built up in square form for drying
siẽʔᴸ	section or natural division, e.g., of garlic, oranges, and other naturally divisible fruit
cî ᴹ	finger width
θáïᴹ	roll, e.g., of twine, wire, vines, 'hand' of bananas

Indivisible classifiers cannot occur with any of the divisors. All the known indivisible classifiers which use the allomorphs *káuᴹ* or *kuᴸ* 'one' are given in (620); most of these classifiers are more obviously mensural in nature than those given in (621).

(620) Indivisible classifiers which take *káuᴹ* or *kuᴸ* one

ciïᴹᴴ	blast of a whistle
huḯᴴ	layers of such things as blankets and clothes
huḯᴹ	trip for sand, firewood, water, or other transportable goods (in the sense of a 'load')
náïʔᴴ	swallow of liquid
ʔeᴴ	cup of liquor, about one *náïʔᴴ*
nióᴸ	group of houses, flock of birds, team of players, pile of coffee
póʔᴸ	strike, blow, peal (of bell) done with an instrument, e.g., a mallet
θiáʔᴴᴸ	bundle of stick-like objects such as sugar cane or firewood

All the indivisible classifiers that have been identified which use the allomorph *káᴹ* 'one' (except for the monetary classifiers; see (622)), are given in (621); most of these classifiers are more clearly sortal in nature than those given in (620).

The Noun Phrase 211

(621) Indivisible classifiers which take ká^M one

ʔmáïʔ^LM	tall and flexible, e.g., maize plant, vine
hēiʔ^LM	turns of a long flexible thing wrapped around something, e.g., a cord wrapped around a wooden handle
máï^L	sphere
máïʔ^LM	fine and long, e.g., wire, thread, vine
mí^Hθiõʔ^H	source, litter, family; if a person, then mí^Hθiõʔ^M includes all that person's descendants
ŋií^H	type, class
tã^L	bush-like, grass-like, e.g., maize plant, bush type bean plant, coffee tree
cu^MH	clutch, e.g., a handful, double handful, armful, a disorderly stack of firewood

There are only two monetary classifiers used when quantifying things such as work, or anything purchased such as fruit, clothing, soap, or kerosene. The first monetary classifier given in (622) uses the allomorph ká^M 'one'; the second classifier occurs only with even numbers, 'two, four', etc.; it is included in (622) since it forms part of the first classifier.

(622) Indivisible monetary classifiers, which take ká^M one

ʔéiʔ^LM kĩeʔ^H	peso's worth
kĩeʔ^H	money, bit, always used in a series of twos and glossed as 'two bits' (twenty-five centavos), 'four bits' (fifty centavos), up to 'twenty bits' (two pesos and fifty centavos)

An example of the use of the monetary classifier is given in (623).

(623) ka^L-ŋií^H-lá^HL   hná^HL   ká^M   ʔéiʔ^LM   kĩeʔ^H   ʔí^Hmiiʔ^MH
PAST-ANDT-buy^TI^IS I   one^IN measure money bread
I went to buy one peso's worth of bread.

Modifiers. A modifier element may optionally occur following the classifier; since all classifiers are inanimate, only the inanimate forms of adjectives occur. The set of adjectives that may function as modifiers in this position appears to be restricted to those which denote size: piʔ^MH 'small', míʔ^H 'little', pa^MH 'big', and hueʔ^LM 'large'.

This same restricted set of adjectives may also occur when there is no classifier. With no classifier (or divisor) present to enumerate, the numeral must agree in animacy with the NP head, the adjective also agreeing in animacy. Examples (624) and (625) illustrate the inanimate and the animate forms of 'big', respectively.

(624) $ʔu^{MH}$ $kǎu^M$ pa^{MH} $ʔná^H$ $ʔmá^M$ $mi^{H}má ʔ^H$ $ʔnú^M$
contain^STI^3 one^IN big^IN despicable wood eye^2 you^s
There is a big wood splinter in your eye.

(625) sa^L $hã^M$ $pã^H$ $ʔná^H$ $tú^Mhue^{LM}$ $hmú^L$
why! one^AN big^AN despicable buzzard (species)

$kuã ʔ^L$ $ciei ʔ^{LM}$ $kio ʔ^{MH}$ $cú^M$
arrive^IA^PAST^3S outside have^STI^3 3
Why, a big ugly buzzard arrived outside his place.

The coordinate amount phrase. The coordinate amount phrase (CRD AMP) has three obligatory constituents: an amount phrase (AMP$_1$), a coordinate conjunction (CONJ), and either a second amount phrase (AMP$_2$) or an indefinite quantifier, as set out in (626).

(626)   COORDINATE AMOUNT PHRASE →

　　　　　　　　　　　　　　　　　　　　　⎰ AMOUNT PHRASE$_2$ ⎱
　　　　　　AMOUNT PHRASE$_1$ CONJ ⎱ INDEFINITE QUANTIFIER ⎰

The absolute amount of AMP$_2$ must always be less than that of AMP$_1$, e.g., in (627), 'tons' of AMP$_1$ is greater than 'kilos' of AMP$_2$.

(627)　　　　　　　　　　Q [SQP[CRD^AMP[[AMP$_1$ [NUM
ka^L-$θiú ʔ^H$　　　　$hná^{HL}$　　　　　　　　$kiǔ^L$
PAST-harvest^TI^1S I　　　　　　　　　　　four^IN

　　　　　　　CLASS]]　　CONJ　[AMP$_2$ [NUM
$tó^Mné^Mla^Hdá^H$　$cí^{MH}$　　$tē ʔ^L$ nio^M $ʔŋia^L$-$láu^L$ $cí^{MH}$
ton　　　　　　plus　　twice times five-twenty plus

　　　　　　　　　　CLASS]]]]] H
kiu^L-kia^L　$ki^Hló^H$ $á^Mřo^Hsá^H$
twenty-ten^IN kilo rice
I harvested four tons and two hundred and thirty kilos of rice.

Only the indefinite quantifiers (INDQ) $ka^Llá^M$ 'some' and $kú^Hpi ʔ^{MH}$ 'a little' can occur in the CRD^AMP. If no other NP constituent occurs after the NP

The Noun Phrase

head, the indefinite quantifier or AMP$_2$ may optionally occur following the NP head, as shown in (628) and (629), respectively.

(628) ka^L-kú^L hná^{HL} tū^L tú^{M}cio^H mï^L ká^{M}fe^{MH} cï^{MH}
      PAST-pick^TI^1S I   two^IN   sack   spherical coffee   plus

      kú^{H}pi?^{MH}
      a^little
      I picked two sacks and a bit of coffee beans.

(629) ka^L-kú?^{M} mï$^{\tilde{a}H}$mí?^{H} ká^M mái^L mï^L ŋií^{H}ráu^L cï^{MH}
      PAST-eat^TI^3   girl   one^IN sphere   spherical   orange   plus

      ká^M θāï?^{MH}
      one^IN   wedge
      The little girl ate one orange and a section of another.

The complex amount phrase. The complex amount phrase (COM AMP) consists of a simple amount phrase (AMP), a partitive element (PRT), and an optional fraction or indefinite quantifier, as set out in (630).

(630) COMPLEX AMOUNT PHRASE →

        AMOUNT PHRASE   PARTITIVE $\left\{\begin{array}{l}\text{(FRACTION)} \\ \text{(INDEFINITE QUANTIFIER)}\end{array}\right\}$

The amount phrase (AMP) is as described above; however, when it occurs in the complex amount phrase, no divisor may occur inside the AMP. There is only one partitive (PR), the word tó^{LM} 'half'. Either the fraction or the indefinite quantifier can occur; both are optional. The indefinite quantifiers are ka^{L}lá^M 'some' or kú^{H}pi?^{HL} 'a little'. When either of these occur as the indefinite quantifier, the meaning of the partitive and the indefinite quantifier elements together is 'almost but not quite one half'.

(631) ?nï^{LM} kua?^{MH} tó^{LM} kú^{H}pi?^{MH}
      three^IN   gourd   half   a^little
      three and a bit gourds-full

The fraction (FR) has two elements: ká^M 'one', followed by one of the divisors. Generally, both constituents are obligatory, yielding the sense of 'one-half'. When the divisor ?ná^H 'section, portion' occurs, ká^M 'one' is optional.

(632) ʔni^LM   li^Htřó^H   tó^LM   (ká^M)   ʔná^H
       three^IN liter   half   (one^IN) portion
       three and one-half liters

When the fraction occurs, the quantity indicated is redundant because it is already indicated by the partitive *tó^LM* 'half'. However, the fraction supplies information as to the shape of the object that is divided in half.

(633)   Q[SQP[COM^AMP[AMP   [NUM   CLASS   ] PR
     ka^L-la^L   cú^M   kấu^M   tú^Mcio^H   tó^LM
     PAST-buy^TI^3   3   one^IN   sack   half

                     FR[one   DIV]]]]   H[   ]
                     ká^M   có^HL   mi^L   ká^Mfe^MH
                     one^IN   half   spherical   coffee
     S/he bought a sack and a half of coffee.

The qualifiers of the specific quantifier phrase. The qualifier elements of the specific quantifier phrase (SQP) precede the quantifier head (QH). There are seven qualifiers, largely independent of one another. They are listed in (634).

(634) QL_1 kó?^L   additionally; lí^L 'more than'
      QL_2 ʔí^H   another
      QL_3 hmá?^L   just
      QL_4 la^L   about, almost, nearly
      QL_5 kū^L   approximately, only, amid
      QL_6 tá^H   together, entire, every
      QL_7 ma^L   by, each, in lots of; ma^L ki^LM ma^L 'every, each separate (one/group of)'

Not all combinations of the seven qualifiers are grammatical. Almost any combination of three qualifiers may occur except when there are semantic restrictions. When *hmá?^L* 'just' of QL_3 occurs, a maximum of four qualifiers may occur. The nonpermissible co-occurrences which have been identified are as follows: The combination QL_2, QL_4, and QL_6 is ungrammatical. *la^L* 'about, almost, nearly' of QL_4 can occur only when the amount phrase expresses a quantity greater or lesser than one. *hmá?^L* 'just' of QL_3 can only occur with *tá^H* 'together, entire, every' of QL_6 or either constituent of QL_7 if *la^L* 'about, almost, nearly' of QL_4 is present.

Example (635) illustrates the co-occurrence of the QL_2 *ʔí^H* 'another' and QL_5 *kū^L* 'approximately' qualifiers.

The Noun Phrase

(635) kuéH ʔɨH kūL ʔŋiáL máïL siɨ́HʔioMH
give^DI^IMP^2>1S another approximately five sphere potato
Give (me) approximately another five potatoes.

Each qualifier is discussed in turn under points 1–7. The relative ordering of the qualifiers is demonstrated in the examples that follow.

1. Two qualifiers can function as the leftmost qualifier QL$_1$: *lḯ*^{L} 'more than' and *kǒʔ*^{L} 'additionally', illustrated in (636) and (637), respectively.

(636) lḯL kūL tūLlóLM mifM máʔL máM ʔṹH cúM
more^than only forty^IN year EXCL PRF be^in^STI^3 3
S/he is now more than only forty years old.

(637) kǒʔL ʔɨH tūL hmuʔL bɨʔH ʔniauʔL
additionally another two^IN panel AFF be^lacking^SII
In addition, another two (fabric) panels are lacking.

2. The second qualifier QL$_2$ is *ʔɨ*^{H}/*ɨ*^{H} 'another'. Its position is QL$_2$ since it follows *kǒʔ*^{L} 'additionally'; see (637) above. The presence of a negative in the verb phrase gives the meaning of 'not even' to *ʔɨ*^{H}, as can be seen by comparing examples (638) and (639).

(638) kuéH ɨH kãuM táuM kiúHL
give^DI^IMP^2>1S another one^IN banana have^STI^1P
Give me (lit., us) another banana.

(639) tiáM kaL-kuéL cúM hnáHL ʔɨH kãuM ʔɨL
not PAST-give^DI^3>1S 3 I not^even one^IN tortilla
S/he didn't give me even one tortilla.

3. The third qualifier QL$_3$ is *hmáʔ*^{L} 'just'. Its position can be seen in (640), where it follows the second qualifier *ʔɨ*^{H}/*ɨ*^{H} 'another'.

(640) kuéH ɨH hmáʔL laL tūL máïL miL máH
give^DI^2>1 another just about two sphere spherical mango

kúʔHL
eat^TI^FUT^1S
Give me just about another two mangoes to eat.

4. The fourth qualifier QL$_4$ is *la*^{L} 'about, almost, nearly'. In (641), *la*^{L} follows *hmáʔ*^{L} 'only, just' of QL$_3$.

(641) hmá?ᴸ laᴸ   káuᴹ ?mï?ᴸᴹ ce?ᴴ háuᴹ bí?ᴴ kï?ᴸᴹ
just almost one^IN clothes old that^IN AFF wear^TI^PRES^3

cáᴹ   ?íᴸ
person that^AN
That person wears almost just that one set of old clothes.

5. The fifth qualifier QL₅ is kũᴸ 'approximately, only, amid'. In (642), kũᴸ follows laᴸ 'about' of QL₄.

(642) ?niáu?ᴸᴹ   háᴸᴹ   áá?ᴸ cúᴹ laᴸ   kũᴸ
be^necessary^SII wait^TI^FUT^3 ASSR 3 about approximately

káᴹ   cáᴴ oᴴráᴴ
one^IN half hour
S/he definitely must wait for approximately a half hour (i.e., at least a half hour, perhaps more).

6. The sixth qualifier QL₆ is táᴴ 'together, entire, every'. In (643), táᴴ follows kũᴸ of QL₅.

(643) tio?ᴸ   kũᴸ   kiaᴸtúᴸ   meiᴹᴴ   ?éi?ᴸᴹ kïeᴸ
contain^SII approximately twelve^IN thousand measure money

kũᴸ   táᴴ   tũᴸ   tu?ᴸᴹ   láᴹ
amid entire two^IN bag   this
These two bags together contain approximately twelve thousand pesos.

7. The members of the seventh qualifier (QL₇) set are maᴸ 'by, each, in lots of' and maᴸ kïᴸᴹ maᴸ 'every, each separate (one/group of)'. Example (644) illustrates maᴸ. When maᴸ occurs with káuᴹ 'one (IN)' or hãᴹ 'one (AN)' the meaning is 'few', as in (645).

(644) kaᴸ-laᴸ   cúᴹ kũᴸ   maᴸ ?ŋiáᴸ máïᴸ ŋiᶦᴹráuᴸ
PAST-buy^TI^3 3 approximately by five sphere orange
They (each) bought oranges in lots of approximately five.

(645) tiᴸlaᴸ maᴸ hãᴹ   cúᴹ kaᴸ-huá?ᴸ
but   by one^AN 3 PAST-say^TI^3
But a few of them said...

The Noun Phrase

When ma^L $kĩ^{LM}$ ma^L is used with numerals greater than one, the sense is 'each separate group of' as in (646) where it follows QL$_6$ $tá^H$. When ma^L $kĩ^{LM}$ ma^L is used with the numeral 'one', the sense is 'each (one)' as in (647).

(647) ʔúʔ^{HL} nú^M kãu^M kú^{M}cia^{H}řá^H mĩ^L lá^M tá^H ma^L
drink^TI^IMP^2 you^s one^IN spoon   medicine this every by

  kĩ^{LM} ma^L kiũ^L o^{H}řá^H
  separate by four^IN hour
Take a spoonful of this medicine every four hours.

(647) ɲiéi^H cú^M ma^L kĩ^{LM} ma^L kãu^{LM} huú^M
go^nonhome^IA^PAST^3 3   each different each one^IN town
He went to each town.

The limiter. The adverb $tá^H$ 'exactly, no more' functions as the limiter element in the specific quantifier phrase. $tá^H$ appears to set the upper limit that is possible for any quantity in the amount phrase; that is, if any amount is proposed, the limiter $tá^H$ marks that amount as the maximum.

(648) kiau^L póʔ^L tá^H mí^{H}ɲií^M kiuʔ^{LM} cú^M
seven^IN peal exactly bell   strike^TI^PRES^3 they
They strike the (death) bell exactly seven peals.

When qualifiers implying some imprecision occur with $tá^H$, the meaning of $tá^H$ is 'no more'.

(649) kũ^L kia^L mái^L tá^H mĩ^L hlái^M bíʔ^H ʔniáuʔ^{LM}
only ten^IN sphere no^more spherical egg AFF be^necessary^SII
Only ten eggs, no more, are necessary.

There appear to be some co-occurrence restrictions between the limiter $tá^H$ and the qualifiers that precede the quantifier head. For example, la^L 'almost' (QL$_4$) cannot occur with the limiter $tá^H$ (a semantic restriction), but if $hmáʔ^L$ 'just' (QL$_3$) occurs with la^L, then together they may occur with $tá^H$. $hmáʔ^L$ probably gives sufficient semantic definiteness to la^L to enable them together to occur with $tá^H$. $kũ^L$ (QL$_5$) 'approximately' can collocate with the limiter $tá^H$ 'exactly, no more', the implication being that the sense of approximation is not great.

6.10 The approximate quantifier phrase

The structure of the approximate quantifier phrase (APP^QP) is given in (650).

(650) APPROXIMATE QUANTIFIER PHRASE →
 (QUALIFIER$_{1-5,7}$) QUANTIFIER HEAD$_1$ (ALTERNATIVE) (QUALIFIER$_x$) QUANTIFIER HEAD$_2$ (LIMITER)

The quantifier head$_1$ (QH$_1$) is a numeral, whereas the quantifier head$_2$ (QH$_2$) is an amount phrase. The quantity referred to by QH$_2$ must be greater than that of QH$_1$.

The majority of the qualifiers of the APP^QP are the same as for the specific quantifier phrase, except that QL$_6$ of the SQP *táʰ* 'together, entire, every' does not occur in the APP^QP. A list of the qualifiers which may occur in the APP^QP is given in (651).

(651) QL$_1$ *kó?ᴸ* additionally
       QL$_2$ *?íʰ* another
       QL$_3$ *hmá?ᴸ* just
       QL$_4$ *laᴸ* about, almost, nearly
       QL$_5$ *kũᴸ* approximately, only, amid
       QL$_7$ *maᴸ* by, each, in lots of; *maᴸ kĩᴸᴹ maᴸ* 'every, each separate (one/group of)'

If a qualifier precedes QH$_1$, it must be QL$_1$, QL$_2$, QL$_5$, or QL$_7$. The occurrence of *hmá?ᴸ* 'just' (QL$_3$) and *laᴸ* 'about, almost, nearly' (QL$_4$) was discussed in the previous section.

Qualifier$_x$ (QL$_x$), which precedes QH$_2$, is essentially a repetition of the qualifier immediately preceding QH$_1$, but QL$_x$ can only be QL$_2$, QL$_5$, or QL$_7$. If *kó?ᴸ* 'additionally' (QL$_1$) immediately precedes QH$_1$, then *cũᴸ* (QL$_5$) must precede QH$_2$. QL$_x$ is optional only if *cũᴸ* immediately precedes QH$_1$; compare (652) and (653).

(652) Q[APP^QP[QL$_5$ QH$_1$[NUM   ]QH$_2$ [NUM   ]]
       kaᴸ-cã̄ᴸ   *kũᴸ*   *gáuᴸ*   *kiũᴸ*
       PAST-die^IA^3P   approximately   three^AN   four^AN

              LIM   ] H
              táʰ   *káʰ?áuᴹ*
              no^more chicken
Approximately three or four chickens died, no more.

The Noun Phrase   219

(653)   Q[APP^QP[QL₅   QH₁[NUM]
   ka^L-kú?^M   cú^M   kū^L   kiũ^L
   PAST-eat^TI^3 3   approximately   four^IN

       QL₅   QH₂[AMP[NUM   CLASS]]]] H[   ]
       kū^L   ?ɲiá^L mái^L   mï^L   má^H
       approximately   five   sphere   spherical mango
   S/he ate approximately four or five mangoes.

The optional alternative (ALT) element is the conjunction ?o^L 'or' (§6.12).
(653) is an example of the APP^QP without the ALT element, while example
(654) has the ALT element.

(654)   Q   [APP^QP[QL₇ QH₁[NUM   ]] ALT QL₇
   hɲií^LM   cú^M   ma^L   hɲiéi^L   ?o^L ma^L
   SOW^TI^PRES^3 3   by   six   or   by

       QH₂[AMP[NUM   CLASS]]] H[   ]
                kiau^L   mái^L   mï^L   kuú^M
                seven^IN   sphere   spherical maize
   They sow maize kernels by sixes or sevens.

The limiter element of the APP^QP is tá̃^H 'no more' (as in the specific
quantifier phrase); because the APP^QP implies approximation, however, the
sense of 'exactly' for tá̃^H does not apply.
  Some of the co-occurrence restrictions of the APP^QP have already been
mentioned. Other restrictions are that only whole units are permissible in the
APP^QP; the divisors cannot co-occur—expressions such as 'about one or one
and a half' are ungrammatical; and when QL₃ and/or QL₄ occur(s), it/they
must be followed either by cū^L 'approximately, only, amid' (QL₅) or by ma^L
'by, each, in lots of' (QL₇), or by both.
  There is one automatic permutation of order among the qualifier elements:
when ?í^H 'another' (QL₂) occurs with hmá?^L 'just' (QL₃) and la^L 'about, almost, nearly' (QL₄), then the order is QL₃ QL₂ QL₄.

6.11 The indefinite quantifier phrase

The structure of the indefinite quantifier phrase (IND^QP) is set out in
(655):

(655) INDEFINITE QUANTIFIER PHRASE →
(QUALIFIER$_a$) (QUALIFIER$_b$) INDEFINITE QUANTIFIER HEAD
(QUALIFIER$_c$) (QUALIFIER$_d$) (CLASSIFIER)

The indefinite quantifiers that can function as the head of the indefinite quantifier phrase are listed in (657); the QL$_{a-d}$ are listed in (659).
The full indefinite quantifier phrase is illustrated by (656).

(656)   Q[IND^QP[QL$_a$ [QL$_b$ IQH   QL$_c$
ka^L-la^L cú^M ka^{L}la^L hlá̰$^{?H}$ ʔliã́u^L lḭ̃^{LM}
PAST-buy^TI^3   3   even^to   really   many^IN   very

QL$_d$ CLASS   ]]]   H[   ]
ku^{L}tí^{HL} (máï^L)   mï^L dú$^{?L}$
absolutely   sphere   spherical   candy
S/he bought an absolutely huge amount of candies.

In both the specific quantifier phrase and the indefinite quantifier phrase, the nature of the NP head determines the presence and choice of the classifier. In the specific quantifier phrase, for enumeration of certain nouns to occur, the presence of a classifier is obligatory; in the indefinite quantifier phrase, however, the classifier is optional for the same nouns. Thus, (656) above is grammatical whether *máï^L* 'sphere' occurs or not.

The head of the indefinite quantifier phrase. There are four indefinite quantifiers (INDQ) that may function as the head of the IND^QP; see (657).

(657) The indefinite quantifiers

	Inanimate	Animate non-1P	Animate 1P
few, little	kú^{H}pi$^{?MH}$	kú^{H}pi$^{?MH}$	kú^{H}pi$^{?MH}$
some	ka^{L}lá^M	ka^{L}lá^M	ka^{L}lá^M
many	ʔliã́u^L	huṍu^{LM}	huóu^{LM}
most, all	hḭ̃^{LM}	hḭ̃^{LM}	hái^{LM}

If the indefinite quantifier *ka^{L}lá^M* 'some' occurs as the head of an IND^QP, none of the qualifiers may co-occur. When the head of the IND^QP is *hḭ̃^{LM}* (*hḭ̃^{LM}* or *hái^{LM}*) 'most, all', then the order of the qualifiers is QL$_b$ QL$_a$, not *QL$_a$ QL$_b$.
None of the forms of the indefinite quantifier *hḭ̃^{LM}*, *hḭ̃^{LM}*, *hái^{LM}* 'most, all' can occur unless one of the qualifiers of QL$_a$, or *lḭ̃^{LM}* of QL$_c$ (or both) also occur; all three forms of 'most, all' have a single variant *hï^L* which occurs only

The Noun Phrase 221

when followed by the QL$_c$ qualifier $lî̂LM$ 'very'. Because of the semantic and phonemic interaction of the variants of 'most, all' with $lî̂LM$ of QL$_c$, and the semantic interaction of these variants with the qualifiers of QL$_a$, the phonemic changes and the connotations have been tabulated in (658), where the sense of 'totality' increases from top to bottom.

(658) $hî LM$ most, all with $lî̂LM$ very

	Inanimate	Animate non-1P	Animate 1P
most, (all)	la^L $hî LM$	la^L $hî̂LM$	la^L $háï LM$
most, (all)	hi^L $li LM$	hi^L $lî̃M$	hi^L la^M
most, (all)	$ka^L la^L$ $hî LM$	$ka^L la^L$ $hî̂LM$	$ka^L la^L$ $háï LM$
all	$ka^L la^L$ hi^L $li LM$	$ka^L la^L$ hi^L $lî̃M$	$ka^L la^L$ hi^L la^M

The qualifiers of the indefinite quantifier phrase. The qualifiers QL$_a$, QL$_b$, QL$_c$, and QL$_d$ are different from the qualifiers of the other quantifier phrase types, hence the different subscripts; see (659). The two qualifiers QL$_b$ and QL$_c$ are largely independent of each other in modifying the head element IQH of the IND QP.

(659) QUALIFIER$_a$ $ka^L la^L$ even to, up to
                   la^L (QL$_4$)   about, almost, nearly (more vague than $ka^L la^L$)
       QUALIFIER$_b$ ma^L (QL$_7$)   in lots of
                   ta^H precisely
                   $hlá ʔ^H$ really
       QUALIFIER$_c$ $lî̃ML$ very (with six variants, conditioned phonemically, pragmatically, or by animacy: $lî̂LM, lî̃MH, lî̂HL, li^M, lî̃M, la^M$)
                   $siï ʔ^H$ quite
                   $ʔlaï ʔ^L, ʔla ʔ^L$ terribly (with an intensifying connotation)
       QUALIFIER$_d$ $ka^L la^M$ rather, somewhat
                   $ku^L tí^L, ku^L tí^{HL}$ absolutely (where the second form is more emphatic)

Examples (660) and (661) illustrate the use of $ka^L la^L$ versus la^L with the quantifier 'most, all'. Example (660) says that every, or nearly every person died, but the meaning of (661) can range from 'most people' to 'all people' bought maize.

(660) kaᴸlaᴸ   hĩ̂ᴸᴹ   cúᴹ kaᴸ-cã̄ᴸ
      even^to most^AN 3   PAST-die^IA^3P
      They all died.

(661) laᴸ   hĩ̂ᴸᴹ   cúᴹ kaᴸ-laᴸ   kuúᴹ
      about all^AN 3   PAST-buy^TI^3 maize
      Most people bought maize.

If either of the other two indefinite quantifiers which can be qualified occurs as the head of IND^QP, only kaᴸlaᴸ can occur. Quite likely laᴸ of kaᴸlaᴸ 'even to, up to' is related to the qualifier laᴸ 'about, almost, nearly', but the meaning of kaᴸ is uncertain.

The classifier constituent of the indefinite quantifier phrase. The classifier constituent of the indefinite quantifier phrase appears to be essentially the same as for the specific quantifier phrase. The sortal classifier is optional in the IND^QP, whereas it is obligatory in the SQP when enumerating certain entities. If a classifier is present in the IND^QP, only inanimate indefinite quantifiers may occur, regardless of the animacy of the head noun. This is because the indefinite quantifier modifies the classifier, all of which are inanimate, and the quantifier plus classifier combination as a whole quantifies the head noun. Examples with inanimate and animate head nouns, respectively, are given in (662) and (663).

(662) Q [INDQ   CLASS] H[   ]
        ʔliắuᴸ   muᴹᴴ   mĩ̂ᴴ siᶠᴹ   ʔnóᴸᴹ   hnắᴴᴸ
        many^IN   leaf   flat book want^STI^IS I
      I want a lot of pages.

(663) Q [INDQ   CLASS] H[   ]
        ʔliắuᴸ   nióᴸ   cắᴹ   kauʔᴸᴹ   mĩ̄ᴸ   láuᴹ
        many^IN   group   person   play^TI^PRES^3 spherical hide

        θiã̄ᴹ
        exist^SIA^3
      There are many teams of basketball players.

If no classifier occurs, then the indefinite quantifier directly modifies the NP head and must agree with the NP head in animateness and, if animate, also agree in person. An indefinite quantifier agreeing with a first-person plural NP head is shown in (664).

(664) huóu^{LM} (lĩ^{LM}) hno$^{?H}$ θiãu^M
many^1P very us exist^SIA^1P
There are (very) many of us.

6.12 Coordination of noun phrases

There are three conjunctions which can connect noun phrases. They are hi^L 'and', ʔo^L 'or', and ʔo^{L}lá^{M}dá^M 'or else'.

If only two noun phrases are conjoined by hi^L, as in (665), then the adverbs ní^M 'too' and siá$^{?L}$ 'also' are optional—either both occur, or neither. If there are more than two noun phrases conjoined, then ní^M and siá$^{?L}$ are both obligatory as in (666).

(665) ŋi^{H}-lá^L hná^{HL} ŋi^H hi^L huĩ^{H}kuú^M (ní^M siá$^{?L}$)
ANDT-buy^TI^1S I salt and sugar too also
I am going to buy salt and sugar (as well).

(666) ŋi^{H}-lá^L hná^{HL} ŋi^H huĩ^{H}kuú^M hmĩ^{M}tiu$^{?MH}$ hi^L
ANDT-buy^TI^1S I salt sugar milk and

ʔmá^{M}ŋi^{H}sĩ^M ní^M siá$^{?L}$
match too also
I am going to buy salt, sugar, milk, and matches as well.

The two disjunctives ʔo^L 'or' and ʔo^{L}lá^{M}dá^M 'or else' are illustrated in (667) and (668); ʔo^L 'or' with more than two nouns is illustrated in (669).

(667) ʔniáu$^{?LM}$ ha^{LM} cú^M tí^M ka^{L}lá^M ŋi^{H}kuú^M ʔo^L
be^necessary^SII spread^TI^3 3 first some pressed^cane or

mu^{MH} ʔmá^M táu^M
leaf^3 tree banana
One must first spread out some pressed sugar cane or banana palm leaves.

(668) ʔnó^{LM} hná^{HL} ká^{M}fe^{MH} ʔo^{L}lá^{M}dá^M hmĩ^{M}ráu^L
want^STI^1S I coffee or^else cordial
I want coffee or else cordial.

(669) ʔnáuʔHL   ʔnúM káMfeMH   hmḭMtauMH ʔoL   hmḭMráuL
 ʔ͡want͡sTI͡2 you͡s coffee   custard   or   cordial
 Do you want coffee, custard, or cordial?[53]

---

[53]The word hmḭMtauMH 'custard' refers to a drink made from ground maize and sweetened with crude sugar.

7
The Prepositional Phrase

The structure of the prepositional phrase (PP) is shown in (670). It can be modified by an adverb, which precedes the PP; see §7.6. There can be no modifier of a prepositional phrase if that prepositional phrase is the complement of a preposition.

(670) PP → PREP $\left\{ \begin{array}{l} \text{PP} \\ \text{NP} \end{array} \right\}$

The prepositions are listed in (671). They are subdivided into four groups according to their semantic function. The following sections deal with the characteristics and co-occurrence of some of these prepositions.

(671) locative

$kã^{LM}$	beside, along
$ká^H\text{?}ŋiu^{MH}$	behind
$ká\text{?}^{LM}$	on the far side of
ciu^L	in, inside, within (a liquid or mass)
$kó^{LM}$	nearby
$\text{?}ŋiu^L$	inside, within
$\text{?}ú^H$	along, on (a trail or road)
ha^H	between, among, within
ho^{MH}	on/at the other side of
$ŋie\text{?}^M$	below, inside
$ŋií^Hkõ^M$	toward, to, from (animate object)

	ci^L	up, up in
	$ku^L\ h\hat{e}i^L$	around
	ta^L	at, nearby (foot)
	$hm\acute{i}ʔ^H$	at the base/bottom of (buttocks)
locative and temporal	$ŋi\acute{\imath}^H$	on, on top of, in, at (face, surface)
	ti^L	at, in, to, from, until
	$la^Lk\tilde{a}u^M$	throughout, in the vicinity of, about
temporal	ha^H	within, during
	$ŋieʔ^M$	before
instrumental	$ki\tilde{o}ʔ^L$	with, by means of
	$k\bar{u}^Lki\tilde{o}ʔ^L$	with, by means of
	hui^{LM}	by, by means of, through

7.1 Inalienable nouns as prepositions

The prepositions ta^L, $hm\acute{i}ʔ^H$, and $ŋi\acute{\imath}^H$ are inalienable nouns which reference body parts and which also function as locative prepositions; the noun gloss for each is given in parentheses in the above chart. The inalienable noun $ŋi\acute{\imath}^H$ 'face' and the preposition $ŋi\acute{\imath}^H$ 'on, at' are shown in (672) and (673).

(672) $hl\acute{a}ʔ^H$ $ki\acute{a}^H$ $ŋi\acute{\imath}^H$ $d\tilde{a}i^M$ $\acute{o}^{LM}$
really be^dirty^sII face^3 baby yonder
That baby's face is really dirty.

(673) $r\acute{o}^{LM}$ $ʔm\acute{a}^M ʔ\tilde{\imath}^{LM}$ $h\tilde{a}u^M$ $ŋi\acute{\imath}^H$ $si\acute{\imath}^M$ $\acute{o}^{LM}$
lie^sII^s pencil   that^IN on book yonder
The pencil is lying on that book.

One way of analyzing the structure in (673) would be to say that inanimate nouns such as $si\acute{\imath}^M$ 'book' function as the possessor of the inalienable noun $ŋi\acute{\imath}^H$ 'face', that is, 'the pencil is lying on that book's face'. Although there is a conceptual relation between the inalienable noun 'face' and the preposition 'surface', there are, however, semantic and syntactic differences.[54]

The syntactic difference is underscored by the fact that the preposition ta^L 'at' can occur with the inalienable noun ta^L 'foot'; and the preposition $ŋi\acute{\imath}^H$

---

[54]Anderson (1989:103–8) refers to such prepositions in Comaltepec Chinantec as "prepositional nouns": inalienable nouns that, when used locatively, have an inanimate possessor instead of the usual animate possessor. In Sochiapan Chinantec there appears to be sufficient grounds for treating such forms as true prepositions rather than as inalienable nouns.

The Prepositional Phrase

'on, at' can occur with the inalienable noun *ɲiɾ^H* 'face', illustrated in (674) and (675), respectively; as would be expected, either preposition can occur with many other inalienable and alienable nouns.

(674) ka^L-di^{L}hɲii^{LM} cú^M ta^L ta^L mi^{L}hmú^L
     PAST-kneel^IA^3 3   at   foot^3   bishop
     S/he knelt at the feet of the bishop.

(675) rṍ^{LM} cí^H ʔmïʔ^{LM} ɲiɾ^H ɲiɾ^H dä́i^M
     lie^SII^s old cloth   on   face^3   baby
     There is a rag lying on the baby's face.

7.2 Co-occurrence restrictions

Certain prepositions are restricted as to their referent, modifier, complement, etc. Each of these prepositions is discussed in turn.

The preposition *ɲiɾ^{H}kõ^M*. This preposition can only have a noun phrase with an animate referent as its object; the object of the preposition can be either source ('from') or goal ('to'), depending on the predicate.

(676) kuá^M-kä́^{H} sii^M lá^M ɲiɾ^{H}kõ^M cá^{M}tä^{MH}
     ANDT^IMP-take^TI^2 letter this   to   authorities
     Take this letter to the (town) authorities.

(677) sii^M nï^M ha^L ɲiɾ^{H}kõ^M tï^{LM} nú ʔ^L
     letter that come^II^PAST^3S from   teacher Arnold
     That letter came from the teacher, Arnold.

The preposition *ku^L héï^L* 'around'. This preposition is the only binomial preposition that has been identified. Only the first element is itself a preposition; most likely it is derived from the preposition *kó^{LM}* 'nearby'. The second element is the noun *héï^L* 'turns, circles'. It cannot have another prepositional phrase as its complement. The only modifier which can collocate with the preposition *ku^L héï^L* 'around' is the adverb *la^L* 'right, even'. The modifier, when present, occurs with both parts of the preposition (as it does with binomial adverbs).

(678) tiõʔ^M ʔliáu^L la^L ku^L la^L héï^L ɲiɾ^{H}ta^{MH}
     be^present^SIA^3P soldier right nearby right circles town^hall
     Soldiers are present right around the town hall.

The preposition *ɲiïH* 'in, on'. When this preposition is used in a temporal sense, it must have as its object a noun phrase whose head is a quantified temporal noun, such as *oHřáH* 'hour', *hmáïH* 'day', *θíʔM* 'month', or *miïM* 'year'.

(679) cắʔLM   cúM ɲiïH hɲiaL hmáïH
      go^home^IA^FUT^3S 3   in   eight day
      S/he will be going home in eight days.[55]

(680) kaL-ciáuLM   hnoʔH ɲiïH máM ʔniïLM hmáïH huúM tuksõ
      PAST-arrive^IA^1P we   on   PRF three   day   town Tucson
      We arrived in Tucson on the third day.

The preposition *tïL* 'at, in, to, from, until'. The meaning of the preposition *tïL* as a locative is determined by the predicate of the clause in which it occurs, as shown in (681)–(683) where *tïL* occurs with a noun phrase object.

(681) maL-cáuHL   tïL siauLM
      EXH-go^nonhome^IA^1P to   other^borough
      Let's go to the other borough.[56]

(682) hãM   cáM   haLM   tïL   hïʔLM bíʔH
      one^AN person come^to^nonhome^IA^PRES^3S from Usila AFF

      niïLM
      that^one
      That person comes from Usila.

(683) róLM   tiúL håuM tïL máʔL
      lie^SII^S rifle that^IN at   mountain
      That rifle is lying at the mountain.

The most common complement of *tïL* 'at, until' as a temporal preposition is a temporal phrase with future reference, such as *kuLléL* 'later', *caLʔáuM* 'tomorrow', or *miïM kắuM* 'next year', as in (684). It is only when *tïL* is modified by *kaLlaL* 'right, even', or *laL* 'right, even', that the other temporal prepositions can occur in a phrase as its complement, as in (685).

---

[55] The Chinantecs count days in the same manner as the Spanish; that is, the first day counted is today. A more precise translation cross-culturally into English of 'eight days' would be to say 'in one week'.

[56] In the town of San Pedro there are two boroughs. Whichever borough one is in, it is possible to refer to the other one simply by the expression *tïL siauLM* 'to/at the other borough'.

(684) tiᴸ kuᴸléᴸ míʔᴴ ŋieᴴ　　　　　　hnáᴴᴸ
　　　at later little go^nonhome^IA^FUT^1S I
　　　I will go a little later.

(685) kaᴸlaᴸ tiᴸ ŋifᴴ kiúᴸ hmáïᴴ máʔᴸ hãuʔᴸ
　　　even at in four^IN day EXCL return^home^IA^FUT^3S

　　　tïᴸᴹ　　ciïᴴ
　　　teacher main
　　　Not until four days time will the principal return!

The preposition *laᴸkãuᴹ* 'throughout, in the vicinity of, about'. This preposition can have either a locative or temporal meaning. Examples (686) and (687) illustrate its locative usage.

(686) kaᴸ-ŋaᴹ　　　　cúᴹ laᴸkãuᴹ　　　　huúᴹ kiuʔᴹᴴ
　　　PAST-pass^by^IA^3 3 in^the^vicinity^of town Puebla
　　　S/he passed by in the vicinity of the town of Puebla.

(687) laᴸkãuᴹ　　　　　máʔᴸ　óᴸᴹ　kaᴸ-hŋiíᴸ　cúᴹ náïᴹ
　　　in^the^vicinity^of mountain yonder PAST-SOW^TI^3 3 weed

　　　hãuᴹ
　　　that^in
　　　S/he sowed that weed (i.e., marijuana) in the vicinity of that mountain.

In its temporal sense, this preposition can take only a noun phrase as its object. It can collocate only with the temporal nouns *θïʔᴹ* 'month' and *mifᴹ* 'year', which offer a more indefinite frame of reference.

(688) kaᴸ-lïᴸ　　　　θiãᴹ　　　cúᴹ laᴸkãuᴹ mifᴹ hãuᴹ
　　　PAST-occur^II exist^SIA^3 3 about year that^IN
　　　S/he was born about that year.

The instrumental prepositions. The semantic difference between *kiõʔᴸ* 'with, by means of' and *kũᴸkiõʔᴸ* 'with, by means of' is not clear. Either preposition can always be substituted for the other, although in some sentences one preposition may be preferred over the other, as in (690), where *kũᴸkiõʔᴸ* is preferred.

(689) máᴹ lį̂ᴹ-hmóuʔᴸᴹ cúᴹ ʔmáᴹsi̯ᴴ nî̯ᴹ kiõʔᴸ hmį̂ᴹtiauᴸ
       PRF HOD-fix^TI^3 3   chair   that with glue
       S/he has just fixed that chair with glue.

(690) kṹᴸkiõʔᴸ   ki̯eᴸ   bíʔᴴ kaᴸ-li̯ãuᴸ   cúᴹ
       by^means^of money AFF   PAST-escape^IA^3   3
       S/he escaped by means of money (i.e., s/he paid a bribe).

The instrumental preposition *hui̯ᴸᴹ* 'by, by means of, through' undoubtedly has as its source the noun *hui̯ᴸᴹ* 'path, trail, road'. This preposition is used only with means of transportation or conveyance, whether real or metaphorical. When means of conveyance are involved, *kiõʔᴸ* or *kṹᴸkiõʔᴸ* 'with, by means of' can be readily replaced by *hui̯ᴸᴹ* 'by, by means of, through', as shown in (691). However, *kiõʔᴸ* and *kṹᴸkiõʔᴸ* cannot always substitute for *hui̯ᴸᴹ*; in (692) and (693), only *hui̯ᴸᴹ* is grammatical; example (693) illustrates the metaphorical use of *hui̯ᴸᴹ* 'by, by means of, through'.

(691) ŋi̯eᴴ   hnáᴴᴸ ŋiᴴkuã́ʔᴹ   kiõʔᴸ/hui̯ᴸᴹ avió
       go^nonhome^IA^FUT^IS   I   Oaxaca   by^means^of airplane
       I will go to Oaxaca (City) by means of an airplane.

(692) cã́ʔᴸᴹ   cúᴹ hui̯ᴸᴹ taᴸ
       return^home^IA^FUT^3S 3   by foot^3
       S/he will return home by foot.

(693) θiaᴸᴹ   ʔiᴸ   kaᴸ-hniaᴸ   hḗi̯ᴸᴹ   hnáᴴᴸ hui̯ᴸᴹ kiᴸθiúᴸ
       exist^SII thing PAST-appear^II experience^TI^IS I   by   dream
       There are things that I saw in my dreams.

7.3 Prepositions with *bíʔᴴ* (affirmation)

When a noun phrase with an inalienable noun as its head is left dislocated to focus position, the illocutionary particle *bíʔᴴ* (affirmation) is grammatical immediately following the inalienable noun; when a prepositional phrase is left dislocated for focus, however, *bíʔᴴ* is ungrammatical immediately following the grammaticalized preposition. An example of the grammaticality of *bíʔᴴ* following left dislocated inalienable nouns is given in (694) and the ungrammaticality of *bíʔᴴ* following prepositions in (695).

(694) nii̯ᴴ   bíʔᴴ meᴴsáᴴ hlã́ʔᴴ   taʔᴴ
       face^3 AFF   table   really be^rough^SII
       The table's face/surface is really rough (in contrast to some other part).

(695) a. *nit^H (*bí?^{H}) me^{H}sá^H ró^{LM} mi^{H}hla^M*
on   AFF   table   lie^sii^s knife
The knife is on the table.

b. *?ŋiu^L (*bí?^{H}) cí^H kuo^M ?ũ^H ká^{H}mí?^{H}*
inside AFF   old box   be^contained^sia^3s baby^chicken
The baby chicken is inside the old box.

Although *bí?^{H}* is ungrammatical following a preposition, it may follow a prepositional phrase, in which case the whole prepositional phrase is in its scope.

(696) *ká^H?ŋiu^{MH} kuá?^{LM} bí?^{H} kuá^H-?o^M sé^{LM} mí?^{H}*
behind   church   AFF   indefinite^PROG-cry^ia^3 Joseph little
(It's) behind the church little Joseph is crying.

7.4 Prepositions with a deictic complement

When the object of a locative preposition is a noun phrase which has a deictic adjective as one of its constituents, the noun phrase elements, apart from the deictic, can be omitted.

(697) *ka^L-kuõ^L nái^M ?la?^{L} ha^H (lí^{HL})   hǎu^M*
PAST-grow^ii weed bad   among flower that^IN
The harmful weeds grew among those (flowers).

(698) *ka^L-hmú^{LM} hná^H ta^{MH} ti^L (má?^{L})   ó^{LM}*
PAST-do^ti^is I   work at mountain yonder
I worked at that (mountain).

Similarly, when the complement of a preposition is a prepositional phrase, the preposition of the second prepositional phrase and all but the deictic element of its noun phrase object, can be omitted.

(699) *ka^L-?ná?^{LM} hná^{HL} ca^{L}kuá^H ?í^L la^{L}kǎu^M (ha^H*
PAST-search^for^ta^is I   horse   that^AN throughout within

?ŋá^H) lá^M
forest this
I searched for that horse throughout this (forest).

7.5 Prepositional phrases as complement

There are two locative prepositions, ti^L 'at, in, to, from' and $la^Lkãu^M$ 'in the vicinity of', which can take a locative prepositional phrase as its complement. Examples of ti^L with phrases introduced by $\eta ie?^M$ 'inside', $\eta i^Hk\tilde{o}^M$ 'towards', and ha^H 'within' are given in (700)–(702), respectively.

(700) $?e^L$ $tio?^L$ ti^L $\eta ie?^M$ $ha?^H$ $n\acute{i}^M$
what? be^contained^SII^3P at inside basket that
What is (contained) in that basket?

(701) $ca^L?áu^M$ hau^L $cú^M$ $?nú^M$ ti^L $\eta i^Hk\tilde{o}^M$ hue^{MH}
tomorrow take^TA^FUT^3>2 3 you^s to towards judge
Tomorrow he will take you before the judge.

(702) ηau^L $cú^M$ ti^L ha^H $huú^M$ $hm\acute{i}^M?iá^{LM}$
go^nonhome^IA^PAST^3S 3 to within town Valle^Nacional
S/he has gone to the town of Valle Nacional.

In (700), ti^L 'at' is essential for the prepositional phrase to be grammatical. In (701) and (702), however, there appears to be little difference in meaning whether ti^L is present or absent.

Examples of $la^Lkáu^M$ 'in the vicinity of' with phrases introduced by ti^L 'at' and ha^H 'among' are given in (703) and (704), respectively.

(703) $má^M$ $kuá^M$-ηi^H-$?nia?^M$ $cú^M$ $ca^Lkuá^H$ $ho?^H$
PRF VEN-ANDT-search^TA^3 3 horse have^STA^3

$la^Lkáu^M$ ti^L $kua^Luóu^M$
in^the^vicinity^of at Quetzalapa
S/he has returned from searching for her/his horse in the vicinity of Quetzalapa.

(704) ka^L-$?na?^M$ $cú^M$ $hó^M$ $la^Lkáu^M$ ha^H $?\eta iú^L$
PAST-search^for^TA^3 3 child^3 throughout among house
S/he searched for her/his child throughout the streets.

A layering effect of three consecutive prepositional phrases can be seen in (705), where $la^Lkáu^M$ has as its complement a prepositional phrase introduced by ti^L 'at' which in turn has a prepositional phrase complement introduced by $k\tilde{a}^{LM}$ 'along'.

The Prepositional Phrase

(705) *kuáᴹ-ŋiíᴴ-kiãuᴹ*   *cáᴹhuúᴹ* *θáïᴹ* *ʔiᴸ* *tioʔᴴᴸ*
VEN-ANDT^PAST-bring^TI^3 townspeople sand COMP be^present^SII^P

laᴸkãuᴹ   *tïᴸ* *kãᴸᴹ* *kuaᴸ*
in^the^vicinity^of at along river
The townspeople went and brought back sand from along the river.

The adverb *laᴸ* 'right' modifying a complex prepositional phrase with *tïᴸ* 'to' is shown in (706).

(706) *kaᴸ-cióᴸᴹ*   *cúᴹ* *laᴸ* *tïᴸ* *taᴸ*   *ŋiíᴴ* *hueᴹᴴ*
PAST-arrive^nonhome^IA^3S 3 right to nearby face^3 judge
S/he stood right before the judge.

7.6 Prepositions with adverbs

There are restrictions as to the adverbs which can occur with the various types of prepositions. There are three adverbs that can occur as modifiers of a locative prepositional phrase: *hmáʔᴸlaᴸ* 'only', *kaᴸlaᴸ* 'right, even', and *laᴸ* 'right, even'.

The adverb *hmáʔᴸlaᴸ* is a compound of the adverb *hmáʔᴸᴹ* 'only' (which cannot modify a prepositional phrase) plus the adverb *laᴸ* 'right, even', which is discussed below. This adverb can modify any locative prepositonal phrase.

(707) *hmáʔᴸlaᴸ* *haᴴ*   *huúᴹ* *bíʔᴴ* *hŋiiᴸᴹ*   *cúᴹ* *háᴴháuᴹ* *pïeʔᴴ*
only within town AFF sow^TI^PRES^3 3 cabbage globe^IN
They sow head cabbage only within the town.

(708) *hmáʔᴸlaᴸ* *tïᴸ* *ŋiíᴴ* *ciéiᴸ* *bíʔᴴ* *θiaᴸᴹ* *mïᴸ*   *huʔᴹᴴ*
only in place hot^IN AFF exist^SII spherical pineapple

káʔᴴ
large^IN^P
There are large pineapples only in hot/tropical places.

(709) *kaᴸ-ʔnauʔᴹ*   *cúᴹ* *taᴹᴴ* *hmáʔᴸlaᴸ* *laᴸkãuᴹ* *huúᴹ* *kiuʔᴹᴴ*
PAST-search^for^TI^3 3 work only throughout city Puebla
S/he searched for work only throughout the city of Puebla.

hmáʔᴸlaᴸ 'only' can modify a temporal prepositional phrase only when *haᴴ* 'during', *ŋieʔᴹ* 'before', or *ŋiíᴴ* 'in' occur as the preposition.

(710) hmá$^{?L}$la^L ha^H niéi^M bí$^{?H}$ $^{?O^M}$ ŋiú^{M}mí$^{?H}$
only during darkness AFF cry^IA^PRES^3 little^boy
The little boy only cries during the night.

(711) hmá$^{?L}$la^L ŋie$^{?M}$ ciu^L?iú^M bí$^{?H}$ híe^L hná^{HL}
only before midday AFF be^free^IA^FUT^1S I
I will be free only before midday.

(712) hmá$^{?L}$la^L ŋií^H hŋia^L hmái^H kué^{LM} cú^M vacuna kio$^{?MH}$
only in eight day give^TI^FUT^3 3 vaccine have^STI^3

cá^{H}mí$^{?H}$
children
They will give the vaccine to the children only in eight days (from now).

hmá$^{?L}$la^L 'only' is the sole modifier of an instrumental adverbial phrase.

(713) hmá$^{?L}$la^L kiõ$^{?L}$ kuo^H θó^{LM} cú^M má^{LM} huú^M lá^M
only with firewood cook^TI^PRES^3 3 food town this
They cook food only with firewood in this town.

The adverbs ka^{L}la^L 'right, even' and la^L 'right, even' are generally interchangeable; when functioning as modifiers of a locative or temporal prepositional phrase, there is no discernible semantic difference between them.[57] Either can modify a prepositional phrase when ti^L is the preposition. Each adverb is shown with locative ti^L.

(714) có^{LM} cú^M la^L ti^L ?ũ^{L}hmái^M ca^L?áu^M
go^nonhome^IA^FUT^3S 3 right to Mexico^City tomorrow
S/he will be going right to Mexico City tomorrow.

(715) ka^{L}la^L ti^L ?ũ^{L}hmái^M ka^L-ŋií^H-ma^{L}ré^M cú^M co^L
right to Mexico^City PAST-ANDT-rectify^TI^3 3 offence
S/he went right to Mexico City to get justice!

The combination of either adverb with temporal ti^L 'at, until' results in the meaning 'not until'.

---

[57] As modifiers of adjectives, ka^{L}la^L means 'even to, up to', and la^L means 'about, almost, nearly'; that is, the latter word is more vague or imprecise.

(716) laᴸ tïᴸ ióᴸᴹ   máʔᴸ hǎuʔᴸ   tïᴸᴹ
even at day^after^tomorrow EXCL return^IA^FUT^3S teacher
Not until the day after tomorrow will the teacher return!

(717) kaᴸlaᴸ tïᴸ mifᴹ kǎuᴹ lïʰᴴᴸ   ʔmáᴹʔõᴹ
even   at year next be^finished^II^FUT^3 bridge
Not until next year will the bridge be finished.

There is a fourth adverb kūᴸ 'about' which occurs only with the preposition ŋifᴴ 'in, on'.

(718) kūᴸ   ŋifᴴ   kúᴹ   mifᴹ máᴹ lïʰᴴᴸ   hmuᴸ   taᴹᴴ
about in   one^IN year PRF be^able^II^FUT do^TI^FUT^3 work

caᴸkuáᴴ   mfʔᴴ nîᴹ
horse   little that
That young horse will finally be able to work in about one year.

8
The Clause

This chapter focuses primarily on the structure of the declarative clause. The Sochiapan Chinantec clause can be characterized as consisting of primary and secondary constituents. In §§8.1–8.6 the primary constituents are discussed; these include the predicate and those nominals for which the verb is indexed. The secondary constituents are those constituents for which the verb is not indexed; these include the source/recipient, benefactive, manner, locative, comitative, temporal, instrumental, illocutionary, and vocative. The secondary constituents are discussed in §§8.7–8.14.

8.1–8.6 The primary constituents

The primary constituents are discussed under the following headings: the predicate, valence, ergativity, direct and inverse cross-referencing, the passive, and the antipassive.

8.1 The predicate

In the Sochiapan Chinantec clause, a predicate can encode action or process with a dynamic verb (§§4.1–4.7), or a description or state with either a state verb (§4.10) or a descriptive adjective (§4.11); the basic word order of the core constituents is predicate-subject-(object). Nonverbal predicates formed with a nominal encode identification. Each type of predicate is illustrated in turn.

Dynamic verbs are the most common predicators.

(719) P   S
      ʔiá^LM   nái^M
      sprout^II^FUT weed
      The weeds will sprout.

(720) P   S   O
      ʔí^LM   cú^M   kïe^L
      count^TI^FUT^3 3 money
      S/he will count the money.

State verbs are predicators in all their occurrences.

(721) P   S   O
      ʔau ʔ^MH   ie ʔ^L   hmï^M kau^LM
      possess^liquid^STI^3 elder kerosene
      The old man has (some) kerosene.

Descriptive adjectives can function predicatively like state verbs.

(722) P   S
      hue ʔ^LM   táu^M nï^M
      be^large^SII hole that
      That is a large hole.

Nominal predicates are usually set off by one of the illocutionary particles such as bí ʔ^H (affirmation) (chapter 11). They cross-reference a single nominal constituent.

(723) P   S
      hla^L cii^L kiu ʔ^MH   bí ʔ^H hlái^M nï^M
      egg^3 DIM   hummingbird   AFF   egg   that
      That egg (is) a hummingbird's egg.

(724) P   S
      tï^LM   bí ʔ^H cá^M   ʔí^L
      teacher AFF   person that^AN
      That person (is) a teacher.

Constructions such as (723) and (724) are functionally equivalent to equative clauses, but are mainly comparative or contrastive in connotation.

The Clause

Equative clauses formed with a copular verb are mainly identificational, generally lacking a comparative or contrastive connotation.

(725) P   S   COMP
       lîˀᴸ   kuáᴴláᴹ   ʔŋiúᴴᴸ   cúᴹ
       beˆɪɪˆPRES brick   houseˆ3   3
       Her/his house is brick.

(726) P   S   COMP
       lîˀᴸ   cúᴹ   tiˡᴸᴹ
       beˆɪᴀˆPRESˆ3 3   teacher
       S/he is a teacher.

Whether a copular verb is indexed for an inanimate or an animate complement, the situation described must be one that has an identifiable starting point; permanent states cannot be referenced by such verbs; instead, a nominal predicate is used, as in (723) and (724). Paired examples of the copular verb and the nominal predicate construction are shown in (727) and (728). The presence or absence of an illocutionary particle such as *bíʔᴴ* (affirmation) cannot make (727a) or (728a) grammatical.

(727) a. *lîˀᴸ   ʔmáᴹ kaᴹ   (bíʔᴴ)   ʔmáᴹ niˀᴹ
           beˆɪɪ tree pine   AFF   tree that
           That tree is a pine tree.

       b. ʔmáᴹ kaᴹ   bíʔᴴ   ʔmáᴹ niˀᴹ
          tree pine   AFF   tree that
          That tree is a pine tree.

(728) a. *lîˀᴸ   cáᴹmiˡᴸ   (bíʔᴴ)   cáᴹ   niˀᴹ
           beˆɪᴀˆ3 woman   AFF   person   that
           That person is a woman.

       b. cáᴹmiˡᴸ   bíʔᴴ   cáᴹ   niˀᴹ
          woman   AFF   person   that
          That person is a woman.

8.2 Valence

The valence of a Chinantec verb is defined syntactically as the number of nominal constituents for which it may be indexed. A verb which is indexed for a single nominal is termed intransitive inanimate (II) or intransitive animate (IA), according to the animacy of its subject. A verb which is indexed for two nominals is termed transitive inanimate (TI) or transitive animate (TA), according to the animacy of the object nominal. Chinantec ditransitives cross-reference up to three nominal constituents directly, without prepositions; such verbs are termed ditransitive inanimate (DI) or ditransitive animate (DA), according to the animacy of the direct object (DO). A few verbs inflectionally differentiate between transitive and ditransitive counterparts. Transitive animate verbs and ditransitive verbs (both animate and inanimate) are also indexed for direct and inverse cross-referencing; see §8.4.

In simple declarative clauses where the subject has not already been established in the discourse, the subject is obligatory even though it may be unambiguously identified by internal inflection.

(729) P   S   L
          $ŋie^H$ $hná^{HL}$ $(tï^L)$ $Ɂŋo Ɂ^L$
          go^nonhome^IA^FUT^1S I   to   Zautla
          I will go to Zautla.

In (729), the form of the irregular verb cau^{LM} 'go (nonhome)' as inflected for the first-person future cannot be confused with any other person or inflectional parameter, or with any other verb; nonetheless, if the first-person pronoun is not present, the construction is ungrammatical. Ellipsis on the basis of the preceding discourse content, however, is possible; see, for example, (744b).

Intransitive verbs. Intransitive verbs may be dynamic or state. Examples of intransitive inanimate and intransitive animate dynamic verbs, respectively, are given in (730) and (731).

(730) P   S
          ka^L-$káu^L$ $Ɂŋiu^{LM}$ $hná^{HL}$
          PAST-burn^II   house^1S   I
          My house burned.

(731) P   S
          ka^L-$kắu^L$ $hná^{HL}$
          PAST-burn^IA^1S   I
          I was burned.

Examples of intransitive inanimate and intransitive animate state verbs, respectively, are given in (732) and (733).

The Clause 241

(732) L P S
ɲii͡ᴴ θioᴴ θeʔᴹ ʔmáᴹsï͡ᴴ
place yonder stand^sɪɪ chair
The chair is standing over there.

(733) L P S
ɲii͡ᴴ θioᴴ θḛ̄ʔᴹ caᴸkuáᴴ
place yonder stand^sɪᴀ^3 horse
The horse is standing over there.

Transitive verbs. Transitive verbs may be dynamic or state. The subject of a transitive verb is normally animate, although inanimate subjects do occur; see §8.4. The unmarked (most common) order of the clause constituents is P-S-O. Examples of transitive inanimate and transitive animate dynamic verbs, respectively, are given in (734) and (735).

(734) P   S O
kaᴸ-kuo͡ʔᴸ cúᴹ ʔnáᴴ ʔmáᴹ
ᴘᴀsᴛ-pull^ᴛɪ^3 3 section wood
S/he pulled the log.

(735) P   S O
kaᴸ-kuó̰uʔᴸᴹ cúᴹ loᴴ
ᴘᴀsᴛ-pull^ᴛᴀ^3 3 mule
S/he pulled the mule.

Examples of transitive inanimate and transitive animate state verbs, respectively, are given in (736) and (737).

(736) P   S O
θéi͡ᴸᴹ   hnáᴴᴸ kǎuᴹ cúᴴliáʔᴹ
possess^upright^sᴛɪ^s^1s I one^ɪɴ clay^water^pot
I have a clay water pot.

(737) P   S O
θéi͡ᴸᴹ   hnáᴴᴸ hãᴹ caᴸkuáᴴ
possess^upright^sᴛᴀ^s^1s I one^ᴀɴ horse
I have a horse.

When transitive verbs are inflected for inverse cross-referencing (§8.4), the order P-S-O is optionally permuted to P-O-S, a permutation not usually available to the direct system (but note (742)).

(738) T　　　　　P　　　　　　　　S　　O
　　　ʔni̵^{LM} hḙi^{LM} ka^L-po^L　　　cú^M hná^{HL}
　　　three times PAST-hit⌒TA⌒3 > 1　3　　I
　　　S/he hit me three times.

(739) T　　　　　P　　　　　　　　O　　S
　　　ʔni̵^{LM} hḙi^{LM} ka^L-po^L　　　hná^{HL} cá^M　ʔi^L
　　　three times PAST-hit⌒TA⌒3 > 1　I　　person that
　　　That person hit me three times.

In (739), the DO is brought into focus by preceding the subject (§12.2). The semantic effect approximates an English passive 'I was hit by that person three times'.

Transitive verbs inflected for the direct system generally permit only a P-S-O order. Examples with both animate and inanimate DO are given in (740) and (741), respectively.

(740) a. má^M ka^L-pá̰^{LM}　　hná^{HL} cú^M
　　　　PRF PAST-hit⌒TA⌒1S　I　　3
　　　　I have hit her/him.

　　　b. *má^M ka^L-pá̰^{LM}　　cú^M hná^{HL}
　　　　PRF PAST-hit⌒TA⌒1S　3　　I
　　　　I have hit her/him.

(741) a. má^M ka^L-pá^L　　hná^{HL} láu^M
　　　　PRF PAST-hit⌒TI⌒1S　I　　skin
　　　　I have played the drums.

　　　b. *má^M ka^L-pá^L　　láu^M hná^{HL}
　　　　PRF PAST-hit⌒TI⌒1S　skin　I
　　　　I have played the drums.

If the DO is inanimate, as in (741b), the utterance can be made grammatical by the addition of the focus particle bíʔ^H (AFF).

(742) P　　　　　　　　　O　　　S
　　　má^M ka^L-pá^L　　láu^M bíʔ^H hná^{HL}
　　　PRF PAST-hit⌒TI⌒1S　skin AFF　I
　　　I have played the drums.

If the verb is inflected for the direct system, however, and the DO is animate, as in (740b), there is no way to make a P-O-S order grammatical.

The Clause

Ditransitive verbs. Only dynamic ditransitive verbs have been found. As with transitive verbs, the subject is normally animate. Examples of DI, DA, and DAI (ditransitive animate inverse) verbs, respectively, are given in (743).

(743) a. *péiʔ^{ML}* spray, splash, splatter (DI)

    P   S   IO   DO
    péiʔ^{ML}   *cú^M* *hmái^M* *lí^{HL}*
    spray^DI^PRES^3 3   water flower
    S/he sprays the flowers with water.

   b. *pḗiʔ^{LM}* spray, splash, splatter (DA)

    P   S   IO   DO
    pḗiʔ^{LM}   *cú^M* *hmái^M* *cá^{H}mí ʔ^H*
    spray^DA^PRES^3 3   water children
    S/he sprays the children with water.

   c. *péiʔ^{LM}* spray, splash, splatter (DAI)

    P   S   DO   IO
    péiʔ^{LM}   *cú^M* *hná^{HL}* *hmái^M*
    spray^DAI^PRES^3>1 3   I   water
    S/he sprays me with water.

In the appropriate discourse context where the speaker assumes that s/he and the addressee have access to the same information, either the IO or the DO may be omitted. Ellipsis of the IO and the DO (together with the subject and predicate) are illustrated in (744b) and (745b), respectively.

(744) a. DO   P   S   IO
    ʔí^M   *cáʔ^M* *lí^M-pḗiʔ^{LM}* *cú^M* *hē^M*
    which^AN? person HOD-splatter^DA^3 3   mud
    Which person did s/he splatter with mud?

   b. DO   P   S
    ŋiú^{M}mí ʔ^H *bí ʔ^H* (*lí^M-pḗiʔ^{LM}*   *cú^M*)
    boy   AFF HOD-splatter^DA^3 3
    (S/he splattered) the boy.

(745) a. IO   P   S   DO
    ʔe^L *lí^M-pḗiʔ^{LM}* *cú^M* *ŋiú^{M}mí ʔ^H*
    what? HOD-splatter^DA^3 3   boy
    With what did s/he splatter the boy?

b. IO   P   S
   hẽ^M bí?^{H} (lĩ^M-péi?^{LM} cú^M)
   mud AFF HOD-splatter^DA^3 3
   (S/he splattered) with mud.

A ditransitive verb in the passive voice (§8.5) permits ellipsis only of the surface IO, however, not the subject.

(746) a. P   S   IO
      hlá?^{H} ka^L-ha^L-péi?^{H} ŋiú^{M}mí?^{H} (hẽ^M)
      really PAST-PASS-splatter^TI^3   boy   mud
      The boy was really splattered (with mud).

      b. P   IO
      *hlá?^{H} ka^L-ha^L-péi?^{H} hẽ^M
      really PAST-PASS-splatter^TI^3   mud
      The mud was really splattered.

Sochiapan Chinantec ditransitives have as their direct object (DO) a semantic patient which may be inanimate or animate, and as their indirect object (IO) a semantic source or goal which may be inanimate or animate, including instrumental, locative, and recipient. Examples of an inanimate DO and an animate DO are given in (747).

(747) a. P   S   IO   DO
      ka^L-hláï^L cú^M mí^H sií^M θíĩ^L lio^{MH}
      PAST-cover^DI^3 3   flat   book   shiny   cargo
      S/he covered the cargo with a sheet of plastic.

      b. P   S   IO   DO
      ka^L-hláï^{LM} cú^M mí^H sií^M θíĩ^L hõ^M
      PAST-cover^DA^3 3   flat   book   shiny   child^3
      S/he covered her/his child with a sheet of plastic.

In (747), note that the identification of the DO and IO is apparent from the form of the verb, which is indexed for the animacy of the DO. The order of the DO and IO is discussed later in this section.

As mentioned above, ditransitive verbs cross-reference up to three nominal constituents directly without prepositions. There are two types of ditransitive verbs, those which are not indexed for the indirect object (IO), and those which are. The former encode instrumental and locative nominals as the IO, the latter encode recipient nominals as the IO. These are discussed in turn below.

The most common case-role encoded in Chinantec IOs is the instrumental.

(748) a. P   S   IO   DO   T
      hiéiʔ^L cú^M mï̃^{L} lí^{HL} ku^{L}lé^L
      spray^DI^FUT^3 3   medicine flower later
      S/he will spray the flowers with medication later.

  b. P   S   IO   DO   T
     hiéiʔ^{LM} cú^M mï̃^{L} ca^{L}kuá^H ku^{L}lé^L
     spray^DA^FUT^3 3   medicine horse   later
     S/he will spray the horse with medication later.

An example of inanimate and animate locative IO as source is in (749).

(749) a. P   S   DO   IO
      ka^L-cii^M cú^M tõ^M kuo^M
      PAST-remove^DI^3   3   thorn   hand^3
      S/he removed a thorn from her/his hand.

  b. P   S   DO   IO
     ka^L-cii^M cú^M ʔa^H ɲiú^{M}mḯʔ^H
     PAST-remove^DI^3 3   shirt   boy
     S/he removed the shirt from the boy.

An example of an inanimate locative IO as goal is shown in (750).

(750) P   S   DO   IO
      ka^L-tã́ʔ^M cá^{M}tã̧^{MH} θié^L lái^H cú^M
      PAST-put^DI^3   authorities   noose   neck^3   3
      The authorities put the noose around her/his neck.

The force of the recipient resembles that of the locative in that the DO may be seen as changing location to or from the IO; however, there is the sense that the IO benefits in some way from the transaction. According to Givón (1984:114), the prototypical benefactive/recipient IO is human, although I see no problem with extending this at least to animate for Chinantec. Examples of human and of nonhuman animate recipients are given in (751) and (752), respectively.

(751) P   S   IO   DO
      ka^L-ʔïe^L cú^M pé^H cá^{M}mï^L ʔí^L
      PAST-show^DA^3   3   Peter   woman that^AN
      S/he presented that woman to Peter.

(752) P   S   IO   DO
      máᴹ lĩᴹ-kuḛᴸ   cúᴹ míᴴtieiᴹᴴ ciiᴸ θúʔᴴ
      PRF HOD-give^DA^3 3   cat   DIM grasshopper
      S/he just gave a grasshopper to the cat.

From (751), it can be seen that where either of the two object nominals could be the recipient, the order IO-DO establishes the first nominal as being the recipient. If the order of the nominals in (751) is reversed, the meaning is that Peter is presented to 'that woman'. In (752) there is only one meaning possible regardless of the order of the object nominals; however, the first object nominal is the more prominent or topical. Some ditransitive verbs inflected for the direct cross-referencing system appear to require a fixed order for the two object elements.

(753) a. DO obligatorily first
         P   S   DO   IO
         máᴹ náᴴ-ciĩᴹ   cúᴹ   séᴸᴹ ʔɲiuᴸmíᴴɲiíᴹ
         PRF PROG^P-remove^DA^S^3 3 Joseph jail
         They are removing Joseph from jail now.

      b. IO obligatorily first
         P   S   IO   DO   T
         ciä̈ᴸ   cúᴹ   ʔéiʔᴸᴹ   míᴹɲiíᴸ   caᴸʔáuᴹ
         put^DA^FUT^3 3   measure pig   tomorrow
         S/he will weigh the pig tomorrow.

The order of the DO and IO, however, appears to be quite flexible for many ditransitive verbs. Generally, the first object nominal is the more prominent or contrastive, depending on the context.

(754) a. P   S   IO   DO
         kaᴸ-maᴸkóʔᴸᴹ   cúᴹ   hmĩᴹhmaᴸ   ceᴸ
         PAST-fill^DI^3   3   potable^water   jar
         S/he filled the jar with water.

      b. P   S   DO   IO
         kaᴸ-maᴸkóʔᴸᴹ   cúᴹ   ceᴸ hmĩᴹhmaᴸ
         PAST-fill^DI^3   3   jar potable^water
         S/he filled the jar with water.

(755) a. P   S   IO   DO
         tĩᴹ hiéiʔᴸᴹ   cúᴹ   hmáïᴹ   cáᴹ   cáuᴴ
         DISC spray^DA^PRES^3 3   water   person   sick
         They used to spray water on sick people.

b. P   S   DO   IO
   tí^M   hiéi?^LM   cú^M cá^M   cáu^H hmái^M
   DISC spray^DA^PRES^3 3   person sick   water
   They used to spray sick people with water.

When ditransitive verbs which take a recipient are inflected for the inverse system, four possible orders of the core arguments are found: P-S-IO-DO, P-S-DO-IO, P-DO-S-IO, and P-IO-S-DO. If the DO of such verbs is inanimate, the verb is indexed for the inanimate DO and for direct/inverse cross-referencing of the IO; however, if the DO of such verbs is animate, the verb is indexed for the animate DO and for direct/inverse cross-referencing of the DO, but not for the cross-referencing of the IO. Nonetheless, when the DO is animate, the permutational possibilities are dependent on the cross-referencing of the IO. Each of the above possibilities is illustrated in turn below.

If the verb is inflected for an inanimate DO and animate-inverse IO, the order of sentence elements may be either P-S-IO-DO or P-IO-S-DO.

(756) a. P   S   IO   DO
          ?ié^LM   cú^M   hná^HL sií^M
          show^DI^FUT^3>1   3   I   book
          S/he will show me the book.

       b. P   IO   S   DO
          ?ié^LM   hná^HL cú^M   sií^M
          show^DI^FUT^3>1   I   3   book
          S/he will show me the book.

If, however, the verb is inflected for an inanimate DO and animate-direct IO, the order of sentence elements is fixed.

(757) a. P   S   IO   DO
          ?ie^H   hná^HL cú^M   sií^M
          show^DI^FUT^1s   I   3   book
          I will show him the book.

       b. P   IO   S   DO
          *?ie^H   cú^M   hná^HL sií^M
          show^DI^FUT^1s   3   I   book
          I will show him the book.

c. P   S   DO   IO
   *ʔieʰ   hná^{HL} sií^M cú^M
   show^DI^FUT^1S   I   book   3
   I will show him the book.

When the verb is inflected for an animate-direct DO, and there is an animate-inverse IO, three options are possible: P-S-IO-DO, P-IO-S-DO, and P-S-DO-IO, the third option being the least common.

(758) a. P   S   IO   DO
         ʔïe^L cú^M hná^{HL} cí^{M}mí$ʔ^H$
         show^TA^FUT^3 3   I   puppy
         S/he will show me the puppy.

      b. P   IO   S   DO
         ʔïe^L hná^{HL} cú^M cí^{M}mí$ʔ^H$
         show^TA^FUT^3 I   3   puppy
         S/he will show me the puppy.

      c. P   S   DO   IO
         ʔïe^L cú^M cí^{M}mí$ʔ^H$ hná^{HL}
         show^TA^FUT^3 3   puppy   I
         S/he will show me the puppy.

When the verb is inflected for an animate-inverse DO and there is an animate-direct IO, three options are again possible: P-S-DO-IO, P-DO-S-IO, and P-S-IO-DO, with the third option being the least common.

(759) a. P   S   DO   IO
         ʔïe^L cú^M hná^{HL} tï^{LM}
         show^TA^FUT^3>1   3   I   teacher
         S/he will introduce me (to) the teacher.

      b. P   DO   S   IO
         ʔïe^L hná^{HL} cú^M tï^{LM}
         show^TA^FUT^3>1   I   3   teacher
         S/he will introduce me (to) the teacher.

      c. P   S   IO   DO
         ʔïe^L cú^M tï^{LM} hná^{HL}
         show^TA^FUT^3>1   3   teacher   I
         S/he will introduce me (to) the teacher.

The Clause   249

In contrast, when the DO is animate-direct and the IO is a pronoun which is animate-direct, only the order P-S-IO-DO is possible.

(760) a. P   S   IO   DO
          ʔĩe^{MH} hná^{HL} cú^M ti^{LM}
          show^TA^FUT^1S I   3   teacher
          I will introduce the teacher (to) her/him.

       b. P   S   IO   DO
          ʔĩe^{MH} hná^{HL} cú^M cĩ^{M}mí̃ʔ^H
          show^TA^FUT^1S I   3   puppy
          I will show her/him the puppy.

       c. P   IO   S   DO
          *ʔĩe^{MH} cú^M hná^{HL} cĩ^{M}mí̃ʔ^H
          show^TA^FUT^1S I   3   puppy
          I will show her/him the puppy.

       d. P   S   DO   IO
          *ʔĩe^{MH} hná^{HL} cĩ^{M}mí̃ʔ^H cú^M
          show^TA^FUT^1S I   puppy 3
          I will show her/him the puppy.

In (760a–b), it can be seen that the third-person pronoun cú^M is identified as the IO regardless of the degree of animacy of the DO (human versus animal); if two noun phrases are used for the DO and IO, however, the sentence is slightly ambiguous when out of context. In (761), the first option is the more likely interpretation. Reversing the order of cá^M ʔí^L 'that person' and ti^{LM} 'teacher' is also slightly ambiguous.

(761) ʔĩe^{MH} hná^{HL} cá^M ʔí^L ti^{LM}
       show^TA^FUT^1S I   person that^AN teacher
       I will introduce the teacher (to) that person. *or* I will introduce that person (to) the teacher.

One final factor which influences the order of the object elements is their relative complexity; generally, the less complex one will be positioned closer to the verb. So long as the complexity of the DO or IO is not too great, however, the factors of prominence or contrastiveness take precedence.

(762) a. P   S   IO   DO
       ka^L-ma^{L}kó$?^{LM}$ cú^M mi̱^{L} ká^{M}fe^{MH} tú^{M}cio^H ?mai̱^{MH} hǎu^M
       PAST-fill^DI^3 3   spherical coffee sack   new   that^IN
       S/he filled that new sack (with) coffee beans.

   b. P   S   DO   IO
      ka^L-ma^{L}kó$?^{LM}$ cú^M tú^{M}cio^H mi̱^{L} ká^{M}fe^{MH} ?i^L
      PAST-fill^DI^3 3   sack sphere coffee   COMP

      ka^L-li̱^{L} hli̱$?^{MH}$ ciáu^L
      PAST-happen^II wet^IN yesterday
      S/he filled the sack (with) coffee beans that had gotten wet
      yesterday.

Some verbs may be used either transitively or ditransitively with no change in the inflectional paradigm or the meaning. An example of a verb with two core and three core arguments, respectively, is given in (763).

(763) a. P   S   DO   L
       má^M dí^H-to$?^M$ cú^M má$?^L$ kuá^L ɲiéi$?^L$
       PRF stand^PROG-put^TI^P^PRES^3   3   squash chilacayote inside

       ?ɲiu^{L}kuî^L
       crib
       S/he is already putting the chilacayote squash in her/his (storage) crib.

   b. P   S   DO   IO
      má^M dí^H-to$?^M$ cú^M θié^L lái̱^{H} ?ái̱^{M}
      PRF stand^PROG-put^DI^P^PRES^3 3   noose neck^3   thief
      He is already putting the nooses around the thieves' necks.

For other verbs, a change in valence results in a change in the inflectional paradigm and/or the meaning (see Foris 1993:375).

8.3 Split-ergativity

Most of the ergative languages that are discussed in the literature utilize a dependent-marked system;[58] that is, the nominals are marked for case. Sochiapan Chinantec nominals are not marked for case; instead, a head-marked system is used, a type which Mallinson and Blake (1981:55, 71) refer to as an

---

[58]The terminology 'dependent-marked' and 'head-marked' is from Nichols (1986:57).

"ergative cross-referencing system"; Mayan and certain northwest Caucasian languages are also representative of this type.

Dixon (1987:3–5) discusses morphological ergativity, syntactic ergativity, and discourse ergativity. This section presents morphological accusativity and ergativity in Chinantec,[59] and briefly explores the possibility of syntactic ergativity.

Morphological accusativity. Chinantec is morphologically accusative in that verbs are indexed for person of subject regardless of transitivity, and IA, TI, and DI verbs are additionally indexed for second-person subject (though TA and DA verbs are not).

The accusative system is seen primarily in the way intransitive, transitive, and ditransitive verbs mark agreement with the person of their subject by a combination of tone and stress. This complex of suprasegmental features is a portmanteau morpheme, marking not only the person of the subject, but also several other inflectional parameters including motion, tense, and mood, as discussed in chapter 4. Thus, for example, the verb cii^M 'remove' (TI⌢s)[60] has the following forms for the four grammatical persons of a class A verb in the present tense.

(764)   3   2   1S   1P
       cii^M $cii{\textipa{?}}^{LM}$ cif^{ML} cii^{LM}

There are some tone-stress paradigms which are unique to intransitive, transitive, and ditransitive verbs, respectively, and there is some correlation between various tone-stress paradigms and a verb's transitivity valence. There are, however, numerous examples of verbs of differing valence which share the same tone-stress paradigm, so that it is apparent that a verb's valence is not the only factor which governs its paradigm. From (764), however, it is apparent that the tone-stress feature is at least marking the subject of the verb—transitive or intransitive—thus following an accusative system.

In addition to indexing of the verb for the person of its subject by tone-stress inflection, certain types of class A and B verbs are indexed for second-person subject by closure of the final syllable with a glottal stop; see (764) above and (765)–(766) below. Class C verbs, apart from a few irregular verbs, use the third-person inflectional form for all grammatical persons and thus are generally not indexed for second person.

---

[59]In describing Comaltepec Chinantec, Anderson states: "as regards the inflection of verbs, an ergative system of agreement exists" (1989:18). The description given by Robbins (1968) for Quiotepec Chinantec, Merrifield (1968) for Palantla Chinantec, and Rupp (1989) for Lealao Chinantec all mention the same system of agreement noted by Anderson and discussed here, but without identifying it as ergative.

[60]The citation form for verbs is the third-person present tense, unless otherwise indicated.

The presence of inherent glottal closure[61] of the syllable masks this indexing; for example, *lauʔ^{LM}* 'bathe (IA)' in (765) and *kúʔ^M* 'eat (TI)' in (766). The classification of glottal closure as inherent or morphemic is determined simply by comparing the 2-PRES form with the citation form, the 3-PRES; if glottal closure of the final syllable is absent in the 3-PRES, then glottal closure for second person is morphemic.

(765)   Examples of IA verbs in the present tense

	sneeze	escape	boast	bathe
3	kué^{ML}	kuõ^M	má^{M}ráu^L	lauʔ^{LM}
2	kuéʔ^{ML}	kuõuʔ^{LM}	má^{M}ráuʔ^{HL}	láuʔ^{ML}
1S	kué^{ML}	kuõ^M	má^{M}ráu^{HL}	lauʔ^{LM}
1P	kué^{ML}	kuõu^{LM}	má^{M}ráu^{HL}	láuʔ^{ML}

(766)   Examples of TI verbs in the present tense

	dispose	throw	clean	eat
3	kuí^{ML}	tó^{LM}	θi^{LM}	kúʔ^M
2	kuíʔ^{ML}	tãuʔ^{LM}	θɨʔ^{ML}	kuʔ^{LM}
1S	kuí^{ML}	tõ^M	θi^{LM}	kuʔ^{LM}
1P	kuí^{ML}	tãu^{LM}	θɨ^{ML}	kúʔ^{ML}

TA and DA verbs, whether inflected for direct or inverse cross-referencing, generally lack morphemic glottal closure, second person being indexed only by tone-stress, as in (767). There are, however, TA and DA verbs with inherent glottal, such as *θã́ʔ^{ML}* 'grab'.

(767)

	appoint	buy	toast	grab
3	ʔiṍ^{LM}	lã́^{ML}	tó^{LM}	θã́ʔ^{ML}
2	ʔiõ^{ML}	lã́^{ML}	tõ^{ML}	θã́ʔ^{ML}
1S	ʔiṍ^{LM}	lã^{LM}	tõ^M	θã^{LM}
1P	ʔiõ^{ML}	lã^{ML}	tõ^{ML}	θã^{ML}

There is a strong tendency to use morphemic glottal to index IA, TI, and DI verbs for second-person subject (77% of 164 verbs without inherent glottal),

---

[61]Both glottal closure of the syllable and nasalization of the syllable nucleus can be either inherent or morphemic. Lexemes contrast by the presence or absence of the glottal phoneme syllable final, and/or nasalization of the nucleus. Examples of minimal pairs are: *ha^{LM}* 'spider', *haʔ^{LM}* 'fist', *hã^{LM}* 'ice', and *hãʔ^{LM}* 'move over (IA)'.

The Clause   253

whereas in TA and DA verbs the lack of morphemic glottal is almost absolute. Thus, the accusative system of indexing verbs for second-person subject shows a split pattern: verbs with an animate object have a neutral system of indexing for second person (that is, neither accusative nor ergative), whereas IA, TI, and DI verbs exhibit accusative indexing for second person.

Morphological ergativity. Chinantec is morphologically ergative in the way verbs are indexed for animacy of the subject and DO, and in the way a few verbs inflect for number (singular versus plural) of the subject and the DO by the use of suppletive forms.

It is necessary to distinguish two subtypes of third person in Chinantec: the third-person proximate (3) and third-person obviative (3^i), where the former is higher on the animacy hierarchy. For Chinantec, the term proximate generally refers to the third-person participant first established as subject in a series of clauses, and obviative refers to the next third-person participant introduced, usually as object, the only exception being when the obviative is inanimate.

In the first of a series of clauses involving two third-person animate participants, only the direct system can occur. If the grammatical relations of the two noun phrases remain the same in successive clauses, then the direct system is used; but if the grammatical relations are switched, then the inverse system is used. The direct and inverse systems are discussed in detail in §8.4.

The inverse system is indicated in examples by the use of an arrow, where the agent is shown to the left of the arrow and the patient is shown to the right; for example, $1S > 2$ means the subject is first-person singular and the DO is second-person; $3^i > 3$ means the subject is third-person obviative and the DO is third-person proximate.

The direct system participants are not indicated in examples since DO is invariably third person. Examples of two third-person participants with the verb $pã^{ML}$ 'hit' inflected for the direct and inverse systems, respectively, are given in (768) and (769). In both examples 'Mary' is the subject and 'Peter' the object in the first clause; the coreferentiality of the third-person pronoun $cú^M$ in the second clause, however, depends on whether the direct or inverse system is being used.

(768) ka^L-$hĩ^L$ $má^M réi^L$ $pé^H$ $ti^L la^L$ $tiá^M$ ka^L-$pã^L$ $iá$ʔ^L $cú^M$
        PAST-scold^TA^3 Mary   Peter but   not PAST-hit^TA^3 ASSR 3
        Mary scolded Peter, but she didn't hit him.

(769) ka^L-$hĩ^L$ $má^M réi^L$ $pé^H$ $ti^L la^L$ $tiá^M$ ka^L-po^L $iá$ʔ^L
        PAST-scold^TA^3 Mary   Peter but   not PAST-hit^TA^3^i > 3 ASSR

       cúᴹ
        3
Mary scolded Peter, but he didn't hit her.

Agreement for animacy operates on an ergative pattern. Intransitive verbs are indexed for animacy of the subject, and transitive/ditransitive verbs are indexed for animacy of third-person DO. In both instances, the indexing for animate S/O consists of nasalization of the nucleus. In the case of third-person subject and third-person DO, the verb is indexed by nasalization only for an animate third-person obviative.

When DO is first or second person, or third-person proximate (that is, the verb is inflected for inverse cross-referencing), the verb is not indexed for animate DO by nasalization, although the person of the DO is marked by the inverse inflection.

Thus, although the direct cross-referencing system of verbs is ergative, the inverse cross-referencing system is morphologically neutral (neither ergative nor accusative); that is, there is no specific marker on the verb for an animate subject or DO, and the cross-referencing system, therefore, exhibits split-ergativity. Dixon remarks, "...absolutive is the unmarked case from an absolutive-ergative system. (I know of no exceptions to this.)" (1987:2). In Chinantec, however, the absolutive S/O is marked by nasalization, while A (transitive subject) has no overt marking. Chinantec, then, offers a counter-example to Dixon's generalization.

Examples of intransitive, transitive, and ditransitive verbs with their inanimate and animate counterparts, respectively, are given in (770)–(772).

(770) a. *súʔᴸᴹ*   *muᴹᴴ ʔmáᴹ*
         fall^down^II^FUT^3P leaf^3 tree
         The tree's leaves will fall (down).

      b. *sũʔᴸ*   *ciiᴸmaʔᴹ*
         fall^down^IA^FUT^3P ant
         The ants will fall down.

(771) a. *súʔᴸ*   *cúᴹ ʔiúʔᴹ ʔẽᴹ*
         cause^fall^TI^P^FUT^3 3   seed chili
         S/he will shake out (the) chili seeds.

      b. *sũʔᴸ*   *cúᴹ ciiᴸmaʔᴹ*
         cause^fall^TA^P^FUT^3 3   ant
         S/he will shake off (the) ants.

(772) a. θió?ᴹᴸ   cúᴹ taᴸ   mïᴸ   láuᴹ
         kick^DI^PRES^3 3   foot^3 spherical skin
         S/he kicks the ball (with) her/his foot.

   b. θió?ᴸᴹ   cúᴹ cáïᴹ   taᴸ
         kick^DA^PRES^3 3   dog   foot^3
         S/he kicks the dog (with) her/his foot.

There are inflectionally related TI and TA verbs in which the animate DO is marked on the TA verb by both nasalization and vocalic change as in (773); however, no examples of inflectionally related II and IA verbs have been found where an animate subject is marked by both features.

(773) a. lauᴴᴸ   cúᴹ tiúᴸ
         buy^used^TI^FUT^3 3   rifle
         S/he will buy a used (formerly purchased) rifle.

   b. lṍᴸᴹ   cúᴹ caᴸkuáᴴ
         buy^used^TA^FUT^3 3   horse
         S/he will buy a formerly purchased horse.

Verbs that are inherently nasalized generally mark agreement for animate S/O by vocalic change and a change in the tone-stress paradigm. Examples of intransitive and transitive verbs are shown in (774) and (775).

(774) a. θä́ïᴹᴸ   kuá?ᴴᴸ
         slip^II^PRES soil
         (The) soil slips (a landslide).

   b. θũᴹ   cúᴹ
         slip^IA^PRES^3 3
         S/he slips.

(775) a. ?uïᴹ   cúᴹ kuúᴹ ne?ᴴᴸ
         peel^TI^PRES^3 3   maize shucks
         S/he peels off the maize shucks.

   b. ?uṍuᴸᴹ   cúᴹ míᴹŋiïᴸ
         peel^TA^PRES^3 3   pig
         S/he skins (the) pig(s).

In summary, regarding agreement as to animacy, indexing of the verb nucleus for animate S/O by nasalization is the norm and inherent nasalization tends not to occur in TA and DA verbs. Split-ergativity occurs on the basis of the animacy hierarchy: verbs inflected for direct cross-referencing are indexed for animate DO, verbs inflected for inverse cross-referencing are not, in which case the indexing is neutral, not accusative.

In Chinantec, there is a limited system of agreement on verbs as to number of S/O. The most common type of verb with an animate subject exhibits a four-way contrast of person: third person, second person, first-person singular, and first-person plural. There are II and IA verbs that have suppletive stems[62] for singular and plural persons, however, resulting in a six-way contrast. For example, the verb $ta?^{LM}$ 'fall' inflected for the present tense has the forms in (776).

(776)   3S   3P
        $ta?^{LM}$ $su?^{LM}$ fall (II)

The majority of IA verbs that have suppletive stems for singular and plural are class C. The singular stem may also be used for the plural, but the plural stem can never be used for the singular. If the speaker uses the singular stem, the individuals are seen as acting independently; if the plural stem is used, the individuals are seen as acting corporately. Generally, the nucleus of the 1P stem differs from that of the 2P/3P. A single tone-stress paradigm pertains to all singular forms, and a different tone-stress paradigm to all plural forms. For example, the verbs $t\tilde{a}?^{LM}/s\tilde{u}?^{ML}$ 'fall' and $h\tilde{u}^{ML}/c\tilde{a}^{M}$ 'die' inflected for the present tense are shown in (777).

(777)   Singular (or plural)   1P   2P/3P
        $t\tilde{a}?^{LM}$ $sau?^{ML}$ $s\tilde{u}?^{ML}$ fall
        $h\tilde{u}^{ML}$ cau^{M} $c\tilde{a}^{M}$ die

Sentential examples based on the singular and plural stems of the verb 'die' in (777) are seen in (778) and (779).

(778) ka^{L}-$h\tilde{u}^{L}$ $c\acute{u}^{M}\ hm\acute{\i}^{fH}$ ka^{L}-$l\ddot{\i}^{L}$ $c\acute{a}u^{H}$
        PAST-die^IA^3S   3   when^PAST PAST-become^II sick
        S/he died when s/he became sick.

(779) ka^{L}-$c\tilde{a}^{L}$ $c\acute{u}^{M}\ hm\acute{\i}^{fH}$ ka^{L}-$l\ddot{\i}^{L}$ $c\acute{a}u^{H}$
        PAST-die^IA^3P   3   when^PAST PAST-become^II sick
        They died when they became sick.

Transitive and ditransitive verbs that are indexed for the number of their object exhibit suppletive stems for singular and plural, and a maximum of a

---

[62]The term 'stem' refers only to the segmental elements, not the tone-stress.

The Clause 257

four-way contrast of subject persons. Example (780) is inflected for the present tense.

(780) *ciĩ*ᴹ   remove (DA^S)
       *ʔuẽ*ᴹ remove (DA^P)

	3	2	1S	1P
Singular object	*ciĩ*ᴹ	*ciĩ*ᴹᴸ	*ciĩ*ᴸᴹ	*ciĩ*ᴹᴸ
Plural object	*ʔuẽ*ᴹ	*ʔuẽ*ᴹᴸ	*ʔuẽ*ᴹ	*ʔuẽ*ᴹᴸ

Sentential examples based on the singular and plural stems, respectively, of the verb 'remove' in (780) are given in (781) and (782).

(781) *má*ᴹ *lĩ*ᴹ-*ciĩ*ᴹ   *cú*ᴹ *cá*ᴹ   *cõ*ᴸ   *ʔŋiu*ᴸ*mí*ᴴ*ŋii*ᴹ
       PRF   HOD-remove^DA^S^3 3   person prisoner jail
       S/he has just removed the prisoner (from) jail.

(782) *má*ᴹ *lĩ*ᴹ-*ʔuẽ*ᴸ   *cú*ᴹ *cá*ᴹ   *cõ*ᴸ   *ʔŋiu*ᴸ*mí*ᴴ*ŋii*ᴹ
       PRF   HOD-remove^DA^P^3 3   person prisoner jail
       S/he has just removed the prisoners (from) jail.

Co-occurrence of ergative and accusative systems. This section discusses the effect that accusative and ergative verb indexing have on each other, specifically the accusative indexing for a second-person subject and the ergative indexing for an animate S/O.

In the accusative system, if an IA, TI, or DI verb does not have inherent glottal closure on its final syllable, then glottal closure of the final syllable functions morphemically, indexing the verb for a second-person subject. TA and DA verbs are generally not indexed by glottal closure for second-person subject.

In the ergative system, the verb nucleus is generally nasalized to index an animate subject in IA verbs and an animate object in TA and DA verbs inflected for direct cross-referencing. Inverse cross-referencing TA and DA verbs are not indexed by nasalization for an animate DO.

In second person, direct cross-referencing animate verbs (TA and DA) are distinguished from inverse cross-referencing animate verbs; and both are distinguished from inanimate verbs (TI and DI) in the following manner: (1) direct cross-referencing animate verbs generally are not indexed for a second-person subject by morphemic glottal, but are indexed for an animate DO by nasalization of the nucleus; (2) inverse cross-referencing animate verbs are neither indexed for a second-person subject by morphemic glottal, nor an animate DO by nasalization of the nucleus; and (3) inanimate verbs, whether direct or inverse, are generally indexed for a second-person subject by morphemic glottal.

From charting the verbs in the corpus for this study, it appears that inherent nasalization of TI and DI verbs tends to interfere with the accusative system of indexing verbs for second person. However, morphemic nasalization of TA and DA verbs (ergative indexing) appears to be an almost total barrier to accusative indexing. Thus, ergative indexing of the verb for animacy appears to take precedence over accusative second-person indexing, and even inherent nasalization tends to interfere with accusative indexing.

Syntactic accusativity and ergativity. With respect to syntactic ergativity, Klaiman remarks that: "Relatively few languages behave ergatively at the level of syntax; those which do also exhibit ergative behavior at the level of morphology. In the majority of languages, ergativity exists exclusively at the level of morphology" (1987:61).

Because of Chinantec's head-marking system, when a nominal is omitted its grammatical person is still marked on the verb. The only constructions in which ambiguity is possible is when there are two third-person participants. For example, (783) is interpreted according to an accusative syntactic pattern, but in (784) and (785) the interpretation tends towards an ergative syntax. The native speaker reaction is that the animal which is bitten would be more likely to run away; however, my personal reaction to the English equivalent would follow accusative syntax; that is, I would equate the subject in both (784) and (785) with the subject of the second clause.

(783) $ka^L\text{-}hie^{LM}$ $cái^M$ $mí^Htiei^{MH}$ $hãu^M$ $ka^L\text{-}kuóu^L$
   PAST-see^TA^3 dog cat   then   PAST-run^IA^3
   The dog saw the cat, then ran away (the dog ran).

(784) $ka^L\text{-}kũ?^M$ $cái^M$ $mí^Htiei^{MH}$ $hãu^M$ $ka^L\text{-}kuóu^L$
   PAST-bite^TA^3 dog cat   then   PAST-run^IA^3
   The dog bit the cat, then ran away (the cat/(dog) ran).

(785) $ka^L\text{-}kũ?^M$ $mí^Htiei^{MH}$ $cái^M$ $hãu^M$ $ka^L\text{-}kuóu^L$
   PAST-bite^TA^3 cat   dog   then   PAST-run^IA^3
   The cat bit the dog, then ran away (the dog/(cat) ran).

If the subject and DO participants occur in a subordinate clause, such as in (786), the identification of the subject in the main clause is ambiguous. In (786), there is a slight preference to identify the subject of the subordinate clause (Peter) with the omitted subject of the main clause; the alternative interpretation is quite acceptable, however.

(786) $hmí^H$ $ka^L\text{-}hí^L$ $pé^H$ $má^Mréi^L$ $ŋa?^L$
   when^PAST PAST-scold^TA^3 Peter Mary   go^home^PAST^IA^3S

The Clause   259

?ɲiúHL
house^3
When Peter had scolded Mary, (Peter/Mary) went home.

From (783)–(785) it appears that Chinantec syntax is accusative unless the choice of verb and arguments and/or the speaker's worldview results in what superficially appears to be ergative syntax. This area of Chinantec syntax merits further research.

8.4 Direct and inverse cross-referencing

Direct and inverse cross-referencing applies only to transitive and ditransitive verbs. The direct and inverse systems can be expressed by the following hierarchies.

(787) Person hierarchy   1, 2 > 3 > 3^i
       Animacy hierarchy   animate > inanimate

In other words, if the subject is higher on the hierarchy than the DO, the direct system is used; the inverse system is used elsewhere.

In the direct system, first person (1), second person (2), or third-person proximate (3) function as the subject argument of the verb, and the third-person obviative (3^i) is the DO argument. A 3 can only be inanimate if 3^i is inanimate; if 3 is animate, 3^i can be either animate or inanimate. In other words, for a verb to be inflected for the direct system, the DO must be third person, either inanimate or animate.

In the inverse system, on the other hand, the subject is equal to or lower than the DO in the hierarchy. When 1 and 2 co-occur, regardless of which is subject or object, the verb is inflected for the inverse system. Generally, both participants in the inverse system are animate, although the subject can be inanimate. If 3^i is the subject, then 1, 2, or 3 may be the DO. A verb inflected for the direct system is usually indexed for second-person subject by glottal closure of the verb nucleus, and for animate DO by nasalization of the nucleus. In comparison, a verb inflected for the inverse system generally exhibits the following features.

1. Lack of indexing of the verb for a second-person subject by means of glottal closure of the final syllable. (Inherent glottal closure is, of course, not affected.)

2. Lack of indexing of the verb for animate DO; that is, if the direct form of the verb has morphemic nasalization, the inverse form will not. (However, inherent nasalization is not affected.)

3. The nucleus of the inverse form frequently differs from that of the direct form of the verb.

Inflection for person-of-subject and person-of-object in the inverse cross-referencing system. The direct and inverse cross-referencing systems are alike in the way they differentiate grammatical persons for class A, B, and C verbs. All class A, B, and C verbs inflected for the direct system invariably have third person as DO. The inverse system, however, references the person of the subject and the object for class A, B, and C verbs in the following manner.

(788) Inverse cross-referencing, class A verbs

third-person obviative subject (3^i)	with third-person proximate (3), second person, or first-person DO
second-person subject	with first-person DO
first-person singular subject	with second-person DO
first-person plural subject	with second-person DO

(789) Inverse cross-referencing, class B verbs

third-person obviative subject (3^i)	with third-person proximate (3), or nonthird-person DO
nonthird-person subject	with nonthird-person DO

(790) Inverse cross-referencing, class C verbs

third-person obviative
subject (3^i)
or nonthird-person subject   > with <   third-person proximate (3),
                                           or nonthird-person DO

In (789) and (790), the nonthird-person subject and nonthird-person DO must not be the same person; nor can 1SG and 1PL ever co-occur as subject and DO. If subject and DO are the same person, the construction is either reflexive or reciprocal; and the form of the verb more closely resembles that of the direct system, but with a different tone-stress paradigm.

Of the eighty-three verbs inflected for the inverse system in the corpus, four patterns emerge: (1) 34 percent exhibit the same tone-stress paradigm as occurs on their direct counterpart; (2) 36 percent exhibit a paradigmatic difference between the direct and inverse tone-stress paradigms only in the 2-PAST; (3) in 18 percent of the verbs, the differences between the direct and inverse tone-stress paradigms range from slight to total dissimilarity in all persons; and (4) in 12 percent of the verbs, the inverse form is indistinguishable from the direct form in all respects. Note that tone-stress difference and vocalic difference are independent features, so even though inflectionally

The Clause   261

related verbs may share identical tone-stress paradigms, they may have different nuclei.

All known verbs which do not differentiate between the direct and inverse system are inherently nasalized, which means the indexing of the TA or DA verb for animate DO is masked by the inherent nasalization, and this nasalization persists with the inverse paradigm. However, inherent nasalization of a verb does not entail identical direct and inverse forms; verbs that are inherently nasalized may distinguish between the direct and inverse forms by vocalic change and/or tone-stress paradigm differences. For example: *ʔmïʔ^{ML}* (TA)/*ʔmaʔ^{ML}* (TAI) 'scratch', *ʔnaʔ^M* (TA)/*ʔnauʔ^M* (TAI) 'search for', and *hã^M* (TA)/*hãu^M* (TAI) 'wait for'.

Comparative examples of the direct and inverse systems, respectively, are given in (791)–(795).

(791) a. *ʔïˆ^L*   *cú^M cá^{M}ʔɲiú^{HL}*
         count^TA^FUT^3 3   inhabitant
         They will count the inhabitants.

      b. *ʔa^L*   *cú^M tï̂^{M} hnoʔ^H*
         count^TA^FUT^3>1 3   first   us
         They will count us first.

(792) a. *ka^L-ʔïʔ^{LM}*   *ʔnú^M cú^M*
         PAST-penetrate^TA^2 you^s 3
         You stabbed her/him.

      b. *ka^L-ʔaʔ^L*   *ʔnú^M cú^M*
         PAST-penetrate^TA^3>2 you^s 3
         S/he stabbed you.

(793) a. *lï̂^{M} pã^L cú^M*
         PROH hit^TA^FUT^2 3
         Don't hit her/him.

      b. *lï̂^{M} po^L hná^{HL}*
         PROH hit^TA^FUT^2>1 I
         Don't hit me.

(794) a. *má^M hɲïʔ^{MH} hná^{HL} cú^M*
         PRF kill^TA^FUT^1s I   3
         I am about to kill her/him.

b. má^M hŋaï?^{MH} hná^{HL} ?nú^M
   PRF kill^TA^FUT^1S>2 I   you^s
   I am about to kill you.

(795) a. ka^L-?ē^{HL} hno?^{H} cú^M ré^M
         PAST-receive^TA^1P we   3   well
         We received her/him well.

    b. ka^L-?e^{HL} hno?^{H} ?no?^{M} ré^M
       PAST-receive^TA^1P>2 we   you^P   well
       We received you well.

Examples involving the third-person proximate and third-person obviative are more complex. A discourse cannot begin with an animate third-person obviative. If the first of two third-person participants to be identified is coreferential with the subject in any successive transitive clause, the direct system is used. If, however, the second third-person participant to be identified is the subject in a subsequent clause where the first third-person participant to be identified is the DO, the inverse system is used. In the gloss of (796), the following notations are used: $_d$ stands for direct inflection, $_i$ stands for inverse inflection, $_p$ stands for proximate, and $_o$ stands for obviative.

(796) hau^L ka^L-kuē^L pé^H tu^{MH} ca^{L}kuá^H ho?^{H}
      two^days^ago PAST-give^DA^3 Peter   Tony   horse   have^STA^3

          háu^M ciáu^L ka^L-θáï^L tu^{MH} ?i^L tiá^M ré^M
          then   yesterday PAST-tell^DI^3^i>3 Tony   COMP   not   well

          hmu^M há?^{L} ta^{MH} háu^M ka^L-θáï?^{L} cú^M tu^{MH}
          do^TI^PRES^3 animal work   then   PAST-tell^DI^3   3   Tony

          ?i^L ?liá^M hmí^H cáu^H bí?^{H} há?^{L} háu^M ku^{L}ca^{LM}
          COMP   because TRM   sick   AFF   animal   then   promptly

          ka^L-he^L bí?^{H} cú^M tu^{MH}
          PAST-scold^TA^3^i>3 AFF   3   Tony

Two days ago Peter$_p$ loaned$_d$ Tony$_o$ his horse; then yesterday Tony$_o$ told$_i$ (him$_p$) that the horse was not working well. So he$_p$ told$_d$ Tony$_o$ that it is because the animal had been sick. Then Tony$_o$ promptly scolded$_i$ him$_p$.

To further illustrate the tracking of participants by means of the direct and inverse systems, the direct cross-referencing form of the verb 'scold' can be substituted in the last sentence of (796) for the inverse cross-referencing form, which results in a switch of the S and O participant; see (797).

(797) háu^M ku^{L}ca^{LM} ka^L-hi̭^{L} bi̭ʔ^H cú^M tu^{MH}
then promptly PAST-scold^TA^3 AFF 3 Tony
Then he$_p$ promptly scolded$_d$ Tony$_o$.

In (798) the third-person proximate is introduced in an intransitive clause. The verb of the second clause is inflected for the inverse system, indicating that the subject of the first clause is the DO of the second clause. If the DO is omitted (as it normally would be), it is recoverable by means of the verbal inflection.

(798) ka^{L}la^L ɲi̭^{H} ka^L-hū^L má̭ʔ^L cú^M ka^L-po^L (cú^M) cáu^M
even^to place PAST-die^IA^3 EXCL 3 PAST-hit^3^i>3 3 people
(Some) people beat her/him to death.

In addition to direct and inverse cross-referencing,[63] Chinantec also makes use of the third-person pronouns cú^M and di̭^{M} for tracking two third-person participants; see the next section.

Generally, ditransitive verbs are indexed for the animacy of the DO, but not for the animacy (and/or person) of the IO. A few verbs, however, have been identified such as hi̭eʔ^{ML} 'return, give back (DI)', kueʔ^{LM} 'give (DI)', and ʔieʔ^{LM} 'show (DI)' which, when indexed for an inanimate direct object, are also indexed for the person of the indirect object. All such verbs encode a recipient IO. In theory, six combinations of animacy and person are possible.

(799) Combinations of DO and IO based on animacy and person

	Direct object	Indirect object
a.	inanimate	third-person
b.	inanimate	nonthird-person
c.	animate third-person	third-person
d.	animate third-person	nonthird-person
e.	nonthird-person	third-person
f.	nonthird-person	nonthird-person

---

[63]Merrifield (1968:48) makes a brief reference to inverse inflection in Palantla Chinantec. In Palantla, evidently, inverse cross-referencing is limited to a first-person DO versus a nonfirst-person DO. Westley (1991:25, 26) describes a similar feature in Tepetotutla Chinantec. Neither author uses the term inverse cross-referencing.

DO is inanimate that the person of the IO is indexed on the verb. As examples of patterns a and b, respectively, compare (800) and (801); note the difference in the verb inflection.

(800) P   S   IO   DO
       ka^L-ʔieʔ^L cú^M rãïʔ^{MH} mí^{H}hla^M kioʔ^{MH}
       PAST-show^DI^3 3   peer^3 knife   have^STI^3
       He showed his companions his knife.

(801) P   S   IO   DO
       ka^L-ʔie^L cú^M hná^{HL} mí^{H}hla^M kioʔ^{MH}
       PAST-show^DI^3>1 3   I   knife   have^STI^3
       He showed me his knife.

Patterns c and d are illustrated, respectively, by (802) and (803). Note in these two examples that, although the person of the IO differs in the manner of (800)–(801) above, there is no change in the verb inflection.

(802) P   S   IO   DO
       ka^L-ʔie^L cú^M pé^H ca^{L}kuá^H hoʔ^H
       PAST-show^DI^3   3   Peter horse   have^STA^3
       He showed Peter his horse.

(803) P   S   IO   DO
       ka^L-ʔie^L cú^M hná^{HL} ca^{L}kuá^H hoʔ^H
       PAST-show^DI^3   3   me   horse   have^STA^3
       He showed me his horse.

Patterns e and f are illustrated, respectively, by (804) and (805). Note that although the person of the IO differs in the manner of (800) and (801), there is no change in the verb inflection, as occurs there; nonetheless, the inflection differs from that of (802) and (803).

(804) P   S   DO   IO
       ka^L-ʔie^L cú^M hná^{HL} tï^{LM}
       PAST-show^DI^3>1 3   I   teacher
       He introduced me to the teacher.

(805) P   S   DO   IO
       ka^L-ʔie^L cú^M hná^{HL} ʔnú^M
       PAST-show^DI^3>1 3   you
       He introduced me to you.

The IO of most ditransitive verbs encodes instrumental case, a few encode locative case. All such verbs have a maximum of three inflectional forms, one for inanimate DO, one for animate DO inflected for the direct system, and one for animate DO inflected for the inverse system.

(806) P   S   IO   DO
      ka^L-sé^L cú^M hmáï^M lí^{HL}
      PAST-sprinkle^DI^3 3 water   flower
      S/he sprinkled the flowers with water.

(807) P   S   DO   IO
      ka^L-sé^{LM} cú^M hmáï^M rāï?^{MH}
      PAST-sprinkle^DA^3 3 water   companion^3
      S/he sprinkled her/his companion with water.

(808) P   S   DO   IO
      ka^L-sé^{LM} cú^M hná^{HL} hmáï^M
      PAST-sprinkle^DA^3>1 3 I   water
      S/he sprinkled me with water.

Tracking third-person proximate and third-person obviative participants with the pronouns cú^M and dí^M. Chinantec has three third-person pronouns, cú^M, dí^M, and di^{LM}. Syntactically, di^{LM} functions identically to dí^M, and is not discussed further in this section; its pragmatic function is discussed in §6.1.

cú^M is by far the most common third-person pronoun. When there are two or more third-person participants in a passage of discourse, dí^M is optionally used to mark the foregrounded (or more prominent) participant, while all other third-person participants are referred to by cú^M (or by other nominals such as proper nouns; or there may be ellipsis of the nominal if the context allows). When the verb is inflected for the direct system, dí^M is used to track the third-person proximate (see (809c)); but when the verb is inflected for the inverse system, dí^M is used to track the third-person obviative (see (810)).

When the speaker assumes (correctly or not) that there is no ambiguity in tracking the third-person participants, dí^M is dispensed with, and cú^M can be used for any third-person participant.

When the verb of the second clause is inflected for direct cross-referencing, dí^M is coreferential with the agent of the prior clause; see (809c). The two proper nouns in the final clause of (809a) may be replaced by the third-person pronoun cú^M, as shown in (809b). Or, more commonly, dí^M is used to track the third-person proximate, in which case cú^M functions as the third-person obviative, shown in (809c).

(809) a. *péʰ   kaᴸ-tḯʰ   kiõʔᴸ   poʰ*
Peter₁ PAST-fight^IA^3 accompany^STA^3 Paul₂

hmḯʰhắuᴹ kaᴸ-ʔliã̄ᴸ   péʰ poʰ
then^PAST PAST-push^TA^3 Peter₁ Paul₂
Peter₁ fought with Paul₂, then Peter₁ pushed Paul₂.

b. *hmḯʰhắuᴹ kaᴸ-ʔliã̄ᴸ   cúᴹ cúᴹ*
then^PAST PAST-push^TA^3 he₁ he₂
Peter₁ fought with Paul₂, then he₁ pushed him₂.

c. *hmḯʰhắuᴹ kaᴸ-ʔliã̄ᴸ   díᴹ cúᴹ*
then^PAST PAST-push^TA^3 he₁ he₂
Peter₁ fought with Paul₂, then he₁ pushed him₂.

When the verb of the second clause is inflected for inverse cross-referencing, *díᴹ* is coreferential with the patient of the prior clause.

(810) *péʰ   kaᴸ-tḯʰ   kiõʔᴸ   poʰ hmḯʰhắuᴹ*
Peter₁ PAST-fight^IA^3 accompany^STA^3 Paul₂ then^PAST

kaᴸ-ʔliauᴸ   díᴹ cúᴹ
PAST-push^TA^3ⁱ>3 he₂ he₁
Peter₁ fought with Paul₂, then he₂ (Paul) pushed him₁.

When the agent/subject of a subordinate clause is coreferential with the agent/subject of the matrix clause, *díᴹ* is used.

(811) *kaᴸ-θáïʔᴸ   cúᴹ cáᴹ ʔíᴸ laᴸ láᴹ hmḯʰ   máᴹ*
PAST-tell^DI^3 he₁ person₂ that^AN idea this when^PAST PRF

lḯᴹ-ciáᴸᴹ   díᴹ réᴹ kïeᴸ   kioʔᴹʰ   cúᴹ
HOD-place^TI^3 he₁ well money have^STI^3 he₂
He₁ gave that person₂ this advice when he₁ had prepared his₂ wages.

If *díᴹ* is substituted for *cúᴹ* in the clause *kïeᴸ kioʔᴹʰ cúᴹ* in (811), then it would be understood to mean: 'He₁ gave that person₂ this advice when he₁ had prepared his₁ (own) money'.

When *díᴹ* occurs in an embedded subordinate clause, it is coreferential with the agent/subject of the highest clause, which may or may not be the same as the agent/subject of the next higher subordinate clause in which it is embedded.

The Clause

(812) kíʰ   cáᴹ   hmuᴹ   ʔíᴸ   laᴸ   hāuᴹ   dáᴹ   ʔnióᴸ
      because person₁ doˆTIˆPRESˆ3 thatˆAN idea thatˆIN VER wantˆSTIˆ3

            COMP [COMP [
            híeᴸ   cáuᴹ   ʔiᴸ   ʔíᴸ   díᴹ
            seeˆTIˆFUT people₂   COMP thatˆAN he₁

                         ]]
            náʰ-máᴹʔīeᴹʰ
            PROGˆP-fastˆIAˆ3

People₁ who act that way want people₂ to see that they₁ are fasting.

An example of an oblique object marked by *dí*ᴹ that is coreferential with a prior subject is given in (813).

(813) hāuᴹ   cáᴹ   ʔíᴸ   ŋaʔᴸ   ʔiᴸ
      then person₁ that goˆhomeˆIAˆPASTˆ3S and

            kaᴸ-ŋiíʰ-ciáᴹ   tíᴸ   haʰ   huúᴹ laᴸ   kūᴸ
            PAST-ANDT-recountˆTIˆ3₁ at within town about only

            ʔíᴸ   máᴹ   líᴹ-hmuᴸ   hāuᴹ   hesús   ŋiíʰkõᴹ díᴹ
            COMP PRF HOD-doˆTIˆ3 thatˆIN Jesus₂ towards he₁

Then that person₁ went back home and recounted in town all about that which Jesus₂ had done to him₁.

In (813), if *dí*ᴹ is replaced by *cú*ᴹ, it becomes ambiguous as to whether Jesus had done something to the man who went back into town, or to some other third person: 'Then that person₁ went back home and recounted in town what Jesus₂ had done to him₁/₃'.

A possessor marked by *dí*ᴹ that is coreferential with a prior subject is seen in (814).

(814) hãᴹ   cáᴹ   faŕiseo   kaᴸ-teʔᴸ   hesús   ʔiᴸ
      oneˆAN person Pharisee₁ PAST-summonˆDAˆ3 Jesus₂ COMP

            caᴸ-hmúᴸ   máᴸᴹ   ʔŋiúʰᴸ   díᴹ
            ANDTˆFUT-doˆTIˆ3₂ food houseˆ3 he₁

A Pharisee₁ summoned Jesus₂ to come eat at his₁ house.

The third-person pronoun *dí*ᴹ tends to be used only while the speaker feels ambiguity may arise, or if the speaker desires to give special prominence to one third-person participant over the other, with *cú*ᴹ being used for the less prominent participant. The speaker may choose to use $cú^M$ rather than $dí^M$, however, when the factors of ambiguity or prominence are considered to be no longer relevant.

(815) ti^Lla^L $hmí^H_i$ ka^L-$ciá^L$ $cá^M$ $ʔí^L$ $cáu^{HL}$
but when^PAST PAST-recount^TI^3 person₁ that^AN crime^3

$cá^M$ $cõ^L$ $né^L$ $tiá^M$ ka^L-$ciá^L$ $iáʔ^L$ $dí^M$
person₂ suspect TOP not PAST-recount^TI^3 ASSR he₁

$cáu^{HL}$ $cú^M$ la^L $kũ^L$ $ʔi^L$ $hmí^H_i$ $lẽ^L$
crime^3 he₂ about only COMP TRM think^TI^PRES^IS

$hná^{HL}$ hmu^L $cú^M$
I do^TI^FUT^3 he₁

But when that person₁ recounted the suspect's₂ crime, he₁ did not recount as his₂ crime that which I had been thinking he₁ would.

In (815), note how the final instance of the pronoun $cú^M$ 'he' is coreferential with the prior $dí^M$ 'he', not the prior $cú^M$. Although the use of $dí^M$ would be grammatical in this (final) position, the speaker evidently feels that there is no longer any possible ambiguity, so discontinues the use of $dí^M$.

A further example of the way a speaker slides between the use of $dí^M$ and $cú^M$ for the same third-person referent is given in (816).

(816) $hmí^Hhã́u^M$ ka^L-$lḯ^{HL}$ $cú^M$ $ʔi^L$ $ma^Lcõ^{HL}$ hesús
then PAST-think^TI^3 they₁ COMP arrest^TA^FUT^3 Jesus₂

$kí^Hʔliá^M$ $má^M$ ka^L-li^L $cḯ^M$ $dí^M$ $ʔi^L$
because PRF PAST-occur^II^3 be^aware^STI^3 they₁ COMP

$hái^{HL}$ ka^L-$tḯ^H$ $ʔmóu^{LM}$ $bíʔ^H$ $dí^M$ $ʔi^L$ $má^M$
word PAST-concern^TA^3 themselves AFF they₁ COMP PRF

li^M-$hmú^L$ $cú^M$ $hã́u^M$ ti^Lla^L $hmí^H$
HOD-make^TI^3 he₂ that^IN but TRM

$huẽ́ʔ^M$ $bíʔ^H$ $cú^M$ $ŋií^Hkõ^M$ $cá^M$
be^afraid^TI^PRES^3 AFF they₁ before people₃

$ná^H$-$ŋíʔ^{LM}$ $ʔí^L$ $ʔi^L$ $hã́u^M$ $kã́u^M$ $lí^H$
PROG^P-gather^IA^3 that^AN₃ and then simply NON

The Clause

    ka^L-lió^{LM}   *bí?^{H} dí^M*   *cú^M*   *kú^{M}hue?^{LM}*   *?i^L*   *hãu^M*
    PAST-release^TA^3   AFF   they₁   him₂   in^preference   and then

    ha^{L}tã?^{MH}
    go^home^IA^3P₁

Then they₁ thought of arresting Jesus₂, because they₁ were aware that the illustration he₂ made was referring to them₁. But they₁ were afraid of those₃ gathered there, so instead they₁ just left him₂ alone and went₁ home.

In (816), note how the first third-person identified is referred to by the pronouns *cú^M*, *dí^M*, *dí^M*, *cú^M*, and *dí^M* in turn.

Inanimate subject cross-referencing. One question that arises from the hierarchy proposed above is: which cross-referencing system is used, direct or inverse, when the subject is inanimate and the DO is animate? The hierarchy predicts that the inverse system would be used. It appears, however, that there is more than one method for encoding such situations, the preferred method being by means of agented passives; see the next section. In the active voice, both the inverse system and the direct system are used.

  The inverse system can be used fairly productively to encode an inanimate subject and animate DO (as predicted by the hierarchy); the subject is regarded as having acquired animate status, however, and the utterance is considered to be slightly humorous, inappropriate to formal situations such as a court case or a town meeting. The inverse system can be employed without first establishing which participants are proximate and obviative.

(817)   *ka^L-hué?^{L}*   *hná^{HL}*   *ki^{L}θiú^L*   *kiõ^{MH}*
     PAST-frighten^TA^3ⁱ>₁   I   dream   have^STI^1S
     My dream frightened me.

(818)   *ka^L-?a?^{L}*   *cú^M*   *mi^{L}kïe^L*
     PAST-penetrate^TA^3ⁱ>3   3   needle
     The needle pricked him.

(819)   *ka^L-hŋa?^{L}*   *cú^M*   *tiú^L*   *kio?^{MH}*
     PAST-kill^TA^3ⁱ>3   3   gun   have^STI^3
     His gun killed him.

(820)   *ka^L-θãu?^{L}*   *cú^M*   *tiá^L*   *co^L*
     PAST-capture^TA^3ⁱ>3   3   firmly   sin
     Sin has gained a firm grip on her/him.

The direct system is not productive in encoding an inanimate subject and animate DO, but is restricted to a small set of verbs, such as 'sprinkle, suffocate, strike, splash, entangle, smear'. All such verbs are transitive and generally have ditransitive counterparts. They are obligatorily P-S-O if the DO is inanimate and obligatorily P-O-S if the DO is animate.

8.5 Passive constructions

There are two passive constructions, the conventional passive and the posture passive. Chinantec has mainly agentless passives; agented passives are restricted to inanimate agents. It also has impersonal passives; these are discussed in this section along with the function of the conventional passive and posture passive constructions, and the types of verbs which permit passivisation.

Both of the Chinantec passive constructions are morphological, not periphrastic. The passives are marked by prefixes, generally in combination with internal inflection (tone, stress, or vocalic change, or a combination thereof).

The more common of the two Sochiapan Chinantec passive constructions uses the directional prefixes, but since there is no longer any sense of direction or motion the term conventional passive (PASS) is used. The second passive construction uses the progressive prefixes; since the sense of posture implicit in the progressive prefixes is retained in this construction, it is called the posture passive (PPAS).

With both passive constructions there is internal inflection of the verb which generally results in a form whose tone-stress and/or nucleus is unrelated to any other form in the verb paradigm. The passive form does not undergo any internal inflection; person is specified by overt nominals without being indexed on the verb, and tense is indicated on the conventional passive by inflection of the passive prefix; the posture passive is found only in the past tense.

For example, the verb hli^{ML} 'cover, wrap up (DA)' exhibits vocalic change only in the passive inflection. The full paradigm is given in (821).

(821) $hl\tilde{i}^{ML}$ cover, wrap up (DA)

	3	2	1S	1P
PRES	hli^{ML}	hli^{ML}	hli^{LM}	hli^{ML}
FUT	hli^{L}	hli^{HL}	hli^{MH}	hli^{HL}
PAST	hli^{L}	hli^{LM}	hli^{LM}	FUT
AMB	hli^{H}	hli^{HL}	FUT	FUT
HORT	hli^{H}	XXX	FUT	FUT
EVID	hli^{H}	AMB	FUT	FUT

The Clause

	3	2	1S	1P
HOD	hlĩʔᴸ	PAST	PAST	FUT
DIR	hlĩʔᴸ	PAST	PAST	FUT
PROH	—	hlĩʔᴸ		
PASS	hláï̃ᴴ			
PPAS	hlãï̃ᴸᴹ			

The passive form of the verb usually resembles that of the direct system more than that of the inverse system; see (822) below and the examples in (823).

A few examples are set out in (822) of transitive and ditransitive verbs inflected for the present tense of the direct system, the directional form for the third-person direct and the third-person inverse, the conventional passive, and the posture passive. The directional forms are supplied to illustrate how the internal inflection of the verb generally disambiguates between direction and passive even though the prefixes are homophonous. Absence of a form is indicated by xxx; all TI verbs lack the inverse form.

(822) Comparison of direct and inverse forms with the passive forms

	Direct present	Direct direction	Inverse direction	Conven. passive	Posture passive
push (TI)	ʔliaᴸᴹ	ʔliáᴹ	xxx	ʔliáᴴ	ʔliáᴴ
push (TA)	ʔliãᴹ	ʔliãᴸ	ʔliauᴸ	ʔliã́ᴴ	ʔliã́ᴴ
join (TI)	ʔlióᴸᴹ	ʔlióᴸ	xxx	ʔlióᴴ	ʔliãuᴸᴹ
sew (TI)	ʔmḯᴸᴹ	ʔmḯᴹ	xxx	ʔmḯᴴ	ʔmḯᴸᴹ
roll (TI)	lĩʔᴹᴸ	lĩʔᴸᴹ	xxx	lĩʔᴸᴹ	lĩʔᴸᴹ
roll (TA)	lĩʔᴹᴸ	lĩʔᴸ	laʔᴸ	lĩʔᴸ	xxx
hit (TI)	páᴹᴸ	paᴸᴹ	xxx	páᴴ	páᴴ
hit (TA)	pã́ᴹᴸ	pãᴸ	poᴸ	pã́ᴴ	pã́ᴴ
call away (TA)	téʔᴹᴸ	tieʔᴴ	tiéᴹ	téᴴ	téᴴ
put in (TI^P)	toʔᴹ	tióʔᴸᴹ	xxx	toʔᴸ	tioʔᴴᴸ
put in (TA^P)	tóʔᴸᴹ	tiõʔᴸ	tiãuʔᴹ	xxx	tiã́uʔᴴ
splash (DI)	séᴹᴸ	séᴸ	xxx	séᴴ	séᴹᴸ
splash (DA)	sẽ́ᴸᴹ	sẽᴸ	seᴸ	sẽ́ᴴ	sẽᴸᴹ

As illustrated in (822), the two passive forms usually exhibit the same stem, although there are exceptions, such as the passives for 'join (TI)' and 'put in (TI^P)'; frequently the forms are identical in all respects. The passive form of TA and DA verbs are always indexed for an animate subject by nasalization. Most verbs which can be inflected for the passive are able to be used in either passive construction; however, some verbs such as 'roll (TA)' and 'put in (TA^P)' exhibit only one of the passive constructions. In (822), the verbs 'roll' illustrate those few verbs which do not differentiate inflectionally between the directional forms and the passive forms of the verb.

As illustrated in (823), the contrast between the direct and inverse systems is neutralized when a verb is inflected for the passive. Sentential examples of 'slash (TI)' and 'slash (TA)', with the latter inflected, respectively, for the direct and inverse systems (823b–c), and for the passive voice (823d–e), are:

(823) a. ka^L-$kie?^L$ $cú^M$ $nái^M$ $ka̱^{LM}$ hui^{iLM}
PAST-slash^TI^3 3   vegetation along trail
S/he cut down the weeds along the trail.

b. ka^L-$kiéi?^{LM}$ $cú^M$ po^H $?ú^H$ hui^{iLM}
PAST-slash^TA^3 3   Paul on trail
S/he slashed Paul on the trail.

c. ka^L-$kiéi?^{LM}$ $cú^M$ $hná^{HL}$ $?ú^H$ hui^{iLM}
PAST-slash^TA^3 >1 3   I on trail
S/he slashed me on the trail.

d. ka^L-ha^L-$kiéi?^H$ $cú^M$ $?ú^H$ hui^{iLM}
PAST-PASS-be^slashed^IA 3   on trail
S/he was slashed on the trail.

e. ka^L-ha^L-$kiéi?^H$ $hná^{HL}$ $?ú^H$ hui^{iLM}
PAST-PASS-be^slashed^IA I   on trail
I was slashed on the trail.

The TA verb 'slash' in (823b) is indexed for an animate subject by vocalic change and changes in the tone-stress with respect to the TI verb in (823a), and by nasalization. The nasalization also marks the TA verb as inflected for the direct system, whereas the TA verb 'slash' in (823c), which is inflected for the inverse system, lacks such nasalization. Comparing (823d–e) it can be seen that the passive forms of the verb 'slash' for both the direct and inverse system are identical.

The two passive constructions are discussed in turn below.

The conventional passive. According to Keenan (1985a:260), the use of a motion verb as an auxiliary to form the passive is rare. Chinantec does not use the motion verbs per se as auxiliaries; but, like the directional prefixes, the prefixes which mark the conventional passive have developed from the verbs of motion. The passive prefixes are given in (824).

The Clause 273

(824) PRES *cá^M*-
FUT *ca^L*-
HOD *há^M*-
PAST *ha^L*-

As can be seen in (824), the passive prefixes inflectionally distinguish between the hodiernal past and past, although the nature of this distinction is unlike the hodiernal past/remote past distinction discussed in chapter 4. The hodiernal past passive is the 'past of today'. The past passive, however, can be used for any past event, whether that of a moment ago, or any point further back in time; it is nonspecific past. The hodiernal passive appears to be used only when the speaker desires to specify that the situation occurred earlier today, or else to indicate that the action/event precedes another past event, but on the same day (that is, past in the past).

(825) *má^M há^M-kuĩʔ^{HL}   cú^M hmĩ^H*
PRF PASS^HOD-be^hurt^IA 3   when^PAST

ká^H-ció^{MH}   hná^{HL}
PAST-arrive^nonhome^IA^IS I
S/he was already hurt when I arrived.

The passive prefixes no longer convey any sense of motion despite their ultimate origin from verbs of motion and their phonological identity to the directional and progressive prefixes. Examples of the verb *ʔó^{LM}* 'bury (TA)' prefixed for future motion and the future passive, respectively, are given in (826). In (826a), the locative 'here' is ungrammatical, whereas in (826b), where no motion is implied, 'here' is grammatical. If the verb itself denotes motion as in (827), then it will continue to do so when inflected for the passive voice (as would be expected).

(826) a. *ca^L-ʔó^{LM}   cú^M ʔla^H   (*ŋif^H lá^M) ca^Lʔáu^M*
ANDT^FUT-bury^TA^3 3   corpse place this   tomorrow
They will go bury the corpse (*here) tomorrow.

b. *ca^L-ʔáu^L   ʔla^H   (ŋif^H lá^M) ca^Lʔáu^M*
PASS^FUT-be^buried^IA corpse place this   tomorrow
The corpse will be buried (here) tomorrow.

(827) *ʔi^L háu^M la^L   háu^M bíʔ^H ca^L-dé^{LM}*
and then way that AFF   PASS^FUT-be^washed^down^II

pí^L   kio?^MH   ?ué^LM
strength have^STI^3 earth
And so then in this way the earth's strength will be washed away.

Examples (826b) and (827) illustrate the future passive. Examples of the present passive, hodiernal passive, and past passive, respectively, are illustrated in (828)–(830).

(828) cá^M-?í^L   lí̃^LM bí?^H kië^L   ɲií^H uṍu?^L
       PRES^PASS-be^expended^II very AFF money place far
       It's expensive to live far away from home.

(829) má^M há^M-?liá^H   ?má^M kã̄^LM huï^LM
       PRF PASS^HOD-be^pushed^II tree   beside path
       The tree beside the path has (just) been pushed aside.

(830) ?ë^L   má?^L ha^L-uõ?^H   cái^M
       EXCM EXCL PASS^PAST-be^cut^IA dog
       The dog was cut terribly!

As mentioned above, neither the motion verbs, nor the past directional prefixes can occur with the hodiernal prefix lí^M-. When the motion verbs or directional prefixes are inflected for the past tense, they can be optionally prefixed with ka^L- (PAST). Similarly, the past passive prefix cannot occur with the hodiernal prefix lí^M-, but can be optionally prefixed with ka^L- (PAST). When ka^L- occurs with the past passive ha^L-, a past more remote than 'yesterday' is implied, although there is no specific time frame.

(831) hlá?^H ka^L-ha^L-?í?^H   tõ^M tã̄^LM hná^HL
       really PAST-PASS-be^penetrated^II thorn foot^IS I
       My foot was badly pricked with (a) thorn(s).

The past passive prefix ha^L- and the hodiernal passive prefix há^M- both have a variant form há^H-. A mid or high tone on the contiguously preceding prefix or verb phrase element perturbs the tone of either passive prefix to a high tone, neutralizing the difference between them. In (832), either temporal adverb (or none at all) is grammatical. If there is no temporal adverb, the degree of time-past is indeterminate.

(832) ka^L-ŋáu^M   mi^L   ?a^MHcií^L hmí̃^H
       PAST-explode^II spherical balloon when^PAST

háH-ʔíʔH   *kiõʔL tõM*
PAST^PASS-be^penetrated^II by   thorn

(máM ʔmäïL/ciáuL)
earlier^today/yesterday
When the balloon was pricked by a thorn (earlier today/yesterday), it exploded.

The posture passive. The posture passive (PPAS) is used only in the past tense. It is formed by the obligatory co-occurrence of three prefixes on the verb root: (1) the remote past (PAST) *kaL-*, (2) the continuous (CONT) prefix inflected for the past tense *taL-*, and (3) either any one of the set of progressive prefixes or the progressive motion prefix *ʔíH-*; see (834) below. Generally, the internal inflection of the verb differs from that associated with the progressive prefixes; consequently, when these prefixes function in the passive construction, they are called posture prefixes rather than progressive prefixes. Sometimes the internal inflection of the verb also differs from that of the conventional passive.

Examples of the verb *toʔM* 'put (TI^P)' inflected for the active voice, conventional passive, and posture passive, respectively, are given in (833). In (833b), the conventional passive indicates only that maize has been put inside the corncrib; there is no indication of whether more maize must yet be put in. In (833c), however, the posture passive construction implies that the task has been completed.

(833) a. *kaL-tóʔL*   *cúM kuúM ɲiéiʔL ʔɲiuLkuîL*
     PAST-put^TI^P^3   3   maize within corncrib
     S/he put the maize inside the corncrib.

    b. *kaL-haL-toʔL*   *kuúM ɲiéiʔL ʔɲiuLkuîL*
     PAST-PASS-be^put^II^P maize within corncrib
     The maize was put inside the corncrib.

    c. *kaL-taL-náH-tioʔL*   *kuúM ɲiéiʔL ʔɲiuLkuîL*
     PAST-CONT-INDEF^P-be^put^II^P maize within corncrib
     The maize was put inside the corncrib.

The set of posture prefixes which are found as the innermost constituent in the posture passive construction are set out in (834).

(834) The posture prefixes

$rá^H$-/$rá^M$-	flat (horizontal) (S)
$dí^H$-	upright (S)
$kuá^H$-	sitting, indefinite (AN S)
$cií^H$-	upright, sustained, indefinite (S)
$ʔú^H$-	contained (S)
$ʔá^H$-	open (IN S)
$ʔí^H$-	moving (S)
$ná^H$-	indefinite (P)

The prefix $rá^H$- is used if the subject immediately assumed a horizontal position after the event, while the prefix $rá^M$- indicates that the event occurred while the subject was horizontal.

When a progressive prefix occurs with a verb in the active voice, the posture indicated is that of the subject/agent. When a transitive or ditransitive verb is inflected for the posture passive, the posture indicated is that of the patient/surface subject, not that of the unexpressed agent. Examples (835) and (836) illustrate a transitive and a ditransitive verb inflected for the active and passive voice, respectively. In (836b), the person would either have received the medication over a prolonged period (for example, intravenous drip), or else the person remained seated for a while after receiving an injection.

(835) a. $ná^H$-$pá^{ML}$ $cú^M$ $hŋiéi^M$
INDEF^P-hit^TI 3   bean
They are (standing) threshing the beans.

b. ka^L-ta^L-$ná^H$-$pá^H$ $hŋiéi^M$ $ŋií^H$ $nái^M$
PAST-CONT-INDEF^P-be^hit^II bean   place ranch
The beans were threshed at the ranch.

(836) a. $kuá^H$-$ʔíʔ^{ML}$ $cú^M$ $mí^L$ $cá^M$ $cáu^H$
sit^PROG-penetrate^TA^3 3   medicine person sick
S/he is (sitting) injecting the sick person (with) medicine.

b. ka^L-ta^L-$kuá^H$-$ʔíʔ^H$ $cú^M$ $mí^L$
PAST-CONT-sit-be^penetrated^IA 3   medicine
S/he was injected (with) medicine (while sitting).

Example (837) illustrates the verb 'count' inflected for the active voice and the posture passive incorporating the prefix $ná^H$- (INDEF^P). In (837b), $ná^H$- (INDEF^P) does not indicate the plurality of the unexpressed agent (the person/people who did the counting), but rather the plurality of the patient/subject.

(837) a. ué^L   bí?^H ka^L-ta^L-ná^H-?ĩ^ML   cú^M ká^Hmí?^H
    lengthily AFF PAST-CONT-INDEF^p-count^TA^3 3 baby^chicken

    ho?^H
    have^STA^3
    They were counting their baby chicks for a long time.

b. ka^L-ta^L-ná^H-?ĩ^H   ká^Hmí?^H
   PAST-CONT-INDEF^p-be^counted^IA baby^chicken
   The baby chicks were counted.

Although the patient/subject of the posture passive can be an inanimate entity, generally animate entities are found as the subject. Inanimate entities are probably uncommon subjects due to the perceived constancy of their posture.

Agented passives. As mentioned above, Chinantec has mainly agentless passives; agented passives are restricted to inanimate agents. The passive construction appears to be the main strategy for encoding inanimate agents.

(838) ka^L-ha^L-tú^H   kuo^M   cú^M kiõ?^L mí^Hhla^M
    PAST-PASS-be^cut^II hand^3 3   by   knife
    Her/his hand was cut by a knife.

In a passive construction such as (838), the preposition kiõ?^L 'by' marks the agent; in an active construction, the preposition kiõ?^L encodes the instrumental 'with', shown in (839).

(839) ka^L-tiú^L   cú^M kuo^M   kiõ?^L mí^Hhla^M
    PAST-cut^TI^3 3   hand^3 with   knife
    S/he cut her/his (own) hand with a knife.

In some passive constructions the prepositional phrase introduced by kiõ?^L may be either agented or instrumental; it appears that the possibility of ambiguity is greater with an animate patient.

(840) ha^L-?ĩ^H   hná^HL kiõ?^L   mi^Lkïe^L
    PASS^PAST-be^penetrated^IA I   by/with   needle
    I was jabbed by a needle. *or* I was jabbed with a needle.

In (840), if the situation described is accidental, then kiõ?^L expresses agency (the needle); however, if there was a human agent (which cannot be expressed in the passive construction), then kiõ?^L expresses instrumentality. Utterances such as (840) are rarely ambiguous when in context.

Both the conventional passive and the posture passive constructions can be agented. The conventional passive with overt inanimate agent is illustrated in (838); an illustration of the posture passive is given in (841), where the posture prefix *dí^H-* indicates the posture of the person, not the affected part of the body. This is further exemplified by (842).

(841) ka^L-ta^L-dí^H-tú^H kuo^M cú^M kiõ?^{L} mí^{H}hla^M kio?^{MH}
       PAST-CONT-upright-be^cut^II hand^3 3   with   knife   have^STI^3
       Her/his hand was cut with her/his (own) knife.

(842) ka^L-ta^L-rá^H-kiú?^{HL} cii^H cú^M kiõ?^{L} tá^{M}ho?^{MH}
       PAST-CONT-flat-be^struck^II head^3 3   with   mammee^fruit
       Her/his head was struck with a mammee fruit (while s/he was lying down).

An example of an animate patient is given in (843), where the posture prefix *rá^M-* is replaced with the prefix *rá^H-*, with the implication that the situation occurred while the person was in a posture other than horizontal, but immediately fell into a horizontal position.

(843) ka^L-ta^L-rá^M-?í?^{H} cú^M kiõ?^{L} mí^{H}hla^M kio?^{MH}
       PAST-CONT-flat-be^penetrated^IA 3 by   knife   have^STI^3
       S/he was stabbed by her/his (own) knife.

Although an animate agent cannot be expressed by a prepositional phrase in a passive clause, the agent can be expressed in an adjoining clause. The passive clause following and preceding the clause in which the agent is expressed is shown in (844) and (845), respectively.

(844) má^M hmu?^{LM} nú^M ?i^L ca^L-?í^L rẽ?^{M}
       PRF   make^TI^2   you^s   COMP   PASS^FUT-be^ruined^IA companion^2

       nú^M
       you^s
       Your companion(s) will be ruined by you.

(845) ha^L-?í?^{H} ?ẽi^H ká^H ?i^L li^M-hmú^L
       PASS^PAST-be^pierced^II stomach^3 Charles COMP   HOD-do^TI^3

       cáu^M
       people
       Charles' stomach was stabbed by someone (earlier today).

The Clause

Impersonal passives. Chinantec has an impersonal passive, but only a few verbs allow such a construction. All the impersonal passive constructions imply a nonspecific animate agent, generally human; and, as noted by Davison (1980:63), they appear to focus on the event rather than the agent. The impersonal passive is only possible with the conventional passive construction, not the posture passive. It appears that the nonspecificity of the agent disallows specification of posture. Such verbs are identified in the glosses as IMPRS (impersonal) in place of the standard transitivity coding such as IA (intransitive animate). All the impersonal passives which have been identified have IA counterparts.

The verb 'scold, yell (at)' has TA and IA forms, both of which have passive counterparts. Examples of each active form, respectively, with its passive counterpart are given in (846) and (847), the latter being an example of the impersonal passive.

(846) a. *hláʔ^H hi^{ML} cú^M ŋiú^{M}mí^{ʔH} nĩ^M*
really yell^at^TA^PRES^3 3   boy   that
S/he really yells at that boy.

b. *hláʔ^H cá^M-hí^H ŋiú^{M}mí^{ʔH} nĩ^M*
really PASS^PRES-be^yelled^at^IA boy   that
That boy is really yelled at.

(847) a. *hláʔ^H hi^{ML} cú^M ni^{fH} má^H ka^L-ʔĩ^{ʔL} má^{M}ciéi^L*
really yell^IA^PRES 3   when^FUT PRF PAST-drink^TI^3   liquor
S/he really yells whenever s/he has drunk liquor.

b. *hláʔ^H cá^M-hí^H ʔŋiú^L ó^{LM}*
really PASS^PRES-be^yelled^IMPRS house yonder
There is a lot of yelling in that house over there.

Impersonal passives generally function evidentially, being used when there is no direct visual evidence for the activity (which would enable specific identification of the agent), but there is auditory evidence; for example (848), where the speaker could hear whistled communication, but was unable to (fully) understand it, nor could s/he determine who the participants were.[64]

(848) a. *hui^{LM} cú^M ʔi^L té^{ʔML} räĩʔ^{MH}*
whistle^IA^PRES^3 3   COMP call^away^TA^PRES^3 companion^3
He whistles to call his companion.

---

[64]The verb *hui^{LM}* 'whistle' denotes communicating in whistle speech; see §2.6.

b. ŋif^H-há^H-huî^H   ha^H   huú^M
   EVID-PASS^PAST-be^whistled^IMPRS among town
   Evidently, there was whistling in the town.

Impersonal passives in the present tense, however, are not restricted to auditory evidentiality, but may refer to any activity which the speaker has heard and/or seen with regularity.

(849) a. ko^M   cú^M kiõ?^L mï^L   láu^M
         play^IA^PRES^3 3   with   spherical hide
         He plays with a ball.

      b. cá^M-káu^H   cií^Mkuá?^LM
         PASS^PRES-be^played^IMPRS church^courtyard
         (Games) are played in the church courtyard.

The function of the passive. In the general linguistic literature, debate is continuing as to whether the passive voice is used primarily to: (1) promote the DO to subject, with a consequent demotion of subject, either to an oblique object or total absence, or (2) primarily demote the subject, with a concomitant promotion of the DO to subject.[65]

Chinantec has ways to emphasize or foreground a noun phrase besides the use of the passive such as the use of illocutionary particles and/or moving the noun phrase to a preverbal position. When the inverse cross-reference system is used, the order can be altered from P-S-O to P-O-S for emphasis of the object. So the passive is not primarily a procedure for promotion of the DO. The main function of Chinantec passives appears to be to background the subject because it is unimportant or unknown; sometimes it is used to purposely avoid specifying an agent. The passive is also the most productive strategy for encoding inanimate agents.

The distinctive features of the conventional passive and the posture passive are summarized in (850); some of the semantic points of difference are then discussed and illustrated.

(850) Conventional passive   Posture passive

       inflected for tense   past tense only
       dynamic   state-like
       neutral as to posture   posture specific for singular
       neutral as to number   ná^H- is P, all others S

---

[65]Siewierska 1984:76–77 supplies a representative list of various linguists who treat the passive primarily as a process of demotion or primarily as a promotional rule, together with a brief discussion of the relative merits of each viewpoint.

The Clause 281

        Conventional passive   Posture passive

        impersonal passive possible   impersonal passive impossible
        IA, TA, TI, DA, DI verbs   mainly TA and DA verbs
        may imply partial affectedness   may imply comprehensive
        or ease of affectedness   affectedness or difficulty of
                                                   affectedness

Depending on the verb, both the conventional passive and the posture passive can be neutral in implication, that is, neither adversative nor positive; the connotation is dependent on the situation.

(851) ka^L-ha^L-$\textrm{?liá}^H$ $\textrm{?má}^M$ $k\tilde{a}^{LM}$ hui^{LM}
       PAST-PASS-be^pushed^II tree   beside path
       The tree was pushed to the side of the path.

(852) ka^L-ta^L-$rá^H$-$\textrm{?liá}^H$ $\textrm{?má}^M$ $k\tilde{a}^{LM}$ hui^{LM}
       PAST-CONT-flat-be^pushed^II tree beside path
       The tree was pushed to the side of the path.

In both (851) and (852), the speaker may be expressing pleasure that something desirable occurred, or else disappointment that something undesirable occurred. The posture passive in (852) does, however, imply a greater degree of difficulty in accomplishing the activity than does the conventional passive construction in (851).

Examples of different degrees of affectedness are shown in (853) and (854). (853) would be used if the person managed to get home on her/his own; in (854), however, it is implied that the person's injury was so severe that s/he required assistance to get home; the combination of the continuous prefix ta^L- with the posture prefix $rá^H$- in (852) indicates that the person was in a horizontal position for a prolonged period.

(853) ka^L-ha^L-$\textrm{?áï}\textrm{?}^H$ $cú^M$ $kiõ\textrm{?}^L$ $tiú^L$ $kio\textrm{?}^{MH}$
       PAST-PASS-be^shot^IA 3   with rifle have^STI^3
       S/he was shot by her/his own rifle.

(854) ka^L-ta^L-$rá^H$-$\textrm{?áï}\textrm{?}^H$ $cú^M$ $kiõ\textrm{?}^L$ $tiú^L$ $kio\textrm{?}^{MH}$
       PAST-CONT-flat-be^shot^IA 3 with rifle have^STI^3
       S/he was shot by her/his own rifle (and became horizontal).

Constraints on the passive. Less than sixty percent of the transitive and ditransitive verbs in the corpus can be inflected for the passive. It appears that mainly prototypical transitive verbs that express impingement exhibit inflection for the passive, that is, verbs that convey a strong sense of an agent actually affecting a patient in some physical way. Verbs such as 'love', which have a passive counterpart in English, lack a passive counterpart in Chinantec. Even many verbs which entail physical impingement on the patient do not inflect for the passive; for example, hmu^M 'do, make (TI)' and $\theta\tilde{a}?^{ML}$ 'grab (TA)'. Nonetheless, it is the case that a few nonprototypical transitive verbs inflect for the passive; for example, $té?^{ML}$ 'call away (TA)' and $ku\tilde{e}^M$ 'give (DA)'. A few verbs which have animate and inanimate counterparts inflect the animate verb for the passive, but not the inanimate counterpart; for example, cii^M (TA)/cii^M (TI) 'remove'.

8.6 Antipassive constructions

A feature of many ergative languages is what has become known as the antipassive construction. Like the passive, there is a loss of transitivity; in the antipassive construction, however, it is the patient rather than the agent that is downgraded to an oblique object (OO) or omitted. Although in Sochiapan Chinantec the antipassive patient is downgraded, it cannot be omitted.

The Chinantec antipassive is restricted to constructions in which the DO of the corresponding ergative clause is animate. (855a–b) illustrate a TA verb inflected for direct and inverse cross-referencing, respectively, followed by the corresponding antipassive with an IA verb in (855c). Note that the distinction between the direct (855a) and inverse (855b) systems is neutralized in the antipassive construction (855c).

(855) a. hi^{ML} $cú^M$ $r\tilde{a}i?^{MH}$
       yell^at^TA^PRES^3 3   companion^3
       S/he (regularly) yells at her/his companion.

   b. he^{ML} $cú^M$ $hno?^H$
      yell^at^TA^PRES^3>1 3   us
      S/he (regularly) yells at us.

   c. hi^{ML} $cú^M$ $\eta i f^H k\tilde{o}^M$ $r\tilde{a}i?^{MH}/hno?^H$
      yell^IA^PRES^3 3   toward   companion^3/us
      S/he (occasionally) yells at/toward her/his companion/us.

As seen in (855c), the verb is IA, and the patient-object is encoded as an oblique object. When both TI and IA counterparts of a verb exist, however, it is the TI counterpart that is utilized in the antipassive, not an intransitive. The animacy of the patient is downgraded by indexing the verb as for an inanimate entity. For example, the TA verb $t\tilde{a}i?^{LM}$ 'defecate on' in (856a) has

The Clause   283

both a TI counterpart *taïʔ^{LM}* illustrated in (856b) and an IA counterpart *táï^{LM}* illustrated in (856c), but it is the TI verb that is used in the antipassive construction in (856d). An attempt to produce an antipassive construction with the IA verb, such as in (856e), is ungrammatical. In (856d), the patient is less affected than in (856a); that is, in (856d) the implication is that the mother got only a slight amount of excrement on her.[66]

(856) a. *ka^L-táïʔ^{LM}*   *dá̰i^M* *mí^{H}θiú^{HL}*
PAST-defecate^TA^3 baby mother^3
The baby defecated on its mother.

b. *ka^L-teʔ^L*   *dá̰i^M* *cḭ́^{H}* *ʔá^M* *kioʔ^{MH}*
PAST-defecate^TI^3 baby old cloth have^STI^3
The baby defecated on its rag.

c. *ka^L-táï^{LM}*   *dá̰i^M* *cíf^{H}ɲif^H* *lḭ́^{LM}* *ciáu^L*
PAST-defecate^IA^3 baby frequently very yesterday
The baby defecated very frequently yesterday.

d. *ka^L-teʔ^L*   *dá̰i^M* *ɲif^{H}kõ^M* *mí^{H}θiú^{HL}*
PAST-defecate^TI^3 baby towards mother^3
The baby defecated (towards) its mother.

e. **ka^L-táï^{LM}*   *dá̰i^M* *ɲif^{H}kõ^M* *mí^{H}θiú^{HL}*
PAST-defecate^IA^3 baby towards mother^3
The baby defecated (towards) its mother.

The Chinantec antipassive construction requires an oblique object for the animate patient of some verbs, such as in (855c). For a few verbs which use the TI counterpart in the antipassive construction, the animate patient can be in either an OO or a complement clause. Examples of a transitive verb inflected for an animate and inanimate object in (857a) and (857b), respectively, followed by an antipassive construction with an OO in (857c), and an antipassive construction with a complement clause in (857d), are:

(857) a. *ka^L-hḭ́e^{LM}*   *cú^M* *cá^M* *cáu^H*
PAST-see^TA^3 3 person sick
S/he cared for the sick person.

---

[66]Traditionally, Chinantecs have not used diapers for their babies. Typically, a baby is carried around in a sling, usually against the mother's (or older sister's) chest or tied to the person's back by means of a shawl. Not infrequently, a mother is defecated on by her baby.

b. ka^L-hǐe^L cú^M lio^{MH} kio?^{MH}
PAST-see^TI^3 3   cargo have^STI^3
S/he saw her/his cargo.

c. ka^L-hǐe^L cú^M ŋií^{H}kõ^M cá^M cǎu^H
PAST-see^TI^3 3   toward sick person
S/he looked at the sick person.

d. ka^L-hǐe^L cú^M kio?^{MH} cá^M cǎu^H
PAST-see^TI^3 3   have^STI^3 sick person
S/he examined the sick person.

If a medical examination was performed, (857a) would indicate a thorough examination, whereas (857d) would indicate checking the person for a specific ailment; however, (857c) would not be used to indicate a medical examination. Neither (857c) nor (857d) imply the intensive or long-term scrutiny of (857a).

The majority of antipassive constructions with a TI verb take only a complement clause; a construction with an OO, as in (858c), is considered ungrammatical.

(858) a. kuá^H-kū?^{M} cú^M huo^{HL}
sit^PROG-eat^TA^3 3   fish
S/he is sitting eating (a) fish.

b. kuá^H-kú?^{M} cú^M kio?^{MH} huo^{HL}
sit^PROG-eat^TI^3 3   have^STI^3 fish
S/he is eating some fish.

c. *kuá^H-kú?^{M} cú^M ŋií^{H}kõ^M huo^{HL}
sit^PROG-eat^TI^3 3   toward fish
S/he is eating some fish.

An ergative clause is illustrated in (859a), followed by examples of the antipassive construction with a complement clause in (859b–c); however, the presence of the complementizer ?i^L (§9.3) is ungrammatical in this construction. In (859a), the connotation is that the person was hit in several places on her/his body, and/or multiple times on a given occasion, and/or on several occasions. In (859b–c), however, in which the antipassive construction is used, the implication is that the person was hit on a single part of her/his body, and/or was hit only a few times, and/or was hit on a single occasion; that is, the antipassive construction implies a lesser degree of affectedness than its ergative counterpart.

(859) a. *ka^L-pã^L*   *cú^M hõ^M*
       PAST-hit^TA^3 3   child^3
       S/he hit her/his child.

   b. *ka^L-pá^L*   *cú^M kio?^{MH}*   *hõ^M*
      PAST-hit^TI^3 3   have^STI^3   child^3
      S/he hit her/his child.

   c. *ka^L-pá^L*   *cú^M kiõ^{MH}*   *hná^{HL}*
      PAST-hit^TI^3 3   have^STI^1S   I
      S/he hit me.

With ditransitive verbs, it is the DI counterpart of DA verbs which is used for the antipassive. (860b) illustrates an antipassive with a DI verb and an OO, and (861b) illustrates an antipassive with a DI verb and a complement clause.

(860) a. *ŋii^L-tiẽ^H*   *hná^{HL} cáu^M sí^M*
       AMB-aim^at^DA^1S I   people light
       I walk around aiming light at (groups of/whole) people (i.e., the light is powerful enough to illuminate the entire body of the individual(s) at once).

   b. *ŋii^L-tiéi^{MH}*   *hná^{HL} sí^M ŋií^{H}kõ^M cáu^M*
      AMB-aim^at^DI^1S I   light towards people
      I walk around aiming light at (individual) people (i.e., the light is a narrow beam that illuminates only part of each individual or part of the group).

(861) a. *ŋií^H-kuẽ^{MH}*   *hná^{HL} pé^H hã^M ká^H?áu^M*
       INT-give^DA^1S I   Peter one^AN chicken
       I intend to give Peter a (whole) chicken.

   b. *ŋií^H-kue^H*   *hná^{HL} pé^H kio?^{MH} ká^H?áu^M*
      INT-give^DI^1S I   Peter have^STI^3 chicken
      I intend to give Peter some chicken.

As mentioned above, all antipassives appear to have a partitive connotation; that is, the patient of the antipassive construction is in one respect or another less affected than the patient of the corresponding ergative clause. This partitive meaning can be seen in (855)–(861) above. Further examples of the partitive function of the antipassive are given in the following pairs of ergative and antipassive clauses, respectively.

(862) a. má^{M}ʔó^L cú^M rāī̃ʔ^{MH}
       assist^TA^PRES^3   3   companion
       S/he (regularly) assists her/his companion.

   b. má^{M}ʔo^L cú^M ɲii^{H}kõ^M rāī̃ʔ^{MH}
      assist^with^TI^PRES^3   3   toward   companion^3
      S/he (occasionally) assists her/his companion.

(863) a. ka^L-kui̯ʔ^L ɲiú^{M}mí̯ʔ^H mí^{H}tiei^{MH}
       PAST-squeeze^TA^3   boy   cat
       The boy squeezed the cat (the whole animal).

   b. ka^L-kui̯ʔ^L ɲiú^{M}mí̯ʔ^H kio?^{MH} mí^{H}tiei^{MH}
      PAST-squeeze^TI^3   boy   have^STI^3   cat
      The boy squeezed the cat (some part of it).

8.7–8.14 The secondary constituents

The secondary constituents of the Chinantec clause include the benefactive, recipient/source, manner, locative, comitative, temporal, instrumental, illocutionary, and vocative constituents. Several of these constituents are expressed by prepositional phrases (chapter 7).

When two or more secondary constituents occur following the primary constituents, the unmarked order is as set out in (864). The superscript ^{n} accompanying the locative, temporal, and vocative constituents indicates that there may be multiple occurrences in an appositive structure. The alternative orders for the DO and the IO represent the fact that certain verbs permit only an IO-DO order, and others permit only a DO-IO order; however, many ditransitive verbs permit either order. The subject, DO, and IO constituents are marked as optional since ellipsis may occur under co-referentiality in discourse.

(864) CLAUSE → (MANNER$_1$) PREDICATE (SUBJECT) $\left\{ \begin{array}{l} \text{(DO) (IO)} \\ \text{(IO) (DO)} \end{array} \right\}$

$\left\{ \begin{array}{l} \text{(RECIPIENT/SOURCE)} \\ \text{(BENEFACTIVE)} \end{array} \right\}$ (MANNER$_2$) (LOCATIVE)^n

(COMITATIVE) (TEMPORAL)^n (INSTRUMENTAL)

(ILLOCUTIONARY) (VOCATIVE)^n

The order of some of the secondary constituents is flexible. Most secondary constituents can precede the predicate, and there is some flexibility of order when they follow the predicate. If two or more secondary constituents occur in a clause, frequently one will be left-dislocated to precede the predicate, and the other(s) will follow the primary constituents, although the vocative constituent, which may occur either clause initial or clause final (usually initial), may occur with one other preceding secondary constituent. The scope of the illocutionary constituent (§8.13) is the whole clause (apart from a following vocative constituent). Illocutionary adverbs and particles are discussed more fully in chapter 11 and §12.2. Each secondary constituent is discussed below, together with its permutability.

8.7 The recipient/source and benefactive constituents

Some verbs encode the recipient as the indirect object (IO) without a preposition, for example, the ditransitive verb $kue?^{LM}$ 'give (DI)'. Transitive verbs, however, encode the recipient as an oblique object (OO). The recipient and source constituents are always introduced by the preposition $\eta i \int^H k \tilde{o}^M$ 'to, towards, from'.

(865) ka^L-$h\tilde{e}^L$ $\quad$ $c\acute{u}^M$ $k\mathring{a}u^M$ $si\int^M$ $\eta i \int^H k \tilde{o}^M$ $hn\acute{a}^{HL}$
PAST-offer^TI^3 3 $\quad$ one^IN book to $\quad$ I
S/he offered a book to me.

(866) ka^L-$?\acute{e}i^{LM}$ $\quad\quad$ $hn\acute{a}^{HL}$ $k\mathring{a}u^M$ $si\int^M$ $\eta i \int^H k \tilde{o}^M$ $c\acute{u}^M$
PAST-receive^TI^IS I $\quad$ one^IN book from $\quad$ 3
I received a book from her/him.

No other secondary constituent can precede the recipient/source when it occurs following the predicate. The recipient/source, however, can be brought into focus by left-dislocation, in which case it is usually followed by one of the illocutionary particles, such as $b i?^H$ (affirmation).

(867) $\eta i \int^H k \tilde{o}^M$ $hn\acute{a}^{HL}$ $b i?^H$ ka^L-$h\tilde{e}^L$ $\quad\quad$ $c\acute{u}^M$ $si\int^M$
to $\quad$ I $\quad$ AFF PAST-offer^TI^3 3 book
(It was) to me s/he offered a book.

The benefactive is expressed by means of a complement clause. Usually, one of the verbs 'have' is used in the complement. Since the same construction is used to express possession of alienable nouns, there is the possibility of ambiguity. The speaker would add the part in parentheses in (868) and (869) only if the context is such that ambiguity is likely. In (868), if the part in parentheses is omitted, the sentence could mean 's/he planted her/his child's coffee trees'. In (869), if the part in parentheses is omitted, the sentence could mean 's/he (just) bought this puppy of mine'.

(868) ka^L-θéi^{PLM} cú^M ʔmá^M ká^{M}fe^{MH} (ʔi^L li^L)
PAST-plant^TI^3 3   tree coffee COMP become^II^FUT

kioʔ^{MH} hõ^M
have^STI^3 child^3
S/he planted the coffee trees for her/his child.

(869) li^M-liā^L cú^M ci^{M}mí$^{?H}$ lá^M (ʔi^L li^L)
HOD-buy^TA^3 3   puppy this COMP become^II^FUT

hoʔ^M hná^{HL}
have^STA^1S I
S/he (just) bought this puppy for me.

The alternative way of expressing the benefactive is with the verb ka^{L}ti^H 'concern, regard'. This verb is always inflected for the past tense, even when the matrix clause is in the future, as in (870); however, it does inflect for person, compare (870) with (871). The complementizer ʔi^L 'that, which' (§9.1) is optional and is usually omitted.

(870) hmu^L cú^M hmái^H (ʔi^L) ka^L-ti^H mí^{H}θiú^{HL}
make^TI^FUT^3 3   fiesta COMP PAST-regard^IA^3 mother^3
They will make a fiesta/party for their mother.

(871) ka^L-hū^L cú^M (ʔi^L) ka^L-ta^H hnoʔ^H
PAST-die^IA^3 3   COMP PAST-regard^IA^1P we^P
He died for us.

8.8 The manner constituents

The manner$_1$ constituent is an adverb; the manner$_2$ constituent may be either an adverb, an adverb phrase, or an adverbial clause.

A few manner adverbs, identified as MA$_1$, must precede the predicate, such as hláʔ^H 'really'. Others, identified as MA$_2$, must follow, such as siá$^{?L}$ 'again'. However, the majority of manner adverbs are able to either precede or follow the predicate; these adverbs are identified as MA$_{1/2}$. The unmarked (most common) position for MA$_{1/2}$ adverbs is following the predicate.

There are numerous manner adverbs, both simple and binomial; for example: ka^{L}lá^M 'moderately, somewhat (MA$_2$)', káu^M 'terrifyingly (MA$_1$)', kú^{H}piʔ^{MH} 'slightly (MA$_{1/2}$)', ku^{L}ti^L 'absolutely (MA$_1$)', ʔí^{M}tái^{LM} 'slowly (MA$_{1/2}$)', siá$^{?L}$ 'differently (MA$_1$)', tiá^L 'forcefully, firmly, rapidly (MA$_{1/2}$)', tē^M 'sluggishly, dimly (MA$_1$)', tia^{L}hui^{LM} 'promptly (MA$_{1/2}$)', tia^{L}siāu^{LM} 'energetically (MA$_{1/2}$)', cif^{H}ká^M cif^{H}tó^{MH} 'closely (MA$_{1/2}$)', and la^{L}ká^H la^{L}híʔ^{HL}

The Clause

'back and forth ($MA_{1/2}$)'. Examples of MA_1 and MA_2 adverbs, respectively, are shown in (872) and (873).

(872) tẽ^M bí?^{H} ?le?^{LM} ie?^{L}
       sluggishly AFF   speak^TI^PRES^3   elder
       The old man speaks sluggishly.

(873) ka^L-kãu^L hná^{HL} ka^{L}lá^M
       PAST-burn^IA^1S   I   moderately
       I was moderately burned.

When the manner$_1$ constituent is a $MA_{1/2}$ adverb, an illocutionary particle such as bí?^{H} (affirmation) usually co-occurs. In (874b), where the manner$_1$ constituent is a $MA_{1/2}$ adverb, the focus is more on the manner of the activity than in (874a).

(874) a. kú?^{M} cú^M má^{LM} ?í^{M}táï^{LM}
         eat^TI^PRES^3   3   food   slowly
         S/he eats food slowly.

       b. ?í^{M}táï^{LM} (bí?^{H}) kú?^{M} cú^M má^{LM}
         slowly   AFF   eat^TI^PRES^3   3   food
         S/he eats food slowly.

The manner$_2$ constituent obligatorily follows the recipient/source constituent and generally follows the benefactive constituent. Examples of each, respectively, are given in (875) and (876). In (875), the manner constituent can precede the benefactive, but it is a less common construction.

(875) P   S   O   RECIPIENT   MAN$_2$
       ka^L-hẽ?^{L} cú^M kãu^M sií^M ŋií^{H}kõ^M hná^{HL} tia^{L}huï^{LM}
       PAST-return^TI^3   3   one^IN letter   to   I   rapidly

       lï̃^{LM}
       very
       S/he returned a letter to me very quickly.

(876) P   S   O   BEN
       kũ?^{L} cú^M kïe^L (?i^L)   ka^L-tï̃^{H} cá^M tia^{L}mii^M
       collect^TI^FUT^3   3   money COMP PAST-regard^IA^3   person poor

       MAN$_2$
       tia^{L}hui̵^{LM}
       quickly
       They will collect money for the poor quickly.

An example of the manner$_2$ constituent preceding the locative constituent is (877). Reversing the order of the secondary constituents would result in an ungrammatical construction.

(877)   P   S   MAN$_2$ LOC
       *ŋi*i^H*-ná*^{H}*-huó?*^{LM} *cú*^{M} *tia^{L}siãu*^{LM} *ti̵^{L} ó*^{LM}
       EVID-PROG^P-discuss^TI^3P 3   energetically at yonder
       It sounds like they are discussing (things) energetically over there.

If there is no recipient/source or benefactive constituent, most MA$_2$ and MA$_{1/2}$ adverbs may occur either immediately following the subject or following all the primary constituents of the clause, with no discernible difference in focus or meaning.

(878) a. P   S   MAN$_2$ DO
          ka^L-hmo?^{L} *huã*^{M}/*cú*^{M} *tia^{L}hui̵*^{LM} *sũ*^{H} *hấu*^{M}
          PAST-fix^TI John/3   promptly radio that^IN
          John/she/he fixed that radio promptly.

       b. P   S   DO   MAN$_2$
          ka^L-hmo?^{L} *huã*^{M}/*cú*^{M} *sũ*^{H} *hấu*^{M} *tia^{L}hui̵*^{LM}
          PAST-fix^TI John/3   radio that^IN   promptly
          John/she/he fixed that radio promptly.

Some MA$_2$ adverbs appear to be sensitive to whether the subject is a pronoun or not, permitting up to three permutations: following all the primary constituents, immediately following the subject, or, if the subject is not a pronoun, immediately following the predicate.

(879) a. P   S   DO   MAN$_2$
          ka^L-hmo?^{L} *huã*^{M}/*cú*^{M} *sũ*^{H} *hấu*^{M} *ka^{L}lá*^{M}
          PAST-fix^TI John/3   radio that^IN   somewhat
          John/she/he fixed that radio somewhat.

       b. P   S   MAN$_2$ DO
          ka^L-hmo?^{L} *huã*^{M}/*cú*^{M} *ka^{L}lá*^{M} *sũ*^{H} *hấu*^{M}
          PAST-fix^TI John/3   somewhat radio that^IN
          John/she/he fixed that radio somewhat.

c. P   MAN₂   S   DO
ka^L-$hmo?^L$ $ka^Llá^M$ $hu\tilde{a}^M$/*$cú^M$ $s\bar{u}^H$ $h\hat{a}u^M$
PAST-fix^TI somewhat John/3   radio   that^IN
John/*she/*he fixed that radio somewhat.

The MA₂ and MA₁/₂ adverbs appear to be quite idiosyncratic with respect to both the permissible permutations and also the normal position in which they occur. The adverb $tia^Lhu\ddot{i}^{LM}$ in (878) is equally acceptable in either position. However, the adverb $ka^Llá^M$ 'moderately, somewhat' in (879) occurs more commonly after the subject (as in (879b)). Of the three possible permutations, (879a) is the least common, regardless of whether the subject is a pronoun or not.

Adverbs are able to modify adverbs, forming a semantic unit, which then modifies the predicate. In (880), the adverb $tiá^L$ 'rapidly' is modified by $hl\tilde{a}?^H$ 'really' forming a semantic unit which is then modified by $ka^Llá^M$ 'somewhat'; the resulting adverb phrase then modifies the verb.

(880) $hl\tilde{a}?^H$ $tiá^L$ $ka^Llá^M$ $\eta\ddot{i}^{LM}$ $ie?^L$ $hu\tilde{a}^M$
      really rapidly somewhat walk^IA^PRES^3S elder John
      Old man John walks really rapidly to a degree.

Manner adverbial clauses which encode comparison are quite common. Comparisons are introduced by a variety of subordinators, such as $la^Lhm\acute{\ddot{i}}^H$ 'like, as' (comparison of equality), la^L $k\acute{o}?^L$ 'more than' (comparison of inequality), and $la^Lhua?^{MH}$ ($dú?^H$) 'like, as if' (counterfactual); see §9.10. The manner adverbial clause normally follows the predicate, as illustrated in (881), but it can precede the predicate, with the exception of the clause introduced by la^L $k\acute{o}?^L$ 'more than', as in (882).

(881) $ku?^{LM}$ $?nú^M$ $la^Lhm\acute{\ddot{i}}^H$ $k\acute{u}?^M$ $h\tilde{a}^M$ $m\acute{\ddot{i}}^Htiei^{MH}$
      eat^TI^PRES^2 you^s like   eat^TI^PRES^3 one^AN cat
      You eat like a cat (eats) (i.e., the person licks his/her fingers like a cat washes its paws).

(882) $t\acute{\tilde{i}}^M$ $cú^M$ $?\acute{\tilde{i}}^{LM}$ $si\ddot{i}^M$ $la^L\char`\^k\acute{o}?^L$ $b\ddot{i}?^H$ $(?i^L$
      be^able^STI^3 3   read^TI^FUT^3 book more^than AFF COMP

      $t\acute{\tilde{i}}^M)$ $ra\ddot{i}?^{MH}$
      be^able^STI^3 companion^3
      S/he is able to read (books) more than her/his companion (is able).

8.9 The locative constituent

The locative constituent may be either an adverb (883), an adverbial clause (884), or an adverbial phrase consisting of a noun phrase or a prepositional phrase. Adverbial clauses are introduced by the locative noun *ɲiɨ^H* 'place, where'.

(883) díɨ^H-te^M hnáɨ^{HL} cá^M θẽʔ^M
       upright^PROG-call^TA^PRES^1S   I   person stand^SIA^3

       káɨ^{H}ʔɲiu^{MH}
       behind^house
       I am (standing) calling the person standing behind the house.

(884) ŋau^L pé^H ɲiɨ^H ʔna^M cú^M ʔíɨ^{H}mii?^{MH}
       go^nonhome^IA^PAST^3S Peter place   sell^TI^PRES^3 3 bread
       Peter went (to) where they sell bread.

Noun phrases and prepositional phrases can function adverbially as locatives. All motion verbs are able to take a noun phrase as the locative constituent, for example, (885). A few nonmotion verbs are also able to take noun phrases as the locative constituent, for example, (886). Locative prepositional phrases may collocate with both motion (887) and nonmotion (888) verbs.

(885) má^M ká^M-híʔ^{LM} cú^M ʔɲiu^{L}má?^{L}
       PRF   PAST-return^IA^3 3   school
       S/he has just gone back (to) school.

(886) má^M kuá^L cú^M ʔŋo?^{L}
       PRF   live^SIA^3 3   Zautla
       S/he now lives (in) Zautla.

(887) ŋau^L cú^M ti^L ciapas
       go^nonhome^IA^PAST^3S 3   to   Chiapas
       S/he went to (the State of) Chiapas.

(888) hláʔ^H ʔíɨ^H-ʔó?^{MH} cá^{H}miʔ^H ha^H ʔɲiú^L
       really MOT-shout^IA^3   children   among   house
       (Some) children are walking along shouting in the streets.

More than one locative constituent may co-occur; when they do, they function appositionally.

The Clause

(889) P   S   LOC   LOC
   ka^L-tã̃ʔ^L   cii^L tã^{LM} ti^L ó^{LM}   kã^{LM} hmí̃ʔ^H ʔmá^M
   PAST-fall^IA^3 DIM bird at yonder beside base^3 tree
   The little bird fell over there beside the tree (roots/base).

The locative constituent can be brought into focus by occurring either contiguously before or after the predicate. When it occurs prior to the predicate, it is usually followed by one of the illocutionary particles such as *bíʔ^H* (affirmation).

(890) kã^{LM} hui^{LM} bíʔ^H ka^L-tã̃ʔ^L   cii^L tã^{LM}
   by   trail   AFF   PAST-fall^IA^   DIM bird
   (It was) beside the trail the little bird fell.

The locative constituent is able to occur between the predicate and the subject only if the verb is IA, compare (892) and (893); the illocutionary particles are optional, compare (891) and (892).

(891) ŋie^H   hmái^H kua^Luóu^M hná^{HL}
   go^nonhome^IA^FUT^1S fiesta Quetzalapa   I
   I will go (to) the Quetzalapa fiesta.

(892) ka^L-kĩ̃ʔ^L   ŋi^H θio^H bíʔ^H hná^{HL}
   PAST-fall^over^IA^1S   place yonder AFF I
   I fell over over there.

(893) *ka^L-kïe ʔ^L   ŋi^H θio^H bíʔ^H hná^{HL} cái^M
   PAST-bite^TA^3>1   place yonder AFF   I   dog
   The dog bit me over there.

An example of the locative constituent following the manner constituent is given in (894). If the order of the manner and locative constituents is reversed, the construction is ungrammatical.

(894) P   MAN₂   LOC
   ti^L ʔó ʔ^{LM}   cú^M citHŋitH   lĩ̃^{LM} ti^L siau^{LM}
   PV shout^IA^PRES^3 3   constantly very at other^borough
   They yell and shout constantly in the other borough.

8.10 The comitative constituent

The comitative constituent (COM) is a transitive clause with the state verb *kiõ ʔ^L* 'accompany' as predicate. The preposition *kiõ ʔ^L* 'with, by', which is used to mark both the instrumental constituent and the inanimate agent of a passive, has most likely been grammaticized from the verb 'accompany'. The structure and use of the comitative and a syntactic/semantic comparison of the comitative verb to the instrumental/agent preposition are discussed below.

Structure and use of the comitative. The verb $kiõ\textit{?}^L$ 'accompany' inflects according to the person of both subject and object. If both subject and object are third person, then $kiõ\textit{?}^L$ is used; both participants must be animate or both must be inanimate. If either subject or object is nonthird person, the form is $kiú\textit{?}^H$; both participants must be animate. The verb $kiõ\textit{?}^L$ can occur in an independent clause.

(895) $dí^H\text{-}kiõ\textit{?}^L$ $cú^M$ $hõ^M$ $\eta if^H ta^{MH}$
upright^PROG-accompany^STA^3   3   child^3   town^hall
S/he is with her/his child in the town hall.

(896) $hmĩ^H$ $kiú\textit{?}^H$ $hná^{HL}$ $bé\textit{?}^L$ $hmĩ^H hãu^M$
TRM   accompany^STA^1S   I   Robert   then^PAST
I was with Robert (at) that time.

Examples of two third-person animate participants in a comitative construction are given in (897) and (898); note (898) where the verb $kiõ\textit{?}^L$ is modified by the terminative adverb $hmĩ^H$.

(897) $kuá^H\text{-}ha\textit{?}^M$ $cú^M$ $\textit{?}io^{MH}$ $kiõ\textit{?}^L$ $\eta if^M kuo^M$
INDEF^PROG-eradicate^STI^3   3   weed   accompany^STA^3   spouse^3
S/he is eradicating weeds with her/his spouse.

(898) $hmĩ^H$ $kiõ\textit{?}^L$ $cú^M$ $\eta if^M kuo^M$ $hmĩ^H$
TRM   accompany^STA^3   3   spouse^3   when^PAST

       $ka^L\text{-}hái\textit{?}^L$ $\textit{?}io^{MH}$
       PAST-eradicate^TI^3   weed
S/he was with her/his spouse when s/he eradicated the weeds (but they are no longer working together).

Examples where one or both participants are nonthird person follow; in (900), the object $sũ^H$ 'song' is normally omitted since it is considered redundant.

(899) ηau^L $hná^{HL}$ $kiú\textit{?}^H$ $hó^{LM}$
go^nonhome^IA^PAST^1S   I   accompany^STA^1S   child^1S
I went with my child(ren).

The Clause

(900) ʔiéHL   hnáHL kiúʔH   ʔnoʔM kuLléL
      sing^TI^FUT^1S I   accompany^STA^1S   you^P later
      I will sing with you later.

Although an inanimate item cannot be encoded as comitative when one of the arguments of the verb $kiõʔ^L$ is animate, nonetheless, the comitative can be used if both arguments are inanimate.

(901) kaL-kuéL   cúM hnáHL tũL   máïL   mehoṙal
      PAST-give^DI^3>1 3 I   two^IN sphere   Mejoral

      kiõʔL   kaLláM hmḯMráuL
      accompany^STI^3   some   refreshment
      S/he gave me two pills of Mejoral (a brand of aspirin) with a soft drink.

An alternative way of expressing accompaniment is with the frozen expression $la^L\ má^M\ kiõʔ^L$ '(mixed) together with, along with', as in (902), where two substances are mixed together.

(902) kaL-áïʔLM   hnáHL hmáïH laL   máM kiõʔL
      PAST-drink^TI^1S   I   water even^to PRF accompany^STI^3

      máHkḯLM
      debris
      I drank the water along with some debris.

Depending on the semantics of the verb in the main clause, if two animate participants are referenced by $kiõʔ^L$ 'accompany', then either accompaniment for the duration of the activity described by the main clause is implied, or accompaniment since the completion of that activity. $la^L\ má^M\ kiõʔ^L$ 'along with', however, can only imply accompaniment for the duration of the activity described by the main clause. In (903), the implication can be either that the person physically accompanied her/his children on the journey, or that s/he went alone first to get things ready, but now they are together in the new location. In (904), the only meaning possible is physical accompaniment on the journey.

(903) ŋauL   cúM kúMhuúM   kiõʔL
      go^nonhome^IA^PAST^3S 3 another^town accompany^STA^3

hõ^M
child$^{\wedge}$3

S/he has gone to (live in) another town with her/his child(ren). *or* S/he has gone with her/his child(ren) to (live in) another town.

(904) ŋau^L cú^M kúi^{M}huúi^M la^L má^M
go$^{\wedge}$nonhome$^{\wedge}$IA$^{\wedge}$PAST$^{\wedge}$3S 3   another$^{\wedge}$town even$^{\wedge}$to PRF

kiõʔ^L hõ^M
accompany$^{\wedge}$STA$^{\wedge}$3 child$^{\wedge}$3

S/he has gone along with her/his child(ren) to (live in) another town.

When the adverb ku^{L}lį^{MH} 'together' occurs without the comitative constituent, the third-person pronoun must be interpreted as plural, as in (905). If ku^{L}lį^{MH} 'together' occurs with the comitative constituent, however, the third-person pronoun subject of the verb reverts to being indefinite as to gender and number. The implication in (906) is that one or more people accompany Peter in some task. If the expression la^L má^M kiõʔ^L 'together with' is used, as in (907), the implication is that two or more people accompany Peter in some task.

(905) hmu^M cú^M ta^{MH} ku^{L}lį^{MH}
do$^{\wedge}$TI$^{\wedge}$PRES$^{\wedge}$3 3   work together
They work together.

(906) hmu^M cú^M ta^{MH} ku^{L}lį^{MH} kiõʔ^L pé^H
do$^{\wedge}$TI$^{\wedge}$PRES$^{\wedge}$3 3   work together accompany$^{\wedge}$STA$^{\wedge}$3 Peter
She/he/they work together with Peter.

(907) hmu^M cú^M ta^{MH} ku^{L}lį^{MH} la^L má^M kiõʔ^L
do$^{\wedge}$TI$^{\wedge}$PRES$^{\wedge}$$^{\wedge}$3 3 work together even$^{\wedge}$to PRF accompany$^{\wedge}STI^{\wedge}$3

pé^H
Peter
They work together, along with Peter.

The comitative constituent is able to be brought into focus by being positioned prior to the predicate. It is usually marked with one of the illocutionary particles, such as bíʔ^H (affirmation).

(908) COM   S
kiõʔ^L cá^M siá̧ʔ^L bíʔ^H cá^{M}mi^L ʔí^L
accompany$^{\wedge}$STA$^{\wedge}$3 person different$^{\wedge}$AN AFF woman that$^{\wedge}$AN

P
ŋauᴸ
go^nonhome^IA^PAST^3S
It was with another man that woman went off.

An example of the comitative constituent following the locative constituent is given in (909). Reversing the locative and comitative constituents would result in an ungrammatical clause.

(909) P   LOC
ŋieᴴ   *hnáᴴᴸ tiᴸ siauᴸ*
go^nonhome^IA^FUT^1S I   to other^borough

COM
kiúʔᴴ   *huãᴹ*
accompany^STI^1S John
I will go to the other borough with John.

Comitative *kiõʔᴸ* versus instrumental/agent *kiõʔᴸ*. It is essential to syntactically distinguish the comitative verb *kiõʔᴸ* 'accompany' from the preposition *kiõʔᴸ* 'with, by'; if *kiõʔᴸ* 'with, by' is a verb and not a preposition, then it would not be possible to say that Chinantec has agented passives since agented passives are oblique objects.

Syntactically, the state verb *kiõʔᴸ* 'accompany' is distinguishable from the preposition *kiõʔᴸ* 'with, by' in the following ways:

1. *kiõʔᴸ* 'accompany', illustrated in (910), can be prefixed with the progressive prefixes and the progressive motion (MOT) prefix *ʔíᴴ*, but *kiõʔᴸ* 'with, by' cannot; see (911). No substitution of progressive prefixes for *díᴴ*- 'upright', nor change of word order, is able to make (911b) grammatical.

(910) a. *kaᴸ-taᴸ-díᴴ-kiõʔᴸ*   *cúᴹ tuᴹᴴ   ciáuᴸ*
        PAST-CONT-upright^PROG-accompany^STI^3 3   Anthony yesterday
        S/he was with Anthony (all day) yesterday.

b. *kaᴸ-taᴸ-ʔíᴴ-kiõʔᴸ*   *cúᴹ tuᴹᴴ   hmíᴴ*
   PAST-CONT-MOT-accompany^STI^3 3   Anthony when^PAST

   ŋauᴹᴴ   *híʔᴸᴹ*
   go^nonhome^IA^PAST^3S Usila
   S/he joined up with Anthony when he was on his way to Usila.

(911) a. kiõ?ᴸ   mí ᴴcif ᴴ bí?ᴴ kiu?ᴸᴹ   cú ᴹ ?má ᴹ
       with axe AFF strike^TI^PRES^3 3   tree
       He chops trees with an axe.

   b. *kaᴸ-taᴸ-dí ᴴ-kiõ?ᴸ   mí ᴴcif ᴴ kaᴸ-kiú?ᴸ   cú ᴹ ?má ᴹ
       PAST-CONT-upright^PROG-with axe   PAST-strike^TI^3 3   tree

       ciáuᴸ
       yesterday
       He was chopping down a tree with an axe (all day) yesterday.

2. kiõ?ᴸ 'accompany' can be made active with the causative má ᴹ-, implying accompaniment partway through a journey, but instrumental kiõ?ᴸ cannot collocate with the causative.

(912) kaᴸ-maᴸ-kiõ?ᴸ   cú ᴹ pé ᴴ   ?ú ᴴ   hui̯ᴸᴹ
       PAST-CAUS-accompany^TA^3 3   Peter along trail
       S/he joined up with Peter along the trail.

(913) a. kiõ?ᴸ   mí ᴴcif ᴴ kaᴸ-kiú?ᴸ   cú ᴹ ?má ᴹ
       with axe PAST-strike^TI^3 3   tree
       He cut down the tree with an axe.

   b. *kaᴸ-maᴸ-kiõ?ᴸ   mí ᴴcif ᴴ kaᴸ-kiú?ᴸ   cú ᴹ ?má ᴹ
       PAST-CAUS-with axe   PAST-strike^TI^3 3   tree
       He cut down the tree with an axe.

3. Some of the verb phrase adverbs (§5) are able to collocate with kiõ?ᴸ 'accompany', but none are able to collocate with kiõ?ᴸ 'with, by'. No matter how (915) is adjusted, the combination of the terminative adverb hmí ᴴ with the instrumental kiõ?ᴸ is ungrammatical.

(914) hmí ᴴ kiõ?ᴸ   cú ᴹ pé ᴴ hmí ᴴ   kaᴸ-kiú?ᴸ   ?má ᴹ
       TRM accompany^STA^3 3   Peter when^PAST PAST-strike^TI^3 tree
       S/he was with Peter when they cut down the tree.

(915) *hmí ᴴ kiõ?ᴸ cú ᴹ mí ᴴcif ᴴ (hmí ᴴ)   kaᴸ-kiú?ᴸ   (cú ᴹ) ?má ᴹ
       TRM with 3   axe   when^PAST PAST-strike^TI^3 3 tree
       S/he had an axe (when) s/he cut down the tree.

The other reasons for distinguishing between kiõ?ᴸ 'accompany' and kiõ?ᴸ 'with, by' are a blend of syntactic and semantic arguments.

The Clause

In Chinantec, an inanimate item must be 'taken' (916). An animate entity can also be 'taken' (917). If the subject and object of *kiõʔᴸ* 'accompany' are animate, accompaniment is always indicated, never instrumentality or agency. (918) cannot be interpreted instrumentally: *'s/he employed John to stab Peter' (see Foris 1988:445).

(916) *kiã̱ᴸ*   *cúᴹ*   *míᴴtáịᴴᴸ*   *hmḭ̂ᴴ*   *ŋauᴹᴴ*
      take^STI^3 3   machete^3   when^PAST   go^nonhome^IA^PAST^3S
      S/he took her/his machete when s/he went.

(917) *kaᴸ-hã̱ᴸ*   *cúᴹ*   *hõᴹ*   *hmḭ̂ᴴ*   *ŋauᴹᴴ*
      PAST-take^TA^3 3   child^3   when^PAST   go^nonhome^IA^PAST^3S
      S/he took her/his child when s/he left.

(918) *kaᴸ-ʔḭ́ʔᴸ*   *cúᴹ*   *péᴴ*   *kiõʔᴸ*   *huã̱ᴹ*
      PAST-penetrate^TA^3 3   Peter   accompany^STI^3   John
      S/he stabbed Peter and John. *or* S/he and John together stabbed Peter.

In the passive voice, if the nominal following *kiõʔᴸ* is animate, the only interpretation is accompaniment as in (919). If the nominal following *kiõʔᴸ* is inanimate in a passive construction, however, the interpretation may be either instrumental or agent, depending on the context, as in (920).

(919) *kaᴸ-haᴸ-ʔḭ́ʔᴴ*   *péᴴ*   *kiõʔᴸ*   *huã̱ᴹ*
      PAST-PASS-be^penetrated^IA   Peter   accompany^STI^3   John
      Peter and John were stabbed.

(920) *kaᴸ-haᴸ-ʔḭ́ʔᴴ*   *péᴴ*   *kiõʔᴸ*   *míᴴhlaᴹ*
      PAST-PASS-be^penetrated^IA   Peter   with/by   knife
      Peter was stabbed with a knife (unexpressed human agency; agentless passive). *or* Peter was stabbed by a knife (accidental; agented passive).

The verb *kiõʔᴸ* 'accompany' inflects to index the presence of a nonthird-person participant, for example, (921). However, the third-person participant cannot be inanimate, cf. (922). If *kiúʔᴴ* of (922) is replaced by *kiõʔᴸ*, as in (923), the construction is grammatical; however, the meaning is instrumental.

(921) *kuã̱ᴸ*   *hnáᴴᴸ*   *kiúʔᴴ*   *péᴴ*
      arrive^here^IA^PAST^1S I   accompany^STA^1S   Peter
      I arrived here with Peter.

(922) *kuã^L hná^{HL} kiũ$?^H$ kã́u^M sií^M
arrive^here^IA^PAST^IS I accompany^STI^IS one^IN letter
I arrived here with a letter.

(923) kuã^L hná^{HL} kiõ$?^L$ kã́u^M sií^M
arrive^here^IA^PAST^IS I by^means^of one^IN letter
I arrived here by means of a letter (of authorization).

In conclusion, there appear to be ample syntactic and semantic grounds for distinguishing the verb kiõ$?^L$ 'accompany' from the homophonous preposition kiõ$?^L$ 'with, by'.

8.11 The temporal constituent

The temporal constituent (T) may be either an adverb phrase, an adverbial clause, or an adverbial phrase. The adverbial phrase can be either a noun phrase or a prepositional phrase. The structure of the temporal adverb phrase is set out in (924).

(924) TEMPORAL ADVERB PHRASE → (INTENSIFIER$_1$) HEAD (INTENSIFIER$_2$)

If only the head element of the temporal adverb phrase occurs, or the head plus one of the intensifier elements, then the temporal constituent may either precede or follow the predicate. If all the elements occur, the temporal constituent must precede the predicate.

(925) T [INTENS$_1$ H INTENS$_2$] P S
hlá$?^H$ ʔú^{M}niéi^M pi$?^{MH}$ ŋau^L cú^M
really early quite go^nonhome^IA^PAST^3S 3

LOC
kua^{L}tá^L
Cuicatlán
Really very early s/he went (to) Cuicatlán.

Two temporal constituents can co-occur; when they do, the second constituent is in apposition to the first, supplying further information.

(926) P S LOC T
lį́^{M}-$?$į^L cá^M ʔái^M ʔŋiú^{HL} hno$?^H$ má^{M}ʔmáï^L
HOD-enter^IA^3S person thief house^IP us earlier^today

The Clause

      T
tá^{H}la^L (?i^L) θiã^{LM} hno?^{H}
while COMP be^absent^SIA^3 us
A thief entered our house earlier today while we were absent.

There can also be two temporal constituents in a given clause, one preceding the predicate, and one following.

(927) *ta^L ?ua^M ka^L-kuǒu^M hná^{HL} cia^L?lo^H*
       while midnight PAST-sleep^IA^IS I   yesterday^evening
       Yesterday evening I went to sleep at midnight.

The temporal constituent can be brought into focus by being left-dislocated, occurring prior to the predicate. Illocutionary particles, such as *bí?^{H}* (affirmation), are optional, but frequently occur.

(928) T   P   S   O
       ha^H niéi^M bí?^{H} ŋií^H-tã^{MH} hná^{HL} kiú^L ?í^L
       among darkness AFF INT-await^TA^IS I   coati that^AN
       I intend to await that coati during the night.

An example of the temporal, comitative, and locative constituents together (illustrating that the temporal follows the comitative) is given in (929). The comitative constituent must precede the temporal constituent, whether or not the locative is present.

(929) P   S   LOC   COM
       ŋie^H hná^{HL} ŋií^{H}kuá?^{M} kiú?^{H}
       go^nonhome^IA^FUT^IS I   Oaxaca   accompany^STA^IS

                        T
       bé?^{L} ca^L?áu^M
       Robert tomorrow
       I will go to Oaxaca with Robert tomorrow.

Temporal and intensifier adverbs. Examples of temporal adverbs are listed in (930).

(930) *hau^L*   day before yesterday
       ciáu^L   yesterday
       cii^L?iú^M   midday
       ?ua^M   midnight
       ca^L?áu^M   tomorrow

ió^{LM}	day after tomorrow
hmí^{H}tį^{M}	previously
má^{M}ʔmáï^{L}	earlier today
ku^{L}lé^{L}	later today
ʔú^{M}niéi^{M}	early
ʔia^{L}háu^{HL}	before

Several of these cannot collocate with one or both of the intensifiers. Sentential examples of temporal adverbs are shown in (931) and (932).

(931) *ka^{L}-kí ʔ^{LM} ʔŋiú^{HL} cú^{M} hau^{L}*
PAST-fall^over house^3 3   day^before^yesterday
Her/his house fell over the day before yesterday.

(932) *tį^{M} ta^{LM} ʔio^{L} ni^{M} ʔmï ʔ^{LM} háï^{L} hmí^{H}tį^{M}*
DISC   weave^TI^3   matron   that   cloth   tunic   previously
That elderly lady used to weave tunics (i.e., the native dress) previously.

The intensifier adverbs are listed in (933). All of the intensifier$_1$ adverbs also function as MA$_1$ adverbs (§8.8). Some of the intensifier$_2$ adverbs are MA$_2$ and some are MA$_{1/2}$ adverbs; *piʔ^{MH}*, however, cannot function as a manner adverb.

(933)

intensifier$_1$		intensifier$_2$	
hláʔ^{H}	really	*lį́^{LM}*	very
ka^{L}la^{L}	exceedingly	*ku^{L}tí^{HL}*	very
ʔú^{H}tá^{H}	definitely	*ca^{L}lá^{M}*	moderately, somewhat
		cú^{H}piʔ^{MH}	slightly
		piʔ^{MH}	quite

Temporal adverbial clauses. Adverbial clauses which are introduced by the subordinators *hmí^{H}* 'when (past)', *ní^{H} má^{H}* 'when (future)', and *ta^{L}* 'while' can also function as the temporal constituent. They are illustrated in (934)–(936), respectively.

(934) *ca^{L}-ʔó^{L} cú^{M} cuú^{M} hmí^{H} ca^{L}-lį^{L} kiéi^{M}*
PAST-harvest^TI^3 3   maize   when^PAST   PAST-become^II   dry
S/he harvested the maize when it became dry.

(935) *rẽ^{L} mí^{H}mí ʔ^{H} ʔa^{H} ní^{H} má^{H} ca^{L}-lį^{L}*
wash^TI^FUT^3   girl   clothes^3   when^FUT   PRF   PAST-become^II

        kiá^H
        dirty^IN
        The little girl will wash her clothes when they have become dirty.

(936)   kua^Lʔã^L   cú^M ʔŋiú^{HL} ta^L tiá^M ʔĩ^M ŋii^{LM}
       leave^IA^PAST^3S 3   house^3 while not anyone know^STI^3
       S/he left her/his house while no one knew.

In addition, the subordinators *ŋieʔ^M (bíʔ^H)* 'before' and *tá^Hla^L* 'while' are obligatorily followed by a complement clause. *ŋieʔ^M* 'before' forms a frozen expression with the illocutionary particle *bíʔ^H* (affirmation); for example, (937). The complement clause following *tá^Hla^L* 'while' generally lacks the complementizer *ʔi^L* 'that, which', although its presence is grammatical; for example, (938).

(937)   ka^L-hmú^L   ʔio^L   má^{LM} ŋieʔ^M bíʔ^H ʔi^L
       PAST-made^TI^3 matron food before AFF COMP

       háuʔ^L   ieʔ^L
       return^home^IA^PAST^3S elder
       The old lady ate dinner before the old man got home.

(938)   ko^M   cá^Hmíʔ^H cieiʔ^{LM} tá^Hla^L (ʔi^L) tiãuʔ^H
       play^IA^PRES^3 children outside while COMP be^present^SIA^3P

       cáu^M   kuáʔ^{LM}
       people church
       The children play outside while (that) people are (present) in church.

Temporal adverbial phrases. One type of temporal adverbial phrase expresses time frequency. It is a quantified noun phrase with the noun *héĩ^{LM}* 'time(s)' as head.

(939)   má^M ca^L-hmoʔ^L   cú^M sũ^H lá^M tũ^L héĩ^{LM}
       PRF PAST-repair^TI^3 3   radio this two^IN times
       S/he has repaired this radio twice.

Another type of temporal adverbial phrase consists of noun phrases which have as their head temporal nouns such as *o^Hrá^H* 'hour', *hmáï^H* 'day, time', *sí^Mma^Hná^H* 'week', *θíʔ^M* 'month', and *miï^M* 'year'; they are obligatorily modified either by the adjective *kãu^M* 'next', as in (940) (except for *hmáï^H* 'day', which cannot collocate with *kãu^M*), or by a relative clause. An expression such as 'last month/year' is formed with a relative clause; see (941) where, although the complementizer $?i^L$ 'that, which' is grammatical, it is never heard in normal speech.

(940) hmu^H hná^{HL} $?\eta i\acute{u}^L$ $?mai^{MH}$ mií^M ką́u^M
make^π^FUT^1S I house new year next
I will make a new house next year.

(941) hlá$?^H$ cau^L hmǐ^L θí$?^M$ ($?i^L$) ka^L-cá^{LM}
really fall^π^PAST rain month COMP PAST-be^finished^π
The rain really came (down) last month.

Examples of prepositional phrases functioning as the temporal constituent are in (942) and (943).

(942) hlá$?^H$ ka^L-$?ó?^{LM}$ lia^M ciu^L nie^M
really PAST-shout^IA^3 owl middle night
The owl screeched in the middle of the night.

(943) la^L kuá^M-ηie^H hmǐ^L ha^H niéi^M
EVID VEN^PAST-go^π rain among darkness
Apparently it rained during the night.

8.12 The instrumental constituent

The instrumental constituent (INST) is a prepositional phrase introduced by the preposition $kiõ?^L$ 'with'; the syntactic and semantic grounds for distinguishing the instrumental preposition $kiõ?^L$ 'with' from the comitative verb $kiõ?^L$ 'accompany' are discussed in §8.10.

The complement of $kiõ?^L$ 'with' must be a noun phrase, the head of which must be an inanimate noun. An animate noun phrase cannot occur as the complement of $kiõ?^L$ 'with'. Compare (944) with (945).

(944) ka^L-hą́u^L hná^{HL} no^M kiõ$?^L$ ką́u^M liá^L
PAST-catch^TA^1S I rat(s) with one^IN trap
I caught the rat(s) with a trap.

(945) ka^L-hą́u^L hná^{HL} no^M kiõ$?^L$ hã^M
PAST-catch^TA^1S I rat accompany^STA^3/*with one^AN

mí^{H}tiei^{MH}
cat
I caught the rat(s) and a cat. *but not* *I caught the rat(s) with a cat.

The Clause

The instrumental constituent can be brought into focus by left-dislocation; when the instrumental constituent precedes the predicate, it is usually modified by an illocutionary particle such as *bí?ʰ* (affirmation).

(946) INST P S O
kiõ?ᴸ mí ʰciíʰ bí?ʰ kaᴸ-?náᴸ cúᴹ ?máᴹ
with axe AFF PAST-cut^transversally^TI^PRES^3 3 tree
He chopped the log in half with an axe.

The instrumental constituent can precede the temporal constituent, but rarely does. The instrumental constituent following the temporal constituent is shown in (947).

(947) P S O T INST
hlíʰᴸ hnáʰᴸ kuoʰ kuᴸléᴸ kiõ?ᴸ míʰ siíᴹ θíᴸ
cover^TI^FUT^1s I firewood later with flat book shiny
I will cover the firewood later with a sheet of plastic.

If the comitative and instrumental constituents co-occur, and both of the comitative arguments are third person, the order of the constituents is fixed, i.e., comitative before instrumental, as in example (948). If the comitative and instrumental constituents co-occur, the order of these constituents may be reversed if one of the comitative arguments is nonthird-person, as in example (949).

(948) P S O COM
kaᴸ-?náᴸ péʰ ?máᴹ kiõ?ᴸ bé?ᴸ
PAST-cut^transversally Peter tree accompany^STA^3 Robert

 INST
 kiõ?ᴸ míʰɲiíᴹháʰ
 with saw
Peter and Robert cut the log in half with a (pit) saw.

(949) P S O INST
kaᴸ-?náᴸ hnáʰᴸ ?máᴹ kiõ?ᴸ míʰɲiíᴹháʰ
PAST-cut^transversally^TI^1s I tree with saw

 COM
 kiúʔʰ bé?ᴸ
 accompany^STA^1s Robert
Robert and I cut the log in half with a (pit) saw.

If the comitative, temporal, and instrumental constituents co-occur, however, the order is obligatorily that way.

(950) P   S   O   COM
       ka^L-ʔná^L hná^{HL} ʔmá^M kiṹʔ^H béʔ^L
       PAST-cut^transversally^TI^1S I   tree   accompany^STA^1S Robert

              T   INST
              hau^M kiõʔ^L mí^{H}ŋií^{M}há^H
              day^before^yesterday with   saw
       Robert and I cut (some) boards two days ago with a (pit) saw.

8.13 The illocutionary constituent

The illocutionary constituent (ILLOC) is a set of illocutionary adverbs and particles which have the entire preceding clause in their scope. Some of the particles can only have a clause in their scope, while others are able to have additional constituents in their scope, such as a noun phrase, a quantifier phrase, the temporal constituent, etc. Illocutionary adverbs and particles are discussed in detail in chapter 11.

An example of the illocutionary particle iáʔ^L (assertion), with the entire clause in its scope is given in (951). By using iáʔ^L the speaker is asserting that s/he is serious in the face of apparent doubt.

(951) [   ] ILLOC
       kuá^M-kiã^M ka^{L}lá^M hmáï^M iáʔ^L
       ANDT^IMP-bring^TI^IMP some   water   ASSR
       Go bring some water!

8.14 The vocative constituent

A vocative phrase (VOCP) can occur as the first or last clause constituent, but it occurs more frequently first than last. It is listed in final position in (864) to show its relation to the other secondary constituents when it occurs following the predicate. If the vocative phrase occurs clause initial, it is set off from the rest of the clause by pause. The use of vocative nouns is discussed in §6.1, and their forms as part of the paradigm of inalienable nouns are discussed in §6.3. The structure of the vocative phrase is given in (952).

(952) VOCATIVE PHRASE → (SECOND-PERSON PRONOUN) HEAD

The Clause

The head element of the vocative phrase can be a proper noun, an inalienable noun inflected for the vocative, or an alienable noun such as ŋiú^{M}mí$^{?H}$ 'boy'.

Example (953) illustrates the vocative constituent preceding the predicate. The optional element of the vocative phrase is one of the second-person pronouns: $?nú^M$ 'you (s)' or $?no?^M$ 'you (P)'. It can occur only when the vocative occurs clause initial, as in example (954).

(953)   tu^{MH} ŋia^{LM} tiá^L ŋií^H lá^M
        Anthony come^IA^IMP^2S SUPL place this
        Tony, please come here.

(954)   ?nú^M pé^H ?e^L ŋii^L-hmu?^{LM} nú^M
        you^s Peter what? INDEF^PROG-do^TI^2 you^s
        Hey Peter, what are you doing?

The vocative constituent may occur as the leftmost element together with one other preceding secondary constituent, for example, (955). When it occurs clause initial, a second noun phrase can occur in apposition, for example, (956).

(955)   mí^H ca^L?áu^M ŋie^H hná^{HL} ŋií^{H}kuá?^{M}
        mom^VOC tomorrow go^nonhome^IA^FUT^1S I   Oaxaca
        Mom, tomorrow I will go (to) Oaxaca City.

(956)   ?nú^M tia^{MH} cá^M ŋií?^{L} ?ŋiu^{L}mí^{L}kuú^M
        you^s dad^VOC person live^SIA^2 heaven
        Heavenly Father, person living (in) heaven

An example of the vocative as the final constituent in (957) also illustrates that the vocative constituent follows the illocutionary constituent.

(957)   O   P   S   ILLOC VOC
        la^L nĩ^M lẽ^L hná^{HL} né?^{H} tia^{MH}
        idea that think^TI^PRES^1S I   COMM dad^VOC
        That's what I think, Dad.

9
Complex and Compound Sentences

The complex constructions include relative clauses, complement clauses, purpose, result, and cause clauses, conditionals, concessives, substitutives, and comparatives; the compound constructions include coordinate clauses, adversative clauses, and alternation.

Chinantec has a morphologically invariant complementizer $\textipa{P}i^L$ (in the sense used by Keenan (1985b:151, 153). $\textipa{P}i^L$ is used to introduce restrictive relative clauses, nonrestrictive relative clauses, and complement clauses. $\textipa{P}i^L$ is also used to introduce certain types of purpose, conditionals, and concessives. This complementizer has most likely been grammaticized from the contingent noun $\textipa{P}i^L$ 'thing'.

9.1–9.2 Relative clauses

The relative clause (RC) is optionally introduced by the complementizer $\textipa{P}i^L$ 'that, which'. It must occur to the right of the domain (or head) noun. Example (958) has two relative clauses, one with and one without the complementizer, respectively; the domain nouns are $\textipa{P}má\textipa{P}^{HL}$ 'gopher' and $\textipa{P}má^M\ táu^M$ 'banana palm'.

(958)	P	S	O[H	DET	RC[COMP	P
	$lí^M$-$hŋí\textipa{P}^{LM}$	$hná^{HL}$	$\textipa{P}má\textipa{P}^{HL}$	$lá^M$	$\textipa{P}i^L$	$hmí^H\ kú\textipa{P}^M$
	HOD-kill^TA^1S	I	gopher	this	that	TRM eat^TI^PRES^3

O[H   RC[P   ]]]]
ʔmá^M táu^M   kiö^MH
tree banana   have^STI^IS

I killed this gopher that was eating my banana palms.

Comrie distinguishes four major types of relative clause formation: "non-reduction, pronoun-retention, relative pronoun and gap" (1989:147). Furthermore, he remarks that "a given language may have more than one type of relative clause construction in its over-all battery of relative clause formation possibilities" (p. 147). Restrictive relative clauses in Sochiapan Chinantec exhibit only the gap strategy. Nonrestrictive relative clauses exhibit the gap and pronoun retention strategies. When the gap strategy is used, the position of the omitted nominal in the relative clause is marked by ∅ in the following examples.

9.1 The restrictive relative clause

The restrictive relative clause, as its name suggests, defines or identifies a subset of the domain noun. As mentioned above, it is optionally introduced by the complementizer ʔi^L 'that, which'. Often, a determiner of the domain noun is also present.

The determiner of the domain noun. If a determiner (DET) of the domain noun is present, it may occur in any of three positions: (1) immediately following the domain noun, (2) following the restrictive relative clause, or (3) within the restrictive relative clause. Examples of all three positions are given in (959). The preference is for the determiner to occur within a restrictive relative clause, as in (959c). The determiner in these examples is the anaphoric deictic adjective ʔi^L 'that (AN)' which is distinct from the complementizer ʔi^L 'that, which'.

(959) a. P   S   O[H   DET   RC[COMP P
         θāï^LM   hná^HL ca^L kuá^H ʔi^L   ʔi^L   hmḯ^H
         like^STA^IS I   horse   that^AN   COMP   TRM

                            LOC   ]]
         θḛʔ^M   ɲi^fH   θio^H
         stand^SIA^3S place yonder

I like that horse that was standing over there.

   b. P   S   O[H   RC [COMP P
      θāï^LM   hná^HL ca^L kuá^H   ʔi^L   hmḯ^H
      like^STA^IS I   horse   COMP   TRM

Complex and Compound Sentences 311

```
                        LOC         ] DET   ]
    θẽʔᴹ            ŋifᴴ  θioᴴ     ʔíᴸ
    stand^SIA^3S    place yonder   that^AN
```
I like that horse that was standing over there.

```
    c. P          S       O[ H        RC [COMP  P
    θãïᴸᴹ       hnáᴴᴸ   caᴸkuáᴴ      ʔíᴸ     hmĩ̂ᴴ    θẽʔᴹ
    like^STA^1S  I       horse         COMP    TRM     stand^SIA^3S

         DET        LOC            ]]
         ʔíᴸ      ŋifᴴ  θioᴴ
         that^AN  place yonder
```
I like that horse that was standing over there.

In (959a) and (959b), the order of head, determiner, and relative clause elements is in accordance with Keenan's typology (1985:145) of the possible orders of the head, determiner, and restrictive clause elements. Although the determiner occurs within the relative clause in (959c), the meaning of (959c) does not differ appreciably from that of (959a) and (959b).

The possibility of a determiner of the domain noun occurring *within* the restrictive clause is not mentioned in Keenan's typology, which makes Chinantec unusual in this respect. Consequently, a fairly lengthy discussion of the determiner follows.

Determiners which occur within the relative clause are not resumptive markers for the following reasons:

1. the determiners are deictic adjectives, not pronouns;
2. the determiner does not mark the position of the omitted nominal; and
3. the determiner never occurs as a constituent of a noun phrase whose head has been omitted due to shared information of speaker and addressee or because of coreferentiality.

With respect to point (1), the spatial deictic adjectives and the anaphoric deictic adjectives have pronominal counterparts, two of which are homophonous with the adjectival deictics. Whenever the adjectival and pronominal forms are distinguishable, however, it is the adjectival forms which occur, whether within or outside the restrictive relative clause. Thus, it can be assumed that it is always the adjectival deictic which occurs.

In (960) the anaphoric deictic adjective $hãu^M$ 'that (IN)' is the determiner of the domain noun si^M 'book' and in (961) the deictic adjective ni^M 'that' is the determiner of the domain noun $ca^Lkuá^H$ 'horse'.

(960) P   S   O[H   RC[COMP   P
     ka^L-láu^H hná^{HL} sii^M ʔi^L hmií^H ʔi^{LM}
     PAST-buy^used^TI^IS I   book   COMP   TRM   read^TI^PRES^3

         DET   S   ]]
         hau^M cá^M ʔi^L
         that^IN person that^AN
     I bought (second-hand) that book which that person was reading.

(961) P   S   O[H   RC[COMP
     lõ^H hná^{HL} ca^{L}kuá^H ʔi^L
     buy^used^TA^FUT^IS I   horse   COMP

         P   DET S   ]]
         dí^H-kõ^{ʔLM} ni^M pé^H
         stand^PROG-utilize^TA^3 that Peter
     I will buy (second-hand) that horse that Peter is working with.

With respect to point (2) above, when a determiner occurs within a relative clause, it does not mark the location of the omitted nominal. The location of the determiner is dictated by the subject of the relative clause, not by the position relativized.

If the subject of the relative clause is a pronoun, the determiner occurs immediately following that pronoun; otherwise the determiner occurs immediately following the predicate of the relative clause. In the examples of relative clauses which follow, the position of the symbol ∅ represents the normal position of the omitted nominal. When the subject is omitted and a determiner occurs within the relative clause, ∅ is placed either before or following the determiner according to whether the omitted subject is pronominal or not.

Compare (962a), in which the subject of the relative clause is a pronoun, with (962b), in which the subject of the relative clause is a lexical noun phrase. In (962a), the determiner hau^M 'that (IN)' coincidentally occurs in the normal position for the object, but in (962b) the determiner occurs immediately following the predicate instead of in the normal predicate-subject-object order.

(962) a. P   S[RC[COMP   P   S   O   DET
        ka^L-háu^M to^M ʔi^L ka^L-la^L cú^M ∅ hau^M
        PAST-break^II   mortar   COMP   PAST-buy^TI^3   3   that^IN

             T   ]]
             ciáu^L
             yesterday
        That mortar that s/he bought yesterday broke.

b. P   S [RC[COMP P   DET   S
   ka^L-háu^M to^M ʔi^L ka^L-la^L hǎu^M mi̋^{H} ró ʔ^L
   PAST-break^II mortar   COMP   PAST-buy^TI^3 that^IN FEM Rose

   O   T   ]]
   ∅   ciáu^L
       yesterday
   That mortar that Rose bought yesterday broke.

With respect to point (3) above, it is unlikely that the determiner is a constituent of a NP whose head noun has been omitted since such a construction is ungrammatical elsewhere in Chinantec syntax. Although the quantifier element of an NP may occur without the head noun when information is shared by speaker and addressee, the deictic element (determiner) of a NP cannot. For example, the response in (963b) to the question in (963a) is grammatical, but the response in (964b) to the question in (964a) is not.

(963) a. kó ʔ^L táu^M ʔnáu ʔ^M ʔnú^M
         how^many?   banana   want^STI^2   you^s
         How many bananas do you want?

      b. kǎu^M bí ʔ^H
         one^IN   AFF
         One.

(964) a. ʔi̋^{M} táu^M ʔnáu ʔ^M ʔnú^M
         which?   banana   want^STI^2   you^s
         Which banana(s) do you want?

      b. *ni̋^{M} (bí ʔ^H)
         that   AFF
         That/those.

Positions which can be relativized. In principal, Chinantec does not have any constraints on the positions which can be relativized; however, the object of temporal prepositions and the object of some locative prepositions cannot be relativized. These are discussed further below.

Starting with (965a), it can be seen in (965b–d) that it is possible to relativize the subject (S), the direct object (DO), and the indirect object (IO), respectively. In (965b), both the complementizer ʔi^L 'that, which' and the determiner are marked as optional. In fact, one or the other must occur, or both may occur; the preferred form is without the complementizer, but with the determiner. In (965c), the preferred construction is with the complementizer, the determiner being optional. In (965d), the complementizer is obligatory and the determiner is optional.

(965) a. ka^L-kué$^{?L}$ ie$^{?L}$ mí^{M}ŋii^L káu^M ?í^{H}mii?^{MH}
PAST-give^DI^3 elder pig   one^IN bread
The old man gave the pig a bread roll.

b. H   RC[COMP P   DET   S   IO   DO   ]
   ie$^{?L}$ (?i^L)   ka^L-kué$^{?L}$ (?í^L)   ∅   mí^{M}ŋii^L ?í^{H}mii?^{MH}
   elder   COMP   PAST-give^DI^3   that^AN   pig   bread
   (that) old man (that) gave the pig a bread roll

c. H   RC[COMP P   DET   S   IO   DO]
   ?í^{H}mii?^{MH} (?i^L)   ka^L-kué$^{?L}$ (háu^M)   ie$^{?L}$ mí^{M}ŋii^L ∅
   bread   COMP   PAST-give^DI^3   that^IN   elder   pig
   (that) bread roll (that) the old man gave the pig

d. H   RC[COMP P   DET   S   IO DO   ]
   mí^{M}ŋii^L ?i^L ka^L-kué$^{?L}$ (?í^L)   ie$^{?L}$ ∅   ?í^{H}mii?^{MH}
   pig   COMP   PAST-give^DI^3   that^AN   elder   bread
   (that) pig that the old man gave a bread roll

When the subject of the relative clause is a noun phrase, as in (965c) and (965d), the determiner (if one is present) is always found immediately following the predicate; however, the determiner follows the subject when it is a pronoun. Compare (966a) with (965c) and (966b) with (965d).

(966) a. H   RC[COMP P   S   DET   IO   DO]
   ?í^{H}mii?^{MH} (?i^L)   ka^L-kué$^{?L}$ cú^M (háu^M)   mí^{M}ŋii^L ∅
   bread   COMP   PAST-give^DI^3   3   that^IN   pig
   (that) bread roll that s/he gave the pig

b. H   RC[COMP P   S   DET   IO DO   ]
   mí^{M}ŋii^L ?i^L ka^L-kué$^{?L}$ cú^M (?í^L)   ∅   ?í^{H}mii?^{MH}
   pig   COMP   PAST-give^DI^3   3   that^AN   bread
   (that) pig that s/he gave a bread roll

When the object of a preposition is relativized, the recipient/source and locative prepositions are stranded in their normal position, and the instrumental preposition is entirely omitted. The object of temporal prepositions cannot be relativized.

Complex and Compound Sentences 315

When the position relativized is a recipient/source noun phrase, the determiner of the domain noun is obligatory; and the recipient/source preposition is stranded in its normal position as in (967b).

(967) a. *ka^L-hē^L*   *cú^M* *ʔmá^Mʔī^{LM}* *ɲiɾ^Hkõ^M* *ɲiú^Mmí^{ʔH}*
     PAST-offer^TI^3 3   pencil   to   boy
     S/he offered a pencil to the boy.

    b. H   RC[COMP P   S   DET   O
     ɲiú^Mmí^{ʔH}   *ʔi^L*   *ka^L-hē^L*   *cú^M* *ʔí^L*   *ʔmá^Mʔī^{LM}*
     boy   COMP   PAST-offer^TI^3 3 that^AN pencil

             RECIPIENT   ]
             ɲiɾ^Hkõ^M   Ø
             to
     that boy who s/he offered a pencil to

When the position relativized is a locative (LOC) noun phrase, the determiner of the domain noun is optional but usually occurs. Generally, the locative preposition is stranded in its normal position as in (968). Relativization of locative noun phrases is not possible when they are the object of certain prepositions such as *tī^L* 'at' and *ciu^L* 'in, inside, within' (a mass or liquid).

(968) H   RC[COMP P   DET   S   LOC   ]
      hē^L   *ʔi^L*   *kuá^H-ʔū^H*   (*ó^{LM}*)   *ká^Hʔáu^M* *ɲieʔ^M* Ø
      bed   COMP sit^PROG-be^within^SIA^3 yonder chicken beneath
      yonder bed that the chicken is sitting beneath

When the position relativized is an instrumental (INST) noun phrase, the instrumental preposition is omitted; a determiner of the domain noun is optional but generally occurs.

(969) a. *ka^L-pā^L*   *cú^M* *cáï^M* *kiōʔ^L* *kāu^M* *ʔmá^M*
     PAST-hit^TA^3 3   dog   with one^IN wood
     S/he hit the dog with a stick.

    b. H   RC[COMP P   S   DET   O   INST]
     ʔmá^M   *ʔi^L*   *ka^L-pā^L*   *cú^M* (*háu^M*) *cáï^M* Ø
     wood   COMP   PAST-hit^TA^3 3   that^IN dog
     that stick that s/he hit the dog (with)

When the possessor (PSR) of an inalienable noun is relativized, a determiner of the domain noun is obligatory. In (970b), the person of the possessor is indicated inflectionally on the inalienable noun *mí^Htái^HL* 'machete (3)'.

(970) a. *ka^L-ʔái^L   huā^M   mí^Htái^H   ŋiú^Mmí^ʔH*
       PAST-steal^TI^3 John machete^3 boy
       John stole the boy's machete.

   b. H   RC[COMP   P   DET   S   PSR]
      ŋiú^Mmí^ʔH   ʔi^L   ka^L-ʔái^L   ʔi^L   huā^M   mí^Htái^HL   ∅
      boy   COMP   PAST-steal^TI^3 that^AN John machete^3
      that boy whose machete John stole

Although the presence of the complementizer *ʔi^L* is grammatical in possessor relative clauses when the domain noun is inanimate, it rarely occurs. If the domain noun is animate, the presence of the complementizer *ʔi^L* is ungrammatical. A determiner of the domain noun is generally optional.

The possessor of an alienable noun can be relativized.

(971) a. *ʔliáu^L   ŋú^L   tō^LM   mú^LM   kioʔ^MH   mí^Htiei^MH*
       much^IN meat be^stuck^to^TI^PRES^3 bone have^STI^3 cat
       A lot of meat is on the cat's bone.

   b. *ka^L-ma^L-hláʔ^H   mí^Htiei^MH ʔi^L   ka^L-ʔái^L   ʔi^L*
      PAST-CAUS-be^angry^IA^3 cat   COMP   PAST-steal^TI^3 that^AN

      cái^M   mú^LM   kioʔ^MH
      dog bone have^STI^3
      That cat whose bone the dog stole got angry.

Multiple relativization. The term multiple relativization refers to the use of more than one relative clause to modify or specify a domain noun. There are two types of multiple relativization: one involves the use of apposition, while the other involves the chaining of relative clauses. The type of multiple relativization used depends on whether or not a determiner of the domain noun is present, and also on the animacy status of the domain noun. Although there are two syntactic constructions, they function the same: they are both used to modify a single entity.

In an appositional construction, there are two or more domain nouns which are coreferential. The second domain noun is either a repetition of the first, or, more commonly, it is an appropriate superordinate noun, such as *cá^M* 'person', *háʔ^L* 'animal', *ŋi^H* 'place', or *huú^M* 'town'.

Complex and Compound Sentences 317

In a chaining construction, more than one relative clause occurs, but there is only one domain noun.

Pause is ungrammatical preceding relative clauses in a chaining construction, whether or not the complementizer $?i^L$ is present; however, pause preceding the second (and successive) domain nouns, is characteristic of appositional relativization, although such pause may be quite abbreviated in fast speech.

When the domain noun is human, and a determiner of the domain noun is present, an appositional construction is required.

(972) P   S[APP₁ [H   RC[COMP
      $má^M$ $lãi^{LM}$ $ŋiú^M mí?^H$ $?i^L$
      PRF   be^recovered^IA^PAST^3   boy   COMP

            P   S DET   ]] APP₂ [H   RC[P
            ka^L-$tá?^L$ Ø $?i^L$ $cá^M$ ka^L-$kué?^L$
            PAST-fall^IA^3   that^AN   person   PAST-give^DI^3

                    S   IO O   ]]]
                    $ie?^L$ Ø $mí^L$
                    elder   medicine

That boy who fell has recovered, (the) person (that) the old man gave medicine (to).

When the domain noun is animate nonhuman, and a determiner of the domain noun is present, an appositional construction is preferred; for example, in (973) if the superordinate noun $há?^L$ 'animal' is omitted (resulting in a chaining construction), the complementizer $?i^L$ becomes obligatory.

(973) P   S   O[APP₁[H   RC[COMP P
      $má^M$ li^M-$?na^L$ $cú^M$ $mí^M ŋi^{iL}$ $?i^L$ $hmí^H$ $θẽ?^M$
      PRF   HOD-sell^TA^3 3   pig   COMP TRM stand^SIA^3

            DET   S   LOC   ]] APP₂[H   RC[COMP
            $?i^L$ Ø $ciei?^{LM}$ $?ŋiú^{HL}$ $há?^L$ $(?i^L)$
            that^AN   outside   house^3   animal   COMP

                    P   DET   S   ]]]
                    ka^L-$kïe?^M$ $?i^L$ $cí^M$ $ŋo^M$
                    PAST-bite^TA^3ⁱ>3   that^AN dog rabid

S/he has sold the pig that previously stood outside her/his house, the animal (that) the rabid dog bit.

Although the complementizer *ʔiᴸ* 'that, which' is optional following most superordinate nouns, such as in (973), *ʔiᴸ* is ungrammatical following *cǽᴹ* 'person', such as in (972). Nor can *ʔiᴸ* 'that, which' be substituted for *cǽᴹ* 'person' in an attempt to produce a chaining construction.

If the domain noun is animate (human or nonhuman), and there is no determiner of the domain noun, then relative clause chaining is required; an appositional construction is ungrammatical.

(974)　P　　　　S[AMP　　　　H　　　RC[COMP　P　　　　　　　O
　　　θiā̃ᴹ　　　*huṍuᴸᴹ*　　*kiúᴸ*　　(*ʔiᴸ*)　　*kúʔᴹ*　　　*kuúᴹ*
　　　exist^SIA^3　many^AN　coati　COMP　eat^TI^PRES^3　maize

　　　　　　　　POSS　　　　　　　　　] RC[COMP　P
　　　　　　　　kiõᴹᴴ　　　　*hnáᴴᴸ*　　*ʔiᴸ*　　*máᴹ*
　　　　　　　　have^STI^1S　I　　　　COMP　PRF

　　　　　　　　　　　　　　　　　　　　　S　　]]
　　　　　ŋiíᴴ-maᴸcǽᴴᴸ　　　　　　　　*hnáᴴᴸ*
　　　　　INT-exterminate^TA^P^1S　I

There are many coati (that are) eating my maize that I intend to exterminate.

When the domain noun is inanimate, the pattern is not as clear. Both types of constructions occur, but if a determiner of an inanimate domain noun is present, an appositional construction is preferred over chaining. For example in (975), if the repeated domain noun *míᴴhlaᴹ* 'knife' is omitted, resulting in a chaining construction, the complementizer becomes obligatory.

(975)　P　　　　　　S[APP₁[H　　　　RC[P　　　　　S　　O]]
　　　kaᴸ-háuᴹ　　*míᴴhlaᴹ*　　*kiõᴹᴴ*　　*hnáᴴᴸ*　Ø
　　　PAST-break^II　knife　　　have^STI^1S　I

　　　　　　　APP₂[H　　　RC[COMP　P　　　　　　　　　DET
　　　　　　　míᴴhlaᴹ　(*ʔiᴸ*)　*líᴴ*　*kaᴸ-kuéᴸ*　　　*háuᴹ*
　　　　　　　knife　　　COMP　NON　PAST-give^DI^3>1S　that^IN

　　　　　S　　　　　DO]]
　　　　míᴹcáuᴹ　Ø
　　　　priest

The knife broke (that) I have, (the knife) (that) the priest gave me as a gift.

Complex and Compound Sentences 319

If there is no determiner of the inanimate domain noun, however, chaining is preferred. For example in (976), if the word *sũ^H* 'song' were to be used in the position marked by #, the construction would then be an appositional one.

(976) P   S   O[H RC[COMP P   S   ]
       θā̈ï^{LM} hná^{HL} sũ^H ʔi^L ʔïe^{LM} cú^M
       likêsTI^ıs I   song COMP   sing^TI^PRES^3 3

         RC[COMP   P   S   ]]
       # (ʔi^L) ka^L-ti^{MH} ʔué^{LM} ʔŋo^{L}hmáï^M lá^M
          COMP   PAST-regard^TI^3   land Mexico   this
       I like the song(s) that s/he sings about this land of Mexico.

9.2 Nonrestrictive relative clauses

A nonrestrictive relative clause "serves merely to give the hearer an added piece of information about an already identified entity, but not to identify that entity" (Comrie 1989:138).

With nonrestrictive relative clauses, if a determiner of the domain noun is present, it occurs immediately following the domain noun.

(977) ka^L-káï^M ŋiú^{H}ʔa^L lá^M ʔi^L ka^L-lá^L hná^{HL} ciáu^L
       PAST-tear^II   tumpline   this   COMP   PAST-buy^TI^ıs   I   yesterday
       This tumpline, which I bought yesterday, tore.

When a nonthird-person pronoun is modified by a nonrestrictive relative clause, an appositional construction is required. The relative clause is introduced by the noun *cá^M* 'person', and the pronoun is obligatorily repeated in the relative clause.

(978) ka^L-kïʔ^H ʔnú^M hmáï^H cá^M ka^L-káu$\!^{\,\text{ʔ}LM}$ cú^M
       PAST-win^TI^2   you^s   day   person PAST-treat^as^TA^3>2   3

       ʔnú^M kú^{M}ŋa^H
       you^s   humorously
       You won the day, you whom s/he treated as a joke.

9.3 Complementation

In Sochiapan Chinantec, only one of the six complement strategies described by Noonan (1985:42) is found, i.e., the sentence-like indicative complement: if the complementizer *ʔi^L* 'that' is removed, the construction usually resembles an independent sentence, except when there is ellipsis under coreferentiality. The complement also has the possibility of having embedded within it other complements.

When a verb has animate and inanimate inflectional counterparts, such as $híe^{ML}$ (TI) and $híe^{LM}$ (TA) 'see', it is always the inanimate form of the verb which takes the complement. For example, (979a) is grammatical, but (979b) is not.

(979) a. ka^L-$híe^{LM}$ $hná^{HL}$ $ʔi^L$ $ŋa^{ʔL}$ $ie^{ʔL}$
        PAST-see^TI^1S   I   COMP go^home^IA^PAST^3S elder
        I saw that the old man went home.

   b. *ka^L-$híe^H$ $hná^{HL}$ $ʔi^L$ $ŋa^{ʔL}$ $ie^{ʔL}$
        PAST-see^TA^1S   I   COMP go^home^IA^PAST^3S elder
        I saw that the old man went home.

The complementizer. Depending on the complement taking predicate, the complementizer $ʔi^L$ is optional to varying degrees. It generally occurs in complements of verbs such as $huáʔ^{ML}$ 'say', $θaïʔ^{LM}$ 'tell', and cia^{LM} 'relate' when the information is given as an indirect quote. Examples of direct and indirect quotes, respectively, are shown in (980).

(980) a. ka^L-$huáʔ^L$ $cú^M$ la^L $lá^M$ $há^{HL}$ $hná^{HL}$ $kuú^M$
        PAST-say^TI^3 3   idea this sow^TI^FUT^1S I   maize

        $ca^L ʔáu^M$
        tomorrow
        S/he said this: "I will sow maize tomorrow."

   b. ka^L-$huáʔ^L$ $cú^M$ $ʔi^L$ $hŋif^{LM}$ $kuú^M$ $ca^L ʔáu^M$
        PAST-say^TI^3 3   COMP   sow^TI^FUT^3   maize tomorrow
        S/he said that (s/he) will sow maize tomorrow.

The complementizer is optional for most complement taking predicates.

(981) $lē^L$ $hná^{HL}$ $(ʔi^L)$ $ŋie^H$ $hmáï^H$
      think^TI^PRES^1S I   COMP go^nonhome^IA^FUT^1S fiesta
      I think (that) I will go to the fiesta.

(982) $hláʔ^H$ $θãï^M$ $hná^{HL}$ $(ʔi^L)$ $kïʔ^{LM}$ $ʔmïʔ^{LM}$ $réʔ^M$
      really like^SII^1S I   COMP wear^TI^PRES^1S clothes green^IN
      I really like to wear green clothes.

Complex and Compound Sentences 321

The complementizer is optional, but usually absent from the complement of a few verbs such as *tį́ᴹ* 'be able (STI)' and *ʔniáuʔᴸᴹ* 'be necessary (SII)'.

(983) *tiáᴹ tį́ᴹ*   *iáʔᴸ hnáᴴᴸ (ʔiᴸ) ʔį́ᴴᴸ*   *ʔiᴸ nįᴹ*
 not be^able^STI^1S ASSR I   COMP read^TI^FUT^1S thing that
 I am not able to read that thing.

Ellipsis. When the subject of the complement clause is coreferential with the subject or indirect object of the matrix clause, ellipsis of the nominal occurs in the complement clause. Nonetheless, the identity of the subject is recoverable by the inflection of the verb; that is, verb inflection in complement clauses is the same as that in independent clauses. Ellipsis of the complement subject when coreferential with the subject of the matrix clause is illustrated in (984b).

(984) a. *ʔnióᴸ*   *cúᴹ ʔiᴸ kiúʔᴴᴸ*   *hnáᴴᴸ ką́ᴴ*
 want^STI^3 3   COMP grind^TI^FUT^1S I   dough
 S/he wants me to grind (maize) dough.

 b. *ʔnióᴸ*   *cúᴹ ʔiᴸ kiúʔᴸᴹ*   *(*cúᴹ) ką́ᴴ*
 want^STI^3 3₁   COMP grind^TI^FUT^3 3₁   dough
 S/he₁ wants to grind (maize) dough.

If the complement subject is coreferential with either the subject of a ditransitive verb as in (985a), or with the IO as in (985b), ellipsis occurs.

(985) a. *kaᴸ-θáiᴸ*   *cúᴹ hnáᴴᴸ ʔiᴸ kiúʔᴸᴹ*   *(*cúᴹ)*
 PAST-tell^DI^3>1S 3₁   I   COMP grind^TI^FUT^3 3₁

 ką́ᴴ
 dough
 S/he₁ told me that (s/he₁) will grind the (maize) dough.

 b. *kaᴸ-θáiᴸ*   *cúᴹ hnáᴴᴸʔiᴸ*   *kiúʔᴴᴸ*
 PAST-tell^DI^3>1S 3   I₁   COMP grind^TI^FUT^1S

 *(*hnáᴴᴸ) ką́ᴴ*
 I₁   dough
 S/he told me₁ to grind the (maize) dough. (lit,. S/he told me₁ that (I₁) will grind the (maize) dough.)

Subject and object complements. Subject complements are not uncommon with intransitive verbs (e.g., (987)), but the only transitive verb noted thus far which permits a subject complement is the verb *hmu*^{M} 'do, make'. If the subject of *hmu*^{M} 'do, make' is a complement clause, the object must be also; the construction is causative as in (986a). Object complements are common, for example, (986b).

(986) a. *ʔi*^{L} *ka*^{L}-*sú*$^{\jmath LM}$ *hȃu*^{M} *cȋ*^{L} *ka*^{L}-*hmú*^{L} *ʔi*^{L} *ka*^{L}-*cú*$^{\jmath M}$
      COMP PAST-fall^II^P then hail PAST-make^TI^3 COMP PAST-break^II

      ʔo^L*tá*^{M}*kié*^{M}
      window
      The falling hail broke the window (lit., that hail fell then made (caused) that the window broke).

   b. *ka*^{L}-*kȋ*^{L} *hná*^{HL} *ʔi*^{L} *ŋiei*$^{\jmath MH}$ *ʔnú*^{M}
      PAST-dream^TI^1S I COMP come^to^nonhome^IA^FUT^2S you^S
      I dreamed that you would come.

The complementizer is optional for most complement-taking predicates.

(987) *tiá*^{M} *ka*^{L}-*lǐ*^{L} (*ʔi*^{L})
      not   PAST-be^possible^II (COMP)

      ŋiʔ^L-*hïe*^{L} *hná*^{HL} *ʔno*$^{\jmath M}$
      ANDT^FUT-see^TA^1S>2 I   you-P
   (It) was not possible that I go see you.

9.4 Purpose clauses

Purpose clauses are usually introduced by the complementizer *ʔi*^{L} 'that', in which case the structure of the purpose clause parallels that of the complement clause; a purpose clause, however, answers the question 'why?' instead of 'what?'. The antecedent action to purpose is called the 'ground'.

(988) GROUND   PURPOSE
      cã$^{\jmath LM}$ *cú*^{M} *ʔŋiú*^{HL} *ʔi*^{L} *cá*^{M}-*hmú*^{L}
      return^home^IA^PRES^3S 3   house^3 COMP ANDT^PRES-make^TI^3

      má^{LM}
      food
   S/he is returning home to prepare the food. *or* S/he is returning to eat a meal.

Sometimes the introducer *ʔi*^{L} 'that' may be omitted from the purpose clause.

(989) GROUND
ɲiéi^H   hnáHL   ha^H   huúM   kaiuka
go^nonhome^IA^PAST^1s I   among   town   Cayuca

> PURPOSE
> (ʔi^L)   ɲif^H-ɲa^HL   hnáHL   mḯMcáuM
> COMP   ANDT^PAST-ask^TI^1s I   priest
> I went to the town of Cayuca to ask the priest...

Although the ground clause generally precedes the purpose clause, it is possible to have the purpose clause precede the ground clause; when this occurs, the purpose must be introduced by the complementizer ʔi^L. In (990), huã^M 'John' is subject of the purpose clause, with ellipsis of the subject occurring in the ground clause.

(990) PURPOSE
ʔi^L   ká^M   lauML   bíʔH   huã^M
COMP   PV^PRES evaluate^TA^PRES^3>1   AFF   John

> GROUND
> haLM   ɲif^H   lá^M
> come^to^nonhome^IA^PRES^3s   place   this
> To thoroughly evaluate (us), John comes to this place.

Negative purpose is introduced by kí^H nî^M lî^H 'lest'; the verb of the negative purpose clause is obligatorily inflected for the remote past tense.

(991) ti^L   koʔL   huïLM   kuîH-ciáHL   dí^M   ʔmá^M   lá^M
      at   upper^side^3 trail   HORT-put^TI^1P   we^INCL   wood   this

kí^H^nî^M^lî^H   kaL-dáʔLM   cáu^M
lest   PAST-trip^IA^3   people
Let's put this log on the trail's upper side lest people trip.

9.5 Result clauses

The clause that describes the result of an action is introduced by hǻu^M 'then, so'. hǻu^M can be optionally preceded by kí^H or ʔi^L, or both: ʔi^L hǻu^M 'then, so', kí^H hǻu^M 'consequently', and kí^H ʔi^L hǻu^M 'consequently'. The introducer ʔi^L hǻu^M 'then, so' is most likely a combination of the contingent noun ʔi^L 'thing' with the inanimate anaphoric deictic hǻu^M 'that', functioning as a kind of summation of the previous proposition in the sense of 'that being the case'. kí^H ʔi^L hǻu^M and kí^H hǻu^M 'consequently' are combinations of *kɨ́ʰ* 'because' with the other two introducers *ʔiᴸ háuᴹ* and *háuᴹ*, respectively. The antecedent action to result is called the ground.

(992)   GROUND   RESULT
       liᴸ   *θiãᴹ*   *hõᴹ*   *cáᴹmïᴸ* *ʔíᴸ*   *ʔiᴸ^háuᴹ*
       occur^ɪɪ^FUT exist^SIA^3 child^3 woman that^AN so

       ŋauᴸ   *tïᴸᴹ*   *mïᵋ*
       go^nonhome^ɪᴀ^PAST^3s master medicine
       That woman is having a baby, and so the doctor has gone (there).

9.6 Cause clauses

Cause clauses are introduced by any one of a variety of clause markers, the nuances of which are not clear; for the present, all cause introducers are glossed as 'because'. *kɨ́ʰ* is the most frequently used introducer; also used are: *ʔliáᴹ*, *ʔiᴸʔliáᴹ*, *kɨ́ʰʔliáᴹ*, *kɨ́ʰ ʔiᴸʔliáᴹ*, *kuᴸŋifʰ ʔiᴸ*, *kɨ́ʰ kūᴸŋifʰ*, *kūᴸŋifʰ ʔiᴸʔliáᴹ*, *kɨ́ʰ kūᴸŋifʰ ʔiᴸʔliáᴹ*, and *kɨ́ʰʔliáᴹ kūᴸŋifʰ ʔiᴸʔliáᴹ*. Regardless of whether the cause clause precedes or follows the effect clause, any of the above introducers may be used.

The following examples illustrate the cause clause following the effect clause.

(993)   EFFECT   CAUSE
       ʔiᴸ^háuᴹ *kaᴸ-haᴸ-ʔíᴸ*   *huúᴹ háuᴹ*   *kɨ́ʰ*
       then   PAST-PASS-be^erased^ɪɪ town that^ɪɴ because

       kaᴸ-ʔiᴸ   *mïᶠᴴuïᴸ*   *kuéʔᴸᴹ*   *bíʔᴴ*
       PAST-enter^ɪɪ^s sickness contagious AFF
       That's why the town was wiped out, because a contagious disease came in.

(994)   EFFECT   CAUSE
       kaᴸ-ŋifᴸᴹ   *hnáᴴᴸ* *ŋifʰ* *háuᴹ* *ʔliáᴹ* *kaᴸ-liᴸ*
       PAST-stay^ɪᴀ^1s I   place that^ɪɴ because PAST-become^ɪɪ

       cáuᴴ   *bíʔᴴ*
       be^sick^SIA^1s AFF
       I stayed at that place because I became sick.

When the cause clause precedes the effect clause, pause occurs between the two clauses, and the effect clause is obligatorily introduced by either

Complex and Compound Sentences 325

hǎu^M 'then, so' or *ʔi^L hǎu^M* 'then, so'. Examples of the cause clause preceding the effect clause are shown in (995) and (996).

(995) CAUSE   EFFECT
 kí^H tiá^M má^{M}tí^{LM} cú^M ʔéiʔ^{LM} kiõ^{MH} hǎu^M
 because not fulfill^TI^PRES^3 3   order have^STI^IS then

 tiá^M lā̃^{HL} iáʔ^L cú^M
 not recover^IA^FUT^3 ASSR 3
 Because s/he is not obeying my orders, s/he is not recovering.

(996) CAUSE
 kū̃^{L}ɲií^H^ʔi^L lǐ^H ha^{LM} mií^L cí^L bíʔ^H dió^{LM}
 because NON come^II^PRES^S compassion heart^3 AFF God

 EFFECT
 ʔi^L^hǎu^M má^M ka^L-liǎu^L hnoʔ^H
 so   PRF PAST-be^saved^IA^1P we
 Because compassion freely comes (from) God's heart, we have been saved.

9.7 Conditional constructions

Reality conditionals, imaginative conditionals, and concessive conditionals are discussed in this section. Reality conditionals include present, habitual/generic, past, and predictive conditionals. Imaginative conditionals include hypothetical and counterfactual conditionals. All reality conditionals are introduced by the subordinator *nǐ^{H}huáʔ^L* 'if'. The imaginative conditionals are introduced by the subordinator *sá^H* or *sá^{H}hmǐ^H* 'if, if only'. Concessive conditionals are introduced by the subordinator *uá^{H}kū̃^{L}* 'even if'.

Reality conditionals. Examples (997)–(1000) illustrate the present, habitual/generic, past, and predictive conditionals in turn.

(997) *nǐ^{H}huáʔ^L lǐ^{ML} nú^M la^L ní^M hǎu^M lǐ^L*
 if   think^TI^PRES^2 you^s idea that then be^IA^PRES^2

 nú^M hā̃^{M} cá^M kǎu^H bíʔ^H
 you^s one^AN person stupid AFF
 If you think that, then you are a stupid person.

(998) *nǐ^{H}huáʔ^L má^{M}tõ^L cú^M mí^{M}ɲií^L kuú^M lǐ^M*
 if   feed^DA^PRES^3 3   pig maize be^able^II^PRES

ʔúʔᴴ   háʔᴸ   tiaᴸhuïᴸᴹ
be^fat^SIA^3 animal rapidly
If one feeds a pig maize, the animal is able to fatten rapidly.

(999) nïʰhuáʔᴸ máᴹ lïᴹ-kiúʔᴸᴹ   cúᴹ ʔmáᴹ táuᴹ háuᴹ
      if   PRF HOD-chop^down^TI^3 3 tree banana then

      lïᴸ   cúᴹ háᴹ   cáᴹ   tiáᴹ ne ʔᴸ   bíʔᴴ
      be^IA^PRES^3 3 one^AN person   not be^obedient^SIA^3 AFF
      If s/he just chopped down that banana palm, then s/he is a
      disobedient person.

(1000) nïʰhuáʔᴸ kaᴸ-háuᴸ   kuáᴴnáïᴹ háuᴹ kúʔᴴᴸ
       if   PAST-be^caught^IA^3   deer   then eat^TI^FUT^IP

       dïᴹ   ɲúᴸ
       we^INCL meat
       If a deer gets caught (in our trap), we'll eat meat.

The subordinator *nïʰhuáʔᴸ* is followed by a complement clause; however, the complementizer *ʔiᴸ* is usually omitted, as in example (1000). An example with the complementizer present is given in (1001).

(1001) lïᴹᴸ   ʔuaᴴ   miᴸ   kuúᴹ   nïʰhuáʔᴸ ʔiᴸ
       become^II^PRES   be^soft^II spherical maize if   COMP

       cióᴹᴸ   cúᴹ hmáïᴹ
       soak^TI^PRES^ 3   water
       Maize becomes soft if one soaks (it) in water.

The apodosis (conclusion) may precede or follow the protasis (condition), as in (1002) and (1003). When the apodosis follows the protasis, it is generally marked by *háuᴹ* 'then', or rarely by *ʔiᴸ háuᴹ* 'then'; when the apodosis precedes the protasis, however, the apodosis is always unmarked. There do not appear to be any restrictions on the tenses in either the protasis or apodosis, and a wide variety of combinations is possible.

(1002) PROTASIS   APODOSIS
       nïʰhuáʔᴸ kaᴸ-ɲiᴴᴸ   cúᴹ háïᴴᴸ (háuᴹ) máᴹ
       if   PAST-understand^TI^3 3   word then   PRF

        ka^L-hã?^{MH}   *bí?^H nú^M*   *cú^M*
        PAST-win^TA^2 AFF you^s 3
        If s/he understood that message, then you have won her/him over.

(1003) APODOSIS   PROTASIS
      ?laï?^L   bí?^H   lí̂^{ML}   *kiõ^{MH}*   *hná^{HL}*   *ní̂^Hhuá?^L*
      bad^IN AFF occur^II^PRES have^STI^1S I   if

      ká̂^{HL}   *lio^{MH}*
      carry^TI^FUT^1S cargo
      It is bad for me if I (should) carry cargo.

A negative conditional is introduced by the same subordinator as a positive conditional, that is, there is no special morpheme such as 'unless'.

(1004) *uí̂^L*   *lí̂^{LM}*   *má?^L la^L*   *kuõu^M*   *mí^Mɲií^L ní̂^Hhuá?^L tiá^M*
      difficult very EXCL EVID grow^IA^PRES^3 pig   if   not

      kue?^{LM}   *cú^M*   *?liã̂u^L*   *kuú^M*
      give^DI^PRES^3 3   much^IN maize
      Evidently, a pig fattens with great difficulty if it is not given much maize.

Imaginative conditionals. Imaginative conditionals include both hypothetical (what might be) and counterfactual (what might have been) conditionals. Generally, the protasis of both hypothetical and counterfactual conditionals is introduced by the subordinator *sá^Hhmí̂^H* 'if, if only'. A complement clause, usually introduced by the complementizer *?i^L*, follows the subordinator; it is rarely omitted. The protasis is optionally closed by the indubitative (INDB) illocutionary particle *dú?^H*. In this context, the meaning of *dú?^H* is 'it's obvious that the opposite is true'. When the apodosis follows the protasis, it is usually introduced by *hãu^M* 'then' as in (1006) or, less commonly, by *?i^L hãu^M* 'then'. Examples of hypothetical and counterfactual conditionals, respectively, are (1005) and (1006). Occasionally, when the apodosis follows the protasis, the apodosis lacks any introducer, as in (1007).

(1005) PROTASIS
      sá^Hhmí̂^H   *?i^L*   *li^L*   *?mu?^{MH}*   *ká^Mfe^{MH}*   *dú?^H*
      if^only COMP become^II^FUT be^expensive^SII coffee   INDB

APODOSIS
hã́u^{M} *hmĩ́*^{H} *lã*^{MH} *hná*^{HL} *hã*^{M} *lo*^{H}
then TRM buy^TA^FUT^1S I one^AN mule
If only coffee would become expensive, I would buy a mule.

(1006) PROTASIS
sá^{H}*hmĩ́*^{H} *ʔi*^{L} *ka*^{L}*-θíʔ*^{HL} *dí*^{M} *ʔŋiú*^{HL} *ŋií*^{H} *nĩ́*^{M}
if COMP PAST-stand^TI^3 we^INCL house^1P place that

APODOSIS
hã́u^{M} *hmĩ́*^{H} *má*^{M} *ha*^{L}*-θã́ĩ*^{L} *bíʔ*^{H}
then TRM PRF PASS^PAST-slip^II AFF
If we had stood our house there, it would have slipped (down the hill).

(1007) PROTASIS APODOSIS
sá^{H}*hmĩ́*^{H} *ʔi*^{L} *tï*^{MH} *huï*^{LM} *dúʔ*^{H} *hmĩ́*^{H} *lá*^{HL}
if COMP reach^TI^FUT road INDB TRM buy^TI^FUT^1S

hná^{HL} *kã́u*^{M} *kařo*
I one^IN truck
If the road were complete, I would buy a truck.

Although the protasis of imaginative conditionals is generally introduced by *sá*^{H}*hmĩ́*^{H} 'if, if only', there are a few examples in the corpus of *sá*^{H}. *sá*^{H}*hmĩ́*^{H} can be readily substituted for *sá*^{H} in any of its occurrences, but not necessarily the other way around. I have not been able to establish any difference in meaning between the two forms when either is grammatical, or why the grammaticality of *sá*^{H} is sometimes equivocal. The apodosis rarely precedes the protasis; when it does, it lacks an introducer. Examples with *sá*^{H}*hmĩ́*^{H} and *sá*^{H} in the protasis are given in (1008) and (1009), respectively.

(1008) APODOSIS
tiá^{M} *hmu*^{M} *iáʔ*^{L} *cú*^{M} *la*^{L} *kũ*^{L} *ʔi*^{L} *hmĩ́*^{H}
not do^TI^PRES^3 ASSR 3 about only COMP TRM

PROTASIS
ʔniáuʔ^{MH} *hmu*^{H} *sá*^{H}*hmĩ́*^{H} *ʔi*^{L} *tĩ́*^{M}
be^necessary^SII do^TI^FUT^3 if COMP be^capable^STI^3

Complex and Compound Sentences

     cú^M
     3
  S/he does not do what s/he ought to do if (it were true that) s/he is capable.

(1009) APODOSIS
  cá^M *hmí*^H *má*^M *?iú*^H *má*^M *cau*^{HL}   *bí?*^H *hnio?*^H
  people TRM PRF PV^FUT PRF die^IA^FUT^1P AFF we

    PROTASIS
    sá^H *?i*^L *tiá*^M *kuā*^L   *?nú*^M
    if COMP not arrive^nonhome^IA^PAST^2S you^s
  We would all now be dying if you had not arrived.

Concessive conditionals. Thompson and Longacre define a concessive conditional declarative sentence as being "like an ordinary conditional sentence in that it may be talking about some 'unreal' event, either predictive or hypothetical, but it is like a concessive sentence...in that its main clause is asserted in spite of assumptions to the contrary" (1985:197). A Chinantec concessive conditional clause is introduced by the subordinator *uá*^H*kū*^L 'even if'. Usually the concessive conditional clause follows the main clause, as in (1010), although it may occur first as in (1011).

(1010) *ŋi*^H*-háï*^{LM}   *hná*^{HL} *ca*^L*?áu*^M *uá*^H*kū*^L *ciau*^M *hmî*^L
   ANDT^FUT-slash^TI^1S I tomorrow even^if fall^II^PRES rain
   I will go slash (a field) tomorrow, even if it rains.

(1011) *uá*^H*kū*^L *hmí*^H *ka*^L*-lau*^M   *cú*^M *tiú*^L *kiõ*^{MH} *hná*^{HL}
   even^if TRM PAST-buy^used^TI^3 3 rifle have^STI^1S I

   tiá^M *hmí*^H *ka*^L*-hāu*^L   *iá?*^L *cú*^M *?ia?*^{LM} *?í*^L
   not TRM PAST-catch^TA^3 ASSR 3 puma that^AN
   Even if he had bought my rifle, he wouldn't have caught that puma.

9.8 Concessive clauses

According to Thompson and Longacre, a concessive clause is one "which makes a concession against which the proposition in the main clause is contrasted" (1985:198). They identify two types of concessive clauses, definite and indefinite. Chinantec has distinct subordinators to introduce these two types of concessive.

Definite concessive clauses. In a definite concessive sentence, there is an expectation that, if the proposition in the concessive clause is true, then the assertion in the main clause would not be true.

Chinantec has three subordinators to introduce definite concessive clauses: *uá^H* 'although', *uá^Hhī?^H* 'even though', and *uá^H hā́u^M la^L hā́u^M* 'in spite of the fact that'. All three subordinators are followed by a complement clause. The complementizer *?i^L* is obligatory following *uá^H* 'although', but is usually omitted following the other two concessive subordinators. The main clause is usually introduced by *kū^Lhā́u^M* 'nonetheless', but not always; cf. (1012) and (1014). The most common of the three concessive subordinators is *uá^Hhī?^H* 'even though'. The order of the main and subordinate clauses appears to be free. In (1012) the main clause precedes the concessive clause; in (1013) the concessive clause precedes the main clause.

(1012) *kū^Lhā́u^M   ka^L-hmú^HL   bí?^H hno?^H ?i^Lráu^L   uá^Hhī?^H*
    nonetheless PAST-make^ʈɪ^1P AFF   we   crude^sugar even^though

    ta^L   ciau^M   hmī̆^L
    while fall^ʈɪ^PRES rain
Nonetheless, we made crude sugar, even though it was raining.

(1013) *uá^Hhī?^H   ló?^LM   cú^M kū^Lhā́u^M   tiá^M li^L*
    even^though bathe^IA^PRES^3 3   nonetheless not   become^ʈɪ^FUT

    kuóu?^L   iá?^L cú^M
    be^cold^SIA^3 ASSR 3
Although one bathes, nonetheless one doesn't become cold.

(1014) *la^L   kū^LM   ?io^L   ká^Mfe^MH   uá^Hhī?^H   tiá^M ré^M má^M*
    EVID pick^ʈɪ^PRES^3 old^lady coffee   even^though not   well   PRF

    huu^M
    be^ripe^ʈɪ^PRES
Apparently, the old lady picks coffee even though it's not fully ripe.

The complementizer *?i^L* occurs following the subordinator *uá^H* 'although' in (1015).

(1015) *uá^H   ?i^L   hmái^H nio^M   tie^L   kū^Lhā́u^M*
    although COMP day   be^present^SII^P tranquillity nonetheless

hmu^M   bí?^H cú^M ta^{MH}
do^TI^PRES^3 AFF   3   work
Although it is a day of rest, s/he still works.

The complex introducer *uá^H hǎu^M la^L hǎu^M* 'in spite of the fact that' is infrequent in the data, but is illustrated by (1016).

(1016) kū^Lhǎu^M   θia^{LM}   ?i^L   kú?^{ML}   dí^M   uá^H   hǎu^M
       nonetheless exist^SII thing eat^TI^PRES^1P we^INCL whether that^IN

       la^L   hǎu^M   θiā^{LM}   hméi^M   dí^M
       idea that^IN be^absent^SIA^3 father^1P we^INCL
       In spite of the fact that our father is absent, nonetheless we have food to eat.

Indefinite concessive clauses. Indefinite concessive clauses "contain some unspecified element, typically an indefinite pronoun or question word" (Thompson and Longacre 1985:198). Chinantec indefinite concessive clauses are introduced by *uá^H ?ī^M mi^L* 'whoever', *uá^H ?ī^M mi^L* 'whichever', *uá^H ?ī^M mi^L ?e^L* 'whatever', *uá^H ?ī^M mi^L hī?^H* 'wherever', and *uá^H lá?^L mi^L* 'however'. In these subordinators, the question words *?ī^M* 'which? (AN)', *?ī^M* 'which? (IN)', *?e^L* 'what?', *hī?^H* 'where?', and *lá?^L* 'how?' occur, respectively. The verb in the subordinate clause is usually inflected for the past tense, although it may be inflected for the present as in (1021); generally, the implication is that the event described in the subordinate clause has occurred before and is likely to occur again, although there need not be a previous occurrence. The main clause is optionally introduced by *kū^Lhǎu^M* 'nonetheless'. Examples of each subordinator in turn are given in (1017)–(1021).

(1017) uá^H   ?ī^M   mi^L cá?^M   ka^L-ma^L
       although which^AN? ever person PAST-ask^for^TA^3 > 1S

       kū^Lhǎu^M   tiá^M   ?ei^{MH}   iá?^L hná^{HL}
       nevertheless not accept^TI^FUT^1S ASSR I
       Whoever proposes to me, nevertheless I will not accept.

(1018) uo^H   hná^{HL} uá^H   ?ī^M   mi^L hmäï^H
       cry^IA^FUT^1S I   although which^IN? ever day

       ka^L-po^L   cú^M
       PAST-hit^TA^3 > 1S 3
       I will cry whenever s/he hits me.

(1019) tiá^M hué?^{HL}   iá?^L hná^{HL} uá^H   ?í^M   mi^L
       not be^afraid^IA^FUT^1S ASSR I   although which^IN? ever

        ?e^L   ka^L-li^L
        what? PAST-happen^II
        I will not be afraid whatever happens.

(1020) ŋii^L-?ẽi^{MH}   cú^M ?ú^Hcií^H uá^H   ?í^M   mi^L hí?^H
       AMB-wear^TI   3   hat   although which^IN? ever where?

        ka^L-ció^{LM}
        PAST-arrive^nonhome^IA^3S
        He walks around wearing a hat wherever he goes.

(1021) cá^M   LM   ku^Ltí^L tiá^M ne?^L   uá^H   lá?^L mi^L
       person yonder truly   not be^obedient^SIA^3 although how? ever

        liéi?^{LM}   cáu^M
        talk^to^TA^PRES^3ⁱ>3 people
        That person over there is not obedient regardless of how people talk to him.

In addition to the above indefinite concessive subordinators, the subordinator *uá^H* 'although', illustrated above with definite concessive clauses, can be used in an indefinite concessive expression involving two subordinate clauses in alternation: *uá^H...uá^H* 'whether...or'. The subordinate clauses in alternation must both be inflected for the same tense.

(1022) uá^H   ?i^L   có^{LM}   uá^H   ?i^L   tiá^M
       whether COMP go^nonhome^IA^FUT^3S whether COMP not

        có^{LM}   cú^M kū^Lhắu^M
        go^nonhome^IA^FUT^3S 3   nonetheless

        ŋie^H   bí?^H hná^{HL} kuá?^{LM}
        go^nonhome^IA^FUT^1S AFF   I   church
        Whether s/he goes or whether s/he doesn't go, nonetheless I'm going to church.

9.9 Substitutive clauses

When an unexpected event replaces an expected one, the clause expressing the expected event is introduced by the subordinator *cia^L* 'rather than'. The verb

Complex and Compound Sentences 333

in the subordinate clause must be inflected for the future and obligatorily occurs with the terminative (TRM) $hmi̊^H$. There is no tense restriction for the main clause; it may come first as in (1023), or the subordinate clause as in (1024).

(1023) $lã^{MH}$ $hná^{HL}$ $hã^M$ lo^H cia^L $hmi̊^H$
       buy^TA^FUT^1S I   one^AN mule rather^than TRM

           $lã^{MH}$ $hã^M$ $ca^Lkuá^H$
           buy^TA^FUT^1S one^AN horse
       I will buy a mule rather than buying a horse.

(1024) cia^L $hmi̊^H$ $ciã^{MH}$ $hná^{HL}$ $tú^M$ $ciã^{MH}$
       rather^than TRM   raise^TA^FUT^P^1S I   turkey raise^TA^FUT^P^1S

       $hná^{HL}$ $ká^Hʔáu^M$
       I   chicken
       Rather than raising turkeys, I will raise chickens.

9.10 Comparative constructions

Comparative constructions are of four types: comparison of equality, inequality, situations across time, or counterfactual comparison. Each is discussed below.

Comparison of equality. When two factual propositions are compared, the standard of comparison is introduced by $la^Lhmi̊^H$ 'like'. The comparative clause usually precedes the clause of the standard. It frequently repeats the verb of the main clause in the subordinate clause, as can be seen in example (1025) with the verb $li̊^L$ 'be'. However, comparisons can be constructed without such repetition as in (1026).

(1025) COMPARATIVE   STANDARD
       $ʔí^Hmiiʔ^{MH}$ $ʔi^L$ hmu^M $ieʔ^L$ $ó^{LM}$ $li̊^L$ $la^Lhmi̊^H$
       bread   COMP make^TI^PRES^3 elder yonder be^II^PRES like

           $li̊^L$ $ki̊^H$ $biʔ^H$
           be^II^PRES rock AFF
       The bread that the old man over there makes is like rock.

(1026)   COMPARATIVE
       $hãu^M$ $tiá^M$ $li̊^H$ $ʔiá^Hʔã^H$ $ʔnoʔ^M$ $ni̊^H$ $má^H$
       then   not NON be^surprised^IA^FUT^2 you^P when^FUT PRF

                            STANDARD
káᴹ-cióᴸᴹ   hmái̧ᴴ hã́uᴹ laᴸhmi̧ᴴ taʔᴸᴹ   kã́uᴹ
PAST-arrive^II time that^IN like   fall^II^PRES^S one^IN

liá̧ᴸ
trap

Then you will not be unduly surprised when that day arrives like the falling of a trap.

Comparisons that involve a stative clause appear to always repeat the state verb or predicating adjective in both clauses, as illustrated, respectively, in (1027) and (1028).

(1027) COMPARATIVE   STANDARD
θi̧ã̧ᴹ   cúᴹ laᴸhmi̧ᴴ θi̧ã̧ᴹ   hã̧ᴹ   mí̧ᴹŋi̧ᴸ bi̧ʔᴴ
exist^SIA^3 3 like exist^SIA^3 one^AN pig   AFF
S/he lives like a pig.

(1028) COMPARATIVE   STANDARD
pi̧ᴸ   cúᴹ laᴸhmi̧ᴴ pi̧ᴸ   hã̧ᴹ ʔi̧aʔᴸᴹ bi̧ʔᴴ
be^strong^SIA^3 3 like be^strong^SIA^3 one^AN puma AFF
S/he is as strong as a puma.

In a negated comparison, the negative *tiáᴹ* precedes the verb in the comparative clause; the clause of the standard is the same as in a positive comparison.

(1029) COMPARATIVE   STANDARD
ti̧ᴸᴹ   ni̧ᴹ tiáᴹ hmuᴹ   laᴸhmi̧ᴴ ti̧ᴹ hmuᴹ   ti̧ᴸᴹ
teacher that not do^TI^PRES^3 like DISC do^TI^PRES^3 teacher

núʔᴸ
Arnold

That teacher doesn't act like the teacher Arnold used to act.

The standard can optionally precede the comparative clause, although it rarely does. When it does, the comparative clause may be unmarked as in (1030) or it may be introduced by *laᴸ hã́uᴹ* 'in the same manner' as in (1031).

(1030) STANDARD   COMPARATIVE
laᴸhmi̧ᴴ hmuᴹ   cái̧ᴹ bi̧ʔᴴ hmuᴹ   cúᴹ
like   do^TI^PRES^3 dog AFF do^TI^PRES^3 3
S/he does/behaves like a dog (i.e., is immoral).

Complex and Compound Sentences 335

(1031) STANDARD COMPARATIVE
  la^{L}hmí^H ka^L-ʔiáu^{LM}   *cú^M hná^{HL} ta^{MH} la^L hấu^M*
  like   PAST-appoint^DA^3 > 1 3   I   work about that

  bí?^{H} ʔiáu^{LM}   *cú^M siá?^{L} ʔno?^{M}*
  AFF appoint^DA^FUT^3 > 2 3   also you^P
  Like he appointed me to hold office, in the same manner he will also appoint you.

Comparisons of inequality. In comparisons of inequality, the comparative clause obligatorily precedes the standard clause. The comparative clause is optionally introduced by *ti^L* 'at', and the standard clause is introduced by *la^L kó?^{L}* 'more than', *kū^L* 'than', or *la^L kū^L* 'than'. The affirmation (AFF) illocutionary particle *bí?^{H}* is obligatory following *la^L kó?^{L}*, but is optional following *kū^L* and *la^L kū^L*. Any one of the three subordinators can be substituted for the other without any apparent difference of meaning. Ellipsis of the verb occurs in the standard clause. Examples of the three subordinators, respectively, are given in (1032)–(1034).

(1032) COMPARATIVE   STANDARD
  (ti^L) ʔliấu^L má^M li^M-kué^{LM} cú^M la^L^kó?^{L} bí?^{H} hi^L li^M
  at more^IN PRF HOD-give^TI^3 3   more^than AFF all^AN very

  cá^M ʔá?^{L}
  person rich
  She has just given more than all the wealthy (have given).

(1033) COMPARATIVE   STANDARD
  (ti^L) ʔấu^H bí?^{H} cú^M kū^L hná^{HL}
  at   be^quick^SIA^3   AFF   3   than   I
  S/he is quicker than I.

(1034) COMPARATIVE   STANDARD
  (ti^L) kú^{H}pi?^{MH} bí?^{H} ku?^{LM} hná^{HL} la^L^kū^L bí?^{H} ʔnú^M
  at small AFF eat^TI^PRES^1S I   than   AFF you^S
  I eat less than you.

Comparison of situations across time. When the present situation of the referent of a subject is compared to a past situation of the same entity (the standard), if there has been no change, the standard is marked in four ways simultaneously: it is introduced by *la^L* 'as', the perfect (PRF) *má^M* must occur with the verb, the anaphoric deictic *hấu^M* 'that (IN)' must occur immediately after the verb, and there is ellipsis of the subject in the standard clause. In addition, the verbs of both the comparative and standard clauses are identical and are inflected for the present tense.

(1035) COMPARATIVE　　　　　　STANDARD
　　　hú?ᴹᴸ　　　　　hnáᴴᴸ laᴸ máᴹ hú?ᴹᴸ　　　háuᴹ bí?ᴴ
　　　cough^ɪᴀ^ᴘʀᴇs^1s I　as ᴘʀꜰ cough^ɪᴀ^ᴘʀᴇs^1s that^ɪɴ ᴀꜰꜰ
　　　I am still coughing as I was (coughing) before.

This construction also has an abbreviated form which consists of the standard clause alone, but with an overt subject. Compare (1036) with (1035).

(1036) laᴸ máᴹ hú?ᴹᴸ　　　háuᴹ bí?ᴴ hnáᴴᴸ
　　　as ᴘʀꜰ cough^ɪᴀ^ᴘʀᴇs^1s that^ɪɴ ᴀꜰꜰ I
　　　I am coughing as before.

If the present situation of the referent of a subject differs from a past situation of the same entity (the standard), both the comparative clause and the standard clause are obligatorily marked in separate ways. The verb of the comparative clause is negated by the interruptive (ɪɴᴛʀᴘ) adverb tiúᴹuúᴹ 'no longer'. The standard clause is introduced by laᴸhmíᴴ 'like', and either the terminative (ᴛʀᴍ) adverb hmíᴴ or the discontinuative (ᴅɪꜱᴄ) adverb tíᴹ must precede the verb of the standard clause. The verb that occurs in the main clause of the comparative is repeated in the standard; in both instances the verb is in the present tense (or else both are state verbs). The order of the comparative and standard clauses cannot be reversed. Examples with the terminative hmíᴴ and the discontinuative tíᴹ are given in (1037) and (1038).

(1037) COMPARATIVE　　　　　　　　　　　　　　　STANDARD
　　　tiúᴹuúᴹ tíᴹ　　　　　hnáᴴᴸ kiẽᴴ　　　　　tūᴸᴹ laᴸhmíᴴ
　　　ɪɴᴛʀᴘ be^able^sᴛɪ^1s I　play^ᴛɪ^ꜰᴜᴛ^1s guitar like

　　　　hmíᴴ tíᴹ　　　　　hmíᴴtíᴹ
　　　　ᴛʀᴍ be^able^sᴛɪ^1s previously
　　　I am not able to play the guitar like I used to be able to previously.

(1038) COMPARATIVE　　　　　　STANDARD
　　　tiúᴹuúᴹ cāᴸᴹ　　　　cúᴹ laᴸhmíᴴ tíᴹ cāᴸᴹ　　　　cúᴹ
　　　ɪɴᴛʀᴘ dance^ɪᴀ^ᴘʀᴇs^3 3　like ᴅɪꜱᴄ dance^ɪᴀ^ᴘʀᴇs^3 3

　　　　　?iaᴸháuᴴᴸ
　　　　　before
　　　They no longer dance like they danced before.

Complex and Compound Sentences 337

Counterfactual comparison. In a counterfactual comparison, the comparative clause is not marked in any way; the standard clause, however, is introduced by $la^Lhua\text{?}^{MH}\ du\text{?}^H$ 'as if, like', which is a frozen formulaic expression composed of the evidential adverb la^L, the verb $hua\text{?}^{ML}$ 'say' (but with a tone-stress that is not part of the verb's inflectional paradigm), and the indubitative (INDB) illocutionary particle $du\text{?}^H$. Unlike the equality comparison construction where the same verb is frequently utilized in both the comparative and the standard clauses, counterfactual comparisons usually do not repeat the verb.

The verb in the standard clause is usually inflected for the third person; there are no person restrictions in the comparative clause. Although it is uncommon, the standard may be inflected for the same person as in the comparative; cf. (1039) and (1040). The standard clause usually follows the comparative clause, but it may optionally precede the comparative clause as in (1041).

(1039) COMPARATIVE   STANDARD
$\text{?}\eta iu\text{?}^{LM}$ $\text{?}nú^M$ $l\hat{i}^L$ $ku^Mdiu^{M\wedge}ku^M\eta ii^M$ $la^Lhua\text{?}^{MH}$ $du\text{?}^H$
house^is you^s be^II^PRES mess   as^if   INDB

$\text{?}i^L$ $tiá^M$ $\text{?}\bar{i}^M$ $\theta i\bar{a}^M$
COMP not anyone be^present^SIA^3
Your home is a mess, as if no one is living there.

(1040) COMPARATIVE   STANDARD
$kuá^H\text{-}\text{?}\eta iei^{MH}$ $hná^{HL}$ $ki\bar{o}\text{?}^L$ $ká^Md\bar{e}^Hná^H$ $la^Lhua\text{?}^{MH}$
sit^PROG-be^bound^IA^is I   with chain like

$du\text{?}^H$ $\text{?}i^L$ $ka^L\text{-}hmú^{LM}$ $hná^{HL}$ co^L
INDB COMP PAST-do^TI^is I crime
I am bound with chains as if I committed a crime (but I am definitely innocent).

(1041) STANDARD
$la^Lhua\text{?}^{MH}$ $du\text{?}^H$ $h\bar{a}^M$ $cá^M$ ηii^{LM} $l\hat{i}^{LM}$ $bi\text{?}^H$
as^if   INDB one^AN person know^STI^3 very AFF

COMPARATIVE
$ka^L\text{-}\text{?}lé\text{?}^L$ $cú^M$
PAST-talk^TI^3 3
S/he talked as if s/he is a person who knows everything (but s/he doesn't know much at all).

9.11 Coordination of clauses

In this section, the following coordinators are discussed: the conjunctives hi^L 'and' and $ʔi^L$ 'and', the adversative ti^Lla^L 'but', and the disjunctives $ʔo^L$ 'or' and $ʔo^Llá^Mdá^M$ 'or else'.[67]

The conjunctives hi^L and $ʔi^L$. If two situations are described where the second is to some degree independent of the first, then either hi^L 'and' or $ʔi^L$ 'and' is grammatical; however, the conjunctive $ʔi^L$ is more common. In constructions where either coordinator is grammatical, frequently both are found together, but only in the order hi^L $ʔi^L$ 'and', as in (1042) and (1043). Note also that when two clauses are in coordination, the adverb $siáʔ^L$ 'also' usually appears in the final clause; however, it is not obligatory.

(1042) hú$ʔ^{ML}$ hná^{HL} ʔi^L/hi^L hni^{LM} siá$ʔ^L$ lé^M
cough^IA^PRES^1S I   and   be^closed^II^PRES also throat^1S
I cough, and also my throat is tight.

(1043) niéi^M ná$ʔ^M$ la^L hí^{LM} hi^L^ʔi^L kuí^H
listen^TI^IMP you^P about all^AN and   HORT

       ŋi^{HL} ná$ʔ^M$ siá$ʔ^L$
understand^TI^FUT^2 you^P also
Listen, all of you, and may you also understand.

Although hi^L 'and' and $ʔi^L$ 'and' are generally interchangeable, as illustrated in (1042), there are some constructions in which only one or the other is grammatical. If two situations are concurrent, only the coordinator hi^L can be used, as in (1044). When two situations are in temporal sequence, only the coordinator $ʔi^L$ is grammatical, as in (1045).

(1044) káu^M ta^{MH} ʔí^H-liú$ʔ^H$ hi^L ti^L ʔó$ʔ^{LM}$
one^IN work MOT-be^annoying^IA^3 and PV^PRES shout^IA^PRES^3

       cá^{H}mí$ʔ^H$ ní^M
children that
Those children only walk around being annoying and constantly shouting.

(1045) ŋiéi^H hná^{HL} ŋi^{H}ta^{MH} ʔi^L
go^nonhome^IA^PAST^1S I   town^hall and

---

[67]Both $ʔi^L$ and hi^L can also be used to express coordination between other parts of speech, such as noun phrases (§6.12); the same is true of $ʔo^L$ and $ʔo^Llá^Mdá^M$ to express alternatives.

Complex and Compound Sentences   339

ka^L-$ŋií^H$-$lẽʔ^H$ $hná^{HL}$ $pí^M déii^H$
PAST-ANDT-speak^to^TA^1S I   president
I went to the town hall and spoke to the president.

The adversative $ti^L la^L$. The adversative coordinator $ti^L la^L$ 'but' marks a following clause as being semantically opposite to the preceding clause in some respect.

(1046) kia^L $ʔéiʔ^{LM}$ $cã^{ML}$ $cú^M$ $ʔŋiú^L$ $lá^M$ $ti^L la^L$ $kiá^{HL}$
       ten   measure   take^TI^PRES^3 3   house   this   but   have^STI^2

       $ʔnú^M$ $kã́^{HL}$ $hná^{HL}$ $ʔŋiá^L$ $bíʔ^H$
       you^s   take^TI^FUT^1S I   five   AFF
They charge ten pesos here, but for you I will charge five.

When $ti^L la^L$ 'but' occurs sentence initial, the material to which it relates as an adversative may be a larger section of discourse than just the preceding sentence, or it may relate to some implicit information such as in example (1047). The speaker here assumes that his audience will expect him to be concerned about his situation, so uses the adversative to express his feelings as being the opposite to the expected.

(1047) $ti^L la^L$ $diá^M$ $ʔi^L$ $hã̌u^M$ $lẽ^L$ $hná^{HL}$ $ʔi^L$
       but   not   thing   that^I   think^TI^PRES^1S   I   COMP

       $ŋau^L$ $cá^M mi^L$ $ʔí^L$ $kiõʔ^L$
       go^nonhome^IA^PAST^3S   woman   that^AN accompany^SIA^3

       $cá^M$ $siã́ʔ^L$
       person   other^AN
But I was not concerned that she went with another man (i.e., she married the other man).

The disjunctives $ʔo^L$ and $ʔo^L lá^M dá^M$. Propositions encoded in two clauses are expressed as alternatives by either the disjunctive $ʔo^L$ 'or' or $ʔo^L lá^M dá^M$ 'or else'. The disjunctive $ʔo^L lá^M dá^M$ is most likely a compound of $ʔo^L$ 'or', the deictic $lá^M$ 'this', and the illocutionary particle $dá^M$ (verification). It functions as a unit phonologically, and its deictic and illocutionary particle components cannot be interchanged with other members of their respective classes.[68]

---

[68]The symbol ⁺ on $má^H$ in (1048) represents a higher than normal high tone (§10.1); and the symbol ? preceding the literal gloss of $má^H ʔma ʔ^H$ represents the presence of question intonation.

(1048) *máʰ+ʔmaʔᴹᴴ*   *díᴹ*   *ʔoᴸ* *tiáᴹ máʰʔmaʔᴹᴴ*
?^pay^TI^FUT^1P we^INCL or   not pay^TI^FUT^1P
Shall we pay or not?

(1049) *lïᴹ-huáʔᴸ*   *tïᴸᴹ*   *mïᴸ*   *ʔiᴸ*   *kuéᴸᴹ*   *kaᴸláᴹ*
HOD-say^TI^3 master medicine COMP give^DI^FUT^3>1 some

        mïᴸ   *ʔoᴸláᴹdáᴹ*   *θeᴸ*   *cúᴹ tïᴸ*   *ɲiʰkuáʔᴹ*
        medicine or^else   send^TA^FUT^3>1 3   to Oaxaca
The doctor just said that he will give me some medicine, or else he will send me to Oaxaca.

Besides connecting two clauses, *ʔoᴸ* 'or' (but not *ʔoᴸláᴹdáᴹ*) can also be used in conjunction with *saᴸ* 'perhaps' to introduce hypothetical situations.

(1050) *tiáᴹ néʰ*   *hnoʔʰ ʔoᴸ saᴸ*   *tũᴸ*   *ʔniᴸᴹ*   *miïᴹ bïʔʰ*
not know^STI^1P we   or   perhaps two^IN three^IN year AFF

        θiãuᴹ
        exist^SIA^1P
We don't know if perhaps we will live two or three (more) years.

10
Interrogative Constructions

The types of interrogatives discussed in this chapter include: yes/no questions, tag questions, information questions, indirect questions, and rhetorical questions.

10.1 Yes/no questions

Yes/no questions are formed either by prefacing a declarative sentence with the query word ʔí^H, or by imposing interrogative intonation on the first syllable of the declarative sentence; the first syllable may be a prefix or the first syllable of a polysyllabic word or it may be the only syllable, i.e., a monosyllabic word. It appears that the interrogative intonation is preferred for sentences which begin with a verb phrase element, and the query word ʔí^H for sentences which begin with a nonverb phrase element. Interrogative intonation affects the normal pitch of the first syllable in the following manner.

1. The mid-falling tone /^{ML}/ becomes high-falling tone /^{HL}/, and the high-falling tone /^{HL}/ becomes a very high-falling tone /$^{HL+}$/, which is symbolized by the plus sign.

2. The low-rising tone /^{LM}/ becomes mid-rising tone /^{MH}/. The mid-rising tone /^{MH}/ with controlled stress becomes a high-rising tone /$^{MH+}$/; however, /^{MH}/ with ballistic stress never occurs on the first syllable of a noninterrogative utterance.

3. In a monosyllabic word with a closed syllable (that is, with final glottal stop), both the low-level tone /^{L}/ and the mid-level tone /^{M}/ associated with controlled stress become high-falling tone /^{HL}/.

4. In a monosyllabic word with an open syllable, both the low-level tone /^{L}/ associated with controlled stress and the low-falling tone /^{L}/ associated with ballistic stress become a high-falling tone /^{HL}/.

5. All other level tones /^{L}/ and /^{M}/ become high-level /^{H}/, and high-level /^{H}/ becomes a very high-level tone /$^{H+}$/.

The effects of interrogative intonation on the first syllable are tabulated in (1051). The symbol + following a tone indicates that that tone is actually higher than /^{H}/. The letters b and c preceding the tone indicate ballistic and controlled stress, respectively. The asterisk indicates that /^{MH}/ with ballistic stress never occurs on the first syllable of a noninterrogative utterance.

(1051) Tone perturbation as a result of interrogative intonation

Nonfinal syllables

H → H+
M → H
L → H

Final syllables (monosyllabic words)

c^H → c^{H+}	c^H? → c^{H+}?	b^H → b^{H+}	b^H? → b^{H+}?
c^M → c^H	c^M? → c^{HL}?	b^M → b^H	b^M? → b^H?
c^L → c^{HL}	c^L? → c^{HL}?	b^L → b^{HL}	b^L? → b^H?
c^{HL} → c^{HL+}	c^{HL}? → c^{HL+}?	b^{HL} → b^{HL+}	b^{HL}? → b^{HL+}?
c^{ML} → c^{HL}	c^{ML}? → c^{HL}?	b^{ML} → b^{HL}	b^{ML}? → b^{HL}?
c^{LM} → c^{MH}	c^{LM}? → c^{MH}?	b^{LM} → b^{MH}	b^{LM}? → b^{MH}?
c^{MH} → c^{MH+}	c^{MH}? → c^{MH+}?	b^{MH} → *	b^{MH}? → *

In the following examples, the tone of the first syllable of an interrogative sentence is written according to the rules given above. Question intonation is indicated in the literal gloss by a '?' immediately preceding the gloss of the first morpheme (which may consist of one or more syllables). In (1052), only the first syllable of $ca^L\textit{ʔau}^M$ 'tomorrow' receives question intonation; in (1053) only the remote past prefix ka^L- receives question intonation.

(1052) $cá^H\textit{ʔau}^M$ $má\textit{ʔ}^L$ $cá\textit{ʔ}^{LM}$ cu^M
?^tomorrow EXCL go^home^IA^FUT^3S 3
Is it really tomorrow that s/he goes home?

(1053) $ká^H\text{-}hui^L$ tu^{MH}
?^PAST-whistle^IA^3 Anthony
Did Tony whistle?

Interrogative Constructions 343

Sets of declarative and interrogative sentences are given below. Interrogative sentences with the interrogative query word *ʔíʰ* and interrogative intonation are illustrated, respectively, following the declarative sentence. If the declarative sentence begins with a verb phrase, no change in the order of sentence constituents is required for the interrogative. There does not appear to be any difference in meaning between (1054b) and (1054c), nor between (1055b) and (1055c).

(1054) a. *háuʔᴸ*   *cúᴹ caᴸʔáuᴹ*
   come^home^IA^FUT^3S 3   tomorrow
   S/he will come home tomorrow.

   b. *ʔíʰ*   *háuʔᴸ*   *cúᴹ caᴸʔáuᴹ*
   QUERY come^home^IA^FUT^3S 3   tomorrow
   Will s/he come home tomorrow?

   c. *háuʔʰ*   *cúᴹ caᴸʔáuᴹ*
   ?^come^home^IA^FUT^3S 3   tomorrow
   Will s/he come home tomorrow?

(1055) a. *máᴹ díʰ-kiáʔᴹ*   *cúᴹ kuoʰ*
   PRF upright^PROG-split^TI^3 3   firewood
   S/he is splitting firewood now.

   b. *ʔíʰ*   *máᴹ díʰ-kiáʔᴹ*   *cúᴹ kuoʰ*
   QUERY PRF upright^PROG-split^TI^3 3   firewood
   Is s/he splitting firewood yet?

   c. *máʰ díʰ-kiáʔᴹ*   *cúᴹ kuoʰ*
   ?^PRF upright^PROG-split^TI^3 3   firewood
   Is s/he splitting firewood yet?

If the constituent being questioned is other than the verb phrase, it must occur prior to the verb in the focus position, and either of the two yes/no question strategies discussed above can be used. A yes/no question formed on the subject is shown in (1056).

(1056) a. *ʔnoʔᴹ bíʔʰ haïʔᴹʰ   huiⁱᴸᴹ néᴸᴹ*
   you^P AFF cut^TI^FUT^2 trail today
   You will be clearing the trail today.

   b. *ʔíʰ   ʔnoʔᴹ haïʔᴹʰ   huiⁱᴸᴹ néᴸᴹ*
   QUERY you^P cut^TI^FUT^2 trail today
   Will you be clearing the trail today?

c. ʔnoʔᴴᴸ haïʔᴹᴴ   huïᴸᴹ néᴸᴹ
   ʔ^you^P cut^TI^FUT^2 trail today
   Will you be clearing the trail today?

An example of a yes/no question formed on the object is shown in (1057).

(1057) a. huãᴹ bíʔᴴ kaᴸ-liéïʔᴸᴹ   cúᴹ ʔúᴴ huïᴸᴹ
         John AFF PAST-speak^to^TA^3 3 on trail
         It was John s/he spoke to on the trail.

   b. ʔíᴴ   huãᴹ kaᴸ-liéïʔᴸᴹ   cúᴹ ʔúᴴ huïᴸᴹ
      QUERY John PAST-speak^to^TA^3 3 on trail
      Was it John s/he spoke to on the trail?

   c. huãᴴ   kaᴸ-liéïʔᴸᴹ   cúᴹ ʔúᴴ huïᴸᴹ
      ʔ^John PAST-speak^to^TA^3 3   on trail
      Was it John s/he spoke to on the trail?

An example of a yes/no question formed on an oblique object is shown in (1058).

(1058) a. cïᴸ ʔmáᴹ bíʔᴴ kaᴸ-táʔᴸ   ŋiúᴹmíʔᴴ
         in tree AFF PAST-fall^IA^3S boy
         The boy fell out of the tree.

   b. ʔíᴴ   cïᴸ ʔmáᴹ kaᴸ-táʔᴸ   ŋiúᴹmíʔᴴ
      QUERY in tree PAST-fall^IA^3S boy
      Was it out of the tree that the boy fell?

   c. cïᴴ ʔmáᴹ kaᴸ-táʔᴸ   ŋiúᴹmíʔᴴ
      ʔ^in tree PAST-fall^IA^3S boy
      Was it out of the tree that the boy fell?

10.2 Tag questions

A tag question is a confirmation question which occurs at the end of an otherwise declarative sentence. The tag question is comprised of the negative adverb *tiáᴹ* with its mid tone perturbed by interrogative intonation to a high tone, and followed by the adjective *cõᴹ* 'true'. Whether the declarative sentence with the tag question is positive or negative, the speaker is expecting confirmation of her/his proposition.

When the expression *tiá^H cõ^M* 'didn't s/he?, isn't that true?' occurs following a positive declarative sentence, the expected response from the addressee is *hã́^{L}* 'yes'. In the following examples, the part in parentheses is optional.

(1059) a. *ciáu^L kuã^L mí^{M}cáu^M tiá^H cõ^M*
yesterday arrive^nonhome^IA^PAST^3S priest ?^not true
The priest arrived yesterday, didn't he?

b. *hã́^{L} (ciáu^L bíʔ^H kuã^L cú^M)*
yes yesterday AFF arrive^nonhome^IA^PAST^3S 3
Yes, (he arrived yesterday).

When the expression *tiá^H cõ^M* 'didn't s/he?, isn't that true?' occurs following a negative declarative sentence, the response from the addressee can be either *hã́^{L}* 'yes', as in (1060b), or *hã́^{H}ʔã^{MH}* 'no', as in (1060c). With either response, the addressee is expressing agreement with the speaker. If the response is *hã́^{L}* 'yes', as in (1060b), any further comment by the addressee is optional; however, if the response is *hã́^{H}ʔã^{MH}* 'no', as in (1060c) or (1060d), something further must be said to explicitly express confirmation. If the addressee disagreed with the speaker, a typical response to (1060a) would be (1060d).

(1060) a. *tiá^M kuã^L iáʔ^L mí^{M}cáu^M ciáu^L tiá^H cõ^M*
not arrive^IA^PAST^3S ASSR priest yesterday ?^not true
The priest didn't arrive yesterday, did he?

b. *hã́^{L} (tiá^M kuã^L iáʔ^L cú^M)*
yes not arrive^nonhome^IA^PAST^3S ASSR 3
Yes, (he didn't arrive).

c. *hã́^{H}ʔã^{MH} tiá^M kuã^L iáʔ^L cú^M*
no not arrive^nonhome^IA^PAST^3S ASSR 3
No, he didn't arrive.

d. *hã́^{H}ʔã^{MH} kuã^L bíʔ^H cú^M*
no arrive^nonhome^IA^PAST^3S AFF 3
No, he did arrive.

10.3 Information questions

Information questions are formed by placing an interrogative word at the beginning of the sentence, followed by the constituent which is being questioned. The intonation is the same as for a declarative sentence. Interrogative words include adjectives, a pronoun, quantifiers, adverbs of place, time, manner, and purpose, and a locative verb.

The interrogative adjectives. The interrogative word $?e^L$ 'what? (IN)' has both adjectival and pronominal functions; the interrogative words $?\tilde{\imath}^M$ 'which? (AN)' and $?\hat{\imath}^M$ 'which? (IN)', however, function only adjectivally.[69]

By using $?\tilde{\imath}^M$ 'which? (AN)' or $?\hat{\imath}^M$ 'which? (IN)', the speaker requests that a selection be made from a definite set: which one(s) of a stated or implied set of animate or inanimate entities, or alternatives. The noun that is modified by either of these interrogative adjectives generally undergoes phonological change. The most common change is glottal closure of the final syllable (if the word does not already end in glottal). In some words there is also change in the nucleus, tone, or stress, or a combination of these; for example, the word $cái^M$ 'dog' becomes $cí?^M$ (or $cái?^M$) following $?\tilde{\imath}^M$ 'which? (AN)'. Compare (1061a) and (1061b).

(1061) a. $?\tilde{\imath}^M$ $cí?^M$ $ka^L\text{-}kïe?^M$ $?nú^M$
which^AN?   dog   PAST-bite^TA^3 > 2   you^S
Which dog bit you?

b. $cái^M$ $ho?^H$ $ŋiú^M$ $rí^H$ $bí?^H$
dog   have^STA^3   MASC   Richard   AFF
Richard's dog (bit me).

The word $hmái^M$ 'water' has a final glottal added to it and there is modification of the nucleus, becoming $hmí?^M$, but the word $hmái^H$ 'day' has only a final glottal added, becoming $hmái?^H$. There are also nouns such as $há?^L$ 'animal' which do not undergo any phonological change; such change is optional for the majority of nouns. The processes involved in these phonological changes await further research.

A noun which is modified by an interrogative adjective must occur immediately following that adjective; that is, the whole of the WH constituent occurs sentence initially. The difference in word order of interrogative and declarative sentences can be seen by comparing (1062) and (1063). In (1063), note also the normal form of the word 'dog'. Example (1064) illustrates $?\hat{\imath}^M$ 'which? (IN)'.

(1062) S[MOD   H   ] P   O
$?\tilde{a}^M$ $cí?^M$ $lí^M\text{-}hŋï?^L$ $ká^H?áu^M$
which^AN?   dog   HOD-kill^TA^3   chicken
Which dog (just) killed the chicken?

---

[69]For some speakers, $?\tilde{\imath}^M$ and $?\hat{\imath}^M$ 'which?' are not differentiated, all being pronounced as either $?\tilde{\imath}^M$ or $?\hat{\imath}^M$.

(1063) lḯᴹ-hŋïʔᴸ   cáïᴹ káᴴʔáuᴹ
       HOD-kill^TA^3 dog chicken
       The dog (just) killed the chicken.

(1064) T[MOD   H   ] P   S
       ʔḯᴹ   hmáïʔᴴ   ŋaʔᴸ   cúᴹ
       which^IN?   day   go^home^IA^PAST^3S 3
       Which day did s/he go home?

The inanimate interrogative adjective ʔeᴸ 'what?' is generally used in reference to quality or character. A noun modified by ʔeᴸ 'what?' does not undergo phonological change as occurs when modified by ʔḯᴹ 'which? (AN)' or ʔḯᴹ 'which? (IN)'. The adjective ʔeᴸ is ungrammatical in (1065b) because the speaker is requesting that a selection be made from a definite set of options. A correct usage is given in (1066), where the speaker is implying 'what is the nature/character of the word/message you bring?'.

(1065) a. ʔḯᴹ   hmaʔᴹ   ʔnáuʔᴹ   ʔnúᴹ
          which^IN? tomato   want^STI^2 you^s
          Which tomato do you want?

       b. *ʔeᴸ   hmaʔᴹ   ʔnáuʔᴹ   ʔnúᴹ
          what?   tomato   want^STI^2 you^s
          What tomato do you want?

(1066) ʔeᴸ   háïᴴᴸ   θiaᴸᴹ
       what?   word   exist^SII
       What message is there?

The interrogative pronoun. The form ʔeᴸ functions not only adjectivally as 'what? (IN)', but also nominally as 'what? (IN)'.

(1067) O   P   S
       ʔeᴸ   hmḯᴴ   ʔnáuʔᴹ   ʔnúᴹ
       what?   TRM   want^STI^2   you^s
       What were you wanting?

In the case of prepositional phrases, a double dislocation occurs relative to the corresponding declarative clause: the prepositional complement which is being questioned occurs to the left of the preposition, and the entire construction occurs at the beginning of the clause. Compare the interrogative sentence in (1068) with the corresponding declarative sentence in (1069).

(1068) OO[COMP   PP[PREP]] P   S   O
       ʔeᴹ   dáᴹ   kiõʔᴸ kaᴸ-kiáʔᴹ   cúᴹ   ʔuéᴸᴹ
       what? ᴠᴇʀ   with   ᴘᴀsᴛ-dig^ᴛɪ^3 3   land
       With what did s/he dig the land?

(1069) P   S   O   OO[PP[PREP COMP   ]]
       kaᴸ-kiáʔᴹ   cúᴹ   ʔuéᴸᴹ   kiõʔᴸ káuᴹ míᴴhmaᴹ
       ᴘᴀsᴛ-dig^ᴛɪ^3 3   land   with   one^ɪɴ shovel
       S/he dug the land with a shovel.

There are examples in which ʔĩᴹ 'which? (ᴀɴ)' appears to function as a pronoun, as in (1070). In all such instances, however, a nominal such as cáʔᴹ 'person' can be readily supplied following ʔĩᴹ; thus, ʔĩᴹ is adjectival, meaning 'which? (ᴀɴ)', with ellipsis of the understood nominal.

(1070) S   P   O
       ʔĩᴹ   kaᴸ-hmúᴸ   ʔéiʔᴸᴹ háuᴹ
       who? ᴘᴀsᴛ-make^ᴛɪ^3 order   that^ɪɴ
       Who gave that order?

The interrogative quantifiers. This section discusses the interrogative quantifiers kóʔᴸ 'how much?, how many? (ɪɴ)', háʔᴸ 'how many? (ɪɴ)', and háʔᴸ 'how many? (ᴀɴ)'. Only kóʔᴸ can modify mass nouns; however, both kóʔᴸ and háʔᴸ can modify count nouns and are generally interchangeable.

The interrogative quantifier kóʔᴸ 'how much?, how many?' can function both adjectivally and nominally. It is limited to quantifying inanimate entities. In its adjectival function, kóʔᴸ can modify both mass and count nouns. Examples of each, respectively, are given in (1071) and (1072). An example of the nominal use of kóʔᴸ is given in (1073).

(1071) kóʔᴸ   kieᴸ   kiáʔᴴ   núᴹ
       how^much? money   bring^sᴛɪ^2   you^s
       How much money did you bring?

(1072) kóʔᴸ   ʔɲiúᴸ   θiaᴸᴹ
       how^many? house   exist^sɪɪ
       How many houses are there?

(1073) kóʔᴸ   réᴹ   núᴹ   kioʔᴹᴴ   huóuᴸᴹ   hnáᴴᴸ
       how^much? owe^sᴛɪ^2   you^s have^sᴛɪ^3   boss^ɪs I
       How much do you owe my boss?

Interrogative Constructions 349

The interrogative quantifiers *há?ᴸ* (IN) and *hã́?ᴸ* (AN) 'how many?', respectively, are shown in (1074) and (1075).

(1074) *há?ᴸ   hmäïᴴ má?ᴸ ?niáu?ᴸᴹ*
how^many^IN? day   EXCL be^lacking^SII
How many more days will it be?

(1075) *hã́?ᴸ   caᴸhaïᴴᴸ   kaᴸ-hã́uᴸ*
how^many^AN? opossum PAST-be^caught^IA^3
How many opossums were caught?

The interrogative adverbs. There are four interrogative adverbs: adverbs of location, time, manner, and purpose/cause.
The interrogative locative adverb *hĩ?ᴴ* 'where?' is usually modified by the adverb *?aᴸ* 'exactly, just'.

(1076) *hĩ?ᴴ   kuáᴸ   ɲiúᴹrẽ?ᴹ   ?núᴹ*
where? live^SIA^3 brother^2 you^s
Where does your brother live?

(1077) *?aᴸ   hĩ?ᴴ   kaᴸ-ɲiíᴴ-?ṍᴹᴴ   ná?ᴹ   cúᴹ*
exactly where? PAST-ANDT-bury^TA^2 you^P 3
Where exactly did you bury her/him?

The interrogative temporal adverb is *lí?ᴸ* 'when?'.

(1078) *lí?ᴸ   θeᴴᴸ   núᴹ   hnáᴴᴸ   kuaᴸtáᴸ*
when? send^TA^FUT^2>1 you^s I   Cuicatlán
When will you send me (to) Cuicatlán?

The adverb *?aᴸ* 'exactly, just' cannot occur with *lí?ᴸ* in direct questions; however, *?aᴸ* is found with *lí?ᴸ* in indirect questions (§10.4).
The interrogative adverb of manner *lá?ᴸ* 'how?' commonly occurs with the state posture verb *rṍᴸᴹ* 'lie', but the expression *lá?ᴸ rṍᴸᴹ* 'how is it (that)?' has become grammaticized, and there is no implication of horizontal posture. *lá?ᴸ* 'how?' is usually preceded by the adverb *?aᴸ* 'exactly, just', similar to the interrogative adverb *hĩ?ᴴ* 'where?'. Compare examples (1079) and (1080).

(1079) *lá?ᴸ   rṍᴸᴹ   kaᴸ-ciã́u?ᴴᴸ   ciĩ?ᴸᴹ   ?no?ᴹ   laᴸ   nĩᴹ*
how? lie^SII PAST-devise^TI^3 head^2 you^P idea that
How is it that you came up with that idea?

(1080) ʔa^L lá́ʔ^L ró^{LM} lîᴹ-ʔúʔ^{LM}   ʔnú^M ŋií^H lá^M
just how? lie^sɪɪ HOD-enter^ᴛɪ^2s you^s place this
Just how is it that you entered this place?

The state verb *ró^{LM}* 'lie' appears to be some kind of grammatical device for highlighting the interrogative. It is restricted to the construction with the interrogative *lá́ʔ^L* 'how?'. Although the frozen expression *lá́ʔ^L ró^{LM}* 'how is it (that)?' is common, *lá́ʔ^L* 'how?' can occur directly with content verbs. In both (1081) and (1082), the expression *lá́ʔ^L ró^{LM}* 'how is it (that)?' could be substituted for *lá́ʔ^L* 'how?'. Although there is generally little difference in meaning between *lá́ʔ^L* and *lá́ʔ^L ró^{LM}*, sometimes *lá́ʔ^L ró^{LM}* indicates a desire for more detailed information.

(1081) lá́ʔ^L hmú^{HL}   dí^M
how? do^ᴛɪ^ꜰᴜᴛ^1ᴘ we^ɪɴᴄʟ
What can we do?

(1082) ʔa^L lá́ʔ^L ŋáïʔ^H   ná́ʔ^M ŋií^Hkõ^M cú^M
just how? respond^ɪᴀ^ꜰᴜᴛ^2 you^ᴘ towards 3
Just how will you respond to her/him?

The interrogative adverb of purpose and cause is expressed by *ʔe^L láïʔ^{LM}* 'why?'. Examples of purpose and cause, respectively, are given in (1083) and (1084). The first part of this expression is the interrogative pronoun *ʔe^L* 'what?', the second part *láïʔ^{LM}* is most likely derived from the verb *láïʔ^{ML}* 'win, gain' (ᴛɪ); however, the tone-stress inflection of *láïʔ^{LM}* is unlike any part of the ᴛɪ verb's paradigm. The form *láïʔ^{LM}* occurs only in the interrogative expression *ʔe^L láïʔ^{LM}*. Since *láïʔ^{LM}* does not inflect, it is glossed as 'be gained' and is categorized as an sɪɪ verb. Since the illocutionary particle *iá^{ʔL}* (ᴀꜱꜱʀ) can occur between the component parts of this expression, *ʔe^L láïʔ^{LM}* is not regarded as a compound, for example, (1085).

(1083) ʔe^L   láïʔ^{LM}   ʔnau^{ʔML}   ʔnoʔ^M hná^{HL}
what? be^gained^sɪɪ search^for^ᴛᴀ^ᴘʀᴇꜱ^2>1 you^ᴘ I
Why are you looking for me?

(1084) ʔe^L   láïʔ^{LM}   hų̄^L   ca^Lkuá^H
what? be^gained^sɪɪ die^ɪᴀ^ᴘᴀꜱᴛ^3 horse
Why did the horse die?

(1085) ʔeᴸ   iáʔᴸ   láïʔᴸᴹ   ʔiᴸ   nḭᴹ   mïʔᴸᴹ   ʔnúᴹ
       what? ASSR   be^gained^SII thing   that   request^TI^PRES^2 you^s
       Why ever are you requesting that? *or* For what purpose are you requesting that?

In Chinantec, when a person does not want to respond to a "why?" question, a commonly heard remark is:

(1086) tiáᴹ   ʔeᴸ   láïʔᴸᴹ
       not   what? be^gained^SII
       For no real reason.

The interrogative locative verb. The interrogative word *néᴹ* 'be where?' is tentatively identified as a (defective) interrogative locative verb. *néᴹ* does not inflect, nor can it be affixed; however, distributionally it is like a verb. The same form is used whether the referent of the subject is inanimate, as in (1087), or animate, as in (1088). In these examples, (b) is given to illustrate how the construction is parallel to that of (a); (b) is not meant to be a typical response to (a).

(1087) a. *néᴹ*   *ʔúᴴciʃᴴᴸ*   *ŋiúᴹmíʔᴴ*
          be^where?   hat^3   boy
          Where is the boy's hat?

       b. *ʔeᴹ*   *ʔúᴴciʃᴴᴸ*   *ŋiúᴹmíʔᴴ*   *ŋiʃᴴ*   *nḭᴹ*
          hang^SII   hat^3   boy   place   that
          The boy's hat is hanging there.

(1088) a. *néᴹ*   *cáïᴹ*   *hoʔᴹ*   *ʔnúᴹ*
          be^where?   dog   have^STA^2   you^s
          Where is your dog?

       b. *θḛʔᴹ*   *cáïᴹ*   *hoʔᴹ*   *hnáᴴᴸ*   *ŋiʃᴴ*   *θioᴴ*
          stand^SII   dog   have^STA^IS I   place   yonder
          My dog is standing over there/yonder.

10.4 Indirect questions

Any interrogative sentence can function as the complement of a complement taking predicate (§9.3); most do not require any change in form.

Indirect questions with *ʔĩᴹ* 'which? (AN)' and *ʔeᴸ* 'what?' are seen in (1089) and (1090).

(1089) tiá^M né^H   hno?^H ?ĩ^M   ka^L-hmú^L   ?ué?^L ó^LM
      not know^STI^1P we   which^AN? PAST-make^TI^3 letter yonder
      We don't know who wrote those letters (i.e., graffiti).

(1090) má^M ŋio^H   hná^HL ?e^L   ŋa^H
       PRF know^STI^1S I   what? reply^IA^FUT^1S
       I now know what to reply.

The interrogative words kó?^L 'how much?', hĩ?^H 'where?', lí?^L 'when?', and lá?^L 'how?' rarely occur in indirect questions without the adverb ?a^L 'exactly, just'. Nonetheless, ?a^L is optional in (1091) and (1092).

(1091) tiá^M ŋii^LM   cú^M (?a^L) hĩ?^H   ŋau^L   hõ^M
      not know^STI^3 3   just where? go^nonhome^IA^PAST^3S child^3
      S/he doesn't know (just/exactly) where her/his child has gone.

(1092) ŋii^LM   cú^M (?a^L) lí?^L   háu?^L   hméi^M
       know^STI^3 3   just when? return^home^IA^FUT^3S father^3
       S/he knows (just/exactly) when her/his father will return.

A yes/no question (§10.1) can also occur as the complement of a cognitive verb to form an indirect question. Generally, the query word ?í^H occurs in indirect questions, but interrogative intonation can also be used. Examples of each method, respectively, are shown in (1093) and (1094).

(1093) cá^H-ne?^MH   dí^M   ?í^H   kuá^H-?ú^H
       ANDT^FUT-see^TI^1P we^INCL QUERY INDEF^PROG-be^contained^SIA^3S

       cú^M ?ŋiu^Lmí^Hŋií^M
       3   jail
       Let's go and see whether s/he is in jail.

(1094) kuá^M-ŋa^L   ŋií^Hkõ^M rí^H   tiá^H   má^M
       ANDT^IMP-ask^TI^2 to   Richard ?^not PRF

       kuã?^LM   ti^LM
       arrive^home^IA^PAST^3S teacher
       Go ask Richard whether the teacher has returned.

Sometimes the yes/no question overtly expresses both alternatives.

(1095) tiá^M ré^M ŋii^LM   cú^M ?í^H há^LM   ?í^H
       not well know^STI^3 3   QUERY come^nonhome^IA^FUT^3S QUERY

tiáM háLM　　　　　　　　tîMmîL
not come^nonhome^IA^FUT^3S doctor
S/he doesn't know whether the doctor will come or not.

10.5 Rhetorical questions

The prototypical rhetorical question does not expect an answer, although a response would be possible. There are three ways in which rhetorical questions can be formed using interrogative words. The first two imply definite agreement by the person(s) spoken to. The third has a scolding implication. In addition, rhetorical questions can be signaled by certain illocutionary particles; see §11.2

1. The interrogative adverb $ʔá^H$ 'really?' can occur with the negative $tiá^M$ 'not' or the contraexpectation negative $h\tilde{u}^L$ 'not as if' to form a rhetorical yes/no question. In rhetorical questions, $tiá^M$ appears to be restricted to collocating with the verb phrase, and $h\tilde{u}^L$ to collocating with the noun phrase.

(1096) ʔáH　tiáM　huéʔM　　ʔnúM　diólM
really? not fear^TA^PRES^2 you^s God
Do you really not fear God?

(1097) ʔáH　hũL　　cáM　óLM　ʔnaʔM　　cúM
really? not^as^if person yonder seek^TA^PRES^3 3
Isn't it really that person they're seeking?

$ʔá^H$ 'really?' is most likely the adverb $ʔa^L$ 'just, exactly', with interrogative intonation overlaid. $ʔa^L$ must be followed by an interrogative word, whereas $ʔá^H$ occurs only in rhetorical questions, such as (1086) and (1087), and no interrogative word can follow. Because of the distributional differences of $ʔá^H$ and $ʔa^L$, they are treated as separate (albeit related) morphemes.

2. There is also a complex interrogative expression $ʔá^H\ h\tilde{u}^L\ huáʔ^{HL}$ 'is it not (true) to say (that)?'. This expression derives from $ʔá^H$ 'really?', the contraexpectation negative $h\tilde{u}^L$ 'not as if', and $huáʔ^{HL}$ 'say', which is inflected as for the third-person hortative. The words $ʔá^H$ and $h\tilde{u}^L$ usually combine phonologically to form the word $ʔãu^{HL}$, although the component parts are distinguishable in slow speech or when the speaker is being emphatic. Examples of the full and reduced forms, respectively, are shown in (1098) and (1099).

(1098) háH^hũL^huáʔHL　ʔnúM　lîM-hïeH　　　hnáHL　haH　ʔmáM
is^it^not^true^that you^s HOD-see^TA^IS>2 I　　among tree

    hā́uM
    that^IN
Aren't you the one I saw among the trees?

(1099) *ʔauHL^huáʔHL laL háïLM bíʔH díM hmuLM ʔiL*
   is^it^not^true^that about all^IP AFF we^INCL do^TI^PRES^IP thing

    ʔlaʔL
    bad^IN
Don't we all do bad things?

  3. Rhetorical questions can also be formed by using the interjection *saL* 'goodness!' immediately following the interrogative expressions *ʔeL láïʔLM* 'why?' or *ʔeL liL* 'what happened?'. The former expression is the more common.

(1100) *ʔeL láïʔLM saL laL nïM náH-lï̂ML ʔnoʔM*
   what? be^gained^SII goodness! idea that PROG^P-think^TI^2 you^P
How could you be thinking such a thing?

(1101) *ʔeL liL   saL lïH kaL-kuïLM ʔnúM*
   what? happen^II^PAST goodness! NON PAST-discard^TA^P^2 you^S

    cïMmíʔH hoʔM
    puppy have^STA^2
Why ever did you abandon your puppies?

11
Illocutionary Adverbs and Particles

In Sochiapan Chinantec, intonation is not a highly developed feature. Possibly, this is because tone has a high functional load elsewhere in the language: tone is used both lexically (§2.5) and to mark the inflection of inalienable nouns (§6.3) and verbs (§4.1). Although Chinantec does make limited use of intonation (§2.7) to indicate attitude or mood, it makes extensive use of illocutionary adverbs and particles, effectively replacing much of what is accomplished in other languages by intonation.

The focus of this chapter is on postpositive illocutionary markers; that is, those illocutionary markers which follow the constituent that lies in their scope. This discussion is by no means exhaustive as to all the parts of speech each illocutionary marker can have in its scope; nor have all the nuances that can occur with positive and negative declaratives and interrogatives been explored. It does, however, demonstrate how the illocutionary markers, both individually and in combination, communicate the Chinantec speaker's attitude to the proposition, and/or towards the addressee.

There are two types of illocutionary markers: adverbs and particles. They are distinguished on the following basis: illocutionary adverbs can have in their scope a verb phrase, a clause, or an entire sentence; illocutionary particles, however, can additionally have in their scope a noun phrase, quantifier phrase, prepositional phrase, adverb phrase, or even certain lexical items such as the adverb $\textit{ʔa}^L$ 'exactly, just', which modifies interrogative adverbs. Neither illocutionary adverbs nor particles can have in their scope prepositions, conjunctions, vocatives, interjections, the query word $\textit{ʔí}^H$, or adverbs that form part of the verb phrase. Certain illocutionary markers are more likely to be used by women than men.[70]

One advantage in having a large set of illocutionary markers is that the Chinantec speaker's attitude is more fully preserved in the written text than is possible in a strongly intonational language. Representing the nuances by English glosses, however, is sometimes problematic; it is often necessary to resort to lengthy explanations to convey the implication of a given illocutionary marker. Further complications are: (1) two or more illocutionary markers may co-occur, each contributing its own nuance, and (2) several of the illocutionary markers shift in their implication when used in a declarative, interrogative, (positive) imperative, or prohibition (negative imperative) sentence.

Chinantec distinguishes between the positive imperative (hereafter simply called imperative; see §4.6) and prohibition (see §5.7) both morphologically and syntactically. Morphologically, the imperative and prohibition are distinguished by different tone-stress inflection of the verb; see §5.6. Syntactically, there are distributional restrictions of the illocutionary markers according to whether the sentence type is imperative or prohibition; see (1102).

In (1102), the illocutionary adverbs and particles are tabulated according to sentence type. The plus symbol signifies a definite occurrence of the illocutionary marker with that sentence type, and the minus symbol signifies a definite nonoccurrence.

(1102) Illocutionary adverbs and particles, and the sentence type with which each may occur

Illocutionary markers		DECL	INTR	IMP	PROH
Adverbs					
$tiá^L$	supplication	+	+	+	+
$né^L$	explication	+	+	+	−
$ne\textit{?}^{MH}$	evaluative	+	+	+	−
$lá\textit{?}^H$	assumption	+	−	+	+
$má^Hna^{MH}$	contraexpectation	+	−	+	+
na^{MH}	assertive	+	−	+	+
$né\textit{?}^H$	commentative	+	−	−	−
Particles					
$bí\textit{?}^H$	affirmation	+	+	+	+
$dá^M$	verification	+	+	+	+
$iá\textit{?}^L$	assertion	+	+	+	+

---

[70]Women and men differ not only in their use of illocutionary adverbs and particles but also in their use of pronouns; see §6.1.

Illocutionary Adverbs and Particles 357

Illocutionary markers		DECL	INTR	IMP	PROH
uá^H	anticipative	+	+	+	+
dúʔ^H	indubitative	+	+	+	−
máʔ^L	exclamative	+	+	−	−
néʔ^H	quotative	+	+	−	−

From this chart it can be seen that all of the illocutionary markers are able to occur in declarative sentences, ten can occur in interrogative sentences, eleven in imperative sentences, and eight can occur in prohibition sentences.

Another way to divide the illocutionary markers is according to the extent of their scope. The four particles *bíʔ^H* (AFF), *uá^H* (ANTP), *máʔ^L* (EXCL), and *néʔ^H* (QUOT) generally have only the immediately preceding constituent in their scope; these are called limited scope illocutionary markers. The other ten illocutionary markers always have within their scope all preceding constituents within the clause; these are called broad scope illocutionary markers. Five of the broad scope markers, the adverbs *né^L* (EXPL), *láʔ^H* (ASUM), *má^Hna^MH* (CEXP), *na^MH* (ASNT), and *néʔ^H* (COMM) occur only sentence final (apart from the vocative constituent which can occur following the illocutionary constituent). The adverb *neʔ^MH* (EVAL) can occur following the predicate or sentence final; and the adverb *tiá^L* (SUPL) generally occurs following the predicate, although it may occur following subjects in their normal post-predicate position. *iáʔ^L* (ASSR) is the only broad scope particle able to occur with a wider variety of constituents than the adverbs, for example, following a left-dislocated object; but when occurring sentence final, it has the entire clause or sentence in its scope, not just the preceding constituent. In the following examples, the scope of an illocutionary adverb or particle is indicated by square brackets.

The particle *bíʔ^H* (AFF) exemplifies the limited scope illocutionary markers in (1103); here it has only the locative constituent in its scope. The speaker is affirming that, of the two or more locations where s/he has cornfields, it is the one on the trail to Quetzalapa that is to be weeded.

(1103) cá^H-haïʔ^MH dí^M ʔiá^H kuú^M [huï^LM kua^Luóu^M]
ANDT^FUT-weed^TI^1P we^INCL weed^3 maize trail Quetzalapa

bíʔ^H
AFF

We'll go weed the cornfield along the trail to Quetzalapa.

The particle *iáʔ^L* (ASSR) exemplifies the broad scope illocutionary markers. Thus, if *iáʔ^L* occurs sentence final, it has the entire sentence in its scope, for example (1104). By assuring the addressee of her/his intent, the speaker is hoping the addressee will agree to accompany her/him in the task.

(1104) [cá^H-haï?^{MH} dí^M ?iá^H kuú^M hui^{LM} kua^{L}uóu^M]
ANDT^FUT-weed^TI^1P   we^INCL   weed^3   maize   trail   Quetzalapa

iá?^{L}
ASSR

Be assured, we'll go weed the cornfield along the trail to Quetzalapa.

Further examples of the variety of sentence constituents and sentence types with which each illocutionary marker may occur are given in the following sections.

11.1 Illocutionary adverbs

Sochiapan Chinantec illocutionary adverbs are listed in (1105) with a gloss that reflects their prototypical usage; other nuances which the adverb may have are discussed in their respective sections following this chart.

(1105) Illocutionary adverbs

né^L	explication	(please) clarify
má^{H}na^{MH}	contraexpectation	to the contrary
na^{MH}	assentive	okay?, eh?
né?^{H}	commentative	you should know that
ne?^{MH}	evaluative	let's see if
lá?^{H}	assumption	really?, right?, okay?
tiá^L	supplication	please

The explication adverb né^L. The explication (EXPL) adverb né^L can occur only sentence final; it has in its scope the entire preceding clause. The implication of né^L varies according to the sentence type in which it occurs: interrogative, declarative, or imperative. (See also §12.1 where né^L functions as a topic marker.)

né^L appears most commonly in interrogative sentences, where it indicates that the speaker is requesting further information: 'answer me!' or '(please) clarify!' as in (1106); there is no pause preceding né^L.

(1106) [?e^L ?i^L ?lai?^{L} má^M ka^L-hmú^L cú^M]   né^L
what   thing   bad^IN   PRF   PAST-do^TI^3   3   EXP
What crime has s/he committed? Answer me!

Illocutionary Adverbs and Particles 359

In a declarative sentence, *né^L* (EXPL) denotes 'really' or 'assuredly'. Generally, either *bí?^{H}* (AFF) or *dá^M* (VER) occur following the verb when *né^L* occurs in a declarative sentence. The effect of the explication and affirmation (or verification) illocutionary markers together is an exclamatory attempt to convince the addressee that the situation is different from the addressee's assumption. In (1107), the implication is 'Don't doubt me!'.

(1107) [*má^M ka^L-ma^L?ma?^{MH} bí?^{H} hná^{HL}*] *né^L*
       PRF PAST-pay^TI^1S AFF I   EXPL
       I have most assuredly paid!

When *né^L* occurs in an imperative sentence, the implication is one of scolding or rebuke. The situation in (1108) involves a disobedient child who has fallen out of a tree which s/he had been told not to climb, and is crying. The parent is in effect saying "Now you have learned your lesson the hard way, let's see if you are brave enough to climb it again. Go ahead and climb it again!"

(1108) [*uí^L siá?^{L}*] *né^L*
       climb^TI^IMP again EXPL
       Go ahead and climb (it) again!

The contraexpectation adverb *má^{H}na^{MH}*. The contraexpectation (CEXP) adverb *má^{H}na^{MH}*[71] occurs only sentence final, and has all of the sentence in its scope. It is found in all but interrogative sentences. (*má^{H}na^{MH}*, like *né^L*, is also used to mark the topic in a topic-comment construction; see §12.1.)

In a declarative or prohibition sentence, *má^{H}na^{MH}* has the force of 'in contradiction to' or 'to the contrary'. In (1109), depending on context, the implication is either 'You are able to play basketball, but, contrary to your expectation, I can't', or 'There are several other games that I am able to play, but, contrary to your expectation, I cannot play basketball'.

(1109) [*tiá^M tî^M hná^{HL} kau?^{MH} mi^L láu^M*]
       not be^able^STI^1S I   play^TI^PRES^1S spherical hide

       má^{H}na^{MH}
       CEXP
       To the contrary, I cannot play basketball.

má^{H}na^{MH} has another, quite uncommon, sense distinction in declarative sentences, which only indirectly fits the notion of contraexpectation. If, for

---

[71] The variant *má^{H}ná^H* is heard with almost equal frequency as *má^{H}na^{MH}*, but I have chosen *má^{H}na^{MH}* as the citation form for the dictionary, and use it consistently in the examples.

example, the speaker has listed several types of music that a person doesn't like, the addressee can respond with a statement such as (1110). The implication is: 'Since you didn't mention that s/he doesn't like guitar music, I presume s/he does.' The speaker here is indicating that it would be contrary to her/his expectation if the referent didn't like guitar music.

(1110) [θai̯^{LM} cú^M tṳ^{LM}]   má^{H}na^{MH}
      like^STI^3 3   guitar   CEXP
      Presumably, s/he likes the guitar.

In prohibitions, the implication of *má^{H}na^{MH}* is that the addressee is being required, contrary to their expectation, to stop doing something that they were doing or not initiate something they had intended to do. In (1111), the addressee has used the radio before, but is told that, contrary to her/his expectations, it is now disallowed.

(1111) [lḭ^{M}uú^M lḭ^H káu$^{\text{ʔ}L}$ sṳ^H nḭ^M]   má^{H}na^{MH}
      CES   NON   handle^TI^PROH^2 radio that   CEXP
      Don't touch that radio any more!

In imperatives, *má^{H}na^{MH}* can signal contraexpectation on the part of either the speaker or the addressee, depending on the context. In (1112), if the addressee is being reminded to do something that s/he has been told to do on previous occasions, *má^{H}na^{MH}* signals that the constant need for reminder is contrary to the expectation of the speaker, who had hoped for better things of the addressee. If the addressee is being told to do something that s/he had not planned on doing, however, then the use of *má^{H}na^{MH}* is an acknowledgment by the speaker that the command is contrary to the addressee's plans or expectations.

(1112) [ráḭ^M ʔã̰$^{\text{ʔ}M}$]   má^{H}na^{MH}
      wash^TI^IMP shirt^2 CEXP
      Wash your shirt!

The assentive adverb *na^{MH}*. The assentive (ASNT) illocutionary adverb *na^{MH}* indicates to the addressee that the speaker requires acknowledgment that s/he has been heard and, depending on the context, the speaker may also be expecting agreement, although not necessarily a simple 'yes'. *na^{MH}* is found in declarative, imperative, and prohibition sentences. Examples (1113) and (1115) illustrate the use of *na^{MH}* (ASNT) in declarative sentences (note the lack of interrogative marking sentence initial; see §10.1).

In (1113), the speaker is making a simple declaration, and uses *na^{MH}* to indicate the desire for acknowledgment from the addressee. This use of *na^{MH}* is characteristic of women's speech. Although the English equivalent requires pause preceding 'okay?' and interrogative intonation, neither occurs with *na^{MH}*. The anticipated response to (1113) could be something like (1114).

(1113) *[tiá^M có^{LM} cú^M ca^L?áu^M] na^{MH}*
  not go^nonhome^IA^FUT^3S 3 tomorrow ASNT
  S/he is not going tomorrow, okay?

(1114) *ré^M bí?^{H} la^L nĩ^M*
  well AFF idea that
  That's fine.

When not only acknowledgment, but agreement, is sought, however, then pause occurs prior to *na^{MH};* such use is found in both men's and women's speech.

(1115) *[cá^H-kiú?^{HL} dí^M ?má^M hãu^M ca^L?áu^M] na^{MH}*
  ANDT^FUT-cut^down^TI^1P we^INCL tree that^IN tomorrow ASNT
  Let's cut that tree down tomorrow, eh?

An example of *na^{MH}* in an imperative sentence is given in (1116). An example of *na^{MH}* in a prohibition sentence is given in (1117). When *na^{MH}* follows an imperative or a prohibition, the effect is more like that of an appeal than a command.

(1116) *[kué^H ku^{L}tiá^L tiú^L kiã^{HL}] na^{MH}*
  give^DI^IMP^2>1 briefly rifle have^STI^2 ASNT
  Loan me your rifle for a while, okay?

(1117) *[su^{L}uú^M lí^H cia^M ?i^L lĩ^M-huo?^{MH} nĩ^M] na^{MH}*
  PREVEN NON relate^TI^PROH^2 COMP HOD-discuss^TI^1P that ASNT

  ɲiú^H
  friend
  Don't talk about that which we were just discussing, okay friend (i.e., keep it a secret)?

The commentative adverb *né?^{H}*. The commentative (COMM) adverb *né?^{H}* indicates that the speaker wants to share some unelicited information that they would like the addressee to pay attention to. *né?^{H}* occurs only sentence final in declarative sentences as in (1118). In (1119) the commentative is followed by a noun functioning as a vocative.

(1118) [má^M kuá^M-ɲiéi^H hná^{HL} ɲii^H kuo^H]   né$ʔ^H$
       PRF VEN^PAST-go^nonhome^IA^IS I   place firewood COMM
       You should know that I have been to get firewood.

(1119) [tiá^M ciú^{LM} hmu^M cú^M la^L nĩ^M] né$ʔ^H$ ɲiú^{M}mí$ʔ^H$
       not good^IN do^TI^PRES^3 3   idea that COMM little^boy
       Little boy, you should know that it's not good to do that sort of thing!

né$ʔ^H$ also functions as a quotative (QUOT) in declarative and interrogative sentences, collocating with a much wider range of clausal elements; see §11.2.

The evaluative adverb ne$ʔ^{MH}$. The evaluative (EVAL) illocutionary adverb ne$ʔ^{MH}$ can occur in declarative, interrogative, and imperative sentences; it most frequently occurs in imperatives. Generally, ne$ʔ^{MH}$ means 'let's see (if)'.

An example of ne$ʔ^{MH}$ (EVAL) in an imperative sentence is given in (1120) where the command is addressed to a small child. In this instance, ne$ʔ^{MH}$ occurs following a verb phrase. It may also occur at the end of a clause, or sentence final; an example of the latter is given in (1121).

(1120) [kuá^M-kã́^{H}]   ne$ʔ^{MH}$ sii^M lá^M ɲii^{H}kõ^M ɲie$ʔ^M$
       ANDT^IMP-take^TI^2 EVAL letter this to   father^2
       Take this letter to your father; let's see (if you can do it).

(1121) [hɲia$ʔ^{MH}$ cii^L tã^{LM} ó^{LM} kiõ$ʔ^L$ kĩ̂^{H}]   ne$ʔ^{MH}$
       strike^TI^IMP DIM bird yonder with stone EVAL
       Strike that bird with a stone; let's see (if you can do it).

In the declarative sentence (1122), only the immediately preceding verb phrase constituent is in the scope of ne$ʔ^{MH}$ (EVAL).

(1122) ʔnó^{LM} hná^{HL} ʔi^L [ʔná$ʔ^H$]   ne$ʔ^{MH}$ ʔnú^M
       want^STI^IS I   COMP cut^transversally^TI^FUT^2 EVAL you^S

       ʔmá^M lá^M
       tree this
       I want you to cut this log transversally (into sections); let's see (if you can do it).

When ne$ʔ^{MH}$ (EVAL) occurs in an interrogative sentence, the indubitative particle dú$ʔ^H$ (§11.2) must co-occur, although not necessarily contiguously.

(1123) [ʔíʰ   líʰᴴᴸ]   neʔᴹᴴ kuʔᴸ   cúᴹ kĩʰ   dúʔᴴ
       QUERY be^possible^II^FUT EVAL   eat^TI^FUT^3 3 stone INDB
       Is it possible for someone to eat stone? Obviously not (let's see what you think).

The assumption adverb láʔᴴ. The assumption (ASUM) adverb láʔᴴ functions in a manner similar to the assentive adverb naᴹᴴ, expecting a positive response, but unlike naᴹᴴ, the anticipated response is a simple 'yes'. By using láʔᴴ, the speaker indicates either that s/he is unsure of what s/he has heard, or is seeking confirmation of her/his own assumption. It occurs in declarative, imperative, and prohibition sentences without any substantial change in meaning; it can occur only sentence final. Generally, láʔᴴ expresses the idea of 'really?', 'right?', or 'okay?'.

Examples of láʔᴴ with positive and negative declarative sentences, respectively, are given in (1124) and (1125).

(1124) [laᴸ   nĩᴹ huáʔᴸ   cúᴹ] láʔᴴ
       idea that say^STI^3 3   ASUM
       That's what s/he is saying, right?

(1125) [tiáᴹ laᴸ tĩᴹ   núᴹ   ʔíʔᴴ   sííᴹ] láʔᴴ
       not EVID be^able^STI^2 you^s read^TI^FUT^3 book ASUM
       You aren't able to read, right?

In (1126) and (1127), the effect of láʔᴴ is to soften the imperative and prohibition, respectively.

(1126) [kueᴴ   kãuᴹ ʔíᴸ   tiᴸ láᴹ] láʔᴴ
       give^DI^IMP^2>1S one^IN tortilla at here ASUM
       Pass a tortilla over here, okay?

(1127) [ʔaᴸ líᴹuúᴹ ʔúʔᴴ   hmáïᴹ] láʔᴴ
       INT CES   drink^TI^PROH^2 water ASUM
       Stop drinking liquor, okay?[72]

The supplication adverb tiáᴸ. The supplication (SUPL) illocutionary adverb tiáᴸ can occur in all four sentence types; it most frequently occurs in imperatives. The verb is always inflected for the second person. Generally, tiáᴸ occurs immediately following the verb phrase. A second-person singular subject is usually omitted in the imperative construction as in (1128).

---

[72]The word hmáïᴹ 'water' is a common euphemism for liquor.

(1128) *[ɲia^LM]*   tiá^L   ʔɲiu^LM   hná^HL
come^nonhome^IA^IMP^2S SUPL house^is I
Please come to my house.

When there is an overt subject, *tiá^L* generally occurs between the verb phrase and the subject; sometimes *tiá^L* occurs following the subject, however. Examples (1129) and (1130) illustrate these two options, respectively.

(1129) *[ʔlé?^H]*   tiá^L   ʔnú^M   ʔi^L   ka^L-ta^H   hno?^H
speak^TI^IMP SUPL you^s COMP PAST-regard^IA^1P we
Please speak on our behalf.

(1130) *[ʔlé?^H   ʔnú^M]* tiá^L   háï^HL   lá^M
speak^TI^IMP you^s SUPL word this
Please speak this message.

An example of *tiá^L* (SUPL) in a prohibition sentence is:

(1131) *[lî^M   ʔlé?^M]*   tiá^L   la^L   nî^M
PROH speak^TI^PROH^2 SUPL idea that
Please don't say those things.

An example of *tiá^L* (SUPL) in a declarative sentence is:

(1132) ʔnó^LM   hná^HL ʔi^L   *[hɲiúʔ^HL   nú^M]* tiá^L   hó^H   ʔmá^M
want^STI^is I   COMP plane^TI^FUT^2 you^s SUPL flat wood

        lá^M   ca^L ʔáu^M
        this tomorrow
I want you to please plane this board tomorrow.

The only type of interrogative sentence in which *tiá^L* can occur is a yes/no question in which the verb is negated and inflected for the future tense.

(1133) *[tiá^H   hmúʔ^HL]*   tiá^L   ʔi^L   ciú^LM
ʔ^not do^TI^FUT^2 SUPL 'thing good
Won't you please do me a favor?

When other illocutionary markers such as the anticipative (ANTP) *uá^H* or the indubitative (INDB) *dúʔ^H/dú^H* occur with *tiá^L*, they must precede *tiá^L*. When *dú^H* (INDB) occurs with *tiá^L* (SUPL), as in (1134), although the speaker is expecting compliance, the effect is that of a courteous request.

(1134) *[ŋiéiʔᴴ   dúᴴ]   tiá̰ᴸ   ʔmá̰ᴸ tḭᴸ hoᴹᴴ kuá̰ᴹ-ciuᴹᴴ*
        extend^TI^IMP INDB SUPL net   at   side hand-good
        Please extend the net on the right side.

tiá̰ᴸ (SUPL) may be modified by the adverb *míʔᴴ* 'kindly', but this use is found only in the speech of the elderly. *míʔᴴ* has probably derived from the adjective *míʔᴴ* 'little'; it collocates only with *tiá̰ᴸ*. As with *dúʔᴴ* (INDB) above, the effect is that of a courteous request.

(1135) *[hmuᴸ]   míᴴ   tiá̰ᴸ   kã̰uᴹ   ʔḭᴸ   ciṵᴸᴹ   kiúᴴᴸ*
        do^TI^IMP kindly SUPL one^IN thing good^IN have^STI^1P
        Please do me a little favor.

11.2 Illocutionary particles

Illocutionary particles are distinguished from illocutionary adverbs on a distributional basis. Parts of speech that cannot occur in the scope of illocutionary adverbs can occur in the scope of illocutionary particles, principally: noun phrases, quantifier phrases, prepositional phrases, and adverb phrases.

Several of the particles have different connotations depending on whether the sentence in which they occur is declarative, interrogative, imperative, or prohibition. These nuances are described, when relevant, in the sections below where each particle is discussed.

The particles *bíʔᴴ* (AFF), *dúʔᴴ* (INDB), and *iáʔᴸ* (ASSR) are addressee oriented; that is, possible or probable doubt on the part of the addressee is assumed, and the speaker is attempting to allay those doubts. (Ultimately, of course, they are still expressing the speaker's own opinion that doubt exists, or potentially exists, in the addressee's mind.)

The particles *dá̰ᴹ* (VER), *má̰ʔᴸ* (EXCL), *néʔᴴ* (QUOT), and *uáᴴ* (ANTP) are speaker oriented; personal attitudes are being expressed without regard to the addressee's attitude.

The affirmation particle *bíʔᴴ*. The affirmation (AFF) particle *bíʔᴴ* is by far the most frequent of all the illocutionary markers. *bíʔᴴ* can occur in declarative, interrogative, imperative, and prohibition sentences.

When glossing examples in which *bíʔᴴ* occurs, sometimes the equivalent of 'indeed' or 'certainly' seems appropriate, and sometimes a cleft sentence best expresses the force of *bíʔᴴ*; however, other times I have not attempted to represent *bíʔᴴ* in the translation of the example, but simply discuss its implication preceding the example.

Examples (1136)–(1139) illustrate the use of *bíʔᴴ* in declarative sentences where a quantifier phrase, a noun phrase, a manner adverb, and a verb phrase, respectively, are in the scope of *bíʔᴴ*. In (1136), with just the quantifier phrase in the scope of *bɨʔᴴ*, the implication is that there was no one else available to go with us; in (1137), however, with the noun phrase in the scope of *bɨʔᴴ*, the implication is that there were others that could have gone with us but didn't. Example (1138) illustrates a manner adverb in the scope of *bɨʔᴴ*. Example (1139), with a verb phrase in the scope of *bɨʔᴴ* (AFF), shows how a clause constituent that is being questioned in the first sentence has that constituent affirmed with *bɨʔᴴ* in the second sentence. This use of *bɨʔᴴ* for focus is discussed further in §12.2.

(1136) *[gauᴸ] bɨʔᴴ hnoʔᴴ ɲiéiᴴ   kuaᴸtáᴸ*
      two^1P AFF we   go^nonhome^IA^PAST^1P Cuicatlán
      Two of us went to Cuicatlán.

(1137) *[gauᴸ hnoʔᴴ] bɨʔᴴ ɲiéiᴴ   kuaᴸtáᴸ*
      two^1P we   AFF go^nonhome^IA^PAST^1P Cuicatlán
      Two of us went to Cuicatlán.

(1138) *hǎᴸ [tiaᴸhuïᴸᴹ] bɨʔᴴ kaᴸ-ʔoᴸ   cúᴹ táuᴹ nïᴹ*
      yes rapidly   AFF PAST-dig^TI^3 3   hole that
      Yes, s/he dug that hole quickly indeed.

(1139) *kuóʔᴴᴸ+   núᴹ caᴸʔáuᴹ*
      ?^go^nonhome^IA^FUT^2S you^s tomorrow

      [ɲieᴴ]   bɨʔᴴ hnáᴴᴸ
      go^nonhome^IA^FUT^1S AFF I
      Are you going tomorrow? I will certainly go.

Examples (1140)–(1143) illustrate the use of *bɨʔᴴ* in declarative sentences where the subject, direct object, oblique object, and temporal clause, respectively, are in the scope of *bɨʔᴴ*. In (1140), the speaker is trying to persuade an employee not to leave, and affirms his intention to take care of all his employee's needs. There is no sense of contrast.

(1140) *[hnáᴴᴸ] bɨʔᴴ kuéᴴᴸ   máᴸᴹ ʔiᴸ kúʔᴴ   núᴹ*
      I   AFF give^TI^FUT^1S food COMP eat^TI^FUT^2 you^s
      I certainly will give you food to eat.

(1141) *[hnáᴴᴸ] bɨʔᴴ kaᴸ-poᴸ   cúᴹ uáᴹhaïᴸᴹ*
      I   AFF PAST-hit^TA^3>1 3 also
      S/he certainly hit me also.

(1142) [kū^Lkiõ?^L   ?i^L   hấu^M]   bí?^H tî^M   hmu^M   cú^M
by^means^of thing that^IN AFF   DISC make^TI^PRES^3   3

?a^H
clothes^3
It was with that that they used to make their clothes.

(1143) [tá^Hla^L   ná^H-hua^{ML}   ?mï?^{LM} hấu^M]   bí?^H cú^M
while   PROG^P-shake^TI^3   cloth   that^IN AFF   3

ka^L-kuõu^L   ŋiú^Mmí?^H
PAST-run^IA^3   boy
It was while they were shaking that cloth (that) the boy ran away.

Although the constituent which comes within the scope of *bí?^H* (AFF) generally occurs sentence initially, as in the examples above, most constituents can occur in their normal position when they come within the scope of *bí?^H* (AFF), such as in (1144).

(1144) lî^M-hǐe?^{LM}   cú^M uõ^M hấu^M   [má^M?máï^L]   bí?^H
HOD-return^TI^3   3   dish   that^IN   earlier^today AFF
It was earlier today that s/he returned that dish.

An example of *bí?^H* in an interrogative sentence is in (1145), where the sentence without *bí?^H* would be a simple request for yes/no confirmation; with *bí?^H*, however, (1145) implies that the speaker has some idea that the addressee may not go, and is seeking clarification.

(1145) [?í^H   kuó?^{HL}]   bí?^H nú^M   ca^L?áu^M
QUERY go^nonhome^IA^FUT^2S AFF   you^s tomorrow
Will you indeed go tomorrow?

An example of *bí?^H* in an imperative sentence is in (1146), where if *bí?^H* is present, the imperative functions as a reminder to the addressee who has either opened or is about to open the bottle; if *bí?^H* is absent, however, the imperative is purely instructional.

(1146) [héi?^H]   bí?^H ?nú^M θí^L   ní^M   kiá^{HL}
shake^TI^IMP AFF   you^s   bottle that have^STI^2
Shake that bottle of yours.

An example of *bí?^H* in a prohibition sentence is:

(1147) [su^Luú^M hmú^M]   bí?^H ?niu^LM la^L ní^M
       PREVEN do^TI^PROH^2 AFF you^s idea that
       Indeed, don't you ever do anything like that!

The verification particle $dá^M$. The verification (VER) particle $dá^M$ is able to occur in all four sentence types. Although verb phrases and adverbs can occur in the scope of $dá^M$, nominals are found more frequently. The constituent within the scope of $dá^M$ generally occurs clause initial. $dá^M$ can occur clause final, but not sentence final.

In a declarative sentence, $dá^M$ (VER) is used to affirm something to be true without making any assumptions as to the possibility of doubt on the part of the addressee, as is the case with $bí?^H$ (AFF) and $iá?^L$ (ASSR). In effect, the speaker is saying 'these are the facts' or 'there is no doubt on my part that'. In some declarative sentences, $dá^M$ conveys some surprise on the part of the speaker that the stated fact is true. Usually $dá^M$ expresses the idea of 'in truth, really, definitely'. Examples (1148)–(1150) illustrate a subject, a locative, and a manner adverb, respectively, in the scope of $dá^M$. Example (1151) has both predicate and object constituents within its scope.

(1148) [cá^M   ?í^L]   dá^M ka^L-ɲif^H-?i^LM   ɲiéi?^L ?ɲiu^LM
       person that^AN VER PAST-ANDT-enter^IA^3S inside^3S house^IS

       hná^HL
       I
       It was (definitely) that person who entered my house.

(1149) [ɲif^H ?liáu^L] dá^M ha^L-?í^L   huú^M hmí^H háu^M
       place many^IN VER PASS^PAST-be^erased^II town time that^IN
       (In truth,) in many places towns were wiped out at that time.

(1150) [tiá^L]   dá^M má^M tiáu?^H   ?no?^M ta^Lné^LM kí^H
       securely VER PRF be^present^IA^PRES^2P you^P now   because
       You are living securely now because...

(1151) [?í^H káu^M ta^MH diá^M tí^M]   dá^M ?no?^M
       even one^IN work not be^able^STI^2 VER you^P
       You (really) can't do a single job.

When $dá^M$ (VER) occurs in an interrogative clause, the speaker is saying 'I really want to know the truth!'. The use of $dá^M$ in interrogatives is characteristic of women's speech, although men occasionally use $dá^M$ for humor.

Illocutionary Adverbs and Particles

dáM (VER) can have in its scope the constituent being questioned in a yes/no question, any of the interrogative words, or the adverb *ʔaL* 'exactly, just'.

An example where *dáM* has in its scope the constituent being questioned in a yes/no question is (1152), and where it follows an interrogative word in (1153).

(1152) *[tiáH máM kaL-lïL   ŋiiLM]   dáM cúM húHcõM*
 ʔ^not PRF PAST-occur^II know^STI^3 VER 3   truth
 Has s/he really not come to know the truth?

(1153) *[ʔeL] dáM ŋiiL-hmuʔLM   núM*
 what? VER INDEF^PROG-do^TI^2 you^S
 What (in truth) are you doing?

If *dáM* (VER) occurs with an interrogative adverb which is modified by the adverb *ʔaL* 'exactly, just', *dáM* usually follows immediately after *ʔaL*, as in (1154). It may occur, however, following a modified interrogative adverb, as in (1155).

(1154) *[ʔaL] dáM hïʔH   ŋauL   tïLM   mïL*
 just VER where? go^nonhome^IA^PAST^3S master medicine
 Really, just where has the doctor gone?

(1155) *[ʔaL hïʔH] dáM kaL-ŋiíH-kiáHL   cáM   óLM   kïeL*
 just where VER PAST-ANDT-bring^TI^3 person yonder money
 Really, just where did that person get his money from?

When *dáM* occurs in an imperative or prohibition sentence, the meaning is more that of an exhortation or plea. This use of *dáM* is more common in women's speech than in men's.

An example of *dáM* in an imperative sentence is (1156); and in a prohibition is (1157) where the implication is that the speaker (most likely a woman) is afraid that something might happen to the people who are preparing to leave on a potentially dangerous task.

(1156) *[tïL óLM] dáM kuáM-náuM   ŋiúMmïʔH*
 at yonder VER ANDT^IMP-stand^IA^2S boy
 Please stand over there, boy!

(1157) *[ʔaL   lïM   kuaLtáuʔH]   dáM ʔnoʔM*
 MODR PROH go^nonhome^IA^PROH^2P VER you^P
 Please don't go!

369

The indubitative particle _dú?ᴴ_. The indubitative (INDB) particle _dú?ᴴ_ usually means 'obviously', 'undoubtedly' or '(but) of course'. _dú?ᴴ_ occurs in declarative and imperative sentence types, but is most common in interrogative sentences. Regardless of the sentence type, _dú?ᴴ_ is more common in women's speech than in men's.

In a declarative sentence, _dú?ᴴ_ indicates that the speaker is aware of the addressee's expectation and is responding with what seems to the speaker as obvious. _dú?ᴴ_ is addressee oriented like _bí?ᴴ_ and _iá?ᴸ_; by its use the speaker seeks to allay any doubts. For example, in (1158), the implication is 'what else would you expect?'.

(1158) *[tiáᴹ ɲioᴴ   niaᴹᴴ]   dú?ᴴ   ɲiúᴴ*
    not know^STI^IS I   INDB   friend
    Obviously, I don't know, friend.

When _dú?ᴴ_ occurs in an interrogative or imperative sentence, it indicates that the speaker is expecting a response from the addressee; that is, s/he expects that the information will be forthcoming, or the command obeyed. An example of _dú?ᴴ_ in an interrogative sentence is in (1159), where the implication is 'undoubtedly you know, so give me the answer'.

(1159) *[?eᴸ   ɲiíᴴ-hua?ᴹᴴ cúᴹ]   dú?ᴴ*
    what? INT-say^TI^3 3   INDB
    What is s/he trying to say?

In a positive yes/no question with _dú?ᴴ_ (INDB), the anticipated answer is 'yes'; for example in (1160), where the implication is 'I didn't realize that you went there (and returned), but based on what you are saying, it appears that you did'.

(1160) *[?íᴴ   kuáᴹ-ɲiéiᴴ   ?núᴹ   ɲiíᴴ   hãuᴹ]   dú?ᴴ*
    QUERY VEN^PAST-go^nonhome^IA^2S you^s place that^IN INDB
    Did you go there then? (obviously you did)

However, the anticipated response to a negative question with _dú?ᴴ_ (INDB) is 'no'; for example, (1161).

(1161) *[?íᴴ   tiáᴹ kuáᴹ-ɲiéiᴴ   ?núᴹ   ɲiíᴴ   hãuᴹ]   dú?ᴴ*
    QUERY not VEN^PAST-go^nonhome^IA^2S you^s place that^IN INDB
    Didn't you go there then? (obviously you didn't)

When _dú?ᴴ_ (INDB) is used in an imperative sentence, the implication is confidence that the request will not be turned down.

(1162) [kiã̂ᴹ]   dú?ᴴ kuᴸtiáᴸ lioᴹᴴ láᴹ kiúᴴᴸ
        takeˆTIˆIMP INDB briefly load this haveˆSTIˆIP
        Carry this load for me for a while (undoubtedly you will).

dú?ᴴ has a variant form *dúᴴ*; there does not appear to be any difference in meaning between the two forms. *dúᴴ* is found most frequently in imperative clauses, for example, (1163), where the supplication adverb *tiáᴸ* could be substituted for or occur with *dú?ᴴ* (INDB). An imperative with *tiáᴸ* is an entreaty; an imperative with *dú?ᴴ*, however, implies that the speaker is expecting compliance. The effect of the sequence *dú?ᴴ tiáᴸ* is a courteous request.

(1163) [kuéᴴ]   dúᴴ   ŋiíᴴ
        giveˆDIˆIMPˆ2>1 INDB salt
        (Please) pass (me) the salt.

dú?ᴴ also has a further variant *díᴴ*, which is used only in interrogative sentences, and only among close friends of either gender. Generally, a positive response is expected, for example (1164), where the implication is that the speaker is somewhat surprised that her/his friend is intending to bathe, possibly because of inclement weather; nonetheless, the intentions of the addressee are obvious.

(1164) [híᴴ   láu?ᴴᴸ   núᴹ   néᴸᴹ] díᴴ
        QUERY batheˆIAˆFUTˆ2 youˆs today   INDB
        Are you going to bathe today?

The exclamative particle *má?ᴸ*. The exclamative (EXCL) illocutionary particle *má?ᴸ* is a limited scope illocutionary like *bí?ᴴ* (AFF), and appears able to collocate with the same range of clause constituents as *bí?ᴴ*. As with *bí?ᴴ*, constituents in the scope of *má?ᴸ* tend to occur clause initially. *má?ᴸ* can occur only in declarative and interrogative sentences.

má?ᴸ (EXCL) expresses a range of attitudes depending on the sentence type and the discourse context: distress, disappointment, frustration, apprehension, consternation, resignation, irritation, surprise, skepticism, and interdiction; the meaning of *má?ᴸ* can often be expressed by 'alas!'. The speaker is expressing a personal attitude, not making assumptions as to the addressee's attitude, as is the case with *bí?ᴴ* (AFF) and *iá?ᴸ* (ASSR).

In a declarative clause, *má?ᴸ* (EXCL) can imply distress, disappointment, resignation, apprehension, frustration, irritation, and/or surprise. For example, the attitude in (1165) is one of distress and disappointment that their father had left so long ago while they were still little and had never returned.

(1165) [hmí͡ʰ   mí?ᴹ]   má?ᴸ hnio?ᴴ   ŋauᴸ   hméi ᴹ
       when^PAST small EXCL we   go^nonhome^IA^PAST^3S father^IP

       hno?ᴴ
       we

Alas, when we were just children, our father went away.

Generally, the constituent in the scope of *má?ᴸ* (EXCL) must occur sentence initial; because *má?ᴸ* is a limited scope illocutionary particle, however, it is possible for *má?ᴸ* to occur sentence final and have only the immediately preceding constituent in its scope such as the temporal in (1166), or have the entire sentence in its scope as in (1167). Evidently, the reason for the limited scope of *má?ᴸ* in (1166) is that there is no reason for surprise that the person's sibling will return. In (1167), since both going to jail and paying the debt are cause for concern, the entire sentence is in the scope of *má?ᴸ*.

(1166) hǎu?ᴸ   rẽ?ᴹ   núᴹ   [laᴸ   ti̠ᴸ   miíᴹ kǎuᴹ] má?ᴸ
       return^home^IA^FUT^3S   relative^2 you^s even   at   year next   EXCL

Not until next year will your brother/sister return.

(1167) [tãu?ᴴᴸ   cúᴹ   ?núᴹ   ?ŋiuᴸmí͡ʰŋiíᴹ kaᴸlaᴸ   ti̠ᴸ
       put^in^TA^FUT^3>2   3   you^s jail   even^to at

       ni͡ʰ   máᴴ   kaᴸ-maᴸ?ma?ᴹᴴ   ?núᴹ   hï̠ᴸ   lïᴸᴹ]   má?ᴸ
       when^FUT PRF   PAST-pay^TI^2   you^s all^IN very   EXCL

They will put you in jail until you have paid everything.

If *má?ᴸ* (EXCL) has a negated declarative verb phrase in its scope, the effect is strong interdiction for example in (1168), where the speaker is stating categorically that the person cannot go.

(1168) [tiáᴹ lí͡ʰᴸ]   má?ᴸ cóᴸᴹ   cúᴹ   néᴸᴹ
       not be^possible^II^FUT   EXCL go^nonhome^IA^FUT^3S   3   today

It is not possible that s/he go today!

The particle *má?ᴸ* can combine with the exclamation (EXCM) word *?é?ᴸ*. Six possible combinations with varying degrees of phonological reduction are: *?é?ᴸ má?ᴸ, ?é?ᴸ maᴸ, ?ē̠ᴸ má?ᴸ, ?ē̠ᴸ maᴸ, ?eᴸ má?ᴸ,* and *?eᴸ maᴸ*. The full form *(?é?ᴸ má?ᴸ)* is the most emphatic, and the most reduced form *(?eᴸ maᴸ)* is the most common and least emphatic. All six variants of this construction are used only

Illocutionary Adverbs and Particles

in declarative sentences and can be expressed by 'wow!'. For example, in (1169), *?eᴸ maᴸ* 'wow!' is conveying an attitude of surprise and dismay.

(1169) *[?eᴸ] maᴸ kaᴸ-sõᴹ ?ma?ᴹᴴ káᴹfeᴹᴴ*
EXCM EXCL PAST-lower^II value^3 coffee
Wow, the value of coffee has (sure) fallen!

The particle *má?ᴸ* also occurs in interrogative sentences. With the interrogative, *má?ᴸ* consistently connotes surprise, astonishment, or incredulity; for example, in (1170), the implication is that the speaker was certain the addressee was unable to speak Spanish and is astonished to find the opposite to be true.

(1170) *[?íᴴ máᴹ tĩᴹ] má?ᴸ núᴹ húᴴmii?ᴹᴴ*
QUERY PRF be^able^STI^2 EXCL you^s Spanish
Are you really able to speak Spanish?

The quotative particle *né?ᴴ*. The quotative particle *né?ᴴ* occurs only in declarative and interrogative sentences. Like the commentative adverb, the quotative particle is used by the speaker to gain the addressee's attention, but when *né?ᴴ* is used as a quotative, the speaker is passing on second-hand information. The following two examples illustrate the contrast between the commentative adverb and the quotative particle, respectively. In (1171), the implication is: 'Listen to what I have to say.' In (1172), however, the implication is: 'This is what I have heard, but who knows if it is true'.

(1171) *[laᴸ nĩᴹ tĩᴹ huá?ᴹᴸ cáᴹdãuᴸᴹ] né?ᴴ*
idea that DISC say^TI^PRES^3 old^person COMM
That is what the old people used to say, pay attention!

(1172) *[laᴸ nĩᴹ] né?ᴴ tĩᴹ huá?ᴹᴸ cáᴹdãuᴸᴹ*
idea that QUOT DISC say^TI^PRES^3 old^person
That, it is said, is what the old people used to say.

In an interrogative sentence, *né?ᴴ* (QUOT) implies that the speaker is puzzled by something that s/he has heard. S/he is not expecting information from the addressee, but simply raising a point for discussion. For example, in (1173), although *díᴴ* normally implies that a positive response is expected, in the context of *né?ᴴ* it implies that the speaker wishes to discuss the matter further.

(1173) *[?íᴴ kaᴸ-híe?ᴸᴹ] né?ᴴ ?uéᴸᴹ ?ŋoᴸhmáiᴹ díᴴ*
QUERY PAST-shake^II QUOT and Mexico^City INDB
Did Mexico City have an earthquake (as I/we have heard)?

The quotative *né?ᴴ* frequently occurs in sentences near the beginning of fables or legends and at points of climax in the storyline. In such instances it may follow the sequential/result marker *(?iᴸ) háuᴹ* 'then, that being the case' as in (1174), which is the second sentence in a fable. In (1175), the story is reaching one of its episodic climaxes; the sun god is about to reward the bat for its help by giving it blood to drink (that is why the bat drinks blood to this day!).

(1174) [*háuᴹ*]   *né?ᴴ*   *ŋauᴸ*   *cúᴹ*   *?úᴹniéiᴹ*   *ĩ̂ᴸᴹ*
       then   QUOT   go^nonhome^IA^PAST^3S 3   early   very
       Then, so it is said, he went very early.

(1175) [*?iᴸ^háuᴹ*]   *né?ᴴ*   *hlá?ᴴ*   *kaᴸ-maᴸ?nioᴸ*   *dióᴸᴹ*   *ŋiɨᴴᴸ*   *?íᴸ*
       then   QUOT   really   PAST-love^TA^3   god   bat   that^AN
       Then, it is said, the (sun) god really loved that bat.

The anticipative particle *uáᴴ*. The anticipative (ANTP) particle *uáᴴ* is found principally in interrogative sentences, occasionally in imperative and prohibition sentences, and only rarely in declarative sentences. It is generally found only in the speech of elderly people.

In an interrogative sentence, *uáᴴ* (ANTP) expresses surprise, but indicates that a 'yes' response is expected.

(1176) [*?íᴴ*   *?núᴹ*]   *uáᴴ*   *kuó?ᴴᴸ*   *caᴸ?áuᴹ*
       QUERY   you^s   ANTP   go^nonhome^IA^FUT^2S   tomorrow
       Are you (the one who is) going tomorrow?

When an interrogative sentence is in the scope of *uáᴴ* (ANTP), it is generally rhetorical. A choice between two options is presented either as a teaching device or to scold the addressee. There is no strict rule as to which option the speaker endorses, but the anticipation is that the astute addressee will discern the correct option. Example (1177) is a rhetorical question where the context is a complaining child who wants to eat immediately. An example of a nonrhetorical question is in (1178).

(1177) [*?îᴹ*   *ŋúᴸ*   *kú?ᴴᴸ*   *núᴹ*   *?íᴴ*   *ŋúᴸ*   *huí?ᴸ*   *?oᴸ*   *ŋúᴸ*
       which^IN?   meat   eat^TI^FUT^2   you^s   QUERY   meat   raw   or   meat

       máᴹ   *kuoᴹ*]   *uáᴴ*
       PRF   cooked   ANTP
       Which meat are you going to eat, raw or cooked?

(1178) [ʔĩᴹ   cáʔᴹ   ʔnúᴹ ʔíᴴ   cáᴹ   hóᴴkuaᴸ   ʔoᴸ cáᴹ
which^AN? person you   QUERY person Retumbadero or   person

ʔáᴹlíᴴᴸ]   uáᴴ
San^Pedro ANTP
Are you an inhabitant of Retumbadero or San Pedro?

Imperatives and prohibitions incorporating *uáᴴ* (ANTP) are relatively more common in women's speech than men's. An imperative sentence with *uáᴴ* (ANTP) results in a plea rather than a true command and usually denotes 'wish'.

(1179) [rǽiᴹ]   uáᴴ uõᴹ nĩ̂ᴹ
wash^TI^IMP ANTP dish that
I wish you would wash those dishes.

An example of a prohibition with *uáᴴ* (ANTP) is (1180) which is more a plea than a stern rebuke or command.

(1180) [lúᴹuúᴹ líᴴ uúᴸ]   uáᴴ ŋiíᴴ nĩ̂ᴹ
CES   NON climb^TI^PROH^2 ANTP place that
I wish you would stop climbing there needlessly.

Declarative sentences with *uáᴴ* (ANTP) are uncommon. By using *uáᴴ*, the speaker indicates to the addressee that something unanticipated by the addressee has occurred.

(1181) [kaᴸ-hmúᴸ] uáᴴ cúᴹ taᴹᴴ hãuᴹ
PAST-do^TI^3 ANTP 3   work that^IN
S/he did that task (even though you thought s/he wouldn't).

The assertion particle *iáʔᴸ*. The assertion (ASSR) particle *iáʔᴸ* can occur with a similar range of constituents as the affirmation particle *bíʔᴴ*. Unlike *bíʔᴴ*, however, *iáʔᴸ* is a broad scope illocutionary marker, having all preceding constituents in its scope; consequently, for *iáʔᴸ* to have any single constituent in its scope, that constituent must occur sentence initially and be followed immediately by *iáʔᴸ*.

In its prototypical use in declarative clauses, *iáʔᴸ* (ASSR) is used by the speaker to give assurance or strong affirmation in the face of perceived doubt. *iáʔᴸ* usually means 'assuredly' or 'be assured (that)'. Examples (1182)–(1186) illustrate the use of *iáʔᴸ* where an entire sentence, a verb phrase, a noun phrase, a quantifier phrase, and a temporal adverb, respectively, are in its scope.

(1182) [la^L hǎu^M ka^L-huá$^{?L}$ cú^M ciáu^L] iá$^{?L}$
    idea that^IN PAST-say^TI^3 3 yesterday ASSR
    Assuredly, that's what s/he said yesterday.

(1183) [má^M ná^H-ha$^{?M}$] iá$^{?L}$ cú^M ʔiá^H kuú^M
    PRF PROG^P-weed^TI^3 ASSR 3 weed^3 maize
    Be assured, they are now weeding the cornfield.

(1184) [mi^L hǎu^M] iá$^{?L}$ hmí^H ʔnó^{MH} hná^{HL}
    medicine that^IN ASSR TRM want^STI^IS I
    Be assured, that medicine (and that alone!) is what I was wanting.

(1185) [ʔí^H hã^M] iá$^{?L}$ cáu^M tiá^M ca^{L}tǎu$^{?H}$ hmái̯^{H}
    even one^AN ASSR person not go^nonhome^IA^FUT^3P fiesta
    Be assured, not even one person will go to the fiesta.

(1186) [ca^{L}ʔáu^M] iá$^{?L}$ hãu$^{?L}$ ɲie$^{?M}$ nú^M
    tomorrow AFF return^home^IA^FUT^3S father^2 you^s
    Be assured, tomorrow your father will return home.

An example of *iá$^{?L}$* in an interrogative sentence is (1187), where if *iá$^{?L}$* occurs, the sentence is a rhetorical question, i.e., the speaker is expressing frustration or concern; without *iá$^{?L}$*, the sentence would be an information question.

(1187) [ʔe^L li^L sa^L tiá^M má^M
    what? happen^II^PAST goodness! not PRF

    kuá^{M}tãu$^{?MH}$] iá$^{?L}$ cá^M hmu^M
    come^nonhome^IA^PAST^3P ASSR person make^TI^PRES^3

    sũ^H
    music
    Goodness, whatever has happened that the musicians have not yet arrived?

The assertion particle *iá$^{?L}$* rarely occurs in an imperative; when it does, the verification (VER) particle *dá^M* often co-occurs. In (1188), for example, *dá^M* softens the imperative to a plea for obedience, whereas *iá$^{?L}$* is an assertion that the request is serious. The use of *dá^M* with *iá$^{?L}$* in the imperative is characteristic of women's speech.

(1188) [kuáᴹ-kiãᴹ   dáᴹ hmáïᴹ] iá?ᴸ
       ANDT^IMP-bring^TI^2 VER water   ASSR
       Go bring water!

An example of *iá?ᴸ* in a prohibition is given in (1189) where, like the imperative, *iá?ᴸ* (ASSR) softens the prohibition to a plea for compliance, and is characteristic of women's speech.

(1189) [?aᴸ   lḯᴹ   kuḯᴴ-lḯᴴᴸ   núᴹ   laᴸ nḯᴹ] iá?ᴸ
       MODR PROH HORT-think^TI^PROH^2 you^s idea that ASSR
       Don't think such a thing!

iá?ᴸ (ASSR) has a variant form *iaᴸ*; there is no apparent difference in meaning between the two forms. Although *iaᴸ* can occur following constituents such as the noun phrase and the verb phrase, unlike *iá?ᴸ*, it never occurs clause final. *iaᴸ* mainly occurs following the interrogative nominals, adjectives, and adverbs.

11.3 Co-occurrence of illocutionary markers

Some of the examples given above have had more than one illocutionary marker in a sentence. Usually there is just one illocutionary marker per constituent; two occasionally occur, and rarely three. When illocutionary markers occur contiguously, the normal order is set out in (1190). Those illocutionary markers which form a substitution set are in the same column.

(1190) Substitution sets of the illocutionary particles and adverbs

1	2	3	4	5	6	7	8	9
bí?ᴴ	má?ᴸ	né?ᴴ	dáᴹ	iá?ᴸ	dú?ᴴ	ne?ᴹᴴ	tiáᴸ	néᴸ
AFF	EXCL	QUOT	VER	ASSR	INDB	EVAL	SUPL	EXPL
	uáᴴ	né?ᴴ					lá?ᴴ	naᴹᴴ
	ANTP	COMM					ASUM	ASNT
								máᴴnaᴹᴴ
								CEXP

The co-occurrence restrictions that have been established are as follows.

1. Although *uáᴴ* (ANTP) can precede either *né?ᴴ* (QUOT) or *né?ᴴ* (COMM), it cannot occur with either *bí?ᴴ* (AFF) or *má?ᴸ* (EXCL). *uáᴴ* has been tentatively assigned to distribution set 2 because it is semantically more like *má?ᴸ* (EXCL), expressing some degree of surprise.

2. *né?ᴴ* (QUOT) can occur immediately before *dáᴹ* (VER) or *dú?ᴴ* (INDB), but *né?ᴴ* (COMM) cannot.

3. *máᴴnaᴹᴴ* (CEXP), like *iá?ᴸ* (ASSR), can occur immediately following *dáᴹ* (VER), but it cannot occur following any of the other illocutionary markers to the right of *dáᴹ*; nor can any other illocutionary marker occur immediately following *máᴴnaᴹᴴ*. It is like *néᴸ* (EXPL) in that they both function as topic markers.

4. *lá?ᴴ* (ASUM) can be followed only by *naᴹᴴ* (ASNT). No other illocutionary marker can occur immediately preceding *lá?ᴴ*. Because *lá?ᴴ* functions as an appeal, not unlike *tiáᴸ* (SUPL), they have been grouped together. (*tiáᴸ* (SUPL) can be immediately followed by *néᴸ* (EXPL) or *naᴹᴴ* (ASNT), and can be preceded by *ne?ᴹᴴ* (EVAL).)

Permutation in the order of certain illocutionary markers is possible without any apparent change in meaning, for example, the normal order of *né?ᴴ* (QUOT) plus *dáᴹ* (VER) can be reversed, the order of *né?ᴴ* (QUOT) plus *iá?ᴸ* (ASSR) can be reversed, and the normal order of *ne?ᴹᴴ* (EVAL) plus *tiáᴸ* (SUPL) can be reversed.

Examples of illocutionary markers occurring contiguously are given in (1191) and (1192). The question in (1191) is rhetorical; the implication is: 'I'm surprised that s/he is still saying those things; s/he shouldn't be speaking that way any longer'. By using *bí?ᴴ* (AFF) the speaker affirms that s/he knows such things are being said, and *má?ᴸ* (EXCL) indicates surprise that such activity is still going on.

(1191) [[*?íᴴ   huá?ᴹᴸ*]   *bí?ᴴ*] *má?ᴸ   cúᴹ laᴸ   níᴹ*
       QUERY say^TI^PRES^3 AFF   EXCL 3   idea that
      Is he still saying that?

Example (1192) is an imperative sentence which would usually be addressed to a child, asking her/him to do an errand. By the use of *dáᴹ*, the imperative has been softened to an appeal. *iá?ᴸ* is assuring the addressee that the request is serious, and *naᴹᴴ* indicates that the speaker is expecting a positive verbal response.

(1192) [[*kuaᴸᴹ*]   *dáᴹ*] *iá?ᴸ*] *naᴹᴴ*
       go^nonhome^IA^IMP^2S VER   ASSR ASNT
      Go, okay?

In (1193), the combination of *bí?ᴴ* (AFF) with *né?ᴴ* (QUOT) has the force of 'according to X it is true that'.

Illocutionary Adverbs and Particles 379

(1193) *[[máᴹ hű̃ᴴ]   bíʔᴴ] néʔᴴ cúᴹ*
        PRF die^IA^HOD^3 AFF   QUOT 3
        S/he has just died, it is said.

The order of illocutionary markers as set out in (1190) is relevant only when they occur contiguously. If, however, two or more illocutionary markers are not contiguous, they have different scopes, and there do not appear to be the same constraints on their order. They can still occur according to the order in (1190), as in (1194), or in a different order as in (1195).

In (1194), *maᴸ* (EXCL) is expressing the speaker's amazement, while *dáᴹ* (VER) is used to verify her/his emotion expressed by the exclamatory *ʔēᴸ* (EXCM) as genuine. *dúʔᴴ* (INDB), which functions separately from these two illocutionary markers, indicates that the speaker feels s/he is stating the obvious.

(1194) *[[[ʔēᴸ]   maᴸ] dáᴹ uóuᴸᴹ kaᴸ-kiúʔᴸᴹ   cúᴹ] dúʔᴴ*
        EXCM EXCL VER pain   PAST-experience^TI^3 3   INDB
        Wow, what pain s/he had, as is obvious.

When *bíʔᴴ* (AFF) and *dáᴹ* (VER) occur contiguously, as in (1195a), *bíʔᴴ* must precede *dáᴹ*; if they have different constituents in their scope, however, as in (1195b), the order may be reversed.

(1195) a. *[[ʔmáᴹsïᴴ hãuᴹ] bíʔᴴ] dáᴹ hmuᴸ   cúᴹ caᴸʔáuᴹ*
            chair   that^IN AFF   VER make^TI^FUT^3 3   tomorrow
            It is the aforementioned chair which s/he will make tomorrow.

       b. *[ʔmáᴹsïᴴ hãuᴹ] dáᴹ hmuᴸ   cúᴹ [caᴸʔáuᴹ] bíʔᴴ*
           chair   that^IN VER make^TI^FUT^3 3   tomorrow AFF
           It is tomorrow that s/he will make the aforementioned chair.

11.4 A comparison of implications

In this section the fourteen illocutionary adverbs and particles are put in a frame to facilitate a comparison of their implications. Not all illocutionary markers are able to occur immediately following the verb, nor are they all able to occur sentence final. Although all illocutionary markers can occur in declarative sentences, the brevity of the frame that has been chosen, and the lack of context, requires the interrogative for (1197j)–(1197l), and the imperative for (1197m) and (1197n). The frame is:

(1196) *kúʔᴹ   cúᴹ lïᴴ*
        eat^TI^PRES^3 3   tepejilote
        S/he eats tepejilote.

The buds and young flowers of the tepejilote palm are edible. Tepejilote has a very bitter taste, somewhat reminiscent of overripe eggplant, but is considered a delicacy by some people.

Without *bíʔ^H* (AFF) in (1197e), the example is grammatical, but somewhat unnatural sounding. In (1197g), if *bíʔ^H* (AFF) does not occur with the contraexpectation adverb *má^{H}na^{MH}*, the out-of-context sentence sounds like a response from the addressee. The supplication adverb *tiá^L* in (1197n) does not fit the substitution frame, so a different verb is required. The implication of each illocutionary marker in turn is shown in (1197).

(1197) a. *kúʔ^M dá^M cú^M lí^H*　　　　　S/he really eats tepejilote.
　　　　(the speaker states a fact of which s/he is certain)

　　b. *kúʔ^M bíʔ^H cú^M lí^H*　　　　　S/he does eat T.
　　　　(the speaker gives affirmation in the face of doubt)

　　c. *kúʔ^M iáʔ^L cú^M lí^H*　　　　　Be assured, s/he eats T.
　　　　(implies: Since s/he eats it, why won't you?)

　　d. *kúʔ^M néʔ^H cú^M lí^H*　　　　　It is said that s/he eats T.
　　　　(the speaker is passing on second-hand information)

　　e. *kúʔ^M bíʔ^H cú^M lí^H néʔ^H*　　You should know that people eat T.
　　　　(the speaker is passing on information that may be of interest to the addressee; there is no implication as to how this information has been acquired)

　　f. *kúʔ^M máʔ^L cú^M lí^H*　　　　　Surprisingly, she eats T.
　　　　(the speaker is surprised, since not everyone likes T)

　　g. *kúʔ^M bíʔ^H cú^M lí^H má^{H}na^{MH}*　　Nonetheless, s/he does eat T.
　　　　(the speaker has listed several food items that the referent doesn't eat, but contrary to what might be expected, the referent eats bitter-tasting T that not everyone likes.)

　　h. *kúʔ^M cú^M lí^H na^{MH}*　　　　　She eats T, okay?
　　　　(after supplying the information, the speaker seeks acknowledgment that the addressee has heard)

i. *kúʔᴹ cúᴹ líᴴ láʔᴴ*   S/he eats T, right?
(the speaker thinks this is true, but seeks confirmation from the addressee)

j. *kúʔᴴᴸ cúᴹ líᴴ dúʔᴴ*   Is it true that people eat T; undoubtedly you know?
(the speaker didn't know that T was edible; s/he is expecting accurate information from the addressee)

k. *kúʔᴴᴸ uáᴴ cúᴹ líᴴ*   Is it true that s/he eats T?
(the speaker is surprised to hear that the referent eats T, nonetheless, a 'yes' response is anticipated)

l. *kúʔᴴᴸ cúᴹ líᴴ néᴸ*   Does s/he eat T then?
(the speaker has heard that s/he doesn't eat certain foods, and is seeking clarification with respect to T)

m. *kíʔᴸ neʔᴹᴴ líᴴ láᴹ*   Eat this T, let's see if you can.
(the addressee has bragged about liking all kinds of food, so the speaker is challenging her/him to try T.)

n. *kiãuᴹ tiáᴸ líᴴ láᴹ*   Please take/carry this T.
(supplication)

12
Topic-Comment and Focus

The function of the Chinantec topic construction corresponds to Chafe's suggestion that: "What the topics appear to do is to limit the applicability of the main predication to a certain restricted domain...Typically, it would seem, the topic sets a spatial, temporal, or individual framework within which the main predication holds" (1976:50).

The Chinantec focus construction, on the other hand, is a means of introducing and emphasizing new information.

12.1 The topic-comment construction

Chinantec topics are marked by either *né^L* (TOP) or *má^{H}na^{MH}* 'contraexpectation topic (CTOP)'. The topic marker follows the topicalized element; there is a pause between the topic and the rest of the sentence. Of the two types of topicalization, contraexpectation is the less common. Although topic is a clearly marked construction in Chinantec, it does not have as high a functional load as the subject-predicate construction. The function of the topic markers is discussed in more detail below.

Topic versus subject. Li and Thompson (1976:461–66) give seven criteria for distinguishing topic from subject. These criteria are discussed briefly below with reference to Chinantec. Although points (2), (3), and (5) are closely related, for completeness, I have followed Li and Thompson's order of presentation.

1. A topic must be definite or generic, whereas a subject need not be. A deictic adjective is found in many Chinantec topic constructions. Those that lack a deictic adjective are still identifiable as definite, having either a proper noun, a generic noun phrase, or a pronoun. Some temporal topics lack a deictic, but they form part of a sequence of events, e.g., hmi^{fH} $má^M$ $ka^L?láu^L$ $né^L$ 'In the afternoon (TOP),...'

In the following examples, the topic is enclosed in square brackets. Example (1198) has a topic with a definite noun phrase, (1199) has a generic noun phrase, and (1200) illustrates that an indefinite specific topic is not grammatical.

(1198) [cái^M lá^M] né^L lí̂^L   ha͂^M   cái^M hɲi?^M   ká^H?áu^M
       dog this TOP be^IA^PRES^3 one^AN dog kill^TA^PRES^3 chicken

       bí?^H
       AFF
This dog (topic), (it) is a dog that kills chickens.

(1199) [ti^Lla^L ca^Lkuá^H] né^L ti^L   hlá?^H ré^M lí̂^M
       but horse TOP more^so really well be^possible^II^PRES

       ta͂^M   bí?^H
       be^tamed^STI^3 AFF
But horses (topic), (they) are able to be tamed much easier.

(1200) *[ha͂^M   cáu^M] né^L hmi̠^fH mi^LM   tu̠^LM   kiá̠^HL
       one^AN person TOP TRM ask^TI^PRES^3 guitar^2 have^STI^2
A person (topic), (s/he) was asking to borrow your guitar.

2. A topic need not have a selectional relation with any verb in the sentence; that is, it need not be an argument of a predicative constituent. In (1201), the topic 'you' is not an argument of the intransitive existential predicate 'live, exist', whereas the subject 'your father' is.

(1201) [ti^Lla^L ?no?^M] má^Hna^MH θia͂^M   bí?^H ɲie?^M ?no?^M
       but you^P CTOP exist^SIA^3 AFF father^2 you^P
But as for you (topic), your father is living.

3. The case role of the subject is determined by the verb, but a topic may be chosen independently of the verb. This is already illustrated in (1201) with a further example in (1202).

(1202) *[háʰháuᴹ pïeʔᴴ láᴹ] néᴸ kóʔᴸ   káʔᴴ   ʔnúᴹ*
cabbage globe this TOP how^much? charge^TI^FUT^2 you^s
This head of cabbage (topic), how much will you charge?

4. The topic serves as the center of attention of the sentence. Subjects, on the other hand, need not play any semantic role in the sentence at all; in many subject-prominent languages, sentences may occur with "empty" or "dummy" subjects. If dummy subjects occur in a language, they generally occur with existential and/or meteorological predicates. Dummy subjects do not occur in Chinantec.

(1203) *hláʔᴴ ʔmïʔᴹᴴ   hmïᴸ*
really be^thick^SII rain
(It) is raining heavily.

5. In many languages, verbs show obligatory agreement with their subject; topic-predicate agreement, however, is rare.

Chinantec verbs exhibit obligatory agreement with their subject, but not with the topic.

(1204) *[caᴸʔáuᴹ] néᴸ ɲiiʔᴹᴴ   hnáᴴᴸ*
tomorrow TOP go^home^IA^FUT^1S I
Tomorrow (topic), I will go home.

6. The surface coding of the topic in all the languages examined always involves the sentence-initial position, and may involve morphological markers. Chinantec topics always occur in the sentence-initial position and are marked by either *néᴸ* (TOP) or *máʰnaᴹᴴ* (CTOP); generally, the topic is set off from the rest of the sentence by a pause. On the other hand, subjects normally occur post-verbally.

7. The subject but not the topic plays a prominent role in such processes as reflexivization, passivization, Equi-NP deletion, verb serialization, and imperativization. Chinantec topics are not involved in any of these processes.

As the preceding discussion has shown, Chinantec topics exhibit almost all of the characteristics of topics identified by Li and Thompson. Their claim, however, that topic-prominent languages tend to be verb-final languages, and that "double subject" constructions always have the order of topic, comment, verb do not hold true for Chinantec. Although some double subject sentences follow this order, as in (1205), the structure of most comments follows the normal unmarked VSO order, as in (1206).

(1205) [lio^{MH} kiõ^{MH}   hná^{HL}]   né^L ʔá̹^{iM} bíʔ^H ka^L-kā̹^L
       cargo have^STI^IS I   TOP   thief AFF   PAST-take^TI^3
       My cargo (topic), a thief stole (it).

(1206) [mí^Htiei^{MH} ʔí^L]   né^L tiá^M héi^{ML}   iá̹ʔ^L cá̹i^M
       cat   that^AN TOP not   like^TA^3ⁱ>3 ASSR dog
       That cat (topic), the dog doesn't like (it).

Characteristics of topic-comment constructions. The characteristics of Chinantec topic-comment constructions are as follows.

1. A Chinantec topic often incorporates a word from the prior clause, or at least information that can be inferred from the prior clause, resulting in a kind of tail-head linkage.[73] Example (1207), from a procedural discourse on how to make crude sugar, illustrates two topic-comment clauses following one after the other. Both topics give the temporal setting for their respective comments. The first topic repeats the NP 'some firewood' of the preceding clause. The first comment makes no further reference to the firewood, but goes on to supply new information—the sugar cane needs to be harvested. The second topic treats the sugar cane as harvested; the noun 'sugar cane' is omitted in both the second topic and comment.

(1207) la^Lŋií^H tí^M   cia^{LM}   cú^M ka^Llá^M kuo^H   [má^H
       first   prior place^TI^PRES^3 3   some firewood   PRF

       ta^L-no^H   hãu^M ka^Llá^M kuo^H] né^L má^M
       CONT^PAST-be^present^3 then some firewood TOP PRF

       kiei ʔ^{LM}   cú^M ʔná^Hkuú^M [ní^H   má^H
       slash^TI^PRES^3 3   sugar^cane   when^FUT   PRF

       ka^L-uóu ʔ^L   hãu^M]   né^L ʔniáu ʔ^{LM}
       PAST-be^cut^II   that^IN   TOP   be^necessary^SII

       hnái̹^{LM}   iá̹ʔ^L cú^M siá ʔ^L
       transport^TI^FUT^3   ASSR 3   too

First of all s/he collects some firewood. Once some firewood has been gathered (topic), s/he will cut down the sugar cane. After (it) has been cut down (topic), s/he will need to transport (it).

2. The frequency with which topic constructions occur varies according to the different genres. Procedural accounts seem to have the most. Reasoned

---

[73]Longacre (1968:1.8–9) discusses tail-head linkage as a discourse feature in various Philippine languages.

Topic-Comment and Focus

argument (monologue) and debate also make extensive use of topicalization. In biographical, autobiographical, and folklore material, topicalization may vary from extensive to minimal, with certain speakers or authors utilizing it more than others. Accounts of customs and beliefs appear to make minimal use of topicalization.

3. One of the most frequent uses of the topic construction is to move the story line on to the next piece of new information by simply saying *(ʔi^L) hãu^M né^L* 'then' or 'that being so'.

(1208) *[ʔi^L^hãu^M]   né^L nɨ^{H}huá^{ʔL} la^L má^M ka^L-ʔéi^M bíʔ^H*
        then   TOP   if   EVID   PRF   PAST-cool^II   AFF

         ʔi^{L}ráu^L hãu^M kãu^M taʔ^{LM} ʔmá^M bíʔ^H cú^M
         crude^sugar   then   simply   pour^DI^PRES^3   wood   AFF   3
         Then (topic), if the crude sugar appears to have cooled, then s/he simply pours (it into) the wooden mold.

4. According to Li and Thompson (1976:469), coreferential constituent deletion is typically controlled by the topic and not the subject. This is true of Chinantec. In (1209), for example, the empty position (∅) is coreferential with the topic 'my dog', and not with the subject 'someone, people'.

(1209) *[cái^M ʔí^L hoʔ^M hná^{HL}]   né^L ka^L-ʔã^L cáu^M*
        dog   that^AN   have^STA^1S   I   TOP   PAST-steal^TA^3   people

         bíʔ^H hãu^M má^M ŋii^L-ʔnaʔ^{MH} hná^{HL} ∅
         AFF   SO   PRF   AMB-search^for^TA^1S   I
         That dog of mine (topic), someone has stolen (it), so I am now walking around searching for (it).

The topic marker *né^L*. When the speaker marks a topic with *né^L*, s/he is alerting the addressee that there is additional information coming up specific to the topic; such information may be either contrastive or noncontrastive/informative, depending on the context. Although there do not appear to be any constraints as to what may serve as the topic constituent marked by *né^L*, the temporal constituent is most commonly topicalized, and the subject constituent is second. Topicalized temporals are rarely contrastive.

An example of a topicalized temporal is given in (1210), and a topicalized subject in (1211). In (1211), if the women were being compared to some other individual(s), the topic-comment construction would be contrastive; in the context in which it occurs, however, there are no other people with which the women are being compared, thus the topic-comment construction is purely informative in function.

(1210) *[hmíʰʰhãuᴹ] néᴸ kaᴸ-ciiᴹ   cáᴹhuúᴹ huɨ̃ᴸᴹ*
       then^PAST   TOP PAST-take^TI^s^3 townsfolk path
       (At) that time (topic), the townsfolk had their procession.

(1211) *[cáᴹmiᴸ ʔíᴸ]   néᴸ kaᴸ-iáᴹʔãʜ   lĩ̂ᴸᴹ bíʔʜ*
       woman that^AN   TOP PAST-be^frightened^IA^3 very   AFF
       Those women (topic), (they) were very frightened.

The direct object can be topicalized, as in (1212), where the more likely meaning is contrastive: my hat was stolen rather than someone else's, or, my hat was stolen instead of something else I own.

(1212) *[ʔúʜciɨᴸᴹ hnáʜᴸ] néᴸ kaᴸ-ʔãɨ̃ᴸ   bíʔʜ cúᴹ*
       hat^IS   I   TOP PAST-steal^TI^3 AFF   3
       My hat (topic), s/he stole (it).

In (1213), an example of a topicalized indirect object, the more likely meaning is contrastive: we were given a parcel of crude sugar, whereas someone else was not (or else they were given something different).

(1213) *[ʔiᴸ hnoʔʜ] néᴸ kaᴸ-kuéᴸ   cúᴹ káᴹ ʔŋieᴹ*
       and we   TOP PAST-give^DI^3>1 3   one^IN parcel

       ʔiᴸráuᴸ
       crude^sugar
       And us (topic), he gave a parcel of crude sugar.

A topicalized locative is given in (1214), where the meaning is purely informative; there is no sense of contrastiveness; and an example of a topicalized instrumental constituent is shown in (1215).

(1214) *[ʔnáʜᴸ láʔʜ hãuᴹ]   néᴸ θiʔᴸᴹ   cúᴹ siáʔᴸ kãuᴹ*
       end^3 trough that^IN TOP stand^TI^PRES^3 3   too   one^IN

       ʔiaᴸᴹ ŋiɨʜ   caᴸ-ʔaᴹʜ   hmíᴹkuúʜᴸ
       vat   place ANDT^FUT-be^contained^II sugar^cane^juice
       At the end of that trough (topic), s/he also stands a vat into which the sugar cane juice goes.

(1215) *[tiᴸlaᴸ kũᴸkiõʔᴸ   ʔiᴸ   hŋiʔᴹ   cúᴹ hãuᴹ háʔᴸ*
       but   by^means^of COMP kill^TI^PRES^3 3   that^IN animal

ʔíL] néL tiL   máM ciauM   bíʔH cîL
that^AN TOP more^so PRF   put^back^II^PRES AFF heart^3

cúM ʔiL   laL   náH-rẽM   bíʔH cúM coL
3   COMP EVID PROG^P-owe^TI^3   AFF 3   sin

But by means of them killing those animals that way (topic), they remember all the more that they are clearly guilty.

Usually, if the topic is coreferential with any of the primary noun phrase constituents, ellipsis of that noun phrase occurs in the comment; see (1211) and (1212). However, a coreferential primary constituent may occur in the comment, for example, (1216), where the topic is coreferential with the pronoun *cúM* 'they' in the comment and (1217), where *hnoʔH* 'we' in the topic is coreferential with *hnoʔH* in the comment.

(1216) [cáM   kaL-θiãuL   ʔíL]   néL maL kĩLM   bíʔH
       person PAST-remain^IA^3 that^AN TOP by   separately AFF

       kaL-ʔáïLM   cúM
       PAST-disperse^IA^3   3

Those people who remained (topic), they went their own separate ways (i.e., those not killed in the epidemic).

(1217) [ʔiL hnoʔH] néL ʔeL   ʔniáuʔLM   hmúHL   hnoʔH
       and we   TOP what? be^necessary^SII do^TI^FUT^IP we

And we (topic), what must we do?

The contraexpectation topic marker *máHnaMH*. When the speaker marks a topic with *máHnaMH*, s/he is alerting the addressee that the comment will contain information that is in some way counter to the known or assumed expectation of the addressee.

In (1218), the speaker assumes that the information contained in the comment is probably contrary to the expectation of the addressee, and so *máHnaMH* is used (for example, if a larger bottle of medicine was cheaper than a smaller). The other topic marker, *néL,* could be used in (1218) if, for example, the speaker wished to compare or contrast two (or more) medications which are similar in size and function, presuming that the addressee had not made any assumption as to the relative expense of each medication.

(1218) [tiLlaL mîL   láM] máHnaMH tiL   sõM   bíʔH ʔmaʔMH
       but   medicine this CTOP   more^so be^less^SII AFF price^3

But this medicine (topic), its price is cheaper.

In (1219), by using *máʰnaᴹᴴ* in the topic, the speaker is warning the addressee that the comment will contain information contrary to the addressee's (probable) expectation, based on the preceding discourse.

(1219) [*tiᴸlaᴸ hméiᴹ cúᴹ*] *máʰnaᴹᴴ laᴸhuïᴸᴹ kaᴸ-θáïʔᴸ cáᴹ*
  but father^3 3 CTOP promptly PAST-tell^DI^3 person

  kiã̄ᴹᴴ laᴸ láᴹ
  servant^3 idea this
  But his father (topic), promptly told his servant this.

The range of elements that can be topicalized by means of *máʰnaᴹᴴ* (CTOP) is the same as that of *néᴸ* (TOP). *máʰnaᴹᴴ*, however, occurs most frequently following topicalized subjects; topicalized temporals are a distant second, which is the opposite of the proportions for *néᴸ*. In these constructions, the topic is usually introduced by *tiᴸlaᴸ* 'but', as in (1218)–(1221), but not always. An example of a topicalized subject with *máʰnaᴹᴴ* is given in (1220).

(1220) [*tiᴸlaᴸ noᴹ ʔíᴸ*] *máʰnaᴹᴴ kaᴸ-liáu̯ᴸ bíʔʰ ɲiˡʰkõᴹ*
  but rat that^AN CTOP PAST-escape^IA^3 AFF from

  cáïᴹ ʔíᴸ
  dog that^AN
  But that rat (topic), (it) escaped from that dog.

An example of a topicalized direct object is given in (1221) where, by using *máʰnaᴹᴴ*, the speaker notifies the addressee that something unexpected happened to the dead animals; the precise information is supplied in the comment.

(1221) [*tiᴸlaᴸ háʔᴸ kaᴸ-cā̄ᴸ ʔíᴸ*] *máʰnaᴹᴴ kaᴸ-hḭ̈ᴸ*
  but animal PAST-die^IA^3P that^AN CTOP PAST-burn^TA^3

  bíʔʰ cúᴹ cieiʔᴸᴹ huúᴹ
  AFF 3 outside^3 town
  But those animals that died (topic), they burned them outside of town.

If the topic noun phrase refers to a different entity than the subject noun phrase, *máʰnaᴹᴴ*, is sometimes simply contrastive rather than contra-expectation; for example, (1222), where *néᴸ* (TOP) can be substituted for *máʰnaᴹᴴ* with no apparent change in meaning.

(1222) *[ʔnoʔᴹ]* máᴴnaᴹᴴ nîᴴhuáʔᴸ cáᴹ   náïᴸᴹ   háïᴴᴸ
       you^P   CTOP   if   person listen^to^TI^PRES^3 word

       kiá̰ᴴᴸ   ʔnoʔᴹ
       have^STI^2 you^P
       You, however (CTOP), if a person listens to your message...

12.2 Focus

Comrie (1989:63) uses the term focus to refer to "the essential piece of new information that is carried by a sentence" and shows how word order can function as a "grammaticalized indication of focus." Focus is accomplished in Chinantec by two methods:
1. by word order, i.e., a left-dislocation of the clause constituent that is in focus, and/or
2. by the use of an illocutionary particle immediately following the constituent that is in focus. If an illocutionary particle is used, there need not be a change from the unmarked word order, but more often than not, the illocutionary particle follows a left-dislocated constituent, resulting in a double marking of focus.

Focus differs from topicalization in the following ways.
1. The constituent which is brought into focus may be indefinite; a topicalized constituent, however, must be definite or generic.
2. Pause occurs following a topicalized constituent, but not a focused constituent.
3. The topic always occurs sentence initial and is obligatorily marked by *néᴸ* (TOP) or *máᴴnaᴹᴴ* (CTOP). Focus is optionally marked if the constituent is left-dislocated, and obligatorily marked if it is in its unmarked/normal position. Some constituents, such as the locative, do not need to be left-dislocated to a sentence initial position, but can occur between the predicate and the subject; see (1223). Since Chinantec is a VSO language, left-dislocation of the predicate is not possible, so a predicate in focus can only be marked by an illocutionary particle.

The most common illocutionary particle used for focus is the affirmation (AFF) particle *bíʔᴴ;* consequently the discussion of focus and the majority of examples are based on *bíʔᴴ*. Other illocutionary particles which can be used for focus are: *dáᴹ* (VER), *máʔᴸ* (EXCL), *uáᴴ* (ANTP), and *iáʔᴸ* (ASSR); see §11.2.

Without knowing the discourse context of a given utterance, a left-dislocated clause constituent within the scope of *bíʔᴴ* (AFF) could be either affirmed, or else new information is in focus. To illustrate the new information that is placed in focus, the following examples are arranged in question and answer sequences. Square brackets are used to enclose the constituent which is in focus.

Focus marked by word order. An example of a locative occurring between the predicate and the subject to mark focus is seen in (1223).

(1223) hĩʔ^H   ciáuʔ^L   nú^M
where? goˆnonhomeˆIAˆPRESˆ2S youˆs
Where are you going?

ŋie^H   [kua^L uõu^M]   ná^H
goˆnonhomeˆIAˆFUTˆ1S Quetzalapa I
I am going to Quetzalapa.

An example of left-dislocation of a temporal to a clause initial position to mark focus is seen in (1224).

(1224) líʔ^L   kuãʔ^L   cú^M
when? returnˆhomeˆIAˆPASTˆ3S 3
When did s/he get back?

[má^M ʔŋiá^L hmái^H]   kuãʔ^L   cú^M
PRF five day returnˆhomeˆIAˆPASTˆ3S 3
It was five days ago s/he got back.

Focus marked by illocutionary particles. A verb phrase that is new information cannot be marked for focus by word order; thus the only way it can be marked for focus is by means of an illocutionary particle, for example, (1225), where the illocutionary particles dá^M (VER) or uá^H (ANTP) can be substituted for bíʔ^H (AFF). With bíʔ^H, the speaker is simply stating a fact; with uá^H, the implication is that the speaker had not anticipated such an action by Peter. With dá^M the speaker (most likely a woman) is expressing some surprise as well as verifying the nature of the action.

(1225) ʔe^L   lĩ^M-hmú^L   pé^H   ŋií^Hkõ^M ca^Lkuá^H
what? HOD-doˆTIˆ3 Peter to horse
What did Peter do to the horse?

[lĩ^M-pã^L]   bíʔ^H cú^M há?^L
HOD-hitˆTAˆ3 AFF 3 animal
He hit it.

A nonverb phrase constituent which is new information may be marked for focus with bíʔ^H without being left-dislocated, for example, (1226), where the illocutionary particle iáʔ^L (ASSR) can be substituted for bíʔ^H (AFF). With bíʔ^H, the speaker is simply affirming the truth that it is a chair s/he is making. With

Topic-Comment and Focus 393

iá?ᴸ, the implication is that the speaker thinks it should be obvious what is being made; the speaker may even be indicating slight annoyance at such a silly, unnecessary question.

(1226) *?eᴸ   ɲiiᴸ-hmu?ᴸᴹ   núᴹ*
 what? sit^PROG-make^TI^2 you^s
 What are you making?

 kuáᴴ-hmuᴹ   hnáᴴᴸ [kǎuᴹ   ?máᴹsïᴴ]   bí?ᴴ
 sit^PROG-make^TI^IS I   one^IN chair   AFF
 It's a chair that I am making.

Focus marked by both word order and illocutionary particles.
Examples (1227) and (1228) illustrate the combined use of left-dislocation of clause constituents together with an illocutionary particle to mark focus. In (1227), the subject is in focus; by using *bí?ᴴ* (AFF) the speaker affirms that Peter was the thief; if *uáᴴ* is used in place of *bí?ᴴ*, the implication is that the speaker had not anticipated such an action by Peter. None of the other illocutionary particles can be substituted. In (1228) a locative is in focus.

(1227) *?ǐᴹ   cǎ?ᴹ   lǐᴹ-?ãᴸ   caᴸkuáᴴ*
 which^AN? person HOD-steal^TA^3 horse
 Who stole the horse?

 [péᴴ] bí?ᴴ lǐᴹ-?ãᴸ   há?ᴸ
 Peter   AFF   HOD-steal^TA^3 animal
 Peter stole it.

(1228) *hǐ?ᴴ   kaᴸ-?ãᴸ   cúᴹ caᴸkuáᴴ*
 where? PAST-steal^TA^3 3   horse
 Where did s/he steal the horse?

 [hóᴴkuaᴸ]   bí?ᴴ kaᴸ-?ãᴸ   cúᴹ há?ᴸ
 Retumbadero   AFF   PAST-steal^TA^3 3   animal
 It was at (the town of) Retumbadero s/he stole it.

In response to questions such as where have you been? or where did you go?, the addressee could supply more new information than just the specific answer to 'where?' as in (1229) and (1230); however, only the information which is germane to the question is marked for focus. The locative can be left-dislocated to a position either pre-subject or pre-predicate, as in (1229) and (1230), respectively. In these examples, the locative Jalapa is the new information in focus and is marked as such by *bí?ᴴ*. The other, voluntarily supplied, new information 'four months' has no special marking. The word order of (1230) places more emphasis on the locative constituent than does the word order of (1229).

(1229) ŋiéi^H   [halapa] bí?^H hná^HL kiũ^L   θí?^M
       go^nonhome^IA^PAST^IS Jalapa AFF   I   four^AN month
       It was to Jalapa I went for four months.

(1230) [halapa] bí?^H ŋiéi^H   hná^HL kiũ^L   θí?^M
       Jalapa   AFF   go^nonhome^IA^PAST^IS I   four^AN month
       It was to Jalapa I went for four months.

Normally, *bí?^H* (AFF) can have only the immediately preceding constituent in its scope. When new information is brought into focus, however, sometimes the scope of *bí?^H* extends beyond the immediately preceding constituent. In (1231), for example, the scope of *bí?^H* includes both the object and the predicate. An alternative way to answer the question in (1231) has only the object in the scope of *bí?^H* in (1232).

(1231) ʔe^L   ta^MH   ŋii^L-hmu?^LM   nu^M   ta^Lné^LM
       what? work   INDEF^PROG-do^TI^PRES^2 you^s   now
       What work are you doing now?

       [kuá^H-hnau^LM   ʔí^L]   bí?^H hná^HL
       INDEF^PROG-form^TI^IS tortilla AFF   I
       I am making tortillas.

(1232) [ʔí^L]   bí?^H kuá^H-hnau^LM   hná^HL
       tortilla AFF   INDEF^PROG-form^TI^IS I
       It's tortillas (that) I am making.

An entire sentence can also be in the scope of *bí?^H* if the whole of the sentence is new information. For example, if a noise was heard and person A goes to investigate, person B could then ask *ʔe^L li^L* 'what happened?'. The entire answer by A would be new information, in which case *bí?^H* occurs sentence final and has the complete sentence in its scope.

(1233) [ka^L-kí?^LM   ʔŋiú^HL   ie?^L   huã^M] bí?^H
       PAST-fall^II house^3 elder   John   AFF
       Old man John's house fell down.

Interrogative words and focus. Comrie (1989:63) points out that English *wh-* interrogatives express focus and must be sentence-initial. Chinantec similarly requires that interrogative words be sentence initial. In addition, one of the illocutionary particles *bí?H/bíH* (AFF), *iá?L/iaL* (ASSR), *má?L/maL* (EXCL), or *dáM* (VER) often occurs immediately following the interrogative word.

In each of the following examples, the focus function of the illocutionary particle is represented in the free translation by 'just'. In (1234), the speaker uses *bí?H* (AFF) to affirm that s/he really wants to know the truth. In (1235), by using *má?L* (EXCL), the speaker is expressing surprise that the addressee has still not done (or begun) what should have been finished by now. In (1236), by using *dáM* (VER), the speaker is verifying her/his desire to know the truth; the use of *dáM* in questions is characteristic of women's speech. In (1237), by using *iá?L*, the speaker is expressing frustration and/or concern.

(1234) *[?eL] bíH ?niáu?LM   hmuH   hnáHL taLnéLM*
       what? AFF be^necessary^SII do^TI^FUT^IS I   now
       (Just) what must I do now?

(1235) *[lĩ?L] má?L kũ?HL   nuM   káMfeMH kiã̰HL*
       when? EXCL pick^TI^FUT^2 you^s coffee   have^STI^2
       (Just) when will you pick your coffee (beans)?

(1236) *[?ĩM]   dáM   cá?M kaL-?ãïL   lioMH kiã̰HL   nuM*
       which^AN? VER person PAST-steal^TI^3 cargo have^STI^2 you^s
       (Just) who stole your cargo?

(1237) *[?ĩM]   iá?L   cá?M   ?áH   ɲïHL   hëH   cuM*
       which^AN? ASSR person PV^FUT understand^TI^FUT^3 word^3 3
       (Just) who will completely understand her/his message?

References

Anderson, Judi Lynn. 1989. Comaltepec Chinantec syntax. Studies in Chinantec Languages 3. Summer Institute of Linguistics and the University of Texas at Arlington Publications in Linguistics 89. Dallas.
Anderson, Stephen R. 1985. Typological distinctions in word formation. In Shopen, 3:3–56. Cambridge: Cambridge University Press.
―――― and Edward L. Keenan. 1985. Deixis. In Shopen, 3:259–308.
Berlin, Brent and Paul Kay. 1969. Basic color terms, their universality and evolution. Berkeley: University of California Press.
Bevan, Bernard. 1938. The Chinantec. México: Instituto Panamericano de Geografía e Historia.
Chafe, Wallace L. 1976. Givenness, contrastiveness, definiteness, subjects, topics, and point of view. In Charles Li (ed.), Subject and topic, 25–55. New York: Academic Press.
Comrie, Bernard. 1989. Language universals and linguistic typology. 2nd ed. Chicago: University of Chicago Press.
Crothers, John. 1978. Typology and universals of vowel systems. In Joseph H. Greenberg (ed.), Universals of human languages, 2: Phonology, 93–152. Stanford: Stanford University Press.
Davison, Alice. 1980. Peculiar passives. Language 56:42–66.
Dixon, Robert M. W. 1987. Studies in ergativity, introduction. Lingua 71:1–16.
Egland, Steven. 1978. La intelegibilidad interdialectal en México: resultados de algunos sondeos. México: Instituto Lingüístico de Verano.

Foley, William A. and Mike Olson. 1985. Clausehood and verb serialization. In Johanna Nichols and Anthony Woodbury (eds.), Grammar inside and outside of the clause, 17–61. Cambridge: Cambridge University Press.

Foris, Christine. 1978. Verbs of motion in Sochiapan Chinantec. Anthropological Linguistics 20:353–58.

Foris, David. 1973. Sochiapan Chinantec syllable structure. International Journal of American Linguistics 39:232–35.

———. 1980. The Sochiapan Chinantec noun phrase. Summer Institute of Linguistics Mexico Workpapers 3:47–76.

———. 1993. A grammar of Sochiapan Chinantec. Ph.D. dissertation. Auckland University.

Givón, Talmy. 1984. Syntax: A functional-typological introduction, 1. Amsterdam and Philadelphia: John Benjamins.

Greenberg, Joseph H. 1966. Some universals of grammar with particular reference to the order of meaningful elements. In Joseph H. Greenberg (ed.), Universals of language, 73–113. 2nd ed. Massachusetts: MIT Press.

———. 1974. Numeral classifiers and substantival number: Problems in the genesis of a linguistic type. In Luigi Heilmann (ed.), Proceedings of the Eleventh International Congress of Linguists, 1972, 17–37. Societā editrice il Mulino Bologna.

Keenan, Edward L. 1985a. Passive in the world's languages. In Shopen, 1:243–81.

———. 1985b. Relative clauses. In Shopen, 2:141–70.

Kikuchi, Atsuko. 1985. Conventional expressions and translation. Te Reo 28:61–79

Klaiman, M. H. 1987. Mechanisms of ergativity in south Asia. Lingua 71:61–102.

Ladefoged, Peter. 1990. The revised international phonetic alphabet. Language 66:550–52.

Li, Charles N. and Sandra A. Thompson. 1976. Subject and topic: A new typology of language. In Charles Li (ed.), Subject and topic, 457–89. New York: Academic Press.

Longacre, Robert E. 1968. Discourse, paragraph, and sentence structure in selected Philippine languages, 1: Discourse and paragraph structure. Washington D.C.: U. S. Department of Health, Education, and Welfare.

Lyons, John. 1968. Introduction to theoretical linguistics. Cambridge: Cambridge University Press.

———. 1977. Semantics, 2 vols. Cambridge: Cambridge University Press.

Mallinson, Graham and Barry J. Blake. 1981. Language typology: Cross-linguistic studies in syntax. Amsterdam: North-Holland.

Merrifield, William R. 1968. Palantla Chinantec grammar. Papeles de la Chinantla 5. Serie científica 9. México: Museo Nacional de Antropología.

Nichols, Johanna. 1986. Head-marking and dependent-marking grammar. Language 62:56–119.
Noonan, Michael. 1985. Complementation. In Shopen, 2:42–140.
Rensch, Calvin R. 1989. An etymological dictionary of the Chinantec languages. Studies in Chinantec Languages 1. Summer Institute of Linguistics and the University of Texas at Arlington Publications in Linguistics 87. Dallas.
Robbins, Frank E. 1968. Quiotepec Chinantec grammar. Papeles de la Chinantla 4. Serie científica 8. México: Museo Nacional de Antropología.
Rupp, James E. 1989. Lealao Chinantec syntax. Studies in Chinantec Languages 2. Summer Institute of Linguistics and the University of Texas at Arlington Publications in Linguistics 88. Dallas.
Schachter, Paul. 1985. Parts-of-speech systems. In Shopen, 1:3–61.
Shopen, Timothy, ed. 1985. Language typology and syntactic description, 3 vols. Cambridge: Cambridge University Press.
Siewierska, Anna. 1984. The passive: A comparative linguistic analysis. London: Croom Helm.
Thompson, Sandra A. and Robert E. Longacre. 1985. Adverbial clauses. In Shopen, 2:171–234.
Welmers, William. E. 1973. African language structures. Berkeley: University of California Press.
Westley, David O. 1991. Tepetotutla Chinantec syntax. Studies in Chinantec Languages 5. Summer Institute of Linguistics and the University of Texas at Arlington Publications in Linguistics 106. Dallas.

Index

A

accompaniment 295, 298–299
accusative 251, 253, 256–259
active 269, 275–277, 279, 298
activizing 125
adjective 81, 121, 132–136, 161, 163–165, 173, 184–188, 192, 211, 237–238, 303, 310–311, 334, 344, 346–347, 365, 377, 384
adjective phrase 184, 187
adverb 81, 98–99, 119, 121, 126–127, 133, 137–140, 142–143, 145–158, 181, 188, 194, 217, 223, 225, 227, 233–235, 274, 287–292, 294, 296, 298, 301–302, 306, 336–338, 346, 349–350, 352–353, 355–363, 365, 368–369, 371, 373, 375, 377, 379–380
adverb phrase 288, 291, 300, 365
adverbial clause 195
adverbial phrase 195, 234, 292, 300, 303
adversative 107, 152, 281, 309, 338–339
affirmation 157, 230, 238–239, 335, 356, 359, 365, 375, 380, 391
agent 32–34, 94–95, 102, 131, 162, 265–266, 270, 276–280, 282, 294, 297, 299
agented passive 269, 277–278, 297, 299
agentless passive 270, 277, 299
agreement 96, 181, 185, 251, 254–256, 385

alienable noun 46, 161, 163, 165, 175, 177–178, 180, 182, 184, 186, 195, 287, 307, 316
alternation 309, 332
ambulative 73, 104–105, 110, 113, 117, 139, 144
anaphora 206
anaphoric deictic 1190
andative 58, 105–08, 111, 113, 117, 120–121, 151, 189
Anderson 42, 44, 97, 125, 137, 167, 181, 226, 251
Anderson and Keenan 189, 193
animacy 55–56, 77, 89, 94, 161, 163, 183–186, 188, 199, 204, 212, 222, 239, 244, 249, 253–255, 258, 263, 282, 283, 316
animacy hierarchy 253, 256, 259, 269
animate 55, 73, 89, 92, 94, 95, 97, 102–104, 112, 128, 130, 135, 163, 175, 183, 185–187, 191–192, 194, 196–197, 199, 201–204, 212, 220–222, 225–227, 239, 240–245, 247, 253–257, 259, 261–263, 269, 270–272, 277–278, 282–283, 294–295, 299, 304, 316–318, 320, 346, 351
anticipative 357, 364, 374
antipassive 237, 282–285

apportional 204–205
apposition 186, 300, 307, 316
appositional 292, 316–319
assentive 356, 358, 360, 363
assertion 306, 330, 356, 375–376
assumption 356, 358–359, 363, 389
attainment 106
attenuative 148, 156–158

B

base root 31
benefactive 237, 245, 286–290
Berlin and Kay 186
binomial 27, 44–46, 48, 53, 162, 166–167
binomial adjective 46–47
binomial adverb 48–49, 227, 288
binomial noun 44, 46
binomial preposition 227
binomial verb 44, 46, 49–50, 55, 126–127, 137, 157–158
borrowed word 20
borrowing 20

C

cardinal number 201
cardinal numeral 200
categorizer 162, 173–175, 206
causative 29, 30, 81, 121, 125, 127–131, 142, 298, 322
cause 309, 324, 349–350
cessative 148, 154–156, 159
Chafe 383
Chinantec 132
class 31, 35, 37, 44, 56, 58–66, 70, 72–76, 78, 80–81, 84–86, 92, 96–97, 99–100, 109, 115–116, 118–119, 128, 147, 163, 204, 251, 256, 260
classifier 173, 198–199, 203–211, 222
clause 89, 95, 125, 137, 145, 149, 151–153, 157–158, 165, 172, 182, 228, 237, 241, 253, 258, 262–263, 265–266, 278, 282–284, 286–288, 290–291, 294–295, 297, 300–302, 306–307, 321, 323–324, 329–332, 334–337, 339, 347, 355, 357–358, 362, 366, 368, 371, 375, 386, 391–393
color 186–188
color hierarchy 186
Comaltepec Chinantec 97, 125, 137, 167, 181, 226, 251
comitative 237, 286, 293–297, 301, 304–306
commentative 356, 358, 361, 373

comparative 238, 309, 333, 336–337
comparative clause 333–337
complement 31, 125, 191, 225, 227–228, 231–232, 239, 283–285, 287, 304, 319–321, 347, 351–352
complement clause 183–184, 303, 309, 321–322, 326–327
complementizer 125, 135–136, 164, 181, 284, 288, 303–304, 309–310, 313–314, 316–323, 326–327, 330
complete-affectedness 46, 51, 126
compound 35–39, 42–44, 46–48, 54, 126, 148, 151, 153–155, 158, 162, 173, 184, 186–187, 194, 200, 233, 309, 339, 350
compound stem 35–36
compound word 36
Comrie 186, 310, 319, 391, 394
concessive 309, 325, 329, 330–332
conditional 309, 325, 327
confirmation 344–345, 363, 367, 381
conjunction 212, 219, 223, 355
conjunctive 338
contingent noun 163–164, 309, 323
continuous 59, 100–101, 113, 121, 123–124, 127–131, 142, 275, 281
contraexpectation 143, 353, 356, 358, 359–360, 380, 383, 389–390
conventional orthography 20
conventional passive 270–272, 275, 278–281
coordinate 42, 44, 309
coordinate phrase 45, 198, 212
coordination 223, 338
copular 239
cranberry morpheme 39
cross-reference 280
cross-referencing 55, 94–95, 162, 237, 240–241, 246–247, 251–252, 254, 256–257, 259–260, 262–263, 265–266, 269, 282
Crothers 11

D

Davison 279
declarative 329, 341, 343–347, 356–357, 358–359, 360–366, 368, 370–375, 379
declarative clause 237, 240
defocusing 167
deictic 105, 107–108, 110, 162–165, 175, 180–181, 188–191, 193–194, 231, 310–311, 313, 323, 335, 339, 384
deictic pronoun 191–192
demonstrative 188
derivation 28

Index

derivational 31–32, 34–35, 121, 127, 141–142
derived stem 27, 29, 32–34
determiner 310–319
diagnostic 63, 101
direct 89, 91, 94–96, 237, 240–242, 246–249, 252–254, 256–257, 259–263, 265, 269–272, 279
direct object 55, 90, 167, 240, 244, 263, 313, 366, 388, 390
direct question 349
direct quote 320
directional 73, 105, 109, 113–114, 139, 144, 151–152, 154, 270–274
directional prefix 58
discontinuative 139, 143, 336
disjunctive 223, 338–339
distribution 107, 147, 377
distribution set 59
disyllabic 9, 18, 57, 75
disyllabic noun 176
disyllabic verb 29, 57, 73, 77–78, 80–82, 121, 123, 127
ditransitive 55, 73, 88–91, 94, 122, 240, 243–244, 246–247, 251, 254, 256, 259, 263, 265, 270–271, 276, 285–287, 321
divisor 198–199, 203–205, 207, 210–211, 213, 219
Dixon 251, 254
domain noun 196, 309–311, 315–319
dummy subject 385
durative 46
dynamic verb 55–56, 59, 62, 64, 77, 84, 88, 97, 101–102, 113–114, 121–125, 127–129, 131, 133, 139, 148, 237–238, 240–241, 243

E

echo 96
effect 324
ellipsis 161, 182, 206, 240, 243–244, 265, 286, 319, 321, 323, 335–336, 348, 389
enumeration 220
equative clause 139, 238
equi-deletion 385
ergative 163, 181, 250–251, 253–254, 257–259, 282, 284–285
ergativity 95, 237, 251, 258
etymology 77, 81, 106, 126
evaluative 161–162, 196–197, 206, 356, 358, 362

evaluative adjective 133, 175, 184, 196
evidential 73, 100, 117–118, 141–142, 280, 337
exclamative 357, 371
exhortative 63–64, 100, 118, 120
existentials 130
explication 356, 358–359

F

falsetto 21
falsetto speech 21
final syllable 9, 16, 18–19, 22, 36, 40, 57, 73, 77–78, 80–81, 94, 99, 150, 158, 176, 252, 257, 259, 342, 346
focus 149, 168, 230, 242, 287, 293, 296, 301, 305, 343, 366, 383, 391–395
Foris 9, 13, 18, 31, 161, 181, 250
formulaic expression 119, 337
fraction 213, 214
future 21, 97–99, 138–140, 144, 149, 152–154, 288, 302, 364
future perfect 142

G

gap strategy 310
Givón 245
grammaticalized 391
grammaticized 102, 106, 108, 121, 125, 294, 349
Greenberg 205–206

H

habitual 97, 98, 104, 106, 141
historic present 117
hodiernal past 29, 61, 63, 65, 73, 115, 121, 123–124, 141, 273
hortative 63–64, 100, 107, 118–119, 151, 155, 168

I

ideophone 39–41
idiom 45, 162, 165, 207
illocutionary 31, 125, 138, 152, 157, 230, 237–239, 280, 286–287, 289, 293, 296, 301, 303, 305–307, 327, 335, 337, 339, 350, 353, 355–360, 362–365, 371–372, 375, 377–380, 391–393, 395
imaginative conditional 325, 327–328

imperative 63–65, 99–100, 107, 109, 118–119, 121, 150–151, 154, 356–363, 365, 367, 369–371, 374–379
impersonal passive 270, 279–281
improbability 144, 148, 151–156
inalienable 227
inalienable noun 30–31, 36, 44, 46, 139–140, 163, 165, 175–178, 226, 230, 306–307, 316, 355
inanimate 36, 55, 61, 63, 65, 73, 76, 83, 89, 94–95, 97, 102–104, 107, 111–112, 125, 130, 135–136, 163, 175, 182–187, 191, 196, 199, 201, 203–204, 206, 211–212, 220–222, 226, 239–42, 244, 245, 247, 253–254, 257, 259, 263–265, 269–270, 277–278, 280, 282–283, 294, 295, 299, 304, 316, 318—320, 323, 346–348, 351
inchoative 141
indefinite 172, 296, 384
indefinite quantifier 212–213, 220, 222
indicative 319
indirect object 90, 167, 244, 263, 287, 313, 321, 388
indirect question 341, 349, 351–352
indirect quote 320
indubitative 337, 357, 362, 364, 370
inflection 57–58, 61, 63–66, 69–70, 72–75, 78, 80, 88–92, 94, 96–99, 101, 108, 112–116, 119, 121, 123, 128–129, 137, 140, 147, 150–151, 154–155, 163, 175–176, 240, 251, 254, 262–264, 270–271, 275, 282, 321, 350, 355–356
inflectional 55–59, 62, 64, 69, 72, 78, 80, 85–86, 96, 123, 141, 240, 250–251, 265, 320, 337
information 143, 161, 300, 313, 319–320, 361, 370, 373, 380–381, 383, 386–387, 389, 390–394
information question 341, 345, 376
inherent glottal 99, 252, 257, 259
inherent nasalization 258–259, 261
injunction 120
injunctive 118
instrumental 226, 230, 234, 237, 244– 245, 265, 277, 286, 294, 298–299, 304–306, 314,–315, 388
intensifier 41, 146, 157, 188, 300, 302
intentive 97, 107, 112–113, 122, 144
interdiction 371–372
interrogative 172, 198–199, 203–204, 341—362, 364–365, 367–371, 373–374, 376–377, 379, 394–395
interrogative adverb 353
interruptive 148, 153, 156, 336

intonation 18, 25, 339, 341–345, 352–353, 355, 361
intransitive 27, 55, 65, 73, 82–83, 88–89, 94, 112, 122, 125, 128, 163, 239–240, 251, 254–255, 263, 279, 282, 321, 384
inverse 55, 89, 91, 94–96, 162, 237, 240–241, 243, 247–248, 252–54, 256–257, 259–63, 265–266, 269, 271–272, 280, 282
irony 167
irregular verb 114
iterative 46, 51–52, 112
iterativity 40, 126

K

Keenan 272, 309, 311
Kikuchi 44–46
Klaiman 258

L

Ladefoged 10, 11
Lealao Chinantec 97, 132, 137, 167, 178, 181, 251
lexical 191
Lexical Formation Strategies 27
Li and Thompson 383, 385, 387
limiter 217, 219
locative 138, 225–226, 228–229, 231–233, 237, 244–245, 265, 273, 286, 290, 292–293, 297, 301, 313–315, 349, 357, 368, 388, 391–393
locative verb 346, 351
Longacre 386
Lyons 181, 205

M

Mallinson and Blake 250
manner 74, 138, 237, 286, 288–291, 293, 302, 349, 365, 368
mensural classifier 163–164, 199, 203, 206–208, 210
Merrifield 17, 96, 150, 181, 251, 263
metaphor 53, 54
moderative 148, 155–158
monosyllabic 16, 18, 20, 61, 162, 200, 341–342
monosyllabic verb 57, 63, 65, 77, 80–81
mood 59, 251
morphemic glottal 252–253, 257
morphemic nasalization 258–259

Index

motion 35, 59, 74–75, 100, 107–108, 110–113, 116, 118, 120, 141, 144, 251, 272–275, 292, 297
motion verb 106, 120

N

nasalization 13–14, 25, 27, 31, 78, 94–95, 185, 187, 254–255, 257, 259, 261, 271–272
negative 37, 137, 140, 147–151, 154–156, 158, 215, 323, 327, 334, 344–345, 353, 355–356, 363, 370
negative adverb 148, 151–153, 155–156, 158, 344
negative phrase 148
negative verb 130
neoteric 146–148
neutralization 14, 36, 42, 44, 135
neutralized 282
Nichols 250
nonentailment 137, 146–147, 158
nonfinal 20
nonfinal syllable 9–11, 16–20, 22, 36, 42, 49, 176, 187, 342
nonrestrictive 309–310, 319
nonverbal predicate 237
Noonan 319
noun 81, 121, 133, 135, 144, 162–166, 173–174, 176–178, 181, 185, 187–188, 196–197, 199, 203, 205–207, 220, 222–223, 226–228, 230, 306–307, 313, 346–348, 361, 365, 384
noun phrase 161, 163, 178, 184, 187, 223, 227–231, 249, 253, 280, 292, 300, 303–304, 306–307, 311–312, 314–315, 353, 355, 365, 375, 377, 384, 389–390
number 56, 74, 81–82, 92, 96, 128, 163, 167–168, 184–185, 253, 256, 296
numeral 146, 163, 193–194, 198–201, 203–207, 211, 217–218

O

oblique object 130, 267, 280, 282–283, 287, 297, 366
obviative 94–95, 253–254, 259–260, 262, 265, 269
optative 144

P

Palantla Chinantec 17, 96, 150, 181, 251, 263
palatalization 11
paradigm 56, 58–60, 62–66, 69–70, 72–76, 78, 80–81, 83–90, 92, 94, 106, 108–109, 115, 119, 165, 171, 176–177, 181, 250–251, 255–256, 260–261, 270, 306, 337, 350
partial affectedness 183, 281
particle 125, 138, 152, 157, 238–239, 242, 280, 287, 289, 293, 296, 303, 305–306, 327, 335, 337, 339, 350, 353, 355–357, 362, 365, 368, 370–377, 379, 391–393, 395
partitive 213–214, 285
part-whole 163, 176, 178, 180, 183
passive 55, 114, 237, 242, 244, 270–275, 277–280, 282, 294, 299
passive voice 276
past 100, 141–142, 144, 146, 342
past tense 109, 115, 118
patient 94–95, 162, 244, 253, 266, 276–278, 282–283, 285
perfect 137, 139–140, 142, 145, 157, 335
perfective 141
permutation 137, 219, 241, 378
person 176
person hierarchy 259
personal pronoun 167, 178–179
phonological modification 36
phonological word 17
phrase 356
pluperfect 145
plural 75, 92, 102, 124, 166–167, 185, 199, 253, 256–257, 296
polysyllabic 10, 16, 20, 341
portmanteau 251
possession 128, 175–176, 178, 180, 182, 287
possessive 175, 177, 183
possessor 161
posture 32, 33, 101–103, 128–129, 134, 275–279, 281, 349
posture passive 114, 270, 271, 275–281
posture verb 132
predicate 132, 145, 227–228, 237–239, 243, 286–287, 290–291, 293, 296, 300–301, 305–307, 312, 314, 320, 351, 357, 368, 384, 391–394
prefix 10, 17, 29, 31, 49, 57, 59–61, 64, 100–108, 115, 118–119, 121, 123–128, 132, 137, 139–142, 144–149, 151–155, 189, 270–276, 278, 281, 297, 341–342
preposition 81, 130, 225–235, 240, 244, 277, 287, 293–294, 297, 300, 304, 313–315, 347, 355

prepositional phrase 225, 227, 230–334, 277–278, 286, 292, 300, 304, 347, 355, 365
present 21, 72, 97, 104, 106, 139–140, 143, 151, 154, 194, 280, 336
presentative 193
preventative 148, 155
preverb 50, 126–127
product-source 176
progressive 32–35, 81–82, 97, 100–103, 105, 111, 114, 124, 128, 130–132, 139, 141, 150, 270, 273, 275–276, 297
prohibition 149, 151, 153, 155, 356–357, 359–361, 363–365, 367, 369, 374–375, 377
prohibitive 59, 63–65, 148, 150–151, 154–157
pronominal 167, 191, 311, 346
pronoun 100, 107, 162–163, 167, 172, 178, 180–181, 183, 192, 240, 249, 253, 263, 265, 267–291, 296, 307, 310–312, 314, 319, 331, 346–348, 350, 384, 389
pronoun retention strategies 310
proximate 94–95, 183, 253–254, 259–260, 262–263, 265, 269
pseudo-activizer 121, 125
punctiliar 40
purpose 309, 322–323, 346, 349–350

Q

qualifier 184, 188, 198, 203, 214–222
quantifier 43, 162–163, 173, 196–198, 203–204, 206, 217–218, 221–222, 313, 346, 348–349
quantifier phrase 164, 197–198, 203, 207, 214, 217–222, 306, 355, 365, 375
query word 341, 343, 352, 355
question 25, 313, 331, 339, 342, 344, 364, 370, 374, 391, 393–395
Quiotepec Chinantec 181, 251
quotative 357, 362, 374

R

ranking 186
reality conditional 325
recipient 89, 95, 237, 244–247, 263, 286–287, 289–290, 314–315
reciprocal 92–93, 260
reflexive 171, 260
reflexive pronoun 92, 171, 179, 180, 183
reflexive verb 91–92

relative clause 161–163, 175, 180–183, 195–196, 303, 309–312, 314, 316–319
relativized 312–316
remote past 29, 88, 115, 123–124, 141, 146, 273, 275, 323, 342
restrictive 309–311
result 309, 323, 374
rhetorical 152, 374
rhetorical question 152, 341, 353–354, 374, 376, 378
Robbins 181, 251
Rupp 97, 132, 137, 167, 178, 181, 251

S

Schachter 39
second-person 58
second-person singular subject 363
semantic 32, 35, 65, 90, 123, 128, 131, 147, 155, 164, 186–188, 204, 214, 217, 221, 225–226, 229, 234, 242, 244, 280, 291, 294, 298, 300, 304, 385
semantic bleaching 32
serial verb 126
Siewierska 280
sociolinguistic factor 167
sortal classifier 164, 173, 199, 206–210, 222
source-product 178, 180, 183
Spanish 11, 15, 20, 37, 39, 83, 98, 176, 186, 202, 208, 228, 373
spatial deixis 189
split-ergativity 250, 253–254, 256
state 103
state verb 55, 81, 121–125, 127–137, 139, 141, 148, 237–238, 240–241, 293, 297, 334, 336, 350
stative clause 334
stative construction 132–133, 135
stem 27, 29, 31–32, 35, 37–38, 40, 61, 74–77, 100–101, 125, 128–129, 139, 162, 187, 256–257, 271
stem class 36
subject 32–34, 43, 55–56, 74–75, 81–82, 89–90, 92, 94, 96, 99, 101–103, 106–107, 110–111, 118, 120–121, 124–125, 128, 149, 154, 162–163, 167, 171, 180–183, 237, 239–244, 251, 252–260, 262–263, 266–267, 269, 271–272, 276–277, 280, 286, 290–291, 293,–294, 296, 299, 312–314, 321, 323, 335–336, 343, 351, 357, 363–364, 366, 368, 383–385, 387, 390–393
subjunctive 64, 119
subordinate clause 145, 258, 266, 330–333

Index

subordinator 291, 302–303, 325–327, 329–332, 335
substitutive 309, 332
superordinate noun 316–318
suppletion 176
suppletive 56, 75–77, 96, 185, 253, 256
supplication 356, 358, 363, 371, 380
syntactic 37, 41, 127, 132–133, 136, 140, 157, 167, 204, 226, 251, 258, 298, 300, 304, 316
syntax 313

T

tag question 341, 344
temporal 98–99, 138, 144, 194–195, 226, 228–229, 233–234, 237, 274, 286, 300–306, 313–314, 338, 349, 366, 372, 375, 384, 386–387, 392
temporal deixis 188, 193–195
temporal noun 193–194
tense 59, 97, 251, 274–275, 280, 288, 326, 331–332, 336, 364
Tepetotutla Chinantec 89, 125, 263
terminative 99, 137, 143–145, 157, 294, 333, 336
third person 108, 115, 179, 253, 260, 267, 294, 305
third-person 58, 86, 95, 106, 155, 168, 172, 180, 182–183, 207, 251, 253–254, 258–259, 262–263, 265, 268–269, 296, 299, 353
Thompson and Longacre 329, 331
tone perturbation 342
tone-stress 46, 63
tone-stress change 36, 38, 115, 150, 173, 176
tone-stress variation 20
topic 359, 378, 383–387, 389–391
topicalization 383, 387, 391
topicalized 387, 388, 390–391
topic-comment 359, 383, 386–387
transitive 27, 29–30, 55, 61, 63, 81, 88–91, 94, 97, 122, 128, 130, 163, 240–243, 250–251, 254, 256, 259, 262, 270–271, 276, 282–283, 287, 293, 321
transitivity 55–56, 73, 88, 96, 122, 251, 279, 282

trisyllabic 9, 40

U

unmarked 43, 137, 140, 154, 166, 181, 241, 286, 288, 326, 334, 385, 391
unstable nucleus 83–84, 87

V

valence 88, 122–123, 237, 239, 251
variant 154–155, 175, 220, 274, 371, 377
venitive 58, 105,–108, 111, 113, 117
verb 43, 55, 56, 62, 102, 207, 237, 239–244, 246–261, 263–266, 270–276, 279, 281–288, 291–296, 300, 304, 320–321, 323, 331, 333, 335–337, 343, 349–350, 352, 355–356, 359, 363, 379, 384–385
verb phrase 57, 126, 137–139, 142–143, 146, 148–153, 157, 181, 215, 274, 298, 341, 343, 353, 355, 362–265, 368, 372, 375, 377, 392
verb serialization 385
verb stem 60
verification 152, 339, 356, 359, 368, 376
vigesimal 200–201
vocalic change 27, 73, 76, 84, 85, 87, 115, 127, 137, 150, 255, 261, 270, 272
vocative 163, 165, 177, 237, 286, 287, 306–307, 357, 361
voice 244, 269, 272–273, 275, 280, 299

W

Welmers 39, 42
Westley 89, 125, 263
WH 346
whistle speech 21–22, 112, 279
women's speech 356, 361, 368–370, 375–377, 395
word class 36
word order 237, 297, 346, 391–394

Y

yes/no question 25, 341, 343–344, 352, 364, 367, 369,–370

www.ingramcontent.com/pod-product-compliance
Lightning Source LLC
Chambersburg PA
CBHW070007010526
44117CB00011B/1456